THE TIMES

GUIDE TO

THE PEOPLES OF EUROPE

CONTRIBUTORS

General Editor:
Felipe Fernández-Armesto
Faculty of Modern History
University of Oxford

Alan R.H. Baker
Head of Department of Geography and
Vice-Master
Emmanuel College
University of Cambridge

Marie Bennigsen Broxup
Editor of the *Central Asian Survey*

Ernst Bruckmüller
Institute of Economic and Social History
University of Vienna

Richard Clogg
Professor of Balkan History
University of London

James Dingley
Senior Lecturer in Russian
School of Slavonic and East European Studies
University of London

Vladimir Dolezil
Lecturer
American College in London

Sir Angus Fraser, K.C.B., T.D.

Lesley Gilbert
Lecturer
University College London

John Haywood

Harry Hearder
Professor Emeritus
University of Wales

Theo Hermans
Reader in Dutch and
Head of the Department of Dutch
University College London

George Hewitt
Reader in Caucasian Languages
School of Oriental and African Studies
University of London

Michael Hurst
Fellow of Modern History and Politics
St John's College
University of Oxford

P.C. Latawski
Associate Professor of International Relations
New England College, Arundel

G.L. Lewis
Emeritus Fellow
St Antony's College
University of Oxford

Anatol Lieven
Deputy correspondent
The Times, Moscow

Bo Lönnqvist
Senior Research Associate
State Commission for Humanist Research
Academy of Finland

Jeremy MacClancy
Research Associate
Institute of Social and Cultural Anthropology
University of Oxford

Ian Murray
The Times, London

Catherine Simpson
British Academy Research Fellow and
Research Fellow
Robinson College
University of Cambridge

Peter Thomas
Senior Lecturer
Department of Geography
Christ Church College of Higher Education
Canterbury

THE  TIMES

GUIDE TO

THE PEOPLES OF EUROPE

Edited by Felipe Fernández-Armesto

TIMES BOOKS

A Division of HarperCollins*Publishers*

Published by
Times Books
A Division of Harper Collins *Publishers*
77–85 Fulham Palace Road
London W6 8JB

© Times Books, London 1994

British Library Cataloguing in
Publication Data
The Times Guide to the Peoples of
Europe:
Essential Handbook to Europe's Tribes
  I. Fernández-Armesto, Felipe
  305.80094

  ISBN 0 7230 0624 5

Typeset by Tradespools Ltd, Frome,
Somerset

Printed and bound in Great Britain by
HarperCollins Book Manufacturing, Glasgow

ACKNOWLEDGEMENTS

Entries on particular peoples are the work of individual contributors who are
specialist academics or journalists with special expertise. Thanks are also owed to
Richard Owen and his staff on the foreign desk of *The Times* and to the academic
consultants who gave generous advice on an earlier project for a survey of
Europe's historic communities: Professor Georges Duby, Dr Robert Evans,
Professor Ernest Gellner, Professor Kirsten Hasdrup, Professor Geoffrey Parker,
Dr Chris Wickham. Thomas Cussans and Philip Parker did coordinating jobs with
flair and acumen. The original concept was Barry Winkleman's. Sole responsibility
for errors and opinions lies with the general editor.

Felipe Fernández Armesto

CONTENTS

INTRODUCTION

The historic communities of Europe are re-emerging. Some peoples have re-discovered or are re-asserting ancient identities. Some have attained devolution, autonomy or independence. Others are calling or fighting for it. The re-drawing of frontiers from above after the First and Second World Wars was no precedent for today's resurgence from below, which shows the amazing tenacity of historic iden-tities in adverse conditions: they incubate under centralizing despotisms and thrive even during federative processes such as that transforming the EC today. When the EC states committed themselves to future unity at Maastricht in January 1992, the world assumed that eastern and western Europe were launched on divergent courses: fission in the east, fusion in the west. In fact, a devolutionary virus is attack-ing big political units all over the continent.

Now and for the foreseeable future, Europe is unintelligible without knowledge of its historic communities: who they are, where they live, what makes them differ-ent from their neighbours, how their people identify themselves, how they fit – and have fitted at successive re-shakings – into the patterns of Europe's political kaleido-scope. *The Times Guide to the Peoples of Europe* is the first attempt to collect the an-swers to these questions, for the benefit of those enmeshed in the tangle of European peoples, and for those who want to make sense of Europeans, or do busi-ness with them, from outside.

In this book, the word 'peoples' is used without the technical meaning it carries in some contexts. We have tried to identify all the extant historic communities likely to be named in media reports or academic work and to give readers a brief guide to their identities. Inclusion is not meant to imply that any group has a right to state-hood, only that it is characterized by a peculiar sense of identity – often compatible with participation in larger communities and allegiance to large states – which the guide tries to define or at least evoke. At the same time, many of the communities listed here are frustrated nations whose self-consciousness is charged with the elec-tricity of an historic identity imperfectly repressed. Where this is the case, the text says so candidly. In some cases, where a case of historic identity seems to be dis-appearing or to have disappeared, the people concerned are dealt with in the entry on a larger group among whom they belong: French and German identities, for in-stance, are amalgamations which include former communities now perfectly assimi-lated. In cases of doubt, however, we have been guided by an inclusive principle. There are separate entries, for instance, for Burgundians as well as Bretons and for Swabians as well as Bavarians. Where the frontiers of Europe fade and blur, we have adopted the broadest possible definitions, including, in the west, island communities from Iceland to the Canaries and, in the east, the Azerbaijanis, who may not take it as a compliment.

There is, however, one big group of omissions: Blacks and recently arrived communities of North African and Asian origin are not covered. This is not meant to imply that they are necessarily 'less European' than longer-established communities. Some relatively recent arrivals – in historic terms – such as the Jews, Magyars and Gypsies have made vital contributions to the formation and development of Europe and there is no reason to suppose that the same will not come to be true of their more recent successors. In practical terms, however, it is not yet possible to make useful generalizations about the identity of so many different groups spread over so many areas at different stages of integration with or self-differentiation from their host communities.

The principle of classification adopted in this guide is geographic. If this is ultimately no less arbitrary than those based on other criteria it has at least the advantage of being morally neutral – and, we hope, somewhat less subjective than political, ethnic, cultural or 'racial' classifications. It also helps draw attention to a marked feature of contemporary Europe: increasing regional association between neighbouring communities on both sides of political frontiers. Within the broad geographical bands among which peoples are grouped, we have not hesitated, where convenient and appropriate, to combine sub-groups on cultural or political lines. Thus most Spanish-speaking communities are treated together, as are most of those which belong to the Italian state: such facts are acknowledged without any implied judgement about the immutability of existing political frameworks. Equally, where geographical divisions cut across state frontiers, no reflection is intended on the integrity of the state concerned. Because of the blurred edges of geographical divisions, and the tug of cultural and political ties, as a matter of common sense some groups belong to more than one region. To avoid repetition, these cases are dealt with by cross-reference.

Sliced how you like, identity is a many-layered cake. A single individual can properly feel both Hungarian and Jewish, Bulgarian and Slav, Catalan and Spanish. A Tatar can feel intense loyalty to the Russian Federation, or a Russian to the Lithuanian state, without sacrifice of cultural allegiance to his particular home-community. In today's conditions of inter-regional economic competition, it is possible to envisage the development of new tiers of fellow-feeling among communities with no previous shared political structures.

The study of identity is not an exact science and readers of this guide are invited to relish the beguiling complexities and contradictions of the evidence. The form and analysis of the various entries and the topics selected for the maps all vary by design from people to people, because all the peoples are different and their individuality is the essential subject of the book. At the same time, it is necessary to be alert to common themes. A question of obvious importance today, for instance, is whether a level of 'European identity' exists in which all or almost all the peoples covered in this guide can participate: the paragraphs that follow below attempt to broach this elusive subject.

Nothing like today's sudden appearance of previously unfamiliar people has happened in Europe since the fall of the Roman Empire. In the familiar Europe of modern history – the arena of states and empires – peoples are kicking up the sand, which is settling in new patterns. Even the language we use to describe the politics of the continent is being revolutionized. Unfamiliar terms – a Europe 'of Peoples' or 'of Regions' or of 'Historic Communities' – have swarmed in like invaders. The names of groups which by the last quarter of the century had become well-known only to folklorists are now key-words of political discourse. The resurgence of historic identities seems to reverse a long-standing trend towards the submersion of small peoples in big states and super-states. Yet in fascinating contrast to earlier upheavals, today's turbulence – the re-drawing of frontiers, the trauma of ethnic cleansing, the development of regional associations across the frontiers of established states – happens in the undertow of European integration. The agglutinative high-politics of Brussels or Moscow, say, are beginning to seem compatible with the amoeba-like micropolitics of the Caucasus or the Pyrenees. The history of Europe since World War II seems to show that the more historic identities are threatened – by attrition and attenuation or by 'homogenization' and 'convergence' – the more they thrive.

Whether Europe is tumbling down or building up, the bricks are showing. The future – whatever it is, whether a federated super-Europe, a well-shaken world of maddeningly complex Bantustans or a revised form of the old state-system, re-forged in crisis – will be constructed from the subject-matter of this guide: the peoples of Europe. Before turning the telescope round and focusing on the details, we must look through the narrow end and try to see 'Europe' whole.

A EUROPEAN IDENTITY? ■

'Europe,' wrote Strabo, 'is both varied in form and admirably adapted by nature for the development of excellence in men and governments.' His confidence has often been echoed but never justified. The term 'Europe' has now been current for at least two-and-a-half millennia yet no agreed definition has been established. As a geographical expression it is of limited usefulness. As the name of a cultural or political reality it inspires hope unsupported by experience. Its potential citizens have fought from within over their rival perceptions of it. Except in resentment or envy, outsiders have rarely seen it whole. Its limits have been expanded or contracted according to the perspective and prejudices of the beholder. Cartographers' projections have been devised to reinforce cultural assumptions or justify short-term policies. Politicians' definitions have been formulated to exclude unwanted peoples, or trump international rivalries. In a guide to European peoples it is chastening but necessary to admit the difficulty of saying what, if anything, being 'European' means. Today's search for a 'European identity' among the peoples who are the subject of this book, is hampered by the difficulties of saying what it is and recognizing it when and if one finds it.

A EUROPEAN CONTINENT? ■

The validity of 'Europe' as a geographical term has been questioned almost since it was first formulated and it is now a commonplace to say that Europe is nothing more than a ragged promontory of Asia. Whereas all other continents are obviously discrete, Europe is separated from Asia by no clear barrier. The Urals are a ridgeless bump. The steppes, which flank them to the south, reach to the Carpathians and the Balkans. The elastic nature of Europe's landward frontier has been illustrated recently by the temporarily successful attempt of Soviet geographers, for political reasons, to supplant the conspicuous Caucasus by the unhappily named Manych Depression.

Within the limits conventionally assigned, Europe can be characterized as a number of regions grouped around a vast arc-shaped lowland which stretches from the Atlantic to the Urals with little interruption. To the south the drainage areas of great river-systems are separated by the Russian uplands and the Carpathian mountains. The highlands that reach from these to the Massif Central fence off the Hungarian Plain and the valleys of the upper Danube and Rhone, while the mountainous south, washed by the Mediterranean, is interrupted by only two broad valleys – those of the Po and Ebro – and is echoed by the lower, older mountains of the northwest fringe of Scandinavia and the British Isles. These mountainous edges are tattered by seas and gulfs. The use of the term 'continent' – sparing but inevitable in this book – is defensible only on grounds of tradition and convenience.

A EUROPEAN RACE? ■

By comparison with native peoples of other parts of the world, the overwhelming majority of Europeans are lightly pigmented with heavy body hair. No other characteristics are sufficiently widespread or sufficiently peculiar to prompt talk of a 'European race'. European expansion has spread these physical characteristics – commonly labelled 'Caucasian' – to other parts of the world: the same type has become preponderant in North America, parts of South and Central America, parts of the Pacific and the vast Russian colony in Asia known as Siberia. There have, moreover, been indigenous Caucasoid peoples outside the commonly assigned frontiers of Europe, while non-Caucasoid communities, especially Blacks, North Africans, Near-Asians and South Asians, are common in Europe and have become increasingly so in the late 20th century. No European identity can be based on a notion of 'race' except in a conscious attempt to exclude such peoples. As the historian H.A.L. Fisher remarked: 'Purity of race does not exist. Europe is a continent of energetic mongrels.'

The preponderance of Indo-European languages as a result of invasions from Asia of perhaps up to about 4000 years ago is a marked characteristic of Europe in historic times. But peoples who have played a conspicuous role in European cultures – including the Basques, Finns, Estonians and Hungarians – speak tongues of quite different ancestry, while Indo-European speakers have also been distributed widely in Asia. Nor is there convincing evidence of the elimination (rather than assimilation) of peoples who preceded the known invasions and migrations, since the extinction of Neanderthal Man more than 30,000 years ago.

Most European peoples have some characteristics in common: high incidence of the Rh negative blood type and the presence of the A2 type in the ABO series – particularly in the case of the Lapps, among whom it attains levels of 50%. Type O is relatively limited, except in peripheral areas, compared with its high levels of occurrence among native peoples of the Americas; and type B is low by the standards of Asia. These patterns have sometimes been used to justify the notion of a European 'race'; but distribution is so erratic, and the diversity within Europe so marked, that the exercise seems valueless except as a cloak for naked racism. European identity cannot be defined in terms of blood type without excluding large numbers of otherwise obviously European individuals and the classification of ethnic groups according to blood depends on the availability of other criteria of differentiation.

A EUROPEAN HERITAGE? ■

In 1991, when 'Ode to Joy' was played at Slovenia's proclamation as an independent state, or the EC flag waved by anti-Soviet demonstrators in St Petersburg, the strength and diffusion of a sense of European identity was startlingly emphasized. Yet at first sight the search for a common European culture seems a hopeless quest. Most of the continent is occupied by peoples long established in their heartlands, with the consequent baffling array of distinctive micro-cultures which characterizes all 'Old Worlds'. Europe is scored, moreover, by long and deep cultural divides, which separate speakers of Romance, Germanic and Slavonic languages, and members of the Roman, Orthodox and Protestant communions. Historic experiences – sometimes centuries-old – have erected 'national' boundaries or barriers of hostility between neighbours of otherwise similar culture – in, for instance, Portugal and Galicia, Norway and Sweden, Serbia and Croatia, Derry and Donegal.

Two sources of cultural unity might have enough spring in them to overcome these differences: first, the sense of inheriting – by a claim which is not exclusive, but which is still unique – the legacy of the civilization of classical antiquity; secondly, awareness of the formative influence of Christianity on most of the cultures of Europe. The first of these is perhaps the more promising. Except to believers in 'Black Athena', Greco-Roman civilization is at least a home-grown European product, whereas Christianity is a religion of near-Eastern origin which became European by accident and universal by design.

Strabo pointed out that most of 'Europe' was under Roman influence. It was a wild exaggeration but, by a curious paradox, it became true after Roman hegemony had collapsed. Within the frontier of the empire, Romanization was an astonishingly potent and pervasive force, even in remote areas where Roman colonization was slight. At Conimbriga (Coimbra in modern Portugal) villas of metropolitan standards of craftsmanship, floored with fine mosaics, defied the Atlantic. The monastery at St Gall housed classical manuscripts which were to fuel a future Renaissance.

In Jarrow, Bede dreamed of Rome and doodled in Greek. Romance speech marks Dacia today, although it was only a briefly occupied outpost of the empire, beyond the normal frontier. The Franks invaded Gaul long after the Romans left but they acquired Latin speech and re-equipped their kings to resemble Roman governors.

At and beyond the extremities of the Roman empire, a sense of continuity with classical civilization has always been sought with extra eagerness and each Renaissance and classical revival has extended the frontiers of classicizing culture. In the midnight of the Dark Ages, classical learning was preserved in Ireland, where Romans never ruled. The earliest of the Renaissances conventionally held to have punctuated the Middle Ages were centred in Northumbria and Aachen, the next – in the 10th and 11th centuries – deep in Saxony where Rome never reached but where Rosvita of Gandesheim wrote comedies in the style of Terence, while Ottonian rulers claimed the legacy of Augustus. In later revivals, Vitegrád housed a reconstruction of Pliny's villa, Prague became the capital of 'Roman' emperors, Moscow the 'Third Rome' and Edinburgh 'the Athens of the North'. Classical taste, 'humanist' values said to derive from classical antiquity, and an education in Greek and Roman letters and history united European élites in the 18th and 19th centuries. It can be objected that the classical heritage has been as much a defining feature of 'western' as of 'European' culture and that one can find neo-classical architecture as fine in Virginia as in Vilnius. Normally, however, the germ of the Greco-Roman past has depended on European carriers for its transmission to a wider world.

However much the classical heritage contributed to the creation of the sense of a shared European culture in the past, it can no longer provide a basis of European identity today. Europeans have been too successful in projecting classicism as a part of the common heritage of mankind to reclaim a proprietary right in it. The relatively sudden near-obliteration of Latin and Greek from the school curriculum has at last made the long-lived languages of antiquity genuinely 'dead'. Post-modernist architecture, with its taste for columns and pediments in unlikely materials, has some claim to be the last classical revival but in most of its exponents the classical influence is so shallow and its lessons so ill-absorbed that it demonstrates the tradition's progressive weakness rather than its abiding strength.

A EUROPEAN ECONOMY? ■

Europe may not make a convincing geographical unit. A common European culture may be elusive or even mythical. But Europe has had a unified network of economies – a 'European economy' – for nearly half a millennium. The European economy was a remarkable achievement. Difficult to contrive, it has had a patchy history and is under threat today. Between Europe's three great axes of long-range exchange – the Mediterranean, the Atlantic and the Volga – communications are hard and distances daunting. The unified economy was forged in two overlapping phases: first, the creation of a western European economy linking those of the Mediterranean and the

Atlantic; then, the incorporation of eastern Europe into this western system. In both processes the smaller economies, based on exchange across Europe's innermost gulfs, the Baltic and the Black Seas, played important parts.

A mountain watershed screens the Mediterranean lands from the vast area of northwest Europe that drains into the Atlantic and the North Sea. From the Castilian plateau and the Cantabrian mountains, along the Pyrenees and Alps, only the Toulouse Gap and the Rhône-Saône corridor provide broad routes of mutual access for carriage in bulk. The only maritime link is between the pillars of Hercules, where the racing current from the Atlantic almost stoppers the Mediterranean. Markedly different sailing conditions along the two seaboards have been, for most of history, a deterrent to shipping. Commercial navigation from sea to sea was practised – probably only on a modest scale – in Roman times but the evidence for it peters out in the early 5th century. When Mediterranean craft resumed large-scale seaborne commerce along the route eight centuries later, they faced enormous problems of adaptation and acclimatization. Heavy seas threatened ships low in the gunwales. Finisterre was their 'cape of no return', beyond which lay a long excursion out to sea around or across the Bay of Biscay. Galleys, which carried much of the trade, depended on huge inputs of victuals and water from onshore. The journey was, in its way, as bold an achievement as the voyages of the age of oceanic adventure. The integration of the northern and southern economies linked by this route depended on geographically specialized production. Italian merchants who carried Mediterranean alum to England and English wool to Italy became bankers to an English king. In the 15th century, Bruges – where the raw materials for the Flemish cloth industry were brought from Phocaea, Burgos and the Lincolnshire wolds – became an entrepôt 'where all the nations of the world meet'.

The arms of this vast commercial embrace extended their reach in the late Middle Ages to include the Baltic and Black Seas. German merchant-colonists who spread along the Danube valley and the Baltic coasts were makers and exploiters of routes of growing importance. Genoese colonies on the northern shore of the Black Sea in the 13th and 14th centuries formed outposts of a trading system which, by way of strategically placed 'branches' of family firms, linked the eastern Mediterranean to England and Flanders.

The Volga had already been a great avenue of commerce in the 10th century, exploited by Rus merchants of Scandinavian origin, who founded a state based on Kiev and exchanged the forest products of the north for the luxuries and exotica of the south: Byzantine coins are plentiful in Polish and Scandinavian hoards of the time. But the links between the Volga basin and the economic zones of western Europe are tenuous: the river flows towards Asia and only hazardous portage links it to the Don. Though navigable to its far northern reaches and along 70 tributaries, its system relies on a land link to the Gulf of Finland. A direct approach across the European mainland is deterred by the vast distances of the Russian uplands and, for most of history, the impenetrable marshlands of the Pripet. The Volga basin's outlets to the world were dislocated or destroyed after the collapse of the Kievan state in

1054 and not restored until after the reconstruction from Moscow of a state which stretched the length of the river – a process only completed in the late 16th century. Even then, it was largely by the northern route that Russian trade met that of western and southern Europe, since the shores of the Black Sea remained in hostile hands from the early 13th to the late 18th centuries.

Even when a European-wide network of exchange was complete and functioning, imperialism and mercantilism kept Europe's national or state-based economies divided from one another by protective barriers and by competition from colonial markets. But the formation of a European economy gave Europe enough experience of long-range trade and geographic specialization to create a basis for early industrialization, which in turn has given Europe a distinct economic character. No continent except North America has a better natural balance of resources and climate for the creation of an industrial economy. Europe's head start – though closely followed by North America and East Asia – shaped the most conspicuous feature of the early 20th-century world: a zone of fairly densely clustered industrial cities from Belfast and Bilbao to Rostov and St Petersburg. Even today the legacy of early industrialization gives the European economy a distinctive profile, with an industrial zone more concentrated than in America and more extensive than in Japan.

This is by nature a diminishing peculiarity and the economic integration of the internal markets of the EC countries will introduce a new economic division of Europe, marked by the Community's tariff barrier. On the other hand, two sources of pressure – the growing strength of popular awareness of European identity from within, the menace of economic competitors from without – suggest that the EC leadership may find the political will to restore European economic unity in the near future.

A SENSE OF EUROPEAN SUPERIORITY? ■

To judge from the evidence of maps, Europe's self-perception was never so modest as in the period between the rise of Islam and the Renaissance, when the ruling convention placed Jerusalem at the centre of the world, preventing the development of a literally Eurocentric image. When the Renaissance revolutionized cartography, along with the other arts, Eurocentrism originated as a strategy for coping with the need to re-arrange the received mental image of the world in response to a double challenge: the uncertainties of an age of discovery, in which the true size of the globe was slowly and painfully established; and the opportunities of an age of conquest, in which European imperialism penetrated much of the rest of the world. In 1610, when the Jesuit missionary, Matteo Ricci, drew his 'Great Map of Ten Thousand Countries', he scandalized his Chinese hosts by putting Europe in the middle. By the end of the century, projects for the exact mapping of the planet were being masterminded from 'meridians of departure' at Paris or Greenwich.

In the same period, 'Europe' as a geographical expression was challenged or supplemented by a new usage in which the term acquired meaning as the name of a culture perceived as distinct and coherent. Queen Christina of Sweden and Peter the Great of Russia wrenched at the cultural frontiers of Europe to include formerly marginal lands. The uniformity of enlightened taste in the 18th century made it possible to glide between widely separated frontiers with little more cultural dislocation than a modern traveller feels in a succession of airport lounges. Mid-way through his *History of the Decline and Fall of the Roman Empire*, Gibbon was able to formulate a 'European ideal' which has survived and been strengthened by Europe's subsequent history of internecine wars and retreat from world hegemony: 'It is the duty of a patriot to prefer and promote the exclusive interest of his native country: but a philosopher may be permitted to enlarge his views, and to consider Europe as one great republic, whose various inhabitants have attained almost to the same level of politeness and cultivation'.

Belief in this common European culture was long inseparable from a conviction of European superiority 'distinguished' – in Gibbon's words – 'above the rest of mankind'. Europeans have been forced to abandon that conviction by the dissolution of their own world-empires, by the economic challenges of other zones and by the collapse of the scientific basis of racism. Today, cartographers are putting Europe back 'in its place' in the world by devising and promoting projections which centre on other areas and emphasise the paucity of Europe's dimensions. Other regions' claims to displace Europe in the centre of our world-picture are impressive: Africa boasts antiquity of human settlement; Asia encloses more mature civilizations; North America is commended by its economic might, South America by its rapid development, the Pacific Rim by economic achievement and promise alike. All this competition has shrunk Europe's share of the map and has forced Europeans into an increased dependence on each other and a patchily enhanced European solidarity. Though not all of them seem to have realized it yet, they can no longer afford the internecine squabbles of the era of European world hegemony.

EUROPEAN INTEGRATION? ■

Europe in the late 20th century is being ground between two vast, slow and apparently contradictory changes: an integrative process, which tends to extend the perceived limits of Europe and the reach of European institutions; and a fissiparous process, which threatens empires and federations with break-up and other states with erosion by devolution.

European institutions were unnecessary while Europe's élites had a shared sense of superiority and were protected from the competition of other continents by colonial supremacy and an industrial lead. In the period of Europe's 'civil wars' of 1917–45, the nature of European civilization was denied or disputed (as never before in the internecine conflicts of the 18th, 19th and early 20th centuries) by advocates of ideologies which claimed to generate distinct cultures of their own. Nazism's racial basis and Communism's class basis were both incompatible with the inclusive concept of Europe inherited from the past.

In 1945 Europe was left divided – apparently for a long time – between armed camps. At the same time, Europe's world hegemony was in a state of collapse: the Dutch, French and British empires had been irremediably damaged by Japanese arms. Colonial nationalisms throve under the impact of war, which bred tough liberation movements.

It took this crisis to give Europe's sagging identity some institutional backbone. The first creative steps in erecting supra-national structures are usually credited to Jean Monnet, a former Cognac salesman who had worked wonders in co-ordinating Anglo-French supply policy during World War II. He proposed a 'High Authority' for coal and steel to overcome Franco-German rivalry. The European Coal and Steel Community was formed, with six countries participating, on 18th April 1951.

In its first years, this European initiative developed all the promise and all the limitations which have continued to characterize it. Member states would not surrender 'an iota of sovereignty'. The 'High Authority' gave way to a Council of Ministers which was in practice an international rather than a supra-national body. A common approach to defence proved unattainable. The Messina Declaration of June 1955 proclaimed it would 'work for ... a united Europe, by the development of common institutions, the progressive fusion of national economies, the creation of a common market and the progressive harmonization of social policies' but the Treaty of Rome, which launched the drive – sometimes more of a drag – towards a common market in 1957, postponed almost everything to a remote future.

Efforts in the 1960s to press towards a 'United States of Europe' were frustrated by the strong nationalist susceptibilities of the French leader General de Gaulle, then slowed in the 1970s and 1980s by the enlargement of the European Economic Community to include twelve member states by 1985. De Gaulle feared that national sovereignty would be undermined and the divisions between western and eastern Europe perpetuated if the Euro-enthusiasts succeeded: a closely integrated western Europe as a 'pillar of the Atlantic alliance' was the fashionable goal of the time. He proposed a vague – and perhaps purely tactical – alternative: 'Europe from the Atlantic to the Urals'. While the Soviet empire remained strong, this looked like a pipe-dream drawn by Magritte.

In the 1980s de Gaulle's role in pouring cold water on Euro-fever was taken up by the redoubtable British prime minister Margaret Thatcher, whose nickname of 'Madame Non' was an echo of de Gaulle's diplomatic language. Her stress on the spread of parliamentary democracy and economic liberalization as pre-conditions for progress in European integration came to seem prophetic as Europe became increasingly 'homogenized' and European institutions 'converged' – not as a result of the efforts of the EC but because of two waves of political and economic re-alignment: first, in southern Europe from 1974 to 1978, when Greece, Portugal and Spain all abandoned authoritarian systems; and again in 1989–92 when most of eastern Europe followed suit.

A EUROPEAN PAST AND FUTURE? ■

These changes have re-created Europe by bringing the historical experiences of European peoples again into alignment – as had been the case in the 18th and 19th centuries. When all the phoney elements routinely said to constitute the basis of European identity have been eliminated – geography, race, language, religion, values – common historical experience remains at the core of the unity or potential unity of Europe. This shared past has made Europe what it is and differentiates European peoples from others. Its ingredients include the Indo-European invasions; the shared legacy or influence of Greco-Roman civilization; Christianization and subsequent centuries of self-differentiation from a pagan world beyond; the cultural exchanges – of colonies, armies, images and words – in the medieval and early modern 'renaissances', the Enlightenment and the romantic and post-romantic eras; a period of partaking in a European culture self-consciously superior to those of the rest of the world; industrialization; and democratization. Some other experiences – participation in confessional struggle, experience of the conflict of absolutism and constitutionalism, participation in nation-states or colonial empires – have been widespread, but not universal. Immigrant-communities of the recent past, who missed some of these experiences, have inherited their effects.

If history is anything to go by (and it probably is not), a strong and widespread sense of European identity is not necessarily favourable to European integration. If progress comes, it will probably be in one of two forms: either a continuation of the old European state-system, with a light confederative dressing, in which the old nation-states of western Europe survive, diminished but not killed, alongside new or emergent nation-states in the east; or else a federal Europe, with a strong 'High Authority', embracing tiers of smaller units which include old states, regional agglomerations and a large number of autonomous historic communities.

Whatever political solutions are adopted, the success of Europe, in a world of competitive regions and increasing economic inequalities, depends on whether the torturous process of economic integration can be developed within the twelve EC states and extended to other parts of the continent. Meanwhile – though small as continents go – Europe has all the characteristics of a giant: poor articulation, lumbering gait, limited intelligent control and enormous reserves of strength.

1
THE MARITIME NORTH

The communities of the maritime north of Europe are grouped around an interconnecting series of seas, partially screened from the Atlantic by islands, straits, winds and ice but joined to the ocean on two fronts: first, below the Arctic circle, by currents and cultural continuities which extend from the western coasts of Scandinavia to embrace Iceland; secondly, from the mouth of the English Channel and the adjacent coasts, to a narrow area of exploitable Atlantic sailing conditions, particularly useful, in the age of sail, as a means of return from the Atlantic to the English Channel and the North Sea. Beyond the limits of Europe as commonly defined, extensions of the same sea-ways lead on to countries founded from maritime northern Europe in Greenland and North America. The cultural heritages which have struggled and mingled in this part of the continent, were evoked in famous lines addressed by Tennyson in 1863 to a Danish princess who married the future King Edward VII of England: 'Saxon or Norman or Dane are we, Teuton or Celt'. The main influence, however, has been exerted by sea-borne conquerors and colonists, chiefly of Scandinavian origin, who set up states or communities in northern Germany, Frisia, Normandy and the British Isles in late antiquity and the early Middle Ages. This was not in itself enough to impose cultural unity: some peoples of the region continued to speak Celtic tongues and others – the Normans – adopted romance; the rest spoke Germanic languages. Nor have the seas ever provided a focus of political unity, though briefly, in the 11th century, under the Danish Knytlinga dynasty, a sea-borne empire of the north seemed to be about to take shape. Today, the Norwegians have tended to hold aloof from European unity; the Faeroese have rejected it; the people of Orkney and Shetland, when last given the chance, voted against it; the Danes have voted for it narrowly and under protest; and the English appear to accept it with reluctance. Still, the seas around which they live have brought these peoples together in trade, and into conflict or co-operation for the exploitation of marine resources. The North Sea has gone from being the communal 'herring-pond' of the dwellers on its shores to being a carefully apportioned oilfield. Before the English Channel became 'a moat defensive to a house', it was the axis of communication of the medieval 'Anglo-Norman' state or the Angevin 'empire'. Continuities of landscape, of farming methods and produce, of migration and, in the early modern period, of Protestant culture have linked the continental Low Countries with East Anglia and Lincolnshire. However, owing in part to the low level of popular acceptance of the European

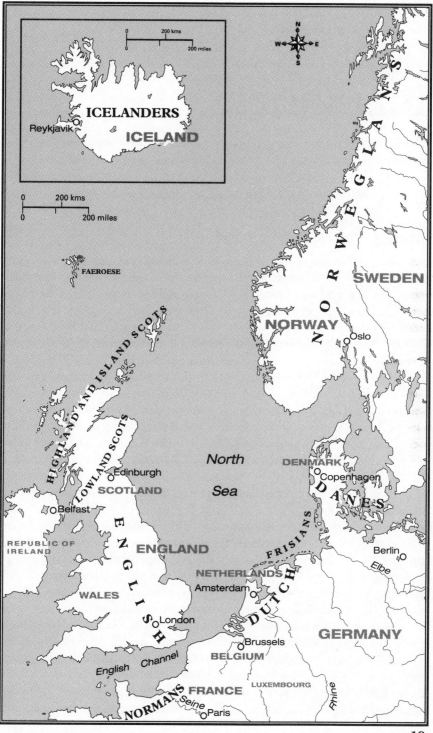

ICELANDERS

ICELAND

Reykjavik

0   200 kms

0   200 miles

FAEROESE

N
O
R
W
E
G
I
A
N
S

SWEDEN

NORWAY

Oslo

HIGHLAND AND ISLAND SCOTS

LOWLAND SCOTS

Edinburgh

SCOTLAND

Belfast

North

Sea

DENMARK

Copenhagen

D
A
N
E
S

REPUBLIC OF
IRELAND

E
N
G
L
I
S
H

ENGLAND

FRISIANS

Berlin

Elbe

NETHERLANDS

Amsterdam

D
U
T
C
H

WALES

London

Brussels

BELGIUM

GERMANY

LUXEMBOURG

English Channel

Rhine

NORMANS FRANCE

Seine Paris

19

Community, regional cooperation is less mature here today than in most of the rest of western Europe.

ICELANDERS

Though the Icelanders have much in common with the other Scandinavian peoples, a separate Icelandic identity, fostered by isolation and distinctive institutions, began to develop soon after the island was settled in the 9th century. Icelanders are intensely proud of their history and many families can still trace their descent back to the settlement period.

HISTORY ■

According to tradition, the settlement of Iceland was begun about AD 870 by emigrants from Norway seeking to escape the oppressive rule of King Harald Fairhair. They were joined by other Norse settlers from Ireland and Scotland who brought with them large numbers of Irish slaves. These were later freed, given land and assimilated to the Norse population. In 930 the settlers founded the Althing, an annual council in which the chiefs met to settle disputes and make laws. In 1000 Christianity was adopted by a majority vote there. In the 13th century, the Althing lost its authority as the leading families fought each other for supremacy. Iceland was saved from anarchy only by a union with Norway in 1263.

In 1380 Iceland came under Danish rule. The next four centuries were ones of extreme hardship: the Black Death and climatic deterioration in the 15th century led to population decline which was accelerated in the 17th and 18th centuries by a series of volcanic eruptions which devastated Icelandic agriculture. The imposition of a Danish trade monopoly stifled economic growth, while power was concentrated in Denmark: the Althing, which had long been powerless, was eventually abolished in 1800.

Recovery began in the early 19th century with the adoption of new farming and fishing methods and, influenced by the European revolutionary and Romantic movements, the Icelanders began to rediscover their sense of nationhood. The diplomacy of Jón Sigurdsson (1811–79) won the restoration of the Althing in 1848 and domestic home rule followed in 1874. Further concessions followed in 1904 and in 1918 Iceland became a sovereign state under the Danish crown.

Following the German invasion of Denmark in 1940, Iceland was occupied by British troops and the forced break with Denmark was made permanent when the Althing declared Iceland a republic in 1944. After the war Iceland became an uneasy member of NATO, although a large minority of Icelanders favoured neutrality. Development of the fishing industry has given the Icelanders one of the world's highest standards of living but the need to protect fish stocks led to disputes with

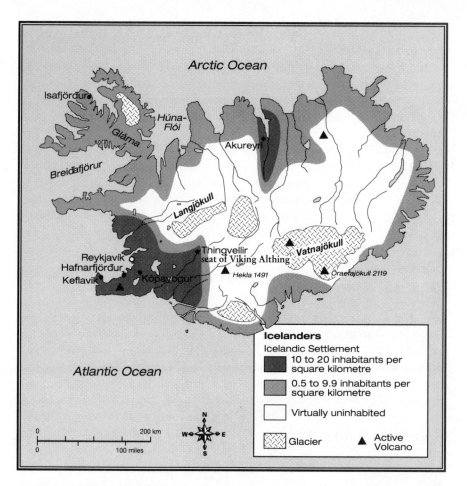

Britain over fishing limits (the so-called 'Cod Wars') in 1952, 1958, 1972 and 1975. Nevertheless, over-fishing threatens Iceland's prosperity and in 1990 Icelanders were forced to accept an 8% cut in their incomes.

LANGUAGE AND LITERATURE ■

Icelandic is descended from the West Norse dialect spoken in Norway in the Viking Age and it has changed little since: the language of the sagas is far closer to modern Icelandic than Shakespearean English is to modern English. The Icelandic language is central to the Icelandic identity and great efforts are made to protect it from 'outlandish' influences. A committee coins Icelandic words for new concepts or inventions, e.g. television becomes *sjornvarp* – 'view casting'. Parents are forbidden to give their children non-Icelandic first names. Related to this is the enforcement of the old Norse tradition of deriving surnames from the father's first name with a suffix

21

indicating the sex of the child, e.g. Jón Sigurdsson's son would have the surname Jónsson, his daughter Jónsdottir.

The Icelanders' pride in their past has always been evident in their remarkable literary tradition. Alone of the Germanic peoples, the medieval Icelanders kept extensive records of the myths and legends of their pagan past – the 'Eddic' poetry. The greatest of Icelandic literature, the terse family sagas, written in the strife-torn 13th century, are historical novels looking back to an Icelandic 'golden age' of the 11th century. The fatalism which pervades the sagas is still in evidence in the modern Icelandic character.

Under foreign rule, Icelandic literature declined but there was a strong revival in the 19th century. Writers like the poet Jónas Hallgrímsson (1807–45) sought inspiration in Iceland's landscape and history, seeking to reawaken the Icelanders' sense of nationhood. These themes have continued to dominate Icelandic literature in the 20th century, for example in the works of the country's most important novelist Halldor Laxness (1902–).

SOCIETY ■

Iceland has a virtually classless society and traditionally everyone, from the president downwards, is greeted on first-name terms. Extremes of wealth and poverty are not marked and Iceland has an advanced welfare state. Women enjoy high status and feminism is a live issue in Icelandic politics: in the 1991 parliamentary election the feminist Women's Alliance party won 5 of the Althing's 63 seats. Most Icelanders are nominally Lutherans but church attendance is low. Icelanders are becoming increasingly urbanized. By the 1980s over half the country's 251,000 people lived in the capital Reykjavik and rural depopulation was causing great concern.

FAEROESE

Though numbering only around 48,000, the Faeroese have a strong sense of national identity. The isolation of the Faeroe Islands – the nearest land is Shetland, 180 miles to the southeast – and the harshness of the environment, which has bred self-reliant communities, are the main causes. However, the unpopular political link with Denmark has also been a focus for the growth of nationalist sentiments.

HISTORY ■

The Faeroese are descended from emigrants from western Norway who settled the islands in the early 8th century. In the 11th century the islands were incorporated into the Kingdom of Norway but in 1380 they came under Danish rule following the union of the Danish and Norwegian crowns. Gradually power was centralized in Denmark and the traditional link with Norway was finally severed in 1814. The 19th

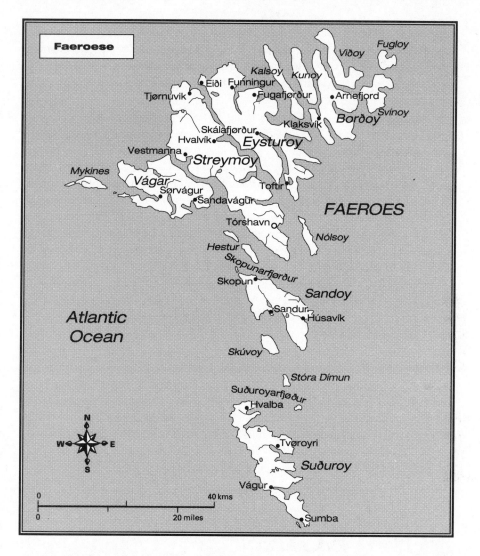

Faeroese

Fugloy
Viðoy
Kalsoy
Eiði Funningur Kunoy
Tjørnuvík •Fugafjørður •Arnefjord
Skálafjørður. Klaksvik Borðoy Svínoy
Hvalvík• Eysturoy
Vestmanna •
Mykines Streymoy
Vágar
Sørvágur Toftir
•Sandavágur
Tórshavn FAEROES
Nólsoy
Hestur
Skopunarfjørður
Skopun•
Sandoy
Atlantic Sandur
Ocean •Húsavík
Skúvoy
Stóra Dímun
Suðuroyarfjørður
•Hvalba
N
W E
S •Tvøroyri
Suðuroy
Vágur•
0 40 kms
0 20 miles Sumba

century saw the awakening of nationalism culminating in a campaign for home rule in the early 20th century. Following the German occupation of Denmark in 1940, the islands were occupied by the British. Under British protection, the Faeroese enjoyed *de facto* home rule and in 1946 the islands' *Løgting* (parliament) declared independence from Denmark. The Danish king dissolved the *Løgting* but in 1948 the Faeroes were granted home rule within the Danish realm. This concession appears to have satisfied the aspirations of most Faeroese but the main divisions in politics still stem from attitudes to the link with Denmark rather than social or economic factors.

Surprisingly, in view of the rich fishing grounds which surround them, the Faeroese have traditionally been a farming people. Though whaling has been practised since medieval times, commercial fishing was only developed in the late 19th century. In the post-war years the fisheries have brought prosperity and the Faeroese enjoy one of the world's highest standards of living. When Denmark joined the EC in 1972, the Faeroese opted to remain outside to protect their fishing grounds.

LANGUAGE ■

Faeroese is closely related to Icelandic and to the dialects of western Norway. In the 16th century, Danish was imposed as the language of administration and of the Lutheran church (to which the majority of Faeroese still belong). Faeroese ceased to be a literary language but a rich tradition of oral literature, in the form of ballads which are still recited at traditional chain dances, continued to flourish. Modern Faeroese nationalism owes much to the struggles of the 19th and 20th centuries to revive Faeroese as a literary language and to replace Danish as the language of government, education and the church. Danish, however, must still be learned by schoolchildren, a cause of some resentment as its usefulness as a second language is limited, and Danish still has equal status with Faeroese in government. Though Faeroese has now achieved international recognition as a literary language, the islands' best-known author, William Heinesen (1900–91), wrote in Danish because he believed it gave him imaginative freedom.

WHALING ■

While the economic importance of the *grindadráp* (pilot whale slaughter) has declined – and opposition from outside has increased – it remains a custom of great importance to the Faeroese. Spontaneous discipline and cooperation are needed to bring off a successful hunt and the whole community shares in the meat, whether or not they have taken part in the hunt. The Faeroese believe the *grindadráp* maintains the bonds of a society which is changing under the impact of high living standards.

NORWEGIANS

The modern state of Norway has been independent for under 90 years and for more than half their recorded history the Norwegians have lived under foreign domination. This, together with the often patronising attitude shown towards the Norwegians by their Swedish and Danish rulers, has bred an assertive patriotism. This manifests itself in the high-profile moral positions adopted by Norwegian governments, supported by public opinion, on issues such as Third World development and the environment. It is also evident, however, in an unwillingness to accept criticism from outsiders as, for example, when Norway faced condemnation by the USA and EC for announcing plans to recommence commercial whaling in 1993.

Social development in the 20th century has been along similar lines to the other Scandinavian countries and Norwegians now enjoy high living standards, an advanced welfare state and one of the world's highest life expectancies.

Though the Norwegian national identity is found only in Norway, the population of the state is not entirely homogenous: in the Arctic north there is a minority population of 20,000 Sami (also known as Lapps, see p. 305). Norwegians are conscious of the common heritage of language, history and culture which they share with the other Scandinavian peoples and relations with them are close and friendly.

THE LAND AND THE SEA ■

Unlike the Danes and the Swedes, who have given their names to their countries, the Norwegians are named after their country Norway – 'the way to the north', from the sea route north around the Norwegian coast. Norway is a mountainous land with a coastline indented with deep sheltered fjords. The mountains have always made overland travel difficult and this has promoted a greater degree of regional identity in Norway than is found in the other Scandinavian countries. The different regions have traditionally had different outlooks. The west coast regions around Trondheim and Bergen have looked west to the British Isles, Iceland and the Faeroes, and, with Bergen, south to Germany. Because of its wide overseas links, Bergen has always been, and remains, Norway's most cosmopolitan city. The main centre in the southeast, around the capital Oslo, has always looked more to Denmark, Sweden and the Baltic. There is still a certain amount of east-west rivalry.

Norway is a large country but its soils are poor and rocky and most of it is too high, wet, cold and windswept to support agriculture. By way of comparison, Denmark, with barely one-seventh the land area, has more than three times as much arable land. Norway has not been self-sufficient in food since the Middle Ages. The Norwegians have suffered hardship as a result on many occasions in their history and modern governments have maximized home food production through heavy subsidies to farmers. The lack of agricultural land made itself felt quickly at times of rapid population growth and was a major factor in two great westward exoduses of Norwegians from their homeland: the first in the 9th century to the British Isles, the Faeroes and Iceland, the second in the 19th century to the United States. Between 1835 and 1935, more than 850,000 Norwegians emigrated, a greater loss in proportion to its population than any other European country except Ireland.

While the mountains were a barrier to overland travel, Norway's sheltered coastal waters made travel by sea relatively safe and easy and it was always quicker to sail across a fjord than walk round it. This led to the development of the adventurous seafaring tradition and shipbuilding skills that in the Viking age allowed Norwegian sailors to cross the North Atlantic to Iceland, Greenland and even North America, and in the 19th century enabled Norway to build and man the world's third largest merchant fleet. The sea has also been an important source of wealth: fish have been

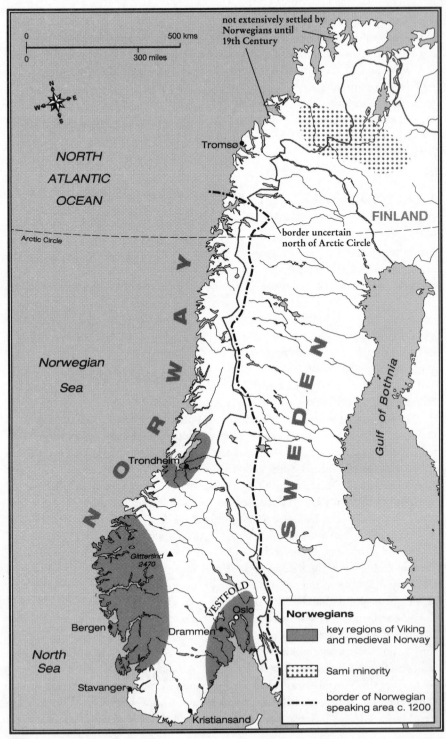

0 / 500 kms
0 / 300 miles

not extensively settled by
Norwegians until
19th Century

NORTH
ATLANTIC
OCEAN

Tromsø

FINLAND

Arctic Circle

border uncertain
north of Arctic Circle

Norwegian
Sea

Gulf of Bothnia

Trondheim

SWEDEN

Glittertind
2470

VESTFOLD

Bergen

Drammen

Oslo

North
Sea

Stavanger

Kristiansand

Norwegians

key regions of Viking
and medieval Norway

Sami minority

border of Norwegian
speaking area c. 1200

important since the Middle Ages; whaling was important in the 19th and early 20th centuries; and in the last 30 years the North Sea has provided oil and gas.

HISTORY ■

When the first Viking raids struck western Europe around 800, there was little to distinguish the Norwegians from their fellow Scandinavians. The English, for example, called all Vikings 'Danes' including those that they knew to come from Norway. Local identities were still strong and authority was exercised by a multitude of chieftains and petty kings. Norwegian Vikings settled in the Faeroes, Orkney and Shetland, Caithness and the Hebrides, Ireland and the Isle of Man in the early 9th century and by its end had also settled in northwest England and Iceland: their raids were even more wide-ranging.

These raids brought wealth into Norway and this was a catalyst for political change. Under its influence regional power centres emerged and sometime towards 900 Harald Fairhair, king of Vestfold (southwest of Oslo), succeeded in unifying a substantial part of Norway for the first time after defeating his rivals in a sea battle at Hafrsfjord near Stavanger. Harald's achievement was superficial and it was the 12th century before the Norwegian kingdom was securely unified. In the 10th century the first attempts were made to convert the Norwegians to Christianity but paganism was still strong and real progress was not made until the 11th century.

The medieval Norwegian kingdom reached its peak during the reign of Haakon IV (1217–63). The Norwegians dominated the North Atlantic: Greenland, Iceland, the Faeroes, Shetland, Orkney, Sutherland and Caithness, the Hebrides and the Isle of Man all came under Haakon's sway. Decline set in in the 14th century. Under a succession of weak kings the Norwegians first lost control of their trade to the German Hanseatic League and, in 1380, lost their independence in a dynastic union with Denmark. The Black Death, which arrived in 1349, also hit Norway hard, depopulating many districts. By the end of the 15th century, the Danes had bartered away Norway's last possessions in the British Isles.

In 1536, following a rebellion, Norway was reduced to the status of a Danish province and, at the same time, Lutheranism was imposed on an unenthusiastic population together with greatly increased use of Danish in church and government. Norway often suffered as a result of Danish involvement in European wars. It lost some of its eastern border territories to Sweden in the 17th century as a result of the Danish-Swedish wars, while the British naval blockade against Denmark, which had allied with France, brought food shortages during the Napoleonic Wars. In 1814, Norway declared its independence from Denmark, but Denmark had been forced to cede Norway to Sweden by the Treaty of Kiel and a Swedish invasion ensured that Norwegian independence was short-lived. The union with Sweden was primarily a dynastic one: Norway did not have independent diplomatic relations but it kept its constitution, parliament and government. The union was never popular and the growth of Norwegian national feeling led the Norwegian parliament to declare the union with Sweden dissolved in 1905, an act which was finally accepted by Sweden three months later. The Norwegians then invited a Danish prince to head a constitutional monarchy under the title Haakon VII. The Swedes did not believe that the Norwegians were capable of handling their own affairs and confidently expected Norway to beg for restoration of the union within a few years. They were disappointed.

Norway managed to remain neutral in World War I but was less fortunate in World War II. German forces invaded in April 1940 and conquered the country in a two-month campaign. However, the king and government escaped to Britain to lead a government in exile, while at home a daring and determined resistance developed. This resistance earned Norway the respect of the world and helped rid the country of the 'little brother' status which the Danes and Swedes had traditionally accorded it. After the war, Norway declined to join a proposed Nordic Defence Union and joined NATO in 1949.

After 1945, the Norwegian economy entered a period of rapid expansion fuelled by shipping, cheap hydro-electric power and, from the 1970s, North Sea oil and gas. For all but 10 years of this period Norway has been governed by centre-left coalitions under Labour Party leadership and has developed an advanced welfare state on similar lines to those of Denmark and Sweden. The fall in oil prices in the mid 1980s adversely affected Norway's economy and unemployment has been a persistent problem. This has greatly reduced support for the Labour Party but, except for 1989–90, it has remained in government, mainly because of the right's inability to form stable coalitions.

In the 1970s Norway negotiated entry to the EC but membership was narrowly rejected by the Norwegian people in a referendum in 1972. Norway's current economic difficulties have put membership back on the political agenda but fishermen and farmers remain fiercely opposed to the EC and the majority of Norwegians still remain sceptical about the benefits of joining.

LANGUAGE ∎

As in all Scandinavian countries, language has been an important factor in the development of the Norwegian national identity. Norwegian began to develop as a separate language in the Viking age from West Norse, a dialect of the original common Scandinavian language. The geography of the country promoted the development of many different regional dialects of Norwegian while the country's relative isolation ensured that the language long remained closer to its roots than Danish or Swedish. However, all three languages remain mutually intelligible.

Two forms of Norwegian are recognized, reflecting a cultural division which was created during the period of Danish rule. Following the Reformation, Danish was imposed on Norway as the language of church, government and education. Danish had little influence on the dialects of western Norway but in the southeast its influence was so strong that a hybrid Dano-Norwegian language developed. In the mid-19th century nationalist reformers sought a 'standard' Norwegian but there were so many dialects that the choice was bound to be controversial. One standard was an adaptation of Danish to the spoken Norwegian of the southeast, which became known as *Riksmål* ('official' Norwegian) or *Bokmål* ('book' Norwegian). The other contender was a new language based on a synthesis of the west coast dialects, which purists regarded as more truly Norwegian, known as *Landsmål* ('country' Norwegian) or *Nynorsk* (New Norwegian). The issue divided Norwegian society on roughly east-west lines. In 1885 both languages were given official status and it was agreed that schools would use whichever language was closest to the local dialect. Though it found favour with poets, *Nynorsk* remained a minority language and there are signs that it is now losing ground to *Bokmål*: though it must be taught as a second language, it is now the language of instruction in only 16% of Norwegian schools. Recent proposals to combine the two languages in a new standard Norwegian, *Samnorsk*, have not found favour.

DANES

Danes share a common cultural heritage with the other Scandinavian peoples yet their geographical position has led them into a much closer involvement with European affairs. Consequently Danish national identity tends to look two ways. Scandinavian sentiments are strong but Danes also regard themselves as the most Europeanized of the Scandinavian peoples. However, Danes also fear a loss of identity in any future European union and their attitude towards their membership of the European Community is distinctly ambiguous. It should not be concluded from this that Danes do not have a clear identity: they do, but might have difficulty defining it. Danes are proud of their country and, despite some social tensions, they continue to be a contented nation and regularly appear in surveys as the world's happiest people.

THE LAND ■

Denmark has the highest proportion of cultivable land in Scandinavia and, as a result, in the Middle Ages was the most populous and wealthy of the Scandinavian states. Unlike Norway and Sweden, there was still room for agricultural expansion even in the late 19th century; consequently relatively few Danes emigrated to North America in this period. The country's controlling position, between the Scandinavian peninsula and western Europe and between the North Sea and the Baltic, has enabled Danes to profit from trade since the Viking age and has fostered a seafaring tradition. It has also left them more open to outside influences than the other Scandinavian countries.

Denmark is low lying with few natural obstacles and has consequently proved

very difficult to defend against foreign invaders. This is particularly true of the short land frontier with Germany across the neck of the Jutland peninsula: though it was fortified as early as the 8th century, Franks, Slavs, Swedes and Germans have all breached it with ease. The sense of vulnerability this has bred has contributed greatly over the years to the Danish fear of loss of cultural and political identity.

HISTORY ■

The Danish identity is an ancient one and had already formed by the time Scandinavia emerged from its prehistoric period around AD 800. At this time the Danes occupied a territory which included the Jutland peninsula as far south as modern-day

Schleswig in Germany, the islands of the Danish archipelago and the provinces of Scania, Halland and Blekinge in present-day Sweden. In the 9th century, Danish Vikings raided western Europe and settled in eastern England and Normandy. Towards the year 1000, the Danes were unified into a single kingdom and began to adopt Christianity. Under Cnut (1018–35), the Danes conquered England and Norway but this empire collapsed on his death. In the Middle Ages a strong nobility and an independent church usually kept the monarchy weak while in the 14th century the German Hanseatic League gained control of Danish trade. By the end of this century, however, Danish power had reached its peak. Through a series of dynastic unions engineered by queen Margrethe I (1375–1412), Denmark gained control of Norway, with its dependencies of Orkney, Shetland, the Faeroes, Iceland and Greenland, in 1380 and in 1397, by the Union of Kalmar, Sweden and Finland came under Danish rule. Much of the force for this union came from a common Scandinavian unease at increasing German influence.

In 1536 the Reformation came to Denmark and the country adopted Lutheranism. Following a short war, Sweden had regained its independence in 1523 but under the charismatic Christian IV (1588–1648) the Danes set about re-establishing their dominance in the Baltic. The attempt was a disastrous failure and by 1660 Scania, Halland and Blekinge were lost to Sweden. The Swedes made great efforts to persuade the Danish population of the conquered provinces to adopt a Swedish identity and had been completely successful by the early 18th century. Denmark's stature was further reduced as a consequence of the Napoleonic Wars. British attacks on the Danish fleet in 1801 and 1807 forced Denmark into a reluctant alliance with France. In 1814 this cost Denmark control of Norway, which was ceded to Sweden by the Treaty of Kiel.

The late 18th century saw the beginnings of reform in Denmark. In 1788 serfdom was abolished and the growth of liberal sentiment in the early 19th century led to the abolition of the absolute monarchy in 1848 and the introduction of parliamentary government. The same period also saw the growth of nationalism which poisoned the dispute over the future of the duchies of Schleswig and Holstein. The duchies, which had a mixed German and Danish population, were united to Denmark through the king, who ruled them as duke. Nationalists urged their full incorporation into Denmark but this alarmed the German population who wanted closer ties with the German Confederation. Danish intransigence led to a crushing defeat by Prussia and Austria in 1864 and the loss of the duchies: Danes concluded that their country was undefendable and have since given defence expenditure low priority. One casualty of the war was Scandinavianism. This had grown up alongside nationalism in the early 19th century but Sweden's failure to support Denmark in the war led to the decline of the movement.

Denmark was neutral in World War I but following Germany's defeat a plebiscite returned predominantly Danish North Schleswig to Denmark, so establishing the present-day border with Germany. Around 50,000 Danish speakers still live in German south Schleswig, while a smaller German speaking minority survives in southern Denmark. The inter-war period was marked by the rise of the Social Democratic party which also initiated the development of Denmark's advanced welfare state.

Danish neutrality in World War II was violated when Germany occupied the country in 1940 to secure its communications for the invasion of Norway. Denmark offered no resistance and was allowed to remain nominally independent as a German protectorate until 1943, when growing grass-roots civil disobedience and acts of sabotage led the Germans to impose direct rule. The resistance's greatest achievement was to smuggle all but 500 of Denmark's 7,000 Jews to safety in Sweden.

After the war, Denmark tried to provide for national security through a Nordic Defence Alliance but negotiations broke down and in 1949 Denmark joined NATO. Until the end of the Cold War took the sting out of the issue, this was a cause of controversy in Danish politics as a large minority of Danes favoured neutrality. A more successful Danish-led Scandinavian initiative was the setting up, in 1952, of the Nordic Council to promote political co-operation between the Scandinavian countries. While also seeking closer ties with the rest of Scandinavia, Denmark's dependence on the British and German markets led to membership of the EC in 1972. However, fears about the loss of traditional ties with other Scandinavian countries and of loss of identity in a European super-state have made the Danes uneasy Europeans, as was made clear in the narrow votes in plebiscites both against the Maastricht Treaty in June 1992 and in favour of it in May 1993.

Denmark has made great economic progress in the 20th century, developing from an agricultural economy in 1900 to become by the 1960s a prosperous developed economy in which light manufacturing and service industries played a dominant role. Despite a considerable debt problem, the Danish economy has performed consistently better than the EC average since the 1980s and currently the Danes enjoy the highest living standards in the EC.

LANGUAGE ■

Danish is descended from a common Scandinavian language, known in the Viking age as the 'Danish tongue' ('*dönsk tunga*'). By the 9th century this had already begun to split into two dialects: West Norse, from which Norwegian, Icelandic and Faeroese developed, and East Norse, from which Danish and Swedish began to develop about 1100. Danes still find it easy to understand both Swedish and Norwegian. From the 13th to the 18th century, Danish was subject to strong German cultural influences and many thousands of German loan words were taken into the language. German even became the language of the court and the army. German was abandoned by the court after the Napoleonic Wars and Danish was actively promoted to help restore the nation's self-respect. This, however, served to alienate the non-Danish speaking populations of Denmark's remaining dependencies, Iceland, the Faeroes and Schleswig-Holstein, leading to the growth of anti-Danish nationalism and independence movements.

In the 20th century it is English that has exerted the strongest influence on Danish and some purists have become concerned that this threatens the integrity of the language. Others consider the fears exaggerated and point out that the influence of English is, as yet, small compared with that of German. The Danes have always been a culturally homogeneous people and with the advent of modern communications the regional dialects are declining, though noticeable regional accents persist.

SOCIETY ■

With its high living standards, classlessness, sexual equality and excellent state provisions for education, health and welfare and corresponding high tax rates, Danish society may superficially resemble Swedish society. However, the Danes are more tolerant of individualism and the high standard of social welfare has been achieved without the intrusions into private life which are a feature of some aspects of the Swedish system. Nevertheless there is a distinct levelling tendency in Danish society which has been satirized as the 'Jante Law' (*Jantelov*), after a fictional village in a novel by Axel Sandemose. In Jante people don't like to draw attention to themselves and don't like it when others rock the boat or get too ambitious: Danes tend to conform.

The Danish social conscience has its origins in the early 19th century when the Danes were coming to terms with defeat in the Napoleonic Wars. Of great significance were the works of the educationalist, theologian and antiquarian, N.F.S. Grundtvig (1783–1872). Grundtvig wanted to see Denmark become a country where 'few have too much but fewer too little'. He attacked the élitism of the education system and inspired the Folk High School movement – voluntary schools which brought an idealistic and patriotic education to country people. This greatly aided the spread of the cooperative movement later in the century which considerably increased the prosperity of the countryside. Though the right of the needy to receive help was written into the 1849 constitution, progress was piecemeal until the Social Reform acts of 1933 introduced comprehensive welfare benefits. A guiding principle of Danish social legislation since then has been that benefits should be sufficient to maintain the dignity of those being cared for and not simply provide for the bare necessities of life. By the 1970s the cost of maintaining the welfare state had become extremely burdensome on the taxpayer but predictions that this would bring an end to the consensus that had supported the social reforms have so far not been fulfilled. Even the centre-right coalition that held power from 1982 to 1993 did not fundamentally depart from the progressive social policies of the 20th century.

The Danes have a not altogether deserved reputation for tolerance: immigration from the Third World has sparked some racial tensions and the right wing anti-tax Progress Party adopted a 'send them back' policy in the early 1980s, with some electoral success. Support for the Progress Party is now in decline, but the problem of integrating a diverse immigrant population remains.

ENGLISH AND LOWLAND SCOTS

English and Scots identity feed off each other. Scots can take as much pleasure in a Scottish victory at Wembley as in a British victory in battle at Waterloo. In crucial ways the most conspicuous cultural division in British history has not been between the English and Scots but between the English and Lowland Scots on the one hand and their Celtic neighbours on the other. The peoples considered together here share a common origin, a common historic experience and elements of a common system of values. Yet the Lowland Scots have wavered between their English brothers and their Highland Scottish cousins. An increasing sense of Scottish solidarity has stimulated a nationalist movement.

HISTORY ■

The common experiences shared by the English and Lowland Scots were political and cultural. The idea that there was a sudden and total replacement of one population by another after the departure of the Romans is unacceptable. The English are not a 'race' formed of Germanic stock, but a people including large numbers of Celts whom Germanic settlers had absorbed into their cultural patterns and drawn into allegiance to their political order. The same is true of the Lowland Scots, though the proportions of Celts in that amalgam may well have been greater.

By the second quarter of the 3rd century AD, the Roman hold on the island of Great Britain had been consolidated south of Hadrian's wall. Above the Scottish lowlands, roughly beyond the line of the River Tay, they did not penetrate at all. The properly 'British' tribes could be defined as those subject to extensive Romanization by about the mid-4th century AD. Their unity, however, was not strong enough to survive Roman withdrawal.

Roman departure from AD 407 on left room for successor-invaders, who had earlier begun to arrive as mercenaries in Roman service. These Germanic newcomers came to be classified as 'Angles', 'Saxons' and 'Jutes'. In the main, the Angles settled in parts of the east of southern Britain, especially in East Anglia; the Jutes in Kent; and the Saxons in what have become the more westerly parts of England. This area, of course, was not one state: amid great instability, early kingdoms included those centred in Kent, East Anglia, Sussex and its westerly neighbour Wessex, the central kingdom of Mercia, and the great realm of Northumbria.

Gradually or fitfully, powerful princes established order in this chaos. Growing political stability – as Northumbria and then Wessex replaced Kent as the leading

English

The Danelaw of England in the 10th Century

Danelaw

kingdom – was not undisturbed. Substantial Danish and Norwegian invasions were launched in the late 9th century: Mercia was almost entirely destroyed and Northumbria damaged. The burden of defending the English fell on the kings of Wessex and in particular on Alfred the Great (877–91). By the Treaty of Wedmore he brought Christianity and political compromise to the Danish leadership, setting up the Danelaw – that is, those areas which Danes were given to settle in and generally to mould. The kingdom of Wessex came close to being an overall English monarchy under Edgar (957–975).

Late Anglo-Saxon England was an imperfect nation state. The Normans who conquered England in 1066 as a small military élite, welded it into an effective political and even economic unit. William the Conqueror (1066–87) turned the country into what was then the largest virtually free-trade zone in Europe. The élite was Normanized and this consistent, close-knit and mutually-supporting political class made England one of the most cohesive states in medieval Europe. From this unified base, for the rest of the Middle Ages and the early modern period, William's successors were able to maintain – and at times intensify – their pressure on the peripheral parts of the island.

Scotland in its formative period can be divided into four areas: the highlands north of the Tay; the Kingdom of Dalriada, in what became Argyllshire and the islands of the southwest; the Strathclyde area, inhabited by Celtic tribes thrust back by Germanic or English invasions; and the southeast, known as Bernicia, which had slipped in and out of Northumbria's sphere. By 855, the king generally acknowledged as the first of Scotland, Kenneth I, had established a looser unity than his English counterparts. His successors recognized English overlords.

Unlike Wales and Cornwall, Scotland found an effective means of resistance through its own growing political unity and the slowly, uncertainly increasing willingness of its kings' subjects to combine in common cause against English pretensions: this was, perhaps, a cause, rather than a result of Scottish 'national' feeling. Indeed – from the perspective of later Scottish nationalism – it is curious to note that there was no convincing basis of Scottish political unity: the ethnic mixture was at least as complex as – and less favourably distributed than – that of England; political traditions and forms of social organization varied widely in different parts of the country; the population was more dispersed. Above all, the political consensus achieved by the Norman conquerors of England had never yet existed in Scotland. If the Scots had an overall consistent character, it was as a group of resisters – people who were at the end of the line and knew it.

This culture of resistance became focused against England thanks in part to the heavy-handed efforts of Edward I of England (1272–1307) to assert his rights as overlord. He twice inflicted military defeats on the Scots, with a stimulating rather than a deterrent effect. In the words of the Scottish national song, 'Caledonia stern and wild' was willing to fight to maintain practical independence. Symbols of future Scottish nationalism date from this period: the blood of William Wallace, hanged in London; the Stone of Scone, coronation-seat of Scottish kings, stolen by Edward and secreted beneath his throne in Westminster; the Arbroath Declaration, in which the lords who repudiated Edward's claims declared themselves Scots with a right to a state of their own. In 1314 followed the greatest event – in Scottish assessment – of Scottish history: the Battle of Bannockburn, where a very large English army was scattered by a small Scottish one. The cultural continuities which embraced lowland Scotland and northern England survived; but in the long period of self-assertive Scots independence which now followed, these tended to diminish or become fossilized; in particular, the language of the Lowland Scots remained outside the process of fusion of English dialects which characterized the late Middle Ages. 'Low Scots' today is recognizably close to English, but is clearly a different form of the language from that which became generalized in England. Recently, there has been a revival of interest in this distinct Scots tongue.

From as early as 1295, Scotland began to look to France for support, and a relationship known as the 'Auld Alliance' developed, which was reflected in French cultural influence, especially in architecture. The era inaugurated at Bannockburn lasted until the Protestant reformation re-made Scottish politics in a direction inevitably looking towards England.

Just as wars against England were a forge of Scottish identity, so English national sentiment was stimulated by wars in France. English began to replace Norman French as a learned and literary tongue in the 1360s; in the law, French was dropped in 1366 except as a language of record. Henry V (1413–22) was probably the first English king habitually to prefer English over French as a language for writing in. The failure of continental ambitions turned English eyes back to their home islands.

The 16th century was a period of political consolidation and religious reformation in both England and Scotland. The foundation of national churches enhanced national feeling. England's reformation was imposed from the throne and continued many features of pre-Reformation doctrine and organization; in Scotland the pace was forced by popular preachers, inspired by the relatively radical reformation of Jean Calvin in Geneva. In both countries, however, the long-term trend was towards the growth of Calvinist influence; and in both the effect of the Reformation was to enrich the élite at the expense of the church: this renewed a measure of common cross-border interest.

SCOTTISH AND ENGLISH UNION ■

In 1603, James VI of Scotland ascended the throne of England as James I. The expression 'King of Great Britain' then became current. Scotland resisted the efforts of his son, Charles I (1629–42) to draw the kingdoms closer together institutionally, but Scots involvement in the English Civil War of 1642–53 proved fatal to Scottish independence. Oliver Cromwell effectively conquered Scotland in the last stages of the war. After that, Scottish independence was only nominal.

The Lowland Scots felt more in common with their English than their highland neighbours; opportunities for commerce and imperial expansion in an enlarged state attracted them. In 1707, the Scottish parliament, dominated by lowland interests, dissolved itself in favour of a union with England. Scotland was recompensed with a disproportionate tally of representatives in the English parliament and in the peerage of the United Kingdom; the integrity of the Scottish legal system and traditions was guaranteed; and the Church of Scotland continued to occupy a privileged position in Scotland, analogous to that of the Church of England in England. The 18th century also saw a cultural renaissance in Scotland. Arts, science and philosophy all prospered.

The English and Lowland Scots seemed to have recovered their common identity as the people of England and of 'North Britain' joined in imposing an emergent

'British' identity on the rest of the British Isles. Lowland Scots only renewed intense, romantic and nationalistic Scots sentiment when their own highlanders were safely repressed (see p. 43). Even after that, the development of the British empire in the 19th century brought English and Scots together in a common imperial venture. It is only, perhaps, as Britain has lost its world role in the late 20th century, and been forced to look inwards on itself, that Scots sentiment has re-emerged most strongly.

POLITICAL CULTURE ■

The peculiar political culture associated with England is perhaps the feature for which the English people are known best world-wide. The British parliament is called 'the mother of parliaments' and, although not the oldest representative legislature in the world, it has perhaps been the most influential as a model. Long and complex though the formation of this political culture was, it was shorter and simpler than that of the British state. The ethos of the English approach to government was associated in the 17th and 19th centuries with institutions, prominently including parliament, which have attained a mythical status in English people's common version of their past and to which a long history, inevitably unfolding, was assigned.

Before the Norman conquest the general appearance of discussion and consensus was part of the political process, though by no means to the extent claimed by celebrators of 'Anglo-Saxon freedom'. After the conquest, government was, more than formerly, directed or dictated from the throne or by royal representatives, and was not so inclined to defer to local customs and sources of authority.

Parliament itself was a royal creation. Its development involved constraints on the crown, but its origins, in the 13th century, were rooted in compromises between kings and aristocratic wielders of local power; even at that early time, towns were contributing a collective voice. Magna Carta itself, the 'Great Charter' of English liberties of 1215, traditionally regarded as the epitome of English political culture, has been derided by many modern commentators, but it did more than merely secure certain narrow interests of the aristocracy, as has been alleged. It defined which subjects had the right to advise the king, and pronounced against arbitrary arrest and summary justice. These guarantees were applicable at all levels of society.

The natural inclination of members of parliament to extend their participation in government developed at times of weak kingship, failure in war and high fiscal demands. Thus the civil wars of the 15th century were a stimulus to parliamentary cohesion and self-consciousness, whereas royal initiative was re-asserted in the peaceful and prosperous conditions which prevailed for long periods in the 16th. At the same time, the need for new laws accelerated: indeed, the main function of government gradually changed from the dispensation of justice to the making of statutes. The reign of Henry VIII was a vital stage in this process, because the English Reformation demanded a vast array of new laws, commanding assent as widely spread as possible.

James I (1603–25) was influenced by continental ideas, stressing the divine inspiration of monarchy; his son, Charles I (1625–42), tended to stress 'Caesar's due' and the subject's duty rather than relying on practical workaday intelligence in teasing and coaxing obedience from his subjects. The long-term consequences of the violent confrontation with parliament which ended his reign included a transition in three stages from a situation in which the crown always had the last word, to one in which the crown sometimes had the last word, to one in which the crown never had the last word.

By the end of the 17th century England was, by some standards of measurement, the richest country in Europe; since, at the end of the day, political power can be bought, this implied a growing political class. By the reign of Queen Anne (1702–14) an active political culture was in place, involving large numbers of educated and modestly propertied men. The beginnings of two parties emerged, which represented tendencies in some ways continuous to this day. In most towns of more than 5,000 people there were usually two newspapers, one 'Whig' and one 'Tory', reflecting the respective party lines.

The beginnings of a constitutional party system enabled England to make an astonishing transformation in the 18th century to a land where political conflict was – on the whole – peacefully resolved; the English could develop their notorious habit of congratulating themselves on the tranquillity of their political evolution towards constitutional and ultimately democratic government, compared with the turbulent histories which took their continental neighbours in the same direction. Until well into the 19th century the stability of the English system did, however, teeter under threat: from dynastic rivalries and the influence of the French Revolution; but it emerged intact and the English with hindsight were able to assign to themselves a unique reputation.

Underlying English political culture is the notion of the rule of law. By the end of the 17th century, this was systematically backed by the power of the state both in England and – by way of different legal and constitutional traditions – in Scotland. England's distinct tradition of 'common law' is rooted in a system of case-precedence – unlike the systems derived from Roman models in Scotland and, ultimately, over most of continental Europe. At the same time inconvenient common-law traditions can be unblocked by act of parliament or by the freedom of judicial innovation conceded in the system to England's highest court of appeal, the House of Lords. The very wide use of juries in criminal cases is a consequence of the evolution of the system which has helped to maximise the liberties of the subject. The effects of the supremacy of law in restraining or preventing tyranny are enhanced by the independence of the judiciary, embodied in terms agreed between crown and parliament after the violent conflicts of the 17th century, and strengthened by stages ever since.

RELIGION ■

In the Middle Ages English Catholicism commanded a high level of respect in Rome. England seemed remarkably resistant to the heresies which sprang up all too frequently on the continent. This reputation was compromised in the very late 14th and 15th centuries by Lollardy – a sort of early Protestantism which began among graduates of Oxford University and which gained a significant following across a wide social spectrum. In the same period the church in England acquired an increasingly national character, reflected in the monopolization of appointments by Englishmen. The reformation in England was not a response to popular demand but a device of the crown to increase its power and of the secular élite to despoil the church. But an English church under the patronage and control of monarch and aristocracy, such as was created between 1533 and 1559, was vulnerable to Protestant doctrines. At first open to Calvinist influences, it was only gradually that the Church of England developed a faith broadly compatible with Catholic tradition. The established church in Scotland, meanwhile, became fixed in a more radical tradition, combining Calvinist theology with a presbyterian system of organization.

This long period of doctrinal uncertainty left two legacies: the Church of England was left wavering between Catholic and Protestant identities, with numerous clergy belonging to each tradition; and many Protestants, despairing of the established church, formed sects of their own. England became a land of many competing churches and chapels, often grouped together around a single square or village green. The pretence that English identity depended on conformity to the official line was often voiced by the clergy and was reflected in civil disabilities inflicted on Roman Catholics and to a lesser degree on Protestant dissenters; but it gradually withered in a society made tolerant by *de facto* religious pluralism.

A further great change occurred in the 1730s and '40s. A Fellow of Lincoln College, Oxford, John Wesley, formed a holy 'club' in the conviction that the official church had grown too far from the people. 'Wesleyanism' became a mass movement with an enormous working-class communion as well as a regional appeal on the western and northern fringes of England and in Wales. In 1843 in Scotland, the majority of ministers seceded on the grounds that they should be chosen by the people, not by patrons. In both kingdoms, the distinction between church folk and chapel folk was henceforth in part a matter of social class. Catholicism, meanwhile, had the virtue of transcending class barriers. Large Catholic urban populations were created by Irish immigration; today, in English towns Catholics number about one in ten of the entire population, in Scotland one in five. This working-class Catholicism was supplemented by converts from the middle and upper classes, who normally worshipped in the same congregations.

ENGLISH SECULAR CULTURE ◼

The secular culture of the English has rarely been thought worthy of study and has been treated as a matter of tea and antipathy, cricket and class-consciousness, clubbability and frosty reserve, restrained gestures and conversation about weather. Most people's secular culture is rooted in their religion and the English are no exception; King James's Bible of 1604, the Prayer Book of the Church of England (essentially complete by 1552) and *Pilgrim's Progress*, John Bunyan's popular handbook of Protestant devotion, were, until the coming of universal education in 1870, the basis of popular literacy. The vivid language of these works characterized the secular literature of their times: Shakespeare's plays, in particular, exercised an almost equal influence on subsequent tradition. Diffused around the world by British imperialism in the 19th century, English language and literature have enhanced British prestige in the eyes of fellow-Europeans and bolstered English self-esteem.

Two secular cults are distinctively English: those of team sports and the countryside. Though sports like football and cricket are presumed to have had popular origins, their modern forms are the gifts to society of a benevolent upper class. Rugby football bears the name of the great school where it was invented; Association football was codified at Charterhouse. Cricket, as well as a school game, was a country house activity mobilizing tenants, servants and masters in shared values of sportsmanship. English self-characterization would be unthinkable without these games: the cults of the gifted amateur, of pluck in adversity, of fair play, of the improvisatory 'spirit of Dunkirk', of battles won 'on the playing fields of Eton' – all these spring from a mentality in which team games are metaphors for life.

A love of the countryside infuses English art and dominates the English way of life. Its most obvious manifestations are a preference for country living over urban living, suburbs over city-centres and small houses with gardens over the convenience of flats. English towns (though not Scottish ones) blend into the countryside, without abrupt outlines.

THE NORTHERN ENGLISH ■

The limit of the Danelaw has remained something of a cultural dividing line in English perceptions between northerners and southerners; while quickly adopting the English language, the Danes contributed some terms to the common tongue and more to northeastern dialects.

Apart from the Scottish border and, perhaps, the limit of the Danelaw, the lines which divide English communities and mark off local or regional identities are very indistinct. Historians in recent times have made much of historic county communities and at some levels county loyalties are important: in once strong but now vanishing ties to county regiments; in cricket fixtures; in county associations formerly maintained by metropolitan exiles. Rarely, however, does county feeling approach the kind of provincialism common in continental Europe: the only possible exception is that of Yorkshire, a uniquely large county, where gentlemen are said to be unwilling to sell property to outsiders and where, until recently, only sons of the county were admitted to the cricket team. Some towns or urban areas enclose strong civic identities, particularly in the north of England: in Manchester, Birmingham or Liverpool, for instance, these have arisen in response to rapid growth and industrialization, and in the course of rivalry to be England's second city. Tyneside is too small to be a region by European standards but is the home of fierce local chauvinism

41

and a lovingly preserved dialect which many other Englishmen claim to find unintelligible.

In addition to these nuances, the English sometimes talk about a 'North-South Divide' – a legacy of England's precocious industrial revolution, which introduced a broad difference of character between an industrialized and a de-industrialized England, north and south of the drainage area of the Thames. The perception clings, and is strongly felt. All in all, the English are, for their size, among the most consistent of European peoples.

CHANNEL ISLANDERS ■

The Channel Islands are the last part of the Norman inheritance of the English crown. During celebrations of the Jubilee of Queen Elizabeth II of the United Kingdom, notices in Guernsey and Jersey shops said, 'Good Health to the Duchess of Normandy'. These people regard themselves rightly as a distinct community among British peoples. Many are of purely French ancestry but their loyalty to the English crown and, in effect, to the British state, has been sustained for over 900 years. They have special forms of government, some of which have still-discernible feudal origins, especially in the small islands of Alderney and Sark. They enjoy a favourable fiscal regime and special, protected markets in the United Kingdom. Their history of prosperity and of urban life is a long one. It is a remarkable fact that in the 19th century, the main towns of Guernsey and Jersey were much bigger than any of those in the maritime counties opposite them on the English shore. In Jersey, a fifth of the population lived in St Peter Port.

Freedom to evade the statutes of the mainland parliament has encouraged the islanders in their cultural preferences. Their culture today is marked by hostility to 'permissive' values prevalent elsewhere and loyalty to private enterprise. In these respects they can claim to have anticipated the 're-modernization' of Britain in the 1980s and 1990s.

HIGHLAND AND ISLAND SCOTS

Conquered and subjected by their Lowland and English neighbours, the Highland and Island Scots have achieved a remarkable cultural counter-conquest supplying modern Scottish identity with its imagery, myths and rituals and contributing to the making of a Scottish nationalism which now unites Scots on both sides of the Highland Line.

HISTORY ■

North of the River Tay, where Roman influence never penetrated, lived Celtic tribes culturally indistinguishable from their southern neighbours until the Romanization of the south left them frozen in their pre-Roman condition. This area, labelled by Roman geographers as 'Pictish' in population, stretched from the north of the great British island to the central valleys of the Tay region. The 'Highland Line' has thus been recognized as a cultural division from antiquity.

In the Middle Ages, it was a line barely crossed by the English-style culture of the Scottish Lowlands. North of the Highland line, speech remained Celtic and society tribal: one's place was determined by kinship with members of a clan rather than by wealth or prowess. In the late Middle Ages, Highlanders and Lowlanders made common cause against England, but the failure of the Scottish Reformation to attract Highlanders' devotion reinforced the cultural divisions. The growing assertiveness of the state centred in the Lowlands was resented in the Highlands as a threat to traditional religion, fiscal practices and methods of landholding. By the late 17th century the pattern was of Highland resistance to Anglo-Lowland aggression.

After the trauma of the uprising of 1745, when a Highlander army almost conquered the rest of Great Britain, the anxious victors inflicted destruction on clans, exile on chiefs, massacres or expropriation on landowners. The 'Highland Clearances' represented the attempted destruction of a whole people by an English and Lowland establishment understandably fearful of a culture of rebelliousness in a society organized for war. The Gaelic tongue was a casualty of the destruction, though it survives as a language of traditional poetry in the Highlands and in small communities, almost all in the Western Isles, as a language of daily use. In parts of Lowland Scotland, however, there has been a revival of interest in Gaelic as a second language, with Gaelic-language television attracting substantial funding and audiences.

SCOTTISH NATIONALISM ■

Today, relative to their neighbours, the Highland and Island Scots have dwindled to small numbers. Even in 1800, almost half the population of Scotland lived north of the Highland Line; by 1914, the proportion was just 9%. The people's identity is also much weakened, partly absorbed in Scottish sentiment which unites Scots in self-differentiation from the English. In the period before the '45, when clan life distinguished the society of the Highlands and islands, the difference between Highlanders and Lowlanders was at least as great as that, say, between French- and German-speaking Swiss. Afterwards, the Highlands were saturated with vast amounts of sustained Presbyterian propaganda. The leaders of society were permanently exiled, or else incorporated into an imperial master-class by university education and enrolment in the service of the state, often in the armed forces or in the government of the growing British empire.

A paradoxical effect of the conquest of the Highlands was a counter-conquest of the Lowlands by Highland culture or, at least, by some of its superficial symbols.

43

Lowland, Highland and Island Scots

MACKAY Major Clan of Scotland

With the Highlanders safely out of the way, Lowlanders could afford the luxury of Scottish sentiment and even, in the long term, of Scottish nationalism, expressed in the imagery of highland tradition, as expounded in the novels of Sir Walter Scott (1771–1832). The equipment includes claymores, kilts, sporrans, bagpipes, bonnets and distinctive tartans invented to perpetuate the sense of lineage of descendants of the old clans. The rituals include highland dancing, 'Caledonian' expatriate re-unions, toasts in malt whisky and the eating of such traditional highland foods as oats and haggis (sheeps' stomachs stuffed with other offal).

Though Highland culture has provided the obvious symbols of modern Scottish nationalism, its hard core is the solid, shrewd, tough wisdom of the Presbyterian kirk. There may be moments, in the depth of the evening, after drams of whisky, when

MacLeod or MacDougall reverts to his Celtic self – sentimental and ebullient – but most of the time he will be indistinguishable from his Lowland colleague, Smith or Brown. The Scots today are indeed a united nation: very few peoples have such a distinct set of uniform notions of themselves. Thrust south to the 'Sassenach' (English) border by Sir Walter Scott and his successors, the Highland Line has become a fiction.

DUTCH

The modern state of the Netherlands has existed within its present boundaries since 1839. However, the country traces its independence as a state back to the revolt against Spanish rule in the second half of the 16th century, which forged an international political identity for the grouping of seven provinces known as the Republic of the United Provinces. Although the United Provinces remained, internally, a federal grouping of fiercely particularist provinces until the dissolution of the Republic in 1795, there can be no doubt that in the two centuries following the break with Spanish rule these provinces forged a cultural, political and economic identity, based on Dutch as the common language, which is at the foundation of the modern state.

GEOGRAPHY ■

As the name implies, the Netherlands occupy a low-lying area on the North Sea around the delta of three major rivers: the Rhine, Maas, and Scheldt. Some 50% of the total land area of 16,040 square miles lies below sea level, protected by dunes and man-made coastal defences and criss-crossed by waterways. Beyond these extremely low-lying, largely clay regions in the west, there are the sandy soils of the east and a pocket of limestone in the far south.

The struggle to survive and make a living in these geographical conditions has, quite literally, shaped the Netherlands. From earliest times settlers threw up artificial barriers, dykes, against the sea and mounds or *terps* to which they could retreat with their beasts and possessions in times of flood. Later, from around AD 1000, quite extensive programmes of drainage and land reclamation were undertaken in the west of the country and dykes were thrown up to protect reclaimed land.

In the 20th century, the latest and largest land reclamation project was undertaken with the closing off of the Zuider Zee, a large sea arm extending into the heart of the county from the north. Once this sea arm had been turned into a lake, the Ijsselmeer, substantial areas of it were drained and reclaimed to provide agricultural land. In recent years, these Ijsselmeer polders have also been used to provide housing and recreation for the people of the heavily-populated western area of the country.

As well as reclaiming land, it has been necessary throughout the centuries for the Dutch to protect it from the sea. The dykes which permitted reclamation work were, in the first instance, intended for this purpose. Advances in technology over the centuries led to improvement in the quality of the coastal defences, but it was not until this century that the technical means were available for major projects of water management like the Delta works, a large-scale project to shorten the coastline around the islands of Zeeland and South Holland. This ambitious plan was undertaken following the serious floods of 1953.

HISTORY ■

In the Middle Ages, the territories of the modern Netherlands were occupied by a variety of small semi-independent states. In the 15th and 16th centuries these were gradually consolidated into a single territorial unit with states to the south, in what are roughly modern Belgium and Luxembourg, under the control of the dukes of

Burgundy. In the second half of the 16th century, these territories passed into the control of the King of Spain, Philip II. Philip's rule provoked increasing opposition because of his centralizing policies and his opposition to Protestantism, which had gained a foothold in various parts of the Netherlands. A revolt broke out in the 1560s, which came under the leadership of a senior nobleman, William of Orange, and by 1609 it was clear that seven provinces in the north, covering most of the territory of the modern Netherlands, had established their independence. From 1648 this independence was recognized by international treaty.

In this long war of independence, the population of the Netherlands was shaken and re-distributed by large numbers of refugees on both sides. Although Calvinists never became a majority, they did become concentrated in the United Provinces, and – like all determined minorities in civil wars – rose to positions of political leadership and cultural influence. The economic context of the northern Netherlands, where the rural hinterland was poor and the aristocracy relatively feeble, while commerce was vital and towns were rich, suited the ascent of civic élites in which Calvinists happened to be well represented. As a result of the war, economic initiatives shifted north with the migrants; Amsterdam replaced Antwerp as the great commercial centre: Holland, indeed, established something like hegemony over most of the other provinces and foreigners came loosely to call the whole state 'Holland' and all its people 'Hollanders'. A relatively small but tightly knit élite – predominantly Calvinist and almost exclusively mercantile – stamped the dominant culture with its values, including godliness, cleanliness and austere moral attitudes. The civic virtues which became part of the Dutch stereotype – religious toleration, civil liberties, press freedom – were unshakeably in place by the early 18th century.

The seven provinces formed themselves into a loose federation with a republican form of government, but for long periods with a descendent of Prince William of Orange functioning as military leader with an influence on policy. In the late 16th and 17th centuries, the newly independent republic experienced a period of tremendous wealth and economic expansion, based on trade, industry and, to a lesser extent, agriculture. It built up a colonial empire in the East Indies and in South America and the Caribbean. The 18th century saw a long period of decline and the republic was in no position to resist the invasion by the forces of revolutionary France, which swept it away in 1795. the Netherlands remained under French control until 1813.

In that year, the son and heir of the Prince of Orange, who had fled into exile in 1795, returned to the country. In 1814, a new unitary constitution was established and the following year William of Orange was made first king of the Netherlands, Belgium and Luxembourg. Belgium broke away in 1830, a situation formally recognized by international treaty in 1839.

The constitution of 1815 gave the king very wide powers but did not establish parliamentary democracy. In 1848 a constitutional revision reduced the powers of the monarch substantially; it increased the size of the electorate and laid the foundations for a modern democracy based on universal suffrage and ministerial responsibility, a process finally completed in 1917. The present head of state is a descendent of the House of Orange: her role is largely titular. By 1917, the Netherlands was beginning to develop a party system. In that year a system of almost pure proportional representation was adopted and is still employed. This system has consistently produced coalition governments since its introduction.

The Netherlands remained neutral during World War I but was less fortunate in World War II. On 19th May 1940 the country was invaded by German troops. The queen and her ministers fled to London and the country remained under German occupation until 5th May 1945. The war caused substantial material damage and loss of life, especially amongst the Dutch Jewish community.

Since the war, the Netherlands has pursued a policy of economic, military and political alliance-building, with the aim of protecting itself against any repetition of the disaster of 1940. It signed the Benelux customs agreement with Belgium and Luxembourg in London in 1944; it was a founder member of the European Coal and Steel Community in 1951 and of the EC in 1957. It was also a founder member of the UN, NATO and the WEU (Western European Union).

FRISIANS ■

During the period of the amalgamation of the provinces into a nation, the most tenacious of the old identities was that of the Frisians, centred on the provinces of Friesland and the town of Groningen. This area was marked off from the rest by its economy, dialect and institutions. Until 1738 it had its own Head of State and, from then until 1815, the offices of Head of State remained separate between Friesland and the rest of the union, though a single individual exercised both.

With origins discerned in the Frisians of antiquity (mentioned by Tacitus and many late Roman writers) and privileges conceded to the people of the region under that name by rulers of the Netherlands in the Middle Ages, the inhabitants of Friesland seemed imperfectly attached to the Dutch state until well into the 19th century. Moreover they could, and sometimes did, claim connections of kinship with communities speaking similar dialects, called 'Frisian' or 'North Frisian', in offshore islands of Germany and Denmark. Today, though the possibility remains of the revival of a sense of being 'Frisian' in parts of the maritime Netherlands and adjacent areas, the success of Dutch state-making seems reflected in the thoroughness with which Frisians have been absorbed.

POLITICS AND RELIGION ■

The political spectrum in the Netherlands extends from a right of centre Liberal party, with its roots in the 19th century economic and political liberalism, via confessional parties representing the various Protestant groupings and the Roman Catholic church in the centre, to a Democratic Socialist Workers' party on the left.

These represent the three major traditional groupings, with origins going back to the last quarter of the 19th century. Until the 1960s, these strands dominated Dutch political and social life through the phenomenon known as *pillarisation*. People attended school, went to a club, belonged to a trades union or employers' organization, read a newspaper, listened to a broadcasting company, belonged to and/or voted for a political party all according to their religious or ethical affiliation. The confessional groupings had the largest number of adherents and, because the Protestant population, which was in the majority, was divided in its allegiance, the largest single grouping was the substantial Roman Catholic minority, based primarily in the south of the country.

Since the 1960s, this picture has begun to alter. Lifelong allegiance to a particular group has largely broken down and the political field has become considerably more complex. To the right and left of the major confessional parties of the centre there are a number of confessional off-shoot parties. Recent economic problems and large-scale influx of migrant workers has caused the rise of a small, but nevertheless worrying number of extreme right-wing groups. In the centre, the left-liberal Democrats '66 party demands radical constitutional reform. To the left of the Social Democrats are various groups with strong environmental and pacifist planks to their platforms. Meanwhile, the three major confessional parties – two Protestant, one Catholic – joined in 1980 to form a Christian Democratic party. This party is now increasingly seen as a secular centre-right option. Finally, like other social democratic parties, the Dutch Social Democratic party has been floundering to find a distinctive voice on the eve of the 21st century.

TRADE AND INDUSTRY ■

The economic situation in the Netherlands after the war has followed the trend of most western economies in basic outline. A period of rebuilding and subsequent economic boom followed the ending of the war. In the Netherlands this period was marked by the rise of Rotterdam to the position of the world's largest port with a pivotal position in the oil trade, a development, however, already foreshadowed in the pre-war years.

Another important development was the discovery of large reserves of natural gas in 1959. The Netherlands has a heavily service-based economy and has a prime role in European freight. Agriculture and fisheries are also major economic activities, stimulated by the Netherlands' early participation in the EC. Like other member states, the Netherlands is now struggling with the consequences of over-subsidy and over-production in these areas.

Following the ending of the long post-war boom, with the oil shocks of the 1970s, the Dutch have had to reappraise their economic position. In particular, they have had to take a look at the heavy expenditure on the highly developed welfare system and take stock of their economy and competitiveness in world markets. As for other western economies, the recent period has been one of difficult transition and review, the outcome of which is not yet certain.

NORMANS

Although many of the regions of France have acquired their distinctive personalities as a result of the marrying of a well-identified physical geography with a powerful cultural history, in the case of Normandy the former brought much less to the alliance than did the latter. Normandy is not a geographical unity, in the way that, say, Brittany may be so described. Geologically, Normandy seems to be sandwiched between the old Armorican massif to the west and the younger, secondary formations of the Paris Basin to the south and east. The valley of the Seine has not served to provide a boundary for Normandy as a territorial unit. Internally, Normandy contains more than a dozen recognizably different geographical localities or pays. *Normandy is an historical creation, a cultural region. By 1066 the name* Normandie *had come to refer more or less to the area thus described today: that is, a maritime province stretching from the vicinity of Dieppe in the east to the borders of Brittany in the west, with the English Channel to the north and its southern frontier defined in places by the alignments of some small river basins, and in other places by the limits of Carolingian administrative districts or* pagi.

HISTORY ■

There was, of course, settlement in Normandy before the arrival of the Northmen themselves, from whom the province acquired its name. Evidence of prehistoric occupation suggests that the area saw some colonization by peoples originating in northern Europe, in Brittany and in the upper Rhineland. During the first millennium the valley of the Seine emerged as a major trading axis, as one of the routes through which tin from Cornwall and amber from nordic areas were carried to the Rhône and the Mediterranean. During the Roman period, the region was designated as the frontier between Belgium to the north and the Celtic tribes of Armorican Gaul to the south; during this period it also acquired some sense of regional and cultural identity, not least in the laying of the enduring foundations of a Christian civilization which, from the 6th century AD, made a distinctive impact with the building of some great abbeys.

Nonetheless, Normandy and the Normans owe their peculiarity essentially to the region's involvement in the waves of migrations of Viking pirates from Denmark and Norway who, during the 9th and 10th centuries, pillaged or occupied many coastal areas of Greenland, the British Isles and western Europe. In the late 9th century Viking bands established permanent settlements in the lower valley of the Seine. Unable to resist the invaders, in 911 the Frankish king Charles the Simple granted the Norwegian chieftain, Rollo, and his band formal recognition of their occupation of the region around Rouen. For their part, the Norsemen agreed

to adopt Christianity and to protect the area from attacks. Receiving further territorial concessions from the kings of France, the Normans extended the area over which they had control: Normandy – the term was first used in the early 11th century – gradually expanded.

The evidence of place-names suggests that Viking settlement was itself dense only in the *pays* of Caux and in the Cotentin peninsula, but the cultural influence of the Norsemen was much more extensive. Nonetheless, the initially massive Scandinavian impact was steadily absorbed into a Frankish society which had survived the invasions. Well before the end of the 10th century, the Vikings had adapted to the Frankish-Gallo-Roman population they had found living in the region. Rollo's family married Frankish princesses and adopted both the Christian religion and the French language. The Vikings had become Normans. In 1066 the duke of Normandy undertook the conquest of England and by the 12th century Normandy itself was more or less the geographical centre of a powerful, rich and stable Anglo-Norman state,

51

extending from Scotland to the Pyrenees, whose acquisition would for a considerable period be a strategic objective of the Capetian kings of France.

When Normandy was conquered by the Capetians in the early 13th century, French rule had little impact upon the political and social structures of the region: Norman nobles with properties in England or in Aquitaine had ownership of their estates assured by the Treaty of Paris (1259), so that they had no need to fight to regain them and the new mercantile and industrial class was more interested in economic development than in affairs of state, so Normandy became part of France without much upset. Local customs were acknowledged in 1250 in the *Grand Coutumier de Normandie* and the region's privileges (including the right to control taxation) were affirmed in the 1315 *Charte aux Normands*. During the Hundred Years' War, Normandy was twice invaded by the English and was under English control from 1415 until 1450, when French authority was reasserted. Thereafter, French power within Normandy grew, despite confirmation in 1458 of the *Charte aux Normands* and the production in 1587 of a new edition of the customs of Normandy. In practice, the charter and the customs were allowed to lapse and the provincial assembly (*Etats*) was consulted less frequently and eventually abolished in 1666. The province, which had been one administrative district, was divided first into two and then into three *généralités* (Rouen, Caen, Alençon) in 1636. After the French Revolution and its programme of administrative rationalization, Normandy was divided in 1790 into five *départements* whose boundaries more or less respected those of the historic provinces. The more recent creation of two economic planning regions – Upper Normandy and Lower Normandy – has partially acknowledged the historic unity of the province. It is certainly the case that the existence of Normandy as a political, historical construction remains alive in the collective consciousness of the inhabitants of the region.

LANGUAGE ■

Although Normandy remained in contact with Scandinavia immediately after the period of initial immigration and colonization, the province did become increasingly absorbed into its Frankish cultural environment to the extent that, by the early 11th century, Scandinavian language had largely disappeared. Most of the Scandinavian settlers were men and their marriage and cohabitation with Frankish women almost certainly led rapidly to the decline of spoken Scandinavian. Norman French (*normand*) soon emerged as a divergent dialect of the French language and was the dialect spoken by the Normans who invaded England in 1066. The cultural adaptability of the Normans has meant that Norman patois has now virtually disappeared and is rarely found in use in public today. Some folklore groups are now resurrecting 'traditional' songs and dances, thereby introducing old Norman to modern Normans.

'NATIONALISM' ■

While retaining through the centuries a clear sense of their own cultural identity, less Latin and Frankish and more Nordic than other Frenchmen, the Normans have also readily recognized their province as being part of France in general and its fortunes as being closely linked to those of Paris. Indeed, the proximity of Normandy to Paris is probably one reason why no separatist movement for the province has been developed by its people. The brief 1793 federalist revolt in parts of Normandy against domination by Paris did not lay the foundations for any similar devolutionist tendencies during the 19th century. In the 20th century, the post-War designation of Normandy as a major economic planning region within France has not led to popular pleas or protests for further autonomy.

PEOPLE AND CULTURE ■

Normans today, reflecting their distant Nordic origins, are often more fair-haired and blue-eyed than people in other parts of France. But they are also said to be both more adventurous, as descendants of seafaring pirates and traders, and more cautious, as heirs of a people who experienced one of the most centralized, systematized and bureaucratic feudal states in medieval Europe.

It is often argued that the early Normans retained the savagery and philistinism of their Viking forebears and that they contributed little to the art of western Europe. Nonetheless, the wealth of medieval Normandy found enduring expression especially in its distinctive religious and military architecture. From the mid-11th century there developed an early-Norman ecclesiastical style which was Romanesque, with massive buildings having rounded arches and a basilica plan; later-Norman churches came to be characterized by more complex articulation of building structures in general and by greater elaboration of towers and spires in particular. This Norman style was a prelude, especially in its use of space and light, to the more generalized adoption of Gothic architecture in western Europe. Advanced in methods of warfare, the Normans also built many solid castles, often sited on vantage points.

In its architecture, Normandy also expresses in its churches and *hôtels* the wealth of its medieval and early-modern urban bourgeoisie and in its rural *châteaux* and manor houses the power of its nobles and lords (*seigneurs*).

More recently, Normandy has produced some very significant contributors to the worlds of fine arts and letters, such as Poussin and Millet, Flaubert and Maupassant, Fontenelle and Tocqueville. Many of the leading Impressionists worked in Normandy, most notably, perhaps, Claude Monet whose water-garden by his home at Giverny has both been wonderfully created and itself helped, along with other artistic and literary representations of the 19th century, to construct an image of Normandy which has come to be cherished by many, not only by Normans.

2
THE ATLANTIC ARC

All the invasions which have contributed to the making of Europe have proceeded from east to west. The Atlantic seaboard has therefore been populated by peoples driven as well as drawn to the resources and opportunities of the ocean. This Atlantic arc from Portugal to Ireland has been the refuge of Celtic peoples driven out by Germanic invaders, of Suevic fugitives in Galicia and Portugal and of the Basques, crowded into their corner by even earlier migrations. When they reached the Atlantic, these peoples were stuck there for centuries, hemmed in by the prevailing westerlies which blow onto all their shores.

Lapped by a single ocean, their homelands were shaped by common environmental features. Atlantic Europe covers a range of climatic zones – sub-Arctic, temperate and Mediterranean – but is unified by high rainfall and a common geological history which, for instance, made the western outposts of Wales, Cornwall, Galicia and Lower Andalusia the metal-rich New World of the ancient Romans. Rivers flow east through low reliefs. These directed ancient commerce into the fairly narrow sea-lanes that skirt the Bay of Biscay, uniting the region like a neighbourhood service road, one that already linked Andalusia to Galicia and both to Cornwall and the Scillies before Phoenician and Greek traders arrived early in the first millennium.

Overwhelmingly, Europe's Atlantic peoples are maritime peoples. The Atlantic has long provided vocations for fishers and seafarers and, once navigational technology permitted, highways of sea-borne migration and empire-building. The Canary Islands, Madeira and the Azores became in the 15th century Europe's first permanent overseas colonies. Breton, Basque and Bristolian fishermen opened up the long-range routes of the North Atlantic. A disproportionate share of the sea-dogs of Elizabethan England were born in the west. Of the European peoples who founded overseas empires in the early modern period, only the Dutch had no direct seaboard on the Atlantic.

Today, the Atlantic communities have been among the first to assert a regional identity, based on geographical unity, transcending the old boundaries of nation-states. The self-defined regional authorities of the Atlantic Bow, which cover the whole of Europe's Atlantic seaboard from Andalusia (see p.161) to Ireland, have had their own assembly since 1989. The attempt to give an essentially geographical group a historic and cultural basis by appealing to a common Celtic allegiance has been unconvincing: most of the peoples of the region have little or no Celtic background. A conviction of

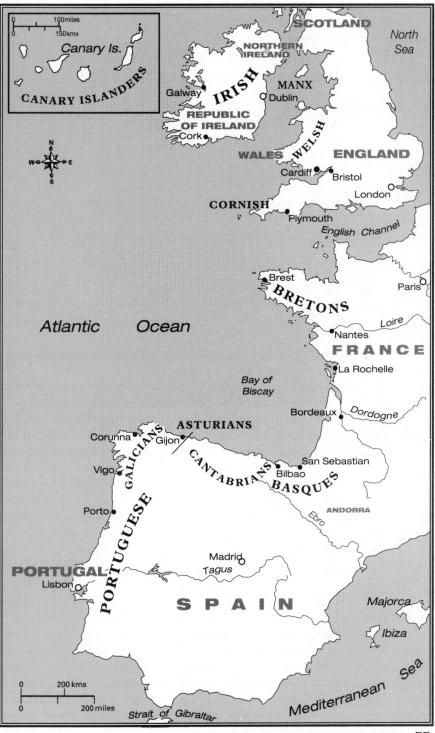

common interest, however, has arisen naturally from their shared habitat
and perspective on the rest of Europe.

PORTUGUESE

*Portugal's distinctiveness is not based on any physical factors. Geographically, it is
merely another part of the Iberian peninsula: there are no natural borders
separating it from Spain nor does it have its own particular climate. What does
mark Portugal out as different from the rest of the peninsula is its historical
evolution as a discrete nation-state with its own past, its own administrative and
legal structures, its own language and its own vigorous cultural traditions.*

HISTORY AND POLITICS ■

Portugal, one of the oldest surviving countries in Europe, came into being in the
12th century thanks largely to the efforts of Afonso Henriques of the House of Burgundy, whose armies, assisted by foreign crusaders, gradually pushed the Muslims
out of much of Western Iberia.

The 'reconquest' from the Muslims of the area which now comprises Portugal
was not, however, completed until the mid-13th century. The independence of the
country from the Spanish Kingdom of Castile was secured in the later years of that
century by Dinis, the first local monarch to encourage a genuinely Portuguese culture. Dinis set up the first national maritime organization, founded the country's university, assisted the expansion of the economic system by establishing large trading
centres, and provided his kingdom with many fine castles, some of which he himself
designed.

His laws were written in Portuguese, which had by now evolved so far from its
cognate, Castilian (the ancestor of modern Spanish), that it was considered a distinct
language. This early form of Portuguese was also the language of the highly influential troubadour culture, which consisted of romantic and satirical poems, penned by
nobles and the king, and sung by minstrels who toured the land. The tradition of
sung courtly verses was to remain the dominant form of literary expression until the
15th century.

The sense of national identity was strengthened during the 15th century by the
gradual development, presided over by the monarchy, of the Portuguese empire.
The first great modern empire of a European power, it came to include important
parts of South America, Africa and Asia. The wealth generated from trading and
from exploitation of foreign resources both helped to stabilize the economy and enabled the monarchy to foster educational reform, while the voyages of discovery
stimulated advances in science and anthropology.

Often hostile relations with Spain remained an almost constant concern. In 1580

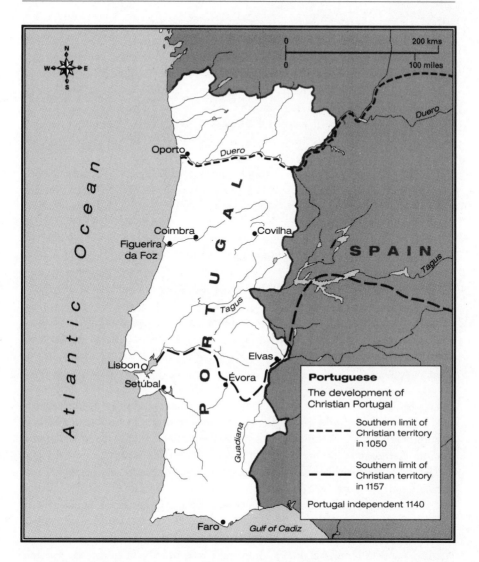

Portuguese

The development of Christian Portugal

- - - - Southern limit of Christian territory in 1050

— — — Southern limit of Christian territory in 1157

Portugal independent 1140

Portugal was left severely weakened by a disastrous military expedition to Morocco in which the king was killed, and was then successfully invaded by its larger neighbour. Though the uprising, 60 years later, which replaced the Spanish administration with a new king was followed by a sustained decline in the national economy and in the extent of its empire, the day of the uprising (1st December) remains an annual cause for the celebration of Portuguese independence.

The discovery, in 1693, of gold in Brazil, part of the Portuguese empire, restored the fortunes of the treasury, but the national administration continued to mismanage the economy and to leave its industrial base undeveloped. It was not until the 1750s, when the king allowed the Marquês de Pombal to take over the reins of government, that effective measures to revitalize the country were carried out. A believer in enlightened absolutism, the marquês curtailed the powers of the nobles and the clergy (and so indirectly aided the rise of the bourgeoisie), improved literacy, reformed the universities and promoted industry. He had Lisbon, devastated by an earthquake in 1755, rebuilt along functional, neo-classical lines. Pombal was a member of the *estrangeirados*, Portuguese educated elsewhere in Europe who wished to modernize their country on a rationalist model. Though there was much resistance to his ideas, his economic and administrative reforms were not reversed following his fall from power on the death of his royal patron in 1777.

Further developments were abruptly halted in 1807, when Napoleon invaded and the royal family fled to Brazil. The British, who forced the French to retreat, then took economic and political advantage of an inept regency government in Lisbon and ran the country as virtually another one of their colonies. Hatred of this tyrannical regime united large sections of the Portuguese people, and under the banner of Liberalism a revolt in 1820 drove out the British.

The liberals, though victorious against the foreign oppressors, were insufficiently powerful to put into effect much of their proposed constitutional reform, which was inspired by the ideals of the French Revolution. For the rest of the century, control of the government oscillated between liberals and conservatives. The need for change, however, was recognized by intellectuals of both political persuasions, who were concerned with the best way of rebuilding their country and of restoring its former glory.

The assassination of the king and his heir in 1908 sounded the death knell for the monarchy and a republic was proclaimed two years later. But the republicans were unable to provide stable government and their attempts to impose anticlerical measures and social reforms were blocked by the conservatives and a revival of support for the church. In 1926 a military coup ended the republican experiment and replaced it with what was to be a remarkably long-lived authoritarian regime led, for more than 30 years, by Antonio Salazar.

Salazar's repressive dictatorship isolated Portugal from much of the rest of Europe. He kept the country undeveloped, supported a reactionary form of Catholicism, and indulged in a backward-looking form of nationalism: Portugal was to be portrayed as a still-imperial power whose coffers were to be filled by the economic benefits of exploiting its overseas territories. But the cost of using the army to deal with the ever-increasing indigenous resistance to this outmoded policy slowly turned management of the once-profitable colonies into a major drain on the resources of the treasury.

As popular discontent over these wars grew, and as Salazar's successor proved incapable of restoring the economy, a widely-supported and nearly bloodless coup toppled the regime in April 1974. The provisional government quickly legalized political organizations and granted the colonies their independence. But the lack of well-established parties and the almost-utopian hopes of many Portuguese, who had been unable to express their views for so many years, was not conducive to a climate of political stability. The left-wing government, brought in by the first democratic elections for over 50 years, passed a socialist-inspired constitution. But it soon fell, leading to a troubled period of short-lived governments. The coalition of the right which came to power in 1978 revised the constitution, divesting it of much of its socialist idealism though retaining its wish for the eventual achievement of a classless society. In recent years, as the electorate has tended to move away from left-wing radicalism, political activity has become much less lively and much more conventional.

With Portugal now a member of the EC, the future and identity of the country is expressed as one of 'catching up' with the rest of industrialized Western Europe, of which it is, should be and will be an integral part. The once-glorious days of its seaborne empire are regarded as now just a part of its distinctive history, not of its destiny. Portugal's dilemma is how to become more European, while at the same time remaining identifiably, and distinctively, Portuguese.

THE PHYSICAL ENVIRONMENT ■

Portugal is a diverse land which in many places along the border is geographically indistinguishable from its neighbour, Spain. The country begins at the western end of the Spanish plain, from which it shelves away, down towards the Atlantic seaboard. The terrain north of the river Tejo is generally hilly, building up into mountains towards the mid-east and the northeastern frontier. In contrast, the region south of the Tejo is flatter and drier. The climate of the country is usually mild, though there are marked regional variations: the western coastline is cooled by seabreezes and is often humid; the mountainous regions are frequently drenched with rain; the hilly areas of the interior are sometimes affected by drought; and the southern Algarve can become very hot during the summer months.

ECONOMY AND SOCIETY ■

Until relatively recently, Portugal's domestic economy relied mainly on agriculture and, to a lesser extent, on fishing. Maize is the major crop in the north and wheat in the central region. Wine production is concentrated in these two areas while olive oil is made throughout the land. Traditional Portuguese industries include the manufacture of cork, the extraction of pine resin, and canning factories for the export of sardines. Though the late industrialization of parts of the country, combined with the phenomenal rise of tourism since the mid-1980s has provided many jobs, both the level of unemployment and the number of migrants seeking work abroad remain very high . Portugal is still in this respect the 'poor man of Europe'.

Despite these recent developments, family ties remain very important. The household, often composed of grandparents, parents and children, continues to be the primary social and economic unit. Many businesses, including even large and new ones, are family-run, while some of the centuries-old companies are still controlled by groups of closely-knit kin.

RELIGION ■

The Catholic Church has had a particularly powerful influence on the lives of the Portuguese at many levels. Perhaps the most notorious example was the Inquisition, which lasted from the mid-16th century to the Liberal revolution of 1820, and which at times exercised more power than the monarchy itself. The association of the church in the political life of the country dates from the beginning of the nation, when Afonso Henriques sought papal recognition of his newly-founded kingdom; the Portuguese empire was represented as a form of divinely-sanctioned crusade, while Salazar justified Portuguese neutrality during World War II by claiming his policy was in accordance with the oracular pronouncements of the Virgin Mary at Fatima.

The Christianity of the country is not uniformly orthodox, however. Despite the continued opposition of the ecclesiastical hierarchy, many popular religious traditions persist, especially in the north, whose inhabitants are much more fervent in their faith than their southern compatriots. These folk practices include measures taken to protect the newborn against the 'evil air' and 'midnight baptisms' held immediately after the birth and without the assistance of a priest. People's relations with specific saints are often very personal. Many saints' shrines, found throughout the land, are ornamented with piles of votive offerings left by grateful supplicants whose prayers have been answered. The most famous, and the most visited, shrine is that of Fatima, where the Virgin supposedly appeared in 1917.

Local Catholicism is inextricably bound up with each community's sense of its own identity. Villagers congregate in their parish church every Sunday; particular holy days are a cause for community-wide celebration, and every year each village or town honours its own particular patron saint in celebrations which may last several days. All Saints' Day and All Souls' Day (1st and 2nd November) are the annual opportunity for members of a community to revisit their tombs, decorating them with flowers and lamps. The community extends beyond the living to include the remembered dead. The departed may not be physically present but nor are they, or their wishes, forgotten.

CUISINE AND WINE ■

Portuguese cooking is distinctive for good historical reasons. The Romans introduced garlic, onions, wheat, olives and grapes, while the Muslims were the first to dig irrigation ditches on a large scale for the production of rice. They also planted almond trees to make marzipan; fig and apricot trees, whose fruits they dried; and groves of lemons and oranges. It was these Islamic colonizers who established the culinary tradition of fish or meat dishes cooked with fruit, and of intensely-sweet egg-based pastries. The national cuisine was further enriched during the days of the empire by explorers who brought spices – cinnamon, cumin, coriander and turmeric – back with them from India. The result of combining these various introduced ingredients with indigenous cereals, local meats and freshly-caught fish is a varied, often highly spicy cuisine, with an elaborate range of sweets.

The most distinctive, and famous, of Portuguese wines are *vinho verde*, 'green wines', which are slightly sparkling and acidic, low in alcoholic content, and made from relatively immature grapes; and port, a fortified – with local grape brandy – wine produced in the Douro Valley.

AZOREANS ■

Further from mainland Europe than any other group of islands in the Eastern Atlantic, the Azores are of volcanic origin and still occasionally experience earthquakes and eruptions. Each of the ten major islands in the group rises steeply from its shore and may reach heights of more than 6,000 feet. The climate is temperate and the flora mostly European. The islands were colonized gradually during the 15th century, beginning in 1439. Though the Marquês de Pombal established a central government for the group in 1766, since 1832 the islands have been divided, for administrative purposes, into three districts. While these districts are treated as an extension of continental Portugal, each has a certain degree of autonomy. In the 1970s some islanders, aided by American businessmen, campaigned for the independence of the Azores, but with little success. The islanders speak an antiquated dialect of Portuguese, and have traditionally relied for trade on the export of pineapples (originally introduced from Brazil), canned fish, hand embroideries and sperm oil from locally caught whales.

MADEIRANS ■

Similar to the Azores, the islands of the Madeira group are of volcanic origin, with mountainous profiles. The interiors of the two main islands (Madeira and Porto Santo) are almost totally uninhabited. Most people live on the lower slopes towards the shore. The climate and vegetation are semi-tropical.

During the 15th century, Portuguese colonizers deforested Madeira and Porto Santo, planting sugar-cane and vines. The land was gradually, but extensively, terraced and an elaborate system of irrigation channels excavated. Besides cultivating the usual vegetables of Europe, islanders grow Pacific taro, sweet potato, gourds, guavas, mangoes, loquats and figs.

The islands, defined by the mainland government as an integral part of Portugal, are administered as a single unit. Islanders have their own dialect of Portuguese, distinct from that of the Azoreans. Traditional rural dress consists of the *carapuca*, a funnel-shaped cap of blue cloth, linen breeches, shirt and a short jacket.

Today much of the economy remains based on the production of sugar and of Madeira, a fruity, very sweet wine fortified with brandy. Other sources of employment include fishing, the cultivation of bananas for export, embroidery – introduced by an Englishwoman in 1850 – and, of long-standing and ever-increasing importance, tourism.

61

GALICIANS

Among the 17 autonomous communities of the Spanish state, Galicians share a special rank with the Basques and Catalans as a people of peculiarly strong historic character. Yet until the Second Spanish Republic of 1931–6, when Galicia obtained a Statute of Autonomy, Galician political history did not reflect the territory's claims to a special identity in the way the Basque and Catalan past did. Unlike Catalonia, Galicia had a long history of submersion in the dominions of the Crown of Castile and the Spanish state. Unlike the Basques, the Galicians did not enjoy a collectively privileged status under the Spanish monarchy. The peculiar position of Galicia depends almost entirely on the distinctiveness of the culture, language and physical environment.

THE LAND ■

Crammed almost four-square into the extreme northwest right-angle of the Iberian peninsula, Galicia can be said literally to occupy a 'corner' of Europe. This has contributed to the way the region has been perceived from outside – inspiring, for instance, the legend that St James the Great could have ended up here in pursuit of the mission, revealed by Christ to the apostles, to preach 'in the four corners of the earth'. It has also helped to mould the Galician self-image, giving a sense of remoteness and isolation, drawing many natives to maritime occupations, and ensuring that past settlers such as the Sueves, and perhaps the Celts, ended up in Galicia because they could escape no further. Geologically, the land is built on some of the oldest rocks in Europe. Granite gives the region a unique feel and look, enhanced by the use of the stone as the main building material; the *rías* or fjords give the coast a flavour unparalleled elsewhere in southern Europe. The high rainfall and varied landscape strikingly differentiate Galicia from most of León and Castile, while, on the whole, the other provinces of the Cantabrian coast have more mountainous characters and more limited hinterlands. The celebrated verdure is a constant motif of the traditional nostalgic and patriotic poetry and song.

THE LANGUAGE ■

Galician (*Galego*) is a romance language which evolved from Latin at an earlier stage – to judge from its many examples of relatively archaic terminology – than other romance tongues of the Iberian peninsula. Terms of Arabic origin occur infrequently by comparison with Portuguese and Castilian. Up to the 14th century, it was a language favoured at the royal courts of León and Castile, especially for poetic expression. Thereafter, the growing prestige and prevalence of Castilian increasingly confined Galician to a limited reach and to low social and educational levels. Few works of literature appeared, except for those of a religious nature, until the 19th

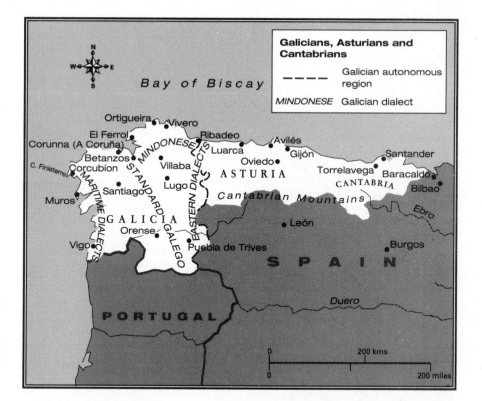

Galicians, Asturians and Cantabrians

– – – – Galician autonomous region

MINDONESE Galician dialect

century, although in the intervening centuries some writers – notably the doyens of the Enlightenment in Galicia, Fathers Feijóo (1676–1764) and Sarmiento (1695–1772) – advocated its merits.

The 19th-century revival of Galician letters owed something to the Catalan example and much to the great poetess Rosalía de Castro (1837–85). Most of her work was written in Castile, in a Galician full of Castilianisms, but it included a spirited advocacy of the language and a defence of its purity. The revival was checked under the dictatorship of Primo de Rivera (1923–30), when Galician was officially regarded as a folksy curiosity, excluded from schools and public occasions and tolerated only 'for purposes of traditional songs, verses and dress'. Under the regime of General Franco (1936–75), it was outlawed in the supposed interests of the political unity of Spain. Propaganda campaigns described it as 'barbarous barking' and invited speakers of it to 'demonstrate their civilization' by abandoning its use.

Towards the end of the Franco regime, restrictions were informally relaxed and with the transition to democracy (1975–8) a Galician-language press and political movement re-emerged into the open. But the fact that Galician had for so long been a language of peasants damaged its prestige with the urban working and lower-middle classes. When autonomous institutions were revived in 1978 and Galician was restored to a place in the school curriculum, a labour of 'recuperation' began which shows remarkable signs of success. According to recent surveys, over 90% of the population in all social classes have a passive knowledge, and over half are at least competent in its active use, although only 36% are native speakers to whom Galician is a first language.

Still, Galician remains limited – or even threatened – by three factors. First, Galicia is committed to a future in the Spanish state, whose official language is Castilian. As in Catalonia and the Basque Country, therefore, the educational system and the inherent pressures of modern life continue to reflect the importance of the state-wide language of communication, especially since Castilian is also a medium of considerable international importance, as the language of most of Latin America and one of the official languages of the European Community. Secondly, unlike Catalan, Galician is not in the fullest sense a 'modern' language, with terms of its own for every category of recent industrial, scientific and technical thought or experience, but a pre-industrial survival, which needs to borrow from Castilian. Thirdly, unlike Basque, Galician is close enough to both Castilian and Portuguese to absorb many alien terms and forms, in all spheres, without the guardians of linguistic purity being able to do much about it.

At the same time, Galician is threatened from within by a struggle over the 'normalization' of a language which, having survived for many centuries without becoming standardized in the usage of a printing trade or of a central élite, has naturally developed a large number of variants. While there is no clear division into regional dialects, there are forms peculiar to some fairly large areas; such peculiarities are particularly numerous, for instance, within the historic diocese of Mondoñedo, which is fairly well-defined by mountainous frontiers.

A fairly fierce division has arisen, in the quest for a 'standard' Galician which can be made mandatory in education, in broadcasting and in the official usage of the autonomous institutions: advocates of a policy of relentless exclusion of Castilianisms in favour of forms which are derived from Portuguese are pitted against 'moderates' who are less anxious to defend Galician against Castilian than to identify authentic forms on strictly scholarly criteria. The official policy of the Galician autonomous government, the Xunta de Galicia, favours the latter course, at the cost of provoking a campaign of agitation, discernible to the visitor in the often unscholarly alteration of road-signs and place-names. Simultaneously, linguistic 'nationalists' campaign against *bilinguismo*, or the parallel use by the government and administration of both Galician and Castilian.

HISTORY AND POLITICAL CULTURE ■

Galician historians and folklorists have focused on belief in a Celtic element in the population, supposedly dating from early in the first millennium AD and said to account for the Roman name of the region, *Gallaecia*. Celtic settlement is presumed to have been widespread in northern and central Spain in the period, but Galicia cannot be shown to have been more Celtic than other parts: terms of Celtic origin are no more common in the language; nor are any distinctive customs particularly Celtic in flavour. Treasure troves establish that pre-Roman Galicia was in contact, probably by land and sea, with the rich, metallurgically inventive civilizations of southern Spain; the workmanship of a royal hoard attributed to the Tartessian civilization (*c*.700 BC) of lower Andalusia, for instance, is echoed in a find near Ourense.

Galician gold may already have been exported before the Roman invaders began to mine it intensively, from the very early 2nd century BC, and to transport it across the peninsula, south along the 'money road' through Mérida for shipment from Cádiz. Lugo retains a complete circuit of walls of the 3rd century AD: clear evidence of the importance of the province in the Roman empire. Despite vast distances and a mountainous frontier, Galicia was fully integrated in the culture of imperial Rome.

Political isolation began in the 5th century, with the erosion of the Roman empire and the creation of a Visigothic kingdom in most of the Iberian peninsula. Galicia, occupied by the Visigoths' Germanic rivals, the Suevi, formed with what is now northern Portugal a distinct state with a much lower level both of material culture and literary and artistic achievement. Documents are rare. When the Suevic kingdom was conquered by the Visigothic king, Leovigild, in the 580s, the local élites do not seem to have been disturbed or displaced.

In the 8th century, Galicia was largely ignored by the Moors who conquered the Visigothic realm: they could not exploit the rainy climate and lacked the technology to resume mining. When the historical thread is resumed in the early 9th century, the descendants of a Romanized native (and perhaps Suevic) aristocracy seem still to have been in place, establishing ever-closer ties with an ambitious royal court in Oviedo. Shortly before 824 an early Christian martyr's burial-place was discovered – reputedly by a miracle – at Santiago de Compostela and proclaimed by the local bishop to be that of St James the Great. The court of Oviedo, where a cult of St James as apostle of Spain was already established, was eager to exploit the opportunity to bind the region more tightly by endowing and publicizing the shrine. By the end of the century the kings of Oviedo were calling themselves Kings of Galicia, and Santiago de Compostela had become a focus of pilgrimage. From the 10th century, at latest, it attracted penitents from the British Isles and even remoter parts of western Christendom. For the rest of the Middle Ages, the pilgrim roads were the cables by which Galicia was tied to the rest of Europe. The first document printed in England, for instance, was an indulgence from which broken vows to St James were exempted.

In relation to the rest of Spain, however, Galicia became a backwater. After the reign of Ferdinand II of León (1157–88), periodic divisions of the royal inheritance undermined Galicia's independence. The aristocracy – in marked contrast to those of the Basque lands, Castile, Catalonia and Portugal – remained at home and failed to profit much from the intra-peninsular wars of the late Middle Ages. By the 16th century, Galicia was of little account in the affairs of the monarchy: collectively represented in the representative assembly by the Castilian town of Zamora, Galicia was without a voice in decision-making. Except in maritime affairs – she built valuable round-hulled vessels and Corunna (Galician: A Coruña) was an important port for Atlantic warfare – she contributed little to imperial needs. The Counter-

Reformation seems to have stimulated the pilgrim trade and the 17th century – normally accounted a period of 'decline' for Spain as a whole – brought some signs of prosperity, still discernible in the baroque monuments of Santiago. Poor communications and inefficient production meant, however, that Galicia found it hard to exploit her considerable potential in agriculture and fishing: late 18th-century legislation allowing her ports to trade directly with the New World came too late and Galicia's reputation was as a country where 'the land is rich and the people are poor'. In the 19th century the region's biggest export was its surplus labour. There are sizeable Galician communities to this day as far apart as Buenos Aires and Merthyr Tydfil. In pre-revolutionary Cuba, Galicians were the biggest ethnic minority.

In the last 100 years, the traditional fishing industry has been revolutionized by canning and freezing and Galician food processing has come to be an important element in the Spanish economy. Agriculture, however, has remained tied to smallholdings, vulnerable to sub-division, and the region's political history has continued to reflect the social and devotional conservatism of the people. Despite Galicians' interest in the republican commitment to autonomy for the region, Galicia was quickly aligned in the civil war with the cause of the Galician-born General Franco. Since the restoration of autonomy in 1978 it has been the only region of Spain governed almost uninterruptedly by Spain's national conservative party, now called the Partido Popular.

POPULAR CULTURE ■

In religion and popular culture, Galicians are traditionalists. The region's coat of arms displays eucharistic symbols. Religious art almost monopolized the great exhibition of the Galician artistic tradition mounted in Santiago by the regional government in 1991. The cult-centres of regional importance are the shrine of the apostle in Santiago and the cathedral of Lugo, where the sacrament is permanently exposed.

Traditional music, cultivated by enthusiasts in every centre of population, has a determinedly rustic character, with a predominance of reed instruments and bagpipes; the strong dance rhythms and habit of singing in unison seem, on the other hand, to belong to an agrarian, village tradition. This is appropriate: like other parts of Cantabrian Spain, Galicia is a land of thickly spread, small communities living in villages and hamlets; outside the ports, there are no big cities. Maritime areas and the city of Santiago have a great reputation for food, thanks to the abundance of shellfish, especially scallops, whose shells became St James's symbols and the inspiration of *coquilles Saint-Jacques* (though the local recipe is less elaborate and calls for grilling with plenty of onions). The distinctive flavours of the food of the inland areas derive from a lightly cured bacon, bitter turnip tops, rancid butter and strong green peppers. High rainfall and long grasses make for better cattle pasture than in most of the rest of the peninsula: hence the renowned cows' cheeses shaped like women's breasts. Galicia does not share the cider-drinking culture of some other regions of Cantabrian Spain. The characteristic wines are *Ribeiro*, fresh and purple, the luscious white *Albariño* and the sweet, pink, foamy Rosal. The viscous grape spirit called *orujo* – heated with coffee and set alight for festive effect – has some claim to be considered the 'national' drink.

ASTURIANS AND CANTABRIANS

Between the Galicians and Basque lands, the Cantabrian coast of Spain is occupied by the autonomous regions of Asturias and Cantabria. Divided by the Cantabrian mountains from the rest of the historic kingdom of Castile, they have some common distinguishing features; rainy climates; high, heavily wooded hinterlands; settlement in numerous small towns and hamlets; cultures of cider and butter or lard. These contrast with the parched tablelands, city life, wine and olives of the rest of Castile (see pp. 160–2). Historically, too, their experience has been distinctive in influential ways. Both areas lay beyond the frontier of Muslim invaders of the Iberian peninsula in the Middle Ages; in partial consequence, they enclosed, in early modern times, communities with historically high numbers of fiscally privileged residents with claims to 'noble' status under the Castilian crown. The Cantabrian town of Santillana del Mar – birthplace of Le Sage's hero, Gil Blas – is the locus classicus *of this world where almost every house, however modest, has a coat of arms engraved over the door.*

ASTURIANS ■

Of the two regions, Asturias has much the stronger regional identity. Like Wales within the United Kingdom, it is a 'principality' – uniquely so called among the autonomous regions of Spain – which supplies the heir to the throne with his title. This has never meant much in institutional terms, but has contributed to the Asturians' sense of being distinct. They also take pride in their instrumental role in Spanish history. In the 8th and 9th centuries, the Kingdom of Asturias was centred on a spectacular court at Oviedo, where a scholarly and artistic culture of great originality and flair flourished, which can still be appreciated in a few surviving buildings and manuscripts. In the 880s, the expansion of this kingdom beyond the Cantabrian mountains was the first step in the makings of the kingdoms of Léon and Castile, which – always including Asturias within their territories – became the hegemonic states of the peninsula and the kernel of the slowly-emerging Spanish monarchy. As a result of this symbiotic process, Asturians' identity depends on, and is enhanced by, their sense of also being Spaniards. There is, therefore, no Asturian separatism, but only a form of regionalist politics typical of other European peripheries. Since the creation of an autonomous region with a cultural budget in 1978, folkloric aspects of culture – regional dress on festive occasions, traditional bagpipe bands – have received official encouragement and some intellectuals have become self-conscious about the use of the dialect, which differs from mainstream Castilian chiefly in suppressing the distinctions between palatalized vowels.

CANTABRIANS ■

Whereas *Asturiano* is a traditional designation for the inhabitants of the principality, no-one called himself 'Cantabrian' before the 1970s. Castile north and south of the Cantabrian mountains was intimately connected, in the Middle Ages, by the mule-train routes which joined the wool-producing lands around Burgos to the ports of Santander and Laredo. Anthropologists favour the region's intimate, isolated valley-communities for field-work on Castilian ethnicity. Since devolution in 1978, however, a sense of peculiar regional interests has become the focus for the promotion, by the autonomous government, of a heightened identity. This has helped to generate some silly pseudo-scholarly theories, such as, for instance, that Cantabria is 'the cradle of mankind' and that the Cantabrians are a lost tribe of Israel. The maritime and industrial economy of Cantabria has much in common with those of its Basque and Asturian neighbours and in any future 'regionalization' of Europe, Cantabria is likely to belong with them in an alignment of Atlantic-side communities.

CANARY ISLANDERS

Arrayed, from east to west, like stepping-stones into the Atlantic, the Canary Islands lie about seven degrees of latitude beyond the rest of Europe's furthermost south. They are 600 miles from Cadiz and within sight, at the nearest point, of the coast of Western Sahara. Yet their European character has been indelibly established: by Spanish conquest in the 15th century; by incorporation in the Spanish state; by colonization – chiefly from the Iberian peninsula and northwest Europe. The Canary current and northeast trade winds make the islands part of the Mediterranean climatic zone, despite their proximity to the Sahara, and kept them easily accessible from Spain throughout the age of sail. The islands' remoteness is enough to ensure a strong collective regional identity, which a peculiar history has strengthened. In addition, the enormous range of micro-climates, reliefs, soils and economic activities across the archipelago, and even within individual islands, has helped breed particularism.

THE NATIVE PAST ■

The intensity of Canarian identity can be measured by its historic myths. The most fundamental is the myth of the survival of the pre-hispanic population. Evidence of

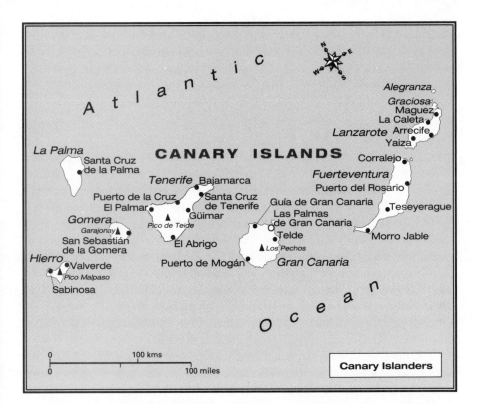

the nature and origins of the aboriginal inhabitants conflicts but they were probably pre-Berber north African peoples similar, perhaps, to the Imraguen of the western Saharan coast today. Never numerous, with a generally low level of material culture, they were astonishingly resilient in resisting late-medieval European conquistadors. This gave them a distinguished reputation in chivalric, pastoral and romantic writings after the conquest and ensured that indigenous blood was a source of pride. To this day, insistence that 'strong native blood runs in the veins of islanders' remains strong. Sometimes, this has been taken to absurd lengths – for instance, by the enthusiasts who invented a 'Canarian language' in the 1960s on the tenuous basis of a few fragmentary survivals of the pre-conquest tongues, or by the small independence party which proclaimed a government in exile in Algeria and applied to join the Organization of African Unity. Universally, differentiation from peninsular Spaniards, called by affectionately offensive names, is the key element in Canarian identity.

Yet the evidence of the obliteration of the natives in the era of conquest and colonization is overwhelming: mass deportations, 'culture shock' and the impact of European diseases reduced them, by the mid-16th century to a few isolated communities on the margins of the colonial society. They were not consciously exterminated, but simply swamped. The evidence in favour of the thesis of native survival can all be better explained in other ways. The peculiarities of islanders' blood-group types, compared with those of mainland Spaniards, are typical of peripheral peoples gener-

69

ally; the supposedly limited range of physical types may be a product of isolation. Remote rural communities, such as Chipude on the island of Gomera, are shown off as nests of indigenous survival, but their primitive air is reminiscent of many isolated peasant villages and it is not clear that their pottery, made in pre-conquest style without a wheel, represents a genuinely continuous tradition.

POPULAR CULTURE ■

Memorials of the pre-conquest past do survive, however, in popular culture. Most of the peculiarities of the Canarian menu can be explained by climate and isolation, but the taste for *gofio* – powdered, toasted grain served in soup or mixed with milk and water – goes back to pre-conquest days. Of the distinctively Canarian games, *vela latina* sailing is a product of the environment and the varieties of stick-fighting are essentially from a tradition common to pastoral societies; but the Canarian 'national' game of wrestling called *lucha canaria* seems a genuine survival from the indigenous past. Most Canarian music and popular verse seems to have developed from Andalusian traditions but an impressive case has been made out for tracing the verse-form called *endechas* to native origins. The most important focus of religious devotion, the Virgin of Candelaria, is traditionally held to have been the miraculous agent of a partial revelation of Christianity to the pre-conquest natives.

The dominant sources of cultural influence, however, have been Spain, and Andalusia in particular, where most settlers came from and with which the closest communications were maintained. Patterns of settlement, ways of life, lay-out of dwellings, structure of families are transplanted from the peninsula. So are the forms of religious devotion, which have all the features of popular Catholicism, although local saints and manifestations of Christ and the Virgin tend to attract more fervour than the universal cults of the Church, and carnival is celebrated with an abandon more reminiscent of Latin America than Spain. The Canarian dialect is very close to Andalusia's, with elongated vowels and swallowed consonants. The ancillary role of other influences is displayed in the rich lexicon with many words of pre-conquest and English origin – the latter reflecting the historic importance of Atlantic trade and British investment.

SPANISH INFLUENCE ■

The second myth which has nourished Canarian identity is of the islands as victims of a colonial relationship with the peninsula. Canarian townscapes have an irresistibly colonial look, with baroque churches surrounded by exotic flora; and their economic history looks like a typical saga of dependency, as one mono-culture has succeeded another: sugar in the 16th century, wine in the 17th and 18th, cochineal in the 19th, bananas, then tourism in the 20th. In reality, however, the islands have always enjoyed a privileged place in the Spanish state. In the era of colonization, settlers were attracted by fiscal concessions. The islands were a crucial staging-post and source of supply for the Spanish empire in the New World. When that empire collapsed, Canarian prosperity followed but was restored in 1852 by the granting of free port status. This brought foreign investment and gave the islands a pivotal role in the west Africa steamship trade, comparable to that they had enjoyed in the sail-borne commerce of the New World.

POLITICS ■

Early in the second half of the 19th century an influential group of intellectuals and antiquarians around Agustín Millares Torres promoted a sense of Canarian identity and denounced Madrid's alleged neglect; a separatist party wanted to follow Cuba to independence in 1898. But the benefits of belonging to Spain seemed incontrovertible and the novelist Pérez Galdós spoke for most of his fellow-islanders when he proclaimed the Canaries 'Spain's advanced guard in the midst of the Atlantic'. Rather than join in confronting the Spanish state, Canarians preferred inter-island rivalry. The proclamation of the Second Spanish Republic in 1931 briefly excited hopes of devolution to a single autonomous region, but the project sank in the Spanish Civil War. Under the rule of General Franco in Spain (1936–75), growing prosperity kept the islands' restiveness appeased and the new democratic constitution of 1978 found a satisfactory formula combining an autonomous government for the archipelago with a regional council for each island. Since Spain joined the European Community in 1982, Canarian solidarity has grown in relation to European institutions which seem remote and a European economic system in which the islands have no obvious role.

The results have included the rise of regional politics, with grumbling at a new form of 'colonial dependency' on Europe; meanwhile, cultural organizations – traditionally rather introspective – have invested heavily in promoting Canarian folklore, food and festivities; and Canarians have become increasingly vehement in exalting *lo nuestro* – their perceived common identity and interests.

BASQUES

The basis of Basque identity is the language known as Euskara, spoken widely throughout Basque areas of Spain and, to a lesser extent, France. Self-conscious Basques (Euskaldunak) include those who, through emigration or assimilation with their neighbours, have lost the use of the language, but who nourish a nostalgic identification with Basque tradition and culture, usually signified by a willingness to learn at least some Euskara. The uniqueness of Western Europe's only non-Indo-European language has led to the disputed inference that the Basques are the remnant of a widespread pre-Indo-European people. A gap in development today divides the heavily industrialized areas from the rural rump. The Basque identity thrives in both environments.

LANGUAGE ■

The use of Euskara in prehistoric times and in antiquity has been ascribed to a vast area as far north as the Loire and as far south as the Strait of Gibraltar. But the historical evidence is limited to areas in and neighbouring the western Pyrenees, between the Garonne and the Ebro. The ruggedness of the country – mountainous and, historically, densely forested – has helped to preserve an array of dialects.

Since 1869, linguists have distinguished eight main dialects – one in each of the political sub-divisions and one in the Roncal Valley, but this is to discern only the patterns of a complex mosaic, not its individual components. Standard Euskara is spread today by television and by the educational policies of the government of Euskadi (the Basque region).

PHYSICAL GEOGRAPHY ■

The Basque lands (Euskal-Herria) comprise the provinces of Álava, Guipúzcoa, Vizcaya and Navarre in Spain, plus Labourd, Soule and Lower Navarre in France. The largest Basque city is Bilbao (Bilbo) the capital of Vizcaya province and one of the main industrial cities in Spain. Although barely 110 miles across, the Basque lands encompass deep oak forests, verdant mountain valleys and a rugged coastal strip along the Bay of Biscay. With the exception of the flat and arid Alava Plain, the Basque region is well watered by the Atlantic rain.

Most Basques (approximately two million) live in the Spanish provinces, and a further 100,000 in France. There are also large Basque communities in Central and South America, the destinations of migrants, both willing and unwilling, during the 18th century.

HISTORY ■

In the 1st century BC, Roman and Greek writers identified numerous Basque tribes. The name of one tribe, the Vascones, gradually became extended to inhabitants of the region generally. Their reputation for fierce resistance to Rome seems exaggerated: Roman remains are common in the lowlands. Latin and Christianity encroached in outlying areas.

In the 7th century, Vascones (probably mercenaries) settled what was to become Gascony, giving the future duchy its name and spreading Basque place-names to the Garonne. Settlements also spread in southern border regions of the Basque lands in the 9th to 12th centuries.

Throughout this era, Basque political culture showed a marked degree of independence. The most famous episode – the slaughter in 778 of Charlemagne's rearguard, which inspired the legend of Roland – may represent the repudiation of Frankish authority by a mountain tribe.

By the mid-9th century, some western communities acknowledged overlords in Oviedo where a kingdom, perhaps of Basque origin, emerged to become the nucleus of the Kingdom of Navarre. Only for a brief spell in the 1020s and 1030s, under King

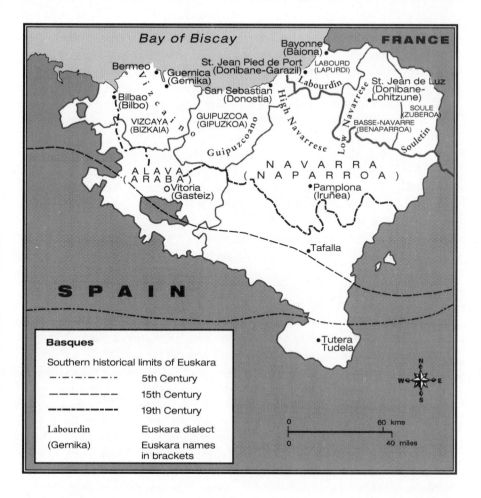

Basques

Southern historical limits of Euskara

–·–·–·–·–	5th Century
––––––––	15th Century
–––––––––	19th Century
Labourdin	Euskara dialect
(Gernika)	Euskara names in brackets

Map labels: Bay of Biscay; FRANCE; Bayonne (Baiona); Bermeo; Guernica (Gernika); St. Jean Pied de Port (Donibane-Garazil); LABOURD (LAPURDI); Labourdin; St. Jean de Luz (Donibane-Lohitzune); Bilbao (Bilbo); San Sebastian (Donostia); High Navarrese; SOULE (ZUBEROA); VIZCAYA (BIZKAIA); GUIPUZCOA (GIPUZKOA); BASSE-NAVARRE (BENAPARROA); Low Navarrese; Souletin; Guipuzcoan; ALAVA (ARABA); NAVARRA (NAPARROA); Vitoria (Gasteiz); Pamplona (Iruñea); Tafalla; SPAIN; Tutera Tudela; 60 kms; 40 miles

Sancho the Great, did a single source of political authority again hold sway throughout the Basque lands. The reconstruction of such a state was dreamed of – by Alfonso the Battler of Aragon in the 12th century, by Basque nationalists in the 19th – but was never again achieved.

In the late Middle Ages, Basque allegiances divided permanently. The warrior aristocracy from the western Basque lands blended into the history of Castile. The Kingdom of Navarre might have become a focus for nascent Basque nationhood – some courtly verse in Euskara was written there in the 15th century; in the 16th century, however, the kingdom was divided between France and Castile.

Within the Castilian monarchy, Basques were a privileged élite, with preferential exemptions and immunities. Some writers supposed that these privileges (*fueros*) derived from a contractual relationship between the Basques and the Crown. Resentment by the monarchs' other subjects complemented a growing Basque sense of identity in the 16th century, when humanists extolled the antiquity of

73

Euskara. The argument that the Basques had preceded other occupants of the Iberian peninsula was first advanced in 1539.

In the 17th and 18th centuries, however, Basques identified with their parent-monarchies, French or Spanish, rather than with each other, or with their several provinces rather than with any pan-Basque sentiment. Particularism continued to make a united Basque region unthinkable. The *fueros* were re-codified, province by province.

POLITICS ■

In the 19th century, foralism – the movement for the defence of traditional privileges against the centralizing policies of the liberal Spanish governments which predominated after 1833 – was boosted in the Spanish Basque lands by a fierce, clericalist Catholicism which spurned the church's own policy of modernization. The result was a militant movement which supported the ousted absolutist pretender to the throne of Spain, Don Carlos. In a series of wars, Carlism defied the Spanish establishment, which favoured state control, and in 1875 a mainly Basque and Navarrese army came within striking distance of Madrid.

Meanwhile the Basques of the French lands had gone their own way and were absorbed into France's unitary state. Basque nationalism thus became a largely Spanish phenomenon. Its growth as a political movement after 1860 was stimulated by scientific racism. Only pure-blooded Basques were admitted to the Basque National Party, founded in 1894. The revival of Basque literature was bound up with reactionary nostalgia and the rejection of Spanish, the language of liberalism.

Paradoxically, Basque nationalism grew when heavy industry came to Bilbao and Vitoria (Gasteiz) – because of local resentment of immigrant workers and the creation of a middle-class movement for regional devolution. In the Spanish Civil War of 1936–9, conservative, clericalist Basques formed an alliance with radicals, secularists and the revolutionary left in exchange for a statute of autonomy.

Defeat by Franco buried the statute for 40 years and inaugurated an era of clumsy, ineffective repression which sustained the old Basque nationalism and created, for the first time, a Basque nationalism of the left. Middle-class *enfants terribles* took to terrorism and acquired, in Franco's last years, a remarkable degree of popular sympathy. The Spanish constitution of 1978, which restored democracy to Spain and granted devolution to Euskadi, left unresolved the questions of the frontiers of the territory and the limits of autonomy. This indecision has kept militant nationalism alive, while the cultural budget of the Basque government has fomented national consciousness. In the last decade or so, a political movement of Basque nationalism has emerged on the French side of the border and the prospect of a re-fashioned federal EC has stimulated hopes of some future pan-Basque entity within a European super-state.

SOCIAL STRUCTURE ■

Matriarchal or, at least, matrilineal principles have been ascribed to the early Basques. The earliest surviving records, from the high Middle Ages, show that, as in many other parts of Spain and southern France, women could own property, head families and contest cases at law.

The relish with which the Romans divided the Basques into tribes does not necessarily reflect the Basques' own perceptions: in many parts of the empire, tribes discerned by the Romans disappeared from the records after the empire's fall and the Basque lands are no exception. It is reasonable to suppose, however, that in the isolated inland valleys groups were defined by ties of kinship and that blood-relationships – whether or not modified by other factors such a wealth or seniority – helped to determine the distribution of authority. Outside the Kingdom of Navarre, no native aristocracy can be discerned until the late Middle Ages. The emergence of conspicuous fortified manor houses, especially in Alava, coincided with an era of opportunity for ambitious warriors in Castile's 14th-century dynastic wars. The victor, Enrique of Trastámara (d.1379), recruited some of his most effective supporters among the Basques.

The chief distinguishing feature of Basque society, compared with neighbouring peoples, was inheritance of the entire property, normally by the first-born son. This may help to account for the large Basque contribution to the internal settlement of the expanding frontiers of medieval Castile and to Spanish overseas imperialism in the 16th century. By favouring the accumulation of capital and encouraging enterprise, it may also have contributed to the commercial and industrial development of the Basque lands in modern times.

RELIGION ■

Despite the evidence of early Christianization of the low-lands, the remote mountain areas were regarded as still virtually pagan by the 12th century. If slow, evangelization was nevertheless thorough in some respects, as the enduring heritage of clericalism and dogmatism shows. Intense spiritual initiatives which have enriched the Catholic world – from the Jesuits to Opus Dei – have been launched by Basques.

Counter-Reformation churchmen were suspicious of alleged witchcraft and pagan survivals in the mountains: in 1610, during a witch-hunt in a Basque-speaking community of northern Navarre, the inquisitor Salazar formulated the theory that witchcraft was a psychological delusion. The fervour with which Basques continue to venerate local cults, often in preference to the universal cults of the Church, continues to shock evangelists to the present day. In the modern and cosmopolitan industrial port of Bilbao (Bilbo), devotion to the image of Nuestra Señora de la Begoña is a badge of civic identity and the football club celebrates its victories at her shrine. Veneration of numinous trees – like the blasted oak of Guernica, almost finished off by German incendiary bombs in 1937, beneath which the *fueros* of Vizcaya were reputedly sworn – has suggested that tree-worship is a tenacious Basque tradition.

POPULAR CULTURE ■

The distinctive elements in Basque popular culture are games, song and verse, and cooking. Competitive sports and games are a conspicuous part of the culture, especially *aizkolari* – wood-cutting and stone-dressing contests – and *pilota*, also known as *frontón* and *jai-alai*, which resembles squash played by teams on a vast court either with a basket-like glove or with a bat. It has become popular wherever colonies of Basques are found. Unlike *aizkolari*, which remains a village or neighbourhood affair, it has developed a formal and professional structure.

The first printed book in Euskara was *Linguae Vascorum Primitiae* (Bordeaux, 1545), a collection of popular religious and amatory rhymes, representative of a corpus of traditional oral literature which is kept alive today by song and dance competitions or *bertsolariuk*. The complex and varied rhythms of the dance *zortzico* and *aurresku* played on the recorder-like *txistu* have given rise to the term *Pas de basque*.

The popularity of societies of gastronomy – almost exclusively for men – attests the importance of Basque cuisine in the rest of Spain. It is rich in dairy products and vegetables. The thin wine known as *chacolí* is served cold in shallow china goblets throughout the Spanish Basque provinces and cider is favoured, except in Alava.

ECONOMY ■

A martime economy, based on fishing, shipping and long-range trade, is well documented from the 15th century onwards, especially in Bayonne (Baiona) and San Sebastián (Donostia). This commercial and maritime tradition, and the availability of coal and iron ore, favoured the development of heavy industry in the Spanish part of the region in the late 19th and early 20th century.

BRETONS

The distinctiveness of Breton society owes much to its development in the remote, northwest peninsula of France, and its relative physical and cultural isolation from the rest of France. The peninsula was recognized by the Gauls as having two distinct personalities: the coastal region was the Armor, the 'country near the sea', while the interior region was Arcoet, the 'country of woods'. First and foremost a peninsula, the whole area became Armorica as part of the Roman Empire. A long, deeply-indented coastline with rugged cliffs and headlands alternating with sandy bays and tidal estuaries fringe a once-forested interior of hills and plateaux derived mainly from hard granite and slate, with intervening depressions formed of softer schists. Not more than 65 miles across, and with that distance effectively reduced by penetrative estuaries, the peninsula favoured the integration of life on

*land and sea. Celtic immigration to the peninsula in the post-Roman period was to
have a profound and enduring impact upon an already-ancient Celtic civilization
in Armorica and it is its powerful Celtic inheritance which differentiates Brittany
fundamentally from the rest of France.*

HISTORY ■

Brittany has been peopled since at least about 700,000 BC. Mesolithic hunters and
gatherers and Neolithic farming communities have left an impressive legacy of mid-
dens, burial chambers and menhirs (standing stones, such as those at Carnac). The
Bronze and Iron Ages saw the exploitation of the peninsula's mineral deposits, the
construction of tumuli and hill-forts and the considerable development of maritime
and inland trade, for example in weapons and tools. Julius Caesar's conquest (57 BC)
of the Armorican tribes saw the Romanization of the peninsula, although it is generally recognized that its economic integration into the Empire proceeded further
than did its cultural assimilation: for example, while towns and some large rural
estates had populations using either debased Latin or Gaulish (or both), the very
large rural population still spoke Gaulish, and Christianity spread only very slowly in
Armorica. When Rome's influence was withdrawn, whereas the peninsula was
hardly touched by the Germanic invasions happening elsewhere in Gaul, it did
become increasingly a refuge for many *Brittones* fleeing from the Anglo-Saxon invasions of Britain during the 5th and 6th centuries AD. *Brittones* merged with the indigenous Armorici to become the Bretons and to create Brittany. This growing
Celtic population and colonization through to the 9th century was associated with
the expansion of Celtic speaking, of Celtic place-names and of Christianity. During
the Dark and Middle Ages, Brittany – first given administrative and political unity in
the 9th century – fought to establish and maintain its independent status, territorially
and politically, but eventually became part of France in 1532. Even then, the province was guaranteed regional privileges and in the succeeding centuries it
continued to resist the centralizing tendencies of the French state. In 1790, the
province was divided into five *départements* and the process of *françisation*
thereafter accelerated.

LANGUAGE ■

As a spoken language, Breton probably reached its apogee in the 9th century, since
when it has declined, being modified and ultimately replaced by French, although
even today it is spoken by about a quarter of the population of Brittany. A Celtic language closely related to Cornish and Welsh, and perhaps to a continental language
spoken in the peninsula before the arrival of the *Brittones*, Breton by the 17th century had developed four dialects (those of Cornouaille, Léon, Trégor and Vannetais).
During most of the Middle Ages, Breton was predominantly an oral rather than a literary language, used for example by jongleurs to tell Arthurian legends and other
stories. Only from the mid-15th century does an extensive Breton written literature

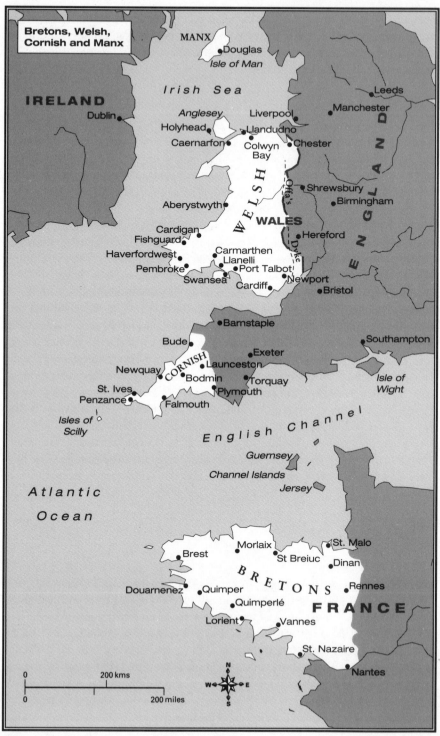

Bretons, Welsh, Cornish and Manx

MANX
Douglas
Isle of Man

Irish Sea

IRELAND
Dublin

Leeds
Manchester

Anglesey
Holyhead
Caernarfon

Liverpool
Llandudno
Colwyn Bay
Chester

ENGLAND

Shrewsbury
Birmingham

Aberystwyth

WELSH
WALES

Offa's Dyke

Hereford

Cardigan
Fishguard
Haverfordwest
Pembroke

Carmarthen
Llanelli
Port Talbot
Swansea
Cardiff
Newport
Bristol

Barnstaple

Bude

Southampton

Newquay
St. Ives
Penzance

CORNISH
Launceston
Bodmin
Falmouth

Exeter
Torquay
Plymouth

Isle of Wight

Isles of Scilly

English Channel

Atlantic Ocean

Guernsey
Channel Islands
Jersey

St. Malo

Morlaix
Brest
St Breiuc
Dinan

BRETONS

Douarnenez
Quimper
Quimperlé
Lorient
Vannes

Rennes

FRANCE

St. Nazaire
Nantes

0   200 kms
0   200 miles

N
W   E
S

appear, in the form of religious and secular poetry, drama, dictionaries and instructional manuals. In the 19th century, a renewed interest in Breton was a reaction to the central government's aim to replace regional languages by French. From having its use prohibited in schools in the 19th century, Breton is now taught in some secondary schools and teacher-training colleges; there is a chair of Celtic Languages in the University of Rennes and there are radio and television programmes in Breton. The maintenance of a living, written language is the objective of authors producing prose, poetry and drama in Breton today. There are, however, no longer any monolingual Breton speakers and even as a second language it is spoken by less than one in five of the population of Brittany.

NATIONALISM ■

Historically, the Bretons have a long-established attachment to conservatism, to religious sentiments, and to the maintenance of traditional social structures. Politically, they have for centuries been opposed to the colonizing and centralizing tendencies of other empires and states. The period of the French Revolution, for example, was particularly marked in Brittany by royalist and counter-Revolutionary movements: participation of Bretons in the peasant uprising of the *Chouannerie*, which originated in the Vendée to the south of the Loire, was suppressed with a savagery which guaranteed the hostility of succeeding generations to the impositions of central governments. This ultimately took political expression with the formation in 1898 of the Union Régionaliste Bretonne, and later of similar organizations, which argued for varying degrees of regional devolution and autonomy. But a plan promoted by the Parti National Breton (founded in 1932) to establish an independent government by negotiation with the Nazis, following the collapse of France in 1940, is the closest Breton autonomist ideas have come to fruition in modern times. Since 1945, separatist groups have proliferated but not gained mass political support, as both French and European Community funds have been provided to meet perceived economic needs in the region.

CULTURE AND CUSTOMS ■

The Celtic heritage of the Bretons includes an attachment to fantasy and to the supernatural, to story-telling and to religion. Alongside the Arthurian legends and the popular stories about magicians, spirits, fairies and demons (often associated with natural physical features, sometimes with prehistoric constructions), are those about numerous 'saints' (most of them not canonized, merely recognized by local bishops or nominated by local people, but almost all represented as painted wooden statues in churches and chapels).

The deeply religious character of the Bretons is expressed in the typical parish 'close', a monumental grouping around a small cemetery of church, triumphal arch, Calvary and charnel-house, and in the *pardon*, a religious procession of people wearing local costumes and head-dresses, carrying candles, banners and statues of saints, and singing canticles, which is then succeeded by a secular celebration involving today both traditional and modern music and dancing, and sometimes sports (formerly wrestling, now usually cycling).

Additionally, today, pan-Celtic festivals bring to Brittany other Celtic peoples and serve both to attract tourists and to revitalize the Breton sense of a non-French identity.

WELSH, CORNISH AND MANX

These three Celtic peoples, who live between the English and the Atlantic, subscribe in varying degrees to the over-arching notion of British identity without sacrifice of their distinct self-perceptions as historic communities. In the Manx case and, to a lesser extent, that of the Welsh, these are backed up by special institutional status.

HISTORY ■

On the higher ground of the west, in the face of the Germanic invasion, British princes, penned or driven, maintained their own self-rule. When the descendants of Kenneth I of Scotland admitted English overlordship by the 12th century, no such admission was made in Wales. There were also Celtic areas, not fully occupied or dominated by English rulers, in what is now called Cornwall. These western Celts, similar to the Welsh and indeed to the Bretons in language, culture and political traditions, maintained their cultural identity even when obliged to submit politically to the kings of Wessex and to take part in the slowly-emerging English state.

From the late 11th century, the peripheral parts of Great Britain were faced with ambitious rulers of a remarkably united English state and a disproportionately numerous English people. Norman ambitions in Wales were less thoroughgoing than those of the Romans. Though they did take steps to colonize Pembrokeshire, they tended, like the English before them, to draw a line at the former Mercian border, at Offa's Dyke, beyond which they were willing to concede peculiar institutions. They did cross the line, install lords, punish enemies and prevent the formation of any potential rival; increasingly in the 12th century, moreover, they selectively enforced their own laws and imposed their own claims to exercise ultimate rights of jurisdiction; but they did not attempt systematic reform of political traditions or extend the English system of administration by counties. Wales was a land of a kind so often found on the continent on the edge of greater states, where lords subordinate to neighbouring kings remained outside those kings' realms. As if to emphasize the distinctiveness of Wales, a special type of county was established along the border, initially in Cheshire, Shropshire and Hereford, regulated with an exceptional degree of military rigour, as a buffer against a turbulent march. Gradually, as the reach of English laws lengthened, counties were removed from this 'palatine' zone and lost their special status and relationship with the crown – first Hereford, then Shropshire, but not Cheshire for some considerable time. In the case of Wales, a gradualist approach led to a total English take-over which reached its climax in the reign of Edward I, between 1280 and 1286. Edward felt that the Welsh had welshified English or Norman lords and that in the northwest of the country Welsh princes were taking on the airs and graces of sovereign rulers. He mounted punitive expeditions, controlled the north of Wales through a formidable series of castles, created counties and treated them as part of his own realm. In the centre and south native lordships remained, but the proximity of the castles was a restraining influence on those inclined to repudiate English overlordship.

For much of the rest of the Middle Ages the English crown was distracted by adventures in France or paralysed by civil wars. In 1485 an era of relative internal peace began when Henry VII seized the crown. His Welsh ancestry and large Welsh following gave his coup a flavour of a Welsh conquest of England; in practice, the consequent integration of the Welsh élite into English life expunged Welsh independence for ever. The sons of Welsh gentlemen began their education at Shrewsbury and ended it at Oxford. In 1536 Henry VIII spread England's uniform system of counties to Wales and the catholic sensibilities of Welsh tradition were swept aside in a religious reformation imposed from Westminster.

RELIGION ■

Medieval Wales and Cornwall were lands of saints and retained redoubts of Catholic resistance long into the era of the reformation. In the 18th century, however, Wales was conquered by distinctively Welsh brands of Protestantism, such as Calvinistic Methodism and Strict Baptism, whose adherents between them came to outnumber those of mainstream Methodism, of the Church of Wales and of independent congregations combined. In 1923 the Welsh majority prevailed and the Church of Wales was disestablished. Radical Protestantism of various kinds has become integral to Welsh identity – a badge of resistance to metropolitan culture.

POLITICS ■

In a land famous for the rolling harmonies of its vast amateur choirs, populist movements, the rhetoric of community, collaborative causes and social issues all command more attention than in England, just as private enterprise and individualism are less highly-prized. The distinctiveness of Welsh political culture is apparent at election times. At every stage of the history of democracy in the country, majorities have been big: first Tory, then Liberal and nowadays in favour of the Labour Party. This is a culture in which consensus is valued and politics is conducted by discussion as much as by debate. The same is true of their fellow-Celts, the Manx and, to a lesser extent, of the Cornish. Nationalism is more widely embraced as a programme of cultural self-assertion rather than as a programme of secession from the United Kingdom, though the Welsh Party (Plaid Cymru) also enjoys a measure of electoral success, especially in the north of the country where industrialization has never penetrated and traditions of allegiance to the British Labour Party have not taken root. The social programme of Plaid Cymru is markedly left-wing, especially by comparison with regional parties in continental western Europe.

LANGUAGE ▪

The Welsh use language differently, even if it is English. Their reputation for skill in oratory, though objectively unverifiable, is supported by universal experience. It has been suggested that the call of the pulpit was important in spreading sectarian protestantism in Wales.

Adept in the use of English, the Welsh have their own Celtic tongue, which has the oldest literature of any language still spoken in western Europe today. This proud heritage is a symbol – as the use of the language is a badge – of nationalism; but it must be admitted that the future of the language is not secure. Its decline began in the late 18th century. Rapid industrialization in south Wales dealt it one blow; schools' tendency to spread the use of English as formal education became widespread was another. Although not actively persecuted, Welsh was forced back into a purely domestic sphere. By 1851, less than half the Welsh spoke Welsh as their first language; today the proportion is only 10%. The last individuals who spoke nothing but Welsh were three sisters in the Caernarvon peninsula who all died before 1950. Nationalists and sentimentalists are putting formidable resources into an attempted revival; like all such exercises, their efforts are criticized because of the need to refine a 'standard' tongue, which almost nobody speaks, out of a linguistic tradition which has got riven into local dialects. With the help of Welsh language broadcasting, there is some prospect that the continuing decline may be arrested.

Hopes of reviving the similar Cornish language are entertained only by committed romantics. It was a minority tongue even in Cornwall by the mid-17th century. The last native speaker, Miss Dorothy Pentreath, died in 1802.

MANX ▪

The traditional rulers of the Isle of Man were the House of Stanley, earls of Derby. In the 18th century, their liberal policies left them unprepared for the impact of the preaching of John Wesley (see p. 40) for whom the island became a great prize, stolen from under the eyes of Tory managers. The industrial revolution was the making of Man, which became a holiday destination for the workers of industrialized Lancashire. Wesleyanism, spanning the water, stimulated this link. The combination of assured prosperity and evangelical religion marked the Manx as prized employees throughout the British isles.

In their home island, a very traditional form of government was preserved.

Surrounded by England, Scotland, Ireland and Wales, Man has never been part of any of them. The antiquity and integrity of its parliament, known as the House of Keys and traced by Manx to Norse origins, are essential tenets of Manx self-pride. They are able to maintain a favourable tax regime and impose strict controls on settlers from outside. Insulated from the social and cultural changes of the 1960s and 1970s – or, at least, from the legislation associated with them – the Manx have been able to congratulate themselves on progressing directly between eras of conservatism. Though subjects of the British government they are not subject to it, except in matters of foreign policy and defence.

IRISH

Ireland has two principal historic communities. In very general terms they are characterized by religion: Catholics, who comprise the vast majority of the Republic of Ireland and around 30% of the population of the province of Northern Ireland (Ulster); and Protestants, who make up the balance of the population of Northern Ireland. More than anywhere else in western Europe, ethnic division in Ireland has given rise to political instability which has continued since at least the middle of the 19th century and which is as far from a lasting solution today as it has ever been. More, too, than in almost any other area of western Europe, the people have a heightened sense of the historical roots of their differences. In Ireland, as in the former Yugoslavia, history can cast a murderous shadow.

To each of the two main historic communities of Ireland, the other's identity is so sharply apparent that terrorists on either side have little difficulty in identifying targets for murder; yet in some ways the two groups are hard to define and even to name. As well as on religious grounds, they can be broadly characterized in terms of culture, political allegiance and ethnic origin, yet none of these categories is watertight. There is a long and respectable tradition of Catholic loyalty to the United Kingdom and there are a few Protestants who are contented citizens of the Republic of Ireland. Sobriety, industry, 'family planning' and divorce are virtues and vices traditionally – but no longer convincingly – associated with the Protestants. Most of the concentrated Protestant communion in northeast Ireland is descended from Scots or other settlers from Great Britain who arrived in the 17th century; yet many are the descendants of assimilated native Irish.

A third community, small in number, was important in Irish history from the 12th to the 20th century. This was an 'Anglo-Irish' élite spread thinly over the island who rejected the Catholicism of native Irish tradition without sharing the radical Protestantism of the northeast. The group included descendants of aristocratic English settlers and, in modern times, those of anglicized native Irish aristocracy: the amalgam shared a distinct Irish identity peculiar to itself. Dethroned by political change, it has almost disappeared today.

EARLY HISTORY ■

In historical times Ireland has always seen a close relationship between the state and religion. The first notable missionary was St Pelagius but from AD 432 his disciple, Patrick, trained at Auxerre in southern France, enormously extended his achievement. He built churches in what became Leinster, Munster and Connaught and the great, central and lasting headquarters of Irish Christianity in Armagh. The church was organized with a degree of cohesion unattainable in the purely political sphere. By about AD 600 there were at least five kingdoms in Ireland and a 'high king' or nominal chairman elected from among them. His seat was usually at Tara (near modern Drogheda): hence its great importance in both religious and secular culture. The five kingdoms were centred in Munster – sometimes divided into two, east and west; Connaught; Leinster, which represented what is now the southern half of the province of that name; Meath, occupying the northern half; and Ulster, the last and most enduringly important. Only 12 miles from Scotland at the nearest point, Ulster at times included part of the kingdom of Dalriada over the water in modern Scotland.

By the 9th century, four provinces of the church were established in a settled system at Armagh, Dublin, Tuam and Cashel. With its great daughter-monastery at Iona, from which much of the island of Great Britain was evangelized, the Irish church maintained, until well into the 8th century, a tradition, allegiance and practice different from those of Rome. Growing acceptance of Rome's lead, however, was espoused with the enthusiasm of converts.

In 701 Norwegian maritime invasions began. One gradual effect of this was the emergence of towns – the lack of which had previously made Ireland seem strange even by the standards of a remote and pastoral society such as that of Scotland. In 840 the town of Dublin was established as a Norse colony. Trouble followed between the domineering Norsemen who controlled long-range commerce – such as it was – and the native Irish. The upshot was that the Norse stayed in their towns, while native kings and high kings ruled the hinterland, unrestrained except by each other's power and the patchy tutelage of the church.

A single Gaelic language prevailed throughout the island, subject to the inevitable variations between districts and tribes. Beneath the kingdoms and provinces was a world of clans, whose heritage can still be perceived in their names, preserved as common Irish surnames. The prevalence and endurance of tribal society, the marginal status and paucity of towns, the pastoral basis of much of the economy – these deep-rooted features of Irish society drew the contempt of some neighbouring European peoples throughout the Middle Ages and early modern period.

Against this background of clan warfare came the first 'English' interference in the island: the English were summoned in 1167 by Dermot MacMurrough, King of

Munster, who, attempting to emulate the territorial kingship of Scotland and England, faced opposition from recalcitrant chiefs, especially in Leinster. Anglo-Norman knights established in Wales (see p. 80) were prominent amongst those who answered his call.

The English king, Henry II welcomed this development as a stage towards what he envisaged as total domination of the British archipelago. He asked the only English pope ever, Hadrian IV, for permission to take over Ireland; the pope agreed – obligingly but perhaps unsurprisingly – to let him take the opportunity; in 1172, after an Anglo-Norman colony had been successfully established by these allies of Dermot MacMurrough, Henry crossed the water himself, to prevent any usurpation of his 'rights'.

Especially in Leinster and Munster, the Anglo-Norman bridgehead developed and prospered spectacularly over the next 200 years. Its builders were frontiersmen, advancing from one marchland in Wales to another in Ireland. The modernization and regularization of laws and institutions and the development of common law, which were proceeding apace in England, were transmitted to Ireland only in distorted or attenuated form. Ireland was not just a frontier, but a frontier beyond a frontier, remote from the fount of authority. 'Going Irish' was a common recourse of invading lords in their efforts to establish a profitable relationship with their indigenous victims, especially in the outlying lands which they gradually penetrated in Connaught and the far west. In the growing prosperity of the 13th century an Irish parliament began to emerge. During the reign of Edward II (1307–27), an attempt by the brother of Robert the Bruce to set himself up as king of a rebel Celtic realm in Ireland in imitation of the Scots who had defeated the English at Bannockburn (see p. 36) failed within two years, even aided by the remoteness of Ulster. Yet this history of gradual, fitful conformity to English plans and models was not to continue. Just as Ireland was politically stricken by the internal divisions of its native people, so – in the process of going native or breaking free from the standards of the Anglo-Norman world – the colonial aristocracy descended into disunity. The Statute of Kilkenny (1366) was a desperate attempt to insulate English families from Irish influence; it established a 'Pale of Settlement' around Dublin, within which inter-marriage or alliance with the native Irish was forbidden. In the reign of Henry V (1413–22), when English power was altogether distracted by war against France, as much as half the Anglo-Norman colony from Ireland took refuge in England. Only when England's civil wars were over, in the reign of Henry VII (1485–1509), was this general anarchy ended. New legislation was introduced to re-fashion the Irish parliament. In 1495, Henry VII induced the parliament to reform itself by a system known as the Poyning's Laws: Irish parliaments were not to take place without leave from London; no legislation could be enacted without approval from London; and statutes made in London were to apply to Ireland automatically.

IRELAND AFTER THE REFORMATION ■

The Reformation destroyed the unanimity so lately imposed and so briefly enjoyed. Henry VIII (1509–47) proclaimed himself King of Ireland. The pope's gift of nearly 400 years before had made English kings 'Lords of Ireland' – a title which implied feudal superiority but not close-in kingly proprietorship. Henry's new initiative was intended to make reformed religion easier to impose. He began his Reformation as a conservative in religious terms – simply quarrelling with the papacy on a specific issue, then on a series of specific issues. When his course seemed to be leading to a general schism, the native Irish élite and many of the colonial aristocracy hesitated to follow. Irish-speaking congregations were outraged by a vernacular they could not understand and had to endure sermons in English. Adherence to the old religion went hand-in-hand with a preference for the old political order and resistance to close political supervision from England. Contacts with France and Spain were sought by those who remained faithful to Rome. The 'Irish problem' had emerged, which is still with us now: a problem of divergence of faiths and of incompatible allegiances.

Resistance was not confined to Celtic areas and the 'old English' families were tenaciously catholic. Latin as a common language of worship kept them united with their Celtic co-religionists. Much of the English crown's effort to anglicize Ireland – building up the 'pale' of English settlement around Dublin – seemed wasted. England contributed too little to Irish welfare for fellow-feeling with the metropolitan community to be sustained. Determined and brutal efforts at reconquest in the late 16th century were only partly successful, though it did force some of the leaders of resistance into exile in France and Spain.

Early in the new century, however, an intensive new programme of settlement helped to retrieve some of the ground lost in the Reformation: or, rather, it shifted the bridgehead from Great Britain to new ground, in Ulster. That remote northern province had always been immune from English rule. The invaders had remained content to cultivate the alliance – rather than exacting the allegiance – of one or two leading chiefs, of whom the greatest was the O'Neill. Committed to their religion, rejoicing in their independence, the Ulster chiefs were actively at war with the English establishment in Dublin by the 1590s: their subjugation inflicted great destruction and devastation on their lands, vacating space which Scots settlers were eager to fill.

For James I of England – the first ruler of the whole of Great Britain – encouragement of settlement in Ireland was a single solution to two problems: on the one hand pacification and repopulation of Ulster; on the other, demilitarization of the Anglo-Scottish border by the export of unruly Scots manpower. All nine counties of Ulster – especially Antrim in the northeast – came to be dotted or, in more central and easterly parts, covered with Scots. Thus the future 'loyalist' community in Ireland was founded: a great colonial bastion peopled by newcomers not beholden to their indigenous neighbours, with no share in the political and religious identity produced by the earlier history of Ireland. It was no longer a question of a privileged colonial elite struggling to coexist with a reluctant population: these new settlers made up every level of society; their self-contained world was proof against the erosion that had befallen earlier colonists' allegiance and identity. The number of native Irish who remained in the area of Scots settlement, adopting the invaders' culture, was probably higher than is usually supposed, especially in Antrim and Down: the clearances and 'ethnic cleansing' were directed against those unwilling to abjure Catholicism. English settlers supplemented the incoming Scots, many of them organised by patrons and investors in the City of London. By the close of this phase of settlement in about 1640, when 30,000 Protestant settlers were slaughtered in a sudden Irish uprising, about 40% of the population of Ulster was English and Welsh and about 60% Scots and native Irish.

The English Civil War of 1642–53 was, for the native Irish, an opportunity to strike back again at the invaders. Their enemies – presbyterians, Scots, the City of London – were arrayed on the parliamentary side of the conflict; the Irish were therefore in the paradoxical position of supporting the crown. The parliamentarians' revenge was terrible. In two major battles Cromwell trounced the upholders of the royal cause and Ireland lay at his feet. His massacre of intractable garrisons remains part of Irish folk memory; the name of Cromwell is still calculated to cheer up an Irish nationalist orator whenever the substance of his case seems to flag. Having also disciplined Scotland, in 1656 Cromwell set up the first state whose institutions encompassed the whole of the British Isles. From 1656 to 1658 Irish representatives sat in a London parliament.

The restored monarchy of 1660 might have rewarded the Irish with emancipation; in the Secret Treaty of Dover of 1670, Charles II promised freedom of worship for Catholics at the first convenient moment; in practice, he never found any moment convenient, but his brother and successor, James II (1685–9) was eager to flaunt his own catholic convictions and to impose religious toleration on his realms. The incumbent élite was loath to admit outsiders to equality; dethroned in 1688, James appealed to the sympathy of his Irish subjects; though they rallied to him in large numbers, they were decisively defeated by an English army at the Battle of the Boyne in June 1690. The Irish capitulated to generous terms of surrender, including freedom of catholic worship, suspension of victimization and leave to depart for would-be exiles; but in 1695 the victors tore up those terms and embarked on a course intended to eliminate the Catholic church in Ireland. New ordinations of priests were forbidden; outside Connaught, Catholic landowners suffered the confiscation of their lands; the community was thus to be deprived of its secular and spiritual leaders. Conceived in alarm, the persecution waned in security. By the 1770s Catholicism no longer seemed a threat to the state and the ban on Catholic officers in the armed forces was relaxed. In the 1790s Catholic suffrage was restored: in consequence, Ireland had probably the broadest electorates in the world outside the United States of America.

Ireland was developing into a kind of proto-America: a western colony, differing from the metropolis in religion, resentful of its modest share in imperial prosperity, toughened by the hardships of the frontier. Complaints against English rule in the mid-18th century came not from woebegone Celtic misfits but from Dublin merchants and landowners in the pale, clamouring for equitable access to British markets. The rebels who defied British rule in 1798 included Catholics and Presbyterians in a common cause. Following the American Revolution, London was obliged to modify Poyning's Law: the Irish parliament was empowered to make statutes of its own, subject to the royal assent. As a result of the French Revolution, which renewed and redoubled English fears for Irish security, William Pitt (prime minister, 1784–1802) conceived an even bolder plan: absorption by union of the colony into the mother country. If this seems a curious idea, it can usefully be compared with the historical process of the formation of the United States of America, where each new frontier of settlement, after a spell of colonial status, was then in its turn incorporated into the union. The Irish already had before their eyes the encouraging precedent of Scotland – brutally transformed but also enormously enriched since its own union with England in 1707. Pitt's vision for Ireland was of a country developed out of bigotry and accelerated into modernity.

In 1800 the Union was passed. 100 representatives went from Ireland to the British House of Commons and 28 to the House of Lords, but not one of them was a Catholic: emancipation had stopped short of this vital right, making reconciliation impossible. The new members fortified the imperial parliament as a bastion of reaction on Irish matters. Full emancipation in 1829 came too late to prevent the entrenchment of enmities in Ireland itself.

THE RISE OF NATIONALISM ■

Lack of natural resources condemned Ireland to exclusion from the strides in prosperity achieved in Great Britain through the Industrial Revolution. A huge increase of population, beginning in the late 18th century left many lacking adequate outlets for employment and, when the potato crop failed, no means of sustenance. In the worst of the famines, in 1845–9, a million died and a million more were forced to emigrate. The average standard of living of an Irish labourer was something like 5 to 10% per cent of that of his mainland counterpart. Ireland got poorer under the union, while her partner-kingdoms grew richer.

From the early 1820s, Daniel O'Connell and his Irish Association began to break landowners' control of the electorate; he took people from low social ranks into the House of Commons to challenge the system: the privileges of the Church of Ireland – a Protestant establishment, living off taxes levied on Catholic people; the conditions of tenancies which favoured Protestant landlords to the disadvantage of catholic tenants; the inequalities in a remote periphery unremedied by an indifferent metropolis. None of these grievances was redressed until their effects had become intolerable.

In the late 19th century, industrial development in central and eastern Ulster, supplied with coal from mainland Britain, opened a gap in prosperity which exacerbated tension between this protestant, 'loyalist', prosperous corner and the catholic, 'nationalist', impoverished rest. With the triumph of democracy in the British Isles as a whole, this ethnic cleavage, reinforced by divergent economic interests and political trends, was bound to split Ireland in two. The Irish National Party succeeded to O'Connell's parliamentary niche with more radical demands: no longer willing to rely on justice from Westminster, it demanded autonomy. 'Home Rule' was viewed sympathetically by a substantial minority in the imperial establishment, but, narrowly defeated in parliament in 1886, it was swept off the agenda for 20 years while Irish resentment continued to incubate. Out of it emerged a republican separatist movement. There was no likelihood that this would triumph: Irishmen in remoter parts of the empire – in Australia and Canada – were happy with dominion status; but its prestige was enhanced by an abortive rising in 1916, under cover of World

War I: the romantic 'martyred' dead of this episode captured the sympathy even of moderate nationalists. The reaction of some opponents of Home Rule was as violent as that of the separatists: as autonomy drew near the paradox of 'loyalist rebellion' disfigured the north.

These bloodlettings were alien to the tradition of British politics. In 1920 the British government espoused a well intentioned but fatal solution: home rule would be the subject of a referendum so regulated as to give the loyalist community the option of parting company with the rest of Ireland. In consequence, in 1922, the Irish Free State, from which were excluded the six counties of the northeast where loyalists at that time formed majorities, became a free dominion within the empire, like Canada. The new state's birth was marred by another civil war between autonomists and separatists, who rejected compromise and abhorred partition; the moderates won, but gradually thereafter separatist electoral success distanced what, in 1932, became the Irish Republic from its former imperial partners. Irish neutrality in World War II was the final, definitive step in the severance of links with the United Kingdom – though even today, Irish citizens enjoy residual rights to live and vote in the mainland.

Since World War II, attitudes in southern Ireland have matured and mellowed, but the six counties still in the United Kingdom have been left with insoluble problems of inter-communal tension. Their relative prosperity also attracted catholic immigrants from the south. The loyalist majority is therefore small and, for demographic reasons, diminishing; yet its sense of identity, forged in colonial times in opposition to a culture which the colony was founded to subvert, seems incompatible with absorption in a united Ireland. Since 1969, the frustrations of this situation have been displayed in exchanges of terrorist outrages between extremists in both communities; every political initiative so far has only tended to make matters worse.

LANGUAGE ■

Irish, the Gaelic language of Ireland, with an ancient and glorious literary tradition behind it, survived centuries of English ascendancy. But an Anglo-Irish literary culture grew up alongside it, embodied early in the writings of Edmund Spenser, and provided with an institutional home with the foundation of Trinity College, Dublin, in 1592. Many of the products of this tradition evince an Irish consciousness. Dean Swift, English-born Dean of St Patrick's Cathedral, Dublin, joined the great 18th-century protest of the Irish colonial mind against the exploitation of the Irish economy for totally British ends, as did his friend and collaborator of Huguenot origin, Molyneux. Conversely, Irish writers in English have been among the most capable wielders of the language: Burke and Sheridan represented the fruitful union of native Irish and Anglo-Irish traditions in the late 18th century. It became increasingly common for contributions of similar quality to come from writers of purely Catholic, native Irish background: William Carlton's stories of the Irish peasantry (1840) are a brilliant account of a level of society previously neglected in literature. Bernard Shaw and Oscar Wilde have been followed by James Joyce and Samuel Beckett from the Celtic cradle – using the English language sometimes even more effectively than the Anglo-Irish, who, as a class, are perhaps the most brilliant of all users of English.

The Irish language had been knocked from its pedestal by the Battle of the Boyne and the clearance of Catholics and native Irish from positions of influence and authority. Yet it had persisted as the vernacular for over three quarters of the ordinary people. The eclipse of Irish at even this level occurred with surprising suddenness towards the middle of the 19th century. Daniel O'Connell, whose family had escaped the hammering of the native gentry, had been brought up by a wet-nurse in a traditional native-Irish household. He had lived among the people as well as in the manor-house. This was the key to his mastery of the electorate, to whom he denounced the iniquities of the union as he toured the country. He understood the force and beauty of the Irish language; yet it was he who urged his fellow-countrymen to adopt English as the language of the future. By the end of the 19th century Irish was confined to the extremities of the west coast and the offshore islands. It was, however, seen by nationalists of the Irish Language Movement and the Sinn Fein Party as a means whereby a screen could be drawn between Ireland and England or between 'Celtic' Ireland and the Ireland of the intruded colonists. In 1932, 16,000 people spoke Irish as their main language out of a population of three million in the newly proclaimed Irish republic. By 1956, after 24 years of all-out campaigns, the corresponding number was 12,000. Today, everybody has to take it as a school subject and everybody has to go through the motions of using it. In the Dáil Éireann, the Irish parliament, speeches are begun in Irish, but speakers rapidly and impressively switch to that hateful, repressive English tongue when the moment arrives to say something.

3

THE CONTINENTAL NORTHWEST

The concept of geographical determinism – the theory that a people's history is the consequence of the environment they inhabit – has played a major part in the historiography of the countries of northwest Europe. French history has often been represented as a quest for 'natural frontiers'; the Germans have been seen as seekers of *Lebensraum* from a position surrounded by enemies with limited access to the seas. The political and cultural divisions of the Netherlands have been traced to geographical features which have made some provinces more defensible than others against rulers and influence from outside.

Yet at another level, the history of this region seems to have defied geography. The distinction between upland and lowland peoples which is a marked feature of Europe further east and south seems to have little relevance here, where the French and Germans – or particular communities within those nations – span both types of environment. The region covered in this chapter therefore includes the westernmost reach of the great plain from the south of southwest France, to the lower Rhineland and the western extension of the upland hoop of Europe from the Massif Central to the northwestern edge of the Bohemian mountains. Of those who belong to the French state, only some maritime and island peoples are excluded: the Corsicans, Provençals, Basques, Bretons and Normans (for these see pp. 174, 170, 71, 76 and 50 respectively); of the rest, the mixture seems sufficiently well stirred for them to be dealt with in two broad categories. Though all German communities are equally German, and politically unity is probably as widely prized in Germany as in any existing European state, for reasons explained on p.111, the cultural diversity and fragmented history of Germany's regions justifies the inclusion here of Franconian and Rhineland Germans, whose route to their present homeland was via the west and who have continued to be influenced from that direction (for other German peoples see pp. 260–1).

93

FRENCH

The French of today are an amalgam of peoples, just as the France of today is an amalgam of places. The planned creation of a French nation and the spontaneous Parisianization of its provinces during the 19th century is usually acknowledged to have been a product of the homogenizing tendencies of military conscription (introduced in the late 18th century, much earlier than in any other European country), of primary schooling (much improved from the 1830s and compulsory, free and secular from the early 1880s) and of improved communications (especially the railways from the 1850s). The effective annihilation of space and time was accompanied by the construction of a national French culture intended to include in its embrace an historically diverse set of peoples and provinces. Nonetheless, however deliberate the process of francisation *came to be in the 19th century, its origins can be traced back to well beyond even the 9th century, to the migrations of barbarian peoples – the Franks – and their creation of a powerful kingdom – Francia – following the collapse of Rome's Western Empire in the 5th century.*

HISTORY ■

The Franks (see p. 117) were one of the groups of Germanic peoples who invaded and conquered the prosperous central provinces of Roman Gaul during the 5th and 6th centuries, establishing what was to become the most powerful of the barbarian kingdoms of Europe after the disintegration of the Roman Empire, and the strongest Christian kingdom of early-medieval western Europe.

The peoples of early-medieval Europe were not racially distinct or ethnically pure: they were instead, for the most part, communities grouped together by their leaders, sharing a common language and culture (although components of that language and culture might have been imposed upon them by another people). The Franks seem to have developed during the 3rd century from the fusion of several Germanic peoples. Two groups of tribes are usually identified: the Salian Franks, established on the river Ijssel, and the Ripuarians, living on the right bank of the Rhine, although this latter group was an inchoate collection of people not perceived as a distinct group until the 8th century. Unsuccessful invasions into Roman Gaul during the second half of the 3rd century led the Salian Franks to recognize Roman authority and to provide soldiers for the Roman army, but as the power of Rome gradually declined, so the degree of independence of the Franks grew and they themselves colonized parts of the Empire. With the collapse of the Empire in 476, the Salian Franks took over most of northern Gaul as far as the Somme and under Clovis I, who ruled from 481 to 511, they both adopted Christianity and moved south to the Seine and then to the Loire, colonizing lands which today comprise Upper Normandy and much of the Paris Basin. During the 6th and 7th centuries the

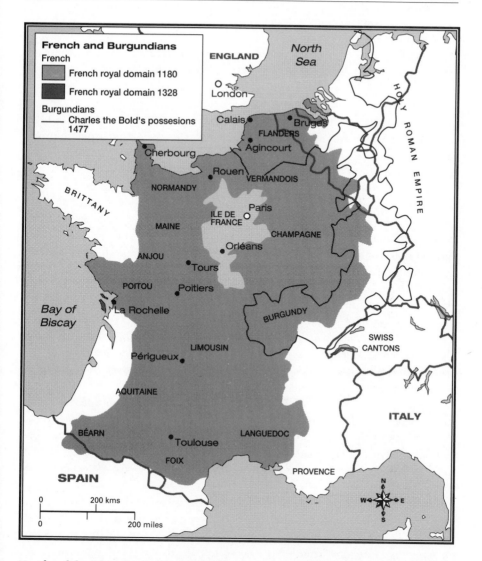

French and Burgundians
French
French royal domain 1180
French royal domain 1328
Burgundians
—— Charles the Bold's possesions 1477

Franks of the Rhineland colonized the left bank of the Rhine as far as the present-day boundary of Latin and Germanic languages and also moved into what is now Flanders, which had been abandoned by the Salian Franks. Not until the 8th century did the Rhineland Franks adopt Christianity.

As the Franks colonized the territories of former Roman Gaul, they mixed and married with the more numerous Gallo-Roman inhabitants of those areas. Unlike the Romans and Goths, the Franks did not prohibit marriage between conquering and conquered peoples, which was one reason for their rapid cultural assimilation with the Gallo-Roman population. In later centuries, the inhabitants of the Frankish kingdom, or France, persisted in calling themselves Franks although the Frankish component of the population had become merged with the Gallo-Roman people.

95

Additionally, the political hegemony of the kings of the Franks began to make their subjects, of whatever origin, consider themselves as Franks and the kingdom of the Franks assumed a political rather than an ethnic connotation.

By the early 6th century Clovis had not only subdued the Burgundians, he had also freed the southwest as far as the Pyrenees from the Visigoths, so that virtually the whole of what is now France was then in Frankish control, even if Frankish settlement itself was mainly in the north and east of the territory. These conquests provided the foundation for constructing the powerful and extensive Frankish empire, which reached its zenith in the reign of Charlemagne (768–814).

With the death of Charlemagne in 814, the great Frankish Empire fragmented and it was to take almost another 1000 years for the political boundary and unity of the modern French state to be established. In 806 Charlemagne had himself proposed partitioning the Empire : *Francia* was to comprise the northern lands, settled by the Franks themselves, while *Aquitania*, to the south, covered what had been the most romanized part of Gaul. Although Charlemagne's proposal was not implemented, that broad bisection of France has come to be regarded as reflecting a fundamental cultural division which persists in some ways through to the present-day. Instead, the partition of the Empire in 843 by Charlemagne's grandsons gave to Louis the German the lands in which a Teutonic language was spoken and to Charles the territories in which Romance was dominant. It was from the lands allocated to Charles that the modern French state was slowly, and with much political turbulence and many political boundary changes, to emerge.

Although the kingdom of France in the 10th and 11th centuries was well-defined, legally and territorially, in practice political power struggles reduced it to a collection of small states, each effectively independent and owing little more than nominal allegiance to the king. France became a bundle of feudal lordships, each in conflict with the others and often struggling also with internal challenges to its authority.

In addition to those provinces occupied by the Bretons, the Normans and the Burgundians (see pages 50, 76 and 102), and of course the Franks, the two most important units of medieval France were Aquitaine and Gascony. The Roman province of *Aquitania*, extending from the Pyrenees to the Atlantic coast and to the Loire river, became part of the Visigothic kingdom in the early 5th century before coming under Frankish control in the early 6th century. Established as a kingdom by Charlemagne in the 8th century, Aquitaine became a duchy under the counts of Poitou during the 9th, 10th and 11th centuries and then, through the marriage of Eleanor of Aquitaine (daughter of the last duke of Aquitaine), to the Plantagenet Henry II of England, a large part of the duchy came under English control as part of the Angevin Empire. It was for centuries a territory whose ownership was disputed between England and France, before it returned definitively to France in 1453. Gascony, situated between the Garonne and the Pyrenees, was part of Rome's Aquitania before being conquered by the Visigoths and then by the Franks. The people, the Gascons, had come from the south (hence the area's name, *Vasconia*, being the Latin for the

Basque lands) and, following the Norman invasions, regrouped into the duchy of Gascony, with its capital at Bordeaux. In the early 11th century Gascony was reunited as a result of a marriage with the duchy of Aquitaine, but it was owned or occupied by the English from 1154 until it again became part of France in 1453. During those 300 years Gascony developed an important trade in wine to England.

The incorporation of Aquitaine and Gascony into the kingdom of France was part of a wider, prolonged process. The effective French royal domain in the 11th century was restricted to the Ile-de-France, focused upon Paris since the establishment there of the court after the accession of Hugues Capet in 987, and thereafter spread only slowly and by no means continuously to encompass by the 17th century most of what is now France. Which is not to say that all of those living within its boundaries had either the ability to use French as a common language or a shared conception of France as a nation.

LANGUAGE ■

France lacked a common language at the time of Charlemagne and even in the mid-19th century one in five 'Frenchmen' still could not speak French and in one in five communes French was not yet the language of everyday use. It took centuries for regional languages and dialects to be replaced by 'standard' French.

During the romanization of Gaul, from the 1st to the 5th century, its inhabitants were also latinized: Latin came to be the language of administration, law, commerce, religion and education, but of course the process was not complete either regionally or socially. With the weakening of Roman influences when the Roman Empire collapsed in the 5th century and the barbarians invaded, spoken Latin in Gaul gradually changed, so that it became differentiated both from classical Latin and from the forms of Latin spoken at the time in other parts of the Empire. Through to the 8th century there gradually developed a differentiation between the language of the north and that of the south, reflecting in part the greater influence and density of colonization by Salian Franks in the former than in the latter. Culturally inferior to the Gallo-Roman population, with whom they inter-married, and rapidly converted to Christianity, the Franks soon abandoned their native language but nonetheless both introduced to the Romance language many words associated with agriculture and with warfare, and influenced pronunciation significantly.

A fundamental linguistic divide, running from the Gironde around the northern edge of the Central Massif to the locality of Lyon, separates the northern dialects of *langue d'oïl* ('hoc illud' in Latin became modern French 'oui') from the southern dialects of *langue d'oc*, sometimes generally referred to as Provençal. The northern dialects included *normand* and *anglo-normand*, *picard* and *wallon*; *champenois*, *lorrain* and *bourguignon*, as well as the dialects of the Paris Basin, among them *francien*, the dialect of the Ile de France from which modern French is essentially derived.

With royal administration centred on Paris from the late 10th century, the *francien* dialect began to acquire a superior status over others and gradually came to be used over a wider geographical area, both as an official and as an increasingly fashionable form of communication. From at least the 13th century, the spoken language of Parisian society was adopted as a model followed by others and there flourished a rich *francien* literature, in verse, in *chansons de geste*, in narratives, didactic texts and histories. Legal documents came increasingly to be written in *francien*. Although by no means all of the years of what came to be called the Hundred Years' War (1338–1453) saw open conflict with England, they did serve to engender a sense of French national identity and promoted still further the use of *francien*, in both spoken and written forms (with, for example, more works being translated into *francien* from Latin). This trend was encouraged by governments during the later Middle Ages and given a major boost under François I with the Ordonnances de Villers-Cotterêts of 1539, which prescribed the exclusive use of *francien* in the courts and in legal documents. The measure was intended in part to protect the rights of individuals unable to comprehend Latin, which remained frequently in use in the courts, in part to provide a single language of administration for the kingdom, and in part to assert the paramount status of the language of the king. Its effect was the increasing relegation of other, regional dialects of French to use principally in speech, and hardly at all in literature where they were ousted by *francien*, which accordingly came to be recognized as standard French.

During the 17th century a classical French was actively promoted, not least by the Academie Française established by Richelieu in 1634 specifically to standardize the usage of French by producing a grammar, a dictionary and a rhetoric of French. A steady flow of similar works were published, diffusing the concept of *le bon français*, although it was still restricted both geographically and socially, focused upon high Parisian society but gradually spreading beyond to other social groups, to the French provinces and to the New France across the Atlantic. From the early 18th century, with the Treaty of Rastatt (1714), French was recognized as an international language of diplomacy. The Revolution of 1789 resulted in a project to eliminate regional languages and dialects and to establish French as the language of liberty and of the nation. From the late 19th century the schooling system sought to impose French as a national language and to eradicate regional linguistic variations, although not until schooling was made compulsory in 1882 could such measures make their full impact. The growth of mass French literacy and of a popular French press and literature during the 19th century virtually concluded a long historical process whereby what had been a regional dialect – *francien* – came to be superimposed on the other regions.

Such a development was perceived in some parts of France as a form of internal colonialism and so was resisted. Whereas in northern France, standard French – as taught in the nation's schools as the language of the educated Parisian and so Frenchmen – has established a hegemonic status, in the Midi a distinct form of southern standard French has emerged and is accorded considerable status. Additionally, in those areas of France where a minority language was or is spoken, such as Brittany, Alsace and much of the Midi, distinctive regional pronunciations of

French have created *français régionaux*. In most such regions there is a degree of bilingualism, with the minority, regional language (Breton, Alsatian, Occitan) used informally with family and friends and French (with a degree of regional pronunciation) used formally with strangers and officials. Nonetheless, although standard French is still not universally and constantly spoken throughout France, it has been gaining ground rapidly during the 20th century and the minority languages and dialects are in serious decline, with knowledge of them being concentrated into a diminishing and ageing component of the population. Endeavours by regionally-minded individuals and groups since the end of the 19th century to ensure the survival of minority languages and dialects have, since the *Loi Deixonne* of 1951, found some public support in a measure designed to encourage the teaching in schools of Basque, Breton, Catalan and Occitan (and, from 1974, Corse) in those areas which use them, but the effectiveness of such measures as attempts to stem a tide of linguistic change is open to question. Indeed, standard French is itself changing even as it is becoming more widely used: it is being transformed by new, popular expressions, by words and phrases which are anglo-american borrowings, by new scientific terms, and by acronyms and abbreviations: in effect, by the internationalization of a regional dialect which had itself been imposed upon a nation.

NATION AND NATIONALISM ■

The identity of France and of the French has been a subject of controversy for centuries and the debate continues today. By the early 7th century most of the people living in northern Gaul might have thought of themselves as Franks and *Francia* as the territory to the north of the Loire. But for much of the Middle Ages, the image of France held by, and promoted by, the intellectual élite was derived from the partitioning of the Empire of Charlemagne after the Treaty of Verdun in 843, which established three kingdoms: a western kingdom (*Francia occidentalis*), a middle kingdom (*Francia media*) and an eastern kingdom (*Francia orientalis*). From the 9th century onwards, western Francia came increasingly to be referred to in literary sources simply as Francia, a kingdom which stretched from Flanders to Roussillon and eastwards to the 'four rivers' of the Rhône, Saône, Meuse and Scheldt; the Eastern Kingdom came to be known as *Germania* and that area of it inhabited by Franks came to be called *Franconia*; the northern part of the Middle Kingdom (following its further partitioning in 855) came to be called Lotharingia (after Lothar II) and then subsequently Lothringen (in German) and Lorraine (in French). Politically, the Western Kingdom or Francia is the direct ancestor of the modern French state and its outline provides an historical underpinning to the popular, if inaccurate image of France today as a hexagon.

Of course, by no means all those living in the new kingdom of France perceived themselves as being French nor, before maps and primary schooling became widely available in the late 19th century, did they have a clear conception of the shape and significance of the French state. Nonetheless, an image of France as a nation and as a country did develop from the late Middle Ages onwards, fostered by a cultural and political élite and gradually diffused more widely throughout society. National sentiment and French nationalism emerged in the 15th century, at the time of the conflict with England, and then strengthened in the 16th century in response to the growth of Spanish power in Europe. The idea of France was promoted from the early modern period by intellectuals, by the makers of ideologies, who sought justification for a French identity in the country's history, with France portrayed as being the heir of Gaul, and in its geography, with France depicted as having natural frontiers defined by coastlines, rivers and mountain ranges. The ethnic and cultural diversity of medieval France was thus subsumed in an image which highlighted its historical and geographical unity.

Views about the historical origins of the Franks have become part of the making of French identity. Some early-medieval historians ascribed a Trojan origin to the Franks, perhaps in order to bestow upon them a cultural equality with the Romans, and until the 18th century, genealogies of French kings taught to French schoolchildren often began with King Priam. Other early historians emphasized the continuity of Gallo-Roman people and culture, minimizing the role of the Frankish invaders, and then from the 16th century it came to be argued that the true origins of France and of the French were to be found in Gaul. The familiar phrase, 'Nos ancêtres, les Gaulois' (Our ancestors, the Gauls), was first used by François de Belleforest (d.1583). The idea gradually developed that the aristocracy were descended from the Franks and the masses from the Gauls, and the Revolution of 1789 was (incorrectly) interpreted by some contemporaries as an ethnic conflict, with the Gauls at last chasing out the Franks and the cock replacing the fleur-de-lys as a national icon. During the 19th century such interpretations acquired more credibility when the new science of physical anthropology was harnessed to explanations of social and racial conflict and of nationalism. After the defeat of France in the Franco-Prussian War (1870), French nationalists seeking to insulate themselves against Germanic influences promoted the Gauls as the true founders of France and portrayed the Franks as barbarian invaders who had destroyed a Gallo-Roman civilization. In addition, the new nation state used the instruments available to it – especially primary schooling – to construct a French national consciousness, but it did so in order to create an awareness of a country with a distinctive history and geography, of a country with a unity of assimilated peoples and of integrated regions.

REGIONS AND REGIONALISM ■

The modernization of France during the 19th and 20th centuries is often assumed to have had associated with it not only the creation of a new national identity but also the destruction of local and regional identities. While there can be no doubt that the ethnically, culturally and socially diverse populations incorporated into the French nation saw much of their individuality eroded, it was not entirely destroyed. Indeed, to some extent the centralizing tendencies of the state created a reaction, a heightened awareness of the different regions of France and a vigorous debate about regional devolution.

The increasing spatial integration of French territory and the growing cultural homogenization of French people, especially from the mid-19th century onwards, was paradoxically accompanied by the birth of modern geography, with its emphasis on regional differences. The most influential of France's geographers, Paul Vidal de la Blache, published in 1903 his *Tableau de la Géographie de la France* as an introductory volume to Ernest Lavisse's comprehensive, multi-volume history of France: it provided a detailed account of the regions of France, emphasizing their individual personalities more than the extent to which they were inter-related. Moreover, Vidal de la Blache portrayed France in terms of its traditional *pays* and provinces, not of its modern *départements*. At that time, too, many schoolchildren were acquiring an idea of France from G. Bruno's *Le tour de France par deux enfants*, a collection of reading passages and lessons told as a story of two children from Phalsbourg in Lorraine who, fleeing their province after its annexation by the Prussians, determined to know and love their own country, France. The book's message is that while each of the regions of France is different, each contributes significantly to the whole that is France. First published in 1877, Bruno's book was monumentally successful, selling 7.4 million copies by 1914, shaping the idea of France and its regions in the minds of generations of schoolchildren. The regions of France – such as the Auvergne and the Dordogne – remain vital to the cultural life of the French today, known and appreciated for their distinctive histories, geographies and life-styles. Reverence for the regions has not been destroyed by the superimposition upon them of either a network of administrative *départements* at the end of the 18th century or a framework of planning regions in the third quarter of the 20th century. The historical and geographical provinces of France have proved to be remarkably enduring.

Late 19th-century France was the birth-place in Europe not only of regional geography but also of regionalism as a political movement. Belief by some Frenchmen that both provincial and national life had come to be excessively concentrated in the national capital resulted in the emergence of a regionalist movement whose objective was the decentralization of administrative, social and economic activities from Paris to the provinces, which in turn would bring about a renaissance of the regions. The regionalist movement aimed ultimately at the creation of entirely new provinces to replace the *départements*, with each new province having a substantial measure of democratic self-government. Many schemes for such regional devolution were propounded and debated in the period immediately before 1914 and again during the 1920s and 1930s. Although the regionalist idea dates from the mid-1860s, from a conference held at Nancy in eastern France, the word *régionalisme* was not coined until the mid-1870s and did not become common political currency until the early 1900s. Only from the 1950s has there been any serious, but limited move towards political, economic and cultural decentralization. Paris remains the centre for the French, as it effectively has been for more than 1000 years.

BURGUNDIANS

*Burgundy (French Bourgogne), an historic region of eastern France, encompasses
a wide variety of physical environments and owes its distinctiveness to its specific
cultural and political history. Its extent and its boundaries fluctuated considerably
before it was incorporated into the French state at the end of the 15th century,
almost exactly 1000 years after the region had first been settled by the
Burgundians, a people of Scandinavian origin who inhabited the islands and
southern shores of the Baltic (where the island of Bornholm – known as
Burgundholm in the Middle Ages – testifies to the general area of their original
homeland).*

HISTORY ■

During the 1st century AD, Burgundians migrated into the lower valley of the Vistula
but, encountering there the more powerful Gepidae, they moved westwards into the
territory of the Roman Empire. Serving first as auxiliaries in the Roman army, they
established a powerful kingdom which, by the early 5th century AD, extended to the
west bank of the Rhine. While endeavouring to move even further westwards, into
Belgium, they were defeated and almost annihilated by the Romans, assisted by the
Huns. The surviving Burgundians were transported to Savoy, from where – with
Rome's grip on its Western Empire weakening – they subsequently spread into the
Saône and Rhône river basins, and as far south as the shores of the Mediterranean.
Then, in the 6th century, the Burgundian kingdom was conquered and occupied by
the more powerful Franks and the remnants of its royal family were destroyed. By
that time, however, the name 'Burgundy' had come to signify a region of France, al-
though its boundaries as a political unit were by no means fixed.

From the mid-6th century, Burgundy's fluctuating boundaries reflected its political vicissitudes. Burgundy was an unstable political construction, rather than a region reflective of its relatively stable physical geography or of the deeply-engrained
culture of its people. In 561, when Clotaire I died, the Frankish kingdom was partitioned and the kingdom of Burgundy was allocated to one of his sons. Gradually the
kingdom was extended to embrace the former Burgundian territories and also a
large part of the southern Rhône valley, of lands to the east of the Alps and even considerable areas in north-central France. As a much-disputed territory, Burgundy was
at times divided into Upper and Lower Burgundy before being united again and
then once more partitioned. This time it was divided into the duchy of Burgundy
(that part to the west of the Saône, which remained part of the Carolingian kingdom
of France) and the Franche-Comté of Burgundy (that part to the east of the Saône,
where the count of Mâcon refused to pay homage to the king, so that his territory
came to be known as the 'free-county' of Burgundy). These two Burgundies were

united under the Valois dukes during the 14th and 15th centuries (1363–1477). The duchy of Burgundy was annexed to France in 1477; Franche-Comté was part of the Habsburg Empire from 1493 until 1678, when it too was annexed by France. In 1790 the province of Burgundy was suppressed, with the former Franche-Comté replaced by three départements (Jura, Doubs and Haute-Savoie) and the former duchy of Burgundy by four départements (Côte-d'Or, Nièvre, Saône-et-Loire and Yonne).

PEOPLE AND CULTURE ■

Given Burgundy's turbulent political history, it is hardly surprising that the term 'Burgundy' has itself often lacked definition and precision, both historically (as was the case, for example, during the 15th century) and at present. Moreover, although the Burgundians have left as a legacy what has become an extremely well-known name for one of France's provincial regions, the inheritance of the *Lex Burgundionem* or *loi gombette*, which permitted marriage between Burgundians and other neighbouring peoples, has been promotion of their cultural assimilation and the undermining of their own distinctive identity, a process encouraged by the role of the Rhône and Saône river valleys as corridors of communication, of the intermixing of peoples and the exchange of ideas and practices.

The survival and persistence of a Burgundian personality derives in considerable measure from the region's economic prosperity during the Middle Ages and from its distinguished contribution to European culture, especially in the realm of architecture and music. During the 11th and 12th centuries there emerged a distinctive Burgundian style of architecture and sculpture which produced some of the outstanding achievements of Romanesque art. The most influential development upon the region's architecture was the building of the third abbey church at Cluny (1088–1130), which was the largest Christian church built in Europe during the Middle Ages. Constructed on a massive elaboration of the traditional basilica plan, Cluny played a key role in the diffusion of Romanesque art, serving as a model for other churches throughout Burgundy, notably that of Sainte-Marie-Madeleine at Vézelay (1150–1215). The essential features of Clunian architecture came to be two towers over the western façade, an octagonal bell-tower over the crossing of the central, vaulted nave and the large transepts; an ambulatory and chapels radiating away from the sanctuary apse; apertures diffusing a serene light; and, of course, the church's immense length and height. Some of these features came to be the fundamental components of European Gothic architecture. In addition, the Burgundy school as directed by the Cluniac order produced some of the outstanding sculpture of medieval Europe. Detailed, lively sculptures on the capital of columns and the tympana of the massive western doors of churches portray, for example, the Last Judgement or the Apocalypse.

Later, during the 15th century, when Burgundy was expanding territorially, its wealthy rulers patronized the arts and in particular music. By promoting composers, singers and instrumentalists they fostered a Burgundian school of music which came to acquire a reputation and influence well beyond the region. During the Hundred Years War, Burgundy was a cultural centre, relatively insulated against the disruptions of war, and Dijon became perhaps the outstanding European court, attracting international artists. The Burgundian school of music advanced the Mass as a musical genre, moving away from the French Gothic tradition, but it was the secular song that became its most significant expression.

BURGUNDY AS A FRENCH REGION ■

Since the annexation of the duchy of Burgundy to France in 1477, the centralizing tendencies of the state have continually eroded the local and regional characteristics of Burgundy as a region and of the Burgundians as a people, increasingly integrating the region into France and its people into Frenchmen. The *burgonde* language has long since disappeared as a commonly-used form of communication. Of course, *bourgogne* as a fine wine – produced and traded in considerable quantities since the Middle Ages – continues to make the region, but not the people, of Burgundy a household name today throughout the Francophone and the Anglophone worlds.

LUXEMBOURGERS

Small, tenaciously self-differentiated historic communities are typical of mountainous regions. The historical geography of the Low Countries, however, shows that introspective identities and peculiar institutions can breed just as effectively around sea-level, if rivers, canals, bogs, shoals and sudden topographical faults conspire to make small territories defensible. In the late Middle Ages, the Low Countries contained almost as many distinct and proudly independent communities as Switzerland; in the 16th century, some of them combined to resist outside control with comparable effect. Since then, their identities have blended in those of larger groups: Walloon (pp. 106–8), Flemish (pp. 109–11), Dutch (pp. 45–9) and Frisian (p. 48). The Luxembourgers remain, however, as a unique survival, unassimilated to broader ranks. As Catholic speakers of a Germanic language different from German, they have much in common with the Walloons – especially with the two Germanic-speaking Walloon communities – and with the Flemings; their economic ties in the Benelux heartland of the European Community amount to a pooling of sovereignty with Belgium and the Netherlands. Their feelings of ease with both French and German language and culture, and their prominent role in international banking and broadcasting, as well as in housing institutions of the European Community, give them a cosmopolitan profile reminiscent of the Swiss. Yet their identity is uncompromised by any of this and they remain resolutely themselves.

In their loyalty to European ideals, their willing immersion in regional co-operation and the tenacity with which they cultivate their identity, Luxembourgers can be said to typify the 'new Europe' of regions and historic communities within a developing overall federal structure, which is said to be replacing, or at least threatening, the 'old Europe' of big, mutually hostile states.

HISTORY ■

Luxembourg's position seems made for independence: perched at the southernmost tip of the Low Countries, where the forests are still dense in places, protected on three sides by the uplands of the Fagnes, the Eiffel and the Hunrück, and on the fourth by the Ardennes, this is the most obviously defensible of all the areas inhabited by Netherlandish peoples. The capital teeters impregnably on a dramatic ravine. Luxembourg – straddling the cultural and political frontiers of France and Germany – seems to distil the quintessence of the medieval ideal of a 'Middle Realm', for which the Emperor Lothair fought and Charles the Bold died. Yet full independence and internal sovereignty are recent prizes, won only in the course of the 19th century.

The House of Luxembourg was established in the 10th century as marcher-vassals of the Holy Roman Empire. Their prominent role in European history in the Middle Ages and early modern periods involved the supply, at various times, of rulers for the empire and for the kingdoms of Bohemia and Poland; from the 14th century, however, the present territory of the Grand Duchy of Luxembourg always formed part of the Burgundian dominions and of Burgundy's successor-states – the Spanish and Austrian Low Countries and the Kingdom of the Netherlands. When the short-lived united Netherlandish state broke up in the 1830s, the Grand Duchy, shorn of what became the Belgian province of Luxembourg, was assigned a unique status under the Dutch crown but outside the Dutch state. King William II of the Netherlands (Grand Duke, 1840–9) is revered by Luxembourgers as 'Founder of the State of Luxembourg'. But the emerging nationalism of this small people owed as much to poetry as to politics; writers like Edmond de la Fontaine, Michel Lentz and Michel Rodange discovered in the Duchy the makings of a national consciousness. The existence of a common frontier with Belgium, Holland, Germany and France invited the attentions of each, but also ensured, at different times, the protection of all. In 1867, to prevent annexation by France, the other neighbouring powers imposed guaranteed neutrality by the Treaty of London. In 1890, on the death of William III, severance of the Dutch connection was formalized by the transfer of the hereditary headship of the state to the House of Nassau.

LANGUAGE ■

Although French and German are universally known in Luxembourg and are used in certain traditional contexts – French in government and the courts, German in church, and both as languages of instruction in schools – the speaking of

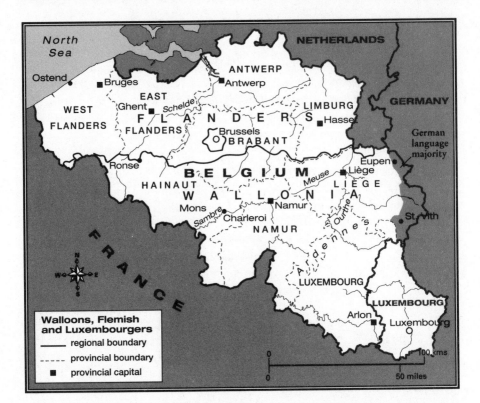

North Sea

NETHERLANDS

Ostend

Bruges

WEST FLANDERS

EAST FLANDERS

Ghent

Schelde

ANTWERP

Antwerp

F L A N D E R S

LIMBURG

Hasselt

GERMANY

German language majority

Brussels

BRABANT

Ronse

B E L G I U M

Eupen

Liège

HAINAUT

W A L L O N I A

LIÈGE

Meuse

Mons

Namur

St Vith

Sambre

Charleroi

NAMUR

Ardennes

Ourthe

F R A N C E

LUXEMBOURG

Arlon

LUXEMBOURG

Luxembourg

Walloons, Flemish and Luxembourgers

— regional boundary
---- provincial boundary
■ provincial capital

0   100 kms

0   50 miles

Letzeburgesch is a mark of national identity. Though its history as a medium for literature has been short so far, it is considered impertinent by Luxembourgers to call their language a dialect of German: though the grammar and accidence are Germanic, the intonation is peculiar – and closer, in many respects, to Dutch than to German – while the vocabulary is heavily influenced by French. The distinctiveness of Letzeburgesch was the basis of the Luxembourgers' successful resistance to Nazi attempts at incorporation of the Grand Duchy into Germany during World War II. In a conscious attempt to consolidate the difference, for new word-coinings Luxembourgers prefer to borrow from French or even English, rather than German.

WALLOONS

The identity of the French-speaking Walloons is elusive and the creation of an authentic Walloon nation has not yet been fully achieved. The French-speaking Walloon population of almost 3 million is found in southern Belgium. Wallonia (Wallonie) won a degree of autonomy in 1980, and this has been extended since 1988, as Belgium has moved towards a federal structure. Regionalist fervour, however, lags behind that in Flanders, where there is strong support for nationalist parties.

Wallonia's population is not entirely French-speaking. Over 5% are Italian; and the foreign population in some urban communes exceeds 25% of the total. There is also a German-speaking minority of 68,000 and German is the official language in a small area around Eupen and St Vith. This area was relinquished to Belgium by Germany after World War I but now has a measure of autonomy in cultural affairs. The Luxembourg dialect (Letzeburgesch) also survives in a few communes near Arlon, though this is not recognized officially. In the bilingual region of Brussels, the majority of the population is French-speaking, although the interests of the Walloons and the Brussels francophones by no means coincide entirely.

LANGUAGE AND LANDSCAPE ■

The northern limit of Walloon territory corresponds to a historic line of division between Romance and Germanic language groups, dating back to Roman times, and the word Walloon (akin to 'Welsh') is derived from a Germanic word meaning 'foreigner'. In the Middle Ages, western Walloon dialects showed affinities with the Picard dialect of French, though further east a stronger Germanic influence was evident. Standard French was, however, also widely used. The use of French was officially encouraged between 1795 and 1815, when Belgium was part of the French state; and, after a period of Dutch rule, French was adopted as the language of government when Belgium achieved its independence in 1830. The use of French throughout Belgium was resisted by the Flemish population (see p. 110), and in 1932 its use was restricted to Brussels and Wallonia, which became a unilingual, francophone region.

The Walloon region is a land of contrasts, extending from the outer suburbs of Brussels to the gorges and wooded uplands of the Ardennes. But almost two-thirds of its population is located along the urban axis of the Sambre-Meuse coalfield, which extends from near Mons through Charleroi and Namur to Liège. The coalfield has a distinguished history, and Wallonia was to become an early cradle of west European industry. The wooded slopes of the Meuse valley offered abundant supplies of charcoal, and metal-working industries were well established by late medieval times, using local ores and water power. After 1795, Belgium's incorporation into France opened up a huge market for armaments and metal goods at a time when French industry was relatively under-developed, and French companies played a part in the rapid development of the coalfield. Coal production reached a peak output of 25 million tonnes in 1927; but mining ceased by 1985 and heavy industries such as steel have also contracted.

WALLOON IDENTITY ■

By the mid-19th century, Wallonia had become the foremost industrial region of continental Europe, and a world leader in sectors such as the manufacture of railway

107

rolling stock. Yet a sense of Walloon regional identity was slow to develop. Although the use of French was a commercial asset, which enabled Walloon manufacturers to penetrate the European market, the Walloon population, unlike the Flemish, did not suffer the suppression of its regional language and so did not achieve a similar sense of unity. Moreover, the ruling élite, which occupied many key positions within the new Belgian state, although French-speaking, was not exclusively Walloon. French had been used among the upper classes throughout Belgium since the 18th century, and the bourgeoisie identified with the culture and ideology of France, rather than with Wallonia.

Despite this, some newspapers were published in the Walloon dialect and a Societé de Littérature Wallonne was founded at Liège in 1856. The symbolist literary review *La Wallonie*, launched in 1886, also attempted to foster a francophone literature which was specifically Belgian, and for a time this became a focus for Walloon consciousness. But many Walloon musicians and writers, including César Franck and Georges Simenon, eventually moved to Paris and were absorbed within the mainstream of French culture. Even today, Belgian art is often equated simply with the Flemish cultural heritage, while the Walloon contribution to French culture is overlooked.

By the late 19th century, industrialization had begun to change the fabric of Walloon society. Although still nominally Catholic, the coalfield towns showed anti-clerical tendencies, and socialism quickly took root. The harsh treatment of the workforce provoked widespread civil disturbances, most notably in 1886, and the solidarity of the industrial working class remained a feature of Walloon society until the 1980s. Following an extension of the franchise in 1893, 28 socialist deputies entered parliament – all from Wallonia. But the momentous appeal for the federalization of Belgium, made in 1912 by the Walloon socialist leader Jules Destrée, was not widely supported, and the separatist parties which emerged in Flanders during the inter-war period had no equivalent in Wallonia.

It was only in the 1960s that a wider sense of Walloon identity emerged and Walloon separatism became a significant force. In 1900, Wallonia accounted for over 40% of the Belgian population; but by 1961, its share had fallen to one-third, owing to a remarkably low birth rate. The demoralization of the Walloon population was reinforced by an economic crisis in the Sambre-Meuse coalfield, and by the language laws of 1963, which satisfied Flemish demands for full linguistic equality within Brussels. In 1961, the *Mouvement Populaire Wallon* was founded as a Walloon federalist party, and its successor, the *Rassemblement Wallon* won 14 seats at the 1971 general election. For the first time, Walloon working-class consciousness had acquired a specifically regional dimension and in 1978 the Walloon socialist party finally separated from its Flemish counterpart. Despite the quickening pace of devolution, the growth of nationalism within Belgium remains asymmetrical. By the early 1980s, the *Rassemblement Wallon* was in decline.

FLEMISH

As currently used, the term 'Flemish' refers to the approximately 6 million Dutch-speakers in Belgium (total population 10 million). They live primarily in Flanders, roughly the northern half of the country.

The Flemish Region is a flat, low-lying, densely-populated and highly urbanized area of some 7,500 square miles. It consists of the provinces of East and West Flanders, Antwerp, Limburg and Flemish Brabant. In addition, several hundred thousand Flemings live in the Belgian capital Brussels, an officially bilingual (Dutch- and French-speaking) enclave in the Flemish Region. In Belgian constitutional parlance the 'Flemish Community' comprises the entire Dutch-speaking population of Belgium, i.e. those inhabiting the Flemish Region as well as those living in Brussels. Brussels also doubles up as the capital of Flanders.

HISTORY ■

The designations 'Flanders' for the whole of the Dutch-speaking area of Belgium and 'Flemish people' for all of Belgium's Dutch-speakers date from the 19th century. They emerged after 1830 in the political and linguistic context of the newly independent Belgian state.

In the medieval period the area now known as Flanders was not politically united. The County of Flanders (roughly modern East and West Flanders plus parts of northern France) had feudal ties with the French crown, while the Duchy of Brabant (roughly modern Brabant, Hainault, Antwerp and Netherlands Brabant) was linked with the German empire. In practice, both Flanders and Brabant enjoyed a large measure of autonomy, and considerable power and prosperity. In the early Middle Ages Bruges and Ghent (in Flanders) were the main economic and cultural centres, a role subsequently taken over by Antwerp and Brussels (in Brabant).

In the course of the 15th and 16th centuries most parts of the Low Countries (i.e. modern Belgium and the Netherlands) were gradually united, first under the Burgundian dukes and then under the Habsburg dynasty. In the latter half of the 16th century the centralist policies of the Spanish Habsburgs and the spread of Protestantism led to a general revolt. Catholic Spanish troops eventually reconquered most of the southern Netherlandish provinces, taking Antwerp in 1585. In the ensuing military stalemate the northern provinces gained independence as the Calvinist-dominated Dutch Republic, while the south – roughly present-day Belgium – returned to Spanish rule. Dynastic control passed from Spanish into Austrian hands early in the 18th century, amid obvious signs of economic and especially cultural decline. Shortly after the French Revolution, the Austrian Netherlands were overrun by French armies and incorporated into France. Following Napoleon's defeat in 1815 the old 17 provinces of the Habsburg Low Countries briefly came together

109

again as the United Kingdom of the Netherlands under the Dutch King William I. But by 1830 an alliance of (partly Flemish) Catholics and (largely Francophone) Liberals instigated a rebellion and subsequently established an independent Belgian kingdom.

During the preceding century-and-a-half the upper classes and the bourgeoisie in the Dutch-speaking provinces of Belgium had increasingly adopted French as their main language. French therefore became the sole language of public life in the new state, even though the majority of the population spoke Dutch. The long Flemish campaign to gain equal rights for the Dutch language in Belgium on a par with French is known as the Flemish Movement, which eventually grew into a major political force. It gave all Dutch-speakers in the country a common identity as one 'Flemish' people, the inhabitants of 'Flanders' in its contemporary sense.

It was not until the 20th century that Dutch was recognized as the exclusive language of public life in Flanders. When Flanders replaced Wallonia (the French-speaking southern half of Belgium) as the country's economically dominant region in the 1950s and '60s, the Flemish also began to cast off their underdog mentality and to call, first for cultural and then also for administrative autonomy. In recent decades a series of constitutional reforms has transformed Belgium into a federal state in which Flanders has become largely self-governing, with its own assembly and executive, fulfilling Flemish aspirations to be regarded as a nation.

LANGUAGE ■

The Flemish speak Dutch, a Germanic language. Most Flemings speak both a local dialect and Standard Dutch, which is also the language of the Netherlands. There are only slight differences in pronunciation, vocabulary and usage between Dutch as used in the Netherlands and in Flanders. Dutch spoken by Flemish people is said to sound softer and more melodious.

However, whereas in the Netherlands the Dutch language is taken for granted, in Flanders the issue of language is always sensitive and politically charged. As a result of the long struggle against French encroachment in Flanders and the adoption of the standard language of the Netherlands as a linguistic norm, Flemings tend to be both proud and defensive about their language. In the past they recognized but resented the social and cultural prestige of French. While accepting Standard Dutch as a linguistic norm, they often proved reluctant to sacrifice their local idiom. For the present generation the Flemish economic and social ascendancy in Belgium and the federalization of the country have led to greater self-confidence and assertiveness.

IDENTITY, PERCEPTION AND SELF-PERCEPTION ■

Flemings will preferably define themselves in relation to their francophone countrymen in the south, the Walloons, and to the Dutch of the Netherlands in the north, whose language they share.

While Wallonia, which was industrialized at an early stage, boasts a long socialist

110

and free-thinking tradition, Flanders remained predominantly rural, Catholic and politically conservative for much longer. But both Flemings and Walloons delight in a relatively carefree, spontaneous lifestyle, often characterized as 'Burgundian' by outsiders. In comparison with the Dutch and their seagoing tradition and Calvinist heritage, Flemings tend to be more provincial and more nationalist, more pragmatic, improvisatory and anarchic.

The self-perception of many Flemings is coloured by the awareness of a long history of living with and under foreign powers, of coming from behind in economic, social, cultural and linguistic terms. This gives them their tenacity, inventiveness and pride. At the same time they feel they are living at the crossroads of the Romance and Germanic cultures of Europe, and this has made them open, forward-looking and ready to absorb elements from foreign cultures.

GERMANS

Germany has no separatist movements to match the Basques or the Corsicans. Rather, the Germans are more obsessed with unification than splitting apart. Moreover, the different characteristics of the original tribes have been watered-down by mass post-war migration by refugees – migration on a scale unknown elsewhere in Europe.

LANGUAGE AND IDENTITY ■

German is the native tongue of more Europeans than any other language except Russian. It spills over into all of the nine countries which border the modern, unified country and it brings with it a cultural sense of ethnic identity which transcends that of ancient tribes and regions. Alone among Europe's nations, the name and concept of Germans – or *das Volk*, as the Germans tend to call themselves – derives from the mother tongue and not from the older tribal or territorial name of the region.

The need to cling to language for unity derives from Germany's geographical position in the middle of Europe, which has meant it has been on the migratory route of so many of the peoples who went on to conquer the rest of the continent. With no obvious geographical borders such as mountains or seas to define the limits of Germany to the east or west, 'the country in the middle' has never stopped changing shape or ethnic mix. What has remained constant are the smaller territorial German regions, which for centuries had largely to fend for themselves while mightier powers fought military or political battles to control them. This meant there was no centralization, no national institutions of government and no need for loyalty to a country. Fellow German speakers were fellow countrymen, wherever they lived.

Successive invasions, settlements and the absorption of different tribes and groups make a nonsense of any idea of a 'pure' German race. Layer upon layer of

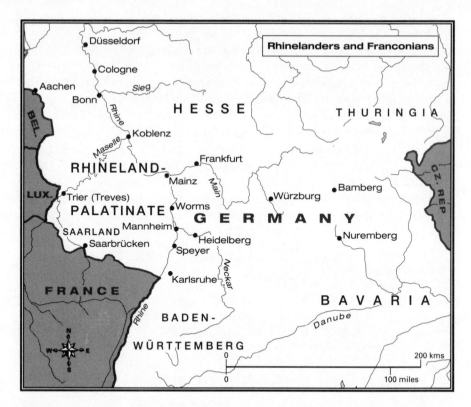

different ideas, personalities and traditions built up everywhere, and language provided the one common thread down the centuries, particularly after Luther translated the Bible into German in 1521, providing a standard literary language. Germany is rich in regional dialects but the language has always been relatively uniform from the Alps to the North Sea and the Rhine to the Elbe, despite the frequent division of the area down the ages.

This constant ebb and flow across the German lands has continued into this century. After World War II, some 12 million ethnic Germans fled to the West from the Soviet-held territories. Later the economic miracle of western Germany was made possible by importing *gastarbeiter*, largely from Turkey. Later again it was the flood of refugees into west Germany through the holes in the Berlin Wall that eventually breached the dam which defended the Soviet empire.

The inevitable consequence of so much turbulence, warfare and migration has been a need by Germans to cling more closely than most peoples to local identities and traditions. This has been the surest way of surviving occupation and ultimately conquering the invader by turning him into a local. Those who refused to integrate – like the Jews – became pariahs.

The concept of *Heimat*, a sort of fancy dress, nostalgic homeland, is both regional and national. Local identities, like so many blocks of Lego, create a single national identity, yet each remains a separate building block, self-contained and capable of standing on its own. In this way Germans are more loyal towards their local town or district than to their state and in turn more supportive of their state than of their nation. They are more concerned by internal borders than by international frontiers – cynics might say that is why they have invaded and occupied adjacent territories so often. *Heimat* comes into being wherever Germans are, regardless of which country they are living in.

This makes it easier for Germans to accept the concept of federalism in Europe, since this is historically all they have ever really known. It also means they have no need to fight for regional autonomy since they have never lost it. The word 'deutsch' in German does not, in fact, have a national so much as a cultural meaning. Although Mozart, for example, is acknowledged to be an Austrian, he is still called 'deutsch' by Germans because of his cultural origins.

UNIFICATION ■

An 'East German' identity may be said to have emerged, or is, perhaps, in course of formation, among Germans – historically belonging to parts of Saxony, Thuringia and Prussia – who formed the Democratic Republic of Germany between 1945 and 1990. The geographical division of the Third Reich after World War II was decided more by the relative claims and military success of the four allies who defeated Hitler than by any real respect for history. Nevertheless the line between east and west – Berlin apart – ran close to that which had divided the Germanic tribes in the west from the Slavs and other northern tribes in the east. The British area largely covered the original homeland of the Saxons. The French area covered much of what had been Swabia and the Americans governed in the old Franconia. The Soviets controlled territory which a thousand years before had been largely controlled by Slavs. In the intervening centuries this area had been germanized by settlement from the west and then conquered and unified by the germanized Prussians from the east. The merger between east and west Germany in 1990 was not a reunification, since many territories east of the Oder-Neisse line were surrendered forever as part of the international deal. It was therefore another unification of some of the German people into a new federal community.

The drive for unification was two-fold. In the first instance it was the desire for democratic freedom which was encouraged by Gorbachev. In the second place, and eventually more importantly, it was the desire for economic equality with the west. The cry of 'We are the people' which brought down the Berlin Wall was replaced by the chant 'We are one people' when east Germans believed unification would provide a short cut to prosperity. The disillusionment in both parts of the country with the consequences of unification has once more divided Germany into disgruntled have-nots in the east and resentful taxpayers in the west. The westerners are seen as occupying conquerors in the east, much as the German settlers were regarded by the Slavs a thousand years ago. The easterners are seen as uncultured layabouts in the west, much as the Slavs were considered. These attitudes look certain to endure for generations and might even, in years to come, give rise to a separatist movement.

RHINELANDERS

The Romans saw the Rhine – which derives its name from the Celtic word for 'current' – as the frontier between the Celts, whom they ruled, and the Germanic tribes, whom they did not. They colonized the western bank, notably building a town for one friendly Germanic tribe which was the birthplace of Julia Agrippana, the wife and murderess of the Emperor Claudius. At her insistence the town was named Colonia Claudia Ara Agrippinensis – Colonia for short – and the name has survived as Cologne. Centuries of Roman occupation gave a Latin character to the people, instilling in them a sense of national identity. This survived their incorporation into the Frankish kingdom after the 6th century, particularly since the Franks integrated easily because by then they had become Romanized themselves.

Down the centuries the area has repeatedly been split between different duchies or swapped back and forth between French and German control, but the river always served as a unifying link between the people, who remain staunchly Catholic, resolutely happy-go-lucky and openly cosmopolitan despite war, invasion and occupation.

HISTORY ■

Copying Roman strategy, the Franks turned the Rhineland into a buffer state, using it as a base for their military and missionary expeditions into Germany. Aachen, at the western rim, became the second city of the revived Holy Roman Empire, and this made Rhinelanders feel more than ever that they were citizens of the most important region in the world.

The church always played a major role in the region, politically as well as spiritually. Cologne became a great international centre of pilgrimage after Frederick Barbarossa donated the bones of the three wise men to the city. Trier, Mainz, Speyer, Worms and Strasbourg were all important players in the medieval power game.

The region was incorporated in its entirety into Napoleon's empire. Yet France was only allowed to keep the Alsatian zone of the river after his defeat. Prussia won back Alsace and Lorraine after defeating France in 1871 and occupied the Rhineland, creating a province which, thanks to its natural wealth in iron and coal, became a major industrial centre and one of the richest areas in Europe.

After World War I the French wanted the Rhineland to revert to its Roman role as a buffer state. In 1919, therefore, capitalizing on anti-Prussian, pro-Catholic feeling and on the fear of Communism, France actively encouraged a separatist movement, which included the young Konrad Adenauer, to create a new republic. Anglo-American pressure forced the French to break this up after only a few hours, but four years later a second Rhineland Republic was declared which survived for a fortnight. French insistence on military occupation of the area until 1930, and on demilitarising it thereafter, channelled the separatist movement into German nationalism, however. When Hitler tore up the Rhineland clauses of the Treaty of Versailles in 1936, the Rhinelanders were out in the streets waving flags to welcome in the German army.

With the end of World War II, the Rhineland once again asserted itself as the heartland of the German nation. Adenauer chose the sleepy riverside university city of Bonn as the temporary capital of divided Germany and the industrial cities of the Rhine and its tributary the Ruhr created much of the wealth which made the nation prosperous again.

THE LAND ■

The Rhineland is in two distinct and contrasting parts. The south, where the river winds through a steep gorge, is wild and sparsely populated. The north is flat, in places marshy, and the site of the largest urban concentration in the entire country.

While the steep valleys of the Rhine and its tributaries in the south are the site of famous vineyards, the lowlands north of Bonn are heavily industrialized. The region owes its wealth and historic importance to its rich mineral deposits. There is coal near Aachen, iron ore near Coblenz and lead in the Eiffel mountains, as well as smaller mines yielding copper, manganese, lime, gypsum and vitriol in commercial quantities.

RELIGION ■

Like the Franconians, the Rhinelanders are devoutly Catholic. Their faith has, perhaps, been strengthened by the existence of so many ancient and wonderful churches and abbeys in the region, which have given them a sense of regional pride allied to their faith. Aachen saw the first domed basilica north of the Alps. Speyer and Maria Laach can boast two of the finest Romanesque churches ever built. Cologne, with its wonderful gilded shrine containing the supposed bones of the three wise men, is home to the most complete Gothic cathedral ever constructed.

FOOD ■

Sauerbraten or beef marinated in wine vinegar with potato quenelles is the favourite dish of Helmut Kohl, who is a proud son of the Rhineland. Stuffed pork belly with pickled cabbage, pork stew thickened with blood and *reibekuchen* – potato pancakes served with apple sauce – are all traditional. Rhine and Moselle wines are of world renown, but less well-known is *federweisser*, a milky coloured partially fermented young wine, which should be accompanied by onion tart.

TOWNS ■

Lively Cologne is the Rhineland capital and the centre of the disparate region, built at the fulcrum between the mountains to the south and west and the lowlands to the north. Situated at the crossroads of important trade routes and with its attraction as a centre of pilgrimage, the city was a power in its own right in medieval Europe. To this day its atmosphere is that of a city state, complete with its own strong dialect – *kolsch* – and beer of the same name. The people seem smaller, wittier and darker-skinned than most Germans and are always ready for a party. The Rhine party-spirit has infected the whole region. Industrious Düsseldorf boasts that its old city is now the longest bar in the world because there are so many cafes working side by side. Koblenz, where the Rhine and Moselle meet, is the site of what used to be Europe's largest fortress – built to keep out the French. Mainz is the centre of Germany's largest wine market and the birthplace of Gutenberg, who gave Europe printing. Aachen, Speyer and Worms are all cities with an important imperial past which permeates their modern atmosphere. Trier dates back to Roman times when it was the meeting place of Celtic, Latin and Germanic civilizations. Despite its age, it still retains the atmosphere of a frontier town, with Belgium, Luxembourg and France all within easy reach. It is not just coincidence, perhaps, that Karl Marx, father of international socialism, was born there.

FOLKLORE ■

The Rhine Valley legends are the most atmospheric of all the many folk stories in Germany. Their inspiration is the river, with its deep gorge the obvious home for dwarves, dragons and heroes. Their modern structure, however, owes a good deal to Gothic ideas and ideals, which swept throughout Germany as a kind of unifying cultural force in the l9th century: Wagner turned them into his Ring Cycle.

The Rhine is also home to the most extravagant and licentious of all the German pre-Lenten carnivals. It actually begins at the eleventh minute of the eleventh hour of the eleventh day of the eleventh month – 11th November. This is when the local carnival committees, each set up with its own uniforms and bands, begin their preparations for the big blow out. In the Rhineland these committees derive in part from the time of the Prussian occupation, when they were used as a way of poking fun at their unwanted rulers. The week-long festivity, when fools are allowed to rule, allows for drunkenness, and gluttony on an heroic scale. It has little to do with Christianity and a great deal to do with paganism.

FRANCONIANS

The Franks, ancestors of, amongst others, the Franconians, first appear in history during the 3rd century AD as a group of three tribes (Salians, Ripurians and Hessians) living on the east bank of the lower Rhine, who tried unsuccessfully to invade the Roman empire to the west (cf pp. 94–9). In the mid-4th century the Salians managed to force their way over to the north, occupying what is today Belgium, extending their influence along the west bank of the Rhine. Today's linguistic frontier in Belgium between French and Dutch – a Germanic tongue – marks the extent of this settlement.

THE LAND ■

The duchy of Franconia was bounded to the west by the Rhine and the east by the Franconian Jura running into the Bohemian Forest near the source of the river Main, which bisects the region. The typical Franconian landscape includes a river, a wooded hillock and a rolling plateau of agricultural land. In the south, where the Rhine meanders through flatlands, the duchy spills over towards France, but in the north, where the river cuts a steep gorge from Mainz to Cologne, the Rhine forms a natural frontier. The plains round the confluence of the two rivers are extensively cultivated, while vineyards both along the Rhine and in the east of the duchy produce many of Germany's best wines.

HISTORY ■

At the end of the 5th century, the Salian leader Clovis set about creating the Frankish empire, compelling the different tribes to submit to his authority and then taking advantage of the disintegrating Roman empire to seize control of northern Gaul. He was strong enough to stop the Alemannic invasions across the Rhine and then he forced his way south to control southern Gaul, consolidating his Frankish kingdom in the north. Mass conversion to Catholicism further unified the Franks and helped them to integrate with the Gallo-Roman population. From this strong power base the Catholic, partly Romanized Franks moved east across the Rhine in the early 6th century into what was to become Franconia. It became an integral part of the Merovingian and then Carolingian empire and when this was split by the treaty of Verdun in 843, it became the nucleus of the East Frankish kingdom. As pagan tribes began to press in from the east, defence was decentralized and military command was left to the strongest local leaders – *duces* in Latin. The success of these dukes won the loyalty of the population, who relied on them for protection and this in turn speeded the disintegration of the authority of the emperor. In the early 10th century, however, the splintered German dukedoms felt the need to elect a single king as leader to increase their security. Conrad, duke of the Franks, was the obvious choice because Franconia was not so exposed to attack from the east, while his continuing links with the western Franks meant he could call on strong allies to help in time of need. Conrad proved unequal to the task, however, and he handed his throne on to the dukes of Saxony when he died. The duchy of Franconia remained vacant thereafter and this led progressively to a fragmentation into many secular and ecclesiastical principalities. These agreed in the mid-14th century to set up their own peace-keeping league. This in turn became the basis of the Franconian administrative district which survived until Napoleon carved it up between the kingdoms of Bavaria and Württemberg.

Franconia's traditional claim to be at the heart of any united Germany was already firmly established when Frederick Barbarossa engineered his election as king of Germany in Frankfurt in 1152, and by 1562 the city had replaced Aachen as the place where Holy Roman Emperors were crowned. The city was the seat of the German federal council which was set up to run the German Confederation of 35 states created at the Congress of Vienna in 1815, after Napoleon's defeat. It was the automatic choice as the meeting place for the first national German assembly in 1848. Goethe, who was born in the city, called Frankfurt 'Germany's secret capital' and its dominant modern role as the country's banking centre means that it does in reality control the national – and European – economy.

CULTURE AND RELIGION ■

Their early history has shaped the character of modern Franconians. Having been Romanized on the way to settling the area, the people have more sophisticated, liberal and fun-loving traditions than the descendants of the purer Germanic tribes who are their neighbours. Perhaps because they were at the first centre of pan-German government, they have a reputation for organizational ability and a strong sense of community.

The Franks were the first of the Germanic tribes to convert to Christianity and Franconia has remained devoutly Catholic. With their more romantic nature, the people preferred the more theatrical and opulent traditions of the Roman church to the spartan style of Protestantism. As the historic centre of the Holy Roman Empire for so many centuries, moreover, loyalty to Rome was natural.

LANGUAGE ■

The Central German, Franconian dialects have formed the basis of modern standard German, partly because it was dominant in Saxony at the time Luther translated the Bible, which became the first widely distributed book in the language. The dialect lengthened and sharpened vowel sounds, striking a balance between the open diphthongs of the south and the more nasal sounds of the north.

FOOD ■

Pork in various guises is a favourite of many recipes and nothing is allowed to go to waste. Pigs ears, trotters and tail served with pickled cabbage and pease pudding is one typical dish. So is a ragout of brains and calves head. Deer, boar and other game are popular and common in season. Sweet potato cake with raisins, liver and onion dumplings and a galantine of pork and beef with liver are found on many local menus. Frankfurter sausages have conquered the world in the guise of hot dogs.

TOWNS ■

Frankfurt, where the kings of Germany were elected and the Holy Roman Emperors were crowned, was to all intents and purposes the capital city of the Germanic tribes. The city retains a feeling of being at the centre of things, with hundreds of foreign banks, a celebrated opera company, arts galleries with important collections and the Zeil precinct, which is arguably the most important shopping street in the entire country. Heidelberg, with its ancient university and imposing ruined castle, was the home of Germany's romantic movement at the beginning of the last century and it is easy to see how its gracious atmosphere inspired poets and artists. In the east, Würzburg, with its baroque churches and castle, containing the largest ceiling painting in the world – by Tiepolo – is a university city with an illustrious past. Bamberg with its fine Gothic cathedral, half timbered riverside town hall and splendid baroque buildings claims to be the most perfect of all Germany's ancient cities.

4
THE ALPINE REGIONS

Mountains breed small, self-contained communities. Sparsity of settlement isolates them from each other; they develop nuances of identity, conflicts of allegiance and differences of language. Upland landscapes – crowding different environments and micro-climates together at different altitudes, or side-by-side in mountains and valleys – encourage economic diversity and divergence of interests. All these effects are multiplied in Europe's highest mountains, the Alps, which form a broad arc from Savoy in the west to Slovenia in the east. The height of the peaks, combined with the exceptional depth and breadth of the valleys and the variety and abruptness of the tectonic divisions makes the Alps a house of many mansions – a home for a large number of small but often fiercely self-regarding groups.

The central, highest zones are occupied by groups of peoples who have come together in modern states of middling size by European standards: the Swiss Confederation encloses tenaciously independent-minded cantons differing in language, religion and institutions, though linked by a strong bond of Swiss identity, while the Austrian Republic is a nation-state characterized by fierce, small-scale provincial loyalties within the over-arching, shared sense of Austrian identity. Accidents of political history have left out of these states two Alpine communities who form part of the Italian state: those of Val d'Aosta (see p. 147), whose individuality is similar in character to that of some Swiss communes, and Trentino-Alto Adige, where the indigenous community is not easily distinguishable from its Tyrolese neighbours across the Austrian border (p. 133). The Friulians, a clearly distinct historic community to the east of Trentino-Alto Adige, inhabit an Alpine landscape but are closely tied, culturally and politically, to their Mediterranean and peninsular neighbours (p. 184). Between the two, the tenacity of mountaineer-cultures is typified by the survival of romance dialects collectively known as Ladin, spoken by a few thousand dwellers at high altitudes, especially in the Garden and Badia valleys, in the midst of German-speaking areas.

The extremities of the Alpine region are occupied by groups of similar character and contrasting fates: in the west, most of the people of Savoy and Piedmont have been divided between France and Italy, gradually merging their identities in those of the larger states. At the opposite end, the Slovenians' strong collective identity has survived centuries of rule from outside and incorporation in Habsburg and Yugoslav super-states: today, Slovenia is an independent state, ethnically homogeneous.

North of the chain of the Alps, in the lands of the Bavarians and Swabians, high foothills and a large upland apron form part of the same

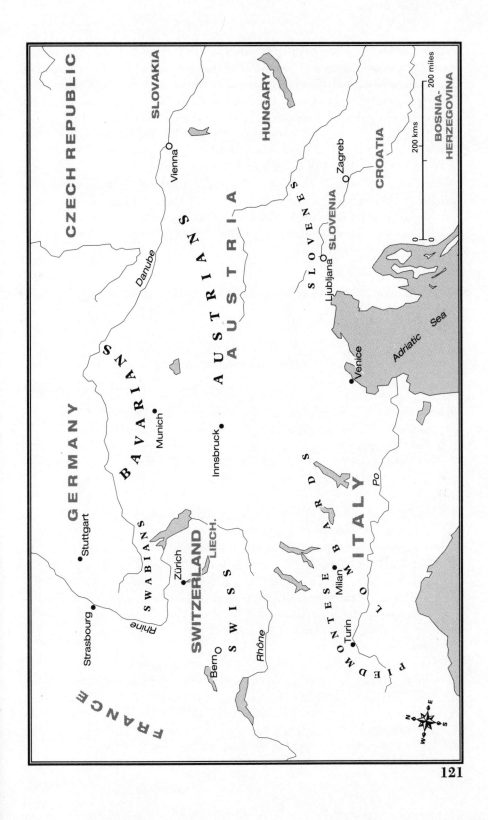

CZECH REPUBLIC

SLOVAKIA

Vienna

HUNGARY

Danube

Zagreb

CROATIA

BOSNIA-
HERZEGOVINA

200 kms
200 miles

AUSTRIANS

AUSTRIA

SLOVENES

Ljubljana

SLOVENIA

Adriatic   Sea

BAVARIANS

GERMANY

Munich

Innsbruck

Venice

Stuttgart

Po

SWABIANS

Zürich

LIECH.

SWITZERLAND

Bern

Rhine

Strasbourg

Rhône

SWISS

LOMBARDS

Milan

ITALY

PIEDMONTESE

Turin

FRANCE

N
W E
S

121

region, linked by strong cultural affinities to Switzerland and Austria: the fact that the Bavarians and Swabians are the most sharply differentiated of the historic communities which combine to form the present German state is a strong testimony to the Alps' magnetic power, drawing in peoples who live in their shadow (for an introduction to the Germans in general, see p. 111). In Alpine and sub-Alpine Italy, though the Piedmontese are well-integrated with their fellow-Italian neighbours, the prevailing direction of trade and commerce has tended to be northward, through the mountain passes, rather than with the rest of the Italian peninsula; this history forms part of the background of the distinctive north-Italian consciousness, which also embraces the Lombards and, less intensely, the Ligurians, and which has inspired a strong regionalist political movement in the area of Italy cooled by the Alps (see p. 151).

SWABIANS

The Alemanni, the ancestors of the Swabians, were among the first German tribes to arrive in what had been an area of strong Celtic settlement. It can be argued that they pre-figured the loose political system which ultimately became the hallmark of modern Germany. Although several tribes were prepared to join forces under the command of a couple of proven military leaders for the duration of a campaign, they found it difficult to work together in time of peace and never had anything like a central government.

THE LAND ■

The Swabian heartland lies between the upper Rhine and the upper Danube, an agricultural country, largely of undulating terraces, through which the Neckar river flows northwards to the Rhine. The original duchy, however, expanded from there in all directions. To the west, the dukes held sway over the mountains of the Black Forest and across the Rhine into modern Alsace. Southwards, Swabia extended round Lake Constance, down past Zurich to the main mountain passes into Italy. To the east it stretched as far as Augsburg, well into what was to become Bavaria. Swabia, however, has come to be identified today with the old duchy of Württemberg, east of the Rhine and Black Forest.

The Swabian Jura stretches across the middle of the region from the southwest to the northeast, while the Adelegg mountains reach down in the southeast to touch the Alps. North of the Jura the land is often rugged, with isolated hills projecting from the plain. South of the range, the plateau of upper Swabia runs smoothly down to Lake Constance and eastwards into Bavaria. Further south again are the mountains and lakes of the Alps. The most fertile area lies between the Jura and the Black

Swabians and Bavarians

Forest, where thickly wooded hills roll down to the Rhine. The forests, though suffering these days from pollution, are still some of the wildest places in western Europe. They induce a good deal of rain, especially in summer.

HISTORY ■

First mentioned by the Romans who attacked them in AD 213, the Alemanni reached the Black Forest region by AD 260. By the late 5th century they had expanded their region into Alsace and northern Switzerland. In 496 they were conquered by the Frankish ruler Clovis and incorporated into his empire, although they were allowed to live under their traditional code of laws, the *Lex Alamannorum* which was deeply rooted in Alemannic tradition.

As the Carolingian empire began to divide and crumble their homeland, Swabia, emerged as one of the five great duchies of the east Frankish kingdom. In 1079 the duke, Rudolf of Rheinfelden, set himself up as a rival German king to Henry IV, who promptly squashed the rebellion by appointing his own son-in-law, Frederick of Hohenstaufen, as duke of Swabia. Frederick's nephew, Frederick Barbarossa, became German king in 1152, establishing one of the most successful dynasties of the early Middle Ages.

When the Hohenstaufen line died out at the end of the 13th century, near-anarchy reigned as the petty nobility fought for power. While the Württemberg

123

family in the centre and east became the most influential, taking over as dukes from the middle of the 14th century, the cities formed a league to support the emperor in return for a promise from him not to mortgage them to any of the petty lords. The Swabian League thus formed was a trend setter, an ancestor of modern German federalism. The idea caught on and was widely copied as a method of banding together autonomous groups with similar interests.

Lutheranism and the Reformation posed a challenge to the League and this increased with the 1525 peasants' revolt which spread from Swabia throughout southern Germany. Although the League suppressed this brutally, the spirit of the Reformation triumphed in the end, and the League disintegrated. The Württembergs returned, by now convinced Protestants, and set about organizing other Lutheran states in a way which made them the natural leader of German Protestantism. This inevitably led to the duchy being ravaged more seriously than most in the course of the Thirty Years War. Over the period the population shrank from 450,000 to 166,000.

This experience burnt itself into the Swabian soul and character: the people to this day have the reputation of being dour, hard working, careful of their money and excessively house proud, with the wry, cynical sense of humour needed to survive in hard times.

A sequence of wars and French invasions was punctuated by a cultural revival at the end of the 18th century, which promoted the arts and sciences and gave the region many baroque masterpieces. The French Revolutionary wars then saw the dukes successively swapping sides to gain territorial advantage. Having opposed Napoleon at the end, the Württembergs emerged from the Congress of Vienna as kings of their province. The family looked askance at the rise of Prussia within the German Confederation and fought with Austria against Bismarck in 1866. That proved such an expensive mistake that the chief minister formed a secret alliance with Prussia and joined in the war against France in 1871.

With integration in the new united Germany, the Swabians began to come into their own again as one of the more inventive, well-ordered and industrious people of the new country. Daimler-Benz, Bosch and Porsche all set up factories there. To this day the region is the high-tech capital of Germany, with electronics, tool-manufacture and precision optical instruments among the products which make it one of the most prosperous in the entire country. The region produces 10% of all capital exports from the EC and has shown itself quicker than most in establishing markets in eastern Europe after the collapse of communism.

RELIGION, LANGUAGE AND CULTURE ■

Swabians are traditionally Protestant, having been influenced both by Lutheranism and, because of their proximity to Switzerland, by Calvinism. However, the modern creation of a federal state linking them to the predominantly Catholic area of Baden in the west has meant that the two Christian churches are increasingly mixed. The compulsory church tax charged by the federal government has also meant that more and more people profess to neither communion since this costs them money – something Swabians are instinctively loathe to tolerate

In the 6th century, the Swabian, or Upper German, dialects began to become distinctive from the language spoken by the other Germanic tribes. Most notably, the consonants became softer with, for example, 'k' sounds becoming 'ch' and 'p' turning into 'f'.

The area is known as a fertile cultural breeding ground, but for pan-German rather than local reasons. It was the birthplace of, among many others, the 18th-century philosopher Hegel, the 19th-century poet Schiller and the 20th-century scientist Einstein.

Swabian food owes something to the cuisines of France and Italy. Typical dishes include snail soup, egg pasta (*spätzle*), *maultaschen* (giant sized pockets of pasta stuffed with meat, brains and spinach), veal in cream sauce. Wine is marginally preferred to beer, and there are many good local vintages. The Baden area specializes in sweet pastries, with Black Forest gâteau the most famous.

FOLKLORE ■

As a front-line state bordering Christian Gaul, the pagan Alemanni and Swabians were prime targets of early missionaries, particularly the Irish, who set about converting them from the 7th century. To do this as quickly as possible they allowed many pagan customs to continue and adapted several of them to fit with Christian festivals. Marriage customs are old Germanic: on the evening before the wedding the couple break glass for luck; on the wedding day the bride is barred from entering the church before being 'stolen' for the ceremony; when a child is born, the umbilical cord is traditionally kept and the afterbirth is buried; death is celebrated with a wake.

The modern festivities surrounding the great Christian festivals of Easter and Christmas probably derive from the pagan rituals in this area. In pagan belief, Yule was the feast of the winter solstice and this translated into a celebration of the heavenly light or the coming of Christ. Since it was the period of slaughter, when animals were killed because they would not survive the winter, it became a period of feasting too. Tree worship, coupled with the custom of using evergreens to scare the devil, persisted as Christmas trees and wreaths. Christmas Eve is the feast of Adam and Eve, and Paradise trees were set up to mark the occasion, hung with apples. Candles were added as a symbol of Christ.

The area also sees some of the most distinctive of the many pre-Lenten carnivals in Germany, with mummers wearing elaborate wooden masks that date back to heathen times in design. Nothing sums up the way Christianity and paganism merged better than the story of Saint Walburga, who ran a monastery at Heidenheim, east of Stuttgart, in the 8th century and whose rocky tomb was supposed to secrete a miracle healing fluid. Not long after she died, her memory became blurred with that of Waldborg, the pre-Christian fertility goddess. On Walpurgis night, the eve of Mayday, when her relics were interred, witches are still said to emerge and rendezvous in the Harz mountains.

Stuttgart, the regional capital, has one of the highest standards of living in the entire country and there is a feeling of royal splendour in the heart of the city, which is built round the baroque palace of the dukes. Ulm, where the *Münster* (cathedral) has one of the tallest spires in the world, was one of Europe's great trading centres in the Middle Ages. Baden-Baden, the archetypal spa town, retains a typical 19th-century feeling.

BAVARIANS

In the absence of credible objective tests, the Bavarians have to be defined in cultural terms: Bavarian is as Bavarian does. The credentials required include a native knowledge of Bairisch *(a form of German very similar to that of Austria and common south of Regensburg); Catholic faith or, at least, a Catholic family background, except around Feldkirchen, which had an exceptionally active Protestant pastorate in the 19th century; and the ability to eat* Lüngerl *without having to ask what it is (a type of lung stew).*

The Bavarians have given their name to the largest Land *of the German federation, but they inhabit only a small part of it. The sudden and substantial expansion of the Bavarian state during the Napoleonic wars added to Bavaria's political legacy areas which had their own distinct culture, including Swabia and most of Franconia. The Upper Palatinate, which has a longer history of entanglement in Bavarian politics, has a culture still its own though modified by Bavarian influence. The heartlands of Bavaria, strictly speaking, are confined to the regions of Ober Bayern (Upper Bavaria) and Nieder Bayern (Lower Bavaria), and although inhabitants of other parts of the* Land *will sometimes use the term 'Bavarian' of themselves, this does not imply adherence to the strong and exclusive identity professed by Bavarians proper. The Bavarians inhabit one of Europe's great cultural frontiers, separated by the Alps and the Bavarian and Bohemian forests from the Latin and Slav worlds. Settlement in a former part of the Roman empire and adherence to the Roman Catholic faith makes it deceptively easy to classify them as the most Latin of the Germans. Their history has little in common with that of other German peoples, neither imperial, like the Austrians, nor martial, like the Prussians, nor commercial like the Rhinelanders and Saxons. It is often said that they became part of the German state reluctantly and by accident. The distinctive political regime of the* Land *they inhabit and the foreign affinities of their art and religion are an inheritance of their peculiar past.*

THE LAND ■

The stereotyped image of Bavarians dressed in *Lederhosen* and alpine hats at least has the merit of marking them out as a mountain people. Almost the whole of Ober

126

Bayern, except for the shallow valley of the Inn, lies more than 3000 feet above sea level. Nieder Bayern, roughly corresponding to the area north of Munich, between the Lech and the Bohemian forest, occupies broad valleys on either side of the Hillertau; a wide, triangular region of the hills between the Danube and the Inn; and the densely forested uplands of the Bayerischer Wald. Except in the Inn valley no part of it is less than 1500 feet above sea level. The mountainous environment makes the Bavarians the most dispersed of Germany's peoples, with population density only half the national average. Proximity to the Alps also imposes a climate of harsh extremes, with fairly hot summers and long winters, and deep snow for three to six months a year.

HISTORY ■

Rome's Danubian frontier collapsed in AD 405, but the Germanic invaders who settled the area of the Roman garrison cities at Augsburg, Regensburg and Passau were not distinguished by the name *Bavarii* in surviving records until the early 6th century. The origins of the name and of the people are unclear. The most favoured theories are that the term was derived from a place-name, bestowed by Frankish neighbours or enemies on a mixed group of settlers or the region, or that the Bavarii were a previously unrecorded tribe which moved into this little-favoured region relatively late in the wake of stronger predecessors. The Bavarians proved tenacious in paganism until the mission of St Boniface from 737 to 748. In 788, Charlemagne overthrew the last of the native Agilulfing dynasty and Bavaria became subject first to the Carolingians, and after 911 a duchy within the Holy Roman Empire. The duchy was dismembered by Emperor Otto II in the 970s, and for 200 years Bavaria survived in name only. In 1180, however, Frederick Barbarossa invested a native magnate, Otto of Wittelsbach, with nominal overlordship of an area enclosed by the Bohemian Forest, the Inn, the Alps and the Lech. The Bavarians were ruled by his direct heirs for the next 738 years. The Duchy of Bavaria, however, proved hard to control effectively: much of its territory was held by individuals or corporations not subject to the dukes – monasteries, episcopal sees, free cities and imperial knights.

In the War of Succession of 1504–6, Duke Albert IV (1465–1508) re-united the parts of this inheritance, with its courts at Munich and Landshut, and introduced primogeniture. This led to a fitful and precarious growth in the dukes' power and prosperity. The 16th-century dukes also profited, through imperial favour and the co-operation of the church, from their tenacious resistance to the Reformation: with the aid of the Jesuits, they recovered ground lost to the reformers in the first flush of Luther's success. With a sparkling court at Munich and an impressive Jesuit university at Ingolstadt, ducal Bavaria became in the second half of the 16th century a model Renaissance state.

Duke Maximilian II (1591–1651) fervently supported the Catholic cause in the Thirty Years' War. His duchy was so ravaged and scorched by French and Swedish invaders as to be rendered, he said, unrecognizable. But like the Napoleonic Wars nearly 200 years later, this disaster proved to be a fortunate opportunity for the ducal house. At the Peace of Westphalia in 1648 Maximilian acquired from his defeated Protestant cousins the territory of the Upper Palatinate, which remained part of ducal Bavaria permanently, and the right to take part, with six other privileged princes of Germany, in imperial elections.

This increase in power proved a source of excessive temptation for his heirs. Charles Albert (1726–45) claimed and lost the imperial crown; Charles Theodore (1777–99) fought a disastrous war for this inheritance which left Bavaria vulnerable to depredations by Austria and France.

Duke Maximilian Joseph (1799–1825) redeemed Bavarian fortunes by a bold alliance – almost unique among princes of the *ancien régime* – with Napoleon. By a timely change of sides in 1813 the Bavarians reaped the benefits alike of Napoleon's rise and fall. The result was a threefold revolution: first, territorial expansion and consolidation; secondly, the transformation of the Bavarian state into a constitutional monarchy with codified laws; thirdly, a unique status for Bavaria within the German *Bund* which replaced the defunct empire, as defender of the smaller constituent states against Prussian ambitions. In a sense, Bavaria has never relinquished this role which has become traditional: in 1850, Bavaria successfully resisted the imposition of a Prussian-inspired constitution; in 1933 Bavaria unsuccessfully opposed Nazi ambitions; in 1946, it was Bavaria that led the demand that states' rights be enshrined in the Federal Republic; in 1972 Bavaria took the central government to court over the constitutional implication of the Basic treaty with the German Democratic Republic.

The aftermath of the Franco-Prussian war of 1870–1 settled Bavaria's permanent place in Germany's future – ensuring both that she would participate in a broad German state in association with her northern neighbours and also that she would be a maverick member of the German community. In 1871, the Kingdom of Bavaria merged her sovereignty in that of the new German Empire, retaining a separate diplomatic corps although without the right to make her own foreign policy. When Bismarck launched the *Kulturkampf* against the Catholic Church, popular reaction was so fierce that Catholicism became for Bavarians more than a just faith, but a badge of identity as well. In 1912 a Catholic party came to power and has been returned in every democratic election since.

The Weimar constitution of 1919, which was too centralist for Bavaria's taste, led to opposition in the region. In 1933 Hitler extinguished such autonomy as Bavaria retained. There was little scope for armed resistance, but the clergy provided a focus of moral opposition. The region suffered relatively little material damage from the conflict of World War II and its combination of dramatic scenery with undamaged art and antiquities has made the *Land* as a whole the most lucrative magnet for tourism in modern Germany. The economic balance of the region – with a few, concentrated heavy industries which have benefited from post-War economic growth, and a large agricultural sector in the hands of small farmers who have been enriched by the EC – has helped to make Bavarians the richest per capita of Germany's peoples today.

The most obvious mark of Bavaria's peculiar contemporary political profile is the fact that it is the only *Land* ruled by a party otherwise unrepresented in national politics. Though the Christian Social Union (CSU) is a partner in the national ruling coalition, the Bavarian government has resisted federal initiatives on a range of issues in recent years, including education, agrarian investment and even foreign policies.

RELIGION AND FESTIVALS ■

Bavarians tend to identify with Catholic devotion rather than Catholic dogma. From 1870 Munich was the home of the Old Catholic schism, which rejected papal infallibility; a small Old Catholic communion survives to this day. The principal shrine, which houses a cult of strongly patriotic Bavarian flavour, is that of the candle-blackened Virgin of Altötting, who is also a focus of devotion for south German and Austrian pilgrims on her feast on 15th August. Despite the crises of the Napoleonic period and the *Kulturkampf*, Bavaria's historic sees and religious communities project an impression of continuity which inspires both regional and religious sentiment. The cathedrals of Passau and Freising, the Cistercians of Ebrach and the Benedictines of Benediktbeuern are particularly marked examples.

In a land of Catholic faith and mountainous country, 'local' religion naturally thrives; a map of Bavarian customs and devotions would be a patchwork-quilt of variety. Christmas customs serve as an example. The *Klopfersnacht*, on the Thursday before the second Sunday before Christmas, is celebrated throughout the region by wassailing children, but in Berchtesgaden the practice is spread over four weeks and accompanied by a fair. The end of the Christmas season is celebrated by chalked invocations to the wise men on doorways. Local patrons, like St Nicholas in Schrobenhausen and St Leonard in Bad Tölz are celebrated with an annual *Dult*, combining feast and fair. No other devotional event rivals the scale of the Oberammergau Passion Play, which is performed once every ten years, the last survivor of a practice common in the 17th century. It seems to have been effective not only in warding off plague – the purpose of the collective vow with which the villagers launched the tradition in 1633 – but also in making Oberammergau Germany's richest village.

Secular festivals are important, too, in what is still a predominantly agrarian land, tied to the rhythm of the seasons. The most elaborate of them tend to be invented traditions; few of them are more than a century old and Munich's renowned *Oktoberfest* began only in 1810.

ART AND ARCHITECTURE ■

There is no peculiarly Bavarian art and architecture but monumental buildings cover a peculiar range, combining the exuberant baroque and rococo characteristic of south German and Austrian Catholic art with the Gothic that represents a national German style. Thus, royal residences range from the restrainedly classical Nymphenburg and Schleissheim to the fairy-tale Hohenschwungau and the Neuschanstein and the theatrically baroque Linderhof and Herrenchiemsee. Most

Bavarian skylines have curious towers and spires topped by onion-tufted, exaggeratedly waisted domes which introduce an exotic flavour.

FOOD AND DRINK ■

'The only Bavarian wine is beer' and the *Land* has more than two-thirds of Germany's breweries: for a visitor, this is the most striking difference between the Bavarians and the wine-drinking Franconians. Lush pastures in the lower-lying areas supply a diet rich in dairy produce: *Kalbsrahmbraten* is braised veal topped with cream; Windbeuteln are cream puffs particularly noted in Berchtesgaden; rich spreads like *Leberkäs*, a spiced potted meat, or Obatze, a confection of cheese and butter, are commonplace. In Munich the *Weisswurst* – a soft white blood-sausage that is kept floating in water and served with sweet mustard – inspires almost mystical raptures and is a symbol of civic pride. The creative use of offal in most traditional meat dishes is a reminder of the poverty of the hill-farming past.

AUSTRIANS

National consciousness amongst the 7,000,000 Austrians is a complex issue. As recently as 1972, the proposition that 'Austrians constitute a nation', was agreed with by only 62% of Austrians taking part in a survey. The population is divided into nine Bundesländer (federal provinces): Burgenland, Carinthia, Lower Austria, Upper Austria, Salzburg, Styria, Tyrol, Vorarlberg and Vienna. The extent of identification with the individual Land (Landesbewußtsein) varies according to the strength of Austrian consciousness (Österreichbewußtsein). Austrian consciousness in Vienna, Lower Austria and Burgenland is markedly stronger than identification with the Land. Both are approximately equally strong in Upper Austria and Salzburg, while in Carinthia, Vorarlberg and the Tyrol identification with the Land rather than with Austria is the primary level of collective consciousness.

These differences reflect historical developments. Until the early 19th century only the inhabitants of the lands of Upper and Lower Austria (of the archduchy of Austria) were regarded as Austrians, with Vienna as their centre and capital city of the Habsburg monarchy. The others were referred to as Styrians, Tyrolese, Carinthians, Vorarlbergers etc, according to the name of their Land. Hence the communities of the Länder, which have long had a strong identification with their home-territories, can be thought of as 'tribes' of the Austrians.

HISTORY ■

From the 8th century onwards, Carolingian feudalism began to dissolve the old tribal system of the Bavarians and Carantians on present-day Austrian territory. In the 12th century, the concentration of fragmented feudal lordships started, leading to the formation of the *Länder* of Austria and Styria, and later of the Tyrol, Carinthia, Salzburg, Upper Austria and Vorarlberg. The *Länder* developed an extraordinary capacity for resistance against all later attempts to subordinate them to the modern concept of a nation-state. The guardians of local consciousness were the Estates, who furnished both advisers and military strength for the Princes. In the late Middle Ages, they increasingly absolved themselves from their military obligations by granting taxation to the monarch instead.

In the territories of present-day Austria, a further process of political concentration began in 1192 with the establishment of the rule of Princes of the Babenberg line over both the *Länder* of Austria and Styria. The Habsburgs took over these two *Länder* in 1282, acquiring in addition in 1335 Carinthia and Carniola (the central part of the present-day republic of Slovenia); in 1363 the Tyrol; and in 1500 Gorizia (parts of which today lie in Italy, Slovenia and Austria).

In 1526 the Habsburgs also became Kings of Hungary and Bohemia, but the administrations in the various Habsburg domains were not thoroughly unified in the following centuries. The Habsburgs' fundamental conservatism meant that they maintained the existence of Estates and Länder, and did not suppress regional tradition. Throughout the period of 'absolutist' rule, the Länder remained in their old form, with their own capitals, their own estates, their own coats of arms and their own mythology.

When the Habsburg monarchy broke apart in 1918, the *Länder* became the constituent elements of the new Austrian republic. Carinthia lost some and Styria lost all of their Slovene-speaking regions; the Tyrol lost not only its Italian-speaking region of South-Tyrol, but also the German-speaking area, which became part of Italy. A new *Land* was added in 1922, the Burgenland, formed from the German-speaking regions of western Hungary.

The *Länder* still have their provincial parliaments (*Landtage*), their own governments, flags and coats of arms, anthems and patrons; very often they have a distinctive Land-costume as well. Inhabitants of each Land are distinguishable too by regional variations in dialect. The *Länder* also carry out an independent foreign policy, working together with non-Austrian regions across the borders in regional groups or associations.

LANGUAGE AND RELIGION ■

The majority of the people speak Bavaro-Austrian variants of the German language, except those in the extreme west of Austria, who – like their Swiss neighbours – belong to the Alemannic linguistic region. Smaller old-established Hungarian, Croatian, Slovene and Czech minorities exist in the east (Burgenland, Vienna) and in the south of Austria (Carinthia). New ethnic minorities have arrived since the 1970s, primarily in Vienna through Turkish and South Slav immigration.

Officially, about 80% of Austrians belong to the Roman Catholic church. Austria is therefore regarded as a Catholic country. Yet Catholicism plays an important role

only for a minority of people (20–30% of the population are active Catholics – more in rural areas than in the cities). In the Austrians' scale of values, religion appears in fifth place after family, job, friends and leisure time. Surveys report that only about 30% regard religion as important.

THE COUNTRY ■

Two-thirds of Austria lies in the Alpine regions. The eastern Alps in Austria are char-acterized by long and wide longitudinal valleys running from west to east. They divide the northern, central and southern Alps. The *Länder* on the Danube (Upper and Lower Austria) also cover a part of the mountain chain (Upper Austria includes Dachstein at about 9000 ft; Lower Austria has Schneeberg at around 6000 ft above sea level). The highest mountain in Austria is the Großglockner (12,500ft) on the frontier between Carinthia and the eastern part of the Tyrol. The geographical pos-ition of Austria is responsible for its character as a pass-country – all the important alpine passes of the eastern Alps lie in Austria – and therefore as a transit-state. Out-side the Alps, plains dominate in the east (Burgenland, eastern Lower Austria), as well as hill-country. These areas – which are quite arid in the east – are used inten-sively for agriculture. In the mountains the breeding of cattle is pre-dominant. An in-dustrial tradition exists in Vienna, Lower and Upper Austria, Styria and Vorarlberg, but Salzburg and the Tyrol too played an important role in industrial development after 1945.

VORARLBERGERS ■

The Vorarlbergers live in the very west of Austria. Their country is situated in the Alemannic-speaking region; their dialects are most closely related to those of the neighbouring Swiss.

In the course of the formation of the Land during the 16th century, the delegates of cities under Habsburg rule and the rural communities (*Ländliche Gerischts-gemeinden*) met together in a Diet (*Landtag*). The lack of nobles and monasteries of any importance in Vorarlberg meant that its Diet was the only one in the Habsburg domains which consisted solely of bourgeois and farming deputies only. This led to an accentuation of democratic traditions and democratic consciousness.

The early and strong industrialization of this Alpine *Land* – especially the development of a textile industry – brought wealth to the country and initiated a self-conscious regionalist tradition among the powerful and rich families of the industrialists. This was complemented by a working class with a generally conservative consciousness, in touch with the peasantry from which it sprang.

TYROLESE ■

Non-Austrians often regard the Tyrolese as the embodiment of Alpine Austria, even as a distinct nation. Even within the borders of Austria itself, the Tyrolese are often seen as especially typical Austrians with a high self-consciousness. Obviously, this notion is closely connected with the tradition of the Tyrol as a highly developed tourist region.

The Tyrol came into existence in the second half of the 13th century. It had an early forerunner of an absolutist system of government. Not only the nobility and the clergy, but also the deputies of the cities and the rural judicial communities took part in the Diets: it was a sign of obligation on urban and rural communities to defend their *Land*. In 1511, this obligation was codified: Tyrolese identification with the Land became very close.

Military conflicts became important for laying the foundations of the modern *Landesbewußtsein*. In 1809 the Tyrolese under Andreas Hofer rebelled, at first with some success, against the forces of the Bavarians, who had ruled the Tyrol since 1805, and the French. The uprising came to a tragic end with the execution of Hofer. The Tyrol, however, reverted to Habsburg rule under the terms of the general peace settlement of 1814.

After World War I (1919) the *Land* was divided. The north became part of the new Republic of Austria, the German-speaking southern part, which was also claimed by Austria, became part of Italy (today's province of Bolzano-Alto Adige). Historically speaking, the Southern Tyrol was the heartland of the Tyrol, and included Tirol Castle, which gave its name to the *Land*. When the Fascists came to power in 1922, a massive programme of Italianization began. After the Hitler-

Mussolini Pact of 1939, the South Tyroleans were faced with the choice either of emigration to Hitler's Reich or accepting further Italianization; the majority opted for emigration. This process was halted during the war, and after 1945 most of those who had opted for emigration (*Optanten*) were given permission to return to their homeland.

The South Tyrol remained Italian after 1945. The region was granted only limited autonomy, which was at first implemented very inadequately. After several attempts, negotiations started in the 1960s, which in 1968 resulted in the so-called *Paket* agreements. These have been implemented on a fairly wide scale, so that today the South Tyroleans possess quite significant minority rights by international standards. Cooperation on an economic level (*Accordino*) exists between the South Tyrol and the North Tyrol, Vorarlberg and the neighbouring province of Trento (the Trentino), with which the South Tyrol forms its own Italian-speaking region. It is not easy to determine if the South Tyrolese are a 'tribe' of their own: they have their own Diet (*Landtag*) in Bolzano (Bozen) and a certain level of autonomy. The region is mostly bilingual – many Italians who live in this region study German, just as the German-speaking Tyrolese study Italian.

SALZBURGERS ■

The Salzburgers only became part of Austria in 1816. By concentrating feudal rights in the heartland of their enormous bishopric, the Archbishops of Salzburg created a principality (*Fürstentum*) of their own, which was regarded as a *Land* from the 14th century onwards with its own Diet. The traditions of the *Land* have been greatly influenced by the clerical princes and their splendid residence, the city of Salzburg. Its integration into the Austrian state meant that Salzburg lost its function as a capital and lost its former importance. However, the beauty of the city and of the countryside was soon discovered both by Austrians and foreigners. Salzburg became one of the main Austrian centres of tourism. The festivals introduced by Max Reinhardt and Hugo von Hofmannsthal after World War I gave tourism in Salzburg a special touch: wealthy opera, music and theatre fans from all over the world began to stream into Salzburg each year. The self-consciousness of the Salzburgers seems less characterized by military and pre-industrial democratic traditions than by the awareness of being the city of Mozart and, in fact, the unofficial cultural capital of Austria.

CARINTHIANS ■

The name of their region imparts to the Carinthians a belief that they have the longest tradition of any Austrian *Land*. It is derived from the Carantians, a tribe which can be traced back to the 7th century and whose members spoke a pre-Slovene dialect. The pre-feudal organization of the Carantians was broken up in the course of feudalization in the same process experienced by the Bavarians, Lombards and Franks. But the name of Carinthia (Kärnten) remained connected with the central part of the older (and bigger) Carantia. In this central area are found the remains of a distinctive medieval constitution: the Stone of Princes (*Fürstenstein*, originally in the

134

Karnburg) and the Seat of Dukes (*Herzogsstuhl*) in the Zollfeld. The ceremonies related to them were preserved until the 15th century: the new duke was first received by a peasant (*Herzogsbauer*) sitting on the stone; only when the duke promised to protect the land would the peasant cede the seat to the duke. These traditions were not forgotten later on, and remained an important part of the Carinthian *Landesbewußtsein*.

In Upper and Middle Carinthia, Bavarian dialects replaced the Slovene language, which was, however, preserved in Lower Carinthia for a long time and survives in some places to this day. By the middle of the 19th century, about 70% of the Carinthians spoke German; the rest spoke Slovene (today the figures are about 96% and 4%). But their *Landesbewußtsein* was a common one. When in 1919 the mostly Slovene-speaking areas were transferred to the new state of the Serbs, Croats and Slovenes, Yugoslav soldiers who began to occupying the territory met with tenacious resistance. An international committee visited the region and finally, in 1920, the treaty of St Germain provided for a plebiscite in the disputed area. The result favoured staying as part of Austria (59% of the votes). The modern *Landesbewußtsein* is not only characterized by old traditions, but also by these more recent experiences. Today Carinthia is well known as a tourist region, popular because of its numerous and splendid old churches and natural beauty.

STYRIANS ■

The *Land* of Styria came into existence in the 12th century as a result of the union of several Carantian and Bavarian regions and expansion and colonization to the east. In 1180, the *Land* became a duchy, and in 1192 the Austrian duke inherited the fledgling state. The rights of the ministers of the duke of Styria outlined in the contract of inheritance of 1186 laid the foundations for the rights of the nobility of the *Land* and formed the basis of continuing autonomy for Styria – despite the almost uninterrupted community with both Upper and Lower Austrians. A unique heraldic animal (the Styrian Panther) is an expression of this autonomy, as is the Diet-Hall (*Landhaus*) of the Estates. In the later Middle Ages and again in 1564 Graz became the administrative capital of the so-called 'Inner Austrian' territories. This gave a special impetus to the cultural and urban development of the city.

Archduke Johann von Habsburg (d.1859) became Styria's most potent symbolic figure. This immensely popular brother of Emperor Francis II of Austria made Styria the focal point of his life. He founded numerous institutions there for the promotion of agriculture, industry, science and education, had Styrian folklore researched, and became an enthusiastic propagator of the grey jacket (*grauer Rock*) and other elements of traditional Styrian costume. Through his marriage to a postman's daughter he finally became the 'Styrian Prince'.

BURGENLANDERS ■

The Burgenlanders are the youngest Austrian tribe. In the counties of western Hungary colonization took place during the High Middle Ages through immigration

135

from the adjoining Austrian and Bavarian areas. After the devastation caused by the Turkish Wars of the 16th and 17th centuries many Croat farmers who had fled also settled here. In today's Burgenland the principal languages in the 19th century were German and Croat, and in some areas Hungarian as well. After the fall of the Habsburg monarchy the representatives of the Germans of this area demanded, and achieved, affiliation with Austria. After a vote, the important centre of Sopron remained Hungarian (1922).

The Burgenlanders lived from wine-growing, farming and cattle breeding. Economic links and trade pointed early on towards Austria. Large noble families, like the Esterházy and Batthyany, dominated the area but they also enriched it culturally – Joseph Haydn was in the service of the Esterházy family for a long time – above all in today's capital, Eisenstadt. Hungarian traditions are more visible in the area's costume (for instance in the men's boots). Historically a part of Hungary, today the Burgenland is one of those areas with the strongest sense of identification with Austria, but also with a clear *Landesbewußtsein*. It makes sense to speak here of a new tribe forming and the Croat- and Hungarian-speaking people can be regarded as an integral part of it.

UPPER AUSTRIANS ■

The Upper Austrians, despite their name which is almost the same as that of the Lower Austrians, have a distinct sense of identity. The *Land* developed in the late Middle Ages, when Diets were introduced for the part of Austria above the river Enns. The cultural elements which form the *Landesbewußtsein* of the Upper Austrians are: the important monasteries (e.g. Kremsmünster, founded in the 8th century); the splendid farmhouses, which in the heartland of the country developed a specific square or rectangular form (*Vierkanter*); and the *Most*, a sort of cider. But Upper Austria is also an important industrial country, whose industry played a crucial role in the modern economic development of Austria.

Upper Austrian identity also reflects the experience of long and bitter peasant wars: the uprising of 1626 was one of the most successful and longest-lived in the whole of the Holy Roman Empire. Nevertheless, quite a settled peasantry developed later demonstrating its wealth by taking the gold caps (*Goldhauben*) of the bourgeois women as part of their own costume.

LOWER AUSTRIANS AND VIENNESE ■

The Lower Austrians and Viennese have the least specific *Landesbewußtsein*, since they have always been seen as the archetypal Austrians; Vienna was the capital of the *Land* of Austria under the Enns (today's Lower Austria) up to the end of World War I, when the town, dominated by the Social Democrats, was separated from the countryside, which was ruled by the Christian Socialists. But in both *Länder*, the lack of *Landesbewußtsein* of their own, results in a strong Austrian consciousness. Lower Austria has only recently got a capital of its own, St Pölten, which should become the focal point of a new *Landesbewußtsein*. In Vienna lie the most Austrian of symbols: St Stephen's cathedral, the parliament, the great museums, the Schönbrunn and the Belvedere castles. Its townscape and its culture indicate larger connections, over the borders of the *Land* and back to the glories of Habsburg Empire, and to its former European importance.

PROSPECTS ■

The Austrian Federal Lands (*Bundesländer*) could play a variety of roles in a Europe of tomorrow: the gradual erosion of national state authorities could give the *Länder* increased importance if their authority is not transferred to some new supra-regional entities.

The demand for supra-regional solutions has already created new initiatives not only in cooperation between the Republic of Austria and its neighbours, but also between single Austrian *Länder* and their non-Austrian neighbours: the Alpen-Adria Association unites Carinthia and Styria with parts of Italy and Hungary and the Republics of Slovenia and Croatia; Upper and Lower Austria as well as Vienna and Burgenland participate in the Danube Lands Association (together with Czech, Slovak, Hungarian and German areas); the Tyrol, Salzburg and Vorarlberg are members of the Alp Association.

The *Länder* as small units offer a good chance for more self-determination for their citizens. Together with small municipalities, the *Länder* are also important regional creators of identity, especially in Austria, where the tradition of certain institutions and symbols has a very long history. If the unifying role of Austria can coexist with new regional cooperation with areas outside Austria, the Austrian *Länder* could also play an exemplary role in the 'Europe of the Regions'.

SWISS

The Swiss must be deemed to be the people who now live in what is now Switzerland. The country was gradually built up from an initial kernel but the consequence was not a bullfrog-state, puffed-up and briefly bulging, but a small, compact, and hard-edged affair, more like a pocket-battleship – secure, well made and seemingly indestructible. Divided into 23 cantons, all with their peculiar identities, traditions and institutions, riven with differences of language, religion and ethnic origins, Switzerland is often said to be an exercise in ethnic co-existence but against the historical background this notion becomes less valid the more it is examined.

The peoples now called Swiss began as various groups of Germanic, Celtic and Italic background. Much of today's German-speaking population is not strictly Germanic in origin but is the result of germanization of Celts. Some French-

137

speakers are partly germanized as well in terms of general culture. The speakers of Italian and Romansch – a romance family of tongues spoken in remote areas of the southeast by just 1% of the population – are by now much affected by the ethos of the rest of Switzerland though their Italian origins and language are undoubted.

HISTORY ■

The process which eventually brought the Swiss together in a shared state began as a feudal quarrel about status when the Habsburg dynasty set out to re-create the ancient duchy of Swabia. In 1291, a moment of Habsburg disarray was exploited by the men of three areas: what were called, misleadingly in many ways, the 'forest cantons' of Schwyz, Uri and Unterwalden. They formed a confederation to resist any Habsburg bid to increase the duchy's power over them. This was not a bid for full, sovereign independence but rather an attempt to freeze feudal power in a fragmentary, undeveloped and comfortably ineffective form. They aimed at establishing a direct relationship with the emperor, without the interposition of an intermediate feudal lord. It was rejection of their moderate aims, and their ability to defend themselves effectively with well-drilled citizen-infantry in their mountain fastnesses which led to a hardening of their political aspirations and an expansion of the fledgling confederation.

Two types of area were involved in this general process. The first was embodied perfectly by the three predominantly-agrarian forest cantons. But they were soon joined by groups that were principally urban, in the sense that whereas the forest cantons were dominated by their valleys and villages, the new recruits were cantons ruled by developed towns. In 1332 the city and area known as Lucerne joined the confederation, followed by Zürich (1351) and Bern (1353), as well as another rural canton, Glarus (1352–88). Together they formed a great bloc of Alpine land, relatively easy to defend but still requiring further expansion for full security. In order to join the confederation, Zürich pushed aside its prince-bishop and replaced him with a committee of lay oligarchs.

The core of confederated cantons acquired allies in the surrounding area, who either joined much later or, in some cases, remained permanently outside the confederation. This cautious growth continued during the 15th and early 16th centuries as the military position of the confederation became increasingly established. A series of remarkable victories obliged the Habsburgs to concede a 24-year truce in 1394. This meant *de facto* group-independence. A confederal Diet had been inaugurated in 1393 though this left the individuality and autonomy of the cantons uncompromised. In extending the security of their own areas outward, Lucerne looked north, Bern to the west and Uri to the south. Subject-areas of individual cantons accumulated: Aargau (1412–15), the Toggenburger regions (1436), Sargans (1440), Thurgau (1460). Allies were acquired: half the Valais in 1416, St Gallen in 1454. The luxury of a civil war between Zürich and some of her neighbours was indulged in from 1436–46, but, considered from one point of view, this was a sign of

138

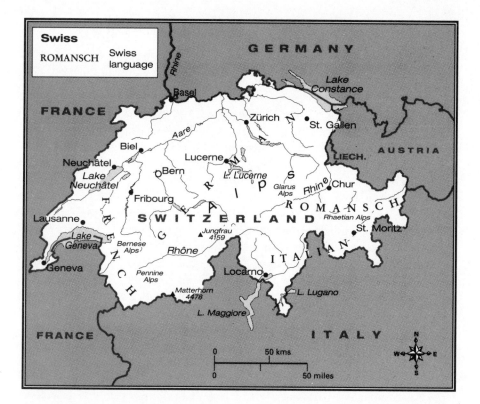

the confederation's growing security and maturity, further demonstrated by Swiss success in wars against Burgundy in 1474–7 and against Milan in 1478. The Swiss had become a major military power with an impenetrable home base, while Swiss mercenaries were a valuable resource for whose services western and central European powers competed.

The union therefore expanded: Fribourg and Solothurn joined in 1481; Schaffhausen in 1501; Basel-stadt in 1501; and Appenzell in the east in 1513. In 1524 the long, hard conquest of the intractable southeastern territory of Graübunden or Grisons was completed. In the French-speaking west, Neuchâtel became an ally in 1495, Geneva in 1526; the bishopric of Basel became allied in 1579. Subject-areas were also added: Thurgau's conquest was complete by 1460; that of Ticino by 1512 and of the Vaud in 1536.

The Reformation had a transforming effect. It led quickly to a division between many of the urban-based cantons, which espoused Protestantism, and their Catholic rural counterparts. In 1524, five cantons – Lucerne, Uri, Unterwalden, Zug and Schwyz – denounced the Reformation which Ulrich Zwingli had launched from Zürich, but in 1528, Bern and Basel-stadt accepted it, while Fribourg and Solothurn backed the pope. In 1531 the dispute reached the battlefield. Initial Catholic success was indecisive; the launch of Calvin's mission from Geneva in 1536 won many souls in the French-speaking west of the Swiss world for a radical form of Protestantism

139

and as a result the common institutions of the confederation were paralysed for over a century.

Despite this long stagnation, international recognition of the full sovereign status of the confederation was included in the general peace which concluded the Thirty Years' War in 1648. In 1655 Zürich proposed a more centralized form for the state but the Catholic cantons rejected the suggestion. The issue was settled in Catholic favour in battle. Thereafter, from 1663 to 1776 the confederal Diet never met – during a period dominated by centralizing and absolutist tendencies in neighbouring monarchies. In the War of the Spanish Succession (1700–14), Swiss troops fought against each other as mercenaries of the opposing sides and, in a development of the conflict, renewed inter-cantonal confrontation ended in Protestant victory in 1712: this was the beginning of a Protestant ascendancy which was never reversed.

Around the middle of the 18th century significant intellectual revivals began in Zürich and Geneva in religion, political philosophy and science. Voltaire was only the most famous of a large number of French political and religious refugees who became residents of Geneva or Neuchâtel, which, like Geneva, had an adventurous and prosperous publishing industry, supplying France with books banned by the French censors.

The French Revolution was the major turning-point in Swiss history. The ruling oligarchies had considered joining Austria and Prussia in a war against revolutionary France but characteristically opted for neutrality in the interests of economy. But in 1792 Geneva was taken over by local revolutionaries who imitated Jacobinism. In 1793 France announced the annexation of the bishopric of Basel. In 1797 Napoleon seized the Valtelline passes – considered, since a costly war of the early 17th century, to be a vital element for Switzerland's defence and Switzerland's prestige. An accelerating pattern of revolutions and annexations led the French to smash the confederation and establish the Helvetic Republic in 1798.

Napoleon, sensing the inapplicability of a centralized model of government, allowed Switzerland to revert to its traditional constitution, with some modifications, in 1802–3. His defeat in 1815 then made possible the restoration of the pre-1797 constitution in its entirety, while at the Congress of Vienna in the same year the major powers of Europe jointly guaranteed Swiss neutrality. Reformers in Switzerland concentrated henceforth not on attempts to centralize but rather on the liberalization of government in individual cantons with calls for equality before the law and extension of the suffrage. This was much needed: in Zürich, for instance, even after a major reconstruction of government along liberal lines in 1848, there were still three levels of treatment for citizens seeking education of their children, depending on where they lived. Yet centralization had not been entirely forgotten. In 1832, the Diet voted to reform the constitution, though no actual programme could be agreed. In the same year, under the Ziebner Concordat, the progressive cantons agreed on the need for a new common decision-making forum.

In 1834, advocacy of a secular state alarmed the Catholics: in 1845 seven Catholic cantons formed a union to fight the tendency. In a war of under three weeks' duration in 1847 this league was forcibly dissolved. The Jesuits were expelled by the victors. In a new mood enhanced by the European revolutions of 1848, the Diet espoused a fresh plan of constitutional reform which involved the establishment of a cabinet, a Diet more or less directly elected by universal male suffrage, a central bank and common coinage, post and telegraphs. The third quarter of the century was one of conspicuous economic progress – especially in railways and industries; the anomalous status of Neuchâtel was ended in 1856, when the Hohenzollern dynasty of Prussia renounced its rights of jurisdiction there.

The main innovation of a more liberalized constitution in 1874 was the referendum, which has remained a distinctive feature of Swiss political culture. Whereas in most democracies referenda have tended to inhibit change, in Switzerland they could be used to promote centralizing measures while the general principle of centralization remained abhorrent. Female suffrage in national elections was not admitted in 1874, nor for more than a century afterwards, but individual cantons, especially the French-speaking ones, did extend votes to women in cantonal and communal elections in the interim. By 1900 even the most conservative cantons had educational systems and standards which were appropriate to a self-conscious participatory democracy.

ETHNIC COMPOSITION AND CULTURE ■

The founding cantons were all German-speaking. Whether true Germans or Germanized Celts, their culture was German and so was their language (Swiss German or *Schwyzertütsch*) – though in a tortured version, to the ears of speakers of the metropolitan language. The dialect is closely related to the speech of western Austria and Baden-Württemberg in Germany. Although standard High German is today used for writing, Swiss German is extensively employed for oral communication. The early urban cantons were German, in the same sense, too. By 1513, when the structure of the confederation was tightened, this German character was only slightly eroded. Fribourg was half-French, half-German; Solothurn, Schaffhausen and Basel-stadt totally German. Even among the allied and subject states, Aargau and Thurgau were totally German as were the Toggenburger and Sargans areas which were added to Glarus. Mulhouse, which never became part of Switzerland but was an ally from the 15th to the 18th centuries, was Alsatian and therefore, at this period, predominantly German, as was St Gallen. Neuchâtel became the first French-speaking ally in 1495, but this was a small community. Among subject-areas, the only really big non-German one was Italian-speaking Ticino. The western half of the Valais – the first to become subject to the confederation – was French, but not until 1536 was a wholly French-speaking area of any great size added. The acquisition of Graubünden, though predominantly German, also brought some Friulian-speakers and the Romansch-speakers into the fold. The bishopric of Basel was another totally German late addition. These non-German communities were acquired in general more as conquests than willing confederates.

Only after the dismantling and reconstruction of the Swiss state in the

Napoleonic wars did the French- and Italian-speaking components come to play a full role. Despite the religious split, the German core of the confederation held together, setting an encouraging example for the closer binding-in of the mostly Protestant French and of the Italians, Catholics or anticlericals in a mutually loyal and tolerant society. The largely uniform educational system, and the existence of great centres of higher learning, like the Technical University in Zürich, which bring together Swiss from all parts of the country, have been instrumental in grafting Swiss identity onto cantonal, communal, linguistic and confessional loyalties.

That a country can successfully incorporate so much ethnic, linguistic and religious diversity, without sacrifice of the identity of any of its parts, is held up as a matter of wonder. In reality, the parts are not as disparate as at first appears. All are united in wishing to belong to Switzerland. Due emphasis should be put on the Swissness of the Swiss, rather than their Frenchness, Germanness or Italianness. Because religious and linguistic divisions cut across one another they tend to establish inter-ethnic links: Protestants, for instance, whether Calvinist or Zwinglian, feel drawn together across the language divide; and the large anticlerical party in the Ticino, though Italian-speaking, supported that coalition in the formative period of the 19th century. Adherence to liberal democracy is a common cause of all the communities and the political parties are not on the whole divided along ethnic lines. The clerical conservative party is in practice mainly Catholic, drawing great strength from the original kernel of Switzerland in the forest cantons, but without affecting a confessional profile. The major parties – liberal, conservative and social-democratic – are usually in coalition.

Swiss self-differentiation from the French and German nations was slow to develop and was in some respects held back by the development of chauvinism in the large neighbour-states during the 19th century. Even in 1914 a large proportion of Swiss university staff was recruited from these 'fatherlands'; this is no longer so and Switzerland is now a big net exporter of academics. Though there was ill feeling between French and German Swiss in World War I, this was not repeated in World War II. Indeed, abhorrence of both Nazism and Fascism consolidated the Swiss as never before and produced in them common pride and deep belief in the superiority of their democracy.

On the political plane, respect for local variety was the hallmark of the Swiss way, in contrast to the roughshod methods favoured by Nazi and Fascist imposers of uniformity. In addition to the three official languages, in 1936–7 Romansch was made a 'national' language, elevated to this status as part of a campaign mounted from inside Switzerland against fascist Italy. The Swiss, indeed, can be said to be united in the celebration of their diversity: in the festive wearing of traditional cantonal costumes; in sporting contests between localities, which constructively affirm particularism; in competitions in singing, shooting and blowing the alphorn.

The campaign for 'Jura Libre' – separate cantonal status for the French-speaking part of Bern – may seem, on the face of it, to be evidence of ethnic tension. It began in the Gaullist era and was sensed as an instance of French interference in Swiss affairs. The result was the creation of a small and impecunious 23rd canton; but it was rejected by the votes of most of the French-speakers of Bern – the prosperous, Protestant community centred on La Chaud-de-Fonds, home of Europe's finest watch-making industry for over 250 years. This outcome seems to affirm rather the Swissness of Switzerland than the supposed tensions of inter-communal rivalry. More recently still, French- and German-speakers have been said to be divided in their attitude to European union, which a Swiss referendum in 1992 narrowly rejected: but this journalistic interpretation is not supported by the statistics which show that Swiss of all descriptions are roughly equally divided on the issue. French-speaking Swiss have perhaps been prone to share the French habit of cultural defe-rence towards Paris, but even this has been countered by 'national' pride in such cul-tural heroes as Rousseau and Le Corbusier. Outside the minor and generally good-natured rivalries perpetuated in sporting fixtures, the main surviving focus of tension is the insistence of some French-speaking Swiss on being dealt with in their own language in German-speaking areas, relying on the 'national' status of the French language.

German numerical preponderance is assured. Their proportion approaches three-quarters of the population. The relative sizes of the French and Italian compo-nents has, however, shifted since the end of World War II when they accounted for about 20% and about 5% respectively. Today the French are down to little more than 17%, while the Italians have gone up to something in excess of 8%, mainly because of the gradual naturalization of immigrant Italian workers. Speakers of Romansch account for the rest.

As well as by education, the consolidation of Switzerland has been favoured through inter-marriage and by the movement of workers between cantons – gener-ally by railways which are vectors of national feeling, just as stations, in rural areas, with their bars and restaurants, are centres of civic life. Above all, Switzerland is united by a concept borrowed, ironically, from the French revolution: that of the people in arms. All males (save a few conscientious objectors, only recently exempted) between 18 and 56 have to serve in some way every year in what is genu-inely a citizen-army. Common endeavour – the Swiss are proudly aware – has brought extraordinary success; a small country has preserved its independence; a land of limited natural resources has achieved the highest standard of living in Europe; the cult of neutrality has not only been a way of defending independence and prosperity but has also served to unite the Swiss in self-differentiation from the political and economic blocs by which they have been surrounded. Outsiders have sometimes denounced this as complacent or smug: yet it coexists with a sense of re-sponsibility to internationalism and the cause of humanity. Not for nothing were the International Red Cross and the League of Nations established in Switzerland.

PIEDMONTESE

The Piedmontese have long felt pride in their political identity as the people who played the greatest role in the unification of Italy. Piedmont provided the nucleus around which the new state coalesced in the 1850s and 1860s, and Turin served as the first capital of a united Italy from 1861 to 1865. Piedmont means 'foot of the hill', and before the 19th century was often referred to as the 'Sub-Alpine Kingdom'. From the later Middle Ages it was identified with the people who were subjects of the Duke of Savoy. This group, as well as the Savoyards, came to include Valdaostans and Sardinians, none of whom would readily have called themselves Piedmontese, and the Piedmontese proper eventually came to inhabit the central and most important part of the duchy. The Piedmontese were less self-consciously 'Italian' than the Ligurians or Lombards, and yet from the early modern period were undeniably Italian in cultural terms. When in 1720 the House of Savoy acquired Sardinia, with the title of King, the state became, in correct diplomatic parlance, 'Sardinia', but Piedmont, rather than the primitive and semi-populated island of Sardinia, clearly remained the political and economic centre, and to overcome the contradiction the term 'Piedmont/Sardinia' was often used.

HISTORY ■

The origins of the Piedmontese ruling house of Savoy lay north of the Alps in a French-speaking duchy. The early dukes ruled an essentially feudal state. While the other parts of central and northern Italy had been based on communes and an urban civilization, with the countryside politically subordinate to the cities, the state of Savoy/Piedmont was more rural in the nature of its power structure, and in this respect more like the other states of western Europe. Amadeo VI (1343–83), the 'Green Count', so-called from the vivid colour of his clothes, ruled a state unique in Europe in that it straddled its highest mountain range, the Alps. The Piedmontese often had to survive at the mercy of one of the great powers – usually France, but sometimes Spain. In the mid-16th century, the duchy was occupied by the French for almost 20 years. The Spanish were victorious in their wars with the French in the first half of the 16th century, and Spanish influence became strong in Piedmont. The French, however, remained in occupation of Turin, and remained a constant military threat to the Piedmontese. Throughout the 17th century Piedmont relied for survival on its diplomacy, sometimes adroit, but occasionally clumsy and also on its small, but never negligible, military strength. In the course of the 18th century the Piedmontese acquired closer economic and cultural links with the rest of the Italian peninsula, but perhaps the most significant development came at the end of the Napoleonic Wars, when Piedmont acquired the considerable port of Genoa. This annexation made Piedmont a maritime country and also, in a fuller sense than

Piedmontese
and Lombards

SWITZERLAND

AUSTRIA

A L P S

FRANCE

L. Maggiore
Verbania
L. Como

Val
Aosta
d'Aosta

Dora Baltea

Como

Legnano

Bergamo

L. Garda

Novara
Ticino
Milan
Brescia

L O M B A R D Y

V E N E T O

I T A L Y

P I E D M O N T

Po

Vercelli

Adda

Pavia

Pinerolo
Turin

Po

Cremona

Torre
Pelice

Alessandria

Piacenza

Po

Tanaro

Alba

Parma

A p e n n i n e s

Cuneo

L I G U R I A

Genoa

FRANCE

Gulf of Genoa

N
W E
S

0   200 kms
0   100 miles

before, an 'Italian' one. Piedmont was henceforth oriented towards the Italian peninsula rather than towards France and Switzerland.

The period from 1815 to 1848 was characterized by revolutionary movements in various parts of Italy, movements aimed at securing constitutions in the individual states, but also, increasingly, with gaining independence from the Austrians. The Piedmontese were joined by considerable numbers of political exiles from other parts of Italy, especially from the Kingdom of Naples after the revolution of 1820–1 and from the Papal States after the revolution of 1831. In 1848 and 1849 the Piedmontese monarchy led a war against Austria, a war in which armies came from the rest of Italy to fight the Austrians. But the Piedmontese and their various Italian allies were defeated. After the reaction of 1849, yet more political exiles arrived in Piedmont. Benedetto Croce suggested that these exiles were the first real 'Italians', in the sense that they could no longer consider themselves citizens of their former states. They were given civil rights by the Piedmontese, could vote (if they were liter-

145

ate and had a given income), sit as deputies in parliament and teach in schools and universities.

In 1858, the Piedmontese Prime Minister Cavour secured an alliance with France, the Austrians were defeated in the war of 1859 and Lombardy was annexed to Piedmont. The rest of the peninsula rapidly followed. The Grand Duchy of Tuscany, the Duchies of Parma and Modena, and much of the Papal States were acquired by Piedmont. In 1860 Garibaldi, a native of the Piedmontese city of Nice led an initially-minute army of volunteers against the old Kingdom of Naples. He rapidly defeated the Neapolitans, and – after a considerable amount of friction with Cavour – handed southern Italy over to the Piedmontese government. Cavour, however, had felt obliged to surrender Savoy and Nice to France to guarantee the French would not interfere while Italy was in the throes of unification. In 1861 the Kingdom of Italy was proclaimed under the Piedmontese king, Victor Emmanuel II, and thereafter the history of Piedmont merged with that of the new nation-state.

LANGUAGE ■

French was the first language of the literate classes in Piedmont during the 19th century, but Italian was their second language. It has been argued that many literate people were not fluent in Italian and wrote it inaccurately: but they also wrote French imperfectly and so not too much French influence can be deduced from this. After Italian unification, Italian came to be increasingly used by the educated classes. Those unable to read and write spoke neither French nor Italian, but a Piedmontese dialect: only as they became literate did they adopt Italian as their written language. In 1858, 35% of the population of Piedmont were literate, and this proportion rose rapidly after Piedmont became part of the Kingdom of Italy. Piedmont thus compared very favourably with the rest of Italy, since estimates of literacy in Italy as a whole in 1861 range from 2.5% to 10%. Italian governments made great efforts to eradicate illiteracy, and their efforts were far more successful in the comparatively prosperous North than in the impoverished South. In the last three or four decades television has been a major factor in leading to the replacement of dialects by the national language. But two regions of the former Piedmont have very distinct dialects of their own: the thinly-populated island of Sardinia; and the Aostans or Valdaostans, living in their Alpine valley and speaking a dialect which has some words of recognizably-French origin. Many of the Valdaostans speak French, and the autonomous Region of Val d'Aosta has been recognized as legally bilingual since its creation; all street signs are written in both Italian and French (see p. 147).

SOCIETY AND ECONOMY ■

The social structure of Piedmont was originally feudal in character, in contrast to the rest of north and central Italy, where power had originally been based in city communes. The rich cultural achievement of the cities of Florence, Milan and Venice have no counterpart in Turin, which was by far the largest of the Piedmontese cities.

146

The link between the existence of the commune, the city state and the great flowering of art and literature in the High Middle Ages and Renaissance is not entirely coincidental. The Piedmontese, however, pride themselves on being quietly civilized and restrained, in contrast to the other peoples of the peninsula. They are, they sometimes say, the English of Italy.

Their agriculture has concentrated on rice, so that risotto is a favourite dish, as in Lombardy. In the 20th century, the car industry has been immensely successful in Piedmont, with the great factories of Fiat sited in Turin. Piedmont has also been in the vanguard of consumer electronics, and Olivetti is a name as familiar to the world as Fiat.

POLITICS ■

Fascism was less successful in Piedmont than in other parts of Italy – Mussolini knew that the working class of Turin hated him. But when he tried to persuade Agnelli, the boss of Fiat, to move his firm to Rome, Agnelli, to his credit, said: 'No. Fiat stays in Turin'. The constitution of the Italian Republic, legally established on 1 January 1948, allowed for regional autonomy: the regions were to have their own budgets, and ultimately their own television channels. But the law was not brought into operation for some years, and the region of Piedmont was perhaps less eager for autonomy than other parts of Italy, with the exception of the Val d'Aosta. In the 1990s, the northern separatist movement of the *Leghe* included the Piedmontese, though they were perhaps a little less enthusiastic about the movement than the Lombards.

RELIGION ■

The Piedmontese were traditionally deeply devout in their Catholicism. But from the 19th century the middle class has become increasingly anti-clerical, without abandoning their formal adherence to the Catholic faith. They are christened, married and given funeral rites in church, but rarely attend mass. In the countryside there is greater respect for the Church, though even there it is declining.

VALDAOSTANS AND WALDENSIANS ■

Piedmont is host to a number of minority communities, descendants of once-widespread sub-Alpine groups, or of more recent immigrants from the north. Whilst most have been assimilated into Piedmontese culture, a few remain distinct.

The Valdaostans (or Valdôtains), who inhabit the autonomous region of Val d'Aosta (or Vallée d'Aoste), have their capital at Aosta. They speak a dialect known as 'Harpeitanya', which has been heavily influenced by French. During the 1930s, both French and Harpeitanya were banned by the Fascist government. The area was granted autonomy in 1948. Recent decades, however, have brought the threat of tourism to local life, as the population can almost double in some communes during the peak skiing season. As elsewhere in the Alps, autonomy has not diminished the pressure to assimilate into larger cultural units.

The Waldensians, some 30,000 strong, are descendants of followers of the 12th-century religious reformer, Pietro Valdo, who fled to the mountainous valleys of Piedmont in the face of persecution. The attentions of the Inquisition in the 14th century, and their vulnerability as an outpost of Protestantism during the Thirty Years War further diminished their numbers. They now inhabit a handful of valleys centred around Torre Pelice, some 230 miles from Turin. Their distinct identity arises from their survival as a 'Protestant' community isolated in a country with a very strong Catholic community. There are also Waldensian communities in North Carolina, Argentina and Uruguay.

LOMBARDS

The Lombards today occupy the richest part of Italy, with its centre in the great city of Milan. Of all Italy's historic communities, they are the only one who took their name from an invading barbarian tribe. The barbarian invasions of the dark ages passed through Italy very quickly: the invaders were generally few in number and did not settle to any great extent. The Lombards were an exception: they arrived in around 568, later than the other barbarians (except the Franks and Magyars). They were only around 200,000 in number, but some of them settled permanently. To the native Italians who had survived since the heyday of the Roman Empire they seemed no less barbaric than the earlier invaders – the Goths and the Vandals. But their legacy endures in the name of the modern province.

PHYSICAL ENVIRONMENT ■

Lombardy is the flattest area of Italy, occupying most of the Po plain. It is bounded on the north by the Alps, and on the south by the Apennines. The mountains are too distant from the centre to relieve the impression that the Lombards, as far as physical features go, inhabit the most boring part of Italy. An exception is the Alpine area to the north of Lombardy, which contains the beautiful lakes of Maggiore, Como and part of Lake Garda.

HISTORY ■

For several centuries after the Lombard invasion, Pavia was the main centre of power. The Lombards quickly acquired the social habits of the native people, living in cities rather than rural fortresses. In the course of the struggle between the medieval German emperors and the Papacy, the Lombards developed something approaching a sense of national identity. When the Emperor Frederick Barbarossa destroyed Milan in 1162, a Lombard League of cities was formed, partly in support of the Pope and his ally the Republic of Venice, but also to maintain Lombard independence from the emperor. The Lombard League became part, not just of Lombard, but of

Italian mythology. The Italian nationalists of the 19th century saw the League as a precedent for an Italian union against the foreigner. More recently, in the 1990s, the phrase 'Lombard League' has again been employed, this time to justify the creation of a political party with separatist ambitions.

During the High Middle Ages and the Renaissance, the Duchy of Milan enjoyed a rich cultural life. The Visconti family ruled the city from 1262 to 1447, and, in spite of wars and the Black Death of 1348, maintained a high level of artistic achievement; but this was surpassed under their successors, the Sforza, who ruled Milan from 1447 to 1500 – the golden age of the Renaissance. Under Francesco, the first Sforza ruler, who died in 1466, the superb *Castello Sforzesco* was built. Its park is still one of the main centres of the city's life. Under Ludovico Sforza, known as Il Moro (1480–1508), the universal genius Leonardo da Vinci was a prominent figure at the Milanese court. He produced many of his finest paintings in Milan, including the *Madonna of the Rocks*, now in the National Gallery in London, and *The Last Supper*, for the refectory of the convent church of Santa Maria delle Grazie. Lombardy effectively lost its independence in 1500, when Louis XII of France conquered Milan. The region then became the battlefield between the French and Charles V, King of Spain and Holy Roman Emperor. In 1521 Charles drove the French from Milan, and the Sforza were briefly restored. But in 1525 Charles won an overwhelming victory at the battle of Pavia, and from then until the 18th century the Spanish were supreme in Lombardy.

Educated Italians of the 19th and 20th centuries came to know the Spanish Lombardy of the 17th century through the novel *I Promessi Sposi*, by Alessandro Manzoni. In view of the popularity of the novel, it was fortunate that it was so accurate in the historical background it provided for its fictional story. Manzoni brought the experience of the plague and the bread riots of 17th-century Milan to Lombards of these later centuries, helped by the genuine historical research that he had carried out in the city archives. But there was a more positive side to the Spanish period of Lombard history. Lombardy was on an important trade route from the Mediterranean to Central and Eastern Europe. Trade in the second half of the 16th and early decades of the 17th centuries was greater than it had ever been, bringing much wealth to the area, although it did decline thereafter.

The War of the Spanish Succession, from 1701 to 1714, marked the end of the Spanish period of dominance in Lombardy. By the Peace of Utrecht in 1714, Milan passed from Spain to the Austrians, who held it until the French Revolutionary Wars. For the last few decades of this period Austria played a central role in the 18th-century Enlightenment. Although the inspiration for the Enlightenment came from French writers, most influential of whom was Voltaire, the most radically-minded of the so-called 'Enlightened Despots' included the Habsburg emperors in Vienna, Joseph II (1780–90) and Leopold II (1790–92). The reforms which the Enlightened Despots carried through were mainly a matter of humanizing laws by getting rid of barbarisms like torture, and introducing religious toleration. A more liberal atmosphere prevailed in Milan and a degree of free thinking was tolerated. Lombardy also produced her own enlightened writers. Pietro Verri (1728–97) advocated free trade, and worked with the Austrian authorities to reform the Lombard administration, the schools and universities. Cesare Beccaria (1738–94) condemned not only torture, but the death sentence. His recommendation that capital punishment be abolished was taken up not by the Austrian government, but by a lesser Habsburg ruler, Pietro Leopoldo, the Grand Duke of Tuscany, who became Emperor Leopold II in 1790.

During the French Revolutionary and Napoleonic Wars, the French occupied Lombardy several times. Napoleon had a grandiose, and tasteless, plan for rebuilding Milan on a massive scale. Fortunately the plan was not carried out, except for a small corner, the Foro Bonaparte, which still stands today, and is completely innocuous. Austria retained Lombardy under the terms of the 1815 Vienna settlement. As the Italian nationalist movement gathered force in the 1830s and 1840s, the Lombard middle and aristocratic classes became increasingly resentful of the Austrian presence. In 1848 the citizens of Milan rose against Austrian rule and drove the Austrian army out of the city during the *Cinque Giornate* – five days of bitter fighting. But the Austrians returned after their victorious wars against the Italians in 1848 and 1849, and remained until 1859, when they were driven out by the Franco-Piedmontese alliance that Cavour, the Prime Minister of Piedmont, had cemented with Napoleon III of France. For the time being, Lombardy was simply annexed to Piedmont, but after the creation of the Kingdom of Italy in 1860–1, the political history of Lombardy lost its independent character. The Italian state was a closely-integrated one: not until after the formation of the Italian Republic was a small degree of autonomy given to the regions, Lombardy among them.

LANGUAGE ■

The written language of the Lombards is Italian, as has been the case for the whole of Italy since the 14th century. But there is a spoken dialect – Lombard. The use of dialect is said to be diminishing with the spread of mass communication, and especially of television. The distinction between a written language and a spoken dialect has, however, sometimes been blurred by attempts to write down the dialect, and these attempts have given rise to or reflected the belief that a distinct language, rather than a dialect, exists. An interesting example of this can be found in Antonio Fogazzaro's novel *Piccolo Mondo Antico* which was published in 1900, but dealt with the Lombardy of the mid-19th century. If his written rendering of the Lombard dialect is roughly correct, it would be undeniably a dialect of Italian, but with a very different vocabulary. Many etymologists, however, maintain that the dialects spoken in Italy – Lombard among them – are far more ancient than Italian, and are in fact distinct Romance languages.

POPULAR CULTURE ■

The eating habits of the Lombards are similar to those of the Piedmontese: rice is a basic food, risotto the most popular first course for those who are rich enough to have more than one course, or the only course for the poor. *Cotoletta alla Milanese* is a

150

particular speciality, not only in Italy, but in Italian restaurants all over the world.

Opera in Italy is a less élitist entertainment than it is in Britain and Europe's most famous opera house is perhaps La Scala in Milan. But love of the opera is something shared by all Italians, not just the Lombards – the same operas are produced in La Scala as in the San Carlo in Naples. Another popular activity the Lombards share with all Italians is an entirely free one, the *passegiata*. At a particular time in the evening, before dark, everyone takes a leisurely stroll in the main thoroughfare, or along the front if the town is on the coast. The crowds enjoying the *passegiata* are well-dressed, and are aware that they are taking part in a social habit of a relaxed, yet vaguely formal, kind. Less relaxed, and certainly less formal, is the Lombard obsession with football. This, again, is a national characteristic. Football takes an even greater share of popular enthusiasm than it does in Britain, and a far greater slice of national investment. Milan's football team is supported with passion, but for the World Cup, Italy is no less passionately followed.

POLITICS ■

In the 1990s, the political situation is one of immense complexity and drastic change. For the Lombards, the most significant development has been the emergence of the Lombard League, which has expanded into a 'League of the North' (Lega del Nord). Its message was initially a separatist one, based on the conviction that the Lombards were hard-working, honest people, whose taxes were squandered on bureaucrats in Rome, or, worse still, fell into the hands of the Mafia in the south. The Lega del Nord has done well in electoral terms, though it has now ceased to demand a complete break with the south, and some of its argument has been undermined by the discovery of widespread corruption in high places in Milan. The League's success is nonetheless a symptom of a growing sense of open identification with the region rather than the nation. The League is now the largest party in a few cities, and holds a strongly-based second place right across Lombardy and the rest of Northern Italy. In Rome, the parliamentary party has grown in a few years from a handful of MPs to a vocal and numerous power bloc, from an irritant for the traditional parties to a force they have to take into account. The League is now pressing for Italy to be transformed into a federation of regions.

SLOVENES

The Slovenes represent 90% of the population of the Republic of Slovenia, the small Alpine state which on 25th June 1991 declared independence from the Socialist Federal Republic of Yugoslavia. The relative ethnic homogeneity of their territory made the break with Belgrade easier to achieve than for Croatia and Bosnia-Herzegovina. There are also Slovene communities in Austria and in the Friuli region of Italy.

THE LAND ■

The Slovenes inhabit a land which is mountainous and wooded with deep fertile valleys and many rivers. Towards the Adriatic and Slovenia's short stretch of coast, the landscape loses its Alpine character and becomes the harsh, inhospitable karst typical of the Istrian peninsula.

LANGUAGE ■

The claim to a separate linguistic tradition has formed the basis of the Slovenes' claims to nationhood and separate national identity. Slovene is a South Slav language, close to the Croatian *kajkavski* dialect but sufficiently removed from the Serbian and Croatian literary standards to be classified as a language rather than dialect. Slovene remains a language of great diversity, since for centuries the Slovenes lived in scattered communities isolated from each other and without any single organization to give them a sense of unity.

The earliest surviving Slovene texts date from around AD 1000 but, unlike the Croats, the Slovenes do not have an unbroken vernacular literary tradition. The Slovene literary standard originated during the Reformation when a leading Protestant reformer, Primož Trubar (1508–86), distinguished the Slovene idiom from the Croatian dialects. The Catholic Counter-Reformation, however, halted the development of the Slovene vernacular. The nobility was Germanized and those who advanced socially took on German culture. At the end of the 18th century, interest in the Slovene language was revived under the influence of German philologists. Slo-

vene grammars were published in 1808 and 1811 and were followed by dictionaries but it was the romantic poet France Preseren (1800–49) who through his poetry established Slovene as a literary language and stirred the longing amongst Slovenes for their own nation.

RELIGION ■

The Reformation claimed converts throughout the Habsburgs' Austrian provinces and Slovenes in Carinthia, Carniola and Styria turned to Protestantism. During the Counter-Reformation, however, the works of the Slovene Protestant reformers were destroyed and those Slovenes who had converted returned to Roman Catholicism. Today Slovenes who practise a religion are almost exclusively Catholic.

HISTORY ■

The Slovenes are the descendants of Slav settlers who settled the eastern Alps in the 6th and 7th centuries, forming a tribal union referred to as 'Carantia'. Most of the Alpine Slavs assimilated to German culture after the 8th-century colonization of the region by the Bavarians, but some retained their Slav culture and were reduced to serfdom by the Germans. In the 11th and 12th centuries, the Alpine Slavs were divided among the marks of Carniola, Carinthia and Styria which became Austrian crown lands in the 16th century and remained under Habsburg rule until 1918. While they remained conscious of being Slav, it was not until the 19th century that they developed a clear sense of a Slovene national community: Slovene only emerged as a national designation during the Slovene national awakening. In 1848, the Slovenes set forth their national programme, demanding a Slovene state within the Habsburg Empire; they reinforced their demands by appealing to the Slovene state tradition stretching back to the 7th century and Carantia.

At the end of World War I, the Slovenes were divided among Italy, Austria and the newly formed Kingdom of Serbs, Croats and Slovenes (later Yugoslavia). Of the non-Serb nations within the Kingdom, the Slovenes were the least resentful at Serb hegemony and prospered during the inter-war period. During World War II, the Slovenes were subject to German, Italian and Hungarian occupying forces. In 1945 the borders between Italy and Yugoslavia were re-drawn so that the Slovenes who had been under Italian rule since the 1920 Treaty of Rapallo were included within the Republic of Slovenia, one of the constituent republics of the Socialist Federal Republic of Yugoslavia.

Slovenia has the most advanced economy of the former Yugoslav republics. Resentment at subsidizing the less developed republics and frustration at the restrictions preventing the free development of the Slovene economy were important factors driving the Slovenes, first to embrace political pluralism and then, in June 1991, to declare independence. The Yugoslav National Army tried to prevent secession in a short campaign which claimed lives on both sides and destroyed property. The Slovenes, however, seem not to harbour any virulent national hatreds and their nationalism is altogether more tepid than the nationalism of the Croats.

ART AND CULTURE ■

Ljubljana, the capital of Slovenia, reflects the Slovenes' centuries-old orientation towards western, more specifically Austrian culture. Baroque churches and town-houses stand alongside 19th-century apartment blocks built in the style common to all the capitals of the Habsburg monarchy. Fine examples of *Jugendstil* decoration are to be found on houses and shops in the centre of the city.

The Slovenes have a long tradition of bee-keeping and the beehives which they decorated with scenes from the Bible and every-day life are a distinctive element in Slovene popular culture alongside dances, songs and costumes which are the cus-tomary ingredients of South Slav folk cultures.

5

THE WESTERN AND CENTRAL MEDITERRANEAN

'We live around a sea,' said Socrates, 'like frogs around a pond.' But since the fall of the Roman empire, the Mediterranean Sea has failed to unite the cultures of the dwellers on its shores. The biggest division can be expressed by a line drawn from the Strait of Gibraltar to Crete and then to the Dardanelles: on one side, the European coasts are occupied by Christians, except in Albania and European Turkey; on the other, the Asian and African shores, except in small Jewish and Maronite patches, are Muslim.

But there are also important vertical divisions, separating the European western Mediterranean from the east. A cultural fault line runs through Dalmatia, between Croatia and Montenegro, separating Latin from Greek Christendom; another, at the eastern edge of the Veneto, separates romance-speakers from others.

Sailing conditions divide the Mediterranean in two at the Straits of Messina, where the sea – in the memorable words of a medieval traveller – 'bursts like a dam and boils like a cauldron'. To the west of this division, a well-unified system of winds and currents linked – sometimes in conflict, sometimes in collaboration or confederation – the coastal and island peoples of the Ligurian and Tyrrhenian Seas in the age of sail. Gradually, and at an increasing pace in the second half of this millennium, political fortunes drew the mainlanders into large hinterland states: on the western rim, speakers of Catalan and its cognates eventually joined Spain; along the northern edge, the Provençals became French; the people of Liguria merged into Italy and the Savoyards were divided between the two. After long hesitancy, the islanders of the central part of the sea were divided between all three states, while the Sicilians and the coastal communities of the Italian peninsula eventually found a political home, in uneasy unity, in Italy. Today, a sense of regional fraternity, muted since the steamship era, is being revived, at least in the northern and western parts of the region, as economic cooperation between local and regional authorities is sought across borders, especially across the Franco-Spanish border, from Marseilles to Barcelona, and, more tentatively, from Genoa to Valencia.

The peoples of this western Mediterranean 'core' are flanked by others, Mediterranean by culture, who have tended to look away from the region, to

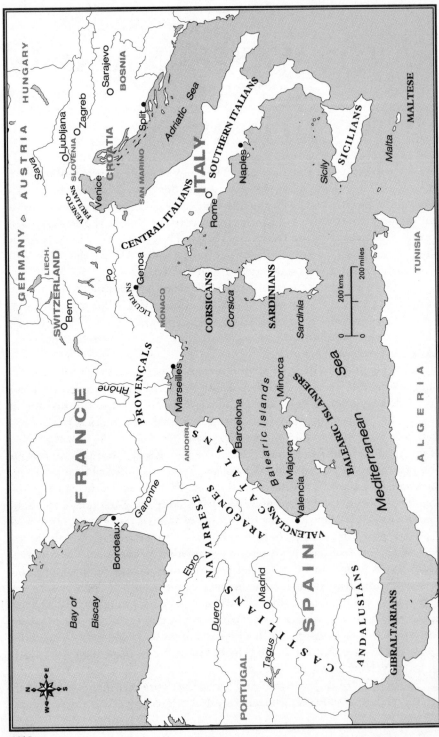

the eastern Mediterranean and the Atlantic. The people of the Veneto have, since the 15th century, forged tenacious links with other north Italians; yet the Adriatic, in terms of geography and navigation, is a gulf of the eastern Mediterranean while the look of Venetian architecture is Byzantine and Venetian history until the late 18th century was linked by trade and politics to 'the gorgeous east'. The Spanish-speaking peoples to the Catalans' west have tended to accept outsiders' classification as 'Mediterranean'. The term is adopted for convenience here, even though most of them have no outlet to that sea, except through neighbours' territory, and inhabit lands which jut into the Atlantic or belong naturally to a 'Pyrenean' region which is neither wholly Mediterranean nor wholly Atlantic but between the two.

SPANISH-SPEAKING COMMUNITIES

Viewed from the outside, Spain looks like a Mediterranean country. From within, for Spain's own historic communities, self-perceptions are more varied. Except for the peoples of the Cantabrian coast, the Spanish-speaking communities of the Iberian peninsula belong, with their Catalan speaking neighbours, to the area of Mediterranean culture – the zone of olives and grapes. Yet only two of those defined as autonomous under the Spanish constitution – the Murcians and Andalusians – have a seaboard on the Mediterranean itself. The peninsula juts far into the Atlantic, a fact which some historically-influential cartographic projections have masked. The main rivers of the Spanish speaking lands – the Duero, the Tagus (Spanish: Tajo) and the Guadalquivir – flow into the Atlantic; and favourable wind-patterns have helped to ensure that the pull of the ocean has been strong, especially for Castilians and Andalusians. Inland in the north, communities with distinct historic identities in Navarra and Aragón look principally neither to the Mediterranean world nor that of the Atlantic but rather to a Pyrenean region shared with communities of the northern slopes who also feel a long way from the sea.

Geography and history have combined to multiply local and regional loyalties. Spain's coasts are short for the size of the country and seem remote and hard-of-access from the centre. Except for the small stretch now occupied by the autonomous communities of Cantabria and Asturias (see p. 67), Spanish-speaking peoples did not occupy the coasts until the late Middle Ages, prolonging a contrast in cultures between periphery and interior which is well documented from pre-Roman times. Spain is ribbed with mountain ranges, which help to define the regions where historic communities took shape. These mountains are densely-

clustered towards the edges: here, relatively small and often defensively-minded peoples have grown up or sought refuge, while in the extensive central tablelands larger groups have tended to share a wider-reaching sense of identity and a more expansive state of mind. The tension between mountains and plateaux accounts in part for the historic complaints of some peripheral peoples against the 'imperialism' of the Castilians of the centre.

The formative period in the history of most Spanish speaking peoples of the peninsula was from the 9th to the 13th centuries AD, an era dominated by the intermittent movement of the frontier southward and the development in the plateaux of an economy based on sheep-rearing. In consequence, a dominant state of disproportionate size, known as Castile, grew up in the tablelands. It absorbed many smaller kingdoms by war or dynastic alliance, and spread the use of the Castilian language, which has come to be known as Spanish, as a first tongue over much of the peninsula (and as a second language over much of the rest). Paradoxically, over the same time and by the same process, strong regional identities among speakers of Spanish were created by sudden extensions of the frontier into regions with peculiar characters, formed or enhanced by geographic seclusion or historic experience. Almost unanimously, peoples throughout the Spanish-speaking lands feel and have felt for most of their history a strong sense of being Spanish, while also subscribing to other levels of identity.

NAVARRESE ■

Often claimed as a Basque province, the Spanish autonomous region of Navarra, around Pamplona, includes a community with a strong sense of its own peculiar identity. Though the Basque language-area formerly stretched into the region, and in the Middle Ages many writers used terms for 'Basque' and 'Navarrese' interchangeably, divergent histories have driven the Basques and Navarrese apart. Neither the Kingdom of Navarre nor its predecessor, documented from the 820s and known as the Kingdom of Pamplona, included the provinces today called the Basque country, except for a brief spell in the late 1020s and early 1030s. As well as Basque-speakers, the medieval kingdom had a population which spoke its own romance language, now called Navarrese by scholars, which developed along lines similar to Castilian. Nowadays, though television in the Basque language is available, Navarra is part of Spanish-speaking Spain and Basque identity is almost entirely confined to immigrants from the Basque country.

Spanish Navarre was incorporated by conquest into the crown of Castile in 1511–14 but retained its own customary laws which have remained at the heart of the Navarrese sense of identity. At the borders of the autonomous region today stand stone pillars inscribed 'Navarra: Territorio Foral' – 'a land with its own laws'. These laws have survived, defended at intervals at the cost of Navarrese blood, attenuated by centralizing Spanish governments during the last three centuries, but never snuffed out. The defensive attitude of the Navarrese towards their own legal tra-

Bay of Biscay

FRANCE

200 kms

100 miles

La Coruña

Santander

GALICIA

ASTURIA

Oviedo

CANTABRIA

Cantabrian Mts.

Bilbao

PAÍS VASCO

Pyrénées

Léon

Burgos

Logroño

Aneto Peak
3404

Ebro

ARAGON

CATALONIA

Duero

Valladolid

Zaragoza

Salamanca

Alcalá de
Hencares

Meseta

VALENCIA

Madrid

Tagus

PORTUGAL

CASTILE

SPAIN

Valencia

Badajoz

Guadiana

Albacete

MURCIA

Mediterranean Sea

Guadalquivir

Murcia

Córdoba

ANDALUCIA

Huelva

Seville

Sierra Nevada

Cartegena

Granada

Gulf of
Cádiz

Mulhacén
3482

Almería

Cádiz

Málaga

Gibraltar (U.K.)

**Castilians, Andalucians,
Aragonese and Gibraltarians**

ditions has been remarkable. The coinage, excise barriers and ancient legislature survived until 1841. Indeed, Navarra retained its status even under the dictatorship of General Franco (1936–75), when all other codes of regional privilege were abolished by a centralizing regime. The reputation of the Navarrese as a people who nurtured a peculiar political culture has been strengthened since 1833 by the extraordinary degree of support in the region for an absolutist dynasty of pretenders to the Spanish throne, the Carlists: since the restoration of regional autonomy in 1978, however, this has dwindled to insignificant proportions. The popularity of dogmatic and traditional Catholicism helped sustain Carlism and, in the second half of the 20th century, has made Navarra the heartland of the conservative Catholic lay-organization Opus Dei.

ARAGONESE ■

Aragón is an autonomous region of Spain on the middle Ebro and the southern Pyrenees, between the Navarrese and Catalan lands. In the Middle Ages the Aragonese had their own romance language, but it was close enough to Castilian to merge indistinguishably into modern Spanish. Their region has also been pulled into the mainstream of pan-Spanish sentiment by the powerful emotional associations of the capital, Zaragoza this is the home of one of the great shrines on which Spanish nationalist feeling has focused, that of the Virgin of the Pillar, whose cult has engaged collective devotion from important nation-wide institutions, such as the armed forces and the para-military Civil Guard. In 1808–9, moreover, Zaragoza heroic resistance to French invasion in sieges in which, reputedly, 40,000 defenders died, made the city a symbol of Spanish national spirit.

At the same time, Aragón has always had a distinctive political culture. The medieval Kingdom of Aragon, documented from 1035, formed a composite state with the Principality of Catalonia from 1134; in the slowly-emerging Spanish state of the early modern era (based on the dynastic union of Aragon and Catalonia with Castile from 1516), Aragon retained some distinctive laws and customs, including fiscal privileges, until 1716. Thereafter, no convincing evidence of Aragonese nationalism can be detected until the late 19th century – a time when renewed appreciation of regional culture in Spain coincided with the growth of regionalist politics. In the 1890s, annual literary and musical gatherings nurtured a sense of a specifically Aragonese heritage – evident especially in forms of dress and dance; Julián Calvo Alfaro dreamed of reviving an 'Aragonese state' but most of his fellow *aragonesistas* professed an overriding loyalty to Spain. The establishment of an autonomous regional government in 1978 was consistent with this tradition.

CASTILIANS ■

The Castilians are the people of the modern autonomous regions of Cantabria, Castilla y León, La Rioja, Castilla-La Mancha, Extremadura, Murcia and (allowing for the colonization of the capital by people from all over Spain), Madrid. By a more comprehensive system of classification, the Andalusians would be included, but their self-perception justifies separate treatment below.

Castilian identity is weak, by the standards of Spain's peripheral peoples, because most Castilians seem for most of the time, if they have thought about it at all, to identify being Castilian with being Spanish. Yet under the influence of Spain's highly devolved system of modern government, a Castilian identity, which never prospered in the old 'imperial' Spain ruled from the centre, is emerging today with increasing force. Its basis is differentiation from other Spanish peoples; the imagery which inspires it is drawn from the distinctive landscapes of the central tablelands of Spain, where the medieval Castilian kingdom, founded under that name in 1035, took shape. The outstanding novelist Miguel Delibes, has been instrumental in formulating it. A fairly well defined range of virtues are said to constitute a 'national character' – perhaps better defined as a collective self-perception – which includes austerity, sobriety, spirituality, hardihood and indifference to practical constraints.

In 1978, the Spanish state made the latest and, apparently, most successful in a long series of experiments in devolved government for regions and historic communities. The need for a flexible and viable settlement led to some anomalies: autonomous governments were established in regions which could hardly be said to enclose communities with strong collective self-consciousness, such as Extremadura and Murcia (respectively in the extreme southwest and southeast of Castile). The rest of Castile was split into three autonomous regions, partly for demographic reasons and partly in order to give the capital a region of its own on a common modern model. The small area of La Rioja, which has oscillated historically between Castile, Aragon and Navarre, became an autonomous region on its own. The luxury of self-government is developing distinctive regional feeling at a marked rate in these areas. New identities are being discovered and old ones revived; the autonomous region of Castilla-León (the more northerly of the Castiles) changed its name to 'Castilla y León' on the grounds, as the slogans said, that 'León is not Castile'; in Extremadura, Murcia and La Rioja regionalist parties have grown up and prospered.

ANDALUSIANS ■

Most of Andalusia was incorporated by conquest into the crown of Castile in the mid-13th century; the rest – the sizable historic Kingdom of Granada in the southeast of the territory – not until the late 15th century. Andalusians have been unconvincingly represented as constituting a distinct ethnic group among Spanish-speakers of the peninsula on the grounds – often asserted but never proved – that they are the product of exceptional levels of intermarriage with African, Jewish or Gypsy immigrant groups in the Middle Ages and early modern period. Nevertheless Andalusians' conviction of their distinctiveness is justified by a peculiar historical experience and a dialect with a distinctive sound. The strength of Andalusian fellow-feeling has often been regarded as influential in Spanish life, from the preponderance of Andalusian artists at the royal court in the time of Velázquez in the 17th century, to the mutually supportive network of Andalusian politicians who dominated the socialist government of the 1980s. As well as the dialect, proudly cultivated, with its suppressed consonants, twangy diphthongs and prolific sibilants, the region's special culture features *flamenco* music – indigenous to no other part of Spain – and fried food, in contrast to the roasting and pot-boiling characteristic of Castilian 'national' cuisine.

The region's great fertility marks it apart from the relatively arid and poor soils of southern Castile, Extremadura and Murcia, but, in an area of sparse settlement, this advantage was under-exploited until well into the present century. Although an aristocratic conspiracy of 1640 is said to have aimed at the creation of an independent Andalusian state, and parts of Andalusia figured prominently in rebellions in the 1870s, regionalist politics had no continuous history until the 1920s, when the

161

concept of Andalusian identity was tirelessly promoted by work of the brilliant publicist, Blas Infante.

The region can be divided into an Atlantic Andalusia, roughly corresponding to the drainage area of the Guadalquivir, centred on Seville (which is also the seat of government of the present autonomous region of Andalucía) and a Mediterranean Andalusia, roughly corresponding to the old Kingdom of Granada, with its focus at Málaga. Overwhelmingly, however, Andalusians look westward – a legacy of the region's preponderance in the maritime history of the Spanish empire between the early 16th and early 19th centuries. A Málaga-born minister in the autonomous government has confessed his despair at Andalusians' indifference to the Mediterranean and most current initiatives in regional cooperation within the European Community are with Atlantic partner-regions.

GIBRALTARIANS ■

Gibraltarians commonly speak of their homeland as a city-state; its official status is that of a self-governing British Crown Colony. Seized by the British as a means of controlling the western approach to the Mediterranean in 1705, the city was transferred to 'the full and entire propriety' of the British crown 'without territorial jurisdiction' under the Treaty of Utrecht (1713), the terms of which still apply. Early British efforts to resolve the ambiguities of the treaty by promoting heavy immigration were unsuccessful. A trickle of Jewish, Genoese, Maltese and Irish Catholic immigrants rose, however, to considerable proportions during a period of prosperity in the early 19th century. Of 17,000 inhabitants in 1830, 1400 were classed as British and a further 6900 as 'recent immigrants'; of the remainder, 1300 were long-established Jewish residents. Though Protestants were – and remain – few in number, the Spanish authorities were always suspicious of the settlement. Yet a constant feature of demographic trends was inter-marriage with women from the Spanish side of the frontier. Spanish-born women, for instance, numbered 10% of the population in 1920. This kept Gibraltar a Spanish-speaking city but did not promote a sense of allegiance to Spain. On the contrary, Gibraltarian interests were too closely bound up with the presence of a British garrison and fleet and with the opportunities created by Britain's global maritime predominance in the 19th century. Gibraltarian commitment to the British Empire was enhanced by the experiences of the world wars, in which Spain remained a non-combatant. After World War II, when the British empire broke up, Gibraltar could not be openly groomed for independence, as that would have been contrary to the terms of Utrecht; but substantial self-government was gradually conceded, feeding and fed by a developing Gibraltarian consciousness. This was well expressed by a local politician, Peter Isola, in submissions to the United Nations in 1960: Gibraltarians, he said, formed a community of their own and Gibraltar belonged to them and no-one else. The Spanish government and public opinion recognize that any closer association between Spain and Gibraltar in the future will have to be adjusted to acknowledge that fact.

CATALANS, VALENCIANS AND BALEARIC ISLANDERS

Catalan identity is found among the Catalan-speaking inhabitants of the Spanish autonomous region of Catalonia (Catalan: Catalunya) and of Roussillon (Rosseló) and Cerdagne (Cerdanya) across the French border; the neighbouring Spanish autonomous regions of Valencia and the Balearic Islands (Balears) were formed as kingdoms in the Middle Ages in a process of Catalan expansion but today house peoples with distinct identities, despite important continuities of culture. Self-styled Valencians are keen to distinguish themselves from Catalans and to resist cultural and political domination from the north. In the Balearic islands, loyalties focused on the archipelago and on individual islands hinder potential fellow-feeling with the mainlanders. In Catalonia proper, however, the Valencians and islanders tend to be seen as sharing in a common Catalan heritage.

LAND AND SEA ■

Speakers of Catalan (Català) – and its dialects and cognate tongues – occupy lands washed by the Mediterranean; until the late Middle Ages they monopolized the routes of access between the Iberian interior and that sea. This has given them some distinguishing characteristics compared with the Castilian-speaking inland peoples; commercial values, big merchant classes, a taste for pasta in Catalonian seafaring élites. At the same time, it has made Catalan- and Castilian-speakers complementary, and even mutually dependent; Spain has always needed the trade of Barcelona and Valencia – cities which in turn have needed Spanish markets. The result has been the sometimes uneasy political collaboration with the rest of Spain which has been the dominant theme of the modern history of the seaboard peoples.

The inhabited areas are narrow, hemmed in by mountains and climatic extremes. Valencia includes large tracts of uninhabitable waste as well as the most fertile soil in Spain. Not only are there two kinds of culture in all these lands – a mountain culture and a maritime culture; there is also a tradition which promotes regional above national identity and puts local interests first. This makes generalization risky and accounts for the peoples' ungovernable reputation.

LANGUAGE ■

In the period from the 9th century to the 12th, the emergence of a form of romance language peculiar to the eastern Pyrenees and the 'Spanish March' of the Frankish empire is hard to separate from the development of Provençal. A translation of a

163

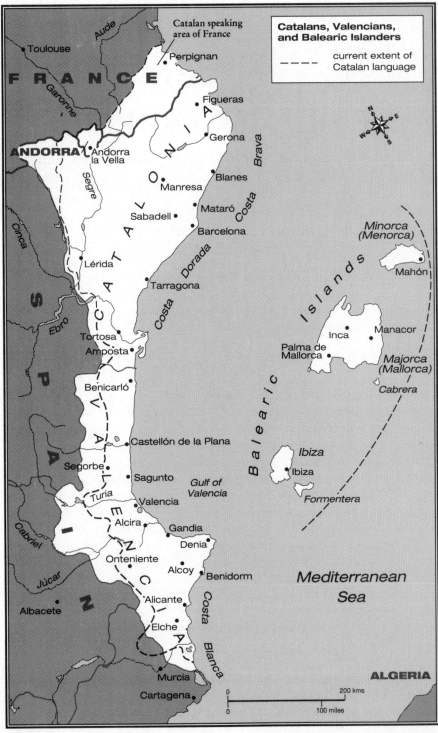

Catalan speaking area of France

Catalans, Valencians, and Balearic Islanders

- - - - current extent of Catalan language

Visigothic law-code of the early 12th century, however, survives in what is recognisably Catalan. Though Provençal was favoured in Catalonia for some kinds of verse until the late 13th century, and the language of Catalan poets continued to be influenced by Provençal throughout the Middle Ages, Catalan developed a distinguished literature of its own, at least equal in range and power to those of other languages of the Iberian peninsula. The period of grandeur of Catalan literature coincided with an era of imperial greatness for the Catalan state: memories of both have nourished Catalan nationalism ever since.

By the 16th century, economic and political changes had virtually eliminated patronage for Catalan literature. Until the 19th century, Catalan survived only as an administrative and spoken tongue and by that time – discouraged or even persecuted by centralizing Spanish regimes that favoured the spread of Castilian as the language of the Spanish state – it was in danger of becoming an ethnographic curiosity. In 1833, however, the movement known as the *Renaixença* began, with the appearance of Carles Aribau's nostalgic poem, *Pàtria*. Every year from 1859 the exponents of the literary use of Catalan met to celebrate *Jocs Florals* in which poets competed for prizes and prestige. Though the early efforts were self-consciously archaic, Catalan rapidly established itself as a suitable medium for inventive writing in every field, including drama, prose fiction, journalism, history and academic, technical and scientific works.

As the everyday language of the people of Barcelona – one of the leading centres in the 19th century of the Mediterranean industrial revolution – Catalan developed a vocabulary abreast of the development of modern life. This gives it unique status among the languages of western Europe's national minorities today, and unique guarantees of survival. Catalan has also preserved a remarkable degree of homogeneity, compared with the other main minority languages of the Iberian peninsula, Euskara and Galego. Traditionally, Catalan scholars divided the language into two main groups of dialects: 'eastern Catalan' was the name applied to forms spoken in the French *pays catalan*, the Balearic Islands, the Catalan colony of Alghero (Catalan: Alguer) in Sardinia, the Spanish provinces of Girona and Barcelona and the eastern half of the province of Tarragona. 'Western Catalan' was the language of the rest of the historic Principality of Catalonia and the Kingdom of Valencia. Sentiment and scholarship in Valencia and the Balearic Islands, however, has claimed that Valencian (*Valencià*) and Majorcan (*Mallorquí*) are independent languages, derived not from Catalan but directly from an intermediate romance language called Limousin (Catalan: *lemosí*), which is also the presumed parent of Provençal. Although this theory has convinced few objective students of the problem, as a matter of courtesy and conviction the speech of Valencia is now commonly designated *valencià*; in the islands, a process of fragmentation has led to further distinctions being drawn between the tongues of Majorca, Minorca and Ibiza with Formentera, but the name *mallorquí* is now generally accepted, at least for the first.

In the present century, the struggle for Catalan was waged against a hostile state during the dictatorships in Spain of Generals Primo de Rivera (1923–31) and Franco

165

(1939–75). The language has also had to contend with the effects of mass immigration from other parts of Spain. Franco's persecution of Catalan-speakers, however, only increased their determination to preserve their cultural heritage. Although substantial numbers of immigrants and their heirs remain outside the majority linguistic communities – exercising, for instance, their right to educate their children in Castilian-speaking schools – the autonomous governments have generally been acclaimed for their success in promoting the use of their official languages through education, broadcasting and the patronage of traditional cultural events. On the French side of the border, and in the tiny Catalan-speaking border-state of Andorra, passions are feebler; but the survival of the language seems guaranteed by the ripple-effect of the efforts of the Catalan government in Spain.

HISTORY ■

The political history of what was to become Catalonia effectively begins in the 870s, when Guifré the Hairy, who was later adopted as a cultural hero by Catalan historians, conquered the Frankish counties south of the Pyrenees. He did not declare independence or transmit a united realm to his heirs, but his was a genuinely 'regional' triumph: a dynasty rooted in the region had definitively ousted 'foreign' rivals. From now on the warrior-aristocrats of the mountains were led by counts who shared their own limited horizons. Guifré left three legacies which profoundly modified the future of Catalonia: the prominence of the county of Barcelona; the survival of an enduring dynasty (known as the House of Barcelona, which ruled until 1412); and his legend as founder of a Catalan state, which was a more powerful stimulant to Catalanist sentiment in modern times than any real achievement of a Dark Age strong man could ever have been.

In the 10th century his inheritance became a sovereign state, now usually called the 'Principality of Catalonia'. Enriched at the expense of neighbouring Muslim states, benefiting from the growth of the western Mediterranean economy, it became, by the early 12th century, a major regional power. The merchants in Barcelona and Tarragona were, however, disadvantaged in competition with their Italian rivals by Muslim control of the Balearic Islands. The conquest of Majorca and Ibiza in the early 13th century was a decisive change of fortune which, owing to the patterns of wind and current, enabled Catalan merchants to dominate western Mediterranean trade. The islands were the springboard for the acquisition of an empire, which, by the mid-14th century, encompassed Sicily, Minorca, much of Sardinia and some commercial outposts on the fringes of the rich trade of the Maghrib.

Although this empire was always rather loosely bound together, its wars created the Catalan national feeling powerfully expressed in the early 14th-century chronicle of Ramon Muntaner, who regarded the Catalans as an uniquely virtuous race, bound together – whatever their political differences – by obligations of kinship. The imperialism of the House of Barcelona exported Catalan speech, culture and colonies. This did not always have enduring effects but the catalanization of the Balearics was thorough and permanent; in the kingdom of Valencia, though the existing Muslim population was at first left largely undisturbed, a Catalan minority was settled which, in the long run – as the Muslims were forcibly converted and at last, in 1609, expelled – was to shape the culture decisively. This is not to say that Valencian and Balearic identities have no independent roots of their own: even when the Catalan empire was at it most well-articulated stage, the kingdoms of Valencia and of Majorca (which comprised all the islands) had distinct institutions and virtual internal sovereignty.

The costs of empire – especially of the brutal war to dominate Sardinia – gradually came to outweigh the profits. Though Catalonia was more robust in the 15th century than is commonly supposed, the richer and more populous neighbouring kingdoms of Castile and France eclipsed her. By the 16th century, dynastic union had transferred the seat of government permanently to Castile. Though Catalonia and the other states of her former empire remained nominally sovereign until 1716, this was the beginning of a long period of resentment of Castile which served to sharpen Catalan identity. Wars of independence in 1640–58 and 1705–15 resulted in defeat and in the attenuation of distinctive laws, traditions and institutions. Armies of occupation were everywhere: Castilian armies in Catalonia and Valencia, French in Roussillon and Cerdagne, British in Minorca (where they stayed from 1705 to 1756, leaving the sash windows of Hanover Street in Mahon [Catalan: Maó] as a lasting souvenir). In the 18th century, Catalonia, Valencia and the Balearic Islands seemed to abandon dissent in favour of collaboration; but the less settled conditions of the 19th century, beginning with the re-assertion of local and regional identities in the resistance against Napoleon (1808–14), showed that the distinct character of the historic communities of the Spanish levant had hibernated, not died.

The 19th-century Catalan cultural revival was accompanied by a political movement, some members of which included all of what were called the *paisos catalans* (Catalan lands) in their aspirations for devolution or separation from the Spanish and French states. Yet the peoples concerned seemed to be on divergent paths. The dominant feature of the history of the lands of the historic Principality of Catalonia was the rapid industrialization of the Barcelona area. In the first half of the century the population doubled. In 1833 Barcelona acquired Spain's first steam-powered factory; in 1836, its shipyards built the first Spanish steamship; in 1848, the country's first railway linked Barcelona and Mataró. Yarn production was almost entirely mechanized by the end of the 1850s. Valencia, meanwhile, remained a centre for the arable produce of its uniquely rich immediate hinterland, the *horta*. Majorca did not experience an industrial revolution until the new century brought rapid take-off: there was a locomotive factory by 1901, a car factory by 1922 and during World War I, Majorcan and Minorcan manufacturers supplied the French army's boots. As a result, radicalism, Catalanism and protectionism throve in the principality while the other lands remained politically cautious and conservative. In Majorca, for instance, during the First Spanish Republic, two-thirds of the adult population subscribed to the petitions of the right-wing Unión Católica, whereas Barcelona welcomed the federal constitutional policies of the new régime.

Whenever Catalan institutions have been revived in the 20th century – from 1911 to 1914, under a limited pooling of provincial resources known as the *Mancomunitat*, from 1931 to 1939 under the second republic and since 1978 under the democratic 'regime of autonomies' – the *paisos catalans* have been separated. The degree of autonomy enjoyed by the principality is even today more privileged than that of Valencia and the Balearic Islands: the regional government there has broader responsibilities and Catalan law takes precedence over that of the Spanish state in some areas.

NATIONALISM ■

In Catalonia, nationalism must be understood as one of the manifestations of Catalanism (Catalan: *catalanisme*) which can itself take many forms: from the sense of being Catalan to the desire to conserve and promote Catalan culture; from sentiments of kinship with other self-confessed Catalans to hostility towards non-Catalans and, in particular, towards the Spanish state; from political programmes embracing devolution, autonomy, federalism or separatism, to 'pan-Catalan' or 'greater Catalan' imperialism which aims to create a Catalan state extending beyond the boundaries of the historic Principality; finally the policy of 'putting Catalonia first' is included – which is as much as 'Catalanists' of the political left today, who reject overtly nationalist language, will admit to.

Historically, nationalism has been divided between loyalties to different concepts of Catalonia, represented by the views of its greatest 19th-century spokesmen. For Josep Torras i Bagès (1846–1916) Catalonia was a community defined by its faithfulness to certain traditional values proper to the country's rural and mountain hinterland – including Catholic piety, allegiance to the old customary laws and codes of privilege which pre-dated the Spanish state, and a language that had always been alive in the mouths of peasants. For Valentí Almirall i Llozer (1841–1904), Catalonia was the embodiment of progress, essentially urban and maritime, secular without being irreligious, with a duty to drag the benighted countryside behind it.

These differences are resolved by self-differentiation from the rest of Spain. No truly satisfying sense of identity can be built up entirely from within: it has to have an excluded 'other', an external point of reference, in this case the Castilians. They represent themselves in their own literature and journalism as commonsensical, practical, industrious, provident, reasonable and scientific, while their stereotype of Castilian weaknesses includes lack of realism, addiction to the useless, laziness, fatalism and uncompromising pride. Political Catalanism has been nourished by a reading of the Spanish past in which Catalan language and liberties are represented as victims of Castilian imperialism. Outright separatism, however, has never commanded much support. The majority party today is in the tradition represented by the slogans of nationalist heroes of the past: 'Spain with Justice' and 'The Spain of All of Us'. Membership of the European Community may have weakened the younger generation's Spanish sentiment and, particularly within the Principality of Catalonia there are now many voices calling for a regional alignment within the Community, in which Catalans might have closer institutional links with French and Italian peoples of the northwest Mediterranean than with the rest of Spain.

Originally an élite – even an arcane – ideal, nationalism attracted a mass vote in every free election from 1898 onwards. It leaped ahead in the early years of the 20th century, when the Spanish state seemed to have failed Catalonia; imperial débacle forfeited markets, while protectionism was resisted from Madrid. The movement's growth was most marked under hostile dictatorships: in an atmosphere of unenfor-ceable repression all forms of forbidden fruit flourished. Nationalism had great diffi-culty, however, in competing for working-class votes with ideologies of the left until the late 1920s, when workers' issues subsided and the Catalanist message could be communicated at every social level. The alliance was cemented by the experience of the Franco years, when tight centralization enhanced the appeal of devolution to voters. When Franco died in 1975 and the President of the Catalan government-in-exile returned to the balcony of the Palau de la Generalitat, the seat of Catalan government, he was cheered by workers and bourgeois, natives and immigrants to Catalonia alike.

Paradoxically, perhaps, the strength of Catalan nationalism has had an inhibiting effect on parallel movements in Valencia and the islands. Valencianism originated as a kind of Catalanist heresy – a protest by the Valencian élite against the vision of a 'greater Catalonia' conceived in Barcelona. Valencia was to have its own revived identity, its own autonomy. Teodor Llorente (1836–1911), first leader of Valencian-ism, claimed that Valencian minstrels of the Middle Ages possessed a different cul-ture from their Catalan counterparts and showed a greater awareness of the unity of Spain. Like most heresies, Valencianism was soon divided by schisms of its own, but it remained a marginal creed, at least for the rest of the 19th century. In 1896, the republican federalist Constantí Llombart complained, 'The Valencian people has failed to respond with the enthusiasm and interest which the glorious cause that is their own ought to have awakened'. This remained broadly true until the Franco era made voters tired of centralization. In the Balearics, nationalism has never caught on electorally; defence of the exceptionally prosperous island economy, rather than an identity or an ideology, is the voters' main priority. The conservative reputation es-tablished in the 19th century continues today, especially in Majorca.

CUSTOMS AND TRADITIONS ■

The custom of primogeniture distinguishes the Catalans from all other peoples of the Iberian peninsula except the Basques. In the remote past, descent through the female line was common, commemorated in some family names today and perhaps in the still-common practice of insisting that husbands incorporate or adopt their wives' patronyms in the absence of a male heir in the wife's family. A strong sense of lineage is also apparent in the small range of baptismal names which tend to be shared among members of a single family. Primogeniture helped shape the Catalan past. While the eldest son (*hereu*) kept the family homestead, siblings were released for the activities which distinguished the Catalan historical experience: commerce, colonialism and – in the last century – industrialization in and around Barcelona.

There are peculiar touches in popular pastimes – Catalonia, for instance, is addicted to building human towers – and distinctive flavours in the cuisine – in Catalonia snails are a common garnish and nuts a basic thickening agent, while Valencia specializes in dishes that use her abundant rice and has many unique sweet drinks and sweetmeats. It cannot, however, be said that food and games have the same place in the Catalan sense of identity as in that – say – of the Basques. In this part of Spain, dance has the defining role: the universal and versatile *contrapàs*, perhaps of liturgical origin; the Catalan *sardana*, which is so strong a symbol of Catalan nationality that Franco banned it; and the dances specific to local festivities, like the *moros i cristians* with which Alcoi or La Vila Joiosa commemorate their reconquest by Catalan armies from the Moors. Popular devotional life is as important as in any part of the Iberian peninsula: the Catalan 'national' shrine of the Virgin of Monserrat, has a special place in Catalanist history, having been identified with the cause by Torras i Bagès; but her cult has spread throughout the whole Hispanic world and she is probably no more popular in Valencia or Majorca than in, say, Valladolid or Mexico City.

PROVENÇALS

People and place have combined in Provence to produce one of the most distinctive, most visited regions of France. By the end of the 2nd century BC, that part of France lying between the Mediterranean and the Rhône river and the Alps had become Gallia Transalpina, the first Roman provincia (and hence the name Provence) beyond the Alps. From that period onwards, Provence developed a distinctive language and history, its own customs and traditions, which have served to differentiate its inhabitants from the rest of France, a differentiation reinforced both by Provence's peripheral location within the country and by its Mediterranean climate.

HISTORY ■

Although there was some pre-historic settlement in Provence, the effective development of the region dates from its colonization by Phocaean Greeks who, around 600 BC, founded trading ports like Massilia (Marseille) and Nikaia (Nice) and taught the native peoples to cultivate vines and olives, to surround their settlements with defensive fortifications and to engage in trade. From about the 4th century BC, Celtic migrants from the north moved into the region to mix with the native Ligurian tribes

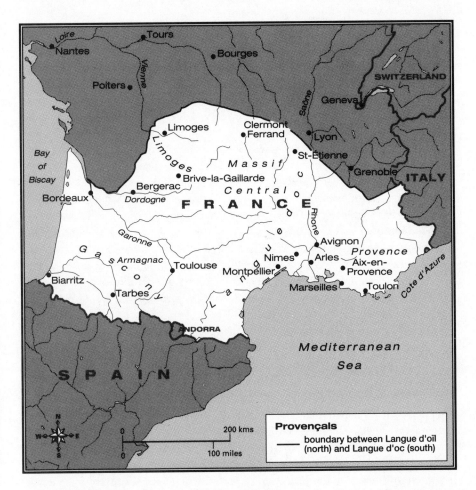

Provençals
—— boundary between Langue d'oïl (north) and Langue d'oc (south)

to form the basis of Provence's population. Threats to the Greek colonies from native tribes led them to seek protection from Rome in 181, in 154 and in 125 BC: on this last occasion, the Romans stayed, establishing their control of the littoral from Italy through to Spain and, in *Provincia Gallia Transalpina*, a base from which to launch the conquest of Gaul.

The Roman occupation of Provence, lasting for nearly five centuries, was to leave an enduring imprint upon its culture and its landscape. It brought Roman law, a Latin language and eventually Christianity, as well as irrigation schemes, villas, roads and monumental towns, with their arenas, temples, baths and theatres. In the 5th century AD, a massive palace was built at Arles, reflecting its role as the administrative centre of the province.

With the collapse of the Roman Empire, Provence was invaded by Visigoths, Burgundians and Ostrogoths and then in 536 it came, at least nominally, under the rule of the Franks. In practice, Provence was not integrated with the northern regions and the cultural impact of romanization persisted. Saracen incursions during

171

the 8th century served to emphasize that by then Provence was more a geographical expression than an historical reality. With the breakup of the Carolingian empire, under the Treaty of Verdun (843) Provence was retained, together with Burgundy and Lorraine, by Lothair, heir to the imperial title, and it became subsequently part of a series of semi-independent kingdoms, one of which (the Kingdom of Arles) became attached to the Holy Roman Empire in 1032. By then, a dynasty of local families who acquired and passed on the title of Count of Provence were its effective rulers: the authority of the Empire was only nominal. With the failure of the male line of this dynasty, Provence passed through the female line in the early-12th century, first to the counts of Toulouse and then to those of Barcelona, and it was then ruled by the Spanish from Catalonia for more than a century. It passed through marriage in 1246 to Charles, Count of Anjou, permitting a northern influence to be extended into Provence. Because they were also kings of Naples, the Angevin dynasty of counts who came to rule Provence at first subordinated it to Italian interests but their reign did ultimately result in the effective administrative and political development of the *comté*, including that of the *Etats*, an assembly for governing the province and securing its privileges and customs, with power to raise taxes and an army.

In 1481 Provence was transferred by will to the King of France, with the firm recommendation that all of the privileges, rights, liberties, laws and customs of the *comté* should be maintained. In practice, thus integrated into France, Provence saw itself increasingly controlled by the crown from the early-16th century onwards. The *Etats* in 1639 declined to raise through taxation the additional money needed by the King for the war against Spain, the King raised funds from elsewhere and the *Etats* were not convened again until 1787, just before the French Revolution. The kings of France were represented in Provence from the 17th century by a *gouverneur*, by a *lieutenant du roi* and – with an increasingly important administrative role – by an *intendant*. At the end of the 18th century, with the Revolution, Provence was finally deprived of its own political institutions: in 1790 it was divided into three *départements* of the new France. Two further *départements* were, in effect, added to Provence during the 19th century. The Niçois joined the Provençals when their territory was transferred to France from Piedmont in return for French help in the Austro-Piedmontese war of 1859 (see p. 146). In 1956 the economic planning region of Provence-Côte d'Azur-Corse was established, comprising seven *départements* ; then in 1970 Corsica itself was given the status of a planning region, leaving Provence as part of the region of Provence-Côte d'Azur.

Ultimately deprived of laboriously-constructed and frequently-contested political unity and never having originally possessed the degree of ethnic integrity found, say, in Brittany, Provence has nonetheless created and maintained its own personality as a distinctive region of France, with an individuality based in part upon its language and literature.

LANGUAGE ■

During the last 100 years or so, spoken Provençal has come to be restricted in its usage to private communications among rural families, having been replaced by French as the official and public language. It was formerly a standard and literary language used widely throughout southern France.

In its widest sense, Provençal is another name for Occitan or *langue d'oc*, a Romance language once spoken in much of southern France, in contrast to the *langue d'oil* of northern parts. In its more restricted sense, Provençal is that dialect of Occitan spoken in the historic province of Provence and even within this narrower usage there exist four principal varieties of the dialect and many sub-varieties (such dialectical diversity reflecting the topographical fragmentation of the region historically into many, relatively discrete localities). There exists a substantial Provençal literature, dating from the 10th century. During the medieval period poetry and songs in Provençal were in the repertoire of jongleurs and troubadours, while prose in Provençal included sermons, translations of the gospels and stories of the lives of troubadours; during the early-modern period there was also a substantial dramatic literature, of mysteries and miracle plays. In the modern period, literature in the Rhône dialect flourished under the influence of the Provençal poet Frédéric Mistral (1830–1914) and his disciples.

REGIONALISM ■

A turbulent political history and the lack of a clear-cut ethnic distinctiveness have meant that opposition to the *françisation* of Provence has tended to take the form not of a separatist nationalism but of a less radical regionalism. Even during the 18th century, in the prelude to the Revolution of 1789, protests about the creeping political enfeeblement of Provence expressed concern for maintaining the distinctive customs and traditions of the region but did not question its being part of the kingdom of France. Equally, during the 19th and 20th century most Provençals have been firm supporters of a patriotic republicanism, while at the same time expressing a clear preference for left-wing political programmes.

The erosion of regional customs and practices did, however, lead to some reaction, notably the foundation in 1854 by seven young Provençal poets (including Mistral) of the *Félibrige* (a borrowing from the title of an old popular song), a movement with defensive, conservative, even nostalgic objectives in relation to the region's language, literature and culture, but it did not produce a movement with a programme for Provençal devolution or autonomy. Provence became, from the mid-19th century, increasingly assimilated into the French nation.

CUSTOMS AND CULTURE ■

Provence witnessed a considerable and precocious conversion to Christianity, influencing deeply not only the collective consciousness of its people, the annual cycle of daily life and the partitioning of space into parishes but also the landscape,

173

which witnessed the early construction and later reconstruction and extension of churches, cathedrals, baptistries and monasteries. An earlier faith of *romanitas* – of belief in the Roman way-of-life – came during the High Middle Ages to be replaced by that of Christianity. It was, of course, in ports of the region that people embarked for the Crusades and in Avignon that the Popes were in residence from 1316 for almost a century. It was also during this period that Provence began to build a new regional self-awareness on the foundations of the former political order. A fervent, Catholic religiosity is one of the characteristics of the Provençals which contributes to the singularity of their region. Encouraged by the Mediterranean climate and influenced by Latin temperament, Provençal religious – as well as secular – festivals and processions are often colourful and exuberant outdoor spectacles.

Not confined to the religious realm, the sociability of the Provençals is to be seen in the range and complexity of their personal social relations and of their public social activities (*la vie collective*). It is also evidenced in their political inclination, since the granting of universal male suffrage in 1848, towards socialism, especially in the towns but also, less expectedly, in the countryside.

Until Provence was linked to northern France, and especially to Paris, by railway from the 1860s its characteristics were not widely known. From then onwards, it became increasingly integrated into the mainstream of French social and economic life and began to acquire its modern, touristic image as a region of bold natural colours and clear light, of historical monuments and geographical wonders, and of a spontaneous, open-air and vibrant life-style, a region with traditional folk-lore and modern artists.

With modernization, many of the traditional practices have in fact been declining for a century or more. The birth of a new Provence has been in parallel with the death of old Provence: it is rarer now to see local women wearing Provençal costumes and head-dresses than it is to encounter topless tourists. On the other hand, many new folklore groups have recently been formed to revive and to preserve old ways, such as dancing the *farandole* to the tune of the *tambourin* (a narrow drum) and the *galoubet* (a flute). When explicitly produced for tourists, history and folklore have become manufactured spectacle. Tradition has persisted of its own accord more visibly in vernacular rural architecture, with its characteristic stone-walled, terracotta roof-tiled farmsteads and villas, often with no doors or windows on the north-facing side as protection against the cold Mistral winter wind. The need for protection of another kind, against political and social insecurity, is evident in the old fortified hill-top villages and towns which punctuate the Provençal landscape.

CORSICANS

Corsican identity has been fostered both by the insularity of Corsica itself and by the island's distinctive cultural history. With an area of only 3368 square miles, Corsica is nonetheless the third largest island in the western Mediterranean, after Sardinia and Sicily, and its more than 600 miles of coastline have offered strategic refuge and trading places to a variety of peoples and powers across the centuries. The most mountainous of the Mediterranean islands, Corsica has been politically a part of France since the mid-18th century, but it is physically much closer to Italy: separated by only 7 miles from the Italian island of Sardinia and by 52 miles from the Italian mainland, Corsica is more than 90 miles from mainland France.

HISTORY ■

The early peopling of Corsica remains enigmatic. It seems that a society of hunters, gatherers and pastoralists existed from the 10th millennium BC and that there was a significant colonization of the island by Ligurians and then by Iberian-Celtic peoples during the second millennium BC. Vestiges of these cultures survive in the present-day landscape as simple dolmens and stone circles, as sculptured menhirs and as fortified camps.

Corsica's long and troubled history as a colony began in the 6th century BC, when the Phocaean Greeks established a trading base at Alalia on the east coast. A struggle for control of the island then ensued among Greeks, Etruscans and Carthaginians. Although the direct impact of these incursions was restricted to the eastern seaboard, they were important in incorporating Corsica into the Mediterranean trading world and in introducing to the island the vine, olives and cereals, as well as prospecting for minerals.

Roman colonization, from the mid-3rd century BC to the mid-5th century AD, left relatively untouched the indigenous Corsican culture of the interior but developed considerably the settlement and economy of the littoral. But the legacy of Rome to the island as a whole was to be significant and enduring: the colonizers imposed their Latin speech, from which *Corse* itself is directly derived; and they permitted the introduction of Christianity. In so influencing the language and religion of the indigenous peoples, Roman occupation of the island fundamentally shaped the culture of the Corsicans. Following the collapse of the Roman Empire, there followed seven centuries marked by waves of invasions and partial occupations of Corsica by Vandals, Ostrogoths, Lombards and Saracens, none of which contributed significantly to the construction of a Corsican identity other than by resulting in a return to indigenous life-styles.

The unstable medieval period witnessed such internal rivalries among Corsican factions and lords that the people turned to the Papacy for relief; at the end of the

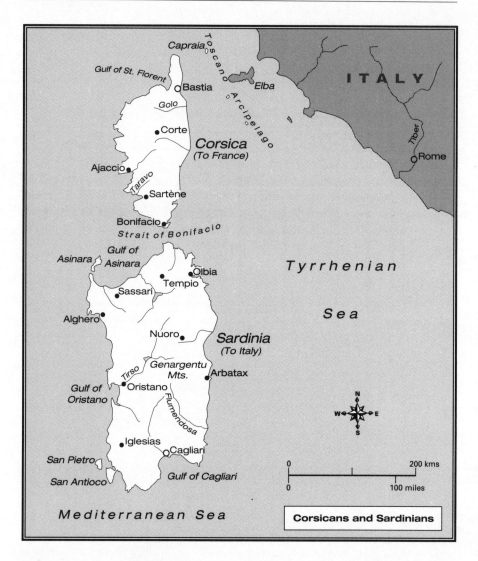

Corsicans and Sardinians

11th century the archbishop of Pisa was appointed to administer the island. The struggle for the control of Corsica between the republics of Pisa and Genoa until 1284 and then between Genoa and Aragon from 1296 until 1434 – with Genoa emerging victorious on both occasions – was accompanied by considerable conflict between Corsican factions, internal rivalries which militated against the emergence of a united Corsican opposition to Genoese rule. Genoese control continued until 1768 but there were before then a number of popular uprisings, notably that in the mid-14th century in the eastern lowlands, a protest against the feudal excesses of the seigneurs which created a short-lived attempt to establish a communalistic and democratic society. In the early 18th century mounting anger about levels of taxation imposed by the Genoese, frustration over the lack of genuine autonomy and resentment at the unwillingness of the Genoese to accord respect to the traditional leaders within Corsican society led in 1729 to the beginnings of a national uprising. The Genoese were driven from the interior almost immediately, and in 1736 there was the astonishing proclamation of a Westphalian adventurer, Théodore de Neuhoff, as King of Corsica (he fled the island after reigning for only seven months). The struggle for independence from Genoa continued. In 1755 a Corsican exile who had been brought up in Naples, Pascal Paoli, was proclaimed 'General of the Nation' and his actions represent the most deliberate effort to change the Corsican people into a modern nation. Paoli provided Corsica with a new, written constitution which established a national legislature elected by universal suffrage, with its own minted money and with its own flag bearing the symbol of the Moor's head. In addition, he established schools and a university in the new capital, Corte, and he promoted economic development. But this experiment in Corsican self-government was shortlived. Genoa ceded Corsica to France in 1769, since when the island has been a part of France (except 1794–96, when it was governed by Britain). Corsicans had warmed to French rule when in the late 1740s, the Genoese had sought assistance from France to run the island and the rise of Napoleon, a native of Corsica, consolidated relations between the island and the mainland, extinguishing separatist aspirations for generations. Corsican loyalty to France was impressively proved in the two World Wars.

SOCIETY ■

Their island birth and their turbulent history give Corsicans a clear sense of their separate identity. Corsicans living in France, *le continent* as it is referred to by islanders, return home in large numbers in vacations and swell electoral registers into lists which are often larger than the census of population. Many return to Corsica permanently on retiring from working in France or elsewhere. They identify not only with the island as a whole but also with their own village, locality or region within it. That close identification is reflected in the many associations or *amicales* which bring together Corsican émigrés.

Corsica to a Corsican is not only a place, it is a people. During the medieval period, marked by political insecurity and discontinuous contact with the continent, there emerged a social structure based on the extended family and the rural clan. A strong social solidarity was accompanied by equally powerful conflicts and enduring vendettas between families and clans. Rural communities developed and jealously guarded their own resources and collective ways of living.

The population of Corsica probably doubled in size during the 19th century, reaching a peak of about 280,000 in 1880. Since then a massive exodus has taken place. Today there are almost as many Corsican-born people living in continental France as there are native Corsicans living on the island. Moreover, about 15% of those now living in Corsica were born in France and a further 20% were born elsewhere (with the former pre-eminence of Italians replaced by North Africans,

177

particularly Moroccans). The 'true' Corsican is an 'endangered species'. Associated with depopulation has been an ageing of the remaining population: the emigrants have tended to be the younger, better educated and more progressive elements of the population.

LANGUAGE ■

The speaking of Corse contributes significantly today to the production and reproduction of a sense of Corsican identity. For most people born and living in the island today, Corse is the everyday, private language while French is the official, public language. It is, however, under threat from French and is spoken more by men than by women, more by parents than by their children, and more in villages than in towns.

Corse is a hybridized Latin language, fundamentally derived from a Tuscan dialect of Italian but in which some terms are pre-Indo-European or pre-Roman in their origins while others are modifications under French influence. While Corse has local variations in dialect within the island – between the *langue du Nord-Est* and the *langue du Sud-Ouest* – it has no defined alphabet, no dictionary and no completely agreed rules of grammar. Until the 19th century, Corse only had an oral expression, with the written, official languages being at first Italian and then French. It would have remained largely an unwritten language but for an upsurge of interest in Corsican culture and folklore in the 19th century. Accorded the formal status of a regional language in 1974, Corse is the medium for folklore and festivals and is itself a field for scholarly enquiry. Some literary periodicals and some journals devoted to history and folklore are published in Corse, but Corse remains essentially a language of the people, widely spoken but little written and little read.

NATIONALISM AND REGIONALISM ■

Corsican 'nationalism' has been less a call for autonomy than a demand for regional devolution. It draws upon the distant past for inspiration and legitimation, but it is essentially a response to the *françisation* of Corsica since the mid-19th century, to the perceived failure of the centralized state to deal effectively with the island's persistent economic and social problems, and to the fear that Corsica was reverting to the status of a colony within metropolitan France. From the early-1960s there emerged groups advocating a strongly regionalist economic programme and then from the late-1960s violent demonstrations and direct action moved the protests into a new phase and with a new emphasis, for some at least, on Corsican autonomy or semi-autonomy. Actions by the central government such as the establishment of Corsica as a separate planning region in 1970 and the granting to it of a degree of political devolution in 1982 have met some, but by no means all, of the demands of those wishing to make Corsica 'Corsican'.

The Corsican national emblem, the Moor's head, is commonplace on the island, used widely as a trade mark on its products, as a decorative motif on objects in daily use as well as on those for selling to tourists, and on its banner. The *Tête de More* is derived from the centrepiece of the heraldic arms of the island which themselves date from an assembly presided over by Paoli at Corte in 1762. The crest itself is much older, probably coming from the heraldic standard of the crusades. The Moor's head was originally blindfolded: Paoli is thought to have removed the band to symbolize enlightenment.

CULTURE AND CUSTOMS ■

Concern with Corsican 'nationalism' has been associated with a vigorous study of, and endeavour to conserve, the island's distinctive cultural heritage. Its archaeology, its history and its ethnology have been intensively studied in recent years; there has been a flowering of writing and publishing in Corse, a revival of Corsican songs and dances, and a 'renaissance' of Corsican traditions and crafts. This included the establishment in 1962 at Palasca, near Belgodere in the Balagne, of *Cyrne Arte*, an artists' village intended to revive rural artisanal crafts and to encourage young painters and sculptors.

Given Corsica's turbulent history, it is not surprising that its culture and customs often focus on death and violence; given its close and enduring reliance upon the Roman Catholic faith, Corsican customs are frequently associated with religious festivals and practices. Holy Week processions held in most parishes typically feature a hooded, chained penitent carrying a cross; they are frequently accompanied by chants of medieval origin and by performance of the *granitola* or snail, a complicated spiralling movement. Most places also celebrate the feast day of their patron saint, as well as that of the Assumption of the Virgin on 15th August, on which Napoleon's birthday is also celebrated. Such festivals involve a mixture of piety, profanity and public spectacle.

Singing and music-making (usually with a guitar) are enjoyed by Corsicans. Behind the modern romantic ballads lie traditional songs like the *lamenti*, sung to mark a death or the departure of menfolk to battle and the *voceri*, sung at the wake of a man who had suffered a violent death and evoking relatives to take revenge. Traditional three-part singing by men – *paghiella* – is now rarely heard except in remote mountain communes.

Corsican concern with violent death also finds expression in the vendetta and banditry. *Vendetta*, meaning vengeance, is the principal contribution of Corse to international language. The vendetta developed in the medieval period as a form of summary justice exacted by vigilantes when official justice was virtually non-existent, slow or corrupt, but it survived as a matter of family or clan honour into the period of the French administration. Bandits emerged from the vendetta, as fugitives from official justice who took to the hills. Banditry, involving robbery and extortion, is an old Corsican tradition which was not effectively suppressed until the 1930s. Nonetheless, firearms and violence remain an integral part of the Corsican way-of-life.

Social and political instability have encouraged architectural forms which provide security, such as hill-top villages and multi-storey buildings. The Genoese

179

constructed many of the island's citadels, fortresses and watchtowers, whereas the most distinctive ecclesiastical buildings of Corsica are the Pisan churches, in the style of the Romanesque basilica. The most significant buildings of Corsica are, in effect, monuments to its early, colonial history. French rule has contributed little of note to the island's ecclesiastical or secular architecture, although it has added engineering features such as railway bridges and viaducts and, more recently, dams. And, of course, Corsica has many visible reminders that it was Napoleon's birthplace: many statues, street-names and hotel-names witness that fact, as do the highbrow Musée Napoléon and the lowbrow souvenir shops selling a range of articles commemorating Napoleon.

SARDINIANS

In modern times, the large island of Sardinia has been thinly populated, in contrast to Sicily, but, as with Sicily, there has long been a strong bandit element in the population, as the remote hills have provided an easy refuge. This rural banditry is sometimes represented as a 'culture of resistance' to outside forces.

HISTORY ■

Sardinia was open to colonization by Phoenicians, Greeks and Romans. It was, in antiquity, an island noted for its populousness, well-integrated in the Roman empire. Its silver and salt made it exceptionally wealthy in the Middle Ages. Yet the Sardinians had a reputation for 'savagery' that exposed them to enslavement and massacre in the Catalan invasions of the 14th century. Their ruling élites all came from abroad – from Pisan or Genoese settlers, or Catalan conquerors. Although tribal chiefs and feudatories from the mainland waged together wars of resistance against the Catalan interlopers for more than a century, there was never any subsequent Sardinian 'national' resurgence. This makes a suggestive contrast with nearby Corsica – a quiescent medieval backwater which has housed a strong identity and fierce regionalist or independence movements in modern times (p. 174).

When the domination of Italy passed from Spain to Austria in 1713, as a result of the War of Spanish Succession, the island of Sardinia too passed from the Spanish Bourbons to the Austrian Habsburgs. But German culture did not have the will or the time to make any impact on the Sardinians, any more than it did on the Lombards. In 1720 the Austrians exchanged Sardinia for Sicily, with Sardinia passing under the sovereignty of the Dukes of Savoy and bringing with it the title of 'King'. The island remained a remote and unimportant part of the Piedmontese kingdom, apart from a brief spell during the Napoleonic wars, when the royal court moved to exile on the island to maintain independence from the French conquerors. The intimacy of Sardinia's symbiosis with the Italian state helps to explain the absence of political separatism.

LANGUAGE AND CUSTOMS ■

The Sardinian dialect – or rather, dialects – are certainly distinct from spoken Italian, but the very fact that more than one dialect existed on the island has made the use of Italian, in recent times, a useful means of communication. The wild island with its brigands was made familiar to the European reading public by the novels of Grazia Deledda, the Nobel prize winner in 1926. Today the coastal areas of the island are being transformed by the increasing numbers of tourists who come, attracted by the spectacular scenery.

LIGURIANS

The Ligurians inhabit one of the most beautiful coastal regions in the world, a region where the mountains come right down to the sea, with dramatic effects. They have seen themselves essentially as Italians rather more obviously than the Piedmontese. Yet their existence has been linked with that of the Piedmontese for nearly 200 years, and with other Italians since the foundation of the Kingdom of Italy in 1861. Although Liguria's historical experience is a strong base for a potentially distinctive identity, the term Ligurian has not become, like Lombard, a political badge.

PHYSICAL ENVIRONMENT ■

Liguria is a narrow coastal strip, lying between the Ligurian Alps and the Apennines to the north, and the Ligurian Sea to the south. The beauty of the coast has made it one of the best-known tourist resorts in Europe – the Italian Riviera. The great port of Genoa divides Liguria into two halves – the Riviera di Ponente, stretching westwards to France, and the Riviera di Levante, stretching eastwards to Emilia-Romagna and Tuscany, which includes the lovely resorts of Santa Margherita, Rapallo, Portofino and Lerici, and the less-lovely naval port of La Spezia.

HISTORY ■

The term Ligurian was very familiar to ancient classical writers. Thucydides even mentions a Ligurian settlement in Spain, and Seneca says that there were Ligurians in Corsica. The Romans reached the Ligurian coast around 200 BC. A reminder of Roman days survives in place-names near Genoa – Quarto and Quinto, which were respectively four and five leagues along the Roman coastal road. In 180 BC, the Romans transported thousands of Ligurians – men, women and children – to a

181

Ligurians, Veneti, Friulians,
Central & Southern Italians

NEAPOLITAN   dialect

PUGLIA   district

settlement in South Italy, near Benevento. Augustus organized Ligurian in an administrative sense: the Ligurian tribes seem to have lived in villages, with Roman settlers in the towns. Under Diocletian, in the late 3rd century AD, Liguria extended as far as Milan, but by the 6th century it was reduced to its familiar modern area. In the 11th century, the Republic of Genoa was established, and in the course of the Middle Ages, became a major power in the Mediterranean. The Genoese even established a settlement in Constantinople, the seat of the eastern Roman Empire. The Genoese part of the city, known as Galata, can still be identified today by its characteristic tower, now a night-club. In the 12th century, the Genoese Republic was at its peak of commercial and naval power, competing with the Republic of Venice. Genoa and Venice were the two largest and most powerful cities on the Mediterranean in the High Middle Ages. By 1200 Genoa probably had a population of some 50,000, and perhaps 100,000 by the mid-14th century. Rivalry with Venice involved the Genoese in warfare in the second half of the 13th century and the Venetians were more often than not victorious. In 1348–9, Genoa passed through one of the grimmest phases of its history. The first year was that of the plague (later known as the Black Death). The pestilence, which reduced the population by at least a third, and perhaps by rather more, struck Genoa in January 1348 – earlier than in most parts of Italy, because the plague spread more quickly to ports than to inland towns. In 1349, Giovanni Visconti became Archbishop of Milan and, as he extended his power in Northern Italy, included Genoa in his conquests.

Perhaps the greatest hero in the history of Genoa and the Ligurians was Andrea Doria (1466–1560), a brilliant admiral who re-established the independent Republic of Genoa in 1528. He preserved Genoese independence through adroit diplomatic dealings with the French and Spanish, in a manner Machiavelli would have approved. Yet already the seeds of the Republic's later economic decline were sown. In the late 13th century Genoese ships had sailed through the Straits of Gibraltar to reach the Netherlands, and – specifically – the great market of Bruges. Genoa and Venice had shared the trade with the English and Flemish markets, but in the 16th century the Italian trades were losing much of their trade on these routes. A real economic deterioration occurred in the course of the 17th and 18th centuries.

In 1797 Napoleon transformed the corrupt and crumbling Genoese Republic into the Ligurian Republic, with a more modern legal system and centralized administration and under French control. At least under Napoleon Genoa did retain the semblance of independence, which was totally eliminated when the Republic was placed under Piedmontese sovereignty in 1815. There is little doubt that the politically-conscious classes were happier when they became part of the Kingdom of Italy in 1861, than they had been as a subordinate part of the Piedmontese monarchy. In 1860 the Piedmontese Prime Minister Cavour gave the most westerly part of Liguria – the province of Nice – to France, in order to retain the goodwill of the Emperor Napoleon III during the process of Italian unification. It was a policy that was bitterly resented by the Ligurians, and not least by Giuseppe Garibaldi, who had been born in Nice and was the city's deputy in parliament. Nice had been Italian in character, and even under French rule in the 20th century had a considerable Italian-speaking colony. The main portion of Liguria has remained an important part of Italy, and since 1948 has been an administrative region.

LANGUAGE ■

Before the arrival of the Romans, the Ligurians almost certainly spoke a distinct Indo-European language, but Latin quickly imposed itself on the local dialect, so that the spoken dialect of Liguria is simply another Romance language. The written language, however, as over the whole peninsula, is Italian, and with the spread of modern communications, especially television, it is rapidly becoming the universally spoken language as well.

POLITICS ■

The flavour of Ligurian politics since the 19th century has been a revolutionary one. Resentment against rule by the Piedmontese monarchy after 1815 developed a republican character under the influence of Giuseppe Mazzini (born in Genoa in 1805). In the 20th century Genoa, like most large ports, has had a strong left-wing working-class population, and the Socialist and Communist parties have always had strong support there.

VENETO-FRIULIANS

Their long maritime history has made the Venetians a people apart from other Italians. The only other comparable group – the Genoese (see p. 181) – had a less powerful and spectacular Mediterranean empire. The Friulians, long united politically with the Veneti, are considered here for convenience, though they have, in some ways, more in common with the culture of the Alpine regions (see p. 122).

HISTORY ■

Many theories have been advanced to explain the origins of the Venetian Republic, more correctly styled 'The Republic of St Mark' because of the highly dubious claim made by the Venetians that they possess the remains of the evangelist. One theory maintains Venice was founded by people fleeing from Attila the Hun and it is probable that the founders of the extraordinary settlement on the lagoons were seeking refuge from one or other of the barbarian invasions. From this bizarre beginning, the Republic of St Mark became a powerful maritime empire in the eastern Mediterranean during the Middle Ages. The Venetians took Cyprus as late as 1489, but as a maritime power the city was already in decline, and was finding compensation by expanding her possessions on the Italian mainland. Thus the lovely cities of Padua and Verona became part of the Venetian Republic, which changed its identity to become a small land empire and an important force in Italian, rather than Mediterranean politics. This area around Venice came to be known as the Veneto. The subsequent decline of the Republic culminated in Napoleon's totally unjustified and immoral occupation. In 1797 he handed Venetian sovereignty over to Austria. At least Wordsworth commemorated the occasion when he wrote a sonnet recognizing the sadness of the extermination of the Republic of St Mark. The peacemakers in 1815 were less sympathetic and confirmed that Venice and the Veneto should remain Austrian. The independent spirit of the Republic of St Mark was not yet dead: when the First War of Italian Independence broke out in 1848, the citizens of Venice rose up in a largely non-violent revolution and persuaded the Austrian authorities to leave. The revived Republic of St Mark held out longer than any other Italian revolution of the years 1848–9, and, indeed, longer than any other in Europe, except that in Hungary. The Venetians faced starvation, cholera and Austrian shelling during a long siege, but the defeat of the Piedmontese in war left Venice isolated and Austrian authority was restored.

The Venetians have traditionally been devout Catholics, and their enthusiasm for the revolutionary nationalist cause in 1848 had partly been conditioned by the fact the Pope, Pius IX, had appeared at that moment to be the leader of Italian nationalism. By the Second War of Italian Independence in 1859, Pius IX had returned to a more traditional papal attitude of hostility to the nationalists. So although the Piedmontese and their French allies were fighting to secure Venetian independence from Austria, the Venetians did not themselves rise in sympathy against the Austrians. In the event, Venice did not secure her independence from Austria until the Third War of Italian Independence in 1866.

CULTURAL ACHIEVEMENTS ■

Perhaps the greatest contribution made by the people of Venice to European culture was their large share in the development of printing. Soon after the invention of printing with a moveable type, a Venetian humanist scholar, Aldo Manuzio (c.1450–1515), founded the famous Aldine press. In the 15th century, a huge proportion of the books printed in the world were produced in Venice. In the three years 1495–7 alone, Venice produced 447 publications out of a world total of just 1821. In the 16th century, Venice was producing three or four times as many books as Rome, Milan and Florence combined. In the visual arts, the principal Venetian achievements came in the 16th century and were in painting. Venetian use of oils enabled more dramatic colours and the technique of *chiaroscuro* to emerge, as typified by the paintings of Giorgione and Titian.

LANGUAGE AND LITERATURE ■

The Venetian dialect was given written form by a great 18th-century dramatist, Carlo Goldoni. Goldoni's first plays – tragedies in Italian – were not successful. He then wrote *Momolo Cortesan* in dialect, and discovered that his real talent lay in the expression of an earthy sense of humour. He went on to write many plays, some in Italian and some in dialect. Perhaps his finest was *La Locandiera* in which his sense of humour is astonishingly modern. The contribution of the Veneto to modern literature came not only from Venice itself. One of the greatest Italian novels of the 19th century was the work of a native of Padua, Ippolito Nievo, who wrote his *Le confessioni di un Italiano* in 1857–8. A sensitive and perceptive work, it was even more modern in spirit than Manzoni's *I Promessi Sposi*. The region of Veneto produced other writers of stature too, including Ugo Foscolo, who grew up in Venice, was a contemporary of Byron and Keats, and was one of the finest lyric poets of his age.

The region to the east of the Veneto, Venezia-Giulia, which includes the Friuli, produced a highly original novelist in Italo Svevo. Discovered and encouraged by James Joyce, Svevo published his finest work, *La Coscienza di Zeno* in 1923, not long after his home-town, Trieste, on the farthest border of Italy, had been acquired from Austria. It is perhaps not a coincidence that in that same period, at the other end of Italy, in Sicily, the Italian language was being employed, also in its purest form, to produce literary masterpieces.

In Friuli, writing was in a dialect very different from Italian. Udine, the capital of the Friuli, had become part of the Venetian Republic in 1420, but it had retained its own totally distinct dialect, *Furlan*, and in more modern times the dialect has been given written form, and so has become a distinct language in which plays are written and produced, Linguists have estimated that 625,000 people speak Friulian, which would make the Friulians one of the largest minority language groups in Italy. The 'Moviment Friúl', founded in 1966, aspires to complete independence for the territory.

SOCIETY ■

Probably no other city in the world is so completely given over to tourism as Venice. It is, in that sense, one vast museum, existing only for its admiring visitors. Even its one industry, that of glass-making, is aimed at the tourist trade, and its products are often in execrable taste, wholly out of tune with the spirit of Italian design. Yet Venice survives all this through its strength of individual character and its vitality. It has been the playground of rich visitors since the 18th century, and has always attracted artists and writes as diverse as Goethe, Byron, Dickens and Thomas Mann. But Venice is also a dormitory for people who work in the industrial town of Mestre on the mainland, at the other end of the causeway connecting Venice with the rest of the Veneto. Mestre is a kind of Caliban to the Ariel that is Venice, and the pollution from Mestre's industry does Venice's ancient buildings no good. Another preoccupation of the Venetians is their falling population; many of the palaces and houses on the canals are owned by foreigners, who are not part of the permanent population, but arrive only for short holiday stays. Their custom is no substitute for a permanent population.

POPULAR CUSTOMS ∎

The carnival is celebrated all over Italy, but in Venice with more colour, enthusiasm and imagination than elsewhere. The practice of wearing masks for the carnival, or heavy but attractive make-up, is very much alive today. A very different kind of festival is the *Biennale*, an exhibition of modern art, in which most countries exhibit major works displayed in national pavilions in a delightful garden setting. The Venice film festival is another international gathering of importance.

CENTRAL ITALIANS

The Central Italians inhabit the regions of: Lazio, around Rome; Umbria, the beautiful hilly region to the northeast of Rome, whose inhabitants like to call it the 'garden of Italy'; the Marche, on the Adriatic; Tuscany, whose capital Florence is, in some ways, the cultural heart of Italy; and Emilia-Romagna, with its ancient university-city of Bologna. Perhaps the most distinctive groups are the Romans, the Tuscans and the Emilians. The region houses some of Italy's finest historical, archaeological and artistic treasures.

HISTORY ∎

Rome is the 'eternal city' in the sense that her Republic and Empire were the centre of the civilized western world for many centuries, and that the medieval Papacy continued this role after the decline of the Roman Empire. The Roman people have shared in this unique experience: they were one among many diverse ethnic groups in the early days of the Republic, but even before Augustus created the Empire, the people of the Roman Republic had come to control the whole of what we now call Italy, and had far surpassed even this achievement. Not only was the Roman Republic the dominant force in the Mediterranean, it had also begun to conquer a great empire to the north. The city of Rome during the late Republic and Empire had a larger population than any city was to have again in Europe until London in the 19th century.

From small beginnings, during the Dark Ages, the medieval Papacy inherited the claims and some of the power of the Roman Empire. From the Reformation however, the Catholic Church went into a relative decline, and with it the influence of Rome. It reached its nadir during the 18th-century Enlightenment, but in the 19th and 20th centuries experienced intermittent revivals of influence. While the Pope has remained the centre of a universal association in spiritual terms, Rome ceased to be the capital of an extensive territorial state in 1870. The Papacy had lost the sympathy of the people in the outlying parts of the Papal States – notably in the

187

city of Bologna – but the people of the city of Rome itself have usually retained much affection and loyalty for the Pope.

The history of the Tuscan people may have lacked the universal significance of Rome, but its cultural achievements were surpassed by no other European people. Yet Tuscany remained a small state, with little military power and not much political influence, from its medieval beginnings to its merger with united Italy in 1861. The Tuscan commune had a form of medieval democracy in the 13th century, and a republican form of government survived until the very end of the 15th century. A genuinely republican regime patronized remarkable artistic achievements in the buildings of the great communal palace, or Palazzo Vecchio, and Florence's cathedral, and a wealth of production in sculpture and painting, even before the successful banking dynasty of the Medici became masters of the city in 1434. Cosimo dei Medici (1434–64) and his grandson. Lorenzo the Magnificent (1469–92), preserved republican forms, remaining commoners themselves, but in fact exercising the powers of enlightened and benevolent despots. Lorenzo dei Medici was successful as a diplomat as well as a political leader and patron of the arts. By his negotiation with the other Italian rulers he gave the peninsula a period of over 20 years of peace, during which the Renaissance enjoyed its most brilliant phase. The death of Lorenzo and the French invasion of 1494 brought an abrupt end to this peaceful and serene age, though individual artists continued their work in the more troubled period that followed in the 16th century. Later Medici rulers of Florence took the title of 'duke' – a step against which Cosimo had always warned. With these later Medici, Florence fell into comparative decline, though the line survived until 1737. A branch of the Habsburgs, the House of Lorraine, ruled Florence from 1737 to 1860. Although absolutists rulers, these Austrian Grand Dukes were on the whole tolerant and openminded, so that Tuscany was regarded with respect by other Italians because of the freedom of expression and the liberal atmosphere its people were permitted. Under the Grand Duke Pietro Leopoldo (the later Holy Roman Emperor Leopold II), the death sentence was totally abolished in 1786.

The peoples of Emilia and Romagna were for many centuries, until the unification of Italy in 1860–1, under the temporal power of the Papacy. Although, of course, remaining Catholics, and so accepting the spiritual authority of the Pope, they became increasingly alienated from clerical control, and in the first half of the 19th century there were several revolutions against papal rule. The revolutionary spirit of the Emilians and the Romagnols survived into the 20th century. The young Benito Mussolini grew up in the radical atmosphere of the Romagna. Further to the north, the fine city of Bologna had been the centre of revolutionary activity in the 19th century, and after World War II became the most solidly communist city in Italy. Bologna and the region of Emilia-Romagna consistently elected communist authorities, who were regarded – and not only by communists – with some respect for their freedom from corruption. Big businesses worked happily with the communist regime and city governments.

LANGUAGE ■

When Metternich in 1847 said that Italy was only a geographical expression, he was overlooking her claim to having had cultural unity, in one important respect, since the 13th century. The written Italian language has existed at least since Saint Francis of Assisi wrote his *Cantico delle Creature* in the mid-13th century, and more significantly, since Dante wrote his masterpiece, the Divine Comedy, at the end of the 13th century. Italy's unity is, in this sense, a far older phenomenon than that of France or England, even if her political unity is far more recent. The Italian language was the creation of the Central Italians, more precisely the Tuscans, and specifically of Dante. But grammarians did have a hand in its creation; Pietro Bembo, at the beginning of the 16th century, codified a language which is remarkably close to today's Italian. Bembo was himself a Venetian, but the language he described had been used by the Tuscans since the 14th century. The role of the Tuscan version of the language in the 19th century has, however, sometimes been exaggerated. Much has been made of the fact that Alessandro Manzoni rewrote his masterpiece *I Promessi Sposi* in 'Italian', by replacing the original version, published in 1825–7, which it is argued, was in 'Milanese dialect', with a revised version in Tuscan Italian, published in 1840. Manzoni's original, however, was in no sense 'translated'. He merely removed a few words of Milanese dialect and some archaic expressions. Today, correct Italian is popularly considered 'Toscano in bocca Romano' (Tuscan as spoken by a Roman), rather as the Queen's English or BBC English is sometimes regarded as the voice of the ruling class in England.

THE ARTS ■

Today's tourists flock to Florence and Rome to see the masterpieces of Renaissance art. In both cities there is also a wealth of early and later medieval art, and Rome is rich in works of the baroque period. Central Italians share with other Italians a refined sense of classical design, which harks back to the artistic achievements of the past. If supremacy in clothes-designing has passed to Milan rather than to Central Italy, Florence still has a deserved reputation for producing shoes that are beautifully designed.

The first great name in Florentine art was perhaps that of Giotto, primarily a painter, but also the architect of the campanile (cathedral bell-tower) in Florence. After Giotto, artists in Siena for a while surpassed Florentine achievements, but the 15th-century Florentine government held open competitions for the design of public buildings and sculptures, and Florence regained its supremacy. To this republican period of the very early Renaissance belong the frescoes of Masaccio, and the architecture of Filippo Brunelleschi, designer of the *duomo* (cathedral) in Florence. To the period of the Medici belong the names of a succession of great artists: Fra Angelico, Donatello, Ghiberti, Botticelli. The High Renaissance in Florence produced artistic geniuses of the stature of Raphael, who died aged just 37, Michelangelo, and Leonardo da Vinci. Michelangelo's major works – the dome of St Peter's and the frescoes in the Sistine Chapel – were accomplished in Rome under the patronage of Pope Julius II.

CUISINE ■

Emilian cooking is perhaps the most-renowned in Italy. Bologna has the culinary reputation in Italy that Dijon has in France. Signs proclaiming 'cucina Emiliana' can be seen all over Italy. Bolognese sauce for pasta has taken the name of Bologna to the far corners of the world, although in its home town is it known as *ragú*.

SOUTH ITALIANS

The conventional wisdom which holds that Southern Italians are poorer then their Northern compatriots is based on fact. There are, however, pockets of prosperity in the South – Naples and Bari have their fashionable areas – just as there are pockets of poverty in the North, though the latter usually correspond to areas where there has been immigration from the South. This economic disparity has led to tensions with the North and charges that large-scale investment in the South has gone to waste through corruption and inefficiency. In the early 1990s Southern Italians were alarmed at the growth of the Lega del Nord which advocated autonomy for Northern Italian regions and de facto abandonment of the South to its own devices.

HISTORY ■

The classical Greeks were amongst Southern Italy's first inhabitants. In the early 8th century BC they settled at Pithecusa on the beautiful island of Ischia in the Bay of Naples. What is now Reggio Calabria was another Greek colony, in an area that came to be called Magna Graecia ('Great Greece'); the remarkable Greek temples at Paestum, south of Salerno, are a reminder that the far south of Italy was inhabited by Greeks long before the Romans arrived.

When the seat of the Roman Empire moved to Byzantium in the 5th century AD, Naples remained nominally under the sovereignty of the Eastern Roman Emperor, but was in reality an independent nation state by the 9th century and minted its own gold coins. Although the medieval Emperor and Italian poet Frederick II founded the University of Naples in 1224, renaissance Naples did not reach the heights of cultural achievement enjoyed by Florence, Rome, Milan or Venice. As the only kingdom in the peninsula, known simply as 'the Kingdom', it was, however, far from being a cultural back-water. Economically, however, there were already signs of a contrast between a prosperous North Italy and a poorer South by the 15th century. The population of the city of Naples itself was growing at the time the Spanish House of Aragon secured their rule over the city in 1435. One of the more remarkable phenomena in the early modern history of Italy has been the huge population of the city of Naples – about 100,000 in 1500, and 245,000 in 1547, which meant she was the second city in Christendom, after Paris. She survived an epidemic of the plague in 1656, though she may then have lost half her population. The numbers were soon replaced.

The Spanish Bourbons ruled Naples from 1735 until 1860, but became increasingly Italian in character. Their rule witnessed a strange paradox in the history of the South Italians. On the one hand the population of Naples soared to immense heights and the city remained the largest city in Europe after London and Paris, and something of an intellectual renaissance occurred, especially in the study of economics. On the other hand, the economy of the Kingdom itself became increasingly depressed. By the time Garibaldi's expedition of 1860 destroyed the ancient Kingdom of Naples, all classes – aristocracy, bourgeoisie and peasants – were suffering economic decline. Even when the South became part of the United Kingdom of Italy in 1861, economic conditions deteriorated as a result of a civil war of great brutality and destruction which lasted four or five years. The economic backwardness persisted into the 20th century. While Mussolini did something to limit the power of the Mafia, he did little, in more general terms, to resolve the sad contrast of rich Northern Italy and a poor Southern Italy. Governments since 1947 have invested considerable sums in the South, but have had no more success than previous regimes in stimulating economic growth there.

LANGUAGE ■

While the Neapolitan dialect is distinctly different from Italian spoken elsewhere, the distinction is perhaps exaggerated by Northern Italians, who are concerned to demonstrate their superiority over Southerners by suggesting that the South is an alien world. Thus the Northerners may make racist remarks about 'our Africa', or refer to the South's union with Italy in 1860 as the 'partition of Africa'. Foreigners are often deceived into thinking that Southerners speak a different language, and are no doubt sometimes surprised to find, on arrival in Naples, that Neapolitans do in fact speak Italian. But there are remote parts of the South where quite distinct dialects – virtually distinct languages – are, indeed, spoken. In remote pockets of Puglia, small communities still speak a Greek that is closer to classical than to modern Greek. Another, equally remarkable, remnant of Magna Graecia survives: in some parts of Puglia, the manual gestures so familiar to peoples all over the Italian peninsula are unknown, and gestures are more akin to those used by Greeks are common.

THE PHYSICAL ENVIRONMENT ■

A sense of territorial unity was preserved for South Italy by the existence of the Kingdom of Naples. One of the last kings, in the 19th century, said that he could keep his kingdom intact, but that he could not expand it, because it lay between 'salt water and holy water' – between the Mediterranean and the Papal States. The kingdom embraced widely differing physical territories, whose characteristics have today been respected by the existence of the Regions. There is the toe of Italy – Calabria, with its granite mountains and long coastline: Puglia (or 'Apulia' in Latin and English), the heel of Italy, even more remote than Calabria, though today also being finally discovered by tourists; Campania, in a sense the heart of the South, since it includes the great city of Naples; Lazio, which has more affinity with Central Italy as it includes the city of Rome; and finally Abruzzi, which, although north of Rome, on the Adriatic side, is undeniably a part of the South. The Abruzzesi are usually considered by other Italians as wild men.

POPULAR CULTURE ■

To have given the world spaghetti and pizza is no small achievement. If the South Italians tend to be shorter in stature than the North Italians, this is almost certainly due to the higher protein content in northern cooking. But the diet of the South, with its lower level of cholesterol, may well be the healthier one. If the Southerner tends to become stout through an excessive consumption of pasta, he may still be treating his heart more gently. The original Neapolitan pizza was not, of course, so varied as the pizza now eaten all over the developed world; it consisted only of dough, cheese and tomato sauce. The tomato itself is an important part of the popular culture of the South, used on pasta as well as on pizza. A more recent part of popular culture is football, as central to the life of the people of Naples as to those of Rome, Milan or Turin, perhaps more so. The footballer Maradonna, although an Argentinian, became a folk hero as popular as Garibaldi had been a century earlier.

SOCIAL STRUCTURE ■

South Italians have been cursed by the phenomenon known as the *latifundia* – huge landed estates – whose owners have often been absentees, and always remote from the peasants who work the land. The peasants themselves have tended not to live on the land they worked, but, with the unemployed, have lived in 'agro-towns', and have had to walk several miles to work each morning. This is partly a manifestation of the urban character of all Italians: they like to live in towns, or preferably cities, where there is a social life which could not be enjoyed in the countryside. An extreme example of this is the city of Naples itself, whose huge population can partly be explained by the Italian love of urban life, but also, more specifically because in the past governments have taxed people in Naples less heavily than those living in the provinces, or because people have sought protection in the city from brigands, or, in still earlier times, from pirates or marauding Turks. The cry of a child threatened by danger remained 'Mamma i Turchi' (Mummy, the Turks!) long after there was any real presence of Turks around the shores of Italy.

POLITICS ■

When the united Kingdom of Italy was created in 1861, it was understandable that a monarchy imposed from the far north-western state of Piedmont would be regarded with suspicion, and sometimes with bitter hostility, by the far South. Yet paradoxically, when the referendum of 1947 was held to see if the monarchy should be preserved, or a republic created, the South, broadly speaking, voted for the monarchy – for the House of Savoy – while the North voted for a republic. Although it seemed for a short while after World War II that the Communist party might gain a hold in the South, in the event the Christian Democrats, and parties further to the right – the Monarchists and the neo-Fascist Missini (Movimento Sociale Italiano) – soon established power bases there. Only in the early 1990s have the Christian Democrats lost ground, partly because of revelations of corruption in their leaders, and even of association with organized crime. Naples has its own version of the mafia – the camorra – an urban criminal organization which still thrives in the city, though it has never had such widespread power as the mafia.

SICILIANS

Sicilians have rarely decided their own destiny. Throughout their long and varied history, they have been ruled by other peoples of immensely varied ethnic origins, religions and cultures. On the one hand this has meant that their 'high' culture – their arts and architectural styles – is a rich one, but on the other hand they have come to regard their government as a remote, alien, hostile and useless one. Governments have rarely been centred in Sicily itself, and have usually been more interested in extracting wealth or securing strategic advantage from the island, rather than in protecting the islanders from domestic crime, or from piracy in the Mediterranean. The Sicilians have been ruled by Greeks, Romans, Arabs, Normans, Germans, Spaniards, Piedmontese, Neapolitans, even, briefly, by the English. While this may have made their history an extremely interesting one, it has not made for any sense of psychological security for the Sicilian people themselves. If ever a people has been the victim, rather than the maker, of its history, it has been the Sicilians.

HISTORY ■

In the 8th century BC, Greek settlers from Euboea in the Aegean founded the towns of Catania and Messina, and later the Greeks of Corinth founded Syracuse, which became the largest Greek city in Sicily or Southern Italy. In 415 BC, at the time of the plays of Sophocles and Euripides, the Athenians tried unsuccessfully to conquer Syracuse. The Romans fought the first Punic war against Carthage for control of Sicily, and primarily of Syracuse. The long and terrible Punic wars ended in a Roman victory and the inclusion of Sicily in the Roman dominions. Much Hellenic culture was to reach Rome through the people of Syracuse.

The Muslims arrived in Sicily in AD 827, and took Palermo in 831. They ruled

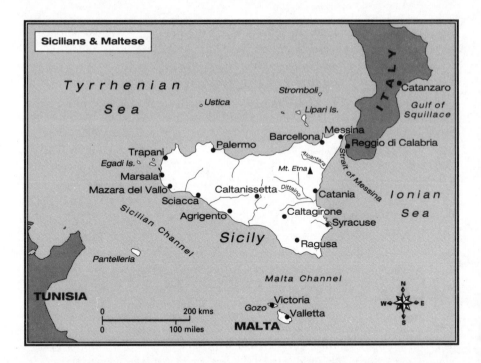

Sicily for 250 years and brought prosperity and comparative peace. Hundreds of mosques were built, and the Muslim style of architecture was to survive the arrival of Christianity. The Normans arrived in Sicily in the late 11th century, as part of the wave of conquests which engulfed England, too. One of the Norman captains was crowned King Roger II of Sicily in 1130. The Sicilians over whom he ruled were a remarkable ethnic mixture and the Normans respected Greek and Arabic, as well as Latin, as official languages. After the fall of the Normans, Sicily eventually passed to a German Imperial line, the Hohenstaufen. But the great Hohenstaufen Emperor, Frederick II made Sicily his base, and became, in effect, an Italian. He was himself one of the first poets writing in an early, but recognizable, form of the Italian language. For a short period in the 13th century, Sicily passed under the French Angevin dynasty who were expelled by a native revolt – the Sicilian Vespers – in 1282, and by the war which followed. The French Angevins were replaced by the Spanish House of Aragon, but Sicily was disputed between rival French and Spanish houses throughout the Renaissance and Counter-Reformation periods, until the Spanish finally prevailed.

The Spanish Bourbons became increasingly Italian in character in the course of the 18th century. Sicily, meanwhile, sank into an ever-deeper economic depression. With the waves of liberalism and nationalism which followed the French Revolution and Napoleonic rule in France, revolutionary movements against the Bourbons in Naples grew frequent; of the many European revolutions of 1848, that in Palermo was the very first. The Bourbons, however, survived until the arrival of Garibaldi and

194

his 'Thousand' irregular volunteers in 1860; the invader was welcomed by the people of Sicily and the Bourbon regime collapsed. Garibaldi's military successes and his popularity made possible the unification of Italy, and from then on the history of Sicily merged with that of Italy. The constitution of the Italian Republic, which took effect on 1 January 1948, allowed for the creation of autonomous regions within an otherwise unitary state. The regional administrations were not immediately introduced throughout Italy – with two exceptions, where a degree of autonomy was demanded. One of these was the Val d'Aosta (see p. 147); the other was Sicily.

LANGUAGE AND LITERATURE ■

The distinction between a spoken and a written language is perhaps more marked in Sicily than in any other part of Italy. The Sicilian dialect is totally different from other Italian dialects, and is often incomprehensible to other Italians. On the other hand, Sicilians writing in Italian have made a huge contribution to Italian literature. The short stories and novels of Giovanni Verga in the late 19th century, the plays and novels of Luigi Pirandello in the early 20th century, and more recently the single masterpiece, *The Leopard* by Giuseppe Tomasi di Lampedusa and the novels of Leonardo Sciascia are of major importance in the development of modern Italian writing. There is a striking similarity with the contribution of Irish writers to literature in the English language in the same period.

SOCIAL STRUCTURE ■

Like Southern Italy as a whole, Sicily has been a land of large estates and poor peasants, but its more significant characteristic has been the existence of the vast criminal organization of the Mafia, which became powerful in the late 19th century and flourished throughout the 20th century. Initially the violence of the Mafia was a weapon used by the landowners against the peasants. The Fascists had some success against the Mafia in the late 1920s, but the evil was not eradicated and grew in strength after World War II. The assault on the Mafia, however, has gathered strength in the early 1990s, accompanied by wave of public repugnance following Mafia violence which claimed the lives of leading anti-Mafia judges, and as part of the general movement against corruption.

POPULAR CUSTOMS ■

Although Sicilians are as preoccupied with television and football as are Italians generally, one popular traditional entertainment has survived: the marionettes known as the *pupi*. These are medieval puppets – such as knights in armour – which constitute a sophisticated kind of Punch and Judy show. One particularly noteworthy traditional dish is *cassata*. This bears little resemblance to what has come to be called cassata in the rest of the world: it is a delicious cake rather than an ice cream. One Sicilian export which has not, however, changed its character is Marsala, the fortified wine, named after the port on the western coast of Sicily from which it comes.

MALTESE

The Maltese have been influenced over the course of centuries by a wide variety of other peoples and nations. Though the islands of the Maltese archipelago (Malta, Gozo, and Comino) are small, they are – unusually for the region – endowed with deep-water harbours and are strategically sited, with Sicily to the north, Libya to the south and Tunisia to the west. Much of Maltese history is, therefore, a catalogue of the impact of the successive powers who have tried to exercise control over the Mediterranean Sea.

HISTORY ■

The prehistoric settlers of Malta appear to have come in waves from Sicily and Southern Italy. They were followed (*c.*1000 BC) by Phoenician colonizers from Carthage, who were later expelled, during the Second Punic War (218–201 BC) when the islanders sided with the Romans. On the collapse of the Roman empire, control of Malta passed to the Byzantine emperors who used it as a base for their reconquest of Northern Africa from the Vandals. Malta's rulers changed again in 870 when Arabs took the Byzantine garrison, and in 1090 when the Normans landed and turned it into part of a kingdom which included Sicily and Southern Italy. The feudal lords subsequently appointed to run Malta taxed the people so heavily that they rose up several times before finally achieving a limited degree of administrative autonomy in 1428.

In 1530, however, the islands were ceded to the Knights of St John, a Catholic military order, who were entrusted with the task of defending them against Ottoman incursions. The Knights had Valletta built as a splendid fortress-city where, together with thousands of armed islanders, they successfully resisted an Ottoman Turkish siege in 1565.

The next invader was Napoleon in 1798, who ejected the Knights. When, in turn, the French were ousted not long after, islanders protested against the proposed return of the Knights. Control of Malta passed instead to the British who developed it as a major naval base. Relations between the islanders and their latest rulers were often troubled, with the British on several occasions granting a certain degree of self-administration and then later revoking it. The Maltese finally achieved full independence, for the first time in millennia, in 1964. Malta is now a sovereign parliamentary state within the Commonwealth.

LANGUAGE ■

Maltese developed from a dialect of Arabic but was also strongly influenced by the version of Romance spoken in Sicily. Until the last century it was only a spoken language, mainly confined to the countryside. Thanks to determined and prolonged efforts by generations of Maltese politicians, philologists and writers, a written version was established in the mid-19th century and it was finally made an official language in 1934. It is the only Semitic tongue officially written in the Roman alphabet.

RELIGION ■

The Maltese, who are among the most regular church-goers in Catholic Europe, were reputedly converted by St Paul when he was shipwrecked on the island in about AD 60. Though the power of the Church has waned somewhat in recent years, it still plays a major role at all levels of Maltese life, from the national government to village politics. Every parish boasts a very large, Baroque-style church, many of them built during the period of prosperity enjoyed under the Knights. Most villages also have several chapels in their streets, as well as statues to the Virgin and to saints, which are used as neighbourhood shrines.

Believers regulate their lives according to the daily and annual rhythms of the Catholic calendar. Church bells mark the divisions of the days, summoning the faithful to Mass and calling them to prayer. Each village stages religious celebrations and processions throughout the year. Greatest effort, however, is spent on the celebration for the village's patron saint, and for that of its secondary saint. There is often fierce rivalry between the village groups who organize these two fiestas, as well as between similar groups in neighbouring parishes.

FOLK CULTURE ■

The traditional dress of Maltese women, today only worn at some village fiestas, consists of a full-length dark dress, an elaborately embroidered bodice, and a broad headdress. The most popular secular festival of the year is that of *Mnarja,* originally a harvest celebration, which now coincides with the feast day of St Peter and St Paul. From the night of 28th June through to the next day, folk groups dance and sing, followed by bareback horse and donkey races. The annual masked Carnival, which celebrates the end of the Ottoman siege in 1565, opens with the *Parata*, a traditional sword dance which re-enacts the Maltese victory over the Turks.

Though the ingredients most commonly used by local cooks are the Mediterranean staples – tomatoes, onions, garlic, peppers, and olive oil – there is still a distinctive Maltese cuisine. The most popular local soup is *minestra*, a bulky version of minestrone, which may include many different vegetables and a generous serving of pasta. Other national dishes include a casserole of home-reared rabbit with vegetables in a thick gravy, *lampuka* (a local fish pie), *bragioli* (a Maltese version of beef olives), and several very rich, sweet puddings, such as *prinjolata* and *kannoli*.

THE ECONOMY ■

The development of local agriculture is hampered by the relative infertility of the soil, a lack of rain and the division of the land into small, terraced plots which cannot be tended or harvested mechanically. Food is imported in large quantities in order to sustain the island, which is one of the most densely-populated areas in the world. The making of lace and the working of silver filigree remain traditional sources of income.

After the departure of the Royal Navy, the government stimulated the tourist and retirement home industries. In a recent effort to diversify the economy, it has also assisted the development of a variety of manufacturing industries. While some Maltese regard the future of their country as lying within the EC, many politicians and businessmen think its prospects would be greater if it became a 'Switzerland of the Mediterranean', an offshore banking and investment centre for the countries bordering the sea which has so influenced the course of its history.

6
THE BALKANS

The volatile and elusive political character of the area treated here as the Balkans – roughly speaking the triangle enclosed by the Drava-Danube corridor, the Adriatic and the Aegean – was epitomized by the novelist Malcolm Bradbury in the fictional setting of his *Rates of Exchange*: a country whose frontiers had changed so often that it occupied none of its historic territory. The history which underlies the region's tragi-comic reputation can be glimpsed in the province of Vojvodina, on the north bank of the Danube, colonized after the Austro-Turkish wars in the 18th century by a patchwork of tiny communities originating from far afield. Today, even after successive experiments in ethnic cleansing, which have virtually eliminated Turks and Jews and greatly reduced the numbers of Croats and Germans, there are still villages crammed within this small area where the local languages include Hungarian, Romanian, Slovak, Czech, Ukrainian, Bulgarian and German as well as Serbian and Croatian (cf p. 243). Between 1771 and 1850, there were even three French-speaking villages. To complicate matters further, at Subotica and near Sombor, some self-classified Serbs of Vojvodina are Catholics, descendants of émigrés from Ottoman rule, although elsewhere Orthodox Christianity is considered a defining characteristic of Serb identity. Throughout the modern history of the region, intricate colonization and unstable political frontiers have combined to produce an ethnic map of bewildering complexity, only one result of which has been spasmodic bloodlettings of inter-communal hatred.

Geographically speaking, the Balkan world occupies a broad peninsula, pinched at the waist, south of which lies Greece, fully Mediterranean by climate and access to the sea, while the northern band, except on the narrow strip of Croatia's coast, is continental in climate and – owing to the extent of the land and the lie of the mountains – out of touch with the sea.

Even in those parts of the region unified by Ottoman rule in the 18th century, diversity was incubating under the shell of unity; the introduction of maize cultivation in mountainous areas enabled independent-minded communities to withdraw beyond the reach of Turkish tax-collectors to upland refuges: thus were sown the seeds of Greek, Albanian, Serbian and Bulgarian self-rule. Today, the most clear-cut cultural divisions separate: the Catholic Croats of the northeast and along the Adriatic coast as far as Dubrovnik, who formed part of the Habsburg empire, from the Muslim and Orthodox areas formerly under Ottoman rule; the non-Slav Albanians from their predominantly Slav neighbours; the Greeks, who can tentatively be defined as users of the Greek alphabet, from their neighbours who use the Roman or

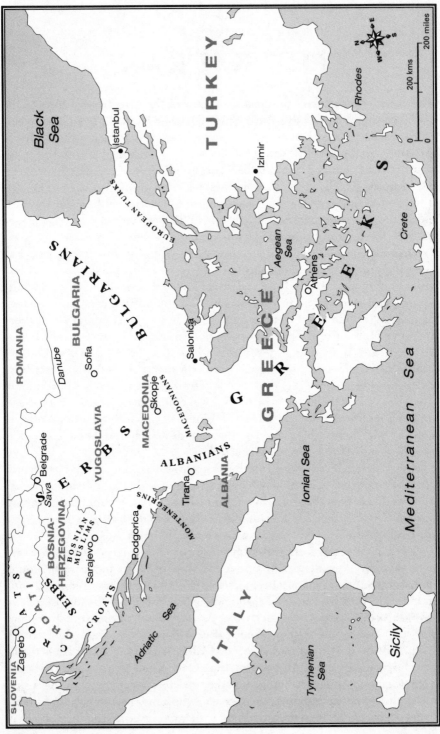

Cyrillic traditions; and the Turks in Turkey's European province of Thrace, distinguished by language and religion from their Bulgarian and Greek neighbours. These relatively clear-cut distinctions mark off peoples of the periphery of the region: most of the rest is an inner 'arena' of conflict or uneasy co-existence between different communities, though the Bulgarian and Macedonian states, the Montenegrin Republic and, less decisively, the Serbian Republic all have distinct ethnic characters while including significant minorities.

TURKS

Although most of Turkey is geographically in Asia, the generality of Turks do not think of themselves as Asian. For well over a century, Turkish intellectuals have looked westwards, and no-one ever called Turkey the Sick Man of Asia. Much debate has been taken up with whether Turks should regard themselves as European, Asian or as occupying a special bridge-position between the two cultures. The westward sweep of Turkish armies, which brought them to control almost the whole Balkans by the 16th century, gave the Turks a formative role in European history, one which, as is demonstrated by their concern for the fate of the Bosnians and other Muslim communities in the area, is continuing today. Their ambiguous position has forced them to fall back on a strong sense of 'Turkishness', which has in the past almost-consciously excluded the possibility of other national groups expressing their own identity.

THE LAND ■

Turkish Thrace (*Trakya*), forming 3% of Turkey's total area of 301,380 square miles, lies in Europe; the remainder of the country, Anatolia (*Anadolu*), forms part of Asia. The northeast of Thrace, bounded by the Black Sea, is mountainous, as is the southwestern coast on the sea of Marmara, most of the rest being lowland. The climate is generally pleasant, with mild but rainy winters and hot, fairly dry summers. It is an excellent wine-producing area, and rice is grown along the river Meriç (Maritsa), which forms its western boundary.

The link between Thrace and Anatolia is Istanbul, no longer Turkey's capital, but still its greatest city. It sits astride the Bosphorus, the waterway which connects the Black Sea and the Sea of Marmara and divides Europe from Asia.

In Turkey as a whole, arable land makes up 32%, pasture 12% and forest 26%. Although half the population is engaged in agriculture and the country is self-sufficient in basic foodstuffs, agricultural produce accounts for less than a fifth of

201

European Turks

The decline of the Ottoman Empire from 1800

- - - - - Frontier of Ottoman empire 1800

—————— Frontier of European Turkey 1923 to present

Turkish exports. Industrial exports include tyres, cement, ceramics, domestic electric and electronic appliances, diesel engines, machine tools and buses.

THE PEOPLE ■

98% of the population (57.7 million in 1993) are Muslims, with Jews numbering some 35,000 and Christians of various denominations, predominantly Greek Orthodox and Gregorian, making up the balance of non-Muslims. The majority of the Muslims are Sunni; the Shi'a, known in Turkey as Alevis, claim to form at least 12% of the population, but there is no statistical evidence by which to judge this claim. Further, the term Alevi covers not only Shi'ites but also adherents of heterodox sects, some of whose practices and beliefs seem scarcely to be Muslim.

Turkey has been secular since 1928, when a constitutional provision declaring Islam to be the state religion was deleted. The constitution forbids discrimination on the basis of language, race, or religion. It also virtually outlaws fundamentalism: 'No one may exploit religion or religious sentiment... for the purpose of personal or political influence or of even partially basing the... order of the state on religious tenets'. Most Turks find no conflict between being citizens of a secular state and Muslims of varying degrees of devoutness. They may have a fellow-feeling towards their co-religionists in Bosnia, just as they do towards those in Central Asia (particularly those who, unlike the Bosnian Muslims, share their language, but their own country's interests come first. There were no protests in March 1949 when Turkey recognized the new state of Israel.

The homogeneity of the nation is an unwritten dogma, although few Turks would seriously maintain that they are a pure race. For thousands of years before their arrival, Anatolia had been the home of Hittites, Phrygians, Lydians, Assyrians and countless forgotten peoples, as well as being a highway into Europe for conquering armies. In that mixture of genes, the Turks were just one more ingredient. Indeed, from the mid-15th century to the mid-17th, it was not easy for Turks to attain high civil or military office, because as a matter of deliberate policy most of the senior civil officials, as well as all the Janissaries, the main military arm of the state, were recruited in boyhood from the Christian subject peoples: of the 215 Grand Viziers who ran the Empire throughout its history, over two-thirds were Christian-born. Moreover, in the multiracial Ottoman Empire, many soldiers and administrators took wives from among the inhabitants of the provinces in which they served.

In the present population, the one large non-Turkish element is the Kurds. Many of them are Turkish-speakers, many have thrown in their lot with the Turks and they are to be found in every walk of life, from farmers and factory-workers to university professors, members of the Grand National Assembly and even of the Council of Ministers. The Kurdish population is concentrated in Southern and Southeastern Anatolia, outside European Turkey. They have been the object of integrationist policies by successive Turkish governments. For many years, some Turkish commentators even denied the existence of a Kurdish people, referring to them instead as 'Mountain Turks'. There is a Kurdish separatist insurgency in the southeast of Turkey, led by the Kurdish Workers' Party (the PKK).

Of the Turks' contributions to civilization, two at least deserve mention: vaccination against smallpox, and their cuisine, one of the seminal cuisines of the world, influencing as it did Greece, the Balkan peninsula, the Middle East, North Africa and Mogul India. Its delicacy and variety owe much to the open-minded acceptance of new raw materials brought to Istanbul by trade and foreign conquest, incorporated in the diet of the capital and then spread throughout the Empire.

As Ottoman rule receded, pockets of Turks were left behind, outside the present frontiers of Turkey. No reliable information exists on their present numbers in Syria,

Egypt or Iraq, but there are probably no more than a few thousands in each of the three countries; the people in northern Iraq sometimes referred to as Turks are in fact Turcomans. The Muslims of Bosnia-Herzegovina and Albania are not Turks but the descendants of 15th-century converts to Islam, linguistically almost indistinguishable from their Christian neighbours. Of the former Ottoman dominions, only Greece, Bulgaria and Cyprus have sizeable Turkish communities. The largest concentration of Turks abroad, however, is in Germany, where they number two million.

The exchange of populations agreed on by Greece and Turkey in 1923 (see p. 214) brought half a million Turks back to the 'motherland' which few of them had ever seen. There are now 110,000 Turks in Greece, mainly in western Thrace.

In 1950 and 1951, to punish Turkey for sending a brigade to join in the United Nations action in Korea, Bulgaria expelled 250,000 'Muslims of Turkish origin', but her relations with Turkey have improved since the fall of communism. The estimated Turkish population of Bulgaria in 1991 was about 900,000.

There were hardly any Turks in Cyprus before the Ottoman conquest in 1571 but in the following year, 1689 Turkish families were moved there from central and southern Anatolia; their number was increased over the next ten years to 8000. The census of 1911 showed 216,300 Greeks and 55,213 Turks. In the Turkish Republic of Northern Cyprus (a state proclaimed in 1983 which has not won international recognition), there are 170,000 Turks, 24% of the island's population.

HISTORY ■

The Turks' earliest recorded home lay in what is now Outer Mongolia. After 744, when their lands were overrun by their Mongol neighbours, the Turks migrated south and west into the Arab Empire. There they gave up their ancestral worship of earth, sky and water, and adopted Islam. They entered the service of the Caliphs as mercenaries and eventually usurped their power. In 1055 Baghdad was seized by Turks led by the family of Seljuk, who then expanded their sway westward into the Byzantine Empire. Within a few years, most of Asia Minor became a Seljuk province, with its capital at Iznik (the ancient Nicaea). As word spread through western and central Asia of the rich pickings to be won by waging war against the infidel in Asia Minor, more and more Turks flooded there. By the time of the Seljuk decline, early in the 13th century, new and vigorous local Turkish dynasties were taking up the heritage of the Seljuks. The most successful of these was the House of Osman, known to the West as the Ottomans, who in 1326 made their capital at Bursa. In 1365, Sultan Murad I shifted the capital to Edirne (formerly Adrianople) and from there campaigns were mounted year after year against Christian Europe. Sofia fell in 1386 and the rest of Bulgaria in 1389, in which year the eastern frontier reached the Euphrates. By 1417 Albania was an ottoman province. The last Byzantine stronghold, Constantinople, was seized by Mehmet II in 1453. Bosnia was incorporated into the ottoman Empire in 1463.

At its greatest extent, in the 17th century, the Ottoman Empire stretched from Algeria to the Crimea and the Caspian, and from Hungary to the far coasts of Arabia.

But the rulers of the Empire were blind to the rapid economic progress of the Christian nations of the West, whose technological advances they dismissed as infidel gimmicks representing no danger to the divinely-protected domains of the Muslim faith. What blinded them was complacency, induced by long years of unchallenged military supremacy and the conviction that God's will, manifested in history, was that the Muslims should always be the dominant power in the world. In 1683 the Ottoman armies were forced to abandon their siege of Vienna and in 1686 the Austrians took Budapest.

The rot continued, in spite of Sultans such as Mustafa III (1757–74), who founded a school of naval engineering with European instructors, Selim III (1789–1807), who tried to reform the army and the administration and was deposed and murdered for his pains, and Mahmud II (1808–39), who committed the blunder of liquidating the undisciplined old army before raising a new one. Rivalries among the European powers in the 19th century prevented any one of them from making an end of the 'Sick Man of Europe', but sometimes they collaborated to strip him of his possessions. The Greeks were the first of the subject peoples to gain their independence, in 1830, with help from Britain, France and Russia. Their neighbours followed their example and by 1878 most of the European provinces were lost. Despite the efforts of reforming sultans and ministers, the Empire's finances steadily weakened. Sultan Abdulhamid II (1876–1909) was saved from total ruin by an offer of credit from the German Kaiser, in the interests of his 'Drive to the East'. This led to an ever-growing Ottoman involvement with Germany, which outlived Abdulhamid. For the revolutionary 'Young Turk' movement which deposed him consisted mainly of army officers who had received German training and saw Germany as Turkey's only true friend. They brought the Turkish Empire into World War I on the side of Germany and her allies, and so to defeat in 1918.

That defeat confronted the Turks for the first time with a problem of identity. The intellectuals and the governing class had regarded themselves not as Turks but as subjects of the universal Islamic state ruled by the Ottoman Sultan; thus those to whom the outside world referred to as 'Young Turks' had called themselves 'Young Ottomans'. While the loss of the European provinces did not change this attitude, the Arab Revolt against the Ottomans and the emergence after World War I of separate Arab states put an end to it for ever.

During the war, in several secret treaties, the Allies had arranged to carve up not only the Turkish Empire but Turkey itself. Now the time had come. Two weeks after the armistice, an Allied force disembarked in Istanbul. Within a few months, French troops occupied Adana and the southeast, Italian troops occupied Antalya and the southwest, and in May 1919 the Greek army mounted a full-scale invasion of Izmir and the west. Although the Sultan's government collaborated with the Allies, the generality of Turks did not accept that they had been conquered. Patriotic groups arose all over the country; soldiers who had been fighting for more than eight years, first in the Balkan wars and then in World War I, stolidly took up their rifles again. Mustafa

Kemal, the hero of Gallipoli and the only Ottoman general never to have lost a battle, organized and assumed command of the resistance.

He made his headquarters in Ankara, an ancient city in central Anatolia, and a natural fortress with excellent communications, where on 23rd April 1920 a Grand National Assembly held its first session, electing Mustafa Kemal as its chairman. His task was formidable: he had to fight several simultaneous wars, not only against foreign invaders but also against those Turks who had been persuaded that loyalty to the Sultan overrode loyalty to their nation. On 11th October 1922 an armistice was concluded which represented a total Allied surrender to the demands of the Ankara government; the document did not even mention the Sultan. The treaty of Lausanne, signed on 24th July 1923, recognized the independence and sovereignty of the new Turkish state. On 13th October the Assembly voted to make Ankara the capital and on 29th October the state was proclaimed a republic, with Mustafa Kemal as its first President.

The task he had set himself was to turn Turkey's face westwards. New legal codes, based on western-European models, replaced the previous mixture of Islamic law and edicts of the Sultans. The wearing of the fez was forbidden (though foreigners may still think it characteristically Turkish, it had been introduced scarcely a century before). A new Latin-based alphabet replaced the Persian-Arabic script. Every family was obliged to choose a surname (the Islamic practice was for people to be known as A, son/daughter of B.). Mustafa Kemal's surname Atatürk, 'Father-Turk', was chosen for him by the Grand National Assembly. Women were given the right to vote and to stand for election to the Assembly (this in 1934, some 37 years before Swiss women were given the vote). Atatürk died in 1938, without seeing the full achievement of his ultimate goal, to make Turkey a parliamentary democracy: this had to await the work of the succeeding generation.

LANGUAGE ■

'Turkish' is the name given to the language of the Republic of Turkey, while the term 'Turkic' is used of the linguistic family to which it belongs, whose territories extend from the Balkans to China and the Pacific. The family has no generally-accepted cognates; even the relationship with Mongolian, once taken for granted, is far from proved, while the 19th-century Ural-Altaic theory, which linked it to Hungarian and Finnish, is no longer widely-accepted. Some members of the family are sufficiently close to Turkish to be called dialects rather than languages; for example the speech of the Gagauz of Moldova (see p.228), the Cypriot Turks, the Kashkai of southern Iran and the Azerbaijanis.

The hybrid known as 'Ottoman Turkish', the official language of the Ottoman Empire, was barely intelligible to Turks who had not had a classical Islamic education. Though essentially Turkish, it was heavily laden with words and grammatical features borrowed from Arabic, the language of religion, and from Persian, which until the 16th century remained the language of literary culture. Indeed, for many years after Ottoman chroniclers had taken to writing in Ottoman Turkish, they persisted in using pure Persian for their chapter-headings. It was only after 1860, with the development of journalism, that writers began to use a simpler Turkish which most people could understand. Efforts to 'purify' the language were effective to the extent that by the 1930s few Arabic or Persian grammatical constructions were in everyday use, though the vocabulary was little changed.

But in 1930, Mustafa Kemal, who regretted that the Turks had ever come under the influence of Islam, delivered himself of the fateful words, 'The Turkish nation, which is well able to protect its territory and independence, must also save its language from the foreign yoke'. The ensuing Language Reform Movement was incomparably more radical than anything of the kind attempted by the Norwegians or Hungarians. The people were mobilized to collect pure Turkish words still current in local dialects, while teams of scholars worked through ancient texts in search of obsolete Turkish words that might replace their Arabic or Persian synonyms. These were publicized through the schools and in the daily press. Since then, so completely has the vocabulary changed that few Turks can comprehend Kemal's own writings in their original form. His six-day Speech (*Nutuk*) on the downfall of the Ottoman Empire and the rise of the republic, which he delivered in 1927, had to be 'translated into modern Turkish' in 1963, and even that version is not entirely intelligible to the youth of today. Many Turks deplore this situation, arguing that the language has become impoverished.

GREEKS

Geography (the conjunction of mountain and sea: no part of the country is more than 60 miles from the coast); poor communications (until recently); lack of natural resources and a dearth of arable land have all played their part in the shaping of modern Greece and the Greeks. But the role of history has been critical. All peoples are burdened by their past, or rather by popular perceptions of their past. The Greeks, however, are particularly weighed down by the impedimenta of a cultural heritage that has for centuries been regarded as the pinnacle of human achievement. Progonoplexia (ancestor obsession) and arkhaiolatreia (excessive reverence for antiquity) are key elements in the modern Greek identity. The quest for a specifically Greek identity and the relationship of the present to the past is a common theme in literature. After all Greece is the only country, Greek the only language and the Greeks the only people that must be qualified by the adjective 'modern' in order to avoid confusion with the past. John Boardman's excellent book The Greeks Overseas *(1964) is not, as its title might suggest, a study of the Greek diaspora that in modern times has extended to the four corners of the globe and the emergence of which is such a significant dimension of Greece's historical experience, but is rather a study of the Greek colonies in the ancient world.*

HISTORY AND RELIGION ■

In 1981 Greece became the tenth member of the European Community, seemingly giving Greeks the reassurance they had sought that they were indeed fully-fledged Europeans. After all, it had been their habit to talk of 'travelling to Europe' as though their country was not in fact a part of it. At the same time, the existing members of the Community were fulsome in acknowledging the Greek roots of western culture. A British foreign office minister, for instance, spoke of Greek entry being a fitting repayment of the 'cultural and political debt that we all owe to a Greek heritage almost 3000 years old'. In doing so he gave powerful reinforcement to a key element in the Greek self-image, namely that there exists an unbroken cultural and indeed racial continuity between the ancient and modern Greeks. When in the 1830s the Austrian Hellenist Fallmerayer suggested that not a drop of pure Greek blood ran in the veins of the modern Greeks he became the object of universal obloquy – to this day he remains a hated symbol of those who would argue that the modern Greeks have little connection with the ancients.

Greek entry into the EC marked a significant turning point not only in the modern history of Greece but in the evolution of the Community itself. For Greece is not only the first east European country to be accorded membership but its double heritage of Orthodox Christianity (the nominal religious affiliation of some 98% of the population) and four centuries of Ottoman rule set it apart from the other member countries whether from the Protestant north or the Catholic south.

Not only is there a strong anti-western dimension to Greek Orthodoxy but the incorporation (with the exception of the Ionian Islands) of the lands inhabited by Greeks into the Ottoman Empire served to insulate them from many of the historical movements that so influenced the evolution of Western Europe. The Renaissance, the Reformation, the Counter-Reformation, the 17th-century scientific revolution, the 18th-century Enlightenment, the French and the Industrial Revolutions passed Greece by. Moreover, the experience of Ottoman rule left its imprint (most obviously in the country's cuisine) on mores and attitudes which in turn helped to shape the political culture of the independent Greek state that emerged in the 1830s. In this respect Greece has more in common with its Balkan neighbours – Bulgaria, Macedonia, Serbia, Albania, Romania and Turkey itself – than with the countries of western or, indeed, of central Europe.

The Greeks have a three-fold historical heritage: that of the pagan world of ancient Greece; that of the Orthodox Christian medieval Empire of Byzantium; and that of the *Tourkokratia*, or period of Muslim Turkish rule. Constantinople fell to the Ottoman Turks on 29 May 1453, a Tuesday; a day of the week still regarded as being of ill-omen in the Greek world. The capture of The City, as the Greeks call Constantinople (Istanbul is a corruption of the Greek *Eis tin Polin* – To the City) sent

Greeks

The Expansion of the Greek State, 1832-1947.

- 1832
- 1881
- 1920

shock waves through western Christendom for, pathetic rump though the Byzantine Empire latterly was, it had symbolized the great bastion against Islam, whose military machine appeared unstoppable. By the Byzantines themselves (Greek by language and culture if not necessarily by ethnic origin), the downfall of their empire was greeted with resignation and, in many cases, with relief. For there was much bitterness at the way in which the Catholic west had sought to blackmail the Orthodox into accepting papal supremacy as the price of military assistance against the Turks and a (not unjustified) feeling that they would be better able to maintain the faith unsullied under the Ottoman dispensation. Some Orthodox divines, indeed, were to argue that the Ottoman Empire had been raised up by God specifically to preserve the Orthodox faith from contamination by the heresies of the West, be they Catholic or Protestant. These kinds of attitudes have nourished a current of xenophobia and anti-Western feeling that is never far beneath the surface. Indeed, it was the political genius of Andreas Papandreou and his Pan-Hellenic Socialist party (PASOK) to have harnessed these xenophobic prejudices to the rhetoric of Third World socialism in his

209

remarkable Short March to power when, after virtually doubling his share of the vote in two successive elections, he swept to power in 1981. The same attitudes underlay the emergence in Greece of a strong current of Orthodox solidarity with the Serbs in the Balkan crisis of the 1990s. The Ecumenical Patriarch Vartholomaios, for instance, declared that 'the cross of martyrdom borne by the people of Serbia calls for universal sympathy from all Orthodox people, who are now facing attacks by dark forces from many directions', a view widely shared in Greece itself.

Nationalist historiography maintains that the Orthodox Church helped to sustain a sense of Greek nationhood during the dark centuries of Turkish rule. To the nascent Greek intelligentsia, however, the Orthodox Church was compromised by its unabashed support for Ottoman power. In the course of their studies in the late 18th and early 19th centuries in European universities, young Greeks became aware of the extent to which they were the heirs to a cultural heritage that was universally admired. On their return to the Greek lands they sought to instil into their compatriots a sense of the past, but they met with opposition from the hierarchy of the Church which equated ancient Greece with paganism. The Church, for instance, was bitterly opposed to the practice that got underway during the first decade of the 19th century, and is now so common, of naming children after the worthies of ancient Greece (eg Aristotle, Aspasia, Leonidas, Themistocles, etc) rather than after Christian saints in the traditional manner.

Greece became independent in 1830 following a protracted war against the Turks that began in 1821. In a symbolic gesture the new state's capital was promptly moved to Athens, then little more than a dusty village, but as the home of the Parthenon forever associated with the glories of the age of Pericles. The educational system of the new state laid a heavy emphasis on the classics, which it has retained until recent times, to the neglect of more practical subjects. A rigidly centralized educational system was to play an important role in instilling a specifically Greek national consciousness in populations which had hitherto been accustomed to think of themselves as Christian rather than Greek and in assimilating, or Hellenizing, minority populations.

This orientation towards the classical past gave rise to the Language Question, the furious, at times violent, debate which has dominated the intellectual life of the independent state. This arose out of disagreement as to the form of the language that was appropriate to a regenerated Greece. Over the three millennia of its recorded history the Greek language has changed remarkably little given the time-span involved. The ancient language stands in relation to the modern much as the language of Piers Plowman does to present-day English. But there were those who thought that the modern language had become debased and should be purified to make it more akin to what was perceived to be its ancient perfection. Hence alongside the ancient language, *katharevousa* (literally purifying) Greek was taught in the schools. This was a stilted construct which differed in vocabulary and syntax from everyday spoken Greek. Not surprisingly generations of school children emerged from school with a confused knowledge of their own language. Only as recently as 1976 was the demotic, everyday spoken Greek, decreed to be the official language of the state.

SOCIETY AND POLITICS ∎

The Greeks were the first of the peoples of the Balkans, indeed of eastern Europe, to gain full independence from the multi-national Empire which ruled over them. But this sovereignty, in practice, was to be a qualified one. For the three Protecting Powers (Britain, France and Russia) who were the guarantors of her independence frequently interfered in Greece's internal affairs. It was they, for instance, who imposed the monarchy, (and a foreign monarch – Otto of the Bavarian Wittelsbach dynasty) on Greece, an institution which, until its final rejection in the referendum of 1974, has made as much for instability as stability. The Greeks may pride themselves on a strong republican tradition but the dynastic element in their politics is strong. Both Konstantinos Mitsotakis and his predecessor and successor, Andreas Papandreou (himself the son of a former prime minister), installed members of their immediate family in the cabinet, while the political pedigree of Giorgios Rallis, prime minister in 1980–1, is impeccable. Both his paternal and maternal grandfathers were prime ministers, as was his father. Close family ties are characteristic of Greek society. Much of the industrial sector consists of small, family run businesses. The huge mercantile marine, one of the largest in the world, is run in the main by a small group of ship-owning clans.

Within a short time of gaining independence, Greece was equipped with the institutions of western parliamentary democracy through the constitution of 1844 (conceded, significantly, after a military coup). But representative institutions did not grow organically over a period of centuries as they had in western Europe. Instead they were adopted wholesale and grafted onto a traditional society, occasioning deep-seated tensions. A weak civil society, with few autonomous institutions and a notably fragmented trade union movement, has opened the way for frequent military interventions in the political process, most recently between 1967 and 1974, the first (and last) such dictatorship to be established in non-communist Europe in the post-World War II period. During the inter-war period the army essentially acted as the arbiter of political life.

Under the Ottomans the Greeks had felt the need for powerful mediators who might offer protection against the institutionalized rapacity of the state. Similar attitudes prevailed in the independent state, which was looked upon as a hostile rather than a benevolent institution, and the formal institutions of parliamentary government proved well suited to the perpetuation of clientelist relations. Through the dispensation of favours and mediation with an overblown, cumbersome and unresponsive bureaucracy, parliamentary deputies were able to build up large voter-clienteles and establish significant local power bases. Political parties were essentially loose collections of notables grouped around powerful and charismatic leaders and, in essence, have remained as such until the present day. Just as Kharilaos Trikoupis and Theodoros Deliyannis dominated the politics of the later 19th century so Konstantinos Karamanlis and Andreas Papandreou have dominated those of the later 20th century. Advanced age has never been an obstacle to political office. In

1989 the prime minister was 85 and the leaders of the three main parties (not so affectionately known as the dinosaurs) were all in their seventies, while the president elected in 1990 was 83.

Such industrialization as has taken place in Greece has been late and on a small scale. The state has remained the major source of employment until the present day and the neo-liberal, Konstantinos Mitsotakis, prime minister from 1990 to 1993, struggled in the face of bitter opposition and without notable success to cut the state down to size. Competition for political power has been particularly intense for this gave control over the vast and hydra-headed state mechanism, a control which was necessary if the insatiable demands of political clients were to be satisfied. Patronage politics continued during the eight-year period of office of the populist PASOK in the 1980s, the difference being that it was now dispensed through the party machine rather than through individual deputies. *Rousfeti*, the reciprocal dispensation of favours that has been the traditional lubricant of society, and *mesa*, the all-important connections, are key words in the country's political vocabulary, even if they are seldom encountered in manuals of modern Greek.

An unusual, and, in the European context, possibly unique, feature of the political process is the way in which incumbent governments, of whatever political hue, tinker with the electoral system to promote their own advantage. One of the last acts of the beleaguered PASOK government in 1989 was to amend the electoral system to make it more difficult for the opposition New Democracy to gain power. Whereas 48% of the popular vote had been enough to ensure a comfortable majority of 172 seats in the 300-seat parliament for PASOK in 1981, a 47% vote for the conservative New Democracy in 1990 scarcely enabled it to scrape into power with 150 seats. True to form, one of the first acts of the incoming New Democracy government was to change the electoral law once again, this time to its own advantage.

THE ERA OF TERRITORIAL EXPANSION ■

The Greek state of the 1830s consisted of the Peloponnese, Attica, central Greece and some of the nearby islands. It contained scarcely a third of the total number of Greeks who had been under Ottoman rule at the outbreak of the armed struggle in 1821. For much of the first century of its existence the policies of the new state were to be dominated by the Great Idea. This, in essence, envisioned the restoration of the Byzantine Empire by uniting all areas of Greek settlement in the Near East into a single state which would have Constantinople as its capital. The discrepancy between the physical resources available to Greece and to the Ottoman Empire, however ramshackle it was in its decline, was striking. As one acute observer noted, Greece in the 19th century had the appetites of a Russia but the resources of a Switzerland. One way in which she sought to achieve her irredentist aspirations was to engage in educational and cultural propaganda among unredeemed Greeks who were scattered throughout the Ottoman domains. Despite the tolerance of the Ottoman authorities, this was an uphill task. Many of the Greeks of Asia Minor, for instance, knew only

Turkish (which they wrote with Greek characters) and had little consciousness of a specifically Greek, as opposed to Orthodox Christian, identity.

The first accessions of territory – the Ionian Islands (since 1815 a British protectorate) in 1864, and Thessaly and a part of Epirus in 1881 – came about through the intervention of the Powers. When in 1897 Greece for the first time went to war with Turkey in support of her irredentist aspirations and in response to the insistent demands of the Cretans for the *enosis*, or union, of the 'Great Island' with the kingdom, she suffered a humiliating defeat.

One of the longer-term consequences of the disaster of 1897 was the military coup of 1909, the first of many such military interventions during the course of the 20th century. This projected the Cretan statesman, Eleftherios Venizelos, to the forefront of the national political stage. Venizelos was well aware that political and economic modernization as well as external alliances were essential if Greece was to have any hope of achieving its grandiose irredentist ambitions.

Together with Serbia and Bulgaria, hitherto Greece's rivals in the increasingly bloody conflict to establish hegemony in Macedonia with its complex and volatile ethnic mix, Greece attacked the Ottoman Empire in October 1912. The allies, whose forces heavily outnumbered those of the Turks, made rapid advances. In November, Greek forces captured Salonica (Thessaloniki), just a few hours ahead of the Bulgarians, who likewise coveted the most important port in the northern Aegean. The largest single element of the population of Salonica were Jews, Spanish-speaking descendants of the Jews expelled from Spain in 1492. The triumphant Greek armies quickly liberated more of Macedonia, Epirus and the islands of the Aegean (with the exception of the Dodecanese which had recently come under Italian rule), a number of which were just miles from the Turkish coast. Crete, after repeated uprisings, was at last incorporated into the Greek state.

Greece was to emerge triumphant from the Balkan wars of 1912–13, her territory enlarged by 70%, her population increased from 2,800,000 to 4,800,000. Under the charismatic leadership of Venizelos she seemed poised to assume the mantle of the Turks in the eastern Mediterranean. Nationalist enthusiasts called (unsuccessfully) for King Constantine on his coronation in 1913 to be crowned not Constantine I but Constantine XII to symbolize that he was the legitimate heir of Constantine XI Palaiologos, the last Emperor of Byzantium.

It is worth noting the Konstantinos Karamanlis, elected president of Greece in 1990, was born in the territories of New Greece when they still formed part of the Ottoman Empire. The fact that so much of the present territory of Greece has been so recently acquired (the Dodecanese Islands were not incorporated into the Greek state until 1947) is one reason for the Greeks' extreme sensitivity over the issue of Macedonia: they fear possible claims by the former Yugoslav republic to Greek territory.

The high hopes engendered by the Balkan wars were destroyed by the schism that divided Greece during World War I into two bitterly divided and, at times, warring camps, consisting of the supporters of Venizelos and of the king. The 'National

Schism' had its immediate origins in the dispute over Greece's participation in World War I (Venizelos was a supporter of the Entente allies, while King Constantine advocated neutrality) but its deeper roots lay in the problems of integrating the newly-liberated, and passionately Venizelist, territories with the conservative and royalist heartland of 'old' Greece. The Peloponnese was the only area of Greece to record a significant vote in favour of the return of King Constantine II in 1974.

France and Britain had no compunction in deposing the king in 1917 and installing Venizelos as the prime minister of a unified, if far from united, Greece. Venizelos' reward for his tenacious support of the Entente was to be allowed to occupy, preparatory to annexing, western Asia Minor with its large Greek population. But the Greek occupation was to end in disaster with the Turkish nationalists, led by Mustafa Kemal (Atatürk), inflicting a crushing defeat on the Greek armies in Asia Minor in September 1922, and thus dealing a mortal blow to the old dream of the Great Idea and bringing an end to a 2500-year Greek presence in Asia Minor.

POPULATION MOVEMENTS ■

Hitherto Greece had been a country much more associated with emigration (principally to the United States) than immigration. Mountainous, with less than 30% of her land area cultivable, Greece had difficulty in supporting her existing population and was ill-prepared to receive an influx of some 1,300,000 refugees (from Turkey, Russia and Bulgaria). These were compulsorily exchanged for some 400,000 Muslims from Greece. Many of the incomers, who were looked upon with suspicion and at times hostility by the indigenous inhabitants, were settled in Greek Macedonia and Thrace, thus substantially reinforcing a Greek claim to these territories that was somewhat shaky on grounds of ethnicity. Having had their worlds turned upside down once, these refugees, and their children, grand-children and great grand-children, were and are disinclined to repeat the process, another factor that helps to explain Greek sensitivities over the Macedonian issue.

Harsh though the human consequences of the exchange of populations were, neither Greece nor Turkey henceforth harboured territorial claims against each other. The decision, however, to exempt from the exchange the Greeks of Istanbul and the Muslims of Western Thrace was to store up future trouble. The Greek minority in Turkey, the victim of an ethnic pogrom in 1955, has dwindled to virtual extinction, although the Ecumenical Patriarchate, whose future is inseparably linked to the future of the minority, remains in Istanbul. The Muslim minority in Greece, however, numbers some 110,000. The Greek government insists on the definition, contained in the Treaty of Lausanne of 1923, of this minority as Muslim rather than Turkish. By the 1990s, however, partly as a consequence of deliberate Greek government policy in the early 1950s when Greek-Turkish relations were very close, most Greek Muslims, irrespective of their true ethnic origin, consider themselves ethnic Turks. In recent years, the status of their respective ethnic minorities has constituted one among a number of sources of discord between Greece and Turkey, perhaps the most intractable of which is the question of Cyprus. Through an accident of history, Cyprus passed from Ottoman to British rule in 1878 and British colonial policy frustrated the desire of the 80% Greek majority on the island for *enosis* (union) with mainland Greece. The elaborate arrangements to share power between the Greek and Turkish communities enshrined in the 1960 settlement, whereby Cyprus became an independent state, soon broke down and ten years of inter-ethnic conflict culminated in the Turkish occupation of some 40% of the island in 1974.

The exchange of populations of 1923–4 resulted in the population of Greece becoming remarkably homogeneous in terms of its ethnic and religious composition. Although the Muslims enjoyed minority rights enshrined in treaties, the Slav-Macedonians and Romanian-speaking Vlachs (see pp. 222, 262) did not and were subject to a process of none-too-benevolent assimilation.

RECENT HISTORY ■

During World War II, Greece was subject to a brutal tripartite occupation by the Germans, the Italians and the Bulgarians. The once flourishing Jewish community of Salonica was virtually wiped out, while in the Bulgarian-occupied area Greeks were uprooted in a form of ethnic cleansing. Memories of the settlement of Bulgarians on Greek soil as recently as 50 years ago contribute to a folk memory which sees a threat to Greece's territorial integrity posed by the Slavs, and particularly by the Macedonians, to the north. Resistance to Axis occupiers was on a large scale but was riven by political dissension. The World War I division between Venizelists and anti-Venizelists (broadly speaking, republicans and monarchists) which cast such a long shadow over the politics of the inter-war period was not overtaken by a bitter and fratricidal confrontation between communists and anti-communists. The British, fearful of a communist take-over in post-war Greece, became enmeshed in the conflict through their support of the anti-communists. The fighting in December 1944 between the communist-controlled resistance and the Greek government and the British forces supporting it was but a stage in the gradual slide of the country into outright civil war.

During the 1946–9 civil war the communists enjoyed the support of the newly established communist regimes on Greece's northern borders (Albania, Yugoslavia and Bulgaria). Only a massive injection of American military and economic aid (but not combat troops) enabled the anti-communists, broadly but not exclusively identifiable with the political right, to prevail. It is sometimes overlooked that by the closing stages of the civil war as much as half of the communist Democratic Army was composed of Slav-speaking Macedonians from the northern provinces, while in 1949 the Greek Communist Party openly, if briefly, advocated the right of the Slav-Macedonian population of Greece to autonomy. This would have entailed the detachment from Greece of Greek Macedonia which had been won at heavy costs during the Balkan wars only 40 years previously and in which large numbers of refugees from Asia Minor had been settled even more recently. When, in 1982, the PASOK government gave blanket permission for the remaining communist refugees to return to Greece from their (frequently bleak) exile in Eastern Europe and the Soviet Union, those of non-Greek ethnic origin, ie the Slav-Macedonians, were explicitly excluded.

The bitterness of the civil war gave way to a period of qualified democracy which paradoxically culminated in the the military dictatorship of 1967–74. Although brutal, absurd and unpopular, the Colonels' regime unwittingly contributed to the healing of the wounds of the civil war; opposition to the dictatorship was manifest across the whole political spectrum from left to right. One of the first acts of the veteran politician Konstantinos Karamanlis, when, in 1974, he was summoned back from a self-imposed exile to clear up the mess left by the Colonels, was to legalize a Communist Party that had been banned in 1947. The brief participation of the Communist Party in a government coalition with the conservative New Democracy in 1989 could be said finally to have exorcized the ghosts of the civil war.

The collapse of the Colonels' regime was followed by seven years of conservative rule which culminated in Greece's entry into the EC in 1981. Greek entry was promptly followed by the election of the first socialist (more accurately populist) government in Greece's history, a government which, moreover, was opposed, at the level of rhetoric at least, to membership of the EC and of the NATO alliance, which Greece had joined in 1951. The PASOK era, which some have taken to calling the lost decade of the 1980s, in the event saw no fundamental changes in Greece's pro-western orientation or market economy.

The peaceful transition from right to left in 1981 and 1993 and from left to right in 1990 appears to indicate a new maturity in Greek political life. The 1974 referendum on monarchy seems to have removed one perennial source of political instability, while the military has shown no inclination to return to the political arena. But if Greece's democratic institutions have demonstrated a new stability, the Greeks currently feel threatened by virtually all their neighbours. The numerous problems in relations with Turkey show no sign of resolution. The collapse of the Yugoslav Federation and the aspirations for independent statehood of the former Yugoslav Republic of Macedonia have re-opened the Macedonian problem in all its old intensity. Relations with Albania are soured by Greek claims of mistreatment of the Greek minority in Albania (estimates of the size of which range from 60,000 to 300,000) and by the flood of illegal Albanian immigrants in Greece.

Greece likes to project itself as an island of stability and prosperity in the turbulent Balkans. Certainly the rate of economic progress since the 1950s is astonishing when contrasted with the economic plight of her neighbours to the north. But it is a stark fact that (apart from the disengagement of the Great Powers) virtually none of the problems which rendered the Balkans such a volatile region on the eve of the World War I, and in which the Greeks were and are so heavily involved, have been resolved in the 1990s.

ALBANIANS

The Albanians in the Balkans are divided between the Republic of Albania (about 3.2 million) and the republics of the former Yugoslavia (about 2 million); in Kosovo, in the south of the Republic of Serbia, they make up over 85% of the population, in Macedonia about 19.8% and in Montenegro about 6.5%. Since the creation of Yugoslavia in 1918, many Kosovan Albanians have settled in Croatia where until recently they had enjoyed good relations with the Croats, typically opening small family-run cafes selling cakes and ice-cream, a legacy of their years of contact with the Turks and Italians.

A number of long-established Albanian communities survive in isolated villages in southern Italy and Sicily and also southern Greece; these villages were founded in the 16th century by Albanian fugitives from Ottoman rule. In the Republic of Croatia, the isolated village of Arbanasi (meaning Albanian) on the Dalmatian coast, was founded in the early 18th century by Albanian refugees. In the 19th and 20th centuries thousands emigrated and there are now more Albanians in North America and Australia than in Europe. After World War II and the establishment of the communist regime of Enver Hoxha, few Albanians had permission to travel and those captured in the act of flight were executed or imprisoned. Since 1989 and the lifting of travel restrictions, thousands have gone to Italy and Greece where their hopes of a better life have quickly faded.

PHYSICAL ENVIRONMENT ■

The Republic of Albania is a mountainous country with alpine pastures and stretches of plain. There is a marked variation in climate between the Adriatic coast and the mountainous interior which is subject to the extremes of a continental climate.

Its great beauty, evoked in the delicate water-colours of Edward Lear, remains largely unspoilt since the poverty of the post-war regime meant that the country was spared the worst excesses of socialist development: during the 1960s Albanians learnt the technique of terracing from the Chinese, with whom they were allied following an acrimonious ending to their relationship with the Soviet Union. They have brought long stretches of mountain-side under cultivation; the other notable post-war additions to the Albanian landscape are the thousands of concrete pill-boxes scattered throughout the country without regard for possible strategy. Few if any artificial fertilizers have been used and the country is in a prime position to exploit the growing European market for organically-grown fruit and vegetables.

LANGUAGE AND ETHNICITY ■

Comparative linguistics and archaeology support the Albanians' claim to being the descendants of the ancient Illyrians. When the Romans founded the province of

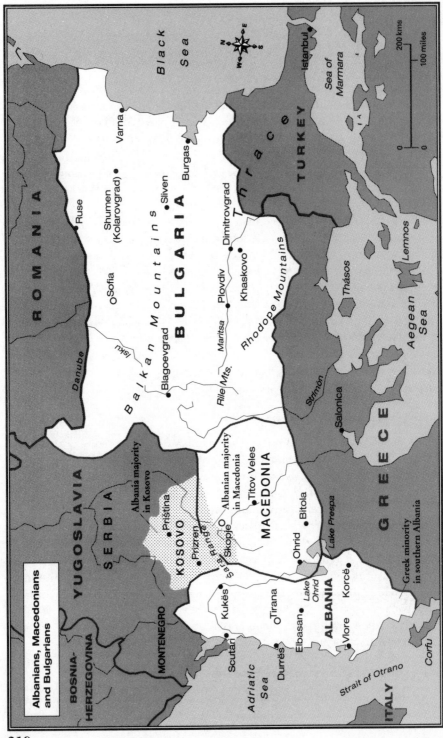

Albanians, Macedonians and Bulgarians

Illyricum, those natives who did not assimilate to Latin culture withdrew into the mountainous region from Krujë north to the Šara range and organized themselves as tribes under highland chieftains. In the 6th and 7th centuries, Slavs passed through the region, those who settled assimilating Illyrian-Albanian culture. Through the centuries, the Albanians have mixed and inter-married with Slavs, Vlachs (see p. 262), Turks, Greeks, Venetians and other Italians.

The early Albanians called themselves the *Arbëni*. The earliest use of this name dates from c.1043 but modern Albanians refer to themselves collectively as *Shqiptari*. There are two major groups of Albanians differentiated by their dialects: the Ghegs in the north and the Tosks in the south, with the river Shkumbin separating the two major groups. The two dialects have been diverging for over 1000 years but the less extreme forms are mutually intelligible. As well as having their own dialects, Ghegs and Tosks have different traditional dress, music and customs. The Albanian enclaves in Greece and Italy speak Tosk.

The Albanian language is clearly of Indo-European origin but is the only survivor of its sub-group and does not display any obvious affinity to any other Indo-European language. It has many archaic traits and in very early times was probably closest to the Balto-Slavic group, including Lithuanian and Latvian. Very few Albanian words are borrowed from ancient Greek, but the Albanians' close contact with the Latin world resulted in many Latin loanwords e.g. *mik*, friend (Latin: amicus) and *librë*, book (Latin: liber). Albanian also has many loan-words from Turkish, Italian, Modern Greek and Macedonian.

During the 19th century, the Ottoman authorities allowed elementary education in national languages. The Albanians, though, were not taught in Albanian since for administrative purposes they were grouped not by nationality but according to religious affiliation (the *millet* system) and so attended Turkish-Islamic, Greek-Orthodox or Italian-Catholic schools; the few who attained literacy, if they wrote Albanian, did so in Arabic, Greek or Latin characters. The decision to use the Latin alphabet for modern standard Albanian was taken in 1908 in the face of vehement opposition from the 'turkicizing' 'Young Turk' regime in Istanbul. The standard orthography issued in 1909 was based on the south Gheg dialect of the town of Elbasan and within Albania was used until World War II. Under Hoxha, who was a Tosk, the basis of literary Albanian was changed to Tosk and a new standardized orthography was produced in 1972. The Albanians in Kosovo, Macedonia and Montenegro have continued to use the Gheg standard.

The earliest surviving piece of literature written in Albanian is the *Liturgy of Don Gjon Buzuk* (*c.* AD 1554) and liturgical and devotional works continued to be produced during the 17th century under the influence of Roman Catholic missionaries. The first purely literary work in Albanian is that of the 18th-century poet Gjul Variboba who lived in Calabria and during the 19th century Italy remained the centre for Albanian literary activity.

RELIGION ■

In keeping with their long history of decentralization, the Albanians are a multi-confessional nation: approximately 70% are followers of Islam, the majority being Sunni Muslims while a small number of Tosks belong to the Bektashi order of dervishes; the remainder in the north are Roman Catholic and in the south, near Greece, Orthodox. More is known about religious affiliation among Albanians outside the Albanian Republic than within; while the majority of the Kosovan Albanians are Muslim, about 50,000 are Roman Catholic, mainly in the region around Skopje, in Vitina, Opština and Prizren, and there are some Orthodox around Lake Ohrid; among the Muslims, dervish orders have made converts and by 1986 there were 53 dervish communities in Kosovo.

HISTORY ■

During the Middle Ages the Albanians fell within the Byzantine and Serb empires. In the second half of the 14th century, the Albanians were grouped in small principalities which were virtually independent of Byzantium but too torn by rivalry and feuds to offer collective resistance to the Venetians who took control of the coastal towns, and the Ottoman Turks who seized their territory from Skadar to Drač. In 1443, Gjergje Kastrioti, known as Skanderbeg, succeeded in rallying the Albanians and in 1449 defeated the army of the Ottoman sultan Murad II; hailed as the saviour of Christian Europe, he was obliged by lack of resources to become a vassal of King Alfonso of Naples (Alfonso V of Aragon). After his death in 1478, Albanian resistance collapsed and the Turks began to establish their effective occupation of the country, a process completed with the Venetian evacuation of Durrës in 1503. Many thousands of Albanians fled to Italy. After initial resistance, the Albanians accommodated themselves to Ottoman rule and in the remote mountainous regions paid their taxes but retained their traditional social organization and a large measure of local self-government. Many converted to Islam. To hasten the process of Islamicization, the Ottoman Sultan Selim II (1566–74) granted exemption from certain taxes to households where at least one male member had converted to Islam, a measure which resulted in mixed Muslim and Christian households. In the 17th and 18th centuries, after the great Serb migrations to Habsburg lands, Muslim Albanians settled in Kosovo, Metohija and western Albania.

In the 19th century, the earliest stirrings of the Albanian national revival were among Albanian intellectuals in Italy who witnessed the *Risorgimento*. Those Albanians under Ottoman rule were content to remain within the Ottoman Empire provided tax demands and centralization were kept to a minimum. It was fear of annexation or partition by Serbia and Greece that prompted Muslim and Christian notables in southern Kosovo to form the League of Prizren (1878–81), but the Turks crushed their movement in April 1881. The Albanian nationalists had hoped that the Young Turk regime which had seized power in Istanbul in 1908, would satisfy their demands for an autonomous and unified Albanian state within the Turkish Empire but instead found themselves threatened with turkicization. After a series of regional revolts which had been swiftly suppressed, the first general Albanian uprising broke out during the First Balkan war (1912), prompted by fears that the neighbouring Christian powers – Bulgaria, Serbia and Greece – would partition their lands.

In 1913, the first independent Albanian state was established whose borders encompassed about 11,000 square miles and about 800,000 Albanians. The new kingdom proved difficult to rule; William of Wied (1876–1945) arrived as prince in March 1914 but despaired of ever governing effectively and left in September the same year.

The Kingdom of Albania disappointed more than it satisfied. One source of continuing strife was the inclusion of Kosovo, which with Prizren had become a centre of Albanian nationalism, within the Kingdom of Serbia. The Kosovan Albanians there found themselves subject to a programme of forced assimilation to Serbian culture and during World War I were slaughtered in great numbers. The Kingdom of Serbs, Croats and Slovenes, founded in 1918, by its very name denied the Albanians' existence as a separate nation within the new state; as non-Slavs, the adoption of the name Yugoslavia was no more satisfactory. The Serb-dominated inter-war regime continued to oppress the Albanians and did its utmost to destabilize the young state of Albania. Many Albanians left Kosovo and formed the Kosovar Committee which organized anti-Serb resistance; during the 1920s and 1930s the *kaçaks* (outlaws) waged a guerilla war in Kosovo, combining a campaign of terror with the traditional Balkan bandit practice of cattle-rustling.

The Albanians within the inter-war Kingdom of Albania lived in a state of near-anarchy. Power passed back and forth between the autocratic Ahmed Bey Zog (King Zog I, 1895–1961) the son of a Muslim chief educated at Istanbul and Fan Noli (1882–1965), a Harvard-educated Orthodox Bishop who tried to introduce land reforms and constitutional rule and was dubbed 'the red Bishop'. Fascinated by Mussolini, Zog clung to power by letting Albania become *de facto* an Italian colony but fled to Britain in 1939 when the Italian army invaded.

During World War II, Kosovo was included within Albania by the Italian regime of Mussolini and its future became a matter of contention between the rival Albanian resistance movements; Enver Hoxha and his communist partisans of the L.N.C. ('National Liberation War'), who had been directed by Tito and the Yugoslav partisans, seized control at the end of the war and returned Kosovo to Tito's Yugoslavia. In January 1946, Albania was declared a People's Republic and, under Hoxha's Stalinist rule, endured the most backward communist regime anywhere in post-war Europe.

RECENT HISTORY ■

The position of the Kosovan Albanians has grown steadily worse since Tito's death in 1980. The Serb nationalist and President of Serbia Slobodan Milošević has portrayed the Albanians as the greatest threat to Serbdom. In 1989 the autonomous status of Kosovo and the province of Vojvodina was withdrawn and many Albanians have lost their jobs, been arrested, beaten and murdered while the Albanian media have been silenced and the universities filled with Serbs.

In the Republic of Albania itself, multi-party elections were held in March 1991 and Albanians are now free to travel and to practise their religion but civil order has broken down and economic advance is slow. The question of Greek claims to protect the ethnic Greek population of Southern Albania (in Greek parlance, Northern Epirus) has resurfaced; since June 1993, relations between the Albanian and Greek governments have deteriorated rapidly after Tirana expelled a Greek Orthodox bishop accused of stirring up *enosis* (desire for union with Greece) among the Greek communities in southern Albania and Athens seized the opportunity to round up and return many Albanian 'economic refugees' settled in Greece. The emergence of a new avowedly-nationalist party in Greece, 'Political Spring', led by former foreign minister Antonis Samaras, did nothing to defuse tension during the 1993 Greek national elections.

MENTALITY ■

The xenophobia and defiant isolationism of Enver Hoxha's Albania had their roots not only in Hoxha's ideology but in the Albanians' national character; for centuries they have lived apart, influenced only by the Ottomans and, to a lesser extent, the Italians and it was not until the establishment of centralized communist rule that they were forced to abandon their traditional tribal way of life and pursuit of the blood feud.

The Kosovan Albanians have found themselves vilified by successive governments in Belgrade as primitive and degenerate. Since the late 1980s, there has been a movement to combat this crude stereotype; heads of families have publicly renounced blood-feuds and in response to the wars in Slovenia, Croatia and Bosnia, an influential Albanian peace movement has grown up.

MACEDONIANS

*Since the 19th century, Macedonia has been synonymous with complexity. Its population is a mixture of Macedonians, Albanians, Bulgarians, Greeks, Vlachs, Jews, Gypsies and Turks – a mixture which has given the French and Italians their words for fruit cocktail (*macédoine *and* macedonia di frutta *respectively). The intense rivalry with which the Serbs, Bulgarians and Greeks have laid claim to Macedonia has been the greatest incentive for the inhabitants of the region to claim separate Macedonian nationhood.*

Modern Macedonian national consciousness is now found in the former Yugoslav Republic of Macedonia and in communities scattered throughout Albania, Bulgaria and Northern Greece. While those who identify themselves as Macedonians are confident that they are a nation, the Greeks refer to them as Slavophone Greeks, claim Macedonia as an exclusively Greek regional name and join the Bulgarians and Serbs in steadfastly refusing to admit the existence of a separate Macedonian nation. The Macedonians' detractors argue that they would have re-assimilated to their pristine national identity had it not been for Tito's determined nurturing of Macedonian nationhood within Yugoslavia; to the Greeks and Bulgarians, Macedonians were instruments of Tito's programme of expansion in the Balkans, to the Serbs, they were part of his policy of undermining the Serb nation.

LANGUAGE ■

The Macedonians' claims to separate nationhood depend heavily upon arguments supporting the existence of a Macedonian language. The South Slav languages are all close and the native idioms used by the Macedonians vary from region to region and can be difficult to distinguish from the vernaculars of their immediate neighbours in Bulgaria and Serbia. The Macedonian literary standard exhibits the characteristics which distinguish Bulgarian from the other Slav languages. It is based on the dialects of the Bitola Veles region which are close to those of western Bulgaria, but since the Bulgarian literary standard has as its basis the dialects of eastern Bulgaria, the two literary standards are sufficiently distinct for Macedonian to be classed as a separate language (cf p. 229).

RELIGION ■

The majority of Macedonians are Orthodox. The Macedonian Church is a source of national pride and is seen by Macedonians as a continuation of the 11th-century patriarchate of the emperor Samuel and therefore older and senior to the Serbian Orthodox Church. The rest of the Orthodox world, however, sees the Macedonian church as a creature of Tito's communist and atheist Yugoslav government and refuses to recognize it. The modern Macedonian Church was separated from the Serbian Orthodox Church in 1958 when the ancient patriarchate at Ohrid was revived, and was declared autocephalous in 1967. It enjoyed good relations with the communist authorities who fostered it as a bulwark against the supposed threat to stability posed by Albanian nationalism and Islam.

Some Macedonians are Muslim; predominantly Sunni with some followers of dervish orders, Muslim Macedonians are referred to as Pomaks (see p. 228), Torbeshes and Poturs. During the 1970s they formed an association to promote their identity and to halt assimilation to the culture of their Albanian Muslim neighbours. The number of Macedonians declaring themselves as Muslim Macedonians rather than Turks, has steadily risen from 1591 in 1953 to 39,555 in 1981.

HISTORY ■

Macedonian rock groups may claim Alexander the Great as a forefather of their nation but even the recent scholarly histories of the Macedonians spanning three millennia are spurious and only lay the Macedonians open to the ridicule of those who would deny their nationhood; the Macedonian regional name is ancient but contemporary Macedonians are among the newest nations in Europe.

The Macedonian Question emerged in the 19th century when the Ottoman Turks withdrew piecemeal from the Balkans and the problem arose of drawing international boundaries across or around Macedonia. Old medieval rivalries re-surfaced as the Bulgarians, Serbs and Greeks, fired with nationalist fervour each claimed for themselves the region and its inhabitants who were of apparently indeterminate Slav nationality.

It was in these conditions that Macedonian national consciousness emerged in the last decades of the 19th century. The original aim of V.M.R.O., the Internal Macedonian Revolutionary Organization, founded in 1893, was to secure the existence of an undivided Macedonia as part of a South Slav federation with Serbia and Bulgaria; the Macedonians identified with the Slav, not the Hellenic, world and of the South Slavs felt most affinity with the Bulgarians. In 1903 the inhabitants of Bitola and Strandiza rose against the Turks in a revolt timed to coincide with an important feast in the Orthodox calendar (the Ilinden, or Elijah-day Rebellion). The rebels were swiftly crushed by the Ottoman authorities using Albanian irregular troops.

Macedonia was finally freed of the Turks at the end of the Second Balkan War (1913) but was divided among Greece (Aegean Macedonia, about 50% of the total area of Macedonia), Serbia (Vardar Macedonia, about 40%) and Bulgaria (Pirin Macedonia, about 10%). Those in Aegean and Vardar Macedonia orientated towards Bulgarian culture suffered as the Greek and Serb governments took revenge upon the defeated Bulgarians. Many thousands fled to Bulgaria.

In 1918 Vardar Macedonia became part of the Kingdom of Serbs, Croats and Slovenes, although the very name of the new South Slav state implicitly denied the existence of a Macedonian nation. The inter-war government in Belgrade ruthlessly pursued a policy of forced assimilation to Serbian culture and, as in Kosovo, aimed to flood the region with Serb settlers. V.M.R.O., which had turned into a more recognizably revolutionary organization, enjoyed the backing of Bulgaria. In 1934 a V.M.R.O. gunman supported by the Croatian Ustaša movement assassinated Aleksander Karadjordjević, the Serb king of Yugoslavia.

Pro-Bulgarian sympathies among the Yugoslav Macedonians were extinguished during World War II when the Bulgarians occupied the region and tried to make it unambiguously Bulgarian in character. The post-war Socialist Federal Republic of Yugoslavia offered the Macedonians, like the Bosnian Muslims, the chance to live unchallenged as a nation. Tito established the Republic of Macedonia with the intention of creating a Macedonian national home within Yugoslavia which would serve as a focus for the national aspirations of the Macedonians. The Greek government, certain that Tito was bent on expansion in the Balkans, settled many thousands of Greeks in Aegean Macedonia to counteract any aspirations among its inhabitants to a nation-state embracing all the Macedonians. Meanwhile the Yugoslav government promoted the new Macedonian language and expounded an official Macedonian history which claimed as Macedonian heroes leading figures from Bulgarian history.

Since the re-emergence of Serbian nationalism, the Macedonians once more feel threatened. Their eagerness in 1992 to follow Slovenia, Croatia and Bosnia in declaring independence has left them prey to Greek nationalism. The Greek government fears that its Slavophone Greeks may yet seek union with the Macedonians in a nation state. The wrangling over the right to use the Macedonian name is not part of a learned academic debate; the Macedonian Question still has the potential to destabilize the Balkans.

THE LAND AND LIVELIHOOD ■

Macedonia is a vast region bordered in the west by lakes Ohrid and Prespa, in the north and east by the Šara and Skopska and Rhodope and Rile mountain ranges. It extends to the south as far as the Aegean coast, Salonica, and the Pindus mountains. The Macedonians within the Republic of Macedonia inhabit the plains which are well-watered and produce early fruit and vegetables, grain, poppies, tobacco and flax. In the past, the Macedonians in the mountainous regions which offered a poor livelihood emigrated or became temporary emigrants *(pečalbari)* travelling through the Balkans as seasonal labourers, pedlars and itinerant metalworkers. The Macedonians dance their own version of the South Slav *kolo* or wheel-dance known as the *oro*. They play their folk music on a wide range of instruments which reflect Turkish musical traditions.

BULGARIANS

The Bulgarians have long lived in the shadow of their powerful neighbours, the Russians and the Turks: their country was among the most obedient of Soviet allies after World War II. Their history of subjection has led them to concentrate on the glories of their medieval past.

HISTORY ■

The Bulgars were first mentioned in extant sources in the early 5th century AD as a people living northeast of the Danube, probably related in some way to the Huns. They were certainly ruled for some timed by a distant relative of Attila's. In 619, Kubrat, a Bulgar khan dominant between the Don and the Caucasus visited Constantinople in pursuit of an alliance against the Avars and became a Christian, though his conversion was without practical consequences for his people.

Early in the second half of the 7th century, a Bulgar war-band migrated into the Danubian region. Victorious against a Byzantine army, they dominated the territory between the Danube and the Balkan mountains, carving their way into the area which is now the Bulgarian heartland. An Asiatic people, they held sway as a territorial élite over a Slav population whose language quickly became that of the state. Bulgaria can therefore be said to be the result of the fusion of a Bulgar military aristocracy with the indigenous Slavs, comparable to that between the Normans and the English after the battle of Hastings (see p. 35–6).

In the 860s Boris I (857–88) introduced Christianity, with a Slavonic liturgy, and the Glagolitic alphabet. His first choice was for Christianity of Roman allegiance but he switched to that of Constantinople because of the Pope's reluctance to grant metropolitan authority to a Bulgarian see. The victories of Tsar Simeon (892–7) made Bulgaria a power whose alliance was coveted and pretensions feared in Byzantium. For nearly a hundred years, however, the Hungarians seemed the major foe of the 'First Bulgarian Empire'. The ambitions of Tsar Samuel (976–1014) overreached Bulgarian power and the state was conquered and, by 1018, annexed by Byzantium, though the victorious Byzantine Emperor Basil II 'the Bulgar-Slayer' prudently conceded autonomy to the native aristocracy and confirmed the status of the church. Some Bulgar leaders were lured to Constantinople and absorbed into its courtly life.

In the 1180s, a 'Second Empire' was created by John and Peter Asen, chiefs from the west of the country, who were perhaps of Vlach rather than Bulgar ancestry. They revived Simeon's title, 'Tsar of all the Bulgars and Greeks' and their successors, especially John II (1218–41) briefly built a Balkan empire of almost commensurate size and splendour. In the second half of the 14th century, however, what was left of it was laid low by the Turks. Remnants of Bulgarian resistance were smashed after long and terrible sieges of Trnovo (1393) and Vidin (1396).

Until the late 18th century there was no hope of autonomy – let alone sovereign independence – for Bulgaria. Periodic appeals to the past by rebel chiefs or romantic proto-nationalists were based on grossly flattering memories of the size and stability of the medieval empires. The population gradually became more mixed. Greek, Armenian and Jewish merchants supplied the place of a middle class – the Jews being admitted into the Turkish quarters of the towns. North of the Balkan Mountains, the only towns were on the Black Sea coast, dominated by Greek citizenry and Turkish garrisons. Even the old towns of Rumelia were hellenized. The native patriarchate – the citadel of Bulgarian identity which had been respected by Byzantine conquerors – was suppressed. The church under Turkish rule was de-nationalized and put firmly under the control of Constantinople; Greek replaced Church Slavonic in its services. Bulgarian imperviousness to religion dates from this period of alienation of the church. The rapid progress of Protestant Evangelism in recent times – in Congregationalist, Baptist and Pentecostal forms – is perhaps another long-term effect.

The Bulgarian people almost disappeared from the map between the end of the 14th century and the end of the 18th. Remnants of Bulgarian tradition were kept alive in secret in monasteries, most notably by Paisii, who as a monk of Athos, wrote a history of his people in Bulgarian in 1762. In the 1830s, the Bulgarians were rediscovered by western Europeans and Americans missionaries who had all-but forgotten their existence; Eli Riggs helped in producing the first Bulgarian bible in 1840.

Further encouragement towards a Bulgarian resurgence came from Russia, where Bulgarian exiles and students were welcomed as potential instruments against the Turks, and where they developed feelings of Slavonic solidarity which have had a continuous history of influence in Bulgaria ever since.

At the same time, Bulgarian sentiment was not altogether unwelcome even to the Turks, who, after Greece won its independence in 1830, could hope to deflect it against the Greeks, who, from a Bulgarian point of view, appeared, by their control of the church and their role in commerce, as oppressors. A plan, urged by Bulgarian patriots and supported by Russia, to restore Bulgarian ecclesiastical autonomy, became increasingly attractive to the Turks.

As Bulgarian political aspirations emerged, the problem of defining the frontiers of a potential Bulgarian area became apparent. On maps of the medieval Bulgarian empires, the state never quite seemed to be the same shape. At its greatest extent it included the whole of the present Macedonian republic and great zones of Serbia, Greece and Albania. For centuries, the cultural centre of the 'Bulgarian' patriarchate was in Ohrid, on the frontiers of Albania. There was no clear linguistic frontier in the west: between the speech of what became western Bulgaria and that of Macedonia or eastern Serbia there was – and to some extent is still – less difference than between the Bulgarian of Rumelia and the coast. When the Turks decided to create a Bulgarian exarchate in 1870, they fixed its limits by plebiscite to include a generous swathe of territory, not much short of medieval Bulgaria at its largest extent.

Revolt in Bosnia-Herzegovina in 1875 provoked similar troubles in Bulgaria the following year, suppressed with great bloodshed by irregular Turkish troops. The ensuing international crisis under the shadow of these 'Bulgarian atrocities' – Gladstone's pamphlet denouncing them sold tens of thousands of copies – produced an unusual degree of unanimity between Britain and Russia. In 1878 the Congress of Berlin agreed the establishment of an autonomous Bulgarian principality, still subject to technical Turkish suzerainty. This partial frustration of Bulgarian aspirations at a time when full independence was granted to the Romanians and Serbs is understandable in the light of British apprehensions about the approach of Russian power towards the Mediterranean. Compared with the 'Great Bulgaria' foreshadowed in the exarchate and advocated by Russia, the new principality was a small affair, confined to the north of the Balkan mountains. Eastern Rumelia remained a Turkish province – though guaranteed a Christian governor and monitored by the supervision of the Great Powers – until a *de facto* union with Bulgaria was achieved by rebels in 1885. The British acquiesced in this adjustment in the hope of weakening Russian influence inside Bulgaria and the new situation was formalized in 1887. Bulgaria was proclaimed and internationally recognized as a fully independent kingdom in 1908.

Bulgaria had no middle class, but its aristocracy was secular-minded and public-spirited. The Germans called the Bulgarians 'the Prussians of the Balkans'. The new state was viewed with suspicion, however, by almost all its neighbours; memories of medieval empires, in which Bulgarians invested much emotion, were a potential threat. In Macedonia, which became in the 1890s a byword for revolutionary terrorism against Turkish rule, the prospects for Bulgarian expansion were enticing for nationalists and alarming to neighbouring countries. When the Balkan states deprived Turkey of most of the rest of her European possessions in 1911–12, the effect of the division of the spoils was further to isolate Bulgaria. In another round of warfare in 1913, her former allies turned on Bulgaria: she lost her hoped-for gains in Macedonia to Greece and Serbia and the southern Dobruja to Romania. When World War I broke out, she therefore sided with Germany and Austria who were prepared to buy her alliance with the promise of restoring these territories.

The bitterness of further defeat, reparations and sacrifices of territory reinforced Bulgarian nationalism. The title of King Boris III (1918–45) was an affected reminder of the First Bulgarian Empire. Communists and peasant revolutionaries were barely contained until Boris imposed a royal dictatorship in 1935. To judge from the large numbers of English and French books from the period in the national library, inter-war Bulgaria was opening up to influence from the west, but these beginnings were disastrously aborted. The start of World War II found the élite divided and the king hesitant. Pressure of early axis victories effectively obliged Bulgaria to throw in its lot with Germany against the western democracies in 1941, though the legacy of pan-Slav sentiment prevented her from declaring war on the Soviet Union.

The genuinely large Communist party welcomed the victory of the Red Army in 1944. Even in 1993 – after three free general elections which followed the collapse of Soviet power in 1989–91 – the leadership of the former Communist party remains in power, thanks in part to communists' experience in manipulating a system of clientage and also – curiously enough – to support from the significant Turkish ethnic minority. To save itself in the period of the downfall of international communism, the Communist party took up xenophobia with enthusiasm. Yet the Turks chose to control this by restoring the communists to power with their votes. By 'Turks' in this context, a variety of communities is understood. It includes ethnic Turks who have become Christian, as well as those who are Turks by both ethnic origin and religion (see p. 202), and the Muslim, Bulgarian-speaking ethnic Slavs, known as Pomaks (see p. 223), who live in the Rhodope Mountains near the Greek border and who, to complicate matters further, have recently been the subject of Roman Catholic evangelization with consequently large numbers of conversions.

PROSPECTS ■

Despite the one-time broad ambitions of Bulgarian imperialism there are few communities outside Bulgaria who could be regarded as proper objects of irredentism. Kindred with the ancient Bulgars has been claimed by, or attributed to, the Chuvash (see p. 364) and the Gagauz, or Bessarabian Bulgars, a community of Turkish-speaking Orthodox who migrated from Bulgaria to Bessarabia and whose language still includes many distinctive Bulgarian terms. Today, numbering about 175,000, they are divided between Moldova and Ukrainian Bessarabia. The biggest external concentration of alleged or would-be Bulgarians is found, owing to the continuities of language, in the present Macedonian republic, where pro-Bulgarian political parties have a meaningful presence and where their representatives in the legislature speak standard Bulgarian in preference to standard Macedonian – though the difference between the two is a much exaggerated feature of south Balkan life.

Bulgarians are much addicted to male voice choirs and the historical theatre, where retrospects on the First and Second Bulgarian Empires predominate over the second most popular theme: the suppression of a worthy people in the period of Turkish rule. The history curriculum in schools is characterized by similar priorities. This overstretch of things Bulgarian is understandable, given the fact that Bulgarians have had so much to struggle for in order to be recognized at all. Bulgarian interests are on the side of international peace in the Balkans and it is likely that the course of westernization, suspended in 1941, will resume and gather pace.

SERBS

Serbian nationalists portray the Serbs as victims throughout their history, from their defeat by the Ottoman Turks in 1389 and subsequent subjection to Turkish rule, to their perceived victimization by the regime of Tito from 1945 to 1980. Past offences are remembered and grudges harboured over centuries. The international isolation of Serbia during the Balkan crisis of the 1990s served only to bolster the Serbs' defensiveness and sense of only being able to rely on themselves.

The greatest concentration of Serbs is to be found in the Republic of Serbia where, according to the 1981 census, they constituted 85.4% of the population (excluding the then autonomous provinces of Kosovo and the Vojvodina). The Serbs also form substantial minorities in Kosovo and the Vojvodina and in the Republics of Croatia, Bosnia and Macedonia; since the rise of Montenegrin national consciousness, their position in Montenegro has become ambiguous.

There are also long-established Serb communities in Hungary, most notably the town of Szentendre, 12 miles outside Budapest, where Serb families found refuge from the Turks in the 14th century and again in the 17th. In the 19th and 20th centuries, the poor opportunities offered by their homeland have driven many Serbs to emigrate to North America, Australia, Germany and Scandinavia.

LANGUAGE ■

Most Serbs use the eastern variant of *Štokavski*, the main dialect of Serbo-Croat but some communities in the Krajina district of the Republic of Croatia have over the centuries of their settlement adopted the western variant more typical of the Croats. As members of the Eastern Orthodox Church, the Serbs have a long tradition of writing in Cyrillic characters but since the 19th century have also used the Roman

Serbians & Montenegrins

The Serbian Population
(Central Bureau of Statistics of the Republic of Croatia, 1991)

over 80% Serbian

30 - 80% Serbian

The Montenegrin Population

Distribution of Montenegrins

alphabet. During the current wave of Serbian nationalist fervour, pressure is being exerted on publishing houses and private individuals to use only the Cyrillic alphabet.

RELIGION ■

The Serbian Orthodox Church has made a decisive contribution to Serbian national consciousness. Founded in the 13th century by Saint Sava, it was the Serbs' only national institution after the fall of the Kingdom of Serbia to the Turks in the 15th century. The Serbs take pride in their steadfast loyalty to Orthodoxy during the years of Ottoman rule when conversion to Islam was the precondition for entry into government and holding land from the Sultan. The sacrifice which their loyalty entailed has

230

coloured their attitude to the Bosnian Muslims and Muslim Albanians who benefited from conversion to the religion of their Ottoman overlords (cf p. 199).

There is a strong anti-western element within all the Orthodox Churches but the Serbs' mistrust of the Western and Catholic world has been fuelled by the memory of the thousands of Serbs in the independent State of Croatia who, during World War II were presented by the Ustaša government with a choice between conversion to Catholicism or death. Any moves by the Serbian Orthodox Church towards ecumenism have been made in the direction of the Protestant Churches.

Since the 1980s and the re-emergence of Serbian nationalism, there has been an upsurge of enthusiasm for Orthodoxy as an expression of Serb national identity. The construction of the vast cathedral of Saint Sava in Belgrade continues, much of the money for the project coming from emigré Serbs.

HISTORY ■

The Serbs settled in the Balkan peninsula in the 7th century and in due course established two provinces under Byzantine suzerainty, Duklja, the core of the Kingdom of Montenegro, and Raška in the southwest of the modern Republic of Serbia. In the late 12th century, under the Nemanjić family, medieval Serbia began to expand from its base in Raška. It came to dominate most of Macedonia and reached the height of its power during the reign of Stefan Dušan (1331–55) who ruled from his capital at Skopje, in modern Macedonia, an empire stretching from the Danube to central Greece, from the river Drina to western Thrace. The memory of this vast medieval state remains a source of pride and inspiration for the Serbs: since the 19th century, Serbian nationalists have dreamt of restoring Dušan's empire.

The battle of Kosovo Polje on 28th June 1389, at which the Serbs were defeated by the Turks, is singled out as the central event marking the end of Serbian statehood. The anniversary of the battle is one of the most potent in the Serb national calendar and in this century it has acquired greater resonance; in 1914 it was the day on which a young Serb assassinated the Archduke Franz Ferdinand at Sarajevo. The observance of the 600th anniversary in 1989 was marked by displays of overtly belligerent nationalism presided over by the Serbian President Slobodan Milošević.

After the Ottoman conquest, many Serbs migrated to areas under Venetian and Habsburg rule. The greatest migrations were in the 17th century after the Habsburg armies had driven the Turks from Hungary. They formed a prosperous emigré community and, unlike those Serbs under Ottoman rule, were open to intellectual and cultural movements in the rest of Europe; in the late 18th and 19th centuries it was among the émigré Serbs under Habsburg rule that the Serbian national awakening began. At the end of World War I, the region of Hungary with the largest Serb minority, known as the Vojvodina, became part of the Kingdom of Serbs, Croats and Slovenes.

Encouraged by the favourable terms offered by the Habsburg emperors, many Serbs settled in the *Vojna Krajina* (the 'military frontier'), a vast buffer zone created between the Habsburg and the Ottoman empires. They took advantage of the opportunities for careers in military service denied them under Ottoman rule and established themselves amid the rough and precarious circumstances of a borderland constantly criss-crossed by raiding parties from both sides. These Serb settlers were the forefathers of the present-day Serbs of the breakaway Krajina district in the Republic of Croatia.

The 19th-century Kingdom of Serbia which formed the core of the modern Serb Republic evolved in stages under the Karadordjević and Obrenović families which had supplied the leaders of the First and Second Serbian Uprisings (in 1804 and 1815). After 1816, although still a province of Turkey, the small state carved out by Miloš Obrenović and his rebels was virtually independent. Formal recognition of autonomy followed in 1829 and of independence in 1878 when the Congress of Berlin also forestalled Serb ambitions for further expansion by granting Bosnia and Herzegovina to the Habsburgs as a protectorate.

In 1844, the Serbian minister of internal affairs, Ilija Garašanin (1812–74) had issued an expansionist programme which aimed at uniting all the Serbs within a Serbian state; because the Serbian nationalist ideologues had taken language as the criterion for determining nationality, Garašanin's programme included areas inhabited by 'Serbs' who had ostensibly lost their Serbian identity; herein lay the seeds of the Serbs' later conflicts with the Macedonians, Bosnian Muslims and Montenegrins. The Yugoslav ideology expounded by some Croatian national theorists which supposed a common South Slav identity transcending individual national identities, found little support among Serbs outside the Habsburg lands.

In 1918, for the Serbs who had fought on the side of the victorious allies, the Kingdom of Serbs, Croats and Slovenes, (later to become Yugoslavia), held out the promise of a Greater Serbia. The inter-war years of misrule by the Serb-dominated Belgrade government turned national rivalries into the hatreds which erupted in World War II and sapped the foundations of Yugoslavia which finally gave way in the 1990s.

The Yugoslav army surrendered to the Axis powers on 17th April, 1941 and a puppet regime was installed in Belgrade. Serb resistance to the occupying forces was divided between the royalist Draža Mihailović and his Četniks, and the followers of the communist Tito and the partisans. Tito strove to gather support among the Serbs, realizing that their backing would be vital for a communist victory throughout Yugoslavia. The Serbs within the independent state of Croatia which had been created by Mussolini fell victim to the programme of genocide executed by the Ustaša leader, Ante Pavelić.

Did the Serbs enjoy favoured status during the years of Tito's Yugoslavia, or were they systematically discriminated against? Tito compensated them by granting the Republic of Serbia small territorial gains but he also established the Vojvodina and Kosovo as autonomous provinces, ever conscious of the need to counterbalance the influence of the Serbs, the largest nation in the Socialist Federal Republic of Yugoslavia.

The current vehement Serb nationalists depict the years of Tito's Yugoslavia as a time when the Serbs were victimized. Political cartoons from the late 1980s and l990s provide a commentary upon current Serb paranoia: the Serbs will soon be over-run by Tito's 'favourite children', the Muslim Albanians; the Croats have reverted to their true type as Ustaša in the pockets of the Roman Catholic Church while the Bosnian Muslims are the agents of fanatical Islam. Serb nationalists have also been able to play upon fears that eastward expansion is again on the Germans' agenda and that recognition of Croatian independence was the first stage in a German-led western conspiracy; International Freemasonry was also credited with an interest in the extermination of the Serbian nation. Slobodan Milošević, the President of Serbia, owed his success not least to his ability to prey upon the Serbs' bitter memories and fears that history may indeed repeat itself.

MONTENEGRINS

The Montenegrins are in the process of establishing a national identity distinct from that of the Serbs. The central element of their identity is the Montenegrin state which they trace back to the province of Duklja, one of two Serb states to emerge in the northwest Balkans during the 11th century. Today, differentiation from the Serbs has a political purpose: Montenegrins have an interest in distancing themselves from the actions of the Serbian government of Slobodan Miloševič in Croatia and Bosnia.

HISTORY ■

While the Kingdom of Serbia fell to the Turks in the 15th century, Montenegro managed to secure special status as an independent princedom, although the Ottomans claimed jurisdiction over it until the Congress of Berlin in 1878. Under the Petrović dynasty of prince-bishops, a strong regional consciousness emerged in Montenegro but the tribes of the principality and their rulers thought of themselves as Serbs and in the 18th and 19th centuries believed it their mission to restore the medieval Serbian Empire. The establishment of the Kingdom of Serbia in the course of the 19th century gave the Serb nation two possible focal points for national unification. Prince Nikola Petrović (1841–1921) of Montenegro hoped to seize the initiative and capitalized upon the rivalry between the ruling and the exiled Serb royal families, marrying his eldest daughter to the emigré Petar Karadjordjević of the ruling line of Serbia proper, while accepting the subsidies which the Austro-Hungarian Empire was prepared to give in order to forestall the combining of the two Serb kingdoms. It was, however, the Karadjordevićs who achieved the political unification not only of the Serbs and Montenegrins but of all the South Slavs; in 1918, the Petrović dynasty was declared deposed by the Montenegrin national assembly and Montenegro ceased to be an independent state and became part of the Kingdom of Serbs, Croats and

Slovenes (later Yugoslavia), under King Aleksander Karadjordjević. In the inter-war years two factions appeared among the Montenegrins: the Whites opposed any distinction between Montenegrin Serbs and the rest of the Serb nation; the Greens resented being lorded over by their fellow Serbs in the Belgrade government, regretted the loss of the Montenegrin state and advocated the re-organization of the kingdom on a federal basis. The two inter-war decades of misrule began the process of alienating the Montenegrins from the Serbs of Serbia; in World War II, Montenegro was a stronghold of the communist partisan resistance rather than of the royalist Serb Četniks. The re-emergence of extreme Serb nationalism under the leadership of Slobodan Milošević drove many more Montenegrins to claim separate nationality in the desire to disassociate themselves from a nation which became an international pariah. One of the ways in which Montenegrinism manifested itself was the petition in 1990 for the restoration of the Montenegrin Orthodox Church which lost its autocephalous status in 1920. In 1993 a faction in the Montenegrin Church did in fact declare itself independent of the Serbian Orthodox Church.

CULTURE AND MENTALITY ■

Like Serbs, the Montenegrins use the Cyrillic alphabet and the eastern variant of Serbo-Croat. They are also members of the Orthodox church. Until the middle years of this century, Montenegrin society was organized on a patriarchal and tribal basis and blood feuds were still continuing in the 1950s. A strong, wiry mountain people and, unlike the Serbs, conspicuously tall, Montenegrins are renowned as fighters and many have followed careers in the army.

THE MOUNTAINS AND THE COAST ■

The Republic is mountainous and little suited to agriculture; since the 19th century many thousands of Montenegrins have left its barren stone wilderness for North America and Australia. The Montenegrin coastline is now a popular holiday-destination for Serbs, who no longer feel welcome in Dalmatia, and includes the sheer cliffs and sinister waters of the fjord-like Gulf of Kotor.

ARCHITECTURE AND TOWNS ■

The inland towns are modern developments replacing earlier settlements built mainly in wood. Cetinje, the seat of the Petrović dynasty, acquired the accoutrements of a royal capital in the 19th century as the Montenegrin rulers tried to play an active role in European politics; it has an attractive complex of palaces and pretty rather than distinguished embassy buildings with brightly painted façades. After World War II, Podgorica was re-born as Titograd and is certainly the most soulless example of socialist-inspired urban planning in the former Yugoslavia. The Venetian Republic governed the Montenegrin coast from the 1420s until 1797 and Kotor and some other coastal towns still have Venetian palaces and towers. The earthquake in 1979 caused irreparable damage to many buildings in Montenegro but it is still possible to find some wooden houses in the Ottoman-Balkan style.

CROATS

The Croats were one of the constituent nations of the former Socialist Federal Republic of Yugoslavia, making up about 70% of the population of the Republic of Croatia and before the war of 1992–3 representing about 18% of the population of the Republic of Bosnia-Herzegovina. In the Burgenland, Moravia, Italy and Slovakia there are small Croatian communities which were founded between the 15th and 17th centuries by refugees from Ottoman rule. In the 19th and 20th centuries, Croats have emigrated to North America, Australia and Argentina; the post-war communist regime in Yugoslavia permitted emigration and many Croats, particularly from the Dalmatian islands, moved to Scandinavia and West Germany. Emigré Croats now play an active role in the Republic of Croatia and since 1991 many young Croats have gone to Croatia, sometimes for the first time, to defend 'their homeland'.

LANGUAGE ■

The Croats use the Latin alphabet and three distinct South Slav dialects known collectively as Serbo-Croat and classified according to the word for 'what'. *Štokavski (što = what)* was chosen in the 19th century as the literary standard for both Croats and Serbs and is used by many Croats and Bosnian Muslims and by all Serbs and Montenegrins. It has two main variants distinguishable by the way in which an early Slavonic vowel sound has developed in the eastern variant typical of the Serbs and the western variant used by most Croats; while a Serb will refer to 'time' as *vreme*, a Croat will say and write *vrijeme*. The diverse cultural influences to which the Croats' and Serbs' separate histories have exposed them are manifest in lexical variations between Serb and Croat *štokavski*-users; for the Croats, bread, drawer and paper are *kruh, ladfca, papir* but for the Serbs *hleb, fioka, hartija*.

The other two dialects used by the Croats are peculiar to them and are difficult for *štokavski*-users to understand, despite the underlying grammatical structure common to all the dialects. *Kajkavski* is used mainly in the northwest of Croatia; *čakavski* principally in the southwest including Istra, the Dalmatian Islands and the Dalmatian coast.

The Croats take great pride in their long vernacular traditions. During the Middle Ages, the Croats used the Glagolitic alphabet to write liturgical and apocryphal literature in the vernacular. Glagolitic had been introduced towards the end of the 9th century by disciples of Saints Cyril and Methodius; the oldest surviving piece of written Croat is the Baška plaque (c. 1100) which is written in Glagolitic script in

Croats

The Croatian population

over 90% of the population

30% - 90% of the population

Central Bureau of Statistics of the Republic of Croatia, 1991.

a mixture of Church Slavonic and the vernacular. Devotional works were still being printed for the Croats in Glagolitic in the early decades of the 19th century and since the 1980s there has been a revival of interest among the Croats in the Glagolitic alphabet as a vital part of Croatian national culture.

The rich body of vernacular literature which the Croats produced during the 16th and 17th centuries was written in Latin characters and in the *čakavski* and *kajkavski* dialects. The Croatian literary standard based on *štokavski* was developed in the 1880s during the Croatian national revival and as part of a programme to promote cultural unity among the South Slavs.

The choice of *štokavski* as the basis for literature made it easier for Croats and Serbs to communicate but has long been regretted by Croat nationalists for contributing to the blurring of distinctions between the Croat and Serb nations and for exposing them to 'serbianization'. Since the 1980s, Croat nationalists have attempted to 'purify' the Croatian language by removing all words perceived as foreign, especially 'Serbian', and finding 'Croatian' words; some of the recommended words are

236

not neologisms in the strictest sense but words coined during World War II by the Ustaša regime of Ante Pavelić.

RELIGION ■

The Croats have remained steadfast in their loyalty to Roman Catholicism and in the 20th century the Catholic Church has played a significant role in their history. Although during World War II some Croatian Catholics had been active in the partisan resistance, the post-war Yugoslav communist regime endeavoured to tar the Catholic Church in Croatia with the Ustaša brush, equating Catholicism and Croatian nationalism with fascism. In 1966, relations between Yugoslavia and the Holy See were normalized but the Catholic Church understood that it operated on sufferance. The 1980s saw a resurgence of Catholicism among the Croats and since Croatia achieved independence the Catholic Church has become a powerful influence in the country, undertaking the 'moral re-armament' of the nation.

HISTORY AND ETHNICITY ■

The Croats were one of several groups of Slav migrants into the Balkans which had set out from different points of departure to arrive in successive waves. These groups remained clearly differentiated so that the first states which emerged in the Middle Ages among the South Slavs were based around the three major groupings of South Slav migrants; the Bulgars, Croats and Serbs. The Croats established their independent principality during the 9th century along the Eastern Adriatic between the rivers Raša and Cetina with their capital at Biograd and later inland at Knin. Under its native dynasty, Croatia became a thriving and expanding maritime power, acquiring the region of Slavonia between the rivers Drava and Sava in the 10th century and Dalmatia in the 11th. When the Croatian ruling house died out, the nobility elected King Kálmán of Hungary as their ruler and the Kingdom of Croatia was annexed to the Kingdom of Hungary, passing to the Habsburgs in 1527. Many of the Croats of the Dalmatian coast and islands, with the exception of the Dubrovnik Republic, became subject to the Republic of Venice from the 12th century and remained so until 1797. From 1815 they were ruled directly by the Habsburgs from Vienna. The many Croats in Bosnia stayed under Ottoman rule until 1878 when the Congress of Berlin placed them under Habsburg protection. Only with the creation of the Kingdom of Serbs, Croats and Slovenes (later to become Yugoslavia) in 1918 did the Dalmatian and Slavonian Croats find themselves united within one state.

NATIONAL IDEOLOGIES: YUGOSLAVISM AND CROATIAN NATIONALISM ■

The Croats have a long history of aspiring to Slavic integration. In the 16th century, Croatian humanists were keenly aware of belonging to the Slavic world and postulated the existence of a single Slav language. In the 19th century, during the early phase of the Croatian national revival, members of the Illyrian movement sought to promote closer cultural ties among the South Slavs, the 'Yugoslavs'. Among the South Slavs in the Habsburg Monarchy, cultural Yugoslavism developed into a political movement with the aim of uniting the Slovenes, Croats and Serbs and Montenegrins within a single state. At the same time, in response to the internationalist Serbian national programme, a rival Croatian national ideology developed which drew upon the Croats' supposed history of unbroken statehood and looked to the assimilation of all the South Slavs, except the Bulgars, to Croatian culture.

During World War I, the Croats' enthusiasm for the creation of a South Slav state was fuelled by optimism that they would enter such a union as equals with the other South Slavs and by fears that Dalmatia with its Croatian population might be awarded to Italy. After 1918, the Croats found themselves caught within a Greater Serbia rather than the Yugoslavia for which they had hoped. Under the Serb-dominated inter-war government, Croats first began to hate the Serbs. World War II brought the Croats the chance to free themselves from Belgrade but at a heavy price. The Independent State of Croatia was a Nazi puppet-state and the Ustaša regime of Ante Pavelić took formal vengeance upon the Serbs of Croatia and Bosnia, killing many thousands alongside Jews, Gypsies and opponents of the regime.

Today, Croatian nationalists look back on the years since 1945 with bitterness for what they see as the long penance which the communist government forced the Croats to pay for the Ustaša regime while disregarding the Croats' contribution to the partisan resistance. Under Tito, any expression of Croatian national sentiment, whether nationalist or not, was swiftly and harshly stifled. In 1990 on the eve of the first multi-party elections in Croatia, a Croatian politician remarked that the gags had at last been removed from their mouths.

The culture of contemporary Croatian nationalists is characterized by their determination to distinguish the Croats from the Serbs while emphasizing their western and European orientation. Croat youths may favour a clean-shaven, 'skin-head' look to contrast with the long-haired and bearded Serbs, thus, often unwittingly, making a distinction which dates back to the early days of the split between the western Roman and the eastern Orthodox churches. National symbols such as the flag and the red and white checked *šaharica* are prominently displayed and the Latin cross too is used as an indicator of national identity.

The Croatian government led by President Franjo Tudjman has done little to allay Serb fears. The Croatian constitution is worded in a way that made the Serbs within the Republic feel excluded; in his zeal to explain the newly independent Republic of Croatia as the re-embodiment of the historic state-tradition of the Croatian nation, Tudjman turned the Serbs within the republic into a veritable fifth column for the Serb president, Slobodan Milošević. Apparently small measures such as the announcement in July 1993 that the currency of Croatia was no longer to be the dinar, a name too long associated with Yugoslavia and hyper-inflation, have played into the hands of those nationalists who work upon the Serbs' fears, since the kuna, as it is now called, was the unit of currency used by the wartime Independent State of Croatia.

TOWN AND COUNTRY ■

It is the life of the town rather than the country that best demonstrates how the Croats belong to the cultural traditions of both central Europe and the Mediterranean, the architecture and town planning still distinguishing the old Habsburg and Venetian spheres of influence. Zagreb has a Baroque quarter equal to that of Prague and Budapest. In the 19th century, the heavy neo-classical and neo-baroque architecture which dominates Vienna was added to the Croatian urban landscape and the lower town at Zagreb was laid out on a grid plan. At the turn of the century, some fine *Jugendstil* façades were inserted and after World War II, work was begun on Novi Zagreb, a bleak vision conjured up by utopian town planners which lies to the south of the former Avenue of the Proletarian Brigades (now renamed Avenue Vukovar in memory of the town in eastern Croatia razed in November 1991). The old city, by contrast, is a lively centre for the art and still retains the café society which sustains itself on spirits, tobacco, coffee and cakes.

The life of the Dalmatian coasts and islands is Italianate. The centuries of Venetian rule are evident in the organization of public spaces and in the tall, austere limestone palaces built around courtyards with carved well-heads, stone balconies and often a carved lion of St Mark. The cathedrals at Trogir and Šibenik, the latter damaged in the recent war, are celebrated as masterpieces of Romanesque architecture. At Zadar, the church of Saint Donat, a two-storey rotunda built on the Roman forum in the late 8th to early 9th centuries is a striking example of the proto-romanesque style; it, too has been damaged and many other proto-romanesque churches have been destroyed and concreted over.

During the years of peace under the post-war communist government, cultural monuments in Croatia suffered not only from years of neglect, but also from an often calculated philistinism in which almost any expression of pride in Croatian culture was stamped out as 'nationalistic'; in the 1980s the country palace of Ban Jelačić, celebrated by the Croats as a national hero, was being used as a turkey hatchery. When Zagreb played host to the Universijade, the international student games in 1947, there was a flurry of restoration work throughout Croatia, but much 'conservation' was ill-conceived, poorly-executed and unsympathetic. The sudden flourishing of civic pride, and still *sotto voce* nationalism, was, even so, conspicuous.

Under communism, 'popular culture', the singing, dancing and craft-work blessed with official encouragement was, as elsewhere in Eastern Europe, impeccably polished but anodyne. Post-communist Croatian popular culture has acquired heavy Catholic overtones but remains too artificial and too political to suggest any genuine creative impulse. Rather the earthiness and spontaneity of the life of the 'folk' has best been expressed in the sophisticated drawings and paintings of a number of brilliant naïve artists whose school was encouraged by the post-war authorities as promising a new art innocent of 'bourgeois' aesthetic criteria. Concerned with rural life, rather than the urban lifestyle aspired to by so many, the work of Croatian naïve artists is characterized by its grotesque portrayal of man set against a natural world which may be the benign pastel visions of Generalić or the altogether more menacing and sometimes desolate landscape created by Ivan Lacković Croata.

BOSNIAN MUSLIMS

The Bosnian Muslims are Slav Muslims descended from Serbs and Croats who converted to Islam while Bosnia was under Ottoman rule (1463–1878). Bosnian Muslim national consciousness is a relatively recent development: it is only since the creation of the first Yugoslav state in 1918 that they have come to identify themselves as a nation. In 1971, Muslims throughout Yugoslavia were recognized by the communist government as a 'Yugoslav nation' and thereafter many chose to register as Muslims in the official census. The war in Bosnia-Herzegovina since 1992 has greatly served to strengthen Bosnian Muslim national consciousness: with the outside world seemingly impotent to assist them, the Bosnian Muslims have had to fall back on their own resources.

Before the outbreak of war in Bosnia and programmes of ethnic cleansing, Muslims constituted 39% of the population of the Republic of Bosnia-Herzegovina. The main concentrations of Bosnian Muslims were around Sarajevo, Mostar, Kordun, to the east of Tuzla and in a long broad band stretching to the north and south of Banja Luka.

The Bosnian Muslims were not the only Slav Muslims in the former Socialist Federal Republic of Yugoslavia; there are long-established Slav Muslim communities in the Sandžak region of southern Serbia, Montenegro and Macedonia, and small numbers of recent settlers in Croatia and Slovenia. The Albanians too are mainly Muslim, but are not Slavs. While Bosnian Muslims are identified by their religion since their language and ethnicity are the same as non-Muslim South Slavs, their sense of nationhood has been strengthened by their peculiar historical experience, particularly since the end of Ottoman rule.

HISTORY ■

It is often claimed that Islam achieved so many conversions in Bosnia and Herzegovina because the region had been a stronghold of Bogomilism (a Christian heresy), but a high-rate of conversion is not necessarily evidence of partial Christianization since the Albanians, who had been distinguished as steadfast Catholics, also converted in great numbers after their conquest by the Turks. As followers of Islam within the Ottoman Empire, the Muslims in Bosnia and Herzegovina were spared the *deverşime* (the recruitment of every tenth boy for Ottoman service), taxed less and allowed a greater measure of self-government than their Christian and Jewish neighbours. Their fiefs became hereditary and a Muslim Slav nobility emerged

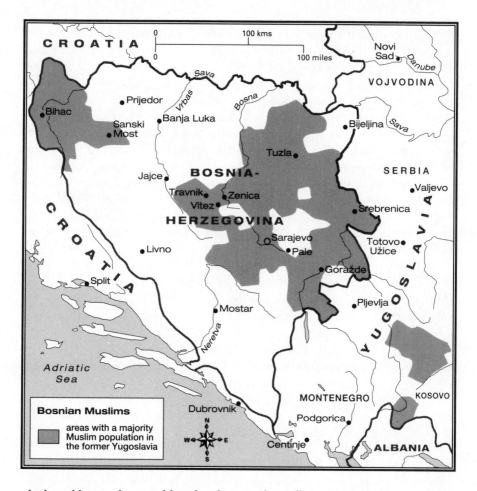

which, unlike Muslim notables elsewhere in the Balkans, continued to speak the vernacular.

In the 19th century, a series of peasant revolts culminated in the mass uprisings of 1875–8 which led to Bosnia and Herzegovina becoming an Austrian protectorate in 1878. The province, with its mixed population of Serbs, Croats and Muslims, was coveted by the Serb government in Belgrade which dreamt of a Greater Serbia and by the Croats who wanted to form a South Slav state within the Habsburg Monarchy. The Austrian minister who governed Bosnia hoped to neutralize, or at least to counterbalance, rival Serb and Croat claims by promoting the idea of *bošanstvo*, of separate Bosnian nationhood. *Bošanstvo*, however, found favour only among the Muslims who felt threatened by Serb and Croat nationalizing programmes and their Christianizing agendas. Muslim national consciousness was very fluid with members of the same family identifying themselves variously as Muslim Croats, Muslim Serbs and simply Muslims.

The defeat of Austria-Hungary at the end of World War I (1918) marked for the

241

Muslims of Bosnia and Herzegovina the end of five centuries of relative security and prosperity. In the period during which the government of the newly formed Kingdom of Serbs, Croats and Slovenes, later Yugoslavia, was establishing control over all its territory, Muslims fell victim to Serb volunteers who pillaged Bosnia and Herzegovina; many fled to their co-religionists in Turkey. Once order was established, they faced the crude propaganda of Serb nationalists which stereotyped the Bosnian Muslims as Asians – idle, effete and in need of re-habilitation if they were ever to recover their pristine Serb identity. Muslim estate-owners had their lands confiscated under a programme of land reform which in 1919 prompted Muslims of all classes to form a united front, the Yugoslav Organization, based at Sarajevo. In 1929, Bosnia was divided into four provinces, so disposed that the Muslims formed a minority in each. Unable to influence the Serb-dominated government, the Bosnian Muslims resorted to supporting Yugoslav unitarism which offered a refuge outside the embattled Serb and Croat political camps.

During World War II, Bosnia and Herzegovina became part of the Independent State of Croatia. The Muslims were ostensibly courted by Pavelić's Ustaša government but these promises turned out to be illusory. Some joined the partisans, the communist-led resistance, but where the Četniks, the royalist Serb resistance, held sway, the Muslims were slaughtered wholesale.

In the post-war Socialist Federal Republic of Yugoslavia, Bosnia was conspicuous as the most enthusiastically communist and 'Yugoslav' of the republics. With its mixed population of Serbs, Croats and Muslims, it was a microcosm of Yugoslavia and welcomed a new Yugoslav identity which promised to transcend and supplant the identities of nations which had been so mutually hostile. The government allowed the practice of religion but on strict terms. Any hostile and counter-revolutionary acts derived from Muslim nationalism were punished with long prison sentences. The Bosnian Muslims grew and prospered neither more nor less than their Serb and Croat neighbours under a regime officially equally hostile to all nationalisms and within an economy lubricated by corruption.

The growth of Muslim consciousness among the Bosnian Muslims had tended towards increased politicization rather than fundamentalism; the Bosnian Sunni Muslims used to appear very lax in their religious observances. In 1990, Alia Izetbegović, a Bosnian Muslim who in the 1980s had been imprisoned for stirring up Muslim nationalism, founded the Party of Democratic Action which had a strong appeal among the Muslims and later that year won a majority in elections to the Bosnian parliament. In 1992, in the wake of the Slovene and Croat declarations of independence, Izetbegović, as President of Bosnia, declared the Republic of Bosnia-Herzegovina independent. Since then Bosnia has become, as one Muslim writer predicted in 1987, the most bloody slaughter-house of nations. The question posed in 1984 by a distinguished Croatian historian when reviewing the inter-war history of Bosnia is today ever-more pertinent: 'Is it strange or queer that in Europe there emerged in the second half of the twentieth century a nation in Europe that no longer wanted to be anything but incongruously Muslim?'

7

THE CARPATHIAN REGION

The communities reviewed in this chapter occupy a region which is ethnically diverse but geographically well defined, lying between the Danube and the Dnestr: a segment of eastern Europe, projecting from the edges of the Germanic world into that of the Slavs, scored by the Danube and the Carpathians and enclosing the Hungarian plain.

Across the Eurasian steppe, the Danube valley has been accessible to migrants from the east: by this route, Magyars and Bulgars came; yet the Danube is a long and navigable river which has been an artery of communication and migration from Germanic central Europe. In partial consequence, the Danube is both a sump for settlers from different directions and a gash across the Slav world: except in patches, where it forms part of the frontier of Slovakia and in Vojvodina, between Batina and Bazias, where it crosses Serbian territory, it has edged purely Slav cultures away from its banks, which are lined with non-Slavs, like the Austrians, Magyars, Romanians or Bulgarians (who have or claim non-Slav ancestors, see p. 199).

The Slovaks, like their Czech neighbours, who inhabit the extreme northwest of the region, are Slavs of markedly 'western' cultural affiliations, occupying part of the heartland of the Habsburg empire, practising Catholic and Protestant forms of Christianity and participating – sometimes close to the fore – in mainstream western-European historical experience, including the Renaissance, the Enlightenment and the Industrial Revolution. The Czechs' self-perception is unequivocally 'western': indeed, Prague is well to the west of Vienna and the river on which it stands flows into the Elbe.

Small-scale river-borne colonization and a modern history of unstable frontiers have both helped to make this a region rich in ethnic minorities, where conflicts of allegiance abound between obligations of citizenship and ties to ethnic groups or extra-territorial nationalities. Except in the lower reaches of the river, where it approaches the Black Sea, the Danube valley and the Hungarian plain are protected to the north by long and barely interrupted ranges – the Carpathian Mountains and the Bohemian and Slovakian uplands. Mountainous areas, which discourage dense settlement, are often cultural dividers: these, however, give the region its unity: they have been the redoubts of some of its peoples and the backbone of its states. The Czech and Slovak republics, Hungary and Romania have all

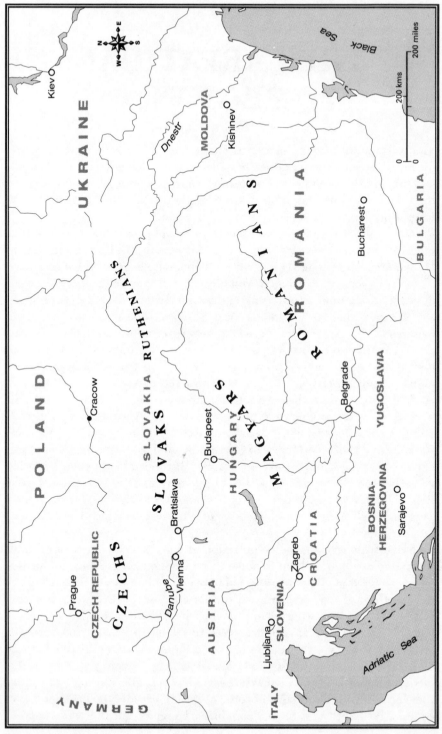

taken shape around or within these uplands. The mountains have been a refuge for many minorities, the most conspicuous case being that of the Ruthenians, themselves an amalgam of various communities.

CZECHS

The Czechs are the people of the Czech Republic, one of the successor states to the former Federal Socialist Republic of Czechoslovakia (Slovakia is the other); the Czech Republic is in the western part of the former federation. They are geographically the most western and culturally perhaps the most westernized of all the Slavic nation, but they have not forgotten their Slavonic roots. The location of the Czech lands, virtually in the centre of Europe, has made their military, political and religious history a turbulent one. The great powers of the region have frequently tried, often successfully, to absorb the Czech lands into their zone of influence. German military strategists in the 19th century claimed that whoever controlled Bohemia, the western part of the Czech lands, controlled Europe. Mindful of its vital strategic position, the modern people of the Czech Republic are having to rethink its political institutions and re-evaluate its economic structures; the process will continue for some years to come.

NATIONAL IDENTITY ■

The Czechs have spent most of their recorded history in the shadow of the German world – an oppressively large neighbour, and at times an unbeatable foe. German and German-Jewish colonization of the towns; the penetration of German language and culture; and, for long periods, the intrusion of German-speaking rulers and élites: all these influences have made Czech identity precious to the Czechs and have inspired, at intervals since the 15th century, movements of national revival and struggles for independence.

The destruction of the Jewish community during World War II and the expulsion of the Germans after it, allowed Czech identity to develop independently of the presence of a sharply-differentiated 'other'. In partial consequence, however, self-differentiation from Slovak neighbours to the east contributed to the break-up of the Czechoslovak federal state in 1993.

During the Post-war period, there has been a visible tendency towards the growth of a separate identity among the inhabitants of Moravia and Silesia, in part encouraged by the authorities in Prague to weight the political machinery of the state against the Slovaks. In 1992 a movement advocating autonomy for Moravia and Silesia gained seats in parliament.

The Czechs and Slovaks, although placed in a common state by treaty arrangements of 1918, had known very different histories. The Czech lands more often

245

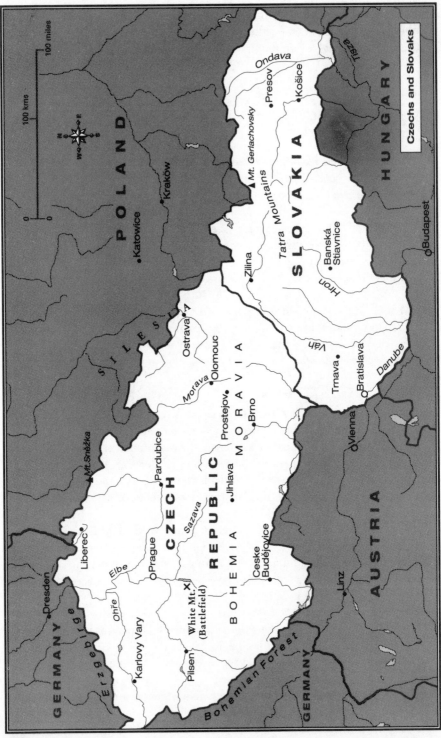

looked west, Slovakia to the east. The Slovaks were colonized by the Hungarians in the 11th century, in part by the Turks in the 16th, while the Czechs were either independent or under Austrian or German rule. With both peoples placed into Czechoslovakia in 1918, there were bound to be tensions between them. When the bonds of central state authority weakened after the collapse of the communist regime in 1989, these broke out into the open. Whereas in the fight to restore democracy, Czechs and Slovaks had worked together, albeit in separate organizations, afterwards many of these groups developed into political parties with a nationalist tinge, especially in Slovakia. By 1992 relations had degenerated to the point where Prague and Bratislava were arguing over whether and where to hyphenate 'Czechoslovakia' to indicate the equality of Czechs and Slovaks. In the end a deep-seated Slovak desire finally to have their own state, and the realization that cutting loose Slovakia's weaker economy would not unduly affect that of the Czech lands, led to the sanctioning, in late 1992 of the 'Velvet Divorce', a sad coda to the 'Velvet Revolution'.

THE LAND ■

The Czech Republic is a land-locked central-European country, with a population of over 10,000,000 (1992). The Republic's largest city is Prague, the capital, with 1,215,000 inhabitants. The second city is Brno (391,000 inhabitants). It has a central-European continental climate with cool winters and warm summers. The highest point is Mount Sněžka (5280ft). The Republic has borders with Poland, Slovakia and Austria and Germany; the latter is the longest. The borders are indefensible, which has helped create a Czech self-perception as peace-loving and politically insecure. The Republic has substantial deposits of black and brown coal and uranium ore.

HISTORY ■

The Czechs were originally one of many tribes which settled the territory and whose names are only remembered in the folklore of the region. They came from Central Asia as part of the massive series of migrations from the 3rd to the 6th centuries AD which overwhelmed the Roman Empire. The first Slav state appeared on the modern republic's territory in the 8th century and soon developed into the 'Great Moravian Empire'. The Empire was converted to Orthodox Christianity in the 9th century by the missionaries Constantine (also known as Cyril) and Methodius, both from Salonica, in a move that was intended to counteract western, Roman Catholic, influence on Central Europe. The two 'apostles of the Slavs' brought with them a new alphabet, Cyrillic, with letters to accommodate the Slavic language; it was based on the Greek alphabet, and a version of it is still used in many Slavic countries.

After the fall of the Moravian Empire, the centre of Czech power moved westward to Bohemia, which was part of the Holy Roman Empire: Prague became a Catholic bishopric in 973. Under the Emperor Charles IV (1355–78), Prague was also capital of the Empire. In the social and religious crisis of the 14th and 15th centuries, Bohemia was aligned early on with the reformers and waged war on the conservatives. Bohemia's was the first national church to secede from the Catholic communion in what became known as the Hussite movement after the reformer Jan Hus. The key tenets of Hussitism were scriptural authority, and lay participation in worship. Following six unsuccessful crusades against the Hussites, the Catholic countries negotiated a compromise (the *Compactata*) with Bohemia in 1433.

After a period of experiment with an elective monarchy, the Czech lands became part of the Habsburg monarchy in 1526. Habsburg rule was marked by progressive centralization in Vienna, the re-imposition of Catholicism and a trend towards absolute monarchy. There was also a marked increase in the numbers of German-speaking immigrants, who were invited by the kings to work in industry, and who increasingly formed their own German enclaves, separate from the Czech majority.

An attempt to break with the Habsburgs by electing a Protestant king was defeated at the battle of White Mountain (1618) by a Catholic Habsburg army. The victory of the Counter-Reformation side was disastrous for some of the independent traditions of the Kingdom of Bohemia; non-Catholic aristocrats were persecuted, some executed and many fled and their property was confiscated and given to Austrian, Italian or Spanish military leaders. Bohemia was declared an Austrian hereditary kingdom, the German language was made equal with Czech, and only the Catholic religion was permitted. For all practical purposes the Czech state had disappeared, to re-emerge only in 1918. Czech cultural life and the notion of Czech statehood were nearly extinguished. This long period is called by the Czechs 'the time of darkness'.

The Czech national revival was made possible by the scientific, philosophical and social revolution associated with the Enlightenment of the 18th century. The Napoleonic wars, the Industrial Revolution, and increased urbanization and the rise of a middle class all fostered nationalist feelings, in which the Czech language played a decisive role. A Chair of the Czech language was established at Prague University, although the University itself remained German-speaking until the second half of the 19th century. The Czech Národní Osvobození (National Liberation) was similar to national liberation movements in other parts of the Austrian empire in the mid-19th century, but achieved few gains and did not benefit from the Austrian defeat by Prussia in 1866. The splitting of the Habsburg lands into two parts, Austria and Hungary, the 'Dual Monarchy', in 1867, in effect ended Czech hopes for an autonomous state under the Habsburgs. The Czech deputies left the Vienna Parliament and returned there only in 1879. The Vienna government did, however, make some concessions: in 1882 the university at Prague was divided into the German Ferdinand and the Czech Charles universities; the Czech language was declared equal with the German in the Civil service; the Czech Academy of Sciences and Arts was founded and the Czech National Theatre was built from private contributions (1883).

The Austro-Hungarian Empire was dissolved after World War I, but the division of successor states along ethnic lines proved an almost impossible task. The Czechs and Slovaks were put together into a common federal state, together with Subcarpathian Ruthenia, where Ukrainian was spoken. The new state, called Czechoslovakia, was established by the Treaty of Trianon in 1920. The election of the Nationalist Socialist German Workers' party in the German Parliament (1933) increased tensions in Europe and the Slav fear of a new German push eastwards. In 1938 the Treaty of Munich, signed by Germany, Great Britain, Italy and France, without the participation of Czechoslovakia, allowed Hitler to occupy the German-speaking parts of Czechoslovakia. In March 1939 the rest of the western part of the country was also absorbed into Germany: Slovakia survived only as a German puppet.

For three years after the end of the war the reconstructed Czechoslovakia survived as a democracy, with the communists doing well in free elections, reaching 38% of the vote. It then followed the standard post-World War II east-European pattern of absorption into the Soviet bloc. In 1948, 12 ministers of the coalition government resigned in protest against the appointment of several security officials; the President of the Republic filled the vacancies with appointees of the Communist party, which, with its allies, from then on held a monopoly on power. In 1968, the government, under Alexander Dubček, reformed itself: inspired by the ideal of 'socialism with a human face', it instituted a period of relative political relaxation known as 'The Prague Spring'. The USSR, however, perceived this as a threat to its interests and Czechoslovakia was invaded by Soviet, Bulgarian, Hungarian, Polish and East German troops. The communist regime survived until 1989, when public anger poured out in 'The Velvet Revolution', and the government which had lasted more than 40 years crumbled in less than two weeks, and was replaced by a movement which combined national sentiment with demands for political and economic freedom.

RELIGION ■

From the 16th to the 19th centuries the Czechs were largely Catholic. In 1918, because of its close relation with the Habsburg dynasty, the Church lost its dominant position in public life. A new national church was established, the Czechoslovak Church, on Hussite principals. Under the communist regime, all religion, however, was persecuted. With the fall of communism, religious life is re-establishing itself: according to the 1991 census, there were over 1,000,000 Roman Catholics, and 175,000 members of the Czech National Church.

LANGUAGE ■

Czech is a West Slavic language, spoken by about 10 million people. It is a phonetic language and the Roman script is used. Czech is closely related to Slovak and the two languages are mutually intelligible. The dialect of Central Bohemia was chosen as the literary standard at the end of the 19th century. Numerous local dialects of Czech survive.

POPULAR CULTURE ■

Folklore played an important role in the 19th century during the national revival of what was overwhelmingly an agricultural and peasant society. With the increasing urbanization of society, and the rise in influence of commercialized performances and the mass media, its importance has declined. In more remote parts of the country, folk culture does survive: folk-songs that have musical value are collected, recorded and published. In Bohemia and Moravia, there exist hundreds of folk museums and scores of song and dance festivals. In southwest Bohemia and southeast Moravia, folk costumes are worn, but only on special occasions, such as marriages.

The national drink in Bohemia is Pilsner beer. In southern Moravia, which is a wine producing area, it is wine. Most recipes for food are very similar to Austrian cuisine, which is in effect partly of Czech origin. Traditional food is rich in calories, with many meat dishes, typical of a hard-working village-society.

TRADE AND INDUSTRY ■

In the 19th century, about 60–70% of the industry of the Austro-Hungarian Empire was located in Bohemia. In 1918 the new Republic of Czechoslovakia had to find new markets quickly. In 1945 the process of adjustment to new conditions had to be repeated. This time, however, for only three years, as in 1949 the country became part of the USSR-controlled organization for the countries of the socialist bloc, the Council for Mutual Economic Assistance (CMEA or Comecon). Trade with the western democratic countries was severely reduced. In 1989 the Czech economy was forced to adjust yet again, this time towards a more free-market system, with a freely-convertible currency. Czech industry was more strongly-placed to recover than many of the industries of other ex-socialist countries in eastern Europe, but the economy is coming to rely heavily on tourism. According to the 1991 census, the level of unemployment had reached just over 4% of the economically-active population.

THE ARTS, ARCHITECTURE AND LITERATURE ■

Prague, with its long, if intermittent, history as a Habsburg court, was a flourishing centre of the arts in international styles from the 14th century. The Emperor Rudolph II was a famous collector of paintings. Prague was also a scientific centre; it was the home of the astronomer Tycho Brahe.

The golden age of visual arts in Prague was in the Baroque period, although many artists were foreigners and the Counter-Reformation forced a concentration on purely ecclesiastical art. Bohemia and Moravia were relatively unscathed by major European wars, so their architectural heritage is a rich one. A self-consciously Czech art began with the national revival of the 19th century. Its greatest expressions were in the music of Smetana (1824–84) and his pupil Dvořák (1841–1904): the former's patriotic opera, *The Brandenburgers in Bohemia*, which contributed to the resurgence of nationalism in 1862, and his symphonic poem, *Ma Vlast*, retain their power to evoke Czech sentiment.

The communist regime once again kept a tight control on artistic expression, and promoted the so-called 'Socialist realist' school. In literature too, political control was firmly exercised, escaping only by limited editions abroad or through clandestine distribution networks (*samizdat*).

SLOVAKS

The Slovaks inhabit the Slovak Republic, one of the newest sovereign states in Europe, which emerged in 1993 as a consequence of the splitting of the Federal Socialist Republic of Czechoslovakia; the Slovaks live in the eastern part of the former federation. It is a small state, geographically open to the south and guarded by high mountains in the north. Their political, economic and cultural history is relatively less complicated than the history of other central European tribes and nations; the land was occupied by the Hungarians early in the 11th century and Slovakia gained effective sovereignty only in the second half of the 20th century – in 1993.

The sort of role played by German threats and presence in forging Czech identity has been performed in Slovak history by the Hungarians. Hungarian rulers and settlers have influenced and, in some ways, shaped Slovak culture, but their chief role has been to provide Slovaks with a yard-stick for their self-differentiation. They are the 'other' against which Slovak identity has been self-defined.

To a lesser extent, Slovaks have formed their self-perception by differentiating themselves from their Czech neighbours, who have also tended to attract resentment as a foreign élite. So despite mutually intelligible languages and many points of common interest, the Slovaks seceded from the Czechoslovak federal state in 1993. By comparison with the experience of former Yugoslavia, this split occurred with remarkably little rancour, and co-operation, especially in sport and trade, continues.

THE LAND ■

Slovakia is a small, land-locked central-European country. The southern part of the Republic is a low-lying plain, less than 650 feet above sea level, which makes up one-quarter of Slovakia's area. The northern part is more mountainous; its highest point is Mount Gerlachovka (8710 feet). This region of Slovakia is rich in mineral resources, including iron ore, copper, lead and lignite. There are deposits of black and brown coal. Slovakia's neighbours are Poland, the Ukraine, Hungary and Austria; its longest border is with Hungary. The country has only two towns of more than 200,000 inhabitants; Bratislava, the capital, with 440,000; and Košice, with 236,000.

HISTORY ■

Before the settling of the Slovak tribes, the territory had been colonized by Celts and after that by Germans. In the 9th century, Slavic tribes, including the Slovaks, formed their first political organization, the Great Moravian Empire, encompassing Moravia, Bohemia, Slovakia, Silesia, Lusatia and Pannonia (the future Hungary). In the mid-9th century, the country was converted to Greek Orthodox Christianity by the missionaries Constantine and Methodius from Salonica. They brought with them a new alphabet, Cyrillic, replacing the Old Glagolitic Slavic alphabet. The present constitution of the Slovak Republic, in its preamble, refers both to the Cyrillic tradition and the Great Moravian Empire. Modern Slovak is, however, written using the Roman alphabet.

After a short interregnum following the fall of the empire in 903, the Slovaks were conquered by the Hungarians in 1025. The Hungarian political and economic domination lasted until 1918, apart from some brief interruptions in the 13th century when the Czech kings ruled Slovakia, and again in the 15th century when the Hussites held sway. Under the long Hungarian dominion, the position of Slovakia, called 'Upper Hungary', varied. While the Turks occupied most of Hungary, Bratislava (the present Slovak capital) became in effect the capital of Hungary: from 1541 to 1784, the kings of Hungary were crowned in Bratislava. When the Turkish threat receded, the Hungarian aristocracy returned to Buda, and Bratislava became a city inhabited mainly by German traders and Jews.

In the 19th century, the Slovak national revival began in Bratislava and the towns in the north along the river valleys of the High Tatra mountains. At that time the Slovak educated classes are estimated to have been just 700 to 1000-strong, most of them Catholic clergy. The threat of magyarization of Slovak culture was a real one, but lessened after Maria Theresa and Emperor Josef II of Austria introduced reforms and religious tolerance in the late 18th century. It increased again, however, in the 19th century as Hungarian aristocrats came to own the majority of the land: landless Slovaks emigrated in large numbers to the USA in the first years of the 20th century. By 1918, Slovakia had a Hungarian minority of over one million.

In 1918 the Czechs and Slovaks formed a common sovereign state in which Slovakia, an economically weaker partner, was promised autonomy. The new country, Czechoslovakia, had its problems with minorities in Bohemia and Moravia, and the situation was no better in Slovakia. In 1938, when the western part of Czechoslovakia was occupied by Germany following the Munich agreement, Slovakia opted for independence as a German puppet-state. After World War II, Slovakia became part of the renewed Czechoslovakia, and became part of the Soviet bloc. After the 'Velvet Revolution' in 1989, when the Communist regime was overthrown,

Slovakia remained an uneasy member of the Czechoslovak Federal State until 1993, when the Czech and Slovak lands split.

RELIGION ■

The Counter-Reformation did not have the same drastic consequences in Slovakia as it had in parts of the Habsburg empire. Some evangelical congregations survived at first, but during the following centuries the Catholic Church re-established itself in 'Upper Hungary' and became an important political force.

LANGUAGE ■

In spite of long efforts by Hungarian governments to magyarize the population, the Slovak language survived, mainly in agricultural and mountainous parts of the country. Its revival and the creation of a literary Slovak date from the 19th century. It is spoken today by about 4.5 million people. Slovak and Czech are mutually intelligible; Slovak is also closely-related to East-Polish dialects.

POPULAR CULTURE ■

The more remote villages, in particular in the south or east of the country, still preserve traditional customs. In general, the country has been more exposed to oriental cultural influence than to that of more western countries. Slovak culture was for long isolated and subject to magyarization. That it survived at all was due, in part, to the geography of the country, with narrow valleys, high mountains and its remoteness from Budapest.

Strong Hungarian influence is still visible: Slovak food and cuisine are similar, if not identical, to their Hungarian counterparts. The national drink – in a wine-producing country – is wine.

Genuine folklore survives largely in the east of the country. Expensively-embroidered costumes, often passed down for generations, are one feature. Another important area is music: large numbers of traditional folksongs were collected by musicians such as Bartók and Kodály. Some surviving customs are of pagan origin, such as the burning of Morena, the goddess of winter, on bonfires in summer.

ECONOMY AND SOCIETY ■

Before World War I, Slovakia (then the Province of Upper Hungary) was not heavily industrialized; trade and industry were mostly in non-Slovak hands. Under the Czechoslovak Republic, the situation changed slowly, partly through the lack of trained personnel, and partly because of the alleged exploitation of the country by the Czechs. After 1945, Slovakia began to industrialize rapidly, and by 1989 the level of industrial production was higher than that in the Czech Republic. Now Slovakia faces the same problems as other post-communist countries; the search for new markets and the need to ensure production is competitive in the free market countries which have replaced its former socialist trading partners from the CMEA (Council for Mutual Economic Assistance). Slovaks have traditionally worked mainly in agriculture or forestry. The situation changed in 1918, and especially after 1945, when the introduction of heavy industry created a powerful industrial working class. In 1991, 11% of the workforce was engaged in agriculture and 32% in industry.

LAW AND POLITICS ■

Before 1918, Hungarian law applied; it differed from Austrian law principally in matters of agriculture and inheritance. After 1918, Czechoslovak law was introduced; after Slovakia gained limited autonomy, some peculiarly Slovak laws were introduced. According to Article 1 of the current Slovak Constitution of 1992, the Slovak Republic is a democratic and sovereign state ruled by law. It is bound neither to an ideology, nor to a religion. The Constitution is an unusual document as it contains provisions on protective rights for citizens that are usually not included in the basic law of western countries.

ARTS ■

Arts flourished in the early Gothic period, in particular in eastern Slovakia, where Gothic art was brought by German settlers. Most artists were foreigners, working for the Hungarian aristocracy, until the rise of a Slovak artistic identity in the second part of the 19th century and after 1918. During the socialist period from 1948 to 1989, the arts were subject to political control.

MAGYARS

The paradox of the Magyars is that as late arrivals on the European scene, who still speak an Asiatic language, they cast themselves as defenders of European civilization against Turkish defenders. They have constituted something of a cultural vanguard as early contributors to some of Europe's major common historic experiences, including the Renaissance, Romanticism, industrialization and democracy.

HISTORY ■

The kingdom created by the ethnic Hungarians (Magyars) was set up over the century following their arrival (c.896) in the central Danube basin. After defeat by the Emperor Otto in 955 had dissuaded them from murderous nomadic thrusts against their neighbours, a series of conscious efforts created a European-style kingdom. They became Christian in the early 10th century under King Stephen I. The Habsburgs long wished to incorporate Hungary and ultimately got their way when the Turks destroyed the united Hungarian state in 1526 and opened the way for Austrian

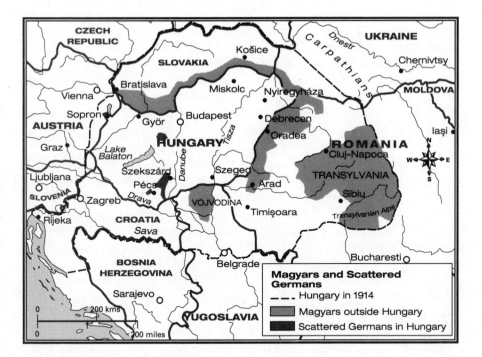

Map legend:
Magyars and Scattered Germans
_ _ . Hungary in 1914
Magyars outside Hungary
Scattered Germans in Hungary

control of the Magyar north and west.

Turkish-controlled Hungary consisted not only of the devastated four *pashaliks* of the centre: there was also the puppet state of Transylvania keeping the idea of Hungarian independence alive; its tradition of practical religious toleration was offensive to the Habsburgs. When thorough-going Austrian reconquest became feasible after a Turkish military debacle in 1683, the Hungarian nobility, used to exercising great authority, faced possible extinction as a force in politics.

The conquerors, moreover, were able to undertake a huge programme of ethnic rebuilding. Until 1526, Magyar ethnic domination had been complete. Especially imported Germans in Polish and Wallachian border areas and in the towns had posed no authority or security problems. Nor was the nobility ethnically exclusive: many non-Magyars within it were willing to learn Magyar and feel a fellow-feeling with Magyar nobles as an order. With the Turks expelled (1699), though Hungary remained a separate kingdom, substantial strips along its borders were put under direct military rule from Vienna and settled with large contingents of Germans, Serbs and Romanians.

The greatest issue was whether the Hungarian nobility could preserve their parliament and county governments or whether, like other Habsburg lands, theirs would be reduced to the level of a province. The reign of Josef II (1780–90) was decisive: his all-out attempt to finish off Hungarian particularism backfired, linked as it was to open germanization of language and administration. Religious toleration only emboldened the toughest Hungarian group – the Calvinist nobility. From a relatively weak, yet clearly indestructible, position, the Magyars began a counter-attack against the Habsburgs.

By 1847, Liberals had won majorities in the legislature from the noble electorate, having secured the substitution of Magyar for Latin as the official national language along the way. Though the nationalist and republican revolutions of 1848–9 were crushed with Russian aid, the Habsburgs were unable to hold their ground. The Compromise of 1867 set up a truly 'dual' monarchy, in which Hungary's own parliament had fiscal responsibility.

In 1828, Magyars made up a mere 38% of the Hungarian population. By 1910 the figure had reached more than 50%. Between 1869 and 1910 those living from industry rose from 12 to 26%. In 1914, Budapest, along with Belfast, was the fastest-growing city in Europe. Political success, magyarization, a higher birthrate and lower emigration rate than their ethnic rivals and co-citizens – all had played into Magyar nationalist hands. Partnership with an increasingly less powerful Austria had proved strengthening for Hungary. The clearest symbol of Magyar achievement during the millennium celebrations of 1896 was the new electric underground railway – the first in continental Europe: soon after, equipment was supplied for the London underground.

World War I demolished Austria-Hungary. By the Treaty of Trianon (1920), Hungary became a virtually ethnically homogeneous state held together by a burning siege mentality. It lost large tracts of territory to Romania and to what was to become Yugoslavia. Even with almost a third of its people living off trade and industry, it depended on agricultural export markets. Depression in 1930–33 knocked the country sideways. Fascist-style politics flourished. Nazi pressure mounted and western links became attenuated. Again on the losing side in World War II, Hungary got no lasting gain from territorial adjustments set in place by the Axis. Occupation by the Red Army in peacetime offered scant hope for the fledgling democracy set up under western auspices. By 1948, the communists were in power. In 1956 the population – hundreds of thousands of ex-communists included, was in revolt. Although, as in 1848–9, the revolution failed, its effects brought a lighter hand from the government and the gradual growth of a sort of Hungarian national conspiracy between much of the Party and most of the people to wriggle through to freedom. When in 1989 the Communist Party effectively decided on suicide there was precious little to kill. As Russia itself seemed to be on a similar track, nothing stood in the way of the present relatively sophisticated liberal democracy. For the first time in virtually 500 years, the Magyars were out from under foreign heels.

Curtailment of the Hungarian state has left Magyar communities raggedly scattered in all the neighbouring states. Some of them, especially in Romania, are far from the Hungarian border, deep in Transylvania where they were formerly known as Szekels and treated under the Hungarian crown as a separate community. The remotest of such communities, the Csangos of Wallachia, occupied a string of villages in the central area of this forest province until World War II. They are Magyar-speaking (or formerly Magyar-speaking) Roman Catholics who originated from occupation groups in the Middle Ages as carters and traffickers between Hungarian territories of Romanian principalities.

LANGUAGE ■

Claims that today's Magyars are an Asiatic people do not hold up. That said, their language is the genuine Asian article. The invading tribes were undoubtedly from Asia, as were various predecessors and successors in the Danubian basin – the Huns, Avars, Pechenegs, and even the Cumans brought in as late as the 13th century to strengthen royal power. Yet the various Germanic, Slavonic, Illyrian and Romanian groups they initially subjected and absorbed, together with the numerous immigrants magyarized over the centuries, were nothing of the kind. There were influences from neighbouring tongues: Slavonic vocabulary might dominate in one sphere (e.g. agriculture), Germanic in another, and Turkish in yet another. But long before Magyar became the official language of the state in 1844 it was clear that its vast body of speakers possessed an instrument for national consolidation far more potent than the Latin it displaced. The illiteracy of the masses was an ally. Latin could only be spread by means beyond their ability. Magyar could be drummed into the non-Magyars by persistent world of mouth.

POLITICS ■

The Magyar nobility created what many would regard as the most distinct Magyar cultural feature – the political tradition. King Stephen (997–1038) created county units the better to govern. In the Middle Ages, the emergence of a Diet representing the whole (and large) nobility (subsequently divided into two Houses) meant there was a central force to combat crown power. Habsburg and Transylvanian Hungary, however imperfectly, operated constitutionally after 1526 and constitutionalism was never destroyed. The Regency government of Admiral Horthy between the World Wars preserved parliament as it had developed under Dualism (with a wider franchise), in the face of huge pressures. Only Stalin finally crushed the democratic parliament in 1945–8. Well before the actual collapse of Communism democratic political parties had re-emerged in Hungary. The choice of constitution was swiftly made and large parties on the British and German model immediately dominated the scene: one Conservative (the Hungarian Democratic Forum) and two Liberal parties appeared – with smaller groups of Christians, Smallholders and Socialists on the fringes. A Conservative-Christian-Smallholder coalition won the first free elections in 1990.

SECULAR CULTURE ■

Hungarian secular culture developed in two waves: in the 1830s Hungary produced great political and philosophical writers like Széchényi ('The Greatest Hungarian'), Eötvös and Kemény, a journalist and statesman in Kossuth, poets and playwrights such as Petőfi, Vörösmar and Arany. The second wave, in the 20 years before 1914,

257

was far broader and far larger. A truly distinguished part of late 19th and 20th century European culture, it contained substantial truly original elements. Bartók and Kodály were the products of long hard work in the music school launched by Liszt as early as 1865. The social scientists too represented a great advance on their predecessors among the intellectual aristocrats. Endre Ady and after him Jószef, along with Babits and Kosztolányi, put Hungarian writing fully on the European, indeed the world map.

POLITICAL CULTURE ■

The establishment of secular marriage in 1894 and the ever more forceful growth of an open-minded debate on almost all fronts were key signs of a continuing basic liberalism built on the assumptions of a liberal magyarization respectful to private property.

World War I, defeat, truncation, Communist revolution (albeit ephemeral), 'White' counter-revolution, and the subsequent kingdom under Regent Horthy would have ripped less powerful cultures totally apart. The new state was more influenced by Budapest's values than the old. But in the provinces, uncompromising nationalism survived, reinforced by the arrival of social élites who had been displaced from the lands Hungary had lost – élites full of new-found bitterness and intensified hate.

RELIGION ■

Despite its Catholic majority, Hungary has a hard-working, Protestant, mentality. The Reformation and Counter-Reformation left west Hungary with a Catholic majority among Magyars and east Hungary with a Protestant equivalent. The Treaty of Trianon did not seriously change that pattern, nor the religious balance overall. Many Catholics were 'Protestantized'; and many Jews converted to Catholicism, Lutheranism or Calvinism. The loss of lands after Trianon meant Lutherans were severely reduced in numbers, though not in influence. Their élitist tendency has persisted to this day and their most important school produced the country's most influential scientists. The Unitarians passed in 1920 to Romania and an intellectually vigorous community was lost to the Hungarian state.

Already by the 1930s the churches had proved little defence against totalitarian trends. Extreme nationalism, the psychological trauma of the Treaty of Trianon, virulent anti-Communism and a highly developed anti-semitism all shaped behaviour from 1930 to 1945. From 1948 to 1989, the churches were undermined by the necessity of living with the communist regime. Not that numerous priests and pastors did not resist the communists (Cardinal Mindszenty not least), but the regime's enforced conformity struck a chord with Catholics, pledged to obedience in a religiously authoritarian body. The mood of moral despair was summed up by the writer Jószef who asserted: 'I have no father, nor mother, I have no god, nor country'.

Yet it was the faithful who led the way in so much of the revival of effective liberal democratic politics. The Calvinist and Lutheran gymnasia in Budapest were the first independent schools to re-open their doors and begin the recreation of a democratic political class. In the first parliamentary by-election to take place under the dying Communist system, it was the Lutheran minister from Gödolo who won the seat for a fledgling Hungarian Democratic Forum.

Within the capital declared Jews outnumbered Protestants by 60% in 1900, and were some 23% of the total population. By 1941 that had dropped to under 16% – an index of prudent conversion and flight; in 1949 to between 6 and 7% – a result of holocaust. Anti-semitic 'Country' interests strong in the towns (above all the gentry-based bureaucracy and officer corps) were well able to attack their ideological opponents – Non-Jewish and Jewish – rousing nationalist socialist-tending workers and the unemployed through the 'Politics of Envy'. To this very day, when the Hungarian role in World War II is being debated more thoroughly than ever before, the anti-semitism of this 'Country' tradition remains influential in political life.

POPULAR CULTURE ■

From Hungarian music emerged a genre now regarded quintessentially Austro-Hungarian, but drawing on Magyar folk music and dances generously on the way. That something was the operetta. The development was initially Viennese, with Johann Strauss in the van. Budapest was nonetheless never backward in furthering the cause of this 'csárdas-valse' cult and incorporating it into theatre. The works of Lehár show it at its most developed. The csárdan craze did much for the popularity of folk music.

What Liszt so erroneously termed gypsy music was nothing of the sort, yet the main interpreters of Magyar folk music to the old upper classes and current upper and middle strata of Hungarian society have long been the gypsy orchestras. Their members were usually the more successful types, whose skill at orchestral adaptation (often on the spot) have long (and deservedly) brought them fame. The 'Country and Eastern' business retains a substantial following among those interested in Magyar folk music and stories.

National dress occupies a unique position in the Hungarian tradition. All social groups had their particular variety, but, as with the language, the upper nobility at least had dropped it before its value as a visual nationalist aid became apparent. The revival began at the very centre of Habsburg power, the court of Maria Theresa, set off by György Bessenyei, one of her famous Hungarian bodyguard. The movement brought solidarity to the Magyar community. It reached its height during the Dual Monarchy and the Horthy regime, much reinforced by formidable folk music and dance developments. Urban growth and industrialization, which accelerated after 1945 and deepened in the wake of 1956, took the edge off the popularity of costumes. The educated classes tend to think and feel like the interwar Czechs, who considered their national identity had no need of dress symbols any more than that of the English. The restored democracy officially takes a more traditional line.

SCATTERED GERMANS

*Numerous German groups existed until the end of World War II in
parts of east-central, eastern and southeast Europe. Some became detached from
the German State, as a result of the Treaty of Versailles, and found themselves in
the new Polish Republic. Others were detached from the former Tsarist Russia in
what became the Baltic States, where, indeed, one group of Germans was known as
the Balts – numerous and important in the élites of Estonia and of some parts of
Latvia and Lithuania. The so-called Volga Germans of south Russia were
descended from migrants encouraged by Catherine the Great (1762–96): they had
never enjoyed the protection of German rule, in any sense, since that time; but now
the unease of their isolation was greater than ever.*

*A further segment of the German diaspora was left high and dry by the collapse
of Austria-Hungary, principally the Sudeten German group in Bohemia, Moravia
and Czech Silesia. Germans made up fully 30% of the population of those three
areas. There were similar but smaller groups in the northern part of what became
Yugoslavia, and a few in what had been Austrian Poland.*

HUNGARIAN AND ROMANIAN GERMANS ■

Of greatest long-term durability were the dispersed German groups of parts of Hungary. The Hungarian state was cut down by almost 70% in the Treaty of Trianon.
Part of the effect was to transfer to Czechoslovak jurisdiction the Germans of Slovakia, who had been prominent in mining since the 18th century and had played a
major role in industrialization in the 19th. The most important of Hungary's Germans, however, were those of Transylvania – Lutheran Saxons by ancestry, who, protected from the effects of the Counter-Reformation, had never been forced back to
Catholicism. They numbered between three and four hundred thousand. Transferred to Romanian sovereignty in 1918–19 they constituted a very exposed group,
along with their Hungarian neighbours, under a potentially hostile regime. Other
Germans were transferred from Hungary in the Banat, an area of the southern part
of the old Kingdom of Hungary, which was divided between the new Yugoslavia and
Romania; others still were to be found in small quantities spread through Croatia
and Slovenia.

The Angst induced by isolation stimulated nationalism among all these groups.
Under the impact of the depression, which was severely felt all over eastern Europe,
they responded favourably, on the whole, to the rise of Nazism in Germany. They
sympathized actively with German initiatives for the acquisition or recuperation of
territory and influence in the region. In World War II they greeted German armies
as liberators and supplied huge numbers of volunteers – especially for S.S. regiments, since they were considered reliable upholders of German race theory and

imperial supremacy. Not surprisingly, this role, in which some of them seemed to revel, outraged nationalists and communists in their host communities. The upshot of German defeat was the expulsion or extermination of many of these German minorities. In Russia and areas absorbed back into the Soviet Union – in the Baltic states, Bessarabia and the Bukhovina – elimination was almost total and in Poland, though the authorities were more selective, the Germans' plight was severe. In Yugoslavia the adult males were usually killed and the women and children expelled. From Czechoslovakia the Germans were almost totally cleared, except for those of exemplary behaviour.

In Hungary and Romania, however, Germans were not eliminated. The post-war pattern of German dispersal was therefore much simplified, with the former scattering reduced to two main groups of survivors. Among the half million-strong German minority in Hungary, however, the tendency to assimilate was keen. They had been divided in their attitudes to the Nazis: urban communities had been warmer than rural ones, while overall the German population had been split about 50–50 in its sympathies. Flight ahead of the Red Army was therefore mainly from large and middling towns, where the Germans' cohesion had been greatest and their cultural centres had been located.

In Romania, the German minority had always been extremely compact inside Transylvania and was preserved almost entire, except for individuals compromised by their commitment to the Nazi cause. They remained at over 300,000 in 1950. Owing, however, to the burgeoning prosperity of the economy of the German Federal Republic in the 1960s and 1970s, many attempted to leave and reclaim a stake in their ancestral homeland. Sometimes emigration was obstructed because of their usefulness to Romania's labour force: people were usually released without question only at 80 years of age, when Romania could benefit from transferring the cost of care and burial. Gradually, however, as conditions were relaxed, more advantage was taken of opportunities to leave so that now the remaining Germans are computed at only about 25,000. It seems likely that soon the 650-year sojourn of Germans in Transylvania will come to an end.

ROMANIANS

Controversy has always surrounded the history of the Romanians. Two rival theories long obtained about their origins: first the theory that when the Roman occupation of Dacia ended, some of the population fell south into Moesia and gradually returned across the Danube later, from the 5th century onwards, after they had experienced protracted Romanization, into the Banat and Transylvania. The rival view, favoured by Romanian historians, is that the Romanians are descended from natives of Dacia who retreated into the Banat and the

Transylvanian mountains after the Romans left, gradually emerging into the plains of Wallachia and Moldavia and parts of Bessarabia. In fact something between the two theories is likely to have been the case.

HISTORY ■

Prior to any Roman occupation there was a powerful kingdom among the people known to the Romans as the Getae and later as the Dacians, adjoining the Roman provinces of Pannonia and Moesia, and occupying what are now Transylvania, a portion of eastern Hungary and the Banat, with an area then called Altenia – roughly the western third of what is now Wallachia. In AD 106 the emperor Trajan decided to annex Dacia in the interests of frontier security. It remained Roman only until the last third of the 3rd century AD. The subsequent differences of opinion about Romanian origins emerged from a protracted dark ages, lasting for centuries thereafter, when the sources are few.

Roman occupation certainly left a rustic form of Latin in the vacated areas. This romance tongue eventually became the hallmark of the Romanians – distinguishing them from their neighbours on all sides. The means by which it survived and was transmitted are, however, unclear. When first recorded in the Middle Ages, 60% of its vocabulary was borrowed from Slavonic languages, or from Greek and Albanian. Turkish terms were later to be added as a result of Turkish occupation. Romanian therefore, while of Latin origins in grammar and accidence, was full of the influence of other languages. Since 60% of Transylvanian place names are of Slav origins, it cannot be true that romance-speaking Dacians continued to dominate throughout the area in the late antique and medieval periods.

It is certain, however, that a people known as the Vlachs emerged into history from Carpathian mountain fastnesses in the 12th century and contributed to the formation of states which became distinguishable in the future Romania in the later Middle Ages; they are commonly described, plausibly but unprovably, as the descendants of Dacians or Getae. Something of their speech and life can be sensed, perhaps, from those of surviving communities of shepherds and hill farmers – today about half a million strong, who, known as Vlachs, Arumans or Armini, retain a romance tongue sometimes classified as Macedo-Romanian in their homes in southern Macedonia and northern Greece (see pp. 215, 222). The romance culture of the medieval Vlachs, on the other hand, may have been owed to – or reinforced by – migrants from Moesia.

After the foundation of a Magyar state in the late 9th century, Hungarians dominated most of what is now Romania. In the early 14th century, an effectively independent Romanian chieftainship – a state in which a romance-speaking élite predominated – can be identified, centred in what is now Moldavia. Around the middle of the century, Wallachia followed suit, taking its name from the Vlachs. These two principalities can be said to have foreshadowed the future Romanian state, together forming what Romanians came to call the *Regat*, or Romanian kingdom.

Romanians and Moldavians

The principality of Moldavia included the whole of Bessarabia and the Bukhovina. It was more extensive but less prosperous than Wallachia. In both Orthodox Christianity prevailed, with – in the late Middle Ages – the Old Church Slavonic rite.

Romanian political success – sustaining the autonomy of their principalities rather than exercising full sovereign independence – depended on playing off Hungarians and Turks. Mircea the Great of Moldavia (d. 1418) recommended to his heirs a rapprochement with the Turks, as did Stephen the Great of Wallachia (d. 1504). An unmistakable national identity had by now emerged, at least among the literate and warrior élites who, distantly influenced by the Renaissance, actually called themselves 'Romans'. But as neighbouring Christian states were conquered – most of Hungary succumbing in 1526 – Romania fell by degrees under Turkish influence.

Despite some spectacular resistance, the succession could hardly ever be secured without Turkish approval or intervention and the general trend of the next two centuries was towards ever closer Turkish control.

In the 18th century, however, this trend was reversed, partly by external events – the liberation of Hungary towards the end of the 17th century and the rise of Russian power under Peter the Great – and partly by the development of highland villages, sustained by maize cultivation outside the effective range of Turkish control. From 1709 the Turks, impatient of the native viceroys, installed loyal Greek overlords from Constantinople to manage the country. So began the notorious 'Phanariot' regimes, which, though regarded as oppressive and exploitative by native Wallachians and Moldavians, lasted unsteadily until the 1820s.

Uncharacteristically, Russia appeared in these provinces in the guise of a liberator, seizing Bessarabia from Turkish control in 1812, and – unable to secure the territories herself – encouraging native resistance movements in the Romanian principalities. The rulers or 'hospodars' who replaced the Phanariots were under Russian patronage. Society was divided between rulers and ruled: the only middle class consisted of foreign merchants – Greeks, Armenians and Jews; but the beginnings of modest prosperity came with the development of grain exports, carried down the Danube and thence, after the Anglo-Turkish Treaty of 1832, on British ships.

By 1848 liberal ideas had penetrated enough to make Romania share in the revolutions which then broke out in many parts of Europe. The nationalist element in the uprising came not from within the Romanian principalities themselves but from Transylvania, the Hungarian part of Romania, where it began among Uniates who wished to assert their identity against Magyar oppression or indifference. Today, despite the strong links between orthodoxy and Romanian nationalism, Transylvania remains the stronghold of Romanian Uniates, who represent about 40% of the Romanian population of that province.

An independent Romania state was an attractive prospect to Britain and France because it would be a useful buffer between Russia, Austria and Turkey and between Russia and the Dardanelles. In the aftermath of the Crimean War, the powers imposed a compromise solution: two autonomous principalities were to have native rulers under nominal Turkish overlordship. The notables of Moldavia and Wallachia foiled this device by both electing the same prince; a native royal family soon proved impractical in the midst of a jealous and quarrelsome noble class and in 1866 a prince of Hohenzollern-Sigmaringen became King Carol I.

By 1914 Romania was the third-largest grain-producer in Europe and most of its exports went to Britain. Yet most investment in railways and in the important oil industry was German; banks were German or Austrian and were often controlled by Jews who had become the economic colonists of the country: 2000 strong in 1800 they had risen to 200,000 by the time of independence. With the native Romanians, these newcomers traded contempt for hatred. It was a German saying that whereas a Wallachian let his hair grow, a Moldavian never cut it. Peasant uprisings in the 1880s and, most severely, in 1907, demonstrated the power of rage against foreign and bourgeois intruders.

The gains were huge from Romania's participation against Germany and Austria-Hungary in the Great War: the whole of Transylvania and a large slice of the Banat were seized from Hungary; and from Russia, Bessarabia was regained. Southern Dobruja – gained earlier from Bulgaria in the Balkan wars – could be safely retained.

Land reform in this 'Great Romania' at last gave the peasantry something to live off. It inhibited efficiency but the peasants were now immunized against Marxism. They were more likely now to be attracted by fascism. Destruction of the landed estates had ruined the old conservative party: the most promising initiatives on the right came from nationalist politicians who had grown up in a Romanian minority under Hungarian rule. Their coalition with peasants in the 'National Peasant Party' was riven with cultural and personal conflicts.

Democratic politics never took hold in the Regat and were impossible in backward Bessarabia, which, seized in tatters from Tsarist and Bolshevik hands, fitted uncomfortably into the union to which it now belonged, like Ireland at the time or East Germany today.

Some of Romania's wealth had been used to educate an upwardly mobile administrative and professorial class for whom nationalism was an alternative to ideology and whose well-intentioned enthusiasm for their own power made them potential servants or masters of totalitarian regimes. The nationalism, for example, of Mircea Eliade, who became one of the world's leading historians of religion, was a sort of homeopathic Bolshevism, harnessing an idealistic social cause for a chauvinistic programme of social revolution within the Romanian nation, reducing an international creed to a national level. This harmonized well with the fashion for fascism.

The depressed economic circumstances of the early 1930s bred popular fascism, which the monarchy tried to control. The infant King Michael's reign from 1927 to 1930 was the first of three accessions he went through – and he may yet manage a fourth if time is on his side. In 1930 his father, Prince Carol, returned from self-imposed exile to reclaim the throne in a country which seemed a happy hunting ground for his unscrupulous ambitions. His experiments in installing dictators whom he could manipulate were unsuccessful: the salon fascism of his professor-nominees lacked the popular appeal of the demagogic fascism of the Iron Guard, modelled on Italian and German examples. In the Iron Guard, King Carol saw the rawest side of Balkan life revealed before him. He struck at it and for a few years contained it by royal dictatorship, thanks to the loyalty of the army officer corps and many civilian politicians. By aborting the elections of 1938 he prevented an Iron Guard victory.

His foreign policy was to appear as all things to all sides. His visit to Britain in 1938 convinced him, however, of the hopeless state of British preparations for war. In the spring of 1939 a pro-German policy alone seemed viable; Romania paid for her lack of commitment to the German cause by the severance of her former gains, with Bessarabia, the Bukhovina, much of Transylvania and the Southern Dobruja redistributed among her neighbours. Greater Romania was now less great. Carol resumed his exile and left the young King Michael as the virtual prisoner of a Nazi-backed dictatorship. To join Germany's war against Russia in 1941 was unavoidable; in the short term, Romania was rewarded with a slice of the Ukraine, dramatically re-named Transnistria, as well as recovering the Bukhovina and Bessarabia.

Defeat for the Germans was catastrophe for the Romanians, with a further round of excisions of territory to the advantage of the Soviet Union. For a moment in 1945–6, Michael's commitment to democracy boded well, but the invading Red Army imposed a tight communist regime on a fiercely anti-communist country which had barely had a Communist Party before. This rapidly revolving history of triumph and humiliation, expansion and dismemberment, left a fierce nationalist legacy. Since then, the damage done by a communist regime to a naturally prosperous country has inflicted starvation on a once-great granary of Europe and poverty on an oil-rich land.

The most awkward legacy of the period of territorial exchanges is perhaps the status of what is now called Moldova. Under Soviet rule, Bessarabia was divided into two parts: the northern part became a Soviet 'People's Republic of Moldavia', while the southern part, between the Dnestr and Danube deltas, was given to Ukraine, where it still remains. The collapse of Communism in the former Soviet Union in 1991 preceded its demise in Romania; Moldavians prudently opted for full independence within the Commonwealth of Independent States rather than re-joining a Romanian state with an uncertain future. Moldova, as the new state is called, has a large Ukrainian minority, which would be a further embarrassment in Romania's ethnic patchwork in the event of re-union; but the Romanian minority cannot yet be said to have evolved a separate identity and, given the traditional strength of Romanian nationalism, reunification is the most likely prospect. The neighbouring states of Russia and the Ukraine have been wary of it. The Romanian government has suspended calls for re-union but frontier controls between Moldova and Romania are deliberately slack.

CULTURE ■

The Romanian tradition is of Orthodox Christianity, led, from the early modern period, when Greek liturgy replaced Old Church Slavonic, by Greek inspiration: it slightly displaced but never completely eradicated the hag-ridden, demon-filled mental world of the peasants, of which the Dracula myth is only the most conspicuous example. Not until 1864 was the Greek Orthodox Church deprived of land-holdings which amounted to a third of the surface of the Regat. Only in 1893 was official funding supplied. The interim period was disastrous for the educational standards of the clergy, who lived as peasants. The secular élite, influenced by French values, with a sophisticated attitude to religion that derived from the Enlightenment, formed only feeble ties with the church.

Romanian culture bears the marks of the country's heritage as a borderland. The ethnographic museum of Bucharest displays traditional houses, mostly of the 18th century, from different parts of the country, on which family names are written in at least three alphabets – Cyrillic, Greek and Roman. On the revolutionaries' flag in 1848, the phrase 'Liberty, Equality, Fraternity' was signified by Cyrillic characters. Through the Slavonic liturgy of the Church, through Russian influence and even – in some small measure – through Bulgarian influence – Romanian had come to be expressed mainly in this alphabet. Only after 1848 did Roman letters gain ground: this was a sure sign of a re-emerging Romanian identity. The use of the Roman alphabet increasingly became part of being Romanian. Huge doses of French and Italian culture began to be swallowed. Widespread illiteracy – as high as 81% in 1899 – eased the task of imposing Romanization.

Imported French books supplied the upper and middle ranges of taste until well into the 20th century. Despite the unique ferocity of Romanian nationalism, the French language was preferred as a means of daily communication by the educated even in the inter-war period. Pronunciation of Romanian could not be warped in a French direction, but Italian, and specifically Tuscan, influence was promoted by official education and broadcasting. The 'standard' intonation was markedly different from that traditional to any of the various dialects. Listening to Romanian radio in the 1930s, one might think oneself in Italy, whereas in northern Romania the speech of the peasants might, at a distance, convey an equal conviction that one was in Poland.

Romanians called in the cultural power of France to bolster their own distinction from the Slavs, Germans and Hungarians who surrounded them. Rather like the Montenegrins who proclaimed, 'With the Russians we are sixty million', so the Romanians seemed to say, 'With the French intellectuals we lead Europe'. The prolonged French influence eventually produced art and literature in which Romanian national consciousness was fulfilled. The 1920s were a decade of breakthrough. The short stories of Marcu Beza associated the Vlachs of Macedonia in an appeal to pan-Romanian sentiment; the novels of Duiliu Zamfirescu, Liviu Rebreanu and the poems of Ion Pillat represented an assertive search for distinctly Romanian themes in town and village life. Romania moved into high culture convincingly, though initially by imitation.

RUTHENIANS

The variety of names for the Ruthenians – Rusyns, Carpatho-Rusyns, Rusnaks – already signifies a problem. The word 'Ruthenian' has a long tradition of denoting the lands of Rus that now form modern Ukraine and Belarus and of the written language employed in the Grand Duchy of Lithuania. In both senses it therefore stands in contrast to 'Russian'. It was also used in 19th-century Austria, although

*not consistently, to refer to Ukrainians. In more modern usage it is used with
reference to the East Slavonic people who live in the Carpathian mountains and
foothills. Once again the term is used alongside 'Ukrainian'; to some the two words
are interchangeable, to others they are mutually exclusive.*

HISTORY AND TRADITION ■

There has never been a specifically Ruthenian state. In theory at least there are over
one million Ruthenians living in several different countries: in one region of Ukraine
(the Transcarpathian province centred on Uzhorod the capital) – 977,000; in Slovakia (the region of Prěsov) – 130,000; in Poland (scattered over the whole country) –
60,000; in northeastern Romania – 1000, according to the 1977 census; Vojvodina
(Serbia) – 30,000; and small communities in Croatia and Bosnia.

The reality is clouded by political considerations. Ukraine does not recognize the
existence of Ruthenian nationality at all. The Czechoslovak census returns of 1991
gave a total of 17,000 living in Slovakia; the same census also showed 14,000
Ukrainians there. Official figures for Vojvodina published in the same year show
21,000. In Poland, the position is made more complicated by the Lemko issue (see
below). The question of who exactly is a Ruthenian is therefore a complicated one.

Ruthenians are in the main Greek Catholics (Uniates); the origin of the problem
is to be sought in those areas of Poland that were populated by eastern Slavs who
were incorporated into the Austro-Hungarian state at the end of the 18th century,
and more specifically into the Hungarian Kingdom after 1848. The Hungarian
authorities were keen that their eastern Slavs should develop a national consciousness separate from the Galician Ukrainians in Austria. Attempts were made in that
direction but with little success; the people simply did not have the necessary intellectual leadership.

Even so, by 1918 the governments of the new states of Hungary and Czechoslovakia deemed it necessary to court the Ruthenian population. The areas they
inhabited were eventually incorporated into Czechoslovakia in a region called
Podkarpatská Rus, which in 1938 was granted full autonomy. It is this area that
eventually came to form part of Soviet Ukraine as the Subcarpathian Region. In the
referendum on Ukrainian independence held on 1st December 1991, 78% of the
population of this region voted for autonomy. The Ukrainian government's refusal to
grant autonomy has led to the setting up of a Ruthenian 'government-in-exile' in Slovakia with representation in Moscow. The Ukrainian authorities appear to regard the
whole affair as pure invention aimed at destabilizing the country and possibly at restoring the eastern frontier of 1938. Only in Vojvodina in the former Yugoslavia has
there been any clear success in establishing a Ruthenian (or Rusyn) identity among
the descendants of farmers who immigrated to the area from the Carpathians in the
second half of the last century. There is also a strong sense of Ruthenian identity
among immigrants in the United States.

One of the factors that has hindered the crystallization of a true national feeling among Ruthenians has been the absence of a unifying literary language. In general they spoke an Eastern Slav dialect influenced by the major language surrounding them. There were moves towards creating a press, national theatre and educational system in Czechoslovakia before the war. Attempts were also made there to use Russian as a means of written communication. After the war, the tendency to use the majority language for cultural purposes has quickened in pace. The one exception is Vojvodina, where a standard form has been developed for use in the press and on the radio; there is also a department of Ruthenian language at the University of Novi Sad.

HUTSULS, BOIKOS AND LEMKOS ■

The Ruthenians themselves comprise several distinct local groups. In the eastern Carpathians live the Hutsuls, a proud mountain people descended from a mixture of shepherds and outlaws (the name is supposed to come from a Romanian word meaning 'brigand'). They represent themselves as the descendants of indomitable Polish aristocrats of the late Middle Ages and early modern period, whose exile to the kingdom's only mountains is seen as proof of uncompromising integrity. They are particularly renowned for their wood-carving and embroidery: the women's distinctive aprons take up to 10 years to make and are treasured heirlooms. West of the Hutsuls, in the lower ranges of the Carpathians, live the Boikos, who probably came into the area from Galicia and Bukhovina. There may be irony in the fact that a major ethnographical study of the Boikos was published in America – in Ukrainian.

Further west still are the Lemkos of Poland. In the 1930s the Polish government was faced with open armed rebellion in its predominantly Ukrainian areas; they sought to solve it by a policy of 'divide and rule' aimed at fostering a sense among the Lemkos that they were quite distinct from the Ukrainians of Galicia, then in eastern Poland. After 1945, the Lemkos remaining within the new Polish borders were deliberately scattered throughout the country. Since 1956 there has been a cultural and educational association for the Ukrainians of Poland, but by no means all Lemkos regard themselves as Ukrainians. Perhaps the independence of a Ukrainian state may prove the catalyst needed to weld together the Ruthenians outside Ukraine.

8
THE NORTHERN PLAIN

Lowlands line the seaboard of continental Europe, along the Atlantic, the English Channel, the North Sea and the Baltic from the Loire to the Volkhov. Between the Artois hills and the Latvian uplands the great plain is hardly disturbed by more than ripples in the landscape. This gigantic arc is bounded on the south by uplands which stretch, with few interruptions except those carved by river valleys, from the Ardennes to the highlands of central Russia. This is one of the world's great avenues of human contact, scored by navigable rivers around which industrious communities have taken shape: the Rhine, Weser, Elbe, Oder, Vistula, Neman and Dvina. Some highly-concentrated industrial zones are located here and the area as a whole is fertile farmland, in which no one crop predominates over a large area but in which many are closely mingled. Especially in the western and central parts of the region, this environment has favoured dense concentrations of population and – until the unification of Germany in the 19th century – relatively small states.

The history of most of the region since the Mongol invasions of the 13th century can be divided into three broad phases. First, in the late Middle Ages, was a period dominated by eastward German expansion, leading to the formation of a relatively large 'Prussian' state, German by culture and control, and to the establishment of German colonies. Then, from the 15th to the 18th centuries, the eastern half of the region was dominated by a big Polish-Lithuanian state. Finally, renewed German expansion from the west coupled with Russian expansion from the east progressively consumed Poland and smothered smaller communities, a phase that has lasted more or less until the late 20th century. Though the collapse of the German and Russian empires in 1917–19 allowed a breathing space to suppressed historic identities, the super-states were soon rebuilt with new political institutions. The grip of Berlin failed definitively with the outcome of the World War II, that of Moscow only with the collapse of the Soviet Union in 1991.

SAXONS

The Saxons can claim to be perhaps the first of the Germanic tribes to have settled in Germany, arriving from Scandinavia and settling along the Baltic coast in the great northern plain in the 2nd and 3rd centuries A.D. This meant they did not mix

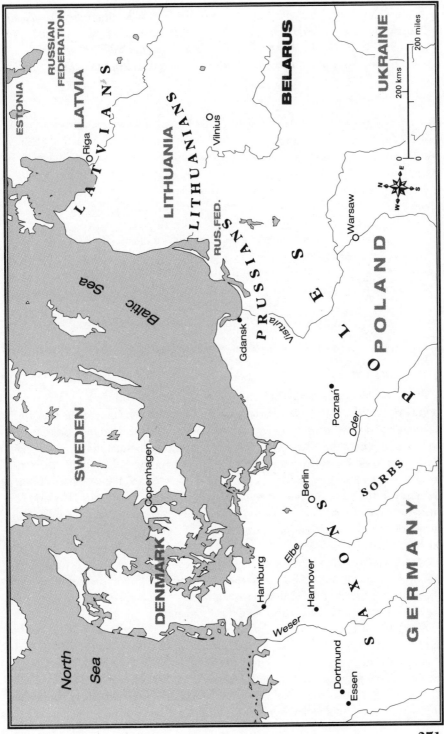

ESTONIA

RUSSIAN
FEDERATION

LATVIA

L A T V I A N S

oRiga

LITHUANIA

LITHUANIANS

Vilnius

BELARUS

UKRAINE

RUS.FED.

Baltic Sea

P R U S S I A N S

Gdansk

Vistula

S I L E S

Warsaw

Copenhagen

SWEDEN

Poznań

Oder

P O L A N D

DENMARK

Berlin

SORBS

Hamburg

Elbe

S A X O N S

Hannover

Weser

North
Sea

Dortmund

Essen

G E R M A N Y

N
W E
S

0

200 kms

0

200 miles

with ethnic groups further south as other tribes did when they migrated westwards and so the Saxons retained the predominantly northern characteristics of blue eyes and blond hair, which the world today regards as being the hallmark of a true German. For an introduction to the Germans in general, see pp. 111–13.

THE LAND ■

The north European plain sweeps right across Germany with its landscape of sand-hills, heathland and moor. Lüneberg Heath in the centre, with its acres of heather, juniper and stumpy trees, remains a spectacular nature reserve even though parts of it were used as a British army tank training ground for over 40 years. The only natural gas and oil reserves in Germany are found not far from the heath, while quarries there have provided much of the gravel used in rebuilding the country.

On the Elbe and along the North Sea dikes and ditches have been built to keep out the sea, but they cannot keep out the winds which often blast across the entire area. The region provides Germany's only outlet to the sea. The country's only deep water port is at Wilhelmshaven, while Bremen and Hamburg owe their existence to their maritime past.

Predominantly agricultural, the lower farmland nearer the sea tend to be dairy farms, while the higher marshlands produce a variety of crops ranging from wheat to sugar beet.

HISTORY ■

With the decline of the Romans from the beginning of the 5th century, the Saxons began to expand along the northern coastline, both into Gaul and across the North sea into Britain. Although their rivals in the area, the Frisians, inhabited the coast from the mouth of the Elbe to the Scheldt, the Saxons dominated them and effectively controlled the entire area. While the Franks and the Allemanni to the south were squeezed between the Huns coming from the east and the vestiges of Roman authority in the west, the Saxons were relatively free from invasion. They also had the advantage of not being landlocked, which increased their independence. They were not only successful as pirates but had an escape route to the west when they were attacked.

It was Charlemagne who eventually conquered them, the best part of three centuries after the romanized Franks to the south had established their empire. They did not surrender their independence easily for it took over three decades before he was able to subjugate and convert them to Christianity.

With the division of the Carolingian empire in 843, Saxony became part of the East Frankish kingdom, an hereditary dukedom with a strong ruling house, the Liudolfings. As late recruits to the empire, the Saxon dukes lost out to the Franks when the first election for king of Germany was held in 911. However the Frankish Duke Conrad made such a poor job of ruling that he himself proposed that when he died the Saxon house should take over and so Henry the Fowler became king.

Saxons

⎯⎯⎯ Saxony in the mid-10th century

This meant that the land of the Saxons became the power base of the kingdom and Henry went on to build his own empire. Unlike Conrad, Henry was a successful military commander and brought Lotharingia back under the control of the East Frankish kingdom. This in turn meant the West Frankish kings became dependent on him. He was equally successful in the east, where he routed the Magyars, who had been ravaging central Europe unchecked for decades. His son Otto I had an even more convincing victory against them in 955 and the Pope rewarded him by making him Holy Roman Emperor.

As emperor, Otto had no time to be duke so he granted the title to Hermann Billung, whose territory on the lower Elbe was a bastion against the pagan Slavs. When the Saxon line of emperors died out and the title passed to the Salian Franks in 1024, the Billung dynasty came to embody Saxon nationalism. As the new line of Salian emperors sought to establish their authority over the Saxons, the Billungs led the opposition against the imperial crown. In 1073 the Saxon nobles started a rebellion against the Emperor, Henry IV, which ended in them forming an alliance with Pope Gregory VII. This sowed the seeds of the conflict which was to break up the empire and the German kingdom with it.

Although the Billung dynasty died out in 1106, the Saxons continued to struggle against imperial rule until the Salian dynasty in its turn died out in 1125 and the new Saxon duke, Lothair, was chosen as king and later emperor. He sought to make his power base impregnable by marrying his daughter to Henry the Proud, a member of the immensely powerful Welf family. That plan backfired because the German nobility and church were so worried by the dominance of the family that they backed the Hohenstaufens of Swabia against the Welfs when Lothair died in 1137.

Power was shared between the two families from 1152 when the new Hohenstaufen emperor, Frederick Barbarossa – whose mother was a Welf princess – gave virtual autonomy to his cousin Henry the Lion, duke of both Saxony and Bavaria. Henry, however, was not prepared to help Frederick exert control over the Lombard League in Italy, which led to an embarrassing defeat for the emperor. He retaliated by outlawing Henry and dividing up his territory.

Henry's fall from grace allowed the Ascanian dynasty to take control of Saxony. They had been leaders of eastward German expansion and had inherited many of the Billung lands, which made them the most powerful family in the duchy. The Ascanian lands were much more extensive than Saxony itself, however, and when the family split in two in the 15th century, the title of duke was retained by the branch ruling in central Germany. The name of Saxony, which was originally that of the tribal lands along the northern coastline, was thus transferred to the landlocked heart of the country.

The blond-haired, blue-eyed Saxon people, however, remained along the coast where they had been for centuries, still fiercely independent and rebellious of central authority by nature. It cannot be coincidence that the most powerful and independent of the German leagues, the Hanseatic states, was set up by the traders in the great sea ports established by the Saxons. To this day Hamburg and Bremen retain their autonomy while cities that were part of the league still take pride in using the title 'Hansa'.

RELIGION ■

The reformation found the native Saxons ready and willing to espouse Protestantism. Instinctively, perhaps, they snapped at the chance to abandon the Catholicism of their traditional rivals the Franconians. The less flamboyant style was perhaps more in keeping with their naturally dour nature.

LANGUAGE ■

Low German, or *Plattdeutsch*, is the most distinctive dialect still used in Germany. It is widely spoken in the north, despite the levelling linguistic effect of broadcasting, and it is both the object of ridicule by those from other areas and of pride by people who live there.

FOOD ■

The sea has an important influence on the cooking in the north, the only area in Germany which is not landlocked. Eel soup, made with prunes, pears, bacon and vegetables is a filling sweet-and-sour winter dish. *Labskaus*, an amazing concoction of beef, pork, salt herrings, potatoes and beetroot topped with gherkins and fried egg tastes a lot better than it sounds. Beer and schnapps are preferred to wine.

TOWNS ■

The great North German cities of Hamburg and Bremen are still city states in their own right, determinedly independent and traditionally more interested in trade than politics. Hamburg was the home of the first German stock exchange in the 16th century. Bremen is the oldest maritime city in Germany, with a cotton exchange as important as Liverpool's and a major share of European coffee imports. Both cities have been rebuilt extensively since the war, when they were heavily bombed. Lübeck, once the chief city of the Hanseatic League, was not so extensively damaged because its commercial importance was outstripped by the other two. It retains its medieval character, with Dutch style architecture; and some of the largest red wine cellars in Europe. Inland, the city of Hanover has converted itself into a major commercial centre and home of Europe's leading trade fair. The baroque gardens of Herrenhausen are the best reminder of the city's illustrious past when it was the capital of a kingdom and home of the British royal family. Hanoverians are supposed to speak the most perfect, accentless German of all.

POLES

For a millennium the Poles have inhabited the portion of the north European plain that sits astride the Vistula and Oder river basins. The Vistula in particular courses through the Polish heartland and brushes up against the most important centres of population. Defining the Polish lands over the past 1000 years has not been a straightforward task. Statelessness in the 19th century and population movements in the 20th have all left their mark on what is understood to be Poland. The Baltic Sea in the north and the Sudeten and Carpathian mountains in the south have been the most stable boundaries of Polish settlement. The same, however, cannot be said of the east-west axis. Although the Poles have clung tenaciously to the lands watered by the Vistula and Oder rivers, it is the eastern and western peripheries of the core area that have seen the most dramatic changes in Polish settlement.

The Poles belong to the western group of Slavs which includes the Czechs and Slovaks. They are the most numerous people among the western Slavs and occupy what is thought to be the original homeland of all the Slavonic peoples. The ancestors of the Poles remained in situ, while the other Slavonic peoples emerged after southward and eastward migrations. The term 'Poles' derives from a tribal group of the western Slavs called the Polanie which means 'people of the plains'. The singular word for Pole, Polak, and its plural, Polacy, are both derived from the word pole meaning 'field'. These linguistic roots of the Poles serve to illustrate their long-standing connection with the environment of the north European plain. The Poles are one of Europe's most integrated nations. Though there are some regional patterns, and the marchland Poles (see p. 320) are separated by their environment and history, there are no distinct communities in the Polish heartlands: the Kashubians – speakers of a cognate but different language, formerly concentrated along the Baltic between Gdańsk and Lake Garden – have become almost totally integrated since their incorporation in the Polish state after World War II.

LANGUAGE ■

The emergence of a Polish literary language mirrors that in other parts of Europe where the civilization of western Christianity held sway. The replacement of the Latin literary language occurred gradually over a period of centuries – it was eventually fully supplanted by the commonly spoken 'vulgar' or 'vernacular' language. Polish was firmly established as a literary language by the end of the 16th century. Literary Polish originated in the dialect spoken in the southern part of the Polish lands in the region known as *Małepolska* – Little Poland. It was the cultural stimulus of the Renaissance and its use as the language of administration which fuelled the rapid development of this particular dialect into a literary language.

HISTORY ■

The baptism of Mieszko I, a Polanian prince into the Roman Church in 966 marked the beginning of the first Polish kingdom. Mieszko I founded a dynasty named after Piast, a figure in the legends of the Polanie and brought his people both into the wider fold of Christendom and into the political mainstream of Europe.

The Piast dynasty ruled between the 10th and 14th centuries over a territory which roughly encompassed the geographical area of present-day Poland. The kingdom was not always united and for nearly a century and a half it dissolved into a collection of feuding principalities. The Piast's major enemies lay to the west and south: the expansionist pressures from the German empire in the west and Bohemia threatened the integrity of the Kingdom. When united, the Piast Kingdom was able to resist its rivals; when politically fragmented, it lost territory to them. The most

276

Poles

German territory awarded to Poland 1945

0   200 kms

0   200 miles

serious loss was Silesia, acquired by the Kingdom of Bohemia in 1335. Another serious threat lay in the influx of the German Teutonic Knights to Prussia – they came at the invitation of a Polish prince. They would be a continuous menace to the kingdom until their final defeat at the Battle of Grunwald (Tannenberg) in 1410.

The most illustrious Piast was Kazimierz Wielki (Casimir the Great), the last king of the line (1333–70). Casimir earned his accolade not as a warrior but as an administrator and diplomat. He restored the unity of the Polish kingdom and consolidated its territory in exchange for yielding Piast claims to lands which for the most part were effectively lost. He codified the law, encouraged the growth of commerce and was an assiduous builder, leaving as visible monuments to his organisational skills an impressive network of stone fortresses. His most notable failure in a life marked by achievement was to die without a heir to his throne.

The extinction of the Piasts marked the beginning of the Jagiellonian dynasty (1385–1572). The consolidated kingdom of the Piasts was quickly transformed into one of the largest dynastic empires in Central and Eastern Europe. The Jagiellonian dynasty was founded on the betrothal of the Polish Queen Jadwyga to a Lithuanian Prince, Władysław Jagiełło. What began as a personal union was eventually transformed into a formal political merger of the two early-modern states at the Union of Lublin in 1569. Poland and Lithuania became a Commonwealth – *Rzeczpospolita*. Although each part kept its own laws and customs, the new kingdom represented an impressive aggregation of dynastic power.

Unlike the preceding dynasty, the Jagiellonians had an orientation toward the east. The defeat of the Teutonic Knights helped stabilize their western borders. In the east, however, it marked the beginning of a period of expansion into what are today the Baltic states, Belarus and the Ukraine. Dynastic union had delivered large portions of this territory; expansionist policies gained even more. At its territorial apogee, the Jagiellonian Commonwealth was one of the largest countries in Europe. It was a place of tolerance in the early-modern period and embraced a colourful mosaic of peoples, languages and religions.

The internal political development of Jagiellonian Poland saw a gradual shift in power in the state from monarch to nobility. The most numerous noble estate in Europe, the *Szlachta* saw its position made more secure in 1425 with the crown's concession of *Neminem Captivabimus*, a form of *Habeas Corpus*. The Polish *Szlachta's* political importance was buttressed by its position of economic and social dominance. As the land-owning class, the nobility's wealth grew with the production and export of grain through the Baltic to other parts of Europe. The extension of serfdom had ensured that the peasantry was tied to the land and served the economic interests of the nobility. In serfdom's perpetuation, however, lay the seeds of an economic and social crisis which undermined the strength of the Commonwealth and left it out-of-step with changes sweeping through Europe.

The last of the Jagiellonian dynasty died in 1572, paving the way for an elective monarchy. Until its demise in 1795, the Polish-Lithuanian Commonwealth was a nobleman's paradise, with the monarch elected by the nobility and subject to severe limitations on his power. Upon election, the King agreed a *Pacta Conventa* which defined and limited his power. Real political power resided in the Diet or *Sejm*, which held the power of the purse strings and where the 'Golden Freedom' of the nobility was zealously guarded. The imbalance between the power of the executive (the monarch) and the legislative (the nobility) began to make the Commonwealth ungovernable. The Diet accepted the introduction in 1652 of the *Liberum Veto*, a procedural device whereby the objection of one member of the Sejm could bring the proceedings to a halt. The Liberum Veto gave the politics of the Commonwealth an anarchic quality.

Compounding the political decay of the Commonwealth was conflict that dominated most of the 17th century and part of the 18th century. The destruction wrought by the Commonwealth's many enemies (Cossacks, Swedes, Russians, Tatars and Turks) reduced the population, disrupted agriculture and threatened the very existence of the state. Although the Commonwealth produced able leaders such as Jan III Sobieski, its strategic position was inexorably eroding.

By the middle of the 18th century, the Commonwealth's neighbours, Austria, Prussia and Russia, were far stronger than it thanks to highly centralized monarchical political structures. They openly meddled in Polish internal politics and contemplated the partition of the Commonwealth. The political crisis facing the Commonwealth produced in the last quarter of the 18th century a burst of creative and reformist energy. The Enlightenment (*Oświecenie*) led to a blossoming of the arts and literature but most importantly to serious political reform. The reform came too late to prevent the Commonwealth's destruction. Its neighbours swallowed Poland in three territorial bites in 1772, 1793 and 1795. The Poles vigorously resisted the third partition under the leadership of Tadeusz Kościuszko, a nobleman who mobilized the nobility and peasantry alike in a bid to stave off disaster. His efforts failed and with the final partition the Commonwealth disappeared from the map of Europe. The destruction of the Commonwealth was the result of a deadly combination; its internal weakness and the rapacity of its stronger neighbours.

THE STRUGGLE FOR NATIONAL LIBERATION ■

The 19th century was characterized by Polish attempts to throw off foreign rule and regain an independent state. The national liberation struggle took place against a pressing need for social reform and economic modernization. In the end, Polish efforts to tackle all of these problems were hostage to the policies of the Poles' political oppressors.

In the course of the 19th century, the Poles staked their fortunes on the politics of one or other European great power in the hope of gaining foreign support for the restoration of Poland. These efforts, however, only achieved partial success. The association with Napoleon led to the creation of the Duchy of Warsaw (1807–1815) and subsequently the Congress Kingdom (1815–1863), which only embraced a portion of the territory of the old Commonwealth. Both of these experiments were swept away by war and Polish insurrections. In the last quarter of the 19th century, the only area in which a Polish administration functioned, albeit in a limited form, was in Habsburg Galicia where the Poles gained a level of autonomy within the Habsburg Empire after 1867.

Polish efforts to regain an independent state by themselves fared even more badly. In 1830 and 1863, the Poles initiated a large-scale rebellion against Russian rule in the Congress Kingdom. The Tsarist government crushed both of these insurrections and in their wake followed oppression and the elimination of any remaining vestiges of Polish political autonomy. In 1846 an abortive uprising against Habsburg rule was defeated by the simple expedient of inciting peasant unrest against the Polish noble insurgents. The revolutionary events of 1848 found their only Polish counterpart in the Prussian partition zone. Like other attempts to forward the Polish cause through armed struggle, it failed. The Polish national movement became more radical with each failure and Poles could be found shedding their blood in revolutionary struggles from Hungary in 1848 to the Paris Commune of 1871. The Polish slogan 'For Your Freedom and Ours', coined in 1830, had a resonance throughout 19th-century Europe.

Social reform and economic modernization came more slowly to the Polish lands than to the western half of Europe. The most pressing social question, the emancipation of the peasantry, took place unevenly with the most progress being registered in the Prussian-controlled part of Poland and the least in the Habsburg Polish territories. Russia emancipated its Polish peasants in the wake of the 1863 uprising, desiring to win their loyalty and so undermine the position of its more rebellious Polish landowning subjects. The industrial revolution had a similarly uneven application in the Polish lands. The Congress Kingdom and Silesia underwent a full-scale industrial revolution while Habsburg Galicia remained agrarian and relatively backward. Although all Poles were touched, to one degree or another, by the forces of modernization sweeping Europe, the degree of change they experienced was shaped by circumstances largely dictated by the policies of the partitioning powers.

POLAND IN THE 20TH CENTURY ■

By the early 20th century, Polish society and politics had been transformed enormously by the events of the previous 100 years. The rise of mass political movements such as nationalist, socialist and peasant parties altered the nature of the Polish struggle for an independent state. The chances for internal development held out greater hope for the national cause than armed rebellion. Ironically, a new Poland emerged in the early 20th century, but it owed its rebirth less to the effort of Poles than to fortuitous geopolitical circumstances.

The disintegration of the Austro-Hungarian Empire, the defeat of Germany and the outbreak of Revolution in Russia at the conclusion of World War I created a political vacuum out of which Poland and other states emerged in East and Central Europe after 1918. Occupying only a portion of the old Commonwealth's territory, the new Poland was multinational in composition and economically weak. The rise of modern nationalism from which the old Commonwealth was immune weakened the historic Polish hold over eastern territories inhabited principally by peoples with their own strong sense of national identity.

Compounding the internal weakness of Poland was the external danger posed by its western and eastern neighbours. Nazi Germany and Soviet Russia never accepted the existence of an independent Polish state; driven by uncompromising totalitarian ideologies, they made Poland's place in the European order precarious. In autumn 1939, on the eve of the outbreak of World War II, they agreed a fresh partition which once again eliminated Poland from the map of Europe.

The occupation of Poland during World War II was particularly tragic for a European people who had already experienced a great deal of misfortune in the previous century. Most tragic of all, Poland was the principal site of the Holocaust of European Jewry; millions of Jewish citizens of Poland perished at the hands of the Nazi occupier in an unparalleled crime against humanity. Poland lost 20% of its pre-war population as a result of the brutal occupation policies. The war also saw heroic resistance to the Nazi occupation – Poland boasted Europe's largest and most elaborate resistance movement, while thousands of Polish soldiers, sailors and airmen fought on many fronts for the liberation of their country.

The end of the war reduced the scale of suffering but failed to restore an independent Poland. The 'liberation' by the Red Army and western indifference delivered the country into the Soviet camp. The Soviet Union also saw to it that the country was remodelled. Poland's borders shifted several hundred miles to the West and, as a result of population transfers and expulsions, emerged from the war a homogeneous state. The country's political, social and economic system underwent a radical transformation in an attempt to make it a mirror image of the Soviet Union.

Communism in Poland never enjoyed substantial support. It faced the redoubtable opposition of the Roman Catholic Church and popular pressures fuelled by an endemic economic crisis. It led to intellectual dissidence which undermined the ideological foundations of the regime. A series of crises threatened communist power in Poland in October 1956, March 1968, December 1970, June 1976 and August 1980. The last crisis heralded the birth of Solidarity, the trade union that transformed itself into a national opposition movement. Led by the charismatic Gdánsk shipyard electrician Lech Wałęsa, it was the most serious postwar threat to Poland's communist regime. The emergence of Solidarity marked the beginning of the end for Polish Communism.

The communist government led by General Wojcich Jaruzelski attempted to crush Solidarity in December 1981. Declaring martial law, Jaruzelski rounded up Solidarity's leadership in an attempt to smash organized opposition to communist political supremacy. For a few years, Jaruzelski succeeded in suppressing dissent. Solidarity, however, managed to transfer its activities underground, adopting a long-term strategy designed to undermine the influence and legitimacy of the regime. Also working against Jaruzelski's regime was the continuing economic crisis. The socialist economy continued to be unreformable despite repeated efforts to make it function more efficiently.

Facing a major shift in Soviet politics when Mikhail Gorbachev signalled the end of a Soviet veto over Polish politics, as well as mounting domestic pressure, Jaruzelski decided to open negotiations with the Solidarity opposition. After Round Table talks which led to partially free elections, Poland saw its first non-communist government formed under the Premiership of Tadeusz Mazowiecki in August 1989. Since then successive post-communist governments of Poland have faced the daunting challenge of reconstructing its political, social and economic system to conform to West European models.

NATIONAL IDENTITY ■

The modern Polish national identity represents a mixture of cultural and political developments over the last millennium. The Polish-Lithuanian Commonwealth bequeathed the strong foundation of Catholicism and the political tradition of the noble class that governed it. From the end of the 18th century, the dominant factor which shaped the development of national identity was Poland's occupation by the partitioning powers and opposition to the various degrees of oppression the Poles had to endure. Moreover, during this period the national identity evolved away from one narrowly defined by membership of an enfranchized noble class to encompass all those who spoke Polish and adhered to Poland's culture.

The Roman Catholic Church has been a powerful element of the Polish national identity. The fact that Christianity arrived in the 10th century from the Latin Church had a profound effect on Polish culture. Religion in the early modern period became important in differentiating the Poles from their neighbours. During the course of the 19th century, the Church gradually assumed the role of depository of national values in the face of German and Russian attempts to eradicate a distinct Polish identity.

By the 20th century, the equation of 'Pole equals Catholic' became a shorthand for the place of the Church in the country's national identity. The relationship of the Church to the nation survived its sternest test during World War II when priests perished alongside their flocks in the face of vicious oppression. The advent of Communism in Poland came at a time when the Church enjoyed a great deal of prestige as a result of its conduct during the war. In the 40 or so years of communist Poland, the Catholic Church represented in the eyes of ordinary Poles a legitimate expression of national values against the alien and foreign import of Communism. The election of a Polish Pope, John Paul II, had particular national significance in the Polish struggle against Communism as it encouraged the development of opposition to the regime that crystallized in Solidarity.

In political terms, Polish national identity rests on three traditions: the legacy of the gentry political nation of the old Polish-Lithuanian Commonwealth, the concept of nationhood grounded in the liberal, romantic nationalism of the mid-19th century and the narrow integral nationalism that emerged at the turn of this century. The first lent the tradition of tolerance and political liberty to the national identity; the second imparted the notion that nations were moral vehicles to promote progress while the third saw nations as ethnically-based organisms in competition with other nations. The first two varieties of nationalism provided important positive national attributes but the third reinforced intolerance most notably illustrated by anti-semitism in Polish society. The present-day national identity amalgamates elements of all three strands of Polish nationalism. There are, however, grounds for considerable optimism that the homogeneous Poland of today will reinforce those positive attributes and discard those that have tarnished the national identity.

LITHUANIANS

The Lithuanians inhabit the southernmost of the three Baltic republics.
Lithuanians themselves form nearly 80% of the total population of the Lithuanian
Republic. According to the 1989 census the total population of the Republic was
3,675,000. The largest national minorities are the Russians (9.4% – many of whom
came to Lithuania along with the Soviet industrialization programme) and the
Poles (7% – who are every bit as indigenous to the region as the Lithuanians). The
higher proportion of indigenous people in Lithuania relative to the two other Baltic
Republics means that, unlike the Latvians and Estonians (see pp. 288, 310), the
Lithuanians do not face the danger of becoming a minority in their own land.

THE LAND ■

Like the other two Baltic Republics, Lithuania is mainly low-lying, with the highest point being 965 feet above sea-level. It is naturally divided into Žemaitija (lowlands – historically known as Samogitia) in the west, and Aukštaitija (highlands) in the east. There are several lakes, and many areas are swampy and difficult of access. This aspect of Lithuania's terrain played an important role in the country's history. The country has two ports on the Baltic: Palanga and Klaipėda (Memel). Some calculations place the geographical centre of Europe close to Vilnius, the capital.

Before World War II, the country was predominantly agricultural, but during the years of Soviet occupation after 1945 the rate of industrialization increased; among the most important sectors of industry are timber, clothing, electronics and food processing. Lithuania is almost totally reliant on imported sources of energy; some peat deposits are exploited, and there may be oil.

LANGUAGE, CULTURE, FOLKLORE ■

The Lithuanian language belongs to the Baltic group of Indo-European, along with Latvian and the now-extinct Old Prussian, and is quite distinct from the Slavonic languages which surround it. The 'discovery' of Lithuanian by German philologists in the early 19th century gave rise to many stories of its antiquity and closeness to original Indo-European. The stories do contain a grain of truth – the language appears to have undergone fewer changes in pronunciation and grammar than its closest relative, Latvian. For most of the time since Lithuanian was first recorded, the language has been used primarily as a means of oral communication.

It is ironic that the first serious study of Lithuanian was undertaken in the 16th century in Königsberg, the capital of Prussia, the home of descendants of the knights of the Teutonic Order who had tried so hard in previous centuries to destroy the Lithuanians. The first book in Lithuanian, the Catechism of M. Mažvydas, was also printed there, in 1547. The Bible was translated by a Lutheran pastor, J. Bretkunas,

283

Latvians and Lithuanians

between the years 1579 and 1590, but no more than the Psalms ever appeared in print. The complete Bible in Lithuanian did not appear before 1735. The first dictionary appeared in about 1620 and the first grammar in 1653. The importance of Prussia, and especially its northern part – the so-called 'Lithuania Minor', roughly identical with the present-day Kaliningrad province of the Russian Federation, in the preservation and study of Lithuanian culture is very great. K. Donelaitis, the first writer of secular poetry in Lithuanian, describes everyday rural life in Lithuania Minor in his *Metai* (The Seasons, published 1760–70). A Lithuanian literary society was founded in Tilsit on the Prussian side of the frontier with the Russian Empire towards the end of the 18th century. During the period of the Tsarist ban on publications in any script other than Cyrillic – from 1864 to 1904 – books and periodicals were printed in Prussia and smuggled over the border.

In Lithuania itself the language was seen as essentially a means of communication for peasants; educated people switched to Polish. The disdain in which Lithuanian was held by the largely Polish clergy can also be explained by the widespread survival of pagan practices in the villages. The situation was rectified in the 19th century by senior Lithuanian clerics who began to make regular use of the language in their sermons and writings. M. Valančius (1801–75), bishop of Samogitia, developed education among the peasants, spread the ideals of temperance, and wrote stories, especially for children. Much work was done throughout the century to study Lithuanian dialects and to use the material to shape a literary language that would be acceptable to all speakers. The linguist J. Jablonskis (1860–1930) is generally regarded as the 'father of the written language'. After 1918 vocabulary was developed to enable Lithuanian to be used in all spheres of activity in a modern state. The loss of Vilnius to the Poles in 1920 meant that the university there – originally a Jesuit Academy founded in 1579 – could not be developed as a truly Lithuanian centre of higher education. This became possible only after 1945, with the proviso that it was Soviet first, Lithuanian second. The government of the newly-independent republic is actively planning the opening of more centres of higher education throughout the country. The prime mover behind the growth of national feeling in the 19th century was without doubt the study of Lithuania's rich and ancient pre-Christian folkloric traditions. Scholars very early on drew attention to the unique melodic patterns found in Lithuanian folk songs (*daina*). Folk traditions also found expression in wood-carving, for which Samogitia is particularly famous.

HISTORY ■

A clear distinction must be made between the modern Lithuanian state and the historical Grand Duchy of Lithuania, a state which for most of its existence was in union with Poland and known as the Polish-Lithuanian Commonwealth (see p. 281). The citizens of the Grand Duchy were often referred to as 'Lithuanians', irrespective of their ethnic origins and language. The history of the Grand Duchy is as much the history of the modern Poles, Belorussians and Ukrainians as that of the Lithuanians.

Nevertheless, the Lithuanians did share in the history of the Grand Duchy. The state probably came into existence when Mindaugas (Mendog) proclaimed himself king in Navahrudak (now in Belarus) in July 1253, with the consent of the Pope, having adopted Roman Catholicism two years earlier. The immediate cause of his action was undoubtedly in-fighting among the Lithuanian nobility resulting from the growing threat from two sources: the Germans (Teutonic knights from Prussia to the west and the Livonian Order from the north) and the Mongols from the east.

Mindaugas' conversion must have had little effect on his countrymen. His successor Gediminas (who reigned in the first half of the 14th century) made two unsuccessful attempts to overcome the resistance of the pagan majority. Expansion of the Grand Duchy to the east and south during the reign of Algirdas (Olgierd), from 1345 to 1377, brought a large Slavonic Orthodox element into the country that came to dominate the Lithuanians in numbers. There must have been considerable concern in the Lithuanian heartland about the danger of being swamped with Slavs. Algirdas' brother Kestutis was not only a stalwart defender of Samogitia against the Germans;

he also held the throne of the Grand Duchy for a time (1381–82) when it appeared that Algirdas' successor Jogaila (better known in the Polish form Jagiełło) was bent on establishing Roman Catholicism as the religion of the Lithuanians and opening up their country to Polish influence. As indeed he was. He married Jadwyga, queen of Poland and established a personal union between the two countries in 1385, and two years later officially converted the Lithuanians to the Roman faith.

The future development of the Grand Duchy was now sealed. It became a powerful player in the European political scene, largely as a rival to Moscow in gathering the lands of Rus that had previously been subordinated to Kiev. This was especially so under Vytautas (Vitovt, Witold) the Great (1392–1430), when the state extended from the Baltic to the Black Sea. But it was also a state in which first Belorussian, and then Polish influence was to grow very rapidly.

Thanks to the degree of autonomy enjoyed by the Duchy of Samogitia, Lithuanian language and traditions were preserved. The threat posed by the Germans receded, especially after their defeat at the battle of Tannenberg (Grunwald) in 1410. However, until the 19th century the history of the Lithuanian people is much more cultural than political. They were absorbed by the Russian Empire at the end of the 18th century, with the Napoleonic invasion providing a short-lived opportunity for the rebirth of the Grand Duchy.

THE NATIONAL REVIVAL ■

The national revival that affected so many parts of Europe in the early 1800s also gave the Lithuanians a chance to assert themselves on the political stage. Here too churchmen and scholars were the most active in the national movement. Simanas Daukantas (1793–1864), the author of the first history of the country in an early form of Lithuanian, was one pioneer of the revival. He was followed by the priest and philologist Antanas Baranauskas (1831–1902), who, despite his use of Lithuanian in his writings, remained a firm supporter of union between Poles and Lithuanians. The most outstanding figure in the national revival was undoubtedly Jonas Basanavičius (1851–1927), who spent much of his life outside Lithuania. His journal *Aušra* (Dawn), although it appeared for only three years from 1883 to 1886, provided the intellectual focus for a true independence movement to develop. Of great importance too was the sizeable Lithuanian émigré population in the United States of America. There the leaders of the community set about winning world support for their country.

Lithuanian territory was occupied by the Germans very early in World War I. The occupying forces were willing to allow the development of national life, so much so that by 1917 they were keen to see a German prince established as ruler in an independent Lithuanian state. Their plans failed after the collapse of the Western Front, and a republic was established. The new state was immediately faced with danger from predatory neighbours. The aftermath of war, break-up of empires and revolution in Russia meant that no effective guarantee of frontiers could be given by the Western powers. There was no real demarcation line between Lithuania, Poland and the Soviet state. Vilnius was a particular bone of contention, because the Poles had good grounds for regarding it as an integral part of their heritage. For a time the Bolsheviks gained the upper hand in Lithuania, and even attempted to recreate in their own fashion the Grand Duchy under the name of the Soviet Socialist Republic of Lithuania and Belorussia, a Leninist experiment that lasted for no more than a few months. The war that broke out between Poland and Soviet Russia led in turn to Polish and then Soviet occupation of Vilnius. A peace treaty between Soviet Russia and Lithuania was signed on 12th July 1920, recognizing the independence of Lithuania with Vilnius as its capital.

LITHUANIA BETWEEN THE WARS ■

The Poles reinvaded and occupied Vilnius in October 1920, at once incorporating the city and the surrounding territory into the Polish state. The Lithuanians were unable to respond militarily and withdrew their capital to Kaunas, although a state of war remained between the two countries until 1939. The loss of Vilnius and its hinterland represented a severe loss to the country's economy as well as a heavy blow to Lithuanian prestige and self-esteem. The addition of Klaipėda (Memel) in 1923 made up for the loss to some extent, at least economically.

A constitution was adopted in August 1922 and land reforms of that year and 1929 were carried through in an attempt to break up the large estates that had been inherited from Tsarist times. The country was, however, unstable politically. A coup by the nationalist Tautininkai party led by A. Smetona in December 1926 led to the establishment of a dictatorial regime in which ordinary political activity was suspended. Life was becoming difficult for small states. The Germans occupied Klaipėda in March 1939, just six months before their invasion of Poland. The simultaneous Soviet invasion of Poland from the east allowed the USSR to perform the magnanimous gesture of formally returning Vilnius to Lithuania according to the terms of the 1920 treaty. The gesture can at best be regarded as cynical; the Lithuanian 'parliament' that was 'elected' in July 1940 formally requested that Lithuania be accepted as a member state of the USSR, amply demonstrating the truth of the old saw 'Vilnius mūsų, Lietuva Rusų' (Vilnius is ours, Lithuania is Russian).

SOVIET LITHUANIA ■

From July 1941 to January 1945, Lithuania was occupied by the Nazis, but liberation from them meant reincorporation into Stalin's USSR. The fact that the West never recognised *de jure* that the Baltic republics were part of the Soviet Union afforded little consolation to those who actually lived there – it is estimated that more than 120,000 people had been deported by 1952. The government of the Lithuanian Soviet Republic carried out a policy of industrialization aimed at tying the country closely to the economic structures of the USSR as a whole. National aspirations were severely curbed and the activities of the Catholic Church restricted. Once again it fell to the lot of the émigré communities to keep traditions alive.

MODERN LITHUANIA ■

Gorbachev's perestroika opened the floodgates of investigation into the Soviet Union's murky past, in particular, as far as Lithuania was concerned, the 1939 pact with Nazi Germany and the illegal absorption of the country in 1940. A Lithuanian Popular Front, Sajudis, was set up in 1988 and in 1990 received 75% of the votes in a general election. On 11–12 March 1990, 135 of the 141 members of the Lithuanian parliament voted in favour of Lithuania's withdrawal from the USSR. (The other six members abstained.) In January 1991 Soviet paratroops occupied key buildings in Vilnius and laid siege to the television station, causing at least 14 deaths.

After the collapse of Soviet power in August 1991 there was no-one in Moscow to dispute the fact of Lithuanian political independence. Economic independence from Russia will take rather longer to secure. Increasing hardship undoubtedly explains why the Sajudis leader Vytautas Landsbergis lost office and was replaced as president by a former communist Algirdas Brazauskas. There can, however, be no doubt of Lithuania's determination to make its mark in Europe.

MINORITY GROUPS IN LITHUANIA: THE TATARS AND KARAITES ■

Two small minorities in Lithuania are especially interesting. Firstly there are the Tatars, totalling 5135 (of whom 32% still claim a knowledge of the Tatar language) – Sunni Muslims living mainly in Vilnius, descendants of the army that settled in the Grand Duchy of Lithuania in the 15th century after their defeat in a civil war within the Tatar Golden Horde (see pp. 355–6).

The Karaites, numbering now no more than 289, are a people some of whom still speak a Turkic language distinct from Tatar and profess non-rabbinical Judaism. Their main settlement is Trakai, just to the northwest of Vilnius, where their ancestors had been employed as guards of the Grand Ducal castle in the lake (see p. 364).

LATVIANS (LETTS)

The collapse of Soviet power in the Baltic states since 1990 has given the Latvian people a chance to regain an independence snuffed out in 1940.

The legacy of the Soviet Union, however, has presented a number of severe problems for the new government. Perhaps most problematically, it must bind together minority groups, most notably the Russians, into a truly Latvian state in which the Latvians themselves will scarcely constitute a majority. Among other pressing difficulties are the need to cope with the pollution caused by Soviet industry; the continued presence of elements of the Red Army; and the need for land reform. These hurdles echo the challenges faced by the governments of the first Latvian Republic (1918–40), to whose constitution the Latvian nationalist movement of the late 1980s looked when seeking to establish the legitimacy of their own renewal of independence on 4 May 1990.

THE LAND ■

The Latvians inhabit a low-lying territory on the western edge of the north European plain – most of the country is no higher than 300 feet above sea-level. The region's many rivers and the Baltic sea have played an important part in shaping the history of the Latvian people. Latvia's main natural resources are peat deposits, industrial dolomite and limestone, and forests. As well as providing timber, the country's forests inspired much of the imagery in its folklore; the oak and lime are seen as sacred.

LANGUAGE AND CULTURE ■

The Latvian language is one of two surviving representatives of the Baltic branch of Indo-European; its closest relative is Lithuanian. In comparison with Lithuanian, however, Latvian shows many innovations which may well reflect the fact that very early in their history people speaking Latvian dialects (the Zemgalians, Latgalians, Couronians and Selonians) came into contact with and absorbed tribes using other Baltic dialects as well as the Finnic-speaking Livs. (As late as 1920 a Latvian census recorded that 830 people regarded themselves as Livs.)

The first recorded written words in Latvian are included in the 13th century Latin chronicle of Henry of Livonia. Lists of guild and trade organizations in Riga dating from the 15th century contain many Latvian personal names. The first printed text in Latvian, a translation of the Lord's Prayer, appeared in Basel in 1550, and the first book, a Catholic Catechism, in 1585 in Vilnius. The first printing shop in Riga, set up in 1590 by a Dutchman, produced 165 books in its 38-year existence, of which only 3 were in Latvian.

The translations of Scriptures and religious songs, together with the use of Latvian in Church sermons, served to level out differences between dialects. The 19th century saw a tremendous upsurge in the use of Latvian in all spheres of activity. This led to further standardization of grammar and spelling, and the creation of a host of new terms. The work of Latvian linguists such as J. Endzelīns was of great importance in achieving this. Writers such as J. Alunāns and J. Rainis also played a part in the development of the language.

The emerging literary language drew heavily on the traditional language of folklore, the first recorded items of which – proverbs, oaths, magic formulae – date back to the 17th century. Modern writers too are drawn back to that source. Over the past

100 years huge collections of folksongs and folktales have appeared which testify to the vigorous survival of old beliefs and traditions among the Latvians. Latvians are mainly Lutheran; there is a lesser number of Roman Catholics and a small number of Orthodox, mainly in the east.

HISTORY ■

The territory was settled in about the 6th century by East Baltic tribes who had been driven westwards by the Slavonic Kryvyčy (the modern Latvian word for Russian, 'krievs', reflects those early contacts).

The areas into which these tribes moved are reflected in the regional and linguistic divisions of modern Latvia: Latgale in the east, Vidzeme around the Gulf of Riga and extending northwards to the Estonian border (the former territory of the Liv people), Zemgale – the most fertile region – in the south, and Kurzeme (Courland) in the west.

Latvia is a country where Western Finns, Balts and Slavs have been in close proximity from very early times. The Baltic Sea and the River Dvina (Latvian: Daugava) formed part of a trade route linking the Viking world with Byzantium. Baltic amber, for example, found its way throughout the Mediterranean world.

Events elsewhere in Europe in the 12th century were to shape Latvian history for the next 800 years. The century saw several major crusades against the Muslims in the Holy Land. The idea of the Church Militant caught on among the Germans who looked to the Baltic as an area ripe for conquest and a crusade was declared by the Teutonic Order. The Bishop of Livonia, Albert, founded Riga in 1201 and the establishment of the German state of Livonia began. It is no exaggeration to say that after this, the history of the Latvian people is essentially the history of the state whose hapless subjects they chanced to be, whether Livonia, Poland, Sweden or, at the beginning of the 18th century, Russia.

The Latvians' religious adherence likewise swayed with the prevailing political wind. At first Catholic in the main (albeit with strong pagan survivals), the Latvians duly submitted to the spread of Lutheranism after Grand Master Albrecht of the Teutonic Order converted in 1525. Albrecht also dissolved the Order and became Duke of Prussia, owing allegiance to the Polish Crown.

Catholicism was re-established towards the end of the 16th century. The Jesuits set up colleges in Daugavpils, Riga and Dorpat (now Tartu in Estonia). The latter was to play an important role in Latvian national life, transformed into a university by order of the Swedish King Gustav II Adolph in 1632.

Latvia was further ravaged by Polish-Swedish wars in the early 17th century. The Treaty of Oliva (1660) led to its division between the two powers; Poland held Latgalia and Sweden took Livonia. In the Swedish-held part of Latvia, Lutheranism once again became the state religion. The fact that numerous laws were passed against black magic and sorcery and that attendance at church was made compulsory suggests that pagan practices were still widespread. Even so, the development of education under Swedish rule means that the period is viewed in some quarters as a 'Golden Age' by comparison with what preceded it and what came afterwards.

LATVIA UNDER RUSSIAN RULE ■

Peter the Great renewed Moscow's westward aggression at the beginning of the 18th century. His war against the Swedes left no more than 90,000 people alive in Swedish Livonia, and 40% of the land uncultivated. Peter's victory over the Swedes and the division of the Polish-Lithuanian Commonwealth at the end of the 18th century gave complete control of the Eastern Baltic seaboard to St Petersburg. Peter restored the rights of the German nobility and reduced the status of the peasants – who were mainly Latvians – to that of land slaves, so bringing them into line with the position of serfs in Russia. By 1772 1.6% of the population lived at the expense of the remainder. This situation was mirrored in 1949, when the ruling Bolshevik party in Latvia had only 31,000 members, of whom 47% were non-Latvians – 1.5% of the population.

18th-century Enlightenment values were brought into Latvia by German Pietist pastors who fostered the use of Latvian. Despite being banned in 1743, the movement attracted many adherents. A peasant revolt near the town of Valmiera – the centre of Pietism – in 1802 was instrumental in persuading the Russian Tsar Alexander I to abolish land slavery in Courland in 1817 and in Livonia two years later. Serfdom persisted in Latgalia until the general abolition throughout the Empire in 1861. A law of 1849 established peasant lands and created a class of small farmers, who by 1914 held 40% of the territory of the future Latvian state.

The intellectual life of the 19th century focused on the germanizing tendencies of the ruling classes and the growing national self-confidence of the Latvian people. Increasing numbers of young Latvians went to study at the university in Dorpat. A higher educational institution, the Riga Polytechnic, was founded in 1862. Three figures are of particular importance: K. Valdemārs, who fought for the rights of small proprietors, founded naval schools on the Baltic coast and was the father of Latvian journalism; K. Barons, a collector of Latvian folklore; and A. Kronvalds, who in 1873 began the tradition of annual song festivals. A reaction under Alexander III launched an active Russification policy. Latvian intellectual leaders were deported to remote regions. Others emigrated to America. By 1900 about 14% of all Latvians lived outside Latvia. The relaxation of that policy after the 1905 revolution made possible the growth of political parties. Among them the socialists were especially prominent, undoubtedly as a result of the development of Riga as a major industrial city.

The start of World War I in September 1914 swiftly brought the Germans close to Riga. In an effort to stem the tide the Commander-in-Chief of the Russian Army ordered the formation of Latvian rifle brigades, using Latvian insignia and the Latvian language for commands. After the Bolshevik Revolution in 1917 some of these brigades were incorporated into the Red Army, others fought against the Reds in Siberia. Latvian independence was declared on 18 November 1918, but the situation

291

was still precarious. The country was not free of its German and Bolshevik occupiers until a treaty was signed with Soviet Russia in August 1920.

INDEPENDENT LATVIA ■

The new state faced enormous difficulties: much of the industrial base had been removed by the Russians in 1915, and the war had cost the country some 27% of its inhabitants. The period of independence (1918–1940) was marked by political instability – between 1918 and 1934 there were 18 cabinets. Moreover, the country was wedged between the growing power of two dictatorships – Hitler's Germany and Stalin's Soviet Union. In May 1934 K. Ulmanis staged a coup d'état, dissolved Parliament and banned political parties.

Nevertheless, the achievements of the Latvian state in this period were considerable. Latvian became the language of government administration and instruction in schools and the university which was founded in 1919. As many books were published in Latvian between 1918 and 1940 as had been published in the preceding 333 years. In 1935 almost three-quarters of the total population were Latvians by nationality. Right from the start the government had addressed the question of land reform, especially the serious discrepancies in the average size of peasant land-holdings – 114 acres in Livonia as against only 27 acres in Latgale. Reform was virtually complete by 1937 with nationalization of the remaining great estates and the redistribution of land, 68% of which land was now in the hands of the peasants. The majority of the population still lived and worked on the land. Only some 17% were employed in industry, although this included a high proportion of women. About 13% of the state budget was set aside for social needs.

The 1940s began with absorption by the Soviet Union and mass deportations, renewed invasion and occupation by the Germans from 1941 to 1944, followed by invasion and reoccupation by the Red Army. The Bolshevik régime introduced collectivization, and set about a policy of rapid industrialization. The work force required for this was largely brought in from other parts of the USSR and by 1989 almost half the population of Latvia were non-Latvians for whom Russian was the mother-tongue. The national spirit of the Latvians was in large measure preserved by song festivals.

SORBS (WENDS)

The Sorbs, also known as Wends or Lusatians, live in two separate regions of Germany: the Upper Sorbs around Bautzen (Sorbian: Budyšin), near the Czech-German border; the lower Sorbs in the areas around Cottbus (Chosebuz), in southeast Germany, near the Polish border. Their number is estimated at between 100,000 and 120,000, about half of them still speaking a dialect of Sorbian. There are more Upper Sorbs than Lower Sorbs, and a trend towards assimilation by the latter is continuing. Almost all Lower Sorbs are Protestants, while a minority of Upper Sorbs are Roman Catholic. Their territory is sometimes known as Lusatia, from luz, the Sorbian for 'meadow'.

HISTORY ■

The Sorbs are the remains of a Slavonic people who settled in the 6th century on the Elbe as far as the River Saale. A group of these Northern Slavs (including the Sorbs, and the now-extinct Polabians, collectively known as the Elbe Slavs), were forcibly converted to Christianity after their conquest by the Germans in 928. In 1002 the Poles took over this territory, known as Lusatia. In 1368–70 it became part of the lands of the Bohemian crown. By the 14th century most of the Elbe Slavs had assimilated to German culture, with the exception of the Sorbs and a group of Polabians, who survived around Hanover into the 18th century. In 1635, Lusatia was ceded to Saxony, and after the Napoleonic Wars, in 1815, became part of Prussia.

During the Prussian occupation, the Sorbs were subject to an intense campaign of germanization, especially in the east, after 1871. Partly as a response, the Sorbs experienced their own national revival. The nationalist organizations *Macica Serbska* (founded in 1847) and *Domowina* (founded in 1912), which is Sorbian for 'Homeland', worked towards increased rights for Sorbs.

In 1919, a proposal that Lusatia be added to Czechoslovakia came to nothing, and it remained as part of Germany. After 1933 the Nazis suppressed manifestations of Sorbian identity, and in 1937 *Domowina* was forced to disband.

After 1945, there was a revival of Sorbian cultural movement. The Sorbs found themselves in the German Democratic Republic, whose government, partly as an easy means of demonstrating to the west its concern for human rights, granted them extensive minority rights. There was a chair of the Sorbian language at Leipzig University. In the united Germany, the Sorbs will, presumably, continue to enjoy those rights, but the pressure to assimilate to German culture will be greater.

LANGUAGE AND LITERATURE ■

There are two main dialects of Sorbian: High (or Upper) Sorbian is spoken around Bautzen, and forms the basis for the literary language; Low (or Lower) Sorbian is dominant around Cottbus. A third dialect, East Sorbian, survives in scattered pockets around Muskau. High Sorbian is close to Czech, Low Sorbian to Polish. The oldest written record in Sorbian dates from the 15th century, although it is clear that Upper and Lower Sorbian had begun to diverge as early as the 13th century. In the 19th century, partly under the influence of the Sorbian national revival, many German loan-words in the languages were replaced with new-coinings or borrowings from Czech.

Sorbian literature developed around the time of the Reformation, but was almost exclusively religious until the 19th century. The first writer of note was the

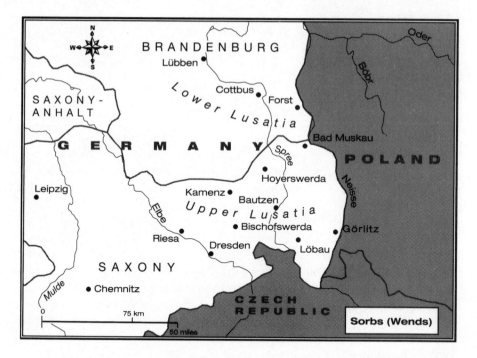

Sorbs (Wends)

poet Handrij Zeljer (1804–72), an Upper Sorb. Jan Arnošt Smoler (1816–84), also an Upper Sorb, collected folk songs. The high-point of 19th-century Sorbian literature was the work of the pastor Jakob Bart-Ćišinki (1856–1909). In the 20th century, Sorbian writers, including the poet Kito Lorenc, have tended to write in German.

PRUSSIANS

It is very difficult to talk about the Baltic Germans or Prussians today. They moved west first by conquest and then by force, and so are no longer resident in their original homeland. With the Pomeranians and the Silesians, they form the vertriebene – the dispossessed – and with unification they lost any hope of ever going home to stay. Within Germany, despite their peculiar origins and history, Prussians identify with being 'German'. For an introduction to Germans in general see pp. 112–13.

THE LAND ■

The most remote and least developed region in Germany, the Baltic coastline has steep cliffs, long, fine beaches and dunes with extensive stretches of marshy moorland. In the centre rises a hilly plateau, studded with over 600 lakes overlooked by

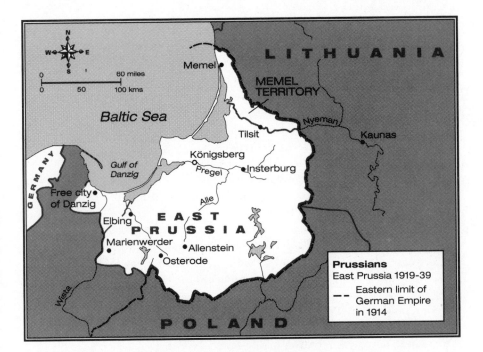

Prussians
East Prussia 1919-39

- - Eastern limit of
German Empire
in 1914

beech forests. In the southwest the soil is poor and sandy, with pine forests and marshy valleys. The former kingdom of Prussia included areas on both sides of the present German frontier, but the original heartland is now almost wholly outside it.

With no mineral resource to exploit, agriculture has become the most important industry, although since unification the remoteness of the unspoilt countryside is expected to make tourism a major money earner. Rostock and Schwerin are the only two cities of any size on the Baltic coast. Both boast fine Gothic cathedrals but both have suffered from wartime destruction and socialist architecture. Berlin, the Prussian and later German capital, is still a divided city, with the more splendid architecture in the east and the prosperity in the west. Potsdam is a baroque jewel in search of a good polishing.

HISTORY ■

The Baltic Germans were scarcely Germans at all in the first place. The Prussians, whose name has become almost synonymous with Germany and German values, were originally Indo-European forest hunters and cattle breeders, obstinately pagan and ferociously resistant to any attempt to occupy and settle their territory in the southeast corner of the Baltic. To the west of them in Pomerania were Slavs, who had ousted Germanic tribesmen from the coast during the 5th century AD to settle between the mouths of the Oder and Vistula rivers.

As the first millennium came to an end, a growing population in the German kingdom meant there was pressure to find more land in the east. It was not until the

12th century that the Saxons succeeded in subduing the Slavs in Pomerania and displacing them. The Prussians proved even more resistant and it took the might and crusading determination of the Teutonic Order to conquer them in the 13th century. The knights, who had been called in by the kings of Poland to protect them from Prussian incursions, were rewarded by being allowed to keep the land. They built castles and brought in German peasants to settle who gradually integrated with the indigenous population. The Old Prussian language survived until the 17th century, but by then the Prussians considered themselves to be German.

Under the strong rule of the Hohenzollern, who became dukes of Prussia when they took control of the territory of the Teutonic Order in 1525, the duchy grew rapidly in importance and influence. After linking with Brandenburg at the start of the 17th century, the dukes were elevated to the status of electors and in 1701 were allowed to call themselves kings of Prussia. By now the population had become staunchly Protestant and had a well-led conscript army and by the time Frederick II the Great died in 1786 Prussia had become a major European power. Prussia's role in ensuring the defeat of Napoleon was rewarded at the Congress of Vienna when the kingdom was given parts of Saxony and the Rhineland.

The dominance of Prussia inside the German Confederation opened the way for its prime minister, Bismarck, to engineer national unity after his army humbled France in 1870 and gained Alsace and Lorraine.

United through war, Germany came to believe in military might as an instrument of policy, with disastrous results. Two world wars later, the original land of the Prussians was lost to the Germans and divided between Poland and Russia. What has survived in Germany, however, is the Prussian inheritance of spartan ideas, strict rules, discipline and courage.

Prussians may lack the imagination and humour of the Rhinelanders – who deeply resented Prussian occupation after the fall of Napoleon – but they personify the qualities of reliability and thoroughness which are seen today as the hallmarks of Germanness. Moreover Prussians, although they were German only by conversion, came to regard the good name of Germany as their personal responsibility. Most of those who took part in the abortive 1944 plot to assassinate Hitler were Prussians, motivated by a sense of duty to rid the nation of someone they realized was shaming the name of their adopted homeland.

RELIGION ■

The Prussians were Protestant but those who remained in East Germany after the war, who grew up with communism, have moved away from organized religion and there has been no great rush back to church since unification.

9
THE NORTHERN BALTIC

The peoples who live around and beyond the northern Baltic are secluded from the world by comparison with the rest of the maritime north (see chapter 1). Narrow straits, often ice-bound in winter, have limited their access to the oceans. As the most southerly and westerly of the peoples included in this chapter, only the Swedes are partly exempt. Their southern shores are hardly ever frozen, though drift ice is a winter hazard on the east coast, and their navigation towards the North Sea is aided by the current – which races out of the Baltic along the Swedish coast in summer. Even the Swedes were able to play only a minor role in modern European overseas expansion, while their neighbours on the opposite shore of the Baltic had no role at all except as migrants in the late 19th and 20th centuries. Rather, the northern Baltic tends to be peopled with the victims of other peoples' imperialism – Swedish, Russian and German – and cultures of resistance to hegemonic powers, and respect for ethnic identities, have developed accordingly.

In the age of sail, the strength of the Baltic current gave this sea almost the character of a monsoonal region, accessible only to seasonal navigation. Freezing weather in winter complemented the inhibiting effects of the summer current. Except to ice-cutting vessels, the Gulf of Finland is normally inaccessible for 150 days a year. The Gulf of Bothnia is scattered with drift ice from November to May. Most of its ports are normally closed for up to 100 days, and sometimes, at the northern end, for over 200 days a year. The 'little ice age' of the late Middle Ages accentuated these effects. In partial consequence, for most of its history, the northern Baltic world has seemed remote from the rest of Europe, introspective and defensive. The region has been a refuge for small and distinctive communities – most of them speaking non-Indo-European languages – and for tenacious traditions.

SWEDES

Culturally and linguistically, the Swedes are most closely related to their Scandinavian neighbours to the south and west, the Danes and the Norwegians (pp. 24–33). However, the Swedes also have strong historical ties with the Finns (pp. 305–8), to the east across the Baltic. The Swedes are the most numerous, as well as the most prosperous, of the Scandinavian peoples and have a tendency, as the Danes and Norwegians see it, to adopt a 'big brother' attitude towards their

297

*neighbours. Physically, the Swedes probably come closest to the stereotype
Scandinavian appearance with some 60–70% of the population being blue-eyed
blonds. All the Scandinavian peoples show clear tendencies towards social levelling
and consensual politics but it is among the Swedes that these characteristics are at
their most pronounced.*

*While the Swedes themselves are very homogeneous, they share their country
with several other ethnic groups. In the far north there are about 10,000 Sami (also
known as Lapps, see p.305) and there is a well-established Finnish minority whose
origins go back to the 16th century. The last 30 years have also seen large-scale
immigration (partly to meet labour shortages, partly because of Sweden's liberal
asylum laws) from southern Europe and the Middle East. Many of the more recent
immigrants have resisted integration into Swedish society, causing increasing
friction with the consensus-minded Swedes: the determination of the Sami to
preserve their traditional reindeer-herding way of life has a similar effect.*

*Finland has a minority Swedish population, mostly concentrated in the Åland
islands, at the entrance to the Gulf of Bothnia between the Swedish and Finnish
mainlands (see p.303). Because of their principally Swedish-speaking population,
the islands have special status within the Finnish state and are largely self-
governing.*

*Although the Swedish government applied to join the EC in 1991, Swedes do
not wholeheartedly support membership. Many fear that the imposition of EC laws
and regulations may lower social and environmental standards and prove socially
divisive. Others fear that future European integration may threaten Sweden's
traditional neutrality.*

THE LAND ■

Although Sweden is the third largest country in Europe, its geography is uncompli-
cated. Mountain ranges to the west, forming a natural frontier with Norway, descend
gradually to lowlands along the Baltic coastline. The only internal physical barriers of
historical significance are the Southern Uplands, in the province of Småland. This
densely-forested hill and lake country formed a natural border between the Swedes
and Danes until the 17th century when the Danish area to the south was conquered
by Sweden.

Despite its size, Sweden is short of agricultural land: only about 10% of its land
area is suitable for farming. Rapid population growth in the 19th century soon outstripped the capacity of the land to support it and between 1851 and 1923 1.3 million
Swedes emigrated to the USA (notably to Minnesota) rather than face grinding
poverty at home. Only Sweden's successful industrialization in the 1920s and 1930s
stemmed the tide.

As with the other Scandinavian countries, the sea has played an important role in
Swedish history. Until the 16th century, Sweden had no west coast ports so Swedish

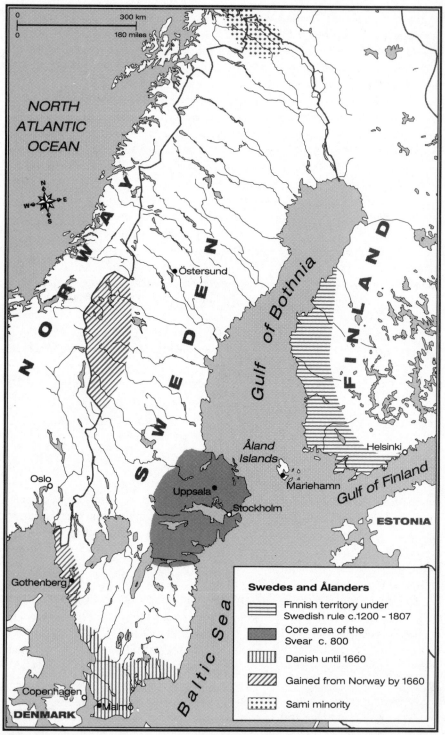

NORTH
ATLANTIC
OCEAN

N
O
R
W
A
Y

S
W
E
D
E
N

F
I
N
L
A
N
D

Gulf of Bothnia

•Östersund

Åland
Islands

Helsinki

Oslo○

Uppsala•

Mariehamn

Gulf of Finland

•Stockholm

ESTONIA

Gothenberg•

Baltic Sea

Copenhagen○

DENMARK

■Malmo

Swedes and Ålanders

Finnish territory under
Swedish rule c.1200 - 1807

Core area of the
Svear c. 800

Danish until 1660

Gained from Norway by 1660

Sami minority

ambitions and security concerns have quite naturally been focused on control of the Baltic Sea.

HISTORY ■

The Swedes get their name from the *Svear* (Sweden or Sverige means 'realm of the Svear'), a Scandinavian tribe who, in the 9th century AD controlled most of central Sweden from a power-base near modern Uppsala. The founder of the Swedish kingdom is held to be king Olof Skötkonung (c. 995–1020) who brought the neighbouring Götar people under his rule.

During the 9th and 10th centuries the Swedes were active as Viking raiders and traders. While Danish and Norwegian Vikings tended to concentrate their activities on western Europe and the North Atlantic, the Swedes looked east across the Baltic and created trade routes along the great rivers of Russia to Constantinople and the Middle East. Along the way they founded the principalities of Kiev and Novgorod and gave their name to Russia – from 'Rus', a corruption of the Finnish name for Sweden. The first attempts at converting the Swedes to Christianity were made in the 10th century but paganism was strong and Sweden was not thoroughly Christian until the 13th century.

In the 12th century the Swedes began a slow conquest of the Finns, a process which was completed in the late 13th century. In the next century, the German Hanseatic League succeeded in gaining control of Swedish (as well as Danish and Norwegian) trade and German cultural and political influence followed. It was partly to resist foreign influence that the Swedes accepted a dynastic union with Denmark and Norway at Kalmar in 1397. However, the Swedes soon found Danish rule disagreeable and after a series of revolts finally regained their independence in 1523 under king Gustav Vasa (reigned 1523–60).

By this time the Lutheran Reformation had come to Sweden and Gustav Vasa pragmatically took the opportunity to fill his coffers at the church's expense. Under Gustav II Adolf (1611–32), Sweden entered its brief age as a great power. Gustav Adolf was one of history's great soldiers and he took the opportunity provided by the outbreak of the Thirty Years' War in 1618 to turn the Baltic into a 'Swedish lake' by conquering Ingria and Latvia and a number of German and Polish ports. By 1660, his successors had added the Danish provinces of Halland, Scania and Blekinge. A policy of integration ensured that the Danish population of these provinces had come to regard itself as Swedish by the early 18th century. Sweden's great-power status was abruptly ended by the Russians in the 'Great Northern War' (1700–21). The Swedes were crushingly defeated and lost all their possessions east of the Baltic except Finland.

In 1805 Sweden joined in the Napoleonic Wars and first lost the last of its German possessions to Prussia (1805) and then Finland and the Åland Islands to Russia (1807). However, Sweden managed to finish the war on the right side and was given Denmark's rights in Norway as compensation for its losses by the Treaty of Kiel in

301

1814. The Norwegians, who had declared their independence, had to be forced to accept the union by a Swedish invasion. The 19th century saw the growth of liberal sentiment and the period saw a succession of social and constitutional reforms. The king retained executive power until 1905 when the Riksdag (parliament) usurped the royal powers following a constitutional crisis caused by Norway's secession from the union.

The turning-point in Sweden's 20th century history came in 1932, when the Social Democratic Party came to power and inaugurated a policy of far reaching social and economic reform which still forms the basic consensus in national politics. Apart from the period 1976–82, the Social Democrats were to remain in power continuously until 1991.

Sweden remained neutral during both of this century's world wars. During World War II, Sweden's neutrality became precarious following the German occupation of Denmark and Norway. The Swedish government made clear that any invasion would be resisted but also appeased Germany by allowing German troops to travel through Sweden to and from Norway – something for which some Norwegians have yet to forgive the Swedes.

In the post-war period Sweden continued its policy of 'armed neutrality', seeking to avoid direct involvement in the superpower rivalry of the Cold War. That neutrality did not necessarily mean immunity was demonstrated by a series of incursions into Swedish territorial waters by Soviet submarines in the early 1980s. Sweden has used its neutrality to act as mediator in international disputes and to take a prominent role in the UN.

Economically Sweden has made remarkable progress in the 20th century. In 1900, 80% of Swedes were peasant farmers, now 85% of the population are urbanized and only 4% work on the land. Sweden began to industrialize in the late 19th century and growth, especially of the engineering industry, became rapid in the inter-war period. In the post-war period, Swedish industry, which had escaped the war unscathed, experienced a boom.

By the late 1980s the Swedish economy had developed serious structural problems of low productivity, high costs and low investment, while the costs of the welfare state began to spiral out of control. This led to a reaction against the Social Democrats which brought a centre-right coalition to power in 1991 on promises of tax cuts and austerity measures. Whether this heralds a significant departure from Sweden's traditional consensus is another matter: the conduct of the centre-right coalition so far indicates that it does not.

THE SWEDISH MODEL ■

The Swedish model of 'humane capitalism', redistributive taxation and cradle-to-grave welfare state has deep roots in the Swedish character which values security and so tends to place the interests of the group over the individual. This tendency is characterised by the concept of *lagom* which might be translated as 'just the right amount', be it of wealth, freedom, or whatever. Hence it is not done to be seen to stray too far from the average. This greatly promotes the achievement of consensus and egalitarianism on which the system depends but it also makes Swedes relatively intolerant of individualism – a majority say they believe that social equality is more important than personal freedom – and social pressures to conform can be considerable.

Two factors have played a part in building the Swedish model. One is the rise to power of the Social Democrats in the 1930s. They eschewed doctrinaire socialism and instead of nationalizing industry, left it in private hands and concentrated instead on ensuring the equal distribution of its profits throughout society. This was to be achieved by a sharply progressive tax system to level inequalities in income and to pay for excellent health, education, pension and welfare facilities. The other factor was a partnership between industry and trades unions. Labour relations in the 1930s were so poor that long-term planning became difficult. A government threat to take control of negotiations persuaded unions and management to reach agreement to regulate collective bargaining and industrial disputes in 1938. This stabilized industrial relations, aided economic planning and restrained both wage demands and inflation. In the intervening years the Swedish economy has become organized to the point where lack of flexibility threatens its competitiveness.

Considerable progress towards egalitarianism has been made. The class system had collapsed by the 1960s, the wages of unskilled workers average only about a quarter less than those of skilled workers and effective equality of opportunity in education has been achieved. Great efforts have been made to achieve sexual equality. Women play a greater role in politics than is usual in most countries and, on average some 30% of MPs and a quarter of cabinet ministers are female. Excellent child-care facilities enable 82% of women to work but, though equal pay for equal work is an established principle, women are still concentrated in lower paid occupations. Recent tax reforms will probably result in the widening of wage disparities.

SWEDISH-SPEAKING FINNS AND ÅLANDERS

These Finnish citizens, most of whom live along the southern and western coast, with Swedish as their mother tongue, enjoy special constitutional status and cultural autonomy. In 1880 they numbered 294,900 (14.3% of the total population of Finland) and in 1990 there were 296,700 of them (5.9%). Though a minority, the Swedish-speaking Finns represent both an élite urban culture and a regional popular culture. The élite culture is well integrated and well-represented in Finnish life. The 1919 Constitution of Finland states that Finnish and Swedish are both national languages of the republic. The Language Act of 1922 refers to the use of both languages within the administration, the use of one or two languages in local government, and the individual citizen's right to use either Finnish or Swedish in communication with the authorities. The historical, social and geographical background of the Swedish-speaking Finns varies. The core population goes back to peasants and fishermen from central and northern Sweden whom the Swedish crown sent over in the 13th and 14th centuries to colonize the south and west coast opposite. There are also some Finns who have become Swedish-speaking over the centuries, as well as more recent immigrants from Sweden, the Baltic countries, Russia and elsewhere. These have learned the Swedish language associated with the Swedish-speaking Finns, and contribute to the heterogeneity of this group, which is both conservative and creative, innovative and avant-garde.

The southerly area of settlement, lying east and west of Helsinki, and in the Turku archipelago and the Åland islands, contains some 190,000 Swedish speakers. The northerly settlement area (Ostrobothnia) has about 100,000 Swedish speakers. Some 175,000 – a high proportion – live in towns.

CULTURE AND LANGUAGE ■

Swedish-speaking business and industry have a bourgeois character, differing from the rest of the country in the prominent role played by trade, industry and shipping. Cultural autonomy is expressed through the schools, which offer teaching in Swedish at all levels, several commercial institutes, a university (Abo Akademi), radio and TV channels using Swedish, a bishopric (Borga), a Swedish military unit (Nylands Brigad), newspapers and periodicals, general and scientific societies, literature, theatres and political organizations. The Swedish People's Party is a bourgeois-liberal party working for the interests of the Swedish-speaking population; it has 10 seats in the Finnish Parliament, not including the Swedish-speaking representatives of left-wing parties.

The Swedish spoken in Finland is an old-fashioned variety of the language and has several dialects with medieval features, which also feature in place names. The State supports cultural autonomy, which is underpinned by private capital with its origins in the late 19th and early 20th centuries. On the other hand, it is increasingly difficult to maintain the country's official bilingualism, owing in part to the predominance of English as the second language in schools and to the relative growth of the unilingual majority of the population.

ÅLANDERS ■

The 23,000 inhabitants of the Åland islands form a special group among the Swedish-speaking Finns. The Åland dialect of Swedish is closer to that of Stockholm that that of the other Swedish-speaking Finns. The League of Nations, in 1923, decided to associate the Åland islands with Finland, which guaranteed the people self-government. By law, Åland is a unilingually Swedish part of the country, with its own parliament, administration and legislation. Only native Ålanders have residential rights, including the right to own land. Åland has separate membership of the Nordic Council; it has had a flag of its own since 1954 and stamps of its own since 1984. Åland comprises an ecologically-unique archipelago of some 6,500 islands with a total land area of 590 square miles. About half of all Ålanders live in the capital, Mariehamn. Shipping and related industries are important to the economy, which also relies on tourism, agriculture and fishing. Cultural life is varied with newspapers, radio, theatres, literature, societies for local culture, and museums. Ethnic identity is strongly-felt and relates to maritime life, the awareness of the islanders' natural environment and their sense of belonging to Swedish history.

LAPPS

The Lapps, or Sami (sabme, sabmelasj), are the aboriginal population of northern Scandinavia and Finland. They inhabit an area extending from the Kola peninsula in the east to northern Sweden and central Norway in the west. The Lapps number some 65,000, of whom 40,000 live in Norway, 17,000 in Sweden, 4,000 in Finland and 1,600 in Russia. Echoing the natural geographic regions, they are divided into four main groups: Sea Lapps on the fjords of northern Norway, River and Lake Lapps in the central part of Finnmarken in Norway and in Swedish and Finnish Lappland, Forest Lapps in Swedish Lappland, and Fell Lapps who herd reindeer for a living in Norway, Sweden and Finland. Two-thirds of the lands of the Lapps (Sameätnam) lie to the north of the Polar Circle, and are covered by snow for eight months of the year.

HISTORY ■

Archaeologically, the Lapps are regarded as descendants of immigrants who moved west during the Stone Age, reaching their present stage of development around 2000 BC. Anthropologically, they have marked features (they are amongst the most shortheaded – brachycephalic – peoples in the world) distinguishing them from their neighbours. Their language is Finno-Ugric and distantly related to the eastern Baltic Finnish languages. It is split up into a dozen different dialects, the main ones being East Lapp, Northwestern Lapp and Southern Lapp. The dialects differ so much as to be mutually unintelligible.

Originally the Lapps were hunters and fishermen hunting animals such as wild reindeer and seal. In 98 AD Tacitus, in his *Germania*, described the Lapps as 'Fenni', a hunting-people. They lived in Lapp villages (*siida*) with a shamanistic and animistic religion focusing, for example, on a bear cult, death rites, sacrifices, holy fells, lakes and stones; traces of these beliefs still remain.

The richly-differentiated Lapps' trade and industry, and their material culture

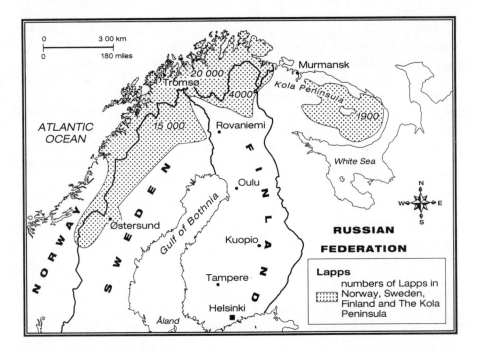

are adapted to ecological conditions in the far North. The Lake Lapps built excellent boats. The reindeer-keeping of the Fell Lapps was taken over in pre-Nordic times from cattle-keeping northerners. Reindeer keeping in the fell region developed into nomadic wanderings over 200 miles or more, between summer and winter residences. At a very early date the Lapps were known for their fur trade and taxed by Nordic kings.

Since the Middle Ages the hunting grounds of the Lapps have been progressively reduced by Norwegian, Swedish and Finnish colonization. When the borders were established between Norway and Sweden in 1751, and Norway and Russia in 1826, the Lapps were accorded certain rights connected with their reindeer-keeping. The survival of this industry, in the 18th century, gave rise to a cultural renaissance marked by silver objects and jewellery. In the 18th century missionaries spread Christianity, and in the 19th century revivalist movements (such as that led by L.L. Laestadius) were strong.

LANGUAGE AND SOCIETY ■

The language of the Lapps has been suppressed, as Norwegian, Swedish and Finnish have dominated in schools up to the present day. Nowadays, the Lapp language is the most important token of identity and is also being used to create a specifically Lapp literature. Lapp may have difficulty in surviving in the 20th century, as there are no words for philosophical and modern technical concepts. Today's schools provide teaching in Lapp, as does the Lapp adult education centre in Jokkmokk.

One of the most important traditions of the Sami is *joik* singing, a simple phrase with a text that is repeated and embroidered upon. The Greek Orthodox Skolt Lapps in Finnish Lapland (600 people) have also retained an ancient dance tradition.

Today Lapp culture is threatened by harsh climatic conditions and over-exploitation due to reindeer herding as well as tourism and sport fishing. Their lands have also been exploited for mining, hydro-electric power, modern forestry and military installations. In Norway and Sweden, the Lapps have exclusive reindeer-herding rights, and Sweden has 40 Lapp villages. Home industries are based on well-preserved textile traditions and ornamental work in wood and horn and other applied arts are among modern sources of income. Many Lapps have, however, moved to towns.

The Lapps have collective organizations such as the Nordic Lapp Council (1956) and the Nordic Lapp Institute in Kautokeino (1973). They have also taken part in international cooperation programmes for Arctic and sub-Arctic peoples. However, internal conflicts have weakened their position. Today, they are consciously striving to retain and strengthen their culture by means of further cultural autonomy.

FINNS

The Finns are a Finno-Ugric people of Uralian origin, numbering some 5,030,000, most of them living in the Republic of Finland. The Finns inhabit an area which is 720 miles long and 340 miles broad; a quarter of Finnish territory lies to the north of the Arctic Circle, at the same latitude as northern Siberia and northern Canada. From an ethnic point of view, the Finns are among the most homogeneous people in Europe.

HISTORY ■

Southern Finland was populated around 7000 BC, as a result of eastward immigration from eastern Poland and Lithuania, and a westward stream with sources in the southern and central Urals. The Finnish language, which could be described as a primitive form of modern Finnish by 1000 BC, bears witness to contacts with primitive Baltic and Germanic groups. By 2500 BC, Finland had a westerly, agrarian form of culture and an easterly hunters' culture. This division of the population into two different groups has been preserved to the present day.

Towards the end of the 16th century, the population numbered around 300,000, but quadrupled between 1750 and 1865. From the 12th century until 1809 Finland was part of Sweden; thereafter, until 1917, it was an autonomous Grand Duchy of Russia. Far from being ground down between Swedish and Russian millstones, Finnish identity was nourished, and nationalism nurtured, by the experience of foreign rule. Finland shared in the experience of cultural renaissance common to many

307

NORWAY

Murmansk

Kirovsk

Kandalaksha

Rovaniemi

Finns, Karelians and Veps

principal areas of
Karelian settlement

principal areas of
Vep settlement

Kola Peninsula

SWEDEN

FINLAND

0   300 km

0   180 miles

White Sea

Archangel

Oulu

Belomorsk

Onega

Gulf of Bothnia

Jakobstad

Lake
Pielinen

RUSSIAN

FEDERATION

Vassa

Kuopio

Medvezh'yegorsk

*Lake
Onega*

Lake
Saimaa

Pori
Lake
Päijänne
Tampere

Petrozavodsk

Kostroma

Rauma

Kota

Lake
Ladoga

Turku
Porvoo

Vyborg

Lake
Beloye

Helsinki

Gulf of Finland

St. Petersburg

Tallinn

Novgorod

ESTONIA

stateless European minorities in the 19th century, stimulated by the publication of
the national epic, the *Kalevala*, in 1835 (see p. 309). Russification, enforced in the
teeth of the Finnish Diet from 1899, bred an intense nationalist reaction, symbolized
by the music of Jean Sibelius (1865–1957) – whose *Finlandia* suite of 1899 drew
tears from early audiences – and the prose of Juhani Aho (1861–1921). Independence was seized from the wreck of the Russian empire in 1917; bloody but successful defence against Russian irredentism in wars of 1918 and 1939–40 impressed the
world with Finnish valour and created a patriotic legend. Feelings of kinship with the
Karelians (see p. 310) who remained inside the Tsarist empire and its Soviet and
Russian successor-states has helped to define Finnish self-perception and maintain
resentment of the Russian bogey.

308

ECONOMY AND SOCIETY ■

Population density is among the lowest in Europe at 39 people per square mile; over half the population live in the southwestern corner of the country. In the 1960s there was a period of intense urbanization, with subsequent major internal migrations. Today, some 80% of the population live in towns. Extensive migration to Sweden has created the largest overseas minority population there, of some 300,000 Finns.

Although the landscape is still mainly rural and agrarian, with villages along watercourses and gravel ridges, only 8% of the Finns depend on agriculture for their livelihood. Farming is largely mechanized these days, and agricultural land covers only 8% of the country's area; large farms only exist in the south and west, and the numerous smallholdings elsewhere are sustained by state subsidies. Two-thirds of the land area is covered by forests. The dominant industries are metal-working, forestry, foodstuffs, chemicals and energy supply.

POPULAR CULTURE ■

Popular culture in western Finland bears the imprint of an agrarian way of life. Christianity was introduced in the 12th century, and this is reflected in buildings and customs, folklore and music. In the 17th century a bourgeois urban culture with elements from Germany and Sweden arose along the coast; this was strengthened in the 19th century, especially with Finland's industrialization in the middle of the century. Finnish became a written language in the 16th century with the first translation of the New Testament in 1548. In the 19th century, influences from St Petersburg were strong, particularly in eastern Finland, where hunting and slash and burn agriculture remained an important means of livelihood into the 20th century, only then being superseded by the rise of the forestry industry.

The first university was founded by the Swedish Queen Christina in Abo in 1640; in 1828 the university was moved to Helsinki, which had become the capital in 1812. In 1863 the Finnish language was given legal equality with Swedish, and the 1919 Constitution states that Finnish and Swedish are the official languages of the independent republic of Finland.

In addition to celebrations for the national poet Johan Ludvig Runeberg on 5th February and for the compiler of the Finnish national epic the *Kalevala*, Elias Lonnrot, on 28th February, the Finns also celebrate Aleksis Kivi Day, remembering the first great writer in Finnish, and Independence Day on 6th December. The birthday of Field Marshal C.G.E. Mannerheim on 4th June is observed as armed forces day. Non-religious celebrations are held on 1st May and at Midsummer, whereas, as for many other Europeans, Christmas has retained Christian features which are now combined with modern consumer culture. During the past 30 years there have been important changes in Finnish culture, appearing in various paradoxes and conflicts, in changing values, and in architecture, food culture, dress and language. Modern media and the consumer culture are mingled with a sporting style of life and a nostalgic idealization of the countryside. The seasons, in particular the long winter, have a great influence on the way of life. The contrasts between town and countryside, ethnic conformity, modern technology and today's consumer culture have all combined to mould modern Finnish culture and create a rich blend of tradition and modernity.

KARELIANS

The Karelians are a Baltic Finnish tribe living immediately east of Finland's border with Russia, between Lake Ladoga and Lake Onega, and northward as far as the White Sea. There is also a more southerly group around Tver (Kalinin), northwest of Moscow. In 1989 there were 131,350 Karelians, of whom 78,900 lived in the northern area and 30,000 in Tver.

HISTORY ■

It is thought that the Karelians arrived in the area between Lakes Ladoga and Onega around 500 AD and then spread to the west and north. They played an important role in the fur trade and developed a well-defined culture, particularly during the Iron Age. In AD 1000–1200 both the Duchy of Novgorod and Sweden made attempts to conquer them. In the 13th century the Karelians were converted to Christianity by Greek Orthodox missionaries, whose influence was strengthened by the founding of the Valamo and Solovetsk monasteries in 1329 and the 1420s, respectively. At the end of the 14th century, Karelia belonged to Novgorod but came under Moscow's control in 1478. After the peace of Stolbova between Sweden and Russia in 1617, many Karelians moved from the Finnish side of the border to Novgorod and Tver (Kalinin) where they still live, their language showing strong Russian influence.

The population of the Karelian isthmus, between Leningrad and Vyborg, was evacuated to Finland in 1940 and 1944, when Finland lost 60 areas with local self-government and three towns. All in all, 400,000 Karelians were settled in small groups all over Finland. They have retained their customs, dress and popular culture. Since 1940 the Karelians have had their own association (*Karjalan Liitto*), which each year gathers together thousands of Karelians at homestead festivals.

The town of Petrozavodsk (Petroskoi) on Lake Onega is the capital of the Russian autonomous republic of Karelia. Here, the last few years have seen a strong revival of language and culture, while Russian influence has receded. The Karelian isthmus, which was evacuated in 1944, now has a Russian population, and Vyborg is a Russian-speaking town.

CULTURE AND LANGUAGE ■

The old Karelian settlements were villages stretching along river valleys or lake shores and gravel ridges. Their architecture is wooden in the north-Russian style, with two-storey houses with rich wood ornaments and people and cattle living under the same roof. Their traditional trades are hunting and fishing, including pearl-fishing, and from the Middle Ages they were also peddlers. Their primitive style of agriculture called for extended families of between 50 and 100 persons to take part. Later, the Karelians turned to handicrafts, seasonal work in St Petersburg and trade. Karelian culture shows strong Russian influence. Culinary traditions are eastern, with dishes cooked in the oven and several fish dishes deriving from Catholic fasting practices, and pastries, mushrooms and tea. On the Karelian isthmus, there was a rich culture of costumes reflecting Renaissance fashions of the 16th century which was retained well into the 19th. In northern Karelia close to the Finnish border (Uhtua, Viena), epic poems in the *runo* metre were written down by Elias Lonnrot in the 1830s; in 1835 he published his collections under the name *Kalevala*. This became the Finnish national epic. In contrast to the Russians, the Karelians have never experienced serfdom. However, Russian was introduced as the official language in the 19th century, even in schools. The Karelian language is divided into north Karelian, which is close to Finnish, and south Karelian, with extensive Russian loans. In the 1930s school books were published in Karelian, but this literature has been superseded by Russian.

Within the Karelian world, broadly defined, are dwindling groups of speakers of what have traditionally been classified as distinct Finnic dialects, such as Votic, Liv (see p. 289) and Ingrian – largely confined to a small area on the Russian-Estonian border.

VEPS

The Veps live to the southwest of Lake Onega, south of the Svir river, and to the northwest of Beloye Ozero, and are counted among the Baltic Finns. Their dispersed villages lie within the autonomous republic of Karelia. In 1931, the Veps were said to number some 35,000, whereas in 1981 there were only around 16,000, about 40% of them speaking Veps as their mother-tongue.

HISTORY AND CULTURE ■

Grave mounds dating back to 950–1100 AD indicate Veps and Karelian settlement in villages in this area. In the 9th century the Veps were involved in the fur trade along the Volga and its tributaries to the East. Adam of Bremen, in 1075, mentions a tribe called the 'Wizzi', and the Russian monk Nestor uses the name 'ves' in his chronicle. After the founding of monasteries in the 12th century, the Veps moved northwest from the Beloye Ozero area, harried by Russians and Christian missionaries. In 1485 their region was included in the Grand Duchy of Moscow.

In spite of strong Russian influence, the Veps have retained a very old-fashioned culture to this day. Their main activities, which also involve the women and children, are fishing on inland lakes and cattle-rearing using dogs. The men were itinerant potters, makers of felt boots, stone-hewers, glassmakers and forest workers, also working in St Petersburg. Even in the 20th century, Veps folk culture retained spinning on spindles, the use of wooden handmills, hollow tree-trunks for boats, and smoke cabins with a stove which could also serve as saunas. Belief in the dead and in spirits and magic, incantations, laments, story-telling, songs and dances are also an integral part of their culture. The Veps are Greek Orthodox.

The Veps language belongs to the northeastern group of Baltic Finnish languages. It is important to Finno-Ugric language history because of the archaic features it retains. There are three main dialects. In 1897 only 14.3% of the Veps could read, but during the Soviet era schooling was arranged in Veps. The central Veps dialect has been a written language since 1932.

ESTONIANS

The Estonians have never been numerically very strong. The country has experienced many wars and periods of occupation which have led to severe population depletion. Estonia has a large Russian minority population; according to the 1989 census, 61.5% of the 1.6 million population are Estonians, 30.3% are Russians. (In 1934 88.2% of the population were Estonians and at that time the most numerous national minorities were Germans and Swedes.) The greatest concentration of non-Estonians is to be found in the more industrialized northeast of the country; the main town of the region, Narva, has only 4% Estonians.

THE LAND ■

The Estonian people inhabit the most northerly of the three Baltic states, all of which are part of the great East European plain stretching as far as the Urals. Estonia itself is situated in a basin containing lakes Peipus (in Estonian Peipsi) and Pskov (Pihkva), which form a natural frontier between the northern corner of the Baltic region and the Russians to the east. The country was always primarily agricultural, although output was adversely affected by collectivization after 1949. The most important natural resources are forests and oil-shale deposits. Severe deforestation took place during the period of Soviet occupation. There are as yet unexploited deep deposits of iron ore. The most important industries are the extraction of oil, petrol and gas from oil-shale, textiles and paper-making.

HISTORY ■

The Estonians are a Finno-Ugric people, most closely related to the Finns (p. 307). Archaeological evidence suggests that their ancestors had settled on the territory at least 9000 years ago. The Finno-Ugric peoples originally occupied an area stretching

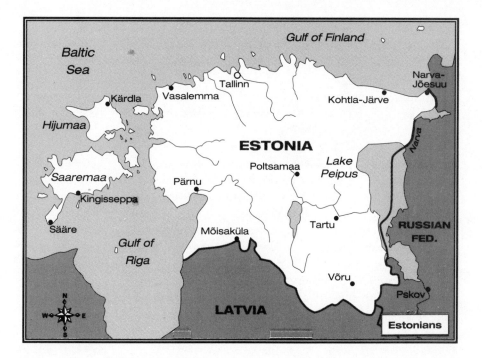

far into present-day Russia. Over centuries they were largely absorbed by new-comers: the Balts, ancestors of modern Latvians and Lithuanians (pp. 283–92), and the Eastern Slav tribes. Throughout their recorded history the Estonians have been subjected to continuous pressure to assimilate to other cultures.

Until the establishment of an independent Estonian state in 1918, the history of the Estonian people is essentially that of a peasant majority ruled by a small foreign minority of landowners, and of the way in which that majority sought to preserve and develop a sense of national identity. In many respects the history of the Estonian people parallels that of the Latvians, with both peoples under pressure from the Germans to the south and the Slavs to the east. The town now known as Tartu was first established as a frontier post by Iaroslav the Wise, prince of Kiev, in the 11th century, when it was called Yur'yev. Like the Latvians, the Estonians received Christianity at the hands of the Knights of the Livonian Order; their turn came after the Germans had subjugated the Livs and the Latgalians to the south. Between the years 1219 and 1346 the Danes were in possession of the northern part of the country. The Danish King Valdemar II called his fortress Reval; the Estonians came to call it Tallinn ('Danish castle'). After 1346 all the Estonian lands formed part of the Confederation of Livonia, including areas directly in the hands of the German Knights, and the Bishoprics of Oesel (Saaremaa) and Dorpat (Tartu).

Just as in Latvia, the period of Swedish rule which followed the collapse of Livo-nia and war between Sweden and the Polish Commonwealth is seen as beneficial. Firstly, after 1645 it brought all Estonians together under one ruler; secondly, the

313

Swedes curbed the power of the German landowners and sought to improve the legal status of the peasants; thirdly, the era marked the beginning of education for Estonians and the establishment in 1632 of a university in Tartu that was in theory at least open to the peasants of Swedish Livonia (Latvians and Estonians).

The history of this university is symbolic of the subsequent history of the country as a whole. Its work ceased when Tartu was razed to the ground by the troops of the Muscovite Tsar Aleksei Mikhailovich in 1656, and did not reopen until 1690. In 1699 it was transferred to Pärnu on the Baltic Coast and closed in 1710 when the whole of the Baltic area fell to the Russians in the Great Northern War. Tsar Peter I reduced the status of the peasants to that prevalent in Russia and reinstated the privileges of the German nobility. The university was reopened, with German as the language of tuition, in 1802. Enlightenment ideas and the progressive views of the young Tsar Alexander I combined to produce an institution that became the leading intellectual centre of the Baltic region. Alexander was also responsible for introducing laws that freed the peasants from serfdom. Eventually it became possible for them to buy land and so form a class of small farmers.

The russification policy of Alexander III affected the university in 1889, when Russian became the language of tuition. By the turn of the century Russian students outnumbered all the rest. During World War I, it was evacuated to Voronezh, deep inside Russia. Following the February Revolution in 1917, which compelled Tsar Nicholas II to abdicate, the Russian Provisional Government granted autonomy to Estonia, and elections were held to form a National Council. The Bolshevik coup d'état in St Petersburg led the Council on 28th November 1917 to declare itself to be the supreme authority in the country. This declaration had little more than symbolic value: the Bolsheviks forcibly disbanded the National Council on the same day. The Germans occupied the country in their turn on 25th February 1918, one day after the National Council had declared full independence.

True independence could not be achieved until the country was free of occupying forces, whether German or Bolshevik. This was achieved with the Peace Treaty of Tartu between Estonia and Soviet Russia in February 1920. Even before passing a constitution the new country's parliament worked on an agrarian law which decreed the expropriation of the large estates and the division of the land into small-holdings. The reopening of Tartu University as a truly national institution of higher education necessitated the finding of highly qualified staff able to teach in Estonian; the achievements of the university in the years to 1940 demonstrate that these efforts were successful.

Independent Estonia suffered the same problem that plagued the other Baltic countries: government instability. Between 1919 and 1933 there were 20 governments under 10 prime ministers. Estonia experienced a period of authoritarian rule under K. Pats between 1934 and 1938, largely the result of economic depression and the growing might of Germany and the Soviet Union. With the adoption of a new constitution in 1938, Estonia seemed to be moving once more in the direction of democracy. Little time was left. The Nazi-Soviet pact left Estonia at the mercy of the

USSR. The new parliament 'elected' in July 1940 voted overwhelmingly for the creation of an Estonian Soviet Socialist Republic and for acceptance of membership of the Soviet Union. In the months preceding the German invasion in June 1941 some 60,000 people were deported.

The Germans offered no support to Estonian national aspirations. Property that had been nationalized under the Soviets was not returned; young Estonians were compulsorily drafted into the German army. Eventually some Estonian national units were formed but were unable to stem the advance of the Red Army in 1944. The re-establishment of Soviet power obviously meant tighter control from Moscow. With its crucial Baltic coastline Estonia became a front-line of defence for the Soviet Union. Industrial development geared to the needs of the whole Union brought an influx of workers from outside Estonia who were not concerned to learn the language or adapt to local conditions. However, the very fact that Estonian is a 'difficult' language gave the Estonians a kind of protection that enabled them to resist russification. Moreover the fact that Estonians could follow Finnish television gave them a window on the outside world.

Mikhail Gorbachev's policy of 'perestroika' was seen in Estonia as an opportunity for national reassertion. In November 1988 the Estonian Soviet Republic was declared a sovereign state within the USSR, and a year later the military acts of the USSR against Estonia in 1940 were declared illegal in international law. In March 1990 the Republic of Estonia formally separated from the Soviet Union and the first six paragraphs of the 1937 constitution were restored. In common with other republics of the former Union, Estonia faces the problems of how to deal with the aftermath of the Soviet system, in particular how to preserve national integrity but at the same time to cope humanely and with due respect for the human rights of a large non-Estonian minority.

LANGUAGE ∎

The Estonian language is completely distinct from the languages of the two other Baltic republics; its closest relative is Finnish; much more distantly-related is Hungarian. The earliest recorded words of Estonian occur in exactly the same source as the earliest words of Latvian, the 13th-century chronicles of Henry of Livonia (see p.289). The oldest printed book is a catechism produced in 1535. This early literature was almost exclusively religious in character and produced by non-Estonians.

From the mid-13th century schools had used Latin as the language of instruction; the first Estonian school primer appeared in 1641; Estonian schools appeared after 1687. It is estimated that in 1688 there were between 45 and 50 such schools attended by about 1100 pupils. The literacy rate, even in the countryside, seems to have been quite high. The New Testament appeared in Estonian in 1686, and the complete Bible in 1739. The Pietist movement of the 1730s was influential in strengthening the position of Estonian as a means of natural discourse in all areas.

As in Latvia, writers and philologists were at the forefront of the national revival in the 19th century. A tradition of Estonian journalism was begun in 1857 by J.V. Janssen; there had been magazines before which were short-lived. Janssen also established the tradition of annual song festivals in 1869. In 1857–61 the wealth of folk tradition was brought together by F.R. Kreutzwald in his *Kalevipoeg* (Son of Kalev), an allegorical epic setting out the history of the Estonian people in a traditional verse form. The dictionary (1869) and grammar (1875) of F.J. Wiedemann were essential to the standardization of the literary language. Estonian in fact offers a unique opportunity to explore the phenomenon of a 'rural language' which develops to the point where it can be used in all spheres of human activity in a modern state.

RELIGION ■

For many years Estonia followed the faith of the ruling classes, while preserving ancient pre-Christian traditions. First came Catholicism with the Danes and the Knights of the Teutonic Order. In the 16th century this was followed by the Reformation and the arrival of Lutheranism, which is now professed by the majority of Estonians. The fact that an Estonian national church was not established until 1917 is evidence of the extent to which church life had previously been dominated by non-Estonian, largely German, clergy. The Orthodox presence in Estonia was strengthened in the 19th century by converts who hoped to better themselves thereby in the Russian Empire. There are also a small number of Roman Catholics.

10
THE EASTERN MARCHES

Between the vast Pripet marshlands and the Urals, eastern Europe's geography is hostile to political continuity. Cut into and crossed by invaders' corridors, its open, flat expanses, its good communications and dispersed populations contribute to an environment in which states can form easily, survive precariously and thrive rarely. It favours vast and fragile empires, vulnerable to external attack and internal rebellion. Volatile hegemonies were established by the Mongols in the 13th century, Poland-Lithuania in the 14th and Muscovy in the 15th. After a long period of relative stability for most of the modern era, the region reverted to its former habits in the 20th century, with the sudden expansion and demise of the Third Reich and the spectacular rise and fall of the Soviet Empire.

Cultural history and demographic change have challenged the dictates of geography by spreading a single religion and a single people over most of the area. The history of empires made and unmade leaves the cultural continuities of the region more conspicuous by contrast. Communist ideology has been a common influence throughout the region in recent times but failed to match the range and durability of older features of shared culture: Russian identity and the Orthodox church. Other identities and – in very small measure – other faiths survive today only in the outlying parts of the Russian region or in pockets and patches within it. Large and self-conscious communities like the Ukrainians, Belorussians and marchland Poles have escaped 'russification', but this is hard for small and isolated groups. However, at the extreme edge of the habitable environment, prospects of survival are typified by the Nenets of the north coast of European Russia – the most westerly of Samoyedic-speakers. For much of this century, improved living conditions for these reindeer-herders and hunters caused a gentle increase in their numbers until the 1980s, when speakers of the Nenets' branches of Samoyedic, were estimated at 28,000.

A further intriguing possibility for the future is the development of quasi-ethnic consciousness in historic regions with their own institutions but no convincing claims, at present, to house distinct ethnicities: Podolia and Volhynia for instance, among Russian and Ukrainian lands, seem to have this potential character.

The Russians are far and away the biggest of European peoples. The history of their formation and expansion along the River Volga – a vast inland avenue of communications between frozen and landlocked seas – has left them limited access to the oceans. In this respect they are like Europe's other large community, the Germans. Both, in partial consequence, have

been feared by their neighbours and have found it hard, in modern times, to associate with neighbouring communities except on terms of dominance. As the end of the millennium approaches, the leaders of both peoples have repudiated this history of conflict and have committed their communities to collaboration on equal terms with others in the European Community, the North Atlantic Treaty Organisation, the Russian Federation and the Commonwealth of Independent States. The progress of Europe depends on how far both are able to forego the advantages of potentially overwhelming numbers in partnership with smaller neighbours, and to foreswear the pattern of the past in favour of prospects for the future.

MARCHLAND POLES

The marchland Poles were always people of the borderlands – the Kresy. *Up to the middle of the 20th century, the marchland Poles were far more numerous than today. In historical terms, the eastern regions of the early modern Polish-Lithuanian Commonwealth, or* Rzeczpospolita *marked out their principal area of settlement. Concentrated in the western reaches of what are today the Baltic states, Belorussia and the Ukraine, the majority of marchland Poles lived in lands where the Catholic, Jewish, and Orthodox faiths intermingled; a multilingual and multicultural panorama that was swept away by the rip tide of Soviet communist ideology and ethnic nationalism in the 20th century. Their surviving settlements are scattered across the western regions of the former Soviet Union.*

HISTORY ■

It was the development of the Polish-Lithuanian Commonwealth which created the large historic Polish communities in the east. Polish expansion eastward into Red Ruthenia (present day western Ukraine) began in the 14th century. The personal dynastic union of Poland and Lithuania in 1385, made into a formal political union in 1413 and later into a Commonwealth by the Union of Lublin in 1569, provided the political and cultural foundation for the establishment of a Polish presence in the east.

The assimilation of the Lithuanian and Ruthenian nobilities into Polish culture provided the core of the marchland Poles. Whether in possession of great estates or petty gentry holding little land, they formed part of a political nation that held sway over vast tracts of Central and Eastern Europe. Urban life similarly acquired a strong Polish overlay which rested alongside the rich cultural inheritance of Europe's largest Jewish community. The Polish nobility and urban classes occupied a dominant political, social, economic and cultural position in the largely agrarian society of the eastern parts of the Commonwealth.

319

Belorussians, Ukrainians &
Marchland Poles

In the countryside, the great Polish landowners also imported Polish peasants to work the land on their estates. Establishing their Polish villages alongside those of the local Lithuanian and Ruthenian peasantries, the Polish peasants counted no more than their non-Polish speaking counterparts in the social order of early modern East Central Europe. Later, however, with the rise of a mass national consciousness, their shared social standing with Belorussian, Lithuanian and Ukrainian peasants counted for less than their identification with the Polish nation.

The partitions of its territory between Prussia, Russia and Austria eradicated the Polish-Lithuanian Commonwealth from the map of Europe at the end of the 18th century and also eliminated the political supremacy of the marchland Poles. Throughout the 19th century, however, they maintained an important social, economic and cultural position in those eastern territories of the defunct Commonwealth which had been incorporated into the Habsburg and Russian empires. In the Habsburg lands, they eventually secured a constitutional arrangement that safeguarded their position as the ruling minority in the eastern half of the province of Galicia. The Russian empire, however, saw them as a threat to Russia's control of its western provinces. The marchland Poles nevertheless managed to retain some of their economic and social position in the face of hostile official policy.

The spread of nationalism among the peoples of the borderlands steadily eroded their dominant position throughout the 19th and early 20th centuries. With the Belorussian, Lithuanian, and Ukrainian national awakenings, the possibility of the marchland Poles regaining their former political ascendency receded in the face of rival nationalisms. The Poles' dominant social and economic position only exacerbated national rivalries.

The rebirth of the Polish state in 1918 gave the marchland Poles an indian summer of political influence. The central political figure in interwar Poland, Józef Piłsudski (1867–1935), was a man of the *Kresy*. The new Poland included a swathe of territory in the east which covered approximately half the old Commonwealth. The Polish government even launched a programme to move Polish settlers to the borderlands. This political renaissance of the marchland Poles was, however, short lived. The outbreak of World War II ended not only this restoration of a political role, but also swept away the centuries-old Polish social, economic and cultural dominance of the borderlands.

Soviet demographic engineering, through wartime deportations and postwar repatriations savagely reduced the size of Polish communities that had been resident for centuries in the east. Between 1939 and 1941 the Soviet authorities transported approximately two million marchland Poles into the depths of the Soviet Union. Postwar repatriation programmes moved nearly two million more marchland Poles to Poland proper. The result of these population changes was to diminish dramatically the size of a historically important community. The last Soviet census (1989) counted a little over one million Poles in the territory of the former Soviet Union. The largest proportion of these remaining marchland Poles resided in Belorussia and the Ukraine.

CULTURAL INFLUENCE ■

Historically, the marchland Poles played an enriching role in the cultural life of Poland. In the 19th century, the romantic poets Adam Mickiewicz (1798–1855) and Juliusz Slowacki (1809–1849) came from the borderlands and their work reflects the cultural influence of their birthplace. Mickiewicz's masterpiece *Pan Tadeusz* (Master Thaddeus) occupies a central place in the Polish literary canon. The borderlands literary tradition extended into the 20th century in interwar Poland with such figures as Bruno Schultz (1892–1942) and Jaroslaw Iwaszkiewicz (1894–1980). In contemporary Poland, the literary tradition of the borderlands survives in Tadeusz Konwicki and the poet and Nobel Prize winning literary scholar Czesław Miłosz. The latter's novel *Dolina Issa* (The Issa Valley) poignantly portrays the multicultural world of interwar Lithuania.

BELORUSSIANS

Belorussian national identity is found among the majority of the population of the newly-independent republic of Belarus formerly the Soviet Republic of Belorussia, and in border areas of Latvia, Lithuania and Poland. There are émigré populations in Western Europe, North and South America and Australia. Belorussians' sense of national identity is often weak, principally because larger and more powerful neighbours to the east and west of Belorussia have for centuries used the country's territory as a cultural, religious and military battleground.

The term 'Belaruś' means literally 'White Ruś'. The colour term may perhaps refer to territory that had not been incorporated by the Mongols into their empire and was therefore not liable to taxation by them.

THE LAND ■

Belorussia occupies a crossroads position in the east of the European plain with no natural frontiers. The highest point in the country is 1135 feet above sea-level. The main rivers are the Dvina (Dźvina), flowing westwards through Latvia into the Baltic, the Neman (Nyoman), which enters the Baltic through Lithuania, and the Dnepr (Dnyapro), which rises in the Valdai hills in Russia and flows southwards through Belorussia and Ukraine towards the Black Sea. The main city is the capital Minsk (Miensk), with more than 1,500,000 inhabitants.

Belorussia, as a geographical term, was originally applied to a wide variety of areas in present-day Russia. Only in the 17th century did it come to refer specifically to the area it now covers. Just to make matters more complex, the territory of modern Belarus, together with the eastern part of modern Lithuania was also referred to historically as '*Litva*' (Lithuania), and its inhabitants as '*litviny*' (Lithuanians). Right into the 20th century one of the most common words used by the people to describe themselves was '*tuteyshyya*' ('locals'), evidence of their failure to identify with the 'high culture' of their neighbours, the Poles and the Russians.

Belarus is not rich in natural resources, although there are oil, shale and brown coal deposits in the south and southeast of the country and some potash and phosphate deposits. Belarus is dependent on imports for its supply of gas and for most of its oil.

LANGUAGE AND CULTURE ■

Belorussian belongs to the eastern branch of the Slavonic group, occupying in many respects a 'half-way house' position between Russian and Polish. The earliest documents with identifiably Belorussian features date from the 13th century. By the end of the 15th century it had replaced Latin as the state language of the Grand Duchy of Lithuania. The most important texts are the law codes (the 'Lithuanian Statutes') of 1529, 1566 and 1588 and the Bible translations and prefaces of Francis Skaryna. The language fell into disuse as a written means of communication after the decision of the Polish parliament in 1696 to use Polish alone as an official language within the Polish-Lithuanian Commonwealth.

The modern revival began in the early 19th century, largely as the result of folklore research conducted among the peasant population of those parts of the Polish Commonwealth that had been absorbed by the Russian Empire. The primary intention of this research, depending upon the nationality of the researcher, was to prove that the indigenous population was either Russian or Polish. Nevertheless the accumulation of a wealth of folkloric and linguistic data led to a realization that the Belorussians were indeed a separate Slavonic people. A literary standard was established with the publication of the newspapers *Nasha Dola* and *Nasha Niva* after 1905 and the emergence of the first really outstanding writers – Kupala, Kolas, and Bahdanovich. The Germans permitted use of the language and the opening of Belorussian schools in their area of occupation in World War I. After 1918 two norms began to develop, one among the Belorussians of Poland, where the centre of Belorussian intellectual life was Vilnius, and the other in Soviet Belorussia.

The belorussification policy in Soviet Belorussia during the 1920s led to the development of terminology in administration, the armed forces and sciences. The reversal of this policy under Stalin in the 1930s brought savage repression and the virtual annihilation of the nation's intellectual life. The 'reform' of the orthography in 1933 included changes in the grammar deliberately aimed at making the literary standard more like Russian. After the war fewer and fewer schools used the language as a teaching medium. People moved away from what was perceived by the authorities as a sub-standard regional dialect to the language of 'high culture', Russian. There was also a danger of being accused of 'bourgeois nationalism' when using Belorussian, with potentially serious consequences. Nonetheless, a few intellectuals began to defend the language actively in the 1970s, most notably the writer V. Karatkyevich. A new young generation of writers is now the guarantee of a genuine cultural revival.

Belorussian is the sole state language in Belarus, but there is continuous pressure to recognize Russian as a second official language. Russian will in any case continue to be the main language of official communication in almost all spheres for many years to come.

The scripts used for writing Belorussian reflect the complex history of the country. Now only the Cyrillic alphabet is in use, although with two standards: pre-1933 (emigré and some internal publications, especially by the young) and post-1933 ('Soviet'), but there is also a standard spelling system in Latin script. The Arabic script was used by Belorussian Tatars (see pp.326, 346–56).

HISTORY ■

Archaeological evidence suggests that the earliest inhabitants of the present territory of Belorussia were Balts, the ancestors of the present-day Lithuanians and Latvians. The northward advance of Slavonic tribes resulted in the expulsion of much of the original Balt population and the assimilation of the remainder. This is still a continuing process; isolated pockets of Lithuanian speakers are still to be found in northwest Belorussia.

The earliest state on the territory of what is now Belorussia was the Princedom of Polatsk (Polack) in the 9th century. It was probably a Scandinavian trading post on the important river route from the Baltic to Byzantium, but a Slavonic element came to predominate very early. Rivalry with the Principality of Kiev, dynastic squabbling, combined with the onslaught of the Teutonic knights from the west and the Mongols from the East led to the demise of Polatsk and the rise of the Grand Duchy of Lithuania.

This state owes its origins to the Lithuanian leader Mindaugas who in 1253 declared himself King in Navahrudak. The town exemplifies perfectly the complex national character of the area. It is now inhabited by Belorussians and Poles, with its greatest claim to fame the fact that the greatest Polish poet Adam Mickiewicz was born nearby. In the 13th century, however, it was right on the border between Slavs and Balts. Before Mindaugas established himself there it had been under the control of the Princes of Volhynia.

From its beginnings the Grand Duchy of Lithuania was ethnically Slavonic rather than Lithuanian in character, spreading to include all of present day Belarus and Ukraine by the 14th century through conquest or alliance (cf pp. 278, 285) Union with Poland in 1385 under Jagiełło established Roman Catholicism as the religion of the Lithuanian state, although Orthodox areas of the Grand Duchy enjoyed considerable autonomy and influence.

At the beginning of the 16th century the Grand Duchy was developing as a major European power in which Catholicism, Orthodoxy and the reformed creeds seemed to be finding a way of living together. An increasing number of towns acquired the autonomous status afforded by the 'Magdeburg law', reflecting their growing economic power. However, the threat posed by the power of Muscovy under Ivan the Terrible compelled the Grand Duchy to enter into close union with Poland in 1569 (the Polish-Lithuanian Commonwealth), and the Counter-Reformation gave new impetus to the spread of Catholicism. The Jesuits founded colleges, in 1579 in Polatsk and in 1644 in Navahrudak. In 1596 the Synod of Biareście established a union of the western-rite Catholic and Orthodox churches in the Commonwealth (the Uniate, or Greek Catholic, Church).

The partitions of Poland in the 18th century between Russia, Prussia and the Austro-Hungarian Empire brought the whole of Belorussia into the Russian Empire. The Uniate Church, which by that time could claim some 75% of Belorussian peasantry, was forcibly suppressed in 1839, and the faithful 'brought back into the fold' of Russian Orthodoxy. The government's russification policies were aimed at stemming Polish cultural influence, but they did little to raise the poverty-stricken level of the vast mass of the ordinary people of the newly-acquired areas. Belorussian units under the leadership of Kastus' Kalinowski participated in the Polish uprising of 1863. Kalinowski also produced the first real newspaper in Belorussian.

A political concept of statehood developed in the early 20th century, culminating in the declaration of the Belorussian National Republic in 1918. With few armed forces of its own, and virtually without recognition, the republic had no chance of survival. In 1921, just before Belorussia was divided between Poland and Soviet Russia, there was one last attempt to establish a national state – a rebellion against Bolshevik rule in the Slutsk (Słuck) region.

The Belorussian Soviet Socialist Republic came to be seen as a centre of Belorussian cultural life by the mid-1920s with the active promotion of the language in all spheres of life. On the Polish side of the frontier some schools were established and national cultural activity conducted in the teeth of opposition from the authorities. Stalin's purges of the 1930s effectively undid all the cultural achievements of the previous decade. Wholesale extermination affected not only the intelligentsia but also the peasants, as the recent discovery of mass graves dating from the period has shown.

The German occupation of 1941–44 saw Belorussia once again become a battle ground, with the population at the mercy of the Germans by day and the Soviet partisans and, in the western part of the country, the Polish Home Army by night. Some national life was permitted by the occupying authorities – Belorussian newspapers were published and national schools were opened; the teachers in them were viewed as prime targets for murder by the partisans.

The re-establishment of Soviet power after 1944 brought an influx of Russians and other nationalities of the USSR to help build new industries and maintain a huge military presence. These newcomers diluted native Belorussian influence. A declaration of sovereignty within the USSR was followed by a declaration of independence on 27th July 1991. Together with Russia and Ukraine, Belarus was one of the founder members of the Commonwealth of Independent States. As for many of the former Soviet Republics, dealing the Russian minority will present a delicate problem for the government of independent Belarus.

CUSTOMS, TRADITIONS, RELIGIOUS BELIEF ■

The rural areas of Belarus are still an acknowledged source of original folklore, although many old customs and traditions have not survived the years of Soviet domination and inevitable urbanization; others have been sanitized for modern performance on the stage. Young nationally-conscious Belorussians are attempting to revive the celebration of *Kupally* at the time of the summer solstice and *Dzyady*, originally a ritual ceremony with special dishes in memory of family ancestors held on All Souls' Day. Traditional patterns of folk-weaving and embroidery are still preserved; particularly noteworthy are the broad woven sashes of Slutsk.

The isolation of the Palyessye (Palešsie) areas in Belarus's southern marshlands had led to the development of traditions that are seen by some as belonging to a distinct nation, the 'Paleshuks'. Attempts have recently been made to develop a separate literary language, but so far without success.

The majority of Belorussians who profess a religious faith are Orthodox. The Orthodox Church in Belarus is administered by the Patriarch of Moscow and does not actively encourage the national revival. There is, however, a Belorussian autocephalous Orthodox church associated with the diaspora. Belorussian Orthodox used to be classified as Russians and Belorussian Catholics as Poles; the Polish church hierarchy, which administers Catholic church affairs in Belorussia, does not readily admit to the existence of Belorussian Catholics. The number of Catholics has been estimated to be as high as 2,000,000, whereas only about 500,000 citizens of Belarus claim Polish nationality. Groups of nationally-conscious Belorussians have recently begun to revive the Uniate church; despite their small numbers they are viewed with great hostility by the Orthodox church authorities. There is as yet no generally-accepted translation of the whole of the Bible into modern Belorussian.

There are settlements of Old Believers (see p. 342) in several areas of Belarus, the most important being Vyetka (Vietka) near Homyel' (Homiel) where their traditions were until recently most strongly maintained. The town has been severely polluted by radiation from the Chernobyl accident. No current population figures are available; in 1913 they numbered about 98,000. Many have come to regard themselves as Belorussian by nationality.

Belorussia was once home to a number of Tatar Muslims (see p. 355–6). There were fifteen mosques in the country in the 19th century. By the beginning of this century there was little to distinguish them from their Christian neighbours. They lost their language, but in the main retained their religion until Soviet domination began to put pressure on all religions. According to the census of 1970, just over 10,031 people regarded themselves as Tatars. There is now an active group of young people seeking to revive their joint Tatar and Belorussian heritage. There is one active mosque, in Iwje (Iŭje), Hrodna (Harodnia) province.

AGRICULTURE AND INDUSTRY ■

Traditional land-owning patterns have been lost for ever as a result of the collectivization of farmland under the Soviets. Deforestation and river pollution have also had a serious impact on rural life. Much agricultural land and forest has been rendered unusable as a result of radiation from the Chernobyl disaster of 1986, which will affect the whole population of the country for decades to come.

Belorussia's industry developed under the central Soviet planning system. The country was accorded the role of end-producer of lorries, tractors and other agricultural equipment, hi-tech and electronic equipment (largely because of the huge military presence), the chemical and petrochemical industries (for which the new town of Navapolatsk (Novapołack) was built – with the accompanying pollution) and consumer goods such as televisions, radios and refrigerators. With the break-up of the traditional economic ties with the remainder of what used to be the Soviet Union, Belorussia is now entering a painful period of readjustment.

UKRAINIANS

The declaration of Ukrainian independence on 24th August 1991 in effect created a huge new state in Europe with a surface area of 233,100 square miles, a population numbering nearly 52 million (according to a 1991 estimate) and four cities with over one million inhabitants: the capital Kiev (Kyyiv), Kharkov (Kharkiv), Dnepropetrovsk (Dnipropetrovs'ke), Odessa (Odesa), Donetsk (Donets'ke). The country has enormous industrial and agricultural potential, and, more alarmingly, a stockpile of nuclear weapons inherited from the USSR, which it could probably acquire the capacity to fire without too much difficulty. Nevertheless, little was known or understood about Ukrainian claims to nationhood, let alone statehood. This can be explained by the fact that almost all constituent parts of the USSR were seen through the Russian prism. Ukraine in particular suffered from this because two centuries of Russian history writing, both before and after 1917, had presented the country as an appendage to Russia. This image was also projected in the West, with the views of émigré Ukrainian scholars being dismissed because of their 'nationalism'. An independent Ukrainian state makes a re-evaluation of old-fashioned russocentric views essential. It also raises a number of questions about who a 'Ukrainian' is.

THE LAND ■

Ukraine covers a range of geographical and climatic conditions. In the centre it consists of steppeland broken by low plateaux and river basins, especially the lowland and plateau of the river Dnepr (Dnipro). To the north it shares the marshlands of the river Pripet with Belorussia. The south comprises a coastal lowland running along the Black Sea and the Sea of Azov. Eastern Ukraine consists of the basin of the river Donets' and the western edge of the Central Russian Upland. The most important feature of Western Ukraine are the Carpathian mountains (highest point: Hoverla, 6762 feet). The Crimean peninsula forms a separate geographical unit. The most important rivers – both flowing roughly north-south into the Black Sea – are the Dnestr and Dnepr.

327

THE PEOPLE ■

Some 73% of the population are Ukrainian by nationality. There are 11.4 million Russians and sizeable numbers of Jews, Romanians, Poles and Hungarians. The east, the main industrial area with its predominantly Russian population, and the south, the traditionally ethnically-mixed Black Sea region, are potential dangers to the country's stability.

The painful history of Ukraine has led to a situation in which large numbers of people who regard themselves as Ukrainian live outside the country; some continue to live in their ancestral regions in neighbouring countries, others were forced out. There are at least 7 million in other republics of the former USSR, especially Russia and the Transnistria region of Moldova. They live in Poland, Slovakia and Romania. There are Ukrainian communities that found refuge after 1945 in Western Europe and both North and South America. In parts of Canada and the USA there are large settlements that date back to the period of mass emigration from Austria-Hungary in the 1880s. These communities in particular, never having known Russian or Soviet hegemony, kept Ukrainian traditions alive which might otherwise have been obliterated, and are now active in supporting the new republic.

The importance of Ukraine for the growing of cereal crops gave rise to the expression, a cliché but true nonetheless, that the country was the 'bread basket of the USSR'. Its industrial base rests on the large iron ore and coal deposits concentrated in the Donets' basin in the east. Iron and steel production for consumer goods and heavy engineering occupies a central place in the Ukrainian economy. There are also deposits of manganese and some oil, but the country is largely dependent on imported sources of energy. One of the home-based energy sources, the nuclear power plant at Chernobyl to the north of Kiev, created horrendous problems when one of its reactors blew up in April 1986; the results of radioactive poisoning will plague Ukraine and its immediate neighbours for decades, if not centuries.

LANGUAGE ■

Ukrainian is an East Slavonic language; its closest relatives are Belorussian and Russian. There are many links in grammar and vocabulary with Polish. The modern literary language is the product of more than a century of both defending the language's right to exist and of reaching a compromise between many different dialects. The Ukrainian of the emigration contains more features of West Ukrainian dialects.

The formation of a literary standard language in the 19th century is an integral part of the process of the formation of the Ukrainian nation. With two intellectual centres in two countries – Kiev in the Russian Empire and L'viv in Austria-Hungary – two standards began to develop. The Kiev 'norm' was above all based on the language used by Taras Shevchenko, the poet who stands at the very heart of Ukrainian national self-esteem. The situation in L'viv was initially made more complex by the support given in some quarters for the use in educated discourse of the mixture of the liturgical language of the Orthodox Church – Church Slavonic – with a large dose of Polish and Latin that had been used for polemical anti-Catholic writings in previous centuries. This mixture was far removed from the way in which the people spoke. There was also the attraction of Polish as a language of high status and culture. In the end the democratic trend prevailed and Ukrainian became established as a means of communication in all spheres of activity.

Its position was strengthened not only by the declaration of the Ukrainian National Republic but also by the language policy pursued by the government of the Ukrainian Soviet Republic in the 1920s. Terminological commissions were set up to propose words for use in the sciences and administration, work was carried out on standardizing the grammar and orthography. All this was undone by Stalin in the 1930s. It became dangerous to promote the language, or stress too strongly its differences from Russian. Ukrainian prisoners of conscience in the Brezhnev era were sent to the gulag as much for daring to write in their own language as for the ideas they expressed. In the current political scene the future of the language is as secure as the independence of Ukraine.

Some outstanding writers have used Ukrainian as their means of artistic expression. Apart from Shevchenko, the 19th century saw two other great poets and writers, Ivan Franko and Lesia Ukrainka. The cultural freedom unleashed by the programme of 'ukrainianization' in the 1920s resulted in much experimentation; an outstanding prose writer of the period was M. Khyl'ovyi. Among many fine contemporary writers, the poet Lina Kostenko stands out.

HISTORY ■

The word 'Ukraine' literally means 'frontier country'. The original sense dates back to the time when the steppe lands of central Ukraine were indeed the frontier separating the Eastern European Byzantine culture of Kiev from Asia and the nomads that sought plunder and space to graze their animals. However it is still appropriate to consider present-day Ukraine as a 'frontier country' in the sense that its borders have been altered by outside powers – principally Moscow – on numerous occasions since its first attempt at modern statehood in 1917, because these frontier changes contain the seeds of potential trouble for the future.

The declaration of independence of the Ukrainian National Republic (or at least autonomy within what was hoped would become a free federation of peoples of the Russian Empire) on 22nd November 1917 soon led to a Bolshevik invasion and the ultimate establishment of the Ukrainian Soviet Socialist Republic. War between Poland and Soviet Russia left the Ukrainian areas of Galicia and Volhynia in Polish hands by the terms of the Treaty of Riga of 1921. Three years later the Ukrainian SSR ceded the areas of Taganrog and Shakhty to Russia. (The National Republic had attempted to establish itself as far east as the Don basin and Kuban' regions.)

In 1940 Romania was forced by the Nazi-Soviet pact to yield territories to the USSR to form the Moldavian SSR. Included in this new entity was territory on the left bank of the river Dnestr, removed from the jurisdiction of the Ukrainian SSR.

(This is now the 'Transnistrian Republic' which is seeking to secede from Moldova.) Romania also lost Northern Bukovyna (now the Chernivtsy region of Ukraine) and Southern Bessarabia (now partly in Moldova, partly in the Odessa region of Ukraine). After 1945 Ukraine received the Subcarpathian region, with its main city Uzhhorod (technically from Hungary, but it had been part of Czechoslovakia before that state was dismantled in 1938). In 1954 Khrushchev made a present of Crimea to Ukraine to mark the 300th anniversary of the 're-unification' of Ukraine with Russia.

Almost without a state history in the generally accepted sense of the term, modern Ukraine has to be seen as resting on the historical and political experience of its people, gained in different states at various times. Ukrainian historians rightly begin their national history with the medieval princedom of Kiev, an ancient city on the Dnepr, standing at the crossroads of trade routes, east-west to and from Europe and Central Asia, and north-south on the river and sea route 'from the Varangians to the Greeks' (ie from the Norsemen to Byzantium). The Norse rulers merged very early into the East Slavonic peoples of the area. Orthodox Christianity was adopted as the official religion in 988 and spread from Kiev northwards and eastwards to the lands of the modern Belorussians and Russians. The word 'Rus' which had earlier referred to a particular kind of Norseman came to signify anyone of the Orthodox faith. Rulers of such major trading and cultural centres as Novgorod and Suzdal' recognized the suzerainty of Kiev, although by the 12th century, dynastic squabbling and rivalry between states severely reduced its authority.

That authority was further undermined by the decline in the city's economic importance; the Dnepr was continually being cut downstream by Turkic nomads. The arrival of the Mongols and the sacking of Kiev in 1240 brought its glory to an end. The centres of political growth were now to be found elsewhere. To the west were the princedoms of Galicia and Volhynia with their close and sometimes hostile relationship with Catholic Poland and Hungary, northwards lay the growing power of the Grand Duchy of Lithuania (which absorbed Kiev in 1362), and in the northeast the Russian princedoms were beginning to expand. At the same time the Mongols and their successors, the Golden Horde, saw trade as a way of revitalizing the Crimea and the Black Sea coast; they encouraged the settlement of merchants, especially Italians from Venice and Genoa.

The economic revival of Kiev got under way during the second half of the 16th century. The Union of 1569 that brought Poland and Lithuania together in one state put all the Ukrainian lands under the direct control of the Polish crown. It was then that the term 'Ukraine' came into use. The result was increased Polish colonization and Roman Catholic influence in church matters.

The Cossacks have an important role to play in the creation of the modern ideal of the Ukrainian state. Originally bands of freebooters and marauders living 'beyond the rapids' of the Dnepr and therefore technically beyond the reach of authority, they came to be regarded as the defenders of the Orthodox faith against the Polish Catholics. An uprising led by Bohdan Khmel'nyts'kyi in 1648 led to the establishment of a Cossack state. The way in which the Cossacks conducted their internal affairs is now seen by some as a model of true democracy (cf p. 338).

The state was unable to survive without allies and in 1654 was compelled to recognize the authority of the Tsar of Muscovy. 'Left-bank Ukraine', ie all the Ukrainian lands to the east of the Dnipro, and Kiev itself entered the Russian Empire, initially with some degree of autonomy. The rest of Ukraine stayed within Poland. A final attempt to assert Ukrainian independence from Moscow occurred under Mazepa who joined the Swedish King Charles XII in his war against Peter the Great. The Russian victory at Poltava in Ukraine in 1709 sealed the country's fate. Cossack institutions were disbanded, although the troops came to serve as special regiments in the Russian army. Ukrainian noblemen began to play an important role in the administration of the Empire, probably because of their higher level of education and more Western outlook. The divisions of Poland-Lithuania that began in 1772 brought almost all of what is now Ukraine under Russian control. The one exception was Galicia in the west which went to Austria. In 1783 Crimea and the Black Sea coast, until then under the control of a vassal of the Ottoman Turks, were incorporated into the Empire.

A strong sense of national identity began to develop in the 1820s and 1830s, fostered mainly by historians and poets. The main difficulty was that this sense was growing in two centres that had at the time little contact with each other – Kiev in the Russian Empire and L'vov in Austrian Galicia. There the Austrian authorities encouraged the Ukrainians in order to offset the growing restlessness of the Poles. The problem was compounded by the inclusion in the Hungarian part of the state a large population that could have come to see themselves as Ukrainians, but who had no contact with Galicia. There were further divisions between the Orthodox in Galicia who favoured a pro-Russian orientation and the mainly Greek Catholic intellectuals who wished to see a united Ukrainian nation. Kiev and L'viv were brought together by the Tsarist ban on the use of Ukrainian in printed material which was in force from 1876 to 1906. Writers from Kiev published their work in L'viv with the result that a sense of common cause developed.

An awareness of common cultural heritage was accompanied by the necessary political will during the upheavals of 1917 to think of Ukraine as a state with a future outside Russia. The declaration of independence in January 1918 had a positive outcome a few weeks later when the Central Powers recognized the existence of the National Republic at the talks which led to the Treaty of Brest-Litovsk. The Republic's existence was extremely precarious, given the presence within its borders of both troops fighting for the restoration of the Russian Empire, and the Red Army intent on establishing Soviet power in Ukraine. Galicia and Volhynia were ceded to Poland in 1921, and a Ukrainian Soviet Socialist Republic – with its capital in Kharkov – was established in the rest of the country.

The new Soviet Republic embarked on a policy of 'ukrainianization' of all spheres of activity. By contrast the Polish authorities discouraged, to the point of persecution, Ukrainian national life. The Soviet Ukrainian experiment petered out by the end of the 1920s to be replaced by Stalinist oppression, first of intellectuals and then from 1932 of the whole population by means of an artificially created famine which killed millions. The Ukrainian response to persecution in Poland was armed struggle that continued throughout the occupation of both countries by the Germans.

The re-establishment of Soviet power in Ukraine after 1944 did nothing to satisfy the aspirations of Ukrainians who sought their country's independence. Only during the Soviet presidency of Mikhail Gorbachev did it become possible to open up painful questions of past history, even though the Ukrainian authorities until 1991 remained firmly 'unreconstructed'. The putsch in Moscow that year changed the whole situation. Ukraine was one of the first republics to declare its independence from the USSR, and in December of that year became one of the founder members of the Commonwealth of Independent States.

Independent Ukraine was immediately faced with the difficult problem of dealing with the nuclear heritage of the USSR and of finding an amicable settlement with Russia on the division of the Black Sea fleet based in Sevastopol in Crimea. There are many loud voices raised in favour of Ukraine's preserving the nuclear weapons on its soil, in the absence of any security agreements in the case of invasion from the most likely enemy, Russia. The whole question of the fleet and the status of Crimea remains unsolved. Ukraine also faces immense economic difficulties. Parliament still has to tackle a whole range of questions connected with the privatization of land and large enterprises. In the wider political arena it has provided a contingent of troops for the UN presence in Bosnia; it is seeking to play a greater role in the affairs of Central Europe by attaching itself to the 'Vyšehrad four' (Poland, the Czech Republic, Slovakia, Hungary). It may also find a role in Black Sea regional cooperation.

RELIGION AND REGIONALISM ■

The majority of Ukrainians who have any religious faith would say that they are Orthodox. However, in the present climate, matters are not that simple. The official church in Ukraine is essentially a branch of the Russian church with a sometimes ambivalent attitude to Ukrainian aspirations. After all Kiev is the city from which Orthodoxy spread to Russia, and it therefore holds a special place in Russian religious consciousness. In the 1920s a specifically Ukrainian autocephalous church was established as part of the process of 'ukrainianization'. It was crushed by Stalin at the beginning of the 1930s but continued to lead a vigorous life in the emigration. It is now in the process of building up its life in Ukraine in parallel to the 'official' Orthodox church.

To this must be added the Greek Catholics or Uniates who have their origin in the union of the Roman Catholic and Orthodox churches promulgated by the Synod of Brest in 1596. Bitterly opposed by Ukrainians in the 17th century, the Uniate church went on to become in Galicia a Ukrainian national church. In 1946 the Uniate faithful were forcibly 'reunited' with their Orthodox brethren in Soviet

Ukraine, but their church continued to exist in the underground, supported by hundreds of thousands of adherents in the emigration. It, too, has returned to Ukraine to claim buildings which were forcibly confiscated and congregations that became Orthodox in name only. Religion has not yet proved to be the cement that will bind Ukrainians together, let alone Ukrainians and Russians within Ukraine.

The almost complete lack of state-building traditions and the absence of any obvious historical continuity which could link all parts of the country have meant that a strong feeling of regional identity has been preserved in many areas of Ukraine, to say nothing of the Black Sea coastal area, Crimea and parts of the industrial east, where the feeling of being a part of the Ukrainian nation is often completely lacking. Among Ukrainians themselves there is an appreciation of the differences between Polishchuks from the Polissia region on the border with Belarus, Volhynians and people from Podillia and Galicia, to name but four regions. History, dialect and folk traditions – tales, songs, embroidery patterns, even the ways in which Easter eggs are painted – all have a role to play. These regional varieties have not produced separate nations and, in the context of an independent Ukrainian state, are most unlikely to do so. However, there is one group which may have claims to a separate non-Ukrainian identity, the Ruthenians (see p. 267).

RUSSIANS

The Russians are one of the most racially varied of all the European peoples – a result of their expansion over more than 1000 years, which has led them to conquer and absorb so many other peoples, above all of Finno-Ugric and Turkic extraction. It is therefore hardly possible to talk of a typically Russian appearance, as one might with qualifications speak of a typically Swedish one. Soviet style has however given Russians, especially from the official classes, certain features in common.

Ethnic Russians make up 82.6% of the population of the Russian Federation (119 million out of 145.3 million in 1987). There are also large groups of ethnic Russians living in other former Soviet republics, totalling approximately 25 million: 11 million in Ukraine; 6.2 million in Kazakhstan; and 2.3 million in the Baltic States. There are also large populations in Uzbekistan and Moldova. More than a million people of ethnic Russian origin also live in the West, descended from people who emigrated after the Russian Revolution or were taken prisoner by the Germans during World War II and chose to remain. The largest Russian émigré communities are in the United States and France.

NATIONAL CHARACTER ■

The Russian national identity today is in a state of flux. Other nations emerged from Communism badly damaged but with their core national traditions and identities intact, since the peoples concerned had devoted much effort, both covert and overt, to preserving those traditions from destruction by Soviet and Communist culture. This was particularly true of the Poles, the Baltic peoples and the Georgians.

The Russian case was different. As the imperial people, they took genuine pride in the Soviet Union as their own state and in consequence absorbed far more of Soviet culture than did the other European nations under Soviet rule: Soviet style debased the Russian language far more than it did Polish. Moreover, Soviet patriotism fed to a considerable extent off the symbols and sentiments of traditional Russian nationalism, and in the process devalued them. Young Russians, having had these national symbols drilled into them all their lives, are much less likely to value them than are other nations, for whom they represent liberation from Communist tyranny. The future character of the Russian people is therefore extremely hard to predict. The old pre-Revolutionary Russia is clearly gone for good, and much of the spirit of the Soviet period is also fading. The old cliché about educated Russians loving to sit and talk endlessly about spiritual matters while drinking tea or vodka no longer holds true. In the past, thanks to the nature of Russian society under the Tsars and the Communists, many of these intellectuals did not have very much work to do: today most are far too busy trying to make money to have much time left over for philosophical speculation.

HISTORICAL CONTROVERSIES ■

As the Russians of today try to reconstruct a national identity on the ruins left behind by Communism, history has become once again a field of vast importance and vast potential for good and harm. Some of the moves to rediscover the national past are beautiful and moving; others, such as the use of tacky Russian imperial symbols in advertisements, are vulgar and pathetic; some, as adopted by the neo-Fascist parties of the hardline opposition, are vicious and dangerous.

Two of the greatest Russian historiographical controversies concern the origins of the Russian nation and state in 10th-century Kiev. One of these is now of mainly academic interest: the question of whether Kievan Rus was founded by Vikings from Scandinavia (the Varangians). For almost two centuries, in the face of all the evidence, many Russian nationalist historians sought to deny this, because of the insulting suggestion that it brings with it that the Russians were not capable of creating a state on their own. The reported petition of the people of Rus for a Varangian ruler, 'Our land is rich but it has no order', has echoed down the centuries as a justification of the need for authoritarian rule in Russia.

The long struggle to show the Slav character of the original Kievan monarchy symbolizes the deep inferiority complex that Russians have long felt towards the west, the fear that they are regarded as barbarians, and the wish to compensate for this is either by superior spiritual values, greater military strength, or bizarre would-be combinations of the two, such as Soviet Communism. At the moment, Russians are more than ever conscious of their inferiority to the west, and many

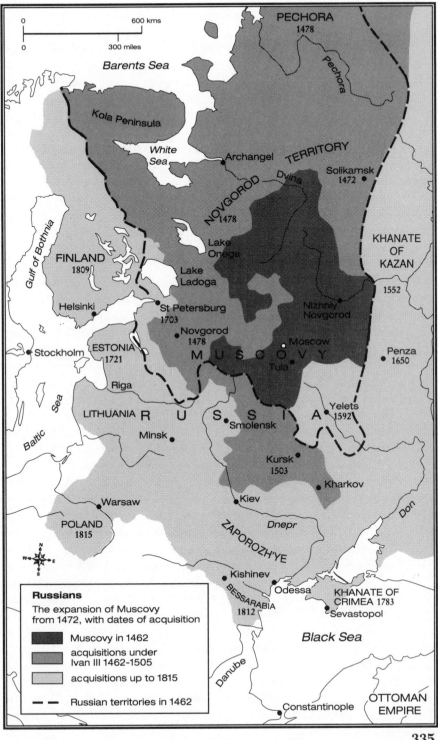

Russians

The expansion of Muscovy from 1472, with dates of acquisition

- Muscovy in 1462
- acquisitions under Ivan III 1462-1505
- acquisitions up to 1815
- – – Russian territories in 1462

Barents Sea

Kola Peninsula

White Sea

PECHORA
1478

Pechora

Archangel

Dvina

Solikamsk
1472

NOVGOROD TERRITORY
1478

Lake Onega

Lake Ladoga

FINLAND
1809

Helsinki

Gulf of Bothnia

KHANATE OF KAZAN
1552

Nizhniy Novgorod

St Petersburg
1703

Novgorod
1478

Moscow

MUSCOVY

Tula

Penza
1650

Stockholm

ESTONIA
1721

Riga

LITHUANIA R U S S I A

Minsk

Smolensk

Yelets
1592

Baltic Sea

Kursk
1503

Kharkov

Warsaw

Kiev

Don

POLAND
1815

ZAPOROZH'YE

Dnepr

Kishinev

Odessa

KHANATE OF CRIMEA 1783

BESSARABIA
1812

Sevastopol

Black Sea

Danube

Constantinople

OTTOMAN EMPIRE

observers have expressed the fear that this will in time lead to some sort of compensatory messianic backlash.

The other great controversy centred on Kievan Rus concerns links between Russian and Ukraine. This is an issue of the most compelling importance today, with the Ukraine newly-emerged as an independent state (see pp. 332). For the vast majority of Russians, Kievan Rus was a Russian state and in consequence, all the lands of Kievan Rus are still today 'Russian lands' – and that includes Ukraine. This attitude presents by far the biggest threat of a really major war on the territory of the former Soviet Union. Differences in Ukrainian language and culture are explained away by most Russians as simply due to the long period of Polish-Lithuanian rule over much of Ukraine, from the 14th to the 18th centuries. 'Ukraine is an artificial country, created by the Communists', and 'Ukrainian is simply Russian spoken with a Polish accent' are frequently-heard phrases, even from moderate Russian nationalists.

KIEVAN RUSSIA AND THE TATAR YOKE ■

The Eastern Slavic tribes who were gathered by the Varangians into Kievan Rus were pagans with a loose tribal form of social organization. Conversion to Orthodox Christianity came in 987, after emissaries of Grand Prince Vladimir were favourably impressed by the glories of Byzantine Constantinople. According to the Chronicles, the Prince turned down Judaism on the grounds that God could not have loved the Jews, or he would not have scattered them over the face of the earth, and Islam on the grounds that the Russian people could not possibly live without alcohol.

Spread as it was over vast distances, Kievan Rus progressively broke up into smaller principalities ruled by descendants of the House of Rurik, owing a more-or-less formal allegiance to the head of the family in Kiev. This city, lying on the edge of the great Eurasian steppe was permanently vulnerable to attack by nomads. In 1237, the greatest nomadic force of all, the Mongols, swept into Russian and brought to an end the Kievan period. Kiev and other cities were destroyed amidst hideous cruelty. One legendary city, Kitezh, was supposedly saved by God by being raised to heaven or drowned in a lake – an image which has become an abiding symbol for Russians of the true Russia, or Russian culture, preserved intact by a miracle despite all the vicissitudes and cruelties of Russian history. The 'Tatar Yoke' period – Tatar, from the Turkic peoples on Russia's eastern frontier who joined the Mongols – has been blamed for much of the subsequent misery of Russian history. It supposedly set back Russian cultural and economic development by hundreds of years, ensuring that Russia would lag behind the West. It is also said to have introduced into Russia the savagely autocratic methods of government so characteristic of later regimes. Recently, some historians have tried to give a more differentiated picture of the Tatar period, but the Tatar Yoke image remains deeply rooted in Russian consciousness. It makes Russians of today react with considerable irritation to claims by the large Tatar population in Russia that they were innocent victims of Russian colonialism. For more than 200 years, Russian princes had to pay tribute to the Tatar Khans and were dependent on them for confirmation of their right to rule. The Tatars played the Russian princes off against each other, and more than one Prince was forced to cross half of Asia to the Great Khan only to be summarily executed when he got there. The Princes of Moscow, hitherto an obscure settlement, rose to prominence largely through their skill in winning Tatar favour.

TSARIST RUSSIA ■

In 1380, on the field of Kulikovo beyond the Don River, Prince Dmitri Donskoy of Moscow defeated a Tatar host, but it was another century before Moscow dared refuse tribute to the Tatars altogether. The Tatar Khanates of Kazan and Astrakhan on the Volga were finally conquered by Ivan the Terrible in the 1550s. The Tatars of Crimea, with Ottoman Turkish backing, held out until the 1780s, and until then much of Southern Russia and Ukraine were open to their raids. Ukrainian historians argue that the Muscovite state which progressively conquered most of the former lands of Kievan Rus from the 14th century to the 20th was not the legitimate de-scendant of the Kievan State, but a completely new foundation. Russian historians have replied by pointing to the descent of the Princes of Moscow from those of Kiev, and to Moscow's role as the new centre of Orthodoxy after Constantinople had fallen to the Turks and Kiev to the Lithuanians. It is certainly true that Muscovite culture was considerably different from that of Kiev: the democratic or at least oligarchical aspects of Russian city states such as Novgorod were suppressed, to be replaced with a rigid autocracy propped up by an equally rigid Orthodox religion.

The old Muscovite monarchy reached both its apogee and its downfall under Ivan the Terrible (1530–84), one of the darkest figures in Russian history. Under his rule, Russia expanded vastly, the first Russian conquerors entered Siberia, and the Russian state sought to break through to the Baltic Sea. In view of this and the Tsar's hatred of the great noble families, Soviet and especially Stalinist historians portrayed Ivan as a modernizing despot, centralizing the Russian state and trying to break down feudal opposition. This was the official thinking behind Eisenstein's great film on Ivan, though the director risked reprisals by also showing some of the more maniacal spirit of the Tsar's later years.

Today, it seems that the comparison with Stalin is apt in another sense. Stalin, in pursuing his personal and communist vision, destroyed many of the best elements in Russian society and despite the appearance of greatly increased power, in fact left the country dreadfully weakened. This is now apparent in the greater difficulty that Russia is experiencing, compared to most East European countries, in struggling out from under communism.

Ivan's monstrous cruelties against his people and finally his own family helped destroy his dynasty. After his death, power fell into the hands of various usurpers, and civil war led to a brief period of Polish occupation of Moscow. This period is known as the 'Time of Troubles', a phrase often invoked to describe the position of Russia today.

Victory over the Polish invaders led to the election by the great nobles of one of their number, Mikhail Romanov, as Tsar of all the Russias in 1613. His dynasty ruled over Russia until 1917 and presided over what is now seen as its most glorious epoch. In the course of the 17th century, Mikhail's successors were able to consolidate the state and took Kiev from the Poles in 1654 – though only after a revolt by the Ukrainian Cossacks which marks the beginning of Ukrainian nationalism. Subsequent Tsars spent generations wriggling out of the concessions made to the Ukrainian Cossacks and nobles in return for their adherence to Muscovy.

In order to organize the population for war, the Russian monarchy sanctioned a vast increase in noble powers over the peasantry, a process which intensified until by the 18th century serfs could be bought and sold like slaves. Serfdom had incalculable effects on Russian history and the Russian national character. To it have been traced a Russian tendency to apathy and acceptance punctuated by bloody revolt, as exemplified by the revolts of Stenka Razin (died 1671) and Pugachev (died 1775). Less-than-enthusiastic Russian attitudes to work have also been traced to the fact that so much of peasant work in the past was forced work for noble masters.

Serfdom played a vital role in preventing the development of a class of private peasant farmers. Instead, peasants remained lumped together in the *Mir of Commune*, the land held in common and periodically redistributed. After the revolution of 1905, the reforming Russian Prime Minister Pyotr Stolypin recognized that a class of peasant proprietors could help prevent revolution and lay the foundation of mass acceptance of private property, but he had too little time. The lack of such attitudes in much of Russian society has been greatly reinforced by Communism, and the tendency of Russians to fall back on ancient populist attitudes to ownership presents a major danger for the growth of a successful capitalism in Russia.

The growth of the Cossacks on Russia's southern and eastern frontiers was to a great extent a result of the expansion of the Russian state and in particular, of state backing for the extension of serfdom. Russian peasants escaping serfdom tended to flee to the frontier, where from the 16th century on they joined the Cossacks, who took their name from a Turkic word meaning nomad or wanderer. The Cossacks were the equivalent of the American frontiersmen. They defended the frontiers against nomad attacks, and in Siberia they performed miracles of exploration, crossing some 4000 miles of uncharted territory in barely 50 years. However, in general, the power of the Russian state and the Russian nobility meant that in contrast to America, the impact of the frontier on Russian culture was limited. It certainly did not lay a basis for 'rugged individualism' and free political institutions.

The reign of Peter the Great (1672–1725) greatly increased state power and brought the beginning of a critical shift in Russian historical development, the effects of which continue to this day. Impressed with the technological and cultural superiority of the West, and determined to make Russia a great power, he embarked on a process of forced westernization, which involved an attempt to sweep away the greater part of the Russian national tradition and replace it with western forms. The greatest symbol of this enterprise was his foundation of a new western-style capital with a western name, Sankt Petersburg, on the shores of the Baltic, to replace Moscow with its medieval and religious associations.

The founding Congress of the main political bloc supporting Russian President Boris Yeltsin in the December 1993 elections, 'Russia's Choice', was dominated by a huge portrait of Peter the Great. This did not greatly encourage western observers concerned about the future of Russian democracy under Yeltsin for while Peter was undoubtedly the greatest westernizing modernizer in Russia's history, his worst enemy would not have thought of calling him a democrat. Tens of thousands of prisoners and serfs died laying the foundations of St Petersburg, and many Russian writers have felt that this placed the city, and Russian history, under a curse.

Peter's reforms made Russia a great power, but they introduced a profound split into Russian society and culture. As the 18th century progressed, the nobility, which at that time constituted virtually the whole 'educated class' in the western sense, became progressively westernized, drawing further and further away from the clergy, merchants and peasantry, who remained tied to their traditional cultures. This alienation of the mass of the Russian people from the state and its élite was a key factor in preparing the way for the revolution of 1917. On the other hand, the realization of 19th century noble writers of their own distance from Russian culture and the Russian people, and their efforts to overcome this alienation, helped produce the greatest glories of Russian literature.

A guilty awareness of their distance from the people helped produce the socialist, anti-government strain which increasingly dominated the Russian intelligentsia as the 19th century progressed. This was also fed by messianic elements in the Russian tradition, which to a greater degree than western churches tended to overlook the problems of life on this earth in favour of contemplating the glories of the courts of heaven and the world to come. Millennial beliefs were also highly characteristic of the various Russian religious sects, some of which emerged in protest against Peter the Great's reforms of the Church (see p. 342). They contributed to a basic dislike of Russian people for the Russian state, which was fed by Peter's westernizing reforms. It is an apparent paradox that a country which produced the most notoriously all-encompassing state of modern times should have been populated by people who hated state power. To some extent, it is precisely the indifference of ordinary Russians to the state which in the past forced the state to organize society and allowed it to act so very brutally. State brutality then alienated ordinary Russians still further.

This religious feeling fed communism, and Soviet rhetoric about the perfect Communist society of the future had unmistakeably religious overtones. A key question for Russia's future is whether the messianic tradition in her culture and politics has been burnt out of her by the cruelties and disappointments of Soviet rule, or whether it will resurface again to trouble the world.

Under Peter the Great and Catherine the Great (1729–96), Russia expanded vastly, swallowing most of Poland and the steppes along the Black Sea Coast. Under their 19th-century successors, the Russian army conquered the Transcaucasus,

Central Asia and the Russian Far East, facing Japan. In 1812, the empire faced its greatest threat since the Time of Troubles when the armies of Napoleon marched as far as Moscow before being destroyed by a mixture of Russian stubbornness and the Russian winter.

THE REVOLUTION AND SOVIET RUSSIA ■

By the later 19th century, however, defeat in the Crimean War and near defeat against the Turks in 1877–8 had led to a renewed awareness of how far Russia still lagged behind Western Europe, and of the threat this presented to Russia's security. The Russian government embarked on a forced process of capitalist economic development, stimulated above all by the construction of railways.

This process led to striking rates of economic growth, which had they continued unchecked would ultimately have made of Russia a prosperous free-market society. They also, however, led to the growth of an impoverished urban proletariat, and when added to the strains of World War I, the social tension produced by economic change destroyed the Tsarist regime and with that the rule of the europeanized upper classes.

What followed was one of the most horrible episodes in human history. Expressing the pent-up bitterness of centuries, both on the part of the descendants of Russian serfs and of ethnic minorities like the Jews, the Communists set about dismantling Russian civilization, both traditional and westernized, and the bases of a dynamic Russian economy. Under Lenin this process was temporarily halted in 1921 by peasant revolts and military mutinies. Under Stalin, it resumed with full force from 1929.

Following the destruction of peasant independence, the intelligentsia was savaged, and the Communist Party itself decimated and reduced to complete subjection to Stalin's will: millions died; the whole of society was dragooned into a totalitarian model later dismally exported to many other states. This was the version in life of the old Russian intellectual dream that the Russian people would one day 'say their word' to the world.

World War II, which was in large part brought about by Soviet Russia's self-imposed isolation from the West, increased further the brutalizing of Russian society. Defeat would have turned Russians into a nation of German slaves. Victory preserved their existence, but also burdened them with an immense and unruly empire in Eastern Europe. The cost of subsidizing and defending that empire drained wealth out of Russia and helped make a true reform of Communism impossible – Russia has still not recovered from Stalinism. The all-encompassing savagery of the process affected almost every family, especially those from the old intelligentsia. On the other hand, for this very reason, educated Russians today seem much less likely to embrace really extreme form of politics than they might otherwise have been. The political effect of the awful memory of Stalin's camps is not as obvious as has been the memory of Nazism in Germany, but it is very powerful nonetheless.

The Leninist and Stalinist record also helped doom Mikhail Gorbachev's attempts at a reformed Communist system. As soon as the full extent of Soviet crimes became known, the attempt to create a respectable Communism collapsed, under the weight of its own sins.

After Stalin, communist rule continued for another 30 years. Political struggles at the top were now conducted without violence on the principle of 'dog does not eat dog'. Dissidents were sometimes severely repressed, but the mass of the population was not terrorized. However, the relentless coarsening of behaviour and morals by the continuous grinding pressure of Soviet life and the odious tone of Soviet mass culture proceeded apace.

For most of the period from 1953 to 1985, a slow but steady rise in living standards, and spectacular achievements in the field of space exploration and military expansion helped remove the sources of discontent. By the start of the 1980s, however, it was clear that the command economy was faltering badly. It could no longer produce even the miserable consumer goods needed to keep the population happy. Nor, much more importantly for the Soviet establishment, could it produce the high-technology armaments needed to continue the arms race with the West.

The result was establishment backing for Mikhail Gorbachev's doomed attempt at economic reform by exhortation from above. This process was to be carried out by the intelligentsia, who in return had to be given the freedom of expression they so desired. This they then turned on the system, and when to their revolt was added that of the subject nationalities and part of the Russian proletariat, the communist system collapsed, taking the Soviet Union with it. With them went the Russian empire, as it had formed from the 17th century onwards. The result was the loss to Russia not just of areas like Ukraine which had been Russian for hundreds of years, but also some 25 million Russians living outside the Russian Federation's borders. Whether the Russian people will accustom themselves to these facts or will seek to overturn them will be one of the greatest defining questions of world politics in the next decades.

At the moment, ordinary Russians are so worn down by economic hardship and the demoralizing effects of Soviet rule that they hardly seem to care very much about the loss of empire. They have reached the same stage of imperial indifference that the British experienced by 1947 or the French by 1963. The difference is that for the Western European imperial states, the loss of empire was softened by economic prosperity. For most Russian, that still seems a distant prospect.

RELIGION ■

Under the Tsars, the identification of 'Russian' and 'Orthodox' was in theory absolute. Under imperial law, ethnic Russians were listed not as Russians but as Orthodox, and anyone from another nationality who converted to Orthodoxy was automatically considered to have become Russian. Ordinary Russian peasants did in fact often address each other collectively as 'Ye Orthodox!'.

The official national slogan of Nicholas I, to which his successors also paid at least lip service, was 'Autocracy, Orthodoxy, Nationalism'. This identification of state and nation with a particular religion and ideology obviously had a major effect in shaping the totalitarian cast of much of Russian thought in the 19th and 20th centuries, and contributed directly to the emergence of Communist rule.

In practice, however this identification was never as absolute as it looked. Until the conversion of 987, the Russian people were pagans, and during their vast territorial expansion from the 10th century on, they assimilated huge numbers of other pagan peoples. The Mordvins (see p. 364), a russified Finno-Ugric people living a bare 200 miles from Moscow, were still worshipping their Bear-God Keremet until well into this century. Various pagan and semi-pagan beliefs remained deeply-rooted in Russian peasant culture and attitudes, and may have contributed to the abundance in pre-revolutionary times of Russian religious sects, some of them with beliefs that appear to have little to do with Christianity.

From 1654, the Russian Orthodox Church suffered a formal schism, with a large part of it breaking away to form the so-called Old Believers. On the surface, this conflict was concerned with small aspects of ritual practice: the Old Believers objected to a Church reform bringing Russian Orthodoxy into line with that of the Greek and Balkan churches, for example that the sign of the cross be made with three fingers rather than two. An obsessive concern with petty dogmatism certainly played a part in the conflict, but it has also been convincingly explained as the first internal conflict resulting from the new imperial policy of the Russian state. Bringing Russia into line with Greek practice was meant to make Russia a more convincing leader of all the Orthodox of the world, and especially the leader of the Balkan Orthodox against the Turks. The Old Believers revolted against this in support of their own more purely Muscovite and Russian culture.

Apart from the monstrous cruelties practised by the state against the Old Believers, the Schism lost to Orthodoxy and the Russian state some of the most dedicated and religiously devout elements of the Russian nation. Like their Methodist equivalents in England, with state service barred to them, their energies came to be concentrated on commercial activity, and most of the great merchant families of late 19th-century Russia were of Old Believer origin.

The closeness of the Orthodox Church to the state was to have fatal effects both under the Tsars and under Communism, especially after Peter the Great abolished the Patriarchate of Moscow and subordinated the Church to a state ministry; priests came to be seen as mere state agents. Under Communist rule, after an initial period of severe persecution, Stalin gave limited toleration to the Church as a force for Russian nationalism during World War II, and used the Orthodox against more dissident churches like the Baptists and the Uniates in Ukraine. The struggle between Orthodox and Uniates in Ukraine is closely bound up with the struggle between Ukrainian nationalism and pro-Russian elements in that country.

The Orthodox Church, and especially its hierarchy, became heavily penetrated by the KGB. The bishops showed a slavish willingness to echo the Soviet official line in international affairs, for example denouncing the alleged imperialism and militarism of the United States. Priests like Gleb Yakunin, who attempted to defend the Church publicly, were not merely persecuted by the state but denounced by their own bishops.

This less than honourable record has sapped the prestige of the Church, and diminished its chances of benefiting from the fall of Communism. Urbanization and modernization, added to Soviet restrictions, also mean that today in Russia, as in the West, although many people profess some kind of Christian belief, actual church attendance is very small.

On the surface, the renaissance of the Church is very visible, with churches being handed back, much state use of religious symbolism and many public appearances by bishops on the state media. In private, however, many ordinary Russians believe in a modern version of semi-magical practices, as witnessed by the striking success of 'faith-healers'. American tele-evangelists, and Orientalist religions like Hare Krishna are also making major inroads, leading to successful calls from the Orthodox hierarchy for laws restricting the activities of 'foreign' religious groups. One of the great dangers facing the Orthodox Church is that such pressures may increase a historical tendency to identify with chauvinist Russian political groups, diminishing its ability to speak for the whole Russian people.

LANGUAGE AND LITERATURE ■

The Russian language is much greater than the Russian state or even the Russian nation. Like the English and French languages, imperial rule by the Russian nation has meant that its language has escaped from its control, and is now used as a literary language by writers whose own origins have nothing to do with Russian ethnicity: men like the Kirghiz Chingis Aitmatov, the Abkhaz Fazil Iskander, and of course very large numbers of Jews. In many cases, these writers or their ancestors saw Russian as a passport to a wider and freer world than the one into which they were born.

For Russian Jewish writers like Osip Mandelstam and Joseph Brodsky, loyalty to the Russian language and Russian literature – in Mandelstam's case, literally unto death – has led to their own kind of literary patriotism, a loyalty not to traditional Russian nationalism, but to their own ideals of Russian culture. One of the questions facing Russian culture today is whether, following the loss of the empire, the Russian language can go on acting as a world language of literature, or whether it will retreat to a more narrow national role – which would be a sad loss for Russia and the world.

The Russian language emerged from the group of Eastern Slavonic dialects which also gave birth to modern Ukrainian and Belorussian. The first language of literature, and indeed the basis of much Russian writing until the 18th century, was Church Slavonic, which was influenced by the language of the Balkan Bulgars, and which in the course of the centuries became progressively more distant from the spoken Russian language.

The Kievan period saw the production of historical chronicles, of the famous *Lay of Igor's Host*, and of *Byliny*, popular epic tales concerned with the Bogatyrs (super-human warriors) and other legendary figures. Throughout the Kievan, Mongol and Muscovite periods, a major literary form was the Lives of the Saints. By contrast to the west, until the reign of Peter the Great and the 18th century, there was no development of modern theatre, of lyrical poetry, or of proto-novels like those of Cervantes and Rabelais.

As far as the nobility were concerned, the fossilized literary tradition was exploded by Peter's westernization, which led to a flood of first German and then French cultural influence. Until well into the 19th century, much of the high aristocracy spoke better French than it did Russian – a situation much satirized by Tolstoy, among others.

The result in the 18th and early 19th centuries was inevitably a highly derivative literature, slavishly obedient to French forms and almost wholly lacking in talent. The 18th century, however, also saw the first formal codification and standardization of the Russian literary language under the great scholar Mikhail Lomonosov. His work laid the foundation for the literary glories of the 19th century. These included the first great Russian modern writer, Alexander Pushkin, a liberal but also a strong Russian patriot, and for that reason extremely popular as an official symbol under Soviet rule.

This pride in Russia among writers was, however, checked both by an awareness of Russian poverty, corruption, cruelty and backwardness, and by a guilty awareness of their distance from the Russian people, and of the artificial nature of their culture. A majority of Russian writers for much of the 19th century were also noble landowners like Gogol, Tolstoy, and Turgenev, guilty of noble exploitation of their serfs, and humiliated by the contrast between their near-absolute power on their own estates and their absolute submission before State and Monarchy. These various tensions can be seen as having played a critical part in producing the unparalleled depth and richness of 19th-century Russian literature.

One feature of this Russian literature and the intelligentsia which produced it, which has recurred in the 20th century is that most of its representatives were oppositionists, critical of the Russian autocratic state. Another strong strand, with deep roots in the Russian tradition, was the frequency of different forms of eschatology – the belief in the possibility of a quite different and better world – associated with either Russian national-religious values, with socialism, or both. Even supporters of the Russian monarchy such as Gogol and Dostoyevsky were often more like religious prophets than pragmatic conservatives in the western sense. This was also true of the utopian Lev Tolstoy.

By the early 20th century, the so-called Silver Age of Russian literature, there were signs that these characteristics of Russian literature were diminishing in the face of a concern with art for art's sake more characteristic of the *fin de siècle* in western Europe. The Russian Revolution, however, ushered in first the triumph and then the utter debasement of the messianic elements in Russian culture. After an initial period of flowering of various modernistic literary and artistic sects – which made

344

ruthless attempts to use Communist power to gain ascendancy over each other – Stalin ushered in the period of socialist realism. As the officially dominant form this persisted until the time of Mikhail Gorbachev, not just because it was the most suitable for state propagandist purposes, but because the sons of workers and peasants who formed the Communist élite actually liked this kind of literature. Their rule also greatly coarsened the Russian language, though the introduction to literature of slang words from the prison camps undoubtedly brought a certain vigour.

A few masterpieces were produced by writers loyal to the regime, most notably the works of Mikhail Sholokhov. The bulk of great Russian writing, however, moved once more into opposition. The difference was that, unlike in Tsarist times, the far greater controls exercised by the communist state meant that in most cases it could not be published in Russia at all. Hence was born *samizdat*, the circulation and copying of works in manuscript, or smuggled in from abroad. The image of Russian intellectuals laboriously copying out such novels – for photocopiers were strictly controlled – is one of the most moving images in the history of civilization.

Precisely for this reason, the end of Soviet dictatorship has left Russian literature very much at sea. It has lost its character as an opposition, and not yet found another role. In the words of the author Viktor Erofeyev, 'Perestroika this time, in contrast with Khrushchev's thaw, proved too bottomless for liberal literature, and in this well many works which yesterday seemed amazingly bold began to drown'. Anti-western conservative nationalist writers, for their part, risk being sucked into becoming mere propagandists for increasingly ugly chauvinist politics.

Partly for financial reasons, and partly in a search for novelty, an increasing number of writers began to turn to popular criminal and pornographic themes. Others became involved in politics, lost their inspiration to write, or failed to gain publishers in a market both increasingly commercial and increasingly poor. Meanwhile, even educated Russians, sated with exposures of Soviet tyranny and harassed by economic hardship, have turned to western potboilers such as Agatha Christie and James Hadley Chase.

Many writers have begun to proclaim the death of Russian literature, following what already seems to be the death of the Russian literary film at the hands of western mass culture. Of course, Russian literature will not die completely. But like the Russian nation, Russian culture is certainly going through one of the most confused patches in its history, a period of turmoil whose outcome cannot be foreseen.

11

THE URALS AND CAUCASUS

This is where doubts multiply. The weakness of 'Europe' as a geographical concept is exposed here, where Europe blends into Asia with no obvious discontinuities. The Urals are modest mountains, with Russians preponderant on both sides; though the Caucasus makes a spectacular frontier zone, it includes no clear dividing line. Compared with the sharp outlines of Africa, Antarctica and the Americas and the divisions which separate Asia from the rest, 'Europe' here looks more like a promontory of Asia than a discrete continent.

Soviet geographers fixed the limit of Europe north of the Caucasus, along the alarmingly-named Manych Depression. Objectively considered, this now looks like a partisan political device to exclude the peoples of the Caucasus from equality of consideration with their neighbours. Even so formidable a mountain range, with relatively few and difficult passes, is an inefficient barrier and many features of the culture straddle the region.

Remote, hard of access and highly defensible, the position of these mountains at the frontiers of Russian, Turkish and Persian empires has made them a refuge for small, tenaciously independent communities and nations; the high altitudes and narrow valleys have encouraged divergent political development; and, especially on the fertile southern elevations, mutually hostile ethnic and religious groups have been inextricably mixed.

In dealing with the non-Russian peoples of the Urals and west to the Volga Valley, soviet ethnography insisted on pedantic divisions, splitting peoples into classifications. Yet most of them have kept a strong and potentially disruptive sense of identity, religious in the Muslim case, ethnic, and principally Finnic, among the non-Muslims.

VOLGA TATARS

Volga Tatars offer an unique example in the history of the Muslim peoples, that of a nation which has survived, maintaining its faith, culture and language, for over four centuries of foreign domination and assimilation policies. The total population of the Republic of Tatarstan in the second half of 1992 was 3,695,900. The Tatars numbered 1,700,110 and the Russians 1,575,361. According to the last 1989 All-

Union Census, the population of the Volga Tatars in the USSR, the only Turkic Muslim diaspora nation, was 6,648,760. In the RSFSR (Russian Republic) according to the same data their number was 5,522,096. They are thus the second largest nation after the Russians in the Russian Federation. The demographic increase of the Tatars between 1970 and 1979, 6.5%, was the lowest of any Muslim nation in the USSR, almost as low as that of the Russians. This exceptionally poor growth may be explained by three factors: the low natural increase of the urban colonies which account for over half of the community; assimilation by the Turkic host nationalities in Central Asia; and the fact that Tatars simply hid their nationality in a Russian milieu for fear of discrimination. Indeed the word 'Tatar' (tatarin) is still used as an insult in the Russian language. The real number of Tatars in the CIS is almost certainly greater than that shown by the official data.

ORIGINS AND TRADITION ■

Despite their modest number in their original homeland, the Tatars of Kazan have played an important role in the cultural, political and religious life of the Muslim nations of the Russian and Soviet empires since the end of the 19th century. They were the initiators of the first religious and educational reforms in the Muslim world and the first to articulate national liberation programmes for the colonial world. However, on the eve of the disintegration of the Soviet Union, the Tatar nation had reached a critical stage and was threatened with 'dying out' through assimilation by Russians or other Turks, and the loss of their language, traditions, culture and iden-tity. Today the Tatars are again in the forefront of national politics through their efforts to gain sovereignty and independence from the Russian Federation, and act as role models for the small republics of the Volga Ural region and other 'autono-mous' regions of the Federation. This virtual renaissance of the Tatar nation is due to the efforts and courage of a handful of intellectuals determined to rehabilitate their national heritage.

The exact origin of the modern Volga or 'Kazan' Tatars is still being debated today. There is a consensus among scholars, however, that they are the descendants of the Bulgars, later intermingled with Turkic tribes of the Golden Horde and East-ern Finns. The ethnic types of the Volga Tatars vary from the Finnic (blond with blue eyes), to the Caucasian and more seldom the mongoloid type close to the Kazakhs. They are an old sedentary nation and have completely lost their tribal and clan struc-ture. In its present form the Tatar literary language dates from the 14th century al-though earliest written monuments go back to the 11th century. The Arabic alphabet was used until 1927, Latin from 1927 to 1940, and Cyrillic from 1940. There is a strong lobby among the intelligentsia to return to the Latin alphabet.

THE LAND ■

The territory of the Republic of Tatarstan, capital Kazan, covers an area of 26,600 square miles. It is a rich agricultural land controlling river communications from

Volga Tartars, Muslim-Turkic and Mongol Peoples of the Volga-Urals and Daghestan

A.R. Autonomous Republic

the Caspian to the Baltic seas. It produces between 20 and 25% of Russia's oil requirements and has a large military industrial infrastructure. The climate is continental northern European.

HISTORICAL BACKGROUND ■

The Bulgar tribes began to arrive in the Middle Volga in the mid-7th century after the Khazars' victory over the Bulgar Union in the Pontic steppes (cf p. 389). At the end of the 9th century, the process of territorial, tribal and political consolidation brought about the emergence of a prosperous Bulgar state. In 922, Ibn Fadlan, the envoy of Caliph Jafar al-Muktadir reached the Bulgar Kingdom. This year marks the official conversion of the Bulgar Kingdom to Islam, although Islam was already widely spread along the Volga.

In 1236 the Mongol army led by Batu conquered and devastated the Bulgar Kingdom. The Mongol conquest provoked a massive population upheaval, but the

349

Bulgar lands soon recovered from the destruction. The conversion to Islam of Khan Berke (1256–1266) intensified the ties between the Golden Horde and the Muslims of the Middle Volga, increasing the interaction between the Turkic peoples of the Horde. For over a century afterwards, the Bulgars were able to benefit from the indirect political rule favoured by the Mongols and the wealth generated by a *Pax Mongolica*.

At the end of the 14th century, the Bulgar lands became the theatre of confrontation between Tamerlane and Tokhtamysh who clashed in 1391 and 1395 for control over the disintegrating Golden Horde. Taking advantage of this struggle, neighbouring Russian princes attacked and devastated the entire region in 1395. The Bulgars then began to move northward and settle along the shores of the Kazanka and Kama rivers. Finally in 1437, the khan of the Golden Horde, Ulu Muhammad, fled his capital, Saray, and his son, Mahmud, took over the throne of Kazan or Bulgar-al-Jadid (the 'new' Bulgar) in 1445.

The new Khanate of Kazan continued the commercial traditions and contacts of the Bulgar Kingdom and the Golden Horde and built a rich market which included Muscovy, the Siberian Khanate, the Caucasus, Persia and Central Asia. Cultural life in the spirit of Islamic tradition and literature flourished and the language of the Tatars took shape as a distinct branch of the Kipchak division of the Turkic language family. Muscovy's dependence on trade with Kazan and the Khanate's alliance with Crimea brought Russian interference in Kazan's domestic affairs, which was facilitated by succeeding dynastic conflicts. It culminated with the conquest and destruction of the Kazan Khanate in 1552 by the army of Ivan IV, the Terrible.

Military conquest was followed by systematic colonization and destruction of Tatar society. The ruling classes were ruined, Tatars were expelled from Kazan, their lands confiscated. As a result, by the end of the 16th century the territory of the former Kazan Khanate already had a mixed Russian/Tatar population and by the end of the 18th century the Tatars became a minority in their homeland. Soon after the fall of Kazan the successor of Ivan the Terrible, Tsar Feodor, launched an energetic missionary campaign as a result of which a relatively large number of Tatars became Christian Orthodox. Religious persecutions, similar to those suffered by the Muslims after the Spanish reconquista of Andalusia, reached a peak in the middle of the 18th century. Results included a massive exodus of the Tatars towards Turkestan, the Kazakh steppes and Siberia, frequent joint armed uprising with the Bashkirs, and active participation in the two great Russian popular rebellions of Stanka Razin and Pugachev (1667–71 and 1773–5 respectively).

Catherine II's favourable attitude to Islam brought a reprieve from the anti-Tatar policy. In 1783 a Central Muslim Spiritual Board was established in Orenburg to serve the needs of the Muslim subjects of the empire, and for a century afterwards the Tatar merchant class cooperated loyally with the Russian government, setting up trading colonies in Central Asia still closed to the Russians in Siberia, and China. The conquest of Central Asia in the second half of the 19th century put an end to this partnership and the Russian government embarked on a new campaign of religious conversion. However, the collaboration encouraged by Catherine II had brought enormous wealth to the Tatar community and encouraged the birth of a vigorous bourgeoisie which allowed them to react to this renewed pressure. Tatar élites understood that in order to survive they had to gain intellectual and economic equality with the Russians, preserve Islam as the basis of their community and reject all internal conflicts. Their efforts to this end gave birth to a modern reformist movement – *Jadidism* – which encompassed all aspects of social life : religion, education, women's liberation and so on. The movement flourished thanks to a remarkable unity of purpose among all layers of society, and on the eve of the revolution the Tatars were a developed nation enjoying a higher degree of literacy than the Russians, with a sophisticated capitalist and industrial experience.

During the October 1917 Revolution and ensuing civil war the Tatars took part in the conflict on the side of the Bolsheviks, lured by Lenin and Stalin's promises of self-determination. The Tatar Mir Said Sultan Galiev became the highest ranking Muslim in Stalin's powerful People's Commissariat of Nationalities. Although accused of nationalist deviation, arrested and executed in the late 1930s, he elaborated a doctrine of 'national communism' for the colonial nations of the East which was to influence the thinking of future leaders such as Mao Tse-tung, Lin Piao, Nasser and Ben Bella. The hopes of the nationalists for a large state on the Volga were crushed with the creation on 23rd March 1919 of the Bashkir Autonomous Soviet Socialist Republic, followed by the Tatar Autonomous Soviet Socialist Republic on 27th May 1920. The borders of the republics were drawn arbitrarily, leaving 75% of the Tatar population outside the boundaries of their namesake republic while in the Bashkir ASSR they represented the ethnic majority.

The Tatars are Sunni Muslims of the Hanafi school. Throughout the centuries they have produced a distinguished school of Islamic theologians. During the Soviet years the practice of Islam was minimal but it remains the basis of Tatar identity. Today, as in the other Muslim regions of the former USSR, there is a revival of Islam but it is imbued with the liberal and enlightened tradition of Jadidism.

POLITICAL SITUATION ■

Perestroika and the debacle of Afghanistan had the effect of a catalyst on the national movements of the USSR. In the Russian Federation the Tatars were the first to raise the question of federalism and sovereignty in the hope of upgrading the status of Tatarstan from 'autonomous' to 'union' republic. Dissatisfaction with the 'second-rate' status of Tatarstan had been endemic since the 1920s. It was brought forward in 1936 when a new constitution of the USSR was being adopted, and again in the 1960s and 1970s resulting in purges of the national élites. In 1988 at the prompting of the Tatar Public Centre, the first important political group to emerge in the Republic after perestroika, the issue came to the fore once again. Tatarstan declared sovereignty on 30th August 1990, the first autonomous republic to do so. The Declaration of Sovereignty limited the application of Russian laws on the territory of the Republic. On 17th March 1991 two referenda were held in the Soviet Union : the ill-fated All-Union referendum on the preservation of the USSR, and the Russian Federation referendum on the institution of the post of a popularly-elected president. Under pressure from the nationalists, the Supreme Soviet of Tatarstan declared on 28th May 1991 that 'The sovereign Republic of Tatarstan will not officially take part in the RSFSR presidential elections' but would instead hold its own presidential elections. These were held on 12th June 1991, the same day as in Russia, and Mintimer Shaymiyev was elected president of Tatarstan. After the CIS had been set up, Tatarstan demanded to be admitted as a founding member of the Commonwealth, a *de facto* call for recognition as an independent state. The following months saw intense political activity, the Tatar nationalist groups demanding a referendum on the status of the republic to decide on its relation with Russia.

The referendum was held on 21 March 1992 despite fierce opposition from Moscow – on 5 March, the Russian Parliament issued an appeal warning about the danger of inter-ethnic strife and separatism; the Constitutional Court ruled that the referendum was unconstitutional; and the day before it was due to be held, President Yeltsin of Russia went on television in a last ditch effort to influence the outcome of the voting, cautioning that it could tear the Russian Federation apart. 82% of the electorate took part in the referendum with 61.4% voting in favour of independence and 'equality' with Russia. These results were held as a minor triumph in Tatarstan because they showed that a significant proportion of the Russian population of the Republic had supported the local government.

In October 1992, Tatarstan adopted a new constitution. Three articles were considered particularly controversial : Article 59 which gave Tatarstan's laws precedence over Russian federal laws; Article 61 which confirmed Tatarstan's sovereignty according to international (rather than Russian) law but made provisions for mutual delegation of powers with Russia to be defined by a future treaty; and Article 62 which allowed Tatarstan to enter into diplomatic and economic relations according to the norms of international law. The Russian federalists, led by former Vice-President Alexander Rutskoy, considered that the implementation of the constitution would be the equivalent of secession and argued that independence and equality with Russia could not be envisaged because, in the absence of a new constitution in Russia, Tatarstan remained a dominion of the Russian Federation. For their part the Tatar nationalists objected to mutual delegation of power which they compared bluntly to 'delegating one's marital rights to a neighbour'

A further blow to Moscow's hegemony was inflicted when Tatarstan refused to sign the Federation Treaty in April 1992, an example which spurred other 'autonomous' republics and regions, Bashkortostan among them, to demand new concessions from the centre. Furthermore, Yeltsin's personal prestige suffered when almost 80% of the electorate of Tatarstan abstained from voting in the referendum of April 1993 called to win support against the now ousted Supreme Soviet – an indifference which can be interpreted as a *de facto* vote of no confidence.

THE ECONOMY ■

Until 1991, the economy of Tatarstan followed the pattern of a classic 'colonial' economy. This was the case for all the former republics of the USSR but, whereas union republics such as the now independent Baltic, Central Asian and Transcaucasian states were allowed to retain approximately 10% of their natural produce, the autonomous republics were further penalized and unable to retain more than 2% of their wealth. Following the Declaration of Sovereignty which decreed that all natural resources should belong to the republic and its peoples, and taking advantage of the 'self-financing' regime encouraged by Moscow, Tatarstan signed an economic agreement with Russia in January 1991. The agreement covered a wide area including oil and industrial enterprises, scientific and technological cooperation, quotas for export commodities, ecology and transportation of goods through the territory of the republic. However, three key fields remained disputed: Tatarstan's unilateral decision to adopt unitary taxation; the oil industry; and the military infrastructure.

Tatarstan contends that Russia has no right to its resources and revenues but is prepared to pay for services provided by Russia such as communications, defence, and so on, which it has estimated at between 4 and 5 billion Roubles in value, a figure which falls far short of the previous 17 billion Roubles in taxation collected by Russia previously. The government of Tatarstan claims to be ready to increase the amount of its contribution if Russia can justify the cost, which it has been unable to do so far. The full details of the oil agreement have remained secret with new quotas agreed annually. In 1991 Tatarstan agreed to supply 50% of its oil extraction to Russia in exchange for refinery and drilling equipment. Tatarstan has since accused Russia of not fulfilling its share of the agreement and falling behind with delivery. On 22nd December 1992, the parliament of Tatarstan voted to reduce the volume of oil extraction from 28 million tonnes to 24.8 million for 1993 and to raise the export quota from 5 million to 10 million. Notwithstanding this, the Russian Ministry of Fuel and Power Engineering set oil extraction for 1993 at 28 million tonnes – a course which would reduce the life span of the oil bearing strata by 10 or 15 years. However, on 28th January 1993, Tatarstan's Prime Minister, Mukhamat Sabirov, declared that a compromise had been reached to reduce Tatarstan's oil production to 25 million tonnes, but declined to reveal the amount of the export quota, saying only that this would be no less than the previous year's 5 million. He added that Tatarstan was sending Russia 2 million tonnes of oil as its share of payment for the foreign debt. With regard to the military infrastructure, Tatarstan wants to close down or transform the military-industrial complex for which it has no need and charge Moscow for the upkeep of the military personnel on its territory.

Negotiations with Russia have been going on since Tatarstan's Declaration of Sovereignty. The negotiating team is Tatar but is led by the republic's Russian vice-president Anatoly Likhachev, a lawyer. All the members of the team have been involved in the talks from the beginning while Russian negotiators change at every round of talks, an obvious delaying tactic. The Tatars are aware of the complexity of their situation because of the republic's position as an enclave. They have skilfully overcome most of Moscow's resistance so far, compromising when necessary, for instance over the language law which allows two official government languages – Tatar and Russian. The achievements on the path to independence obtained so far are substantial and correspond to *de facto* if not *de jure* sovereignty. They have been gained for the republic by the Tatars alone, who have regained virtual control of their homeland for the first time since the fall of Kazan despite initial strident opposition from the local Russian community. The government has approached privatization and the market economy cautiously and gradually with the result that the republic is emerging as the most stable and solid economy of the region. This has brought the Russian population, encouraged by Moscow to adopt radical nationalist and anti-sovereignty views, to reconsider the benefits of independence. It is generally accepted that the day Russia agrees to sign an inter-state treaty with Tatarstan, thus recognizing its independence, or merely acquiesces to its 'asymmetrical' status within the federation, will also mean the end of Russia's control over its other colonial dominions in the Volga-Urals, Siberia and the North Caucasus. The Tatars themselves, however, believe that, as they were the first to be colonized, they will be the last to be free.

TATAR SUB-GROUPS ■

Excluding the Crimean Tatars whose history and identity differs substantially, a distinction is made between the Volga or Kazan Tatars, the Siberian Tatars, the Astrakhan Tatars and the Lithuanian Tatars (see p. 288), although the last decade has seen a political and cultural consolidation around Kazan. In their original territory, the Middle Volga and Urals, the Tatars generally constitute rural communities. In their other native historical homelands such as Siberia and Astrakhan, they represent small minorities with a high proportion of rural dwellers. Urban colonies exist everywhere in the former Soviet Union from the western borderlands to China. Between 1959 and 1979, the Tatars continued migrating from the Middle Volga towards Leningrad and Moscow (which saw a 36% increase in the Tatar population over these years), the Central Asian republics, Western Siberia (Tyumen and Omsk oblasts with an increase of 42% and 22% respectively), and the Lower Volga – Kuybyshev (26% increase), Saratov (27%) and Volgograd (32%). This trend was due to a discriminatory policy during the whole of the Soviet period which sponsored a massive Russian immigration to provide manpower to the defence industry and the industrial cities of Naberezhnyye Chelny and Nizhnekamsk while preventing Tatars from re-settling in the cities of their republic. This demographic policy resulted in a dangerous polarization of society in Tatarstan where the Tatars represented mainly the rural peasant communities and the Russians the urban industrial workers and political and technical cadres. This trend has been reversed since the collapse of the USSR and the encouragement of the government of the Republic of Tatarstan for Tatars to return to their homeland.

The Volga or Kazan Tatars proper also include:

The Mishars who are turkicized Eastern Finns. They were converted to Islam at the time of the Bulgar Kingdom and of the Golden Horde. They have preserved their ethnic type and speak a dialect of the Kazan Tatars. They are essentially a peasant community living between the Oka and Volga rivers in the Southern region of the Tatar, Chuvash and Mordovian republics. In 1912 the Mishars numbered some 200,000 but they have been listed since 1926 as Tatars. However, they are still a distinct ethnic group.

The Teptiyars are Volga Tatars who migrated eastwards after the 1552 conquest of Kazan and settled among the Bashkirs. Despite several centuries of association with the Bashkirs they have preserved their Tatar identity. They speak a dialect combining Kazan Tatar and Bashkir. They numbered 300,000 in 1912.

The Kryashens are Volga Tatars converted to Orthodoxy. A distinction is made between the *Starokryashens* (i.e. old Kryashens) converted in the 16th century and the *Novokryashens* (i.e. new) converted in the 18th century. The majority of the New Kryashens returned to Islam after the religious liberalization in 1906. The Kryashens speak a dialect of Tatar with very few Arabic or Persian loan words and before the 1917 Revolution they had their own written language using the Cyrillic alphabet and not Arabic. According to the 1926 Census they numbered 101,477 and were considered a separate nationality. They are rejected by the Muslim Tatar community and are steadily being assimilated by the Russians with whom they frequently intermarry.

Other groups of Tatars include:

Siberian Tatars whose Khanate of Sibir fell to the Russians in 1582. They were converted to Islam in the 14th and 15th centuries. The Siberian Tatars maintained their tribal and clan structure and did not mix with the Volga Tatars until the Revolution. They number approximately 150,000.

The Astrakhan Tatars' forefathers established the Khanate of Astrakhan, which was destroyed in 1556. They mixed with the Nogays whom they assimilated. There is nothing to distinguish them today from the Volga Tatars.

The Kasymov Tatars are the descendants of refugees from the Kazan Khanate who followed the Chingizide Khan Kasym and settled in the region of Ryazan. The khans of Kasymov became vassals of Moscow and served as distinguished military commanders for the Russian army. They had the title of 'tsar' and for a short time (1575–6) the khan of Kasymov, Sain Bulat, sat on the throne of Moscow when Ivan the Terrible decided to abdicate in his favour. Isolated among non-Muslims, the Kasymov Tatars nevertheless maintained their identity through a firm attachment to Islam. In 1970, the total number of Tatars in Ryazan was 4,000.

The Lithuanian Tatars, also called Polish or Belorussian Tatars, descend from a small Nogay Horde to whom Grand Duke Vytautas applied for assistance in his struggle against the Teutonic Order. After their victory at the battle of Grunwald (or Tannenberg) (1410) they were invited to settle in Lithuania. They have intermarried with local women and lost their language but remained faithful to Islam. Today they are scattered between Poland (around 2000 families), Lithuania (see p. 288) and Russia where they probably number around 5000.

MUSLIM-TURKIC AND MONGOL PEOPLES OF THE VOLGA-URALS AND DAGHESTAN

BASHKIRS ■

The territory of the republic of Bashkortostan (55,400 square miles), is situated to the East of Tatarstan and is separated from Kazakhstan by a narrow strip of land, formerly Tatar-Bashkir lands, annexed by Russia when the Soviets set up the Bashkir Autonomous Soviet Socialist Republic on 23rd March 1923.

According to the 1989 Census, the Bashkirs in the USSR numbered 1,449,462. In their republic they account for approximately one third of the population (3,848,000 in 1979). The majority of the Bashkir peoples live in their ancestral homeland in the Southern Urals but only about 70% in their national republic. The capital, Ufa, has nearly doubled its population since World War II, from 547,000 in 1959 to 969,000 in 1979, mainly through Russian immigration. It ranks amongst the most disastrously polluted cities in the former Soviet Union; its water is poisoned. Compared to the other Turkic nations of the former Soviet Union, their demographic increase has been relatively modest – 25% between 1959 and 1970, and 19.6% between 1970 and 1979.

The Bashkirs are Sunni Muslims of the Hanafi school. Unlike the Tatars, they were not subjected to Orthodox missionary pressure and as such their Islam is less defensive and less deeply rooted than Tatar Islam, especially among the southern formerly nomadic tribes.

The main difference between the Bashkirs and the Tatars is social and economic rather than ethnic : the Bashkir peasantry was liberated from serfdom in the 18th century, and until the Revolution the Bashkirs preserved their tribal aristocracy and never developed a merchant bourgeoisie. Before the Russian Revolution, the Bashkirs – mountain highlanders as opposed to the lowlands Tatars – were considered as a simple ethnic group of the Tatars, speaking several dialects slightly different from Volga Tatar. The written language used by the Bashkirs was Tatar. The Bashkir nation was 'created' in 1923 when Bashkir became a literary language. Had these two nations been left to develop naturally without the social and ethnic engineering imposed in the Soviet period, they would probably have gradually consolidated as one nation sharing a common literary tradition and history.

The ancestors of the northern and western Bashkirs were Finnish tribes, turkicized and islamicized during the rule of the Golden Horde and Khanate of Kazan. Like the Volga Tatars, they are a sedentary people who have lost their clan and tribal structure. The southern and eastern Bashkirs, on the other hand, are the descendants of Turkic nomadic tribes closely related to the Nogays and the Kazakhs. Before the Russian conquest, the Bashkirs' allegiance was divided between the Khanate of Kazan for the westerners, the Khanate of Sibir and subsequently to the Kazakh hordes for the easterners, and the Great Nogay Horde for the southerners. These former nomads belong to the same tribes which can be found throughout the Turkic world – Mangit, Naiman, Kipchak, Jalair and Tabyn, and they have preserved the memory of their clan origin. The sense of kinship with central Asian nomads, cutting across national divisions, remains strong in particular among the intelligentsia and explains why, despite Soviet efforts to this end, Bashkir national sentiment has not really consolidated. Similarly the Bashkirs are relatively indifferent to their official national language which remains semi-literary as many continue to use Tatar, although the proportion who declared Bashkir to be their mother language has increased slightly since the 1960s. Their oral literature and epic songs are the same as that of the Tatars.

In the 17th and 18th century the warlike Bashkirs clans opposed Russian occupation almost uninterruptedly between 1662 and 1774. They took part in Razin's and Pugachev's uprisings – Pugachev's most able lieutenant, Salavat Yulaev, was a Bashkir. In 1919 the president of the Bashkir government, Zeki Velidi Togan, played a decisive role in the outcome of the civil war on the Volga. He defected to the Bolsheviks, after having initially sided with the counter-revolution. He brought his Bashkir National Regiment to the Reds – 2000 experienced and disciplined fighters – an important force at the time. However, disenchanted with the Bolsheviks, he fled to Turkestan and joined the uprising of the Basmachis. This heroic anti-Russian fighting tradition probably forms the core of Bashkir identity.

Following the collapse of the USSR the national movement of the Bashkirs has been slow in asserting itself. This is understandable because of their near minority status in their own Republic where they do not even control parliament. Furthermore, Moscow attempted to undermine the republic by promising Bashkortostan economic and political concessions as long as it agreed to sign the Federation Treaty of March 1992. However, Moscow's promises have failed to materialize and a national opposition is growing which is questioning the wisdom of further reliance on the centre. Bashkortostan has since followed Tatarstan's example deciding to adopt unitary taxation and demanding 'special status'. Furthermore, the republic added the following proviso to Yeltsin's referendum of April 1993, thus limiting the political damage it incurred by signing the treaty: 'Do you agree that the Republic of Bashkortostan must have economic independence and treaty-based relations with the Russian Federation on the basis of the Federation Treaty and Appendix to it, in the interests of all the peoples of the Republic of Bashkortostan?'. Cooperation grew between Tatarstan and Bashkortostan during 1993, in particular in the oil industry with Bashkortostan providing the refining facilities which the Tatars lack, thus freeing them partially from dependence on Russia, in exchange for agricultural produce in surplus in Tatarstan. The idea of resurrecting the short-lived (1918) Tatar-Bashkir Republic has been raised by the nationalists of both republics.

NOGAYS AND KALMYKS ■

The Nogays numbered 75,564 in the North Caucasus according to the 1989 Soviet Census. Approximately half of the population lives in the Nogay steppe in the north of Daghestan between the Terek and Kuma rivers. They are the second largest Turkic nationality in Daghestan. Smaller groups can also be found in Kizlyar, Babayurt and Khasavyurt districts of Daghestan. Outside Daghestan, according to the 1979 Census, Nogay communities live in the Stavropol' *Kray* (22,402), in Mineral'nyye Vody *Kray*, in Chechenia (5,534) and in Karachay-Cherkessia (1,093). The Nogays of Astrakhan and Crimea were assimilated by the Volga Tatars in the 19th century. Between the censuses of 1979 and 1989 they have shown some signs of demographic recovery with an increase of 26.9% as opposed to 15% between 1970 and 1979.

The Nogays are the descendants of the Turko-Mongol nomads of the Golden Horde who moved into the steppe area of the North Caucasus. They are divided into two groups: the Qara ('Black') Nogays of Daghestan, formerly nomadic cattle breeders, and the Aq ('White') Nogays of the Stavropol' *Kray*, former sedentary farmers. The division corresponds to the historical distinction between the Greater Nogay Horde (Qara) in the east and the Lesser Nogay Horde (Aq) in the west. In the 15th century, the Great Nogay Horde was the most powerful military force in Eastern Europe, able to mobilize an army of 100,000 horsemen. At the time of the fall of Kazan, it was still the mightiest Muslim military power in the region. The chief of the Nogay Horde was the brother-in-law of Ivan the Terrible, and many Nogay noblemen were present at his court. A century later, war with the Buddhist Mongol Dzungarians and Kalmyks established in the lower Volga since 1613, brought the Turkic Kazakh and Nogay tribal federations to a state of total impotence. Between 1783, when Russia set out to conquer the North Caucasus, and 1914 most of the Nogays emigrated to the Ottoman Empire as did the Circassians and the Crimean Tatars. The Kalmyks were depleted by an heroic but, for many of them, fatal migration to their ancestral Dzungaria and back in 1771, and by Soviet persecution, culminating in the mass deportation of 1943 (see p. 376). But as many as 150,000 are said to survive or to have returned to their lowlands west of the lower Volga, still mainly practising Buddhism and speaking Mongolic dialects.

The Nogays are divided into four major tribes – the Bujak, Edisan, Jambulak, and Edishkul – and five lesser ones – the Mansur, Kipchak, Karamurza, Tokhtam and Novruz. The feeling of tribal kinship is stronger than national identity. This explains why the Nogay tribes have recently appealed to President Nursultan Nazarbayev of Kazakhstan to accept them as citizens of Kazakhstan. Despite a common faith with their Caucasian neighbours – they are Muslims of the Hanafi school – they remain an alien element in the North Caucasus although the Confederation of the Peoples of the Caucasus has made efforts to include them in their Assembly. Their features are mongoloid resembling the Kazakhs.

The Qara and Aq Nogays speak different languages. Various unsuccessful attempts have been made since the 16th century to endow the Nogays with a written language using the Arabic script. In 1928 two different literary languages were introduced using the Latin script. They belong to the Kipchak division of the Turkic languages. They were replaced by a single language based on Aq Nogay with Cyrillic script in 1938.

KUMYKS ■

The Kumyks are the descendants of the Kipchaks (Polovtsy). They are the largest Turkic nationality in Daghestan and the third 'Daghestani' nationality after the Avars and Dargwans (See p. 377). They are established in the lowlands of northern and northeastern Daghestan. Together with the Avars and the Dargwans, they are a 'dominant' nationality and have been assimilating their weaker neighbours, the Nogays and the Laks. Their features are Caucasian and cannot be distinguished from their Ibero-Caucasian neighbours. The Kumyks numbered 282,178 in 1989. They live in the lowlands of northern and northeastern Daghestan. They are also found in the mountain range of central Daghestan and in all the cities of the Republic. They form the majority in seven districts : Khasavyurt, Babayurt, Kizilyurt, Buynaksk, Karabudakhkent, Kayakent and Kaytag.

The Kumyks are divided into three historical groups : the central Kumyks – the most important group – who formed the Shamkhalat of Tarku; the northern Kumyks; and the southern mountain Kumyks who belonged to the principality of the Utsmi of Kaitag before the Russian conquest. The Kumyks have a high proportion of city-dwellers, including a relatively important number of industrial workers in the Caspian Sea ports. They have possessed a literary language with Arabic script since the 19th century, adopting Latin scripts in 1928 and Cyrillic in 1938. Before the Revolution, Arabic and Volga Tatar were commonly used among Kumyks as literary languages. Between 1923 and 1928, the communist leaders of Daghestan tried to unify Daghestan linguistically around a Turkic language, Azeri or Kumyk. Kumyk, an Oghuz language of the Turkic language family, was then used in inter-tribal relations. It was the second most commonly spoken language and was in the process of becoming the main written language of Daghestan. In 1933, out of 12 newspapers published in Daghestan, 7 were in Kumyk. However, after 1934, against the wishes of the national Daghestani leadership, Moscow opted for a policy of linguistic pluralism condemning Daghestan to linguistic division. Like the other Daghestani nations, the majority of the Kumyks are Muslims of the Shafi'i school.

Unlike their traditional adversaries, the Avars, the Kumyks had a complex and rigid feudal class system strictly upheld by the *adat* – customary law. The highest social class consisted of the princely clan who alone could accede to supreme power. The second rank of the nobility was made up of children of members of the princely clan and women who belonged to the nobility of an inferior rank – the *chanka*. The third class consisted of agriculturists, vassals of the Shamkhal, themselves divided in several classes from nobles or freemen (*uzden*) to serfs. The Shamkhals, who claimed Syrian Arab ancestry, were considered from the Mongol period onwards to be the masters of Daghestan. They were granted the title of *vali* (governor) by the khans of the Golden Horde, like the great princes of Moscow at the same time. Before the Russian conquest the political organization of Daghestan did not correspond to its social, ethnic and linguistic structure, and the Kumyk Shamkhal principality also included Lak, Chechen and Avar minorities organized in free *jemaat* (societies), and Nogays. The principality remained unified until 1574 when, on the death of Shamkhal Surhay, the territory was divided between his sons to form tiny rival *beyliks*. The *beyliks* often fought each other and united only when threatened from abroad, as during the Russian campaigns of 1594, 1604 and 1605 when they sided with the Ottomans and the Crimean Tatars to repel the army of Boris Godunov and stem Russian advances towards the Caucasus for another century. By the end of the 17th century, the Shamkhalat had lost control over the mountains of Daghestan. From the end of the 18th century, resistance to the Russian advance was assumed by the mountain Avar, Dido, Andi and Chechen tribes (see pp. 375, 377). The northern Kumyks took part in the Caucasian War (1825–1859) under the leadership of the imams of Daghestan, Ghazi Muhammad, Hamzat Bek and Shamil, the central Kumyks sided with the Russian and the southern Kumyks remained neutral during the conflict.

The Kumyks, unlike the other Daghestani nations have a national movement, 'Tengliq', which has been active in the last few years. When the official Moscow-sponsored Muslim Religious Board of the North Caucasus and Daghestan collapsed in 1989, the Kumyks elected their own mufti and have refused to accept the authority of Avar religious leaders. Several territorial disputes – a left-over of the Russian and Soviet policies of displacing mountain peoples into the lowlands and deporting nationalities – oppose the Kumyks to the Avars, Laks and Chechens. These disputes have always so far been settled peacefully by the elders of these nations, but they have been used as a pretext by Moscow since 1990 to concentrate some 80,000 troops in and around Daghestan and impose military rule and curfews. Today, the 19th-century Caucasian War – the national liberation struggle common to all the Ibero-Caucasian Muslim nationalities – provides the cornerstone of Pan-Caucasian unity. The Kumyks' less active participation in this epic conflict, their distinct social structure, and Turkic identity, sets them apart from their fellow Daghestanis and North Caucasians and they are somewhat torn between their Turkic and Caucasian identities.

NON-MUSLIM PEOPLES OF THE VOLGA-URALS

In what is now the central part of the territory of the Russian Federation, between the Urals and the uplands of Mordovia on the west bank of the Volga, speakers of Finnic languages still live in what is generally regarded as their 'original' homeland, where archaeological evidence of their occupancy extends back to the 3rd millennium BC. *They can be considered – without necessarily reflecting their own self-perceptions – in two groups: a northern group consisting of the Komi and Udmurt, speaking languages classified in the Permian branch of Finnish; and the Mari and Mordvins of the southwest of the region, traditionally classed together as 'Volga Finns'. Between these last two peoples is sandwiched the homeland of the Chuvash, a nation hard to classify, who speak an aberrant language of Turkic type but whose long, close relationship with their neighbours, especially with the Mari, justifies their treatment alongside the others.*

All these peoples are dispersed over a wide area, with many overlaps and spillages into neighbours' heartlands; all have become interspersed with Russian settlements. Yet all retain at least some elements of their traditional culture and have kept their sense of identity sharp. Though the northernmost of them, the Komi, were protected by their remote and hostile environment from Bulgar and Tatar rule in the Middle Ages, all have shared major elements of their historical experience, including: incorporation into the empires of Muscovy and its successor-states; and imperfect evangelization by orthodox missionaries in the late Middle Ages, which has left these peoples with a sinister reputation in Russian eyes for residual paganism and magic, shamanism and animism.

They could develop as disruptive forces within the present Russian Federation. At the break-up of the Russian empire in 1917, most of them were kept inside the Russian political orbit only with difficulty. Among the Chuvash, for instance, calls were heard for the revival of a long-lost 'Bulgar' state in central and southern Russia. The Udmurt and Mari were granted autonomous regions of their own in 1921–2 to forestall the spread of pan-Finnic nationalism among them. This potentially dangerous movement was particularly strong among the Komi, who claimed the legacy of a medieval Finnic state known as Biarma *and looked to Scandinavia as their historic and cultural centre; visions were evoked of a 'Greater Komi' state including the Udmurts and perhaps the Nenets (p. 30). Komi resistance to Russian rule rumbled on during the 1920s with protests against 'foreigners' exploiting the mineral resources of the area; the new ethnographic map published by the Moscow authorities in 1929 represented an attempt to isolate and belittle the Komi. Only the Mordvins seemed unequivocal in rejecting pan-Finnic sentiment or*

361

calls for secession from the Russian political world: in consequence, they were ignored by the Moscow authorities and not given an autonomous region until 1928.

Nevertheless, by the standards of other ethnic minorities of the former Russian empire and Soviet Union, these peoples have been and continue to be willing to co-operate in large multi-national states. Their potential as disruptive nationalities has been overlooked in recent debates on the future of the Russian Federation, or, at least, overshadowed by the more urgent problems and more insistent voices found elsewhere; but, since all have inherited from Soviet times devolved political institutions – shared with Russian settlers of their regions – which could be used in future as openings for separatism, the likelihood that they will display ever sharper political profiles cannot be discounted.

KOMI AND UDMURTS ■

The Permian branch of Finnic languages has developed away from related tongues for literally thousands of years. Its surviving forms and dialects are now spoken as first languages by nearly a million people. An ancient written form, known as Old Permic, survives in religious texts from the late 14th century, when the peoples concerned were superficially evangelized by St Stephanus; Russian scholars published grammars of the two main linguistic sub-divisions of the group, Komi and Udmurt, in 1775. By then, the historic isolation of this region was becoming thoroughly penetrated by Russian immigrants drawn by mining ventures.

Speakers of Udmurt, known as Udmurts or Votyaks, are concentrated near the middle Volga, around and between the lower Kama and Vyatka Rivers; their reputation as 'the most red-headed men in the world' was celebrated by Victorian ethnographers and may have inspired Conan Doyle's idea for his fictional 'Red-Headed League'. Their environment was heavily forested and included lime trees whose blossom made them famous for bee-keeping; as with the Mordvins, bees figure prominently in their poetry and song; their traditional way of life was in tribal villages of about 40 households which were re-sited when the land became exhausted. Broadly speaking, this semi-nomadic character was shared until well into the 20th century by all these forest peoples.

Speakers of the Komi family of tongues extend north into the lands of the Nenets. Their heartlands are between the upper Dvina, Pechora and Kama rivers. The largest group, dominant in the Komi autonomous republic, speaks Zyryan; to their south are speakers of Permyak, which has been various classified as a dialect of Zyryan and as an intermediate Permian language between Zyryan and Udmurt; some scholars distinguish two dialects within Permyak – northern (Kosinko-Kama) and southern (Inven), which is the basis of the literary language, written since 1920 in Cyrillic script. The unity of the Komi people is a dearly-held tenet among them (cf the Mordvins, below, p. 364, who are equally keen on emphasizing distinctions between their major sub-groups) and speakers of Permyak resent attempts to classify their speech apart from their neighbours' as a politically motivated and divisive ruse

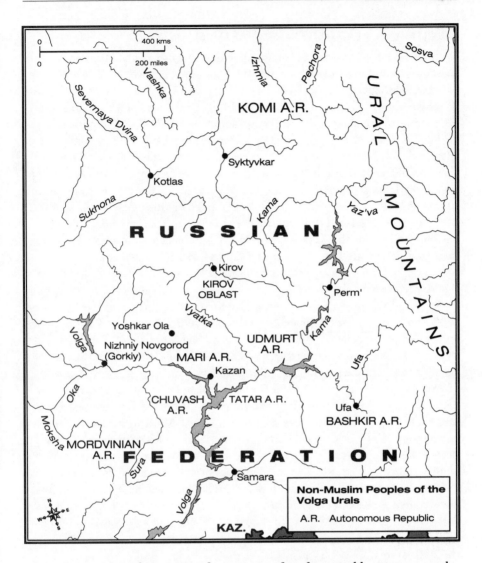

of Moscow's. Somewhat separated groups are found in neighbouring areas: the Zyuzda, 7,000 strong, are normally classified as Permyak despite speaking Zyryan and live in the Zyuzdinskiy district of Kirov Oblast. The Yazwa, now only about 4,000 strong, live in the Yaz'va valley, on the west slopes of the Urals, beyond and between Perm Oblast and the Komi autonomous republic and speak a distinct Zyryan dialect. The 10,000 or so Izhmi or Izva Tas are tundra-dwellers between the Pechora and Izhma Rivers, whose dialect has some claim to be considered a third major branch of Komi, though views on this may, again, be partisan.

MORDVINS, MARI AND CHUVASH ■

With the possible exception of some settlements of Mishars, the Mordvins are the most southerly of surviving Finnic peoples. They have long been recognized by outsiders as a distinct nation – indeed, the term 'Mordeni' had been coined by the time of Jordanes, the mid-6th century historian of the Goths, evidently from the Permic *murt* or *mort*, meaning 'man'. The large autonomous Mordovian republic on the middle Volga, where about half of them live and where they constitute about 35% of the population, is named for them. Yet their identity is made elusive by the fact that they have no common name for themselves. They are divided, in their own perception, in two groups, spread between the Oka and Volga Rivers: the Erzya, in the northwest, towards the Oka and the Moksha, around the River Sura, in the southeast of the area, distinguished from one another by dialects which are markedly distinct and, in the case of the Moksha, by what is traditionally said to be darker pigmentation. There are twice as many Erzya as Moksha. The two groups tend to be mutually aloof and there are no mixed villages. These divisions have helped to make the Mordvins vulnerable to acculturation by Russian and Tatar neighbours. A third group, called Karaites, was formerly found in Kazan, scattered among the Tatars (see p. 346–56): they are now confined largely to three settlements in the Tatar Republic and are Tatar-speaking (see p. 288). The Teryukhan Mordvins of Gorkiy have lost their sense of Mordvin identity: they speak Russian and call themselves Russian. The same erosion continues to threaten other Mordvins.

Although neglected by grammarians until the late 18th century, when the Mordvin languages, like other marginal and minority tongues of Europe, became the passionate concern of philologists and ethnographers, Mordvin literature is ancient and distinguished; the heroes of traditional songs and poems are national heroes, especially King Tushtyan, ally of Ivan the Terrible. Mordvins were the sappers of the latter's campaigns against Kazan: a reputation for excellence in wood-cutting and carving continues to distinguish Mordvins and to recall their traditional forest environment. Collaboration in crusades against neighbouring Muslims was no guarantee of the purity of the Mordvins' own Christianity and clerical denunciations of syncretic idiosyncrasies and reversions to paganism were common, well into the 20th century.

This is even more the case with the Mari or Cheremi (as the Russians formerly called them), whose identity is closely connected with the practice of a syncretic religion peculiar to themselves, which emerged in the last third of the 19th century. Known as the cult of *Kuga Sorta* or 'Big Candle', it developed against a background of Russian immigration, russification and urbanization, against which the native people reacted by reviving traditional elements of their religion. Its rites are celebrated, for preference, in forest glades; priests are excluded and icons redundant. Nature rather than a transcendent deity is the immediate object of devotion; offerings are made of animals and flowers. Christ is relegated to the rank of the greatest of prophets. Rejection of manufactured foodstuffs and medicines has made this religion interesting to outsiders with ecological priorities. Neither the contempt of the Soviet government nor the efforts of the orthodox clergy were able entirely to root it out.

With increasing pace in the early modern period, the oak forests which were the traditional Mari habitat retreated before Russian settlers, leaving cleared valleys between Mari communities. Nevertheless, the keenness with which Mari identity is preserved and projected today is aided by their relatively compact distribution in the Mari El autonomous republic, within the triangle formed by the cities of Kazan, Kirov and Nizhniy Novgorod. Here, they are normally classified in two sub-groups according to dialect: those of 'Meadow' (Olyk Mari) and 'Mountain' (Kuryk Mari) are split by the Volga. Their dialects, written in Cyrillic character since 1821 and the mid-19th century respectively are mutually unintelligible but have been used to record a common corpus of folklore and legendary history. Beyond this heartland there are small numbers of speakers of a third, 'Eastern' dialect (Üpo Mari) on the Kama River and in small numbers around Ufa: they are the descendants of migrants located here from the right bank of the Volga in the 18th century.

They are renowned as carvers in stone as well as wood and for the lavish embroidery, also produced in similar elaborate styles by the Mordvin women. The continued importance of forestry and animal husband in their economy is reflected in the curricula of the agricultural schools of their capital at Yoshkar Ola.

The left bank of the Volga, where the Chuvash or Tavas live, slopes upwards towards the Mordvins' highlands. Despite centuries of exchanging brides with the Mari, the Chuvash are among the most self-aware of the national minorities still remaining inside the Russian Federation. In part, this is a consequence of their numerical preponderance within the autonomous republic which bears their name: over half of them live within its borders where they make up about 70% of the population. They are, moreover, a highly distinctive people, sometimes classified in two groups according to dialect as Viryal (Upper) and Anatri (Lower) Chuvash. Their unique language, of which the favoured literary form has been based on the Amatri dialect and written with Cyrillic characters since the 1870s, was an irresistible puzzle to 19th-century philologists: its Turkic affinities are no longer in doubt but it does not fit into any of the established Turkic families. Chuvash legend derives the origin of the people from the Volga Bulgars who emerge in recorded history in the 4th century BC and this has prompted speculation about the possible affinities of Chuvash with the vanished ancient Bulgar language (cf pp. 225, 349).

PEOPLES OF THE CAUCASUS

The relatively narrow isthmus that divides the Black Sea from the Caspian Sea is a fabled land of stupendous snow-capped mountains (including Mt Elbrus, Europe's highest peak), lush valleys, fast-flowing rivers and rolling meadows, encompassing a variety of micro-climates. The economy is largely land-based, with important oil-production in Azerbaijan and Chechenia. This is Europe's most complex region in terms of ethno-linguistic composition. The Greater Caucasus chain runs for some 500 miles between the two seas and is often regarded as Europe's natural southern boundary. However, the content of the present section is determined by the alternative view, whereby Asia is deemed to begin only with the crossing of the former Soviet Union's Transcaucasian frontiers. Until the collapse of the USSR, it was almost impossible for Westerners to gain permission to visit any part of the North Caucasus, and so the learning-process must be bi-directional: the West of the (North) Caucasus and the (North) Caucasus of the West.

The Caucasus is home to: firstly, the indigenous peoples themselves, who collectively speak some 40 languages, divided into certainly three and possibly four language-families (Daghestanian, or Northeast Caucasian; its clear relative North Central Caucasian; Northwest Caucasian, all three families perhaps deriving from a single, very remote ancestor; South Caucasian, or Kartvelian, which has no demonstrable genetic links with any of the northern groups let alone any other language or language-family); secondly, speakers of a number of Indo-European languages (namely Ossetes/Ossetians, Tats, Talysh and Kurds, all four of whom speak languages related to Persian; Armenians; Greeks; Gypsies; and, of course, Russians and other Slavs including the Cossacks, who first appeared in the Caucasus area only in the second half of the 16th century); a variety of Turkic-speaking peoples such as the Turks themselves, Turkmens, Karapapaks and the Azerbaijanis in Transcaucasia, plus the Karachays and Balkars in the northwest Caucasus, and the Nogays and the Kumyks in the northeast; north of Daghestan are the Mongol Kalmyks; fourthly, the Caucasus is the home of several Semitic peoples (a small Assyrian group in Georgia, and Jews, amongst whom the Mountain Jews of Daghestan speak Tat).

This section concentrates on those peoples whose main homeland is the Caucasus and is sub-divided by language-group, even if there is no precise correspondence between language and ethnicity. Apart from the Nogays with their Mongol features (see p. 358), all native Caucasians manifest the physical characteristics of the southern branch of the European peoples; dark tints in the eye and hair predominate with an almost total lack of concave forms to the nasal bone. In general, the Circassians are perhaps the fairest skinned, the Armenians especially swarthy. Generous hospitality (even by eastern standards) towards guests is characteristic of all the indigenous peoples, as is respect for the dead and the resting-places of ancestral bones. The traditional male tunic (cherkesska), usually black with cartridge-pockets along the breast and never worn without the dagger (khinjal), was taken over by the Cossacks but is really only seen today adorning members of national folk-dance troupes. The blood-feud was the age-old custom of settling scores and has survived vestigially to the present day in places (perhaps to re-surface as the social order collapses). Emerging from 70 years of Soviet rule these peoples are all faced with demanding struggles to re-shape their societies from the very top to the very bottom; even ethnic identity may be uncertain, let alone such peripheral features as educational, judicial and political systems. Had the West taken a genuine interest in understanding and helping the Caucasus in the dying days of Soviet power, some of the awful conflicts that have disfigured the region, such as those in Nagorno-Karabakh and Georgia, might well have been avoided.

SOUTH CAUCASIANS: GEORGIANS, MINGRELIANS AND SVANS ■

Of the four Kartvelian peoples, the Georgians, Mingrelians and Svans live almost exclusively within the Republic of Georgia (Georgian *sakartvelo*, capital Tbilisi), whilst the fourth, the Laz, live mainly in their traditional homeland along part of Turkey's Black Sea coast, with only negligible numbers resident in Georgia. The final Soviet census (1989) gave a total population for Georgia of 5,400,841 of whom 3,787,393 (70.1%) were listed as 'Georgians'. However, it has been the practice since around 1930 to inflate the number of so-called 'Georgians' artificially by officially classifying under this term all Mingrelians and Svans. Thus, not only have all post-1926 censuses been effectively biased but the true demographic picture for Georgia remains a mystery; equally uncertain is the state of first- and second-language knowledge among the Kartvelians – there may, for example, be as many as a million ethnic Mingrelians, who traditionally live in Western Georgia's lowlands (capital Zugdidi) forming a buffer between the Abkhazians and the Georgians proper, but not all will necessarily speak Mingrelian.

Nestling above Mingrelia in a mountain-fastness of unsurpassable beauty that is covered by a thick blanket of snow for over half the year lies Svanetia (capital Mest'ia), which prior to the calamitous winter of 1986–87 could boast a population of perhaps over 50,000, though later almost half of the residents of Upper Svanetia reportedly moved to the relative safety of lowland districts, where nationalists proposed they be resettled among some of the non-Kartvelian citizenry of Georgia so as to help spread knowledge of Georgian.

Of the four sister-languages, only Georgian has literary status. Under the Soviet system this meant that it was both written and taught – indeed, as the chief language

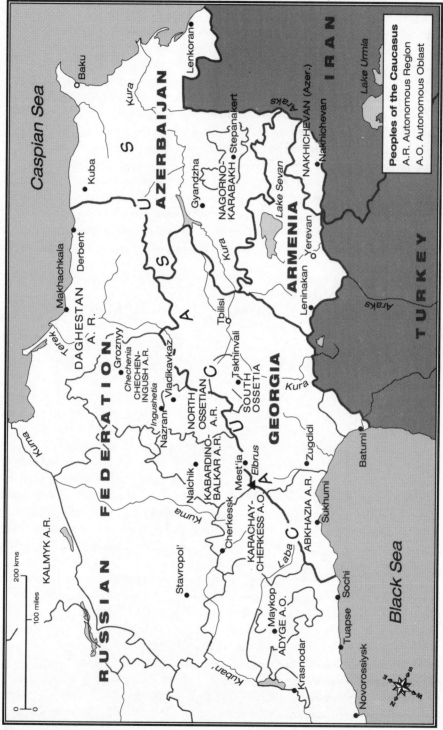

Peoples of the Caucasus
A.R. Autonomous Region
A.O. Autonomous Oblast

of a union-republic it could have served as the language of tuition from nursery through university for anyone educated at a Georgian-language school, as all Svans and most Georgians and Mingrelians were. Russian-language schools tended to be used by Georgia's non-Kartvelians, though the first few grades of schooling might have been in another of the USSR's literary languages, which explains why knowledge of Georgian among the republic's non-Kartvelians was never widespread. The clearly-stated intention to make knowledge of Georgian universal in an independent Georgia, coupled with the lack of concern in Tbilisi for the welfare of any of the republic's other languages helps to explain some of the difficulties that began to mar Georgia's moves towards independence as early as 1989. Attempts by the Russians at the end of the 19th century to create an alphabet for Mingrelian based on Cyrillic along with a Mingrelian liturgy were strongly opposed. Equally hostile was the reaction from Georgians (and even some leading Mingrelians) to calls in the 1920s for a Mingrelian script based on Georgian characters, though the early 1930s did see a daily Mingrelian newspaper produced for the region's capital.

Georgia's conversion as a state to Christianity by St Nino is dated to the 330s, though missionaries had already converted some of the coastal Greek colonies in Abkhazia, Mingrelia and Lazica, which together roughly formed the land the ancients knew as Colchis. The invention of the unique and handsome script, of which three variants have been used down the centuries, is assumed to have occurred a few decades later in order to facilitate the dissemination of church-literature. A writing tradition of 15 centuries has provided Georgia with a wealth of literature, sadly little known outside Georgia itself, for all genres (the study of Old Georgian is important for anyone concerned with the transmission of Biblical texts). The Georgian Church is an autocephalous branch of Eastern Orthodoxy, though during Georgia's subordination to Tsarist Russia its church, too, became subject to the Russian branch of Orthodoxy. Following the Council of Chalcedon's proclamation on the dual nature of Christ (451) the Georgian Church (along with that of the Armenians and the 'lost' Caucasian Albanians, the third Christian nation located in the east of Transcaucasia, with their own script and history, who simply disappeared from the pages of history) defended the monophysite (single-nature) view, but in 607 Georgia broke with its neighbours and adopted the diophysite (dual-nature) position. Some ethnic Georgians in those areas bordering Turkey converted to Islam at the height of Ottoman Turkish influence; today Muslim Georgians live primarily in the province of Ach'ara (Ajaria), whose capital is Batumi. Nationalists tend to regard adherence to any religion other than Georgian Orthodoxy as essentially counter to the spirit of being a Georgian. In November 1944 over 100,000 Muslims from the neighbouring border-region of Meskheti were deported to Central Asia. Their return has always been blocked by the Georgian authorities, and the ethnic status of the majority – whether they are islamicized Georgians or ethnic Turks – is hotly debated.

Heavily influenced by Greeks, Romans, Persians and Arabs, who entered eastern Georgia in 655 and eventually established an emirate in Tbilisi that lasted until 1122,

Kartvelian lands plus some neighbouring territory were unified in 975 under Bagrat III. The Seljuk Turks, recently arrived from their Turkestan homeland, attacked Georgia in 1065, and it fell to David IV, the Builder (1089–1125), to secure the frontiers, setting the seal for the Golden Age under Queen Tamar (1184–1213). Her reign saw the creation of the national epic, Shota Rust(a)veli's *Man in the Panther's Skin*, consisting of some 1,600 end-rhyming quatrains. Political power and cultural activity were soon extinguished with the appearance of the Mongols; many treasures, including manuscripts, were secreted in Svanetia. After this threat subsided, Georgia fragmented into small kingdoms and princedoms, which became prey to Ottoman Turks in the west from 1510 and to the Persians in the east. The Treaty of Giorgievsk (1783) with Russia led to the annexation by Russia of Eastern Georgia in 1801; Mingrelia followed in 1803 and the western kingdom of Imereti in 1804. Georgian language and culture were repressed for most of the century, and it was only the activity of such intellectuals as Prince (now Saint) Ilia Ch'avch'avadze (1837–1907) that bred a renewed sense of national self-awareness.

Independent under a Menshevik government (1918–1921), Georgia was forced into the Soviet Union by the decisions and actions of the Georgians Joseph Jughashvili (aka Stalin) and Sergo Orjonik'idze. Fiercely nationalistic, anti-Russian and adept at playing the system, the Kartvelians, though not immune to the Terror of the 1930s, lived extremely well by Soviet standards, and Georgian language, literature and arts flourished, with the Rustaveli Theatre Company under Robert St'urua, the Sukhishvili-Ramishvili Dance Ensemble and the local film-industry gaining thoroughly deserved world-wide reputations. The waning of Soviet power was accompanied by a deplorable descent into chauvinism, which was calamitous in such a demographically heterogeneous republic (indeed shortly before his death Andrei Sakharov described Georgia as one of the USSR's 'little empires'), with significant minorities dotted around its borders – as late as 1900 Tbilisi itself was largely an Armenian-Russian town. Wars between Kartvelians and both South Ossetians and Abkhazians scarred the immediate post-Soviet period. An intra-Kartvelian conflict broke out in the autumn of 1993, between Mingrelian supporters of the ousted (Mingrelian) president Zviad Gamsakhurdia and followers of his arch-enemy Eduard Shevardnadze, the notoriously pro-Russian Party boss in Georgia (1972–85), all of which points to the essentially illusory nature of the century-old dream of a united Georgia. Rabidly anti-Russian, the Georgians rejoiced in their long refusal to join the post-Soviet Commonwealth of Independent States, though the parlous situation of the Georgian state forced reconsideration of this policy in late 1993.

The provinces, as is typical of a mountainous country, have developed sharply-differentiated dialects and local varieties of traditional dress, food, architecture, dance, music and regional temperament – Gurians (in the west), whence hails Eduard Shevardnadze, are viewed as even more fiery-tempered than the rest of a volatile race; Rach'ans (northwest) as slow-witted; K'akhetians as laid back; Imeretians as eloquently fast-talking; Mingrelians as simpletons. Kartvelian music is intricately polyphonic, Svan songs mirroring mountain-conditions in their austerity, whilst complex Mingrelian harmonies so intrigued Stravinsky that he claimed to want to be reborn a Mingrelian!

Georgia has a basically rural economy (citrus, viticulture, maize, tea, animal-husbandry, wool and textiles), but some mountainous regions (such as Khevsureti) have been depopulated by urbanization.

Georgia historically had a higher percentage of nobility than other areas of the Caucasus, but relations with the peasantry were cemented by the practice of foster-ing aristocratic children among peasant-families – indeed, networks of relatives, friends and acquaintances have remained pivotal for the running of society even through the Soviet period. Kartvelians' celebrated bonhomie (though Svans tend to be more diffident) may conceal from casual observers such less appealing aspects of their character as an over-developed sense of ethnic superiority, an unwillingness to accept criticism, and, in the words of England's first professor of Georgian studies, the late David Lang, 'a proneness to harbour rancour'. Rich in folklore, the Geor-gians' Prometheus-figure is called Amiran, whilst the main figure in Mingrelian demonology is the *očok'oči* (monster-man); important to the Svans are the fertility-deity *barbal* and the goddess of the hunt *däl*. All Kartvelians share a love of the feast (*keipi*), where such delicacies as *xač'ap'uri* (cheese-bread), *k'ak'lis muraba* (walnut-preserve), and *čurčxela* (string of walnuts coated in dried grape-juice) are eaten and a multiplicity of local wines (so crucial to the ritual of seemingly-endless toasting) imbibed, amongst which pride of place surely belongs to (K'akhetian) Kindzmarauli or (Rach'an) Khvanch'k'ara, Stalin's favourite.

NORTHWEST CAUCASIANS: ABKHAZ-ABAZINIANS AND CIRCASSIANS ■

This small group comprises Abkhaz-Abazinians, Circassians and Ubykhs, though no Ubykh has lived on native soil (centred around the Black Sea resort of Sochi) since 1864, and the language became extinct in October 1992 with the death of the last speaker, Tevfik Esenç, in Turkey. Northwest Caucasian territory once stretched from the banks of the Kuban (and possibly the Don) in the Northwest Caucasian plains across the mountains and along the coast of Abkhazia down to the frontier with Mingrelia – place-names hint at an even earlier presence further south in Geor-gia. The Russo-Caucasian war of the 19th century decimated these peoples, leaving merely a rump-population in the Caucasus and producing a tragic diaspora that remains almost totally unknown to the Western world.

Christianity, largely supplanted by Islam, never wholly displaced certain pagan beliefs, and a special affection for trees still survives. In the Caucasus itself neither Christianity nor Islam has today any significance. The Abkhaz word for 'God' (*Anc'a*) can be interpreted as the plural of 'mother' (*an*) and may indicate a one-time matrili-neal society, perhaps reflected in the predominant role of the heroes' mother Sata-nay Gwasha in the Abkhaz version of the pan-North Caucasian folk-epic *The Narts*. The Abkhazian Prometheus is *Abrsk"əl*. The traditional moral code of the

371

mountaineer is strong among Northwest Caucasians: Circassians are renowned for their honesty throughout the Near East – in Jordan they form the king's ceremonial bodyguard. Respect for the elderly and closely-knit extended families are still the norm, marriage with anyone sharing the surname of either parent being forbidden. Skill in horsemanship served the men in battle and the hunt, secret hunting languages once being used to prevent the prey understanding the hunters' intentions. Intricate designs in embroidery and carving are found in Circassia. Maize-mush is the staple food (Abkhaz *abəsta*, Circassian *mamrəs*). Pre-revolutionary Abkhazian society was rigidly hierarchical: before 1864 Circassia had no central authority; the Abzakhs, Shapsughs and Natukhays having a republican system, the remaining tribes clinging to feudalism.

In 1989, 93,267 Abkhazians, famed for their longevity and love of yoghurt, lived in Georgia's Autonomous Republic of Abkhazia (capital Sukhumi, in Abkhaz Aq''a), representing a mere 17.8% of Abkhazia's population. Across the Caucasus in Russia's Karachay-Cherkess Autonomous Region (capital Cherkessk) there were 27,475 Abazinians (6.5% of the population). There were some 125,000 Western Circassians (Adyghes), of whom 95,439 constituted 22% of the population in the Adyghe Autonomous Region (capital Maykop), most of the others living in the Krasnodar District, including 10,000 Shapsughs around Tuapse ('Two Rivers' in Circassian). East Circassians are divided between Karachay-Cherkessia, where they are termed Cherkess and numbered 40,230 (9.6% of the population) in 1989, and the Kabardino-Balkar Autonomous Republic (capital Nalchik), where they are termed Kabardians and numbered 363,351 (48.2% of the population). The North Caucasian administrative units were granted republican status by the post-Soviet Russian Federation. Circassian women have long had a reputation for great physical beauty and were prized in the Turkish harems. It is believed that over one million Circassians and maybe 500,000 Abkhazians live in Turkey and other areas of the Near East.

All three languages in the group are mutually unintelligible and notorious for their fearsome phonetic and structural complexity. Apart from occasional word-lists going back to the 17th century, documents in these languages are no older than the mid-19th century, when first attempts were made to write Circassian and then Abkhaz. The early Soviets created four literary languages: Abkhaz (based on the Abzhwa dialect), Abaza (based on T'ap'anta), West Circassian (based on Temirgoi), and East Circassian (based on Kabardian). The first Soviet script for Abkhaz continued the Cyrillic-based version already employed, which yielded to a Roman form in 1928 during the Soviet latinization-drive. When most of the USSR's 'Young Written Languages' shifted to Cyrillic scripts in 1936–8, Abkhaz significantly had to adopt a Georgian-based alphabet, which was abandoned after the death of Stalin in favour of today's Cyrillic-based variant. Abaza had a Roman script created in 1932 but went over to a Cyrillic variant (different from that in use for Abkhaz) in 1938. West Circassian used a form of Arabic script until replaced by a Roman version in 1928, which yielded to today's Cyrillic-based orthography in 1938. Kabardian replaced Arabic with Latin in 1924, adopting a form of Cyrillic (different again from West

Circassian!) in 1936. None of the current scripts is user-friendly, and there is the possibility of a new reversion to Roman script: ideally one universal alphabet should serve all branches of Northwest Caucasian.

Abkhazians make their first indisputable appearance in history under the classical term 'Apsilian' – they call themselves *Apswa*. The Abazinians, then still living in Abkhazia, were the Greeks' Abazgians. A series of contacts with Lazica and Byzantium saw Christianity introduced under Justinian (543–46) and led in the late 8th century to Leon II establishing the Kingdom of Abkhazia, which incorporated the whole of western Georgia, so that from 780 to 975 the term Abkhazia actually referred to all this territory.

In the 14th century the first wave of Abazinians crossed the Klukhor Pass into the North Caucasus, the rest following after the 17th century. When Georgia fragmented in the wake of the Mongol invasions, Abkhazia became a separate princedom under the Chachba (Shervashidze) family. Subsequent centuries witnessed Abkhazia either at war or in alliance with the Mingrelia of the Dadiani princes. Ottoman Turkish influence led to part of the population adopting Islam.

In 1810 Abkhazia entered the protectorate of Tsarist Russia but administered its own affairs until 1864. It is estimated that the Russians, especially after 1864 and the Russo-Turkish war of 1877–8, expelled over 120,000 Abkhazians to Ottoman lands, which caused wholesale depopulation and the start of an influx of non-natives which is still going on. The Soviets gave Abkhazia full republican status in 1921, and in 1922 Abkhazia entered the Transcaucasian Federation in special treaty-alliance with Georgia, the other two members of the Federation being Armenia and Azerbaijan; this Federation formed a block within the USSR until 1936, when the three Soviet republics of Armenia, Azerbaijan and Georgia were awarded separate status. In February 1931 Stalin reduced Abkhazia's status to that of a mere autonomous republic within Georgia. His Mingrelian lieutenant Lavrent'i Beria then began a georgianization-drive, which included wholesale swamping of the Abkhazians on their native soil by forced importation, largely of Mingrelians, replacement in 1945 of all Abkhaz-language schools by Georgian-language schools plus a ban on Abkhaz publications. Whilst Abkhazians living alongside Mingrelians tend to speak Mingrelian, essentially only those educated during the 1940s know Georgian. Memories of this period, the renewed chauvinism in Georgia from the late 1980s and Georgia's annulment of all Soviet legislation, which defined Abkhazia's subordination to Tbilisi, led to Abkhazian attempts to safeguard their language and culture by temporarily reinstating their 1925 constitution on 23rd July 1992 and seeking to secure a new federative treaty with the Georgians. Their reward was to be invaded by order of Eduard Shevardnadze on 14th August 1992. The subsequent year's war of atrocities must place any new cooperation with Tbilisi in grave doubt.

Christianity came to Circassia at the same time as to Abkhazia, just as the Ottoman Turks eventually sought to convert both to Islam. Circassians had links with Byzantium and, from around 1175, trading and cultural ties with Italy. Circassia did not suffer as much as other Caucasian regions under the Mongols but was invaded by

Tamerlane at the close of the 14th century, while trade with Italy ceased with the fall of Constantinople to the Ottoman Turks in 1453. Population-movements following the waning of Mongol power brought Circassians further to the southeast, pushing the Ossetes eastwards in the process. The 13th and 14th centuries also probably saw the formation and settlement high in the Caucasus of the Karachay-Balkars, supposedly a mixture of Caucasian, Iranian Alan, and Turkic Kipchak stock. The Karachay-Balkars, though separated by Mount Elbrus and divided into different administrative regions, share a common language, which was given a Cyrillic script in 1936 and is of the Kipchak Turkic variety, closely related to Kumyk and Nogay (see pp. 358–60).

The first contacts between Circassians and the Russians on their relentless advance southwards occurred in the 16th century when the first Cossack stations were planted as bulwarks against the mountaineers – Ivan the Terrible married a Kabardian princess. Matters came to a head with the Treaty of Adrianople in 1829, when Turkey ceded 'her' Caucasian territories to Russia – the Circassians never acknowledged Turkey's suzerainty and thus her right to hand their land to the Russians. The horrors of the war that then developed and intensified can be seen in the vivid and strangely moving contemporary descriptions of British travellers such as James Bell, Edmund Spencer and J. Longworth. Final defeat came in 1864, when perhaps half of the Northwest Caucasians (mainly Circassians, all the Ubykhs, and many Abkhazians, who were the only Transcaucasians to fight against Russian seizure of the Caucasus) preferred Ottoman exile to Russian domination, thousands perishing in the hasty, ill-organized exodus southward. Once-fertile Circassian mountain-slopes turned barren in the hands of Slavs, ignorant of the special techniques of cultivation.

Remembrance of this shared tragedy conditioned the Circassian (and indeed pan-North Caucasian) support for the Abkhazians in the face of the renewed Georgian threat in 1989, when the Assembly (Confederation as of November 1991) of Mountain Peoples of the Caucasus was formed. Volunteers from this semi-official organization of 16 peoples proved a crucial counterweight to the Georgian forces in the Abkhazian war of 1992–3. Both Circassians and Abkhazians hope for a large-scale return to the homeland from their diaspora-communities to help in both post-Soviet reconstruction and consolidation of their fragile cultures. The Confederation, which while incorporating some Muslim peoples should not be regarded as Muslim in orientation, has not been joined by the North Caucasian Turkic peoples, and the desire expressed by the Karachays and Balkars to re-establish states independent of their (East) Circassian neighbours, as a possible preliminary to Karachay-Balkar unification, is yet another ominous sign for any future united and secular North Caucasus itself independent of Russia.

NORTH-CENTRAL CAUCASIANS: CHECHEN, INGUSH AND BATS ■

This group comprises Chechens, Ingush and Bats. It is sometimes referred to as Nakh (or Veinakh), meaning 'people' (or 'our people'). The Chechens' self-designation is *Noxčuo*, that of the Ingush *Ghalghai*, that of the Bats *Bacav*, the better known designations for the first two deriving from Russian adaptations of names of two local villages (*auls*). Chechenia (capital Groznyy) and Ingushetia (capital Nazran) together formed the Chechen-Ingush Autonomous Republic before the break-up of the USSR, though they were separate in the early Soviet period. In 1989 the Soviet Chechen population was 958,309, whilst that of the Ingush was 237,577, of whom 734,501 Chechens and 163,711 Ingush lived in their autonomous republic, constituting 70.7% of its population. Chechen villages are also to be found in Turkey and Jordan. No official figures are available for the Bats, who reside in a single village, Zemo Alvani, in the Eastern Georgian province of K'akheti, where they all also speak Georgian; earlier they lived in the mountainous region of Tusheti, from which comes their Georgian designation of Ts'ova Tush. They number perhaps 5,000 and have been classified as 'Georgians' in recent censuses. Their language is unwritten, has been heavily influenced by Georgian and is destined for extinction, unless the Georgian authorities take steps to save it – an unlikely scenario.

The various dialects of Chechen and Ingush are mutually intelligible, and yet both exist as separate literary languages. First attempts to write Chechen employed Arabic characters. In 1925 a Roman script was introduced, replaced in 1938 by Cyrillic. A new Roman version was introduced by the Dudaev regime in 1993. Ingush used Roman as a base for its script from as early as 1923, shifting to Cyrillic in 1938.

Fundamentally pagan, the Chechen-Ingush experienced some Christian influence from Georgia after the 10th century, but Chechenia gradually yielded to Islam (Sunnis of the Hanafi school), slowly introduced by Avars and Kumyks from the 16th century; it was only in the latter half of the 19th century that the Ingush were converted by Sufi Qadiri missionaries. The Sufi *tariqa*, a most conservative form of Islam, partly defines their self-identity to the present day, and the organization of the Sufi order blends well with the prevailing social structure, based on the all-pervading system of clans (*taipa*), which often cuts across the Chechen vs Ingush divide. Folklore in Georgia is replete with battles with the Kist's, as Georgians term the Chechen-Ingush just over their border. Religious fervour combined with the mountaineers' love of liberty has defined relations with Russia (Tsarist, Soviet, post-Soviet) for over two centuries.

The great North Caucasian insurrection against Russian encroachment in 1783 was led by the Chechen Naqshbandi Sheikh Mansur. The Chechens were particularly fierce in their resistance during the long 19th century war, losing much of their forests to wilful Russian destruction in the process. Continuing resentment of foreign (now Soviet) control along with actual rebellions in the 1920s and 1930s resulted in their most recent tragedy. Falsely accused of collaboration with the Nazis, who were keen to gain control of the Groznyy (and Baku) oil-fields, the Karachays (Oct-Nov 1943), the Chechen-Ingush (Feb 1944) and the Balkars (March-April 1944) (plus the Koreans, Volga Germans (see p. 260), Kalmyks (see p. 358), Crimean Tatars and the Meskhians) were transported in their entirety to the wastes of Central Asia.

It was as though these peoples had never existed, their territories disappearing from Soviet maps; most of Karachaia (not linked to Cherkessia at the time) and parts of both Kabardino-Balkaria and Chechen-Ingushetia were bestowed by Stalin upon his native republic, Georgia, whilst the Ingush Prigorodnyy Raion went to North Ossetia. Teaching of their native languages during the Central Asian exile was prohibited. It was only in the late 1950s that these peoples (though not the Germans, Tatars or Meskhians) were allowed to return home by Krushchev and their territories largely restored. Georgia, no longer with so eminent a Kremlin patron, gave up all territorial gains, though Karachaia was forced into union with the so-called Cherkess. North Ossetia, however, was allowed to retain control of its extra land, even though Ingush were permitted to resettle there. Many Chechens and Ingush are still to be found in Central Asia. Given this recent history, it is hardly surprising that the post-Soviet Dudaev regime took the earliest opportunity to declare independence from Moscow. The Ingush subsequently broke away from the Chechens, believing that Moscow would then view with greater favour their claims for return of their lost land – it did not, and reunion with Chechenia is a distinct possibility: the ongoing Ingush dispute with North Ossetia has cost many lives since 1991 and is the greatest single internal problem for the North Caucasian Confederation, which counts both Ingush and Ossetes as members. The Chechens' territorial difficulty with Daghestan, another inheritance of the deportations, has been peacefully resolved. Relations between Chechenia and Georgia are complicated by the Chechens' unfailing support for Abkhazia and by the fact that Zviad Gamsakhurdia, ousted as president of Georgia in January 1992, took refuge in Groznyy as guest of President Dudaev.

Chechens (along with the Georgians) have the reputation of being the prime movers in the organized crime networks that are flourishing all over former Soviet territory. Western media reinforce these stereotypes by emphasizing the number of expensive limousines and weapons openly flaunted on the streets of Groznyy. Reports even circulate, probably emanating from anti-Dudaev (if not anti-Chechen) sources, of the government itself siphoning off oil-revenues and thus impoverishing the state. A representative of the other side, with little opportunity to put its case, offered this defence in June 1993: 'Every Caucasian male regarded it as his birthright to possess both a gun and an eye-catching horse, no matter what the cost; it is not the possession but the (mis)use of weapons that should occasion criticism. The modern equivalent of the horse is the car, and making sacrifices to purchase an attractive one does not necessarily imply involvement in racketeering. In a land-locked country the only outlet for the basic export, oil, is the railway-link through Russia, so that all sales are controlled by the very (Russian) authorities who, in response to

Chechenia's unwelcome declaration of independence, imposed a financial blockade, refusing to pay its own huge oil-debt to Chechenia.'

NORTHEAST CAUCASIANS: AVARS, LAK, DARGWA AND LEZGIANS ■

Daghestan (capital Makhachkala) is indeed a veritable 'Mountain of Tongues', as the Arabs styled it. Multi-lingualism is common throughout the Caucasus but can take formidable proportions in Daghestan, where it has been noted that denizens of the highest areas usually also speak the language of the group living beneath them, and so on down to the lowlands. The indigenous languages, some of which extend south-wards beyond Daghestan itself, are given below, with 1989 census-data in brackets – where no figures appear, this is because the speakers, who may number anything from a few hundred to a few thousand, classify themselves according to the ethnic group of one of their other languages (e.g. 'Avars' include all speakers of both the Andic and Tsezic languages). Soviet literary languages are asterisked:

Avaro-Ando-Tsezic group, comprising: Avaric: *Avar (604, 202); Andic: Andi, Bot-likh, Godoberi, Karata, Akhvakh, Bagvalal, Tindi, Chamalal; Tsezic: Tsez (Dido), Khvarshi, Hinukh, Bezhta, Hunzib

Lako-Dargic group, comprising: Lakic: *Lak (118,386); Dargic: *Dargwa (365,797), Kubachi, Chirag.

Lezgic group, comprising: *Lezgian (466,833), *Tabasaran (98,448), Rutul (20,672), Tsakhur (20,055), Agul (19,936), Udi (8,849), Archi, Budukh, Khinalug, Kryz.

Some Avar, Lak and Dargwa materials were written in Arabic script from the 19th century, but generally the literary languages were given (Roman) scripts only in 1928, shifting to Cyrillic in 1938. The Tabasaran script, however, was created in 1932. Attempts to provide Rutul, Tsakhur and Agul with alphabets failed, though there seems to be a renewed attempt to write these languages today. The Udi, whom some scholars view as the remnants of the 'lost' Caucasian Albanians, were even offered an alphabet in the 1930s, although the language is spoken in only three vil-lages (two in Azerbaijan, one in Georgia). Before the Soviet period, Arabic, Avar and Azeri were common *linguae francae*. The early Soviets tried to wean locals away from Arabic with its religious connotations by supporting the Turkic Kumyk in the north and Azeri in the south, but from the 1930s Russian has been the main inter-communal language outside the mountain-settlements, where there is strong adher-ence to native tongues.

Islam came to Daghestan with the Arabs in the 8–9th centuries, and Daghestan, where the indigenous peoples listed above are Sunnis of the Shafi'i school, was a recognized centre of Arabic learning with some 2,000 Koranic schools before the Revolution. The Udis are, however, Orthodox (Armenian Orthodox in Azerbaijan, Georgian Orthodox in Georgia). Religious sentiment remains strong today, though the degrees of attachment differ, strongest amongst the Avars and Laks, weakest amongst the Lezgic sub-groups in the south. As in neighbouring Chechenia, there is a harmony between Islam and the traditional organization of a society based on clan and village.

The most celebrated period in the history of Daghestan (especially that of the Avars) was their great resistance to the Russians during the 19th century Caucasian War, particularly under the charismatic if unbending leadership of their third Imam, the Avar Shamil (b.1797 Gimri-aul, d.1871 Medina), one of the most successful guerilla-leaders in history. Dargho and Vedeno were his main bases in Chechenia, though forced eventually to Ghunib in Avaria, where he was finally compelled to surrender on 25th August 1859, after which the Tsar's forces were able to concentrate their full attention on the West Caucasian front. Had Shamil been able to unite Daghestanian and Circassian resistance in the 1840s, the outcome of the Caucasian War might well have been different – the Western powers were too concerned with the Balkans in the 1850s to bother about events in the Caucasus (just as today) – but Christian Ossetia's non-adherence to the cause and something less than total commitment on the part of the Kabardians in the central Caucasus meant that East and West Caucasia had to fight an unco-ordinated and thus less effective campaign. Losing his eldest son, Jemal-Ed-Din, as hostage to the Russians in 1839, Shamil secured his release only in 1855 after carrying off as counter-hostages two Georgian princesses with members of their household. Their months of captivity in Shamil's mountain-serail have been described by the French governess, Ana Drancy. Reared in the Tsar's court and unfamiliar with the languages and life-style of Daghestan, Jemal-Ed-Din was dead within the year. Later, Daghestan's anti-Bolshevik uprising in 1920–1 was cruelly crushed.

For all its diversity, there has been little sign of trouble in post-Soviet Daghestan. Accommodation has been found for those Avar-speakers 'persuaded' to vacate Eastern Georgia by Georgian nationalists. There are reports of some dissatisfaction with the ever growing religious and linguistic pre-eminence of the Avars, but the main potential problem concerns the Lezgians. Their homeland extends from Southern Daghestan into Northern Azerbaijan (where perhaps as many as 130,000 plus 45,000 Avars reside), crossing what is no longer a relatively meaningless Soviet administrative division but an internationally recognized border between the Russian Federation and independent Azerbaijan. It remains to be seen what the outcome will be of the calls for a united Lezgistan by the movement *Sadwal* 'Unity', though a rival *Samur* party evidently advocates integration with Azerbaijan.

OSSETES ■

The Ossetes are descendants of the Alans, related to the Scythians and Sarmatians, who in antiquity extended over Russia's southern steppe. Ossetic belongs to the northeastern branch of the Iranian languages: place-names testify to its one-time greater range (e.g. *don* is Ossetic for 'water, river'). Most specialists accept that the pan-North Caucasian heroic sagas known as the *Narts* are of Ossetian origin. In 1989 the 597,802 Ossetes were mainly concentrated in both the North Ossetian Autonomous Republic (capital Vladikavkaz, Russian for 'ruler of the Caucasus'; formerly Ordzhonikidze), where 334,737 constituted 53% of the population, and Georgia. 164,009 then lived in Georgia, 65,195 in the South Ossetian Autonomous Republic (capital Tskhinvali), which is divided from North Ossetia by the main Caucasus chain and where they formed 66.2% of the population in 1989.

The two dialects in the north are Iron (eastern) and Digor (western) – that in the south is somewhat distinct and has been heavily influenced by Georgian, which testifies to a long period of symbiosis. The precise date when Ossetes settled the southern flanks of the Caucasus became a point of heated controversy as nationalist fervour fouled Georgia's road to independence. The most extreme suggestion advanced by some Georgians was that the bulk of the Ossetes simply followed the Bolsheviks into South Ossetia in 1921. Some (non-Ossete) Iranologists have suggested dates from the 6th century BC to the 1st century AD; even objective Georgian historians accept that significant numbers have been in the area since the 13th century – Queen Tamar was herself half-Ossete. Abuse led to clashes, clashes to open war after President Gamsakhurdia of Georgia abolished South Ossetia's autonomous status following a declaration in Tskhinvali of South Ossetia as an independent republic in December 1990. Thereafter it became the norm for Georgians to refer to the region in public as *Shida Kartli* ('Inner Kartli'), *Samachablo* ('Fiefdom of the Machabelis'), or at best so-called South Ossetia. The bloody war that ensued caused tens of thousands of refugees on both sides and so destroyed any trust South Ossetes may have had in Tbilisi that over a year after the ceasefire negotiated in the summer of 1992 and policed by tri-partite Russian-Ossetian-Georgian patrols there had been no political settlement and Ossetian leaders still called for a total break with Georgia and union with North Ossetia.

The first printed book in Ossetic appeared in 1798 using a Cyrillic alphabet. Publications in the 19th century used either Cyrillic or Georgian. Some Digor material in Arabic script also appeared. A Roman script was introduced in 1923. In 1938 Ossetic in North Ossetia adopted a Cyrillic script, whereas in South Ossetia a Georgian alphabet was re-introduced, the northern Cyrillic model finally being adopted after the death of Stalin. Digor was abolished as a literary language in 1939.

Being the one firm centre of Christianity in the North Caucasus (Eastern Orthodoxy came in the 6th century from Byzantium, although in the 17–18th centuries Islam was introduced to the Digors from Kabardia) no doubt conditioned closer relations with Russia than exists for any other North Caucasians with their shared northern neighbour. This surely explains why the Ingush Prigorodnyy Raion was left in Ossetian control even after the Ingush returned from Central Asian exile. Ossetian (and Cossack) loyalties will be put to the test if and when the North Caucasus as a whole seeks to follow Chechenia's lead in attempting to break away from the Russian Federation.

AZERBAIJANIS ■

Of the 6,791,106 Azerbaijanis in the USSR in 1989, 5,800,994 lived in the Republic of Azerbaijan (capital Baku), where they constituted 82.6% of the population. There are at least as many Azerbaijanis living over the border in the northwestern region of Iran; this division of Azerbaijani territory between (Tsarist) Russia and Persia was formalized by the treaties of Gulistan (1813) and Turkmanchay (1828). The now-independent, former-Soviet Azerbaijan has expressed no wish to unify Azerbaijani lands. Initially in favour of joining the Commonwealth of Independent States, membership was never ratified by the Baku parliament, though under the restored former Party Boss, Haidar Aliev, Azerbaijan seemed to change its policy in late 1993. Lying along the Caspian Sea, Azerbaijan (along with Daghestan) has a keen interest in the future of the caviar-trade. Three quarters of Azerbaijanis are Shi'a Muslims, the remainder, predominantly in the north of the republic, are Sunni of the Hanafi school. Fertility-rates, though high, tended to be among the lowest in the USSR's Muslim republics. Azerbaijanis are also less russified than other (former Soviet) Turkic peoples. Little seems to remain of the old clan-system.

The Azeri language belongs to the southwestern (Oghuz) branch of Turkic and is close to Turkish. It became a literary language in the 14th century and was written for centuries in the Arabic script. Widespread as a *lingua franca* in Daghestan even before Soviet times, Azeri was actively promoted in the early 1920s, but this policy went into reverse after 1928 when pan-Turkism became a new bogey for the Soviet leadership. Azeri is, however, still known in Daghestan, especially in the south. The script was latinized in 1929 and became Cyrillic-based in 1939. A Roman alphabet has now been reintroduced.

The ethnic origins of the Azerbaijanis are thought to be a mixture of Caucasian Albanians with various Iranian- and Turkic-speaking tribes (Cimmerians, Scythians, Huns, Bulgars, Khazars, Oghuz, Pachaniks), the consolidation taking place in the 11–13th centuries with the admixture of the new wave of Seljuk Turks. The Red Army put an end to Azerbaijan's few post-Revolutionary years of independence on 28th April 1920.

When the Soviet borders between the Transcaucasian republics were established, Azerbaijan was given two provinces which had Armenian majorities at the time: Nakhichevan (capital Nakhichevan), from which it is totally separated by Armenia; and Nagorno-Karabakh (in Armenian *Artsakh*, capital Stepanakert); the Zakatala region, where the Muslim Georgian Ingilos live, was also placed under Baku's control. In 1989, the Nakhichevan Autonomous Republic had an Azerbaijani population of 281,807 against a mere 1858 Armenians, whilst the Nagorno-Karabakh Autonomous District had 145,450 Armenians against 40,632 Azerbaijanis. The Armenians of Karabakh took advantage of perestroika to express their dissatisfaction with Baku's restrictions on their culture and called for union with Armenia. This led to an all-out war, which is still ongoing. The subsequent massacres of Armenians in and around Baku led to virtually all Azerbaijan's Armenians (those outside

Karabakh) fleeing to Armenia (in 1989 a total of 390,505 Armenians lived on Azerbaijani territory) and vice versa.

For a time in 1989 Georgians were publishing criticisms of Baku's treatment of
the Ingilos (e.g. restricting their language-rights, refusing expeditions from Georgia
permission to visit archaeological sites in the region) as well as charging Georgia's
Muslims (in essence its Azerbaijani minority, which numbered 307,556, concentrated in the southern districts of Marneuli and Dmanisi) with reproducing at such a
rate as to place in jeopardy Georgians' majority-status in Georgia. Not surprisingly,
clashes occurred in early July 1989 in southern Georgia, which reportedly involved
fatalities. These problems, though, were quickly overtaken by Georgian-Abkhazian
fighting. The present state of relations between Georgians and Georgian Azerbaijanis is uncertain – this is the area where the oil- and gas-pipeline running through
Georgia to Armenia has repeatedly been blown up, a fact which suggests that the
Georgians are either unwilling or unable to police the area effectively. On the other
hand, the logical alignment between the two oldest Christian states in the world,
Armenia and Georgia, seems to be frustrated not just by long running rivalries over
such trivial questions as to which of their scripts is the older but by realpolitik: Azerbaijan has oil, Armenia has nothing; furthermore, support for Armenia over Karabakh would weaken Georgia's arguments for retaining control of Abkhazia and
South Ossetia. A similar dilemma undoubtedly faces Russia over Abkhazia: open
support for the considerable Russian minority there, who sympathize with the
Abkhazians (being equally alarmed at Georgian chauvinism), would render Russian
retention of its own numerous colonies less secure, whereas to abandon Abkhazia
completely would surely lead to rebellion across the whole North Caucasus, a danger
that remains very real. What relations independent Azerbaijan will establish with its
Georgian, Daghestanian and Russian minorities remains a question for the future.

ARMENIANS ■

Armenian, though long regarded as a sub-type of Iranian because of the large number of Iranian loan-words it contains, was finally demonstrated to represent an independent branch of the Indo-European language-family in the late 19th century.
Christian (of the monophysite Orthodox variety) since 301, Armenians developed
their unique, angular script later in the 4th century and have enjoyed a continuous
literary tradition ever since. A small group of Armenians were islamicized; they were
called Hemshinli. Hemshinli in southwest Georgia and Armenia were exiled to Central Asia along with the Meskhians in 1944, as were a number of other small Muslim
groups from these areas.

The present Republic of Armenia (capital Yerevan) is only a tiny fraction the size
of the land once inhabited by Armenians, historical Greater Armenia, which incorporated a large swathe of present-day eastern Turkey. Part of this territory was the
home of the ancient kingdom of Urartu. Around 600 BC Urartu was invaded by certain Iranian tribes and a people from Anatolia called Hayasa – the Armenians call

themselves *Hayk* and their land *Hayastan*. Within one hundred years Persians and Greeks were referring to a people they called *Armina* and *Armenioi* respectively.

Armenia had relations with Rome and Byzantium, but the people who were to play the most fatal role in the history of the Armenian nation were the Turks, who first arrived in the region in the first half of the 11th century. Their assaults on Armenian towns led eventually after the battle of Manzikert in 1071 to a mass-migration from part of the homeland to the province of Cilicia, which was to become the most important Armenian centre in medieval times. Some Armenians went north to settle in the Crimea, southern Russia, Romania and even Poland. Armenia did not escape the effect of the Mongols, but from the 16th century Karabakh under the Meliks became a stronghold of Armenian culture until the capture of eastern Armenia by Tsarist Russia early in the 19th century. The creation of the nationalist *Dashnakt-suthiun* (or Alliance) Party late in the century was unwelcome both in Russia and Turkey. In 1895 the Turkish ruler, Abdul Hamid, decided on action and a series of officially sanctioned massacres were committed, Turkish hatreds being fuelled by added resentment of the financial acumen of an urbanized (and Christian) Armenian community – this is what caused Gladstone to talk of 'the unspeakable Turk'. Many deaths occurred in fighting between Armenians and Azerbaijanis in the wake of the Russian Revolution of 1905. Then during World War I, the Young Turk nationalists saw their opportunity to finish the job Abdul Hamid had begun and embarked on what the Armenians refer to as 'The Genocide'. It is estimated that over a million Armenians perished; the Armenian population of Turkey was in essence liquidated and the diaspora-communities in Syria, France, England and America created. Turkey has never officially acknowledged, let alone apologized for, these incidents. Many fled over the border into Russian Armenia, where further misery (e.g. lack of food, clothing and housing) awaited.

Independent for three years after the Russian October Revolution, Armenia had high hopes of recovering some of the lost Turkish *vilayets* (districts), bolstered by what proved to be grandiose but vain promises from such Western leaders as Lloyd George, Clemenceau and Woodrow Wilson. In 1920 the British abandoned even the Baku oilfields, and Armenia was doomed to fall to the Red Army, which was victorious in late 1920. Armenia was conquered a second time after a rebellion while the Red Army was otherwise occupied in gobbling up Georgia, and the Soviet Armenian Republic was declared on 2nd April 1921. With the loss of Nakhichevan and Karabakh, Soviet Armenia was even smaller than the already reduced independent Armenia had been. Armenia also lost the dispute with Georgia over the provinces of Lori and Borchalo in Georgia's southwest.

Armenians of the diaspora tend to have the reputation of making successful entrepreneurs – names such as Gulbenkian have made this trait known to the wider world. They are a numerous and important lobby for Armenia, though not as united and thus not as powerful as the diaspora-Jews are for Israel. They do, however, provide a lot of humanitarian relief for their homeland, as was apparent to whole world after the 1988 earthquake. Wherever in the world they live, they tend to keep very much to themselves, marrying within the community and thus preserving their language and culture.

Armenia is ethnically the most homogeneous republic in the Caucasus (and indeed among the former Soviet republics in general), even though it also has the highest proportion of its people (even excluding the Western diaspora) living outside the republic. In 1989 the Soviet Armenian population stood at 4,627,227. Of these 3,081,920 lived in Armenia itself, constituting 93.2% of the total population, a proportion which will now have increased, given the inflow from Azerbaijan and the outflow of the local Azerbaijanis. The lack of internal division has not, of course, meant that Armenia is flourishing after the collapse of the USSR. The earthquake of 1988 levelled whole towns (such as Leninakan), and the war with Azerbaijan, which all Armenians support, has resulted in a total blockade of supplies from Azerbaijan. Turkey is the western neighbour. Georgia to the north should have been a secure source of supply, but the Georgian railway-network to Russia was frequently blocked from early 1992 by Gamsakhurdia-supporters in Mingrelia, the Mingrelian problem being subsequently compounded by the effect of the war in Abkhazia. This leaves only a road-link (the Georgian Military Highway) through Georgia to Russia, which is not open at the height of winter, plus Iran to the south.

Given this highly precarious situation, it is perhaps not surprising that everything possible is done to avoid open disputation with the Georgians, where in 1989 437,211 Armenians lived (11,000 fewer than in 1979), concentrated in the southwest of the republic, though of this total 76,541 lived in Abkhazia (3,000 more than in 1979). The Armenians have had difficulties with Georgian chauvinism, regarding such questions as the ownership of churches in the southwest, the ethnicity of Gamsakhurdia's local prefects and the number of hours their children are allotted at school for learning Armenian. Little public fuss, however, is made of these difficulties. Significantly, though, inside Abkhazia the local Armenians largely support the Abkhazians – when in 1989 the local Kartvelians refused to have anything more to do with the Abkhazian State University, where they and the Russians formed the two largest sections, and set up the rival 'Branch of Tbilisi University', the Abkhazians immediately created an Armenian section to replace the lost Georgian one.

If Georgia fragments, as it is showing every likelihood of doing following the Ossetian, Abkhazian and Mingrelian conflicts, it is highly probable that the Armenians in the southwest will strive to unite with Armenia, just as the neighbouring Azerbaijanis will seek to unite with Azerbaijan. If Georgia somehow manages to survive its present crisis, Armenians will no doubt seek continuing friendly relations with their old northern rivals.

TATS ■

In 1989 the USSR had a Tat population of 30,817, largely split between Azerbaijan and Daghestan. Their language belongs to the Iranian family of Indo-European, and a Hebrew-influenced dialect of it is spoken by the Caucasus' Mountain Jews, of whom there were 19,516 in 1989. Only this latter variety has literary status, the Hebrew script having been used prior to the Revolution, Roman from 1929, and finally Cyrillic from 1939. Tats are mainly Shi'a Muslims, though monophysite Christians are also found amongst them. Tats also live in Iran. Culturally and in life-style they resemble the Azerbaijanis.

TALYSH ■

Between the 1926 census and that of 1989 the Talysh were classified as 'Azerbaijanis'. In 1989 21,914 (almost all in Azerbaijan) declared themselves to be Talysh – in 1926 there had been 77,000. This means either that there has been an intense process of assimilation at work or that for some reason members of the Talysh community may have been reticent about re-classifying themselves after 63 years of indoctrination to regard themselves as Azerbaijanis (cf. a parallel problem for the Mingrelians and Svans in Georgia p. 367)); a recent article from Azerbaijan suggested that the Talysh community may actually number between 200,000 and 250,000. The language is another member of the Iranian family and enjoyed a 9-year period as a literary language when it was given a Roman alphabet in 1930. They are Shi'a Muslims and live in the southernmost part of Azerbaijan (and in northern Iran).

KURDS ■

In 1989, 152,952 Kurds lived in the USSR, two-thirds in the Transcaucasus: 56,028 in Armenia (part of whom are Yezidis, so-called 'Devil-Worshippers'), 33,327 in Georgia, 12,221 in Azerbaijan. They are Sunni Muslims and speak an Iranian language (see also p. 203).

ASSYRIANS ■

The Assyrians are descendants of the Aramaeans and speak a Semitic language, which for a time at least during the Soviet period was actually taught in some Georgian schools. The total Soviet population in 1989 was 26,289, of whom 6,183 lived in Armenia and 5,286 in Georgia. They are Christians (Jacobites, Nestorians, Catholics or Orthodox).

12
DISPERSED PEOPLES

The epithet 'wandering' has traditionally been applied to Gypsies and Jews. It is an unfortunate usage: Jews have always formed stable communities except when forced to re-locate by persecution or expulsion; Gypsies, though formerly nomadic, have tended increasingly to practise transhumance within a very limited area and, in the recent past, to adopt a sedentary way of life. The perception of them, however, as fluid and shallow-rooted – slipping without mingling between other communities – helps to explain the distinctive experience they have shared among European peoples, never acquiring a homeland within Europe and trapped by their own exclusiveness and others' rejection of them.

Other peoples – especially, until the recent reversals and retreats which drove them back on their heartlands, the Germans (see p. 260), and, in the Middle Ages, some Italian groups – have also become widely dispersed around the continent. Other communities have arrived from outside more recently and settled in patches, especially Blacks, North Africans and some communities of Asian origin. The Jews and Gypsies remain distinctive, however, for a peculiar combination of features: the antiquity of their incorporation in Europe, the breadth of their dispersal and their want of a national home. The authenticity of their European credentials, after such a long time in the continent, and such copious contributions to European civilization, are beyond doubt. Their status is an object lesson to other European peoples, almost all of whom, as far as we know, came to the continent from elsewhere in the world, and a reminder that the formation of Europe is never likely to be over, as new migrants arrive and old communities are re-fashioned.

JEWS

European Jewry is riven into tendencies and communities by historic divisions, religious schisms, geographical separation and – over the last two centuries – assimilation into the national groups and states amid which Jews live. For many purposes, it is more useful to represent Jews as sub-sets within the English, French, Germans and so on than to think of European Jews as a distinct historic community of their own. On the other hand, Jewishness is a powerful extra layer of identity, forged from four main ingredients: first, the peculiar Jewish self-consciousness

North Sea

NORWAY
725
1000

FINLAND
11
2000

SWEDEN

Baltic
Sea

BALTIC
STATES
216,000
25,000

GREAT
BRITAIN
0
450,000

DENMARK
77
5500

SOVIET UNION
1,000,000
2,000,000

NETHERLANDS
106,000
20,000

POLAND
3,000,000
233,000

BELGIUM
24,000
40,000

GERMANY
160,000
330,000

CZECHOSLOVAKIA
217,000
44,000

LUXEMBOURG
700
1000

AUSTRIA
65,000
7000

HUNGARY
200,000
200,000

FRANCE
80,000
200,000

SWITZ

ITALY
8000
35,000

ROMANIA
530,000
430,000

YUGOSLAVIA
67,000
12,000

BULGARIA
50,000

SPAIN

ALBANIA
200
200

TURKEY

Mediterranean
Sea

GREECE
69,250
12,000

Jews

Numbers killed during the Holocaust
1939-45 and survivors

24,000 Approximate number of Jews
murdered 1939-45

2000 Number of survivors and
those who returned

░░ neutral countries

described below under Religion and 'Race'; *secondly, the long and abiding history of anti-semitism, which has made it impossible for Jews to forget their heritage, even in individual cases of deliberate evasion; thirdly, Zionism – the search for and defence of a Jewish homeland or state – which has been one of the major themes of Jewish history for over a century and which has gradually come to provide almost all Jews with a common focus of sentiment; finally, a sense of collective mission, confided by Providence in the course of a long and adverse 'sacred history', which has been represented in Jewish tradition as a series of 'trials of faith'. In modern times it has been reinforced by the extraordinary contributions made by individual Jews – out of all proportion to the people's numbers – to the thought, arts and sciences of mankind.*

RELIGION AND 'RACE' ■

The Jewish people is almost unique in modern times in being virtually identifiable with the adherents of a single religion. Like other religions, Judaism can be defined in theological or sociological terms, but it is probably most useful to define it as reverence for a particular body of tradition. The kernel of the tradition is 'the Law and the Prophets' – scriptures of immense antiquity which began to be compiled in written form perhaps as early as the 10th century BC. In its surviving form the Torah or 'law', comprising the first five books of the Bible, is of primary importance. It establishes a principle of 'righteousness': adherence to both a practical civil code and a programme of ritual observance. This includes the dietary laws – abstention from blood and 'unclean' meats – which have continued to be badges of Jewish identity, as well as injunctions to other familiar features of Jewish life like circumcision of infant males, Sabbath-day observance and penitential sacrifice. The Torah also begins the sacred history of the Jews – a story of divine election, of persecution and wandering, of trials of a faith sometimes found wanting, of progress to a 'promised land'. The same books disclose the unique Hebrew concept of God: a universal creator who made everything from nothing; a stern judge of mankind according to the criterion of righteousness; a 'tribal' God of a 'chosen people' and a cosmic provider with an elusive plan for the whole of creation.

Where religion and identity are held to be co-terminous the question naturally arises of the status of the Jew who has lost his faith. Many Jews, from the apostles of Jesus Christ to Benjamin Disraeli and Bishop Hugh Montefiore, have considered Christianity – which originated as a Jewish heresy – to be the culmination of Jewish tradition and therefore consistent with Jewishness; however, in a test-case, a religious Carmelite who sought Israeli citizenship was disqualified for apostasy. In the 19th and 20th centuries, Jews prominent in science and the arts have often slipped in and out of Christianity, agnosticism and atheism; yet, for example, Heinrich Heine (1797–1856), for whom Christian baptism was 'a ticket into European culture', filled his poetry with Jewish self-awareness and Karl Marx (1818–83), who emphatically repudiated his Jewish origins, has continued to be classified as Jewish – even in some ways 'typically Jewish' – by the rest of the world.

From such dilemmas has arisen the paradox that, though Jewishness can be forfeit in cases of apostasy, it is nevertheless transmissable 'in the blood' – through the female line, according to rabbinical tradition. This in its turn creates problems concerning the status of converts, but, because Jews have no habit of proselytization, numbers of these have generally been very small. A further, more sinister paradox is that this people, who have been the worst victims of racism in modern times, have a doctrine of racial exclusiveness imbedded in their self-perception.

In the early 19th century, a social trend among European Jews provoked a religious split. Part of Jews' self-emancipation from the ghettos in which they had formerly lived was the adoption of the dress and manners of their host-societies and conformity, without necessary sacrifice of traditional faith and morals, to a secular way of life. A 'Reform' movement, generally held to have originated in Seesen, near Hildesheim, in 1810, brought these new ways into the synagogue, introducing organ music, singing in melodic unison, and sermons. Some congregations even switched the sabbath to Sunday and one of the acknowledged leaders of the reformers, Samuel Holdheim (1806–60), was willing to abandon circumcision. The result of these convulsions was the emergence of three main schismatic traditions, usually now called 'liberal', 'united' and 'conservative', according to their degree of conformity to the ways of the world.

LANGUAGES ■

The primary language of European Jews today is that of the country or society in which they live; this is a measure of the progress of assimilation in modern times. Competence in the liturgical use of Hebrew is, in practice, a universal religious obligation, at least – in conservative communities – for menfolk. The peculiarly Jewish languages of Europe, Yiddish and Ladino, as well as Knaanic, a Jewish dialect of Slav origins displaced by Yiddish in the Middle Ages, have increasingly fallen into disuse. They have, however, rich histories and interesting literatures and are subjects of academic study and sentimental revival. Yiddish, a Germanic language normally written in Hebrew characters, is found in surviving biblical glosses from as early as the 12th century and in printed books – notably metrical versions of Bible stories – in many examples from the 1530s onwards. This made it remarkably standardized, especially in view of the dispersal of its speakers; creative literature, however, cannot be said to have flowered in it before the late 19th century. It is said to survive as the first language of some Jews in the United States (through whom it has loaned some expressive and popular terms to English). The European Yiddish press, published in Paris, has today a circulation of about 30,000; yet before World War II, it was the common tongue of over 10 million people. In central and northern Europe, Hungary and Romania it was, until the catastrophic disruption of Jewish life in the present century, the most common Jewish language of religious instruction, into which boys had to translate sacred texts; and over much of the same area it also served as the medium of everyday communication. In communities originating in medieval Spain, similar functions were performed by Ladino, a romance language very close to Castilian and normally written in Arabic or Hebrew characters; isolated terms are found in poetry from as early as the 10th century. It remains a living language among small groups in Bulgaria and Turkey, and survives as a tradition maintained in particular families, but the last large community of Ladino-speakers disappeared when the Jews of Salonica, 60,000 strong, were wiped out in World War II.

HISTORY ■

Though theories abound, no-one knows for certain how or when Jews arrived in Europe. Their numbers, diversity and broad geographical spread demand explanation and have prompted curious hypotheses, notably Arthur Koestler's suggestion that some European Jews must have descended from the Khazars – a nomadic people of Asiatic origin living on the northern shore of the Black Sea, whose rulers embraced Judaism for political reasons in the 8th century. The dispersal of Jews from their biblical heartlands in the Middle East has frequently been connected with cataclysmic events of the 'sacred history', such as the Babylonian and Roman conquests of ancient Jewish kingdoms, but it is as likely that migration happened slowly and fitfully over a very long period of time. Dispersion in the central and eastern Mediterranean had begun before apostolic times. An isolated text locates Jews as far away as Cologne as early as AD 321. Continuous evidence of Jewish settlement in Europe, however, begins in the late antique period, when Jewish communities were widely dispersed over the European coasts and hinterlands of the Mediterranean. Here – like other migrants from the east, such as Greeks, Syrians and, later, Arabs – they were an urban and often a commercial people, self-regarding and aloof from their host-societies. The *Itinerary* of the Jewish merchant Benjamin of Tudela, of 1168, describes their close-knit world, in which a structure of family firms and the fellow-feeling of co-religionists gave Jews a commercial advantage and helped them to trade between hostile Christian and Muslim worlds.

Mediterranean communities may have been the springboard for Jewish colonization of northern European cities between the 6th and 11th centuries AD, by which time there were numerous communities on the Garonne, Loire, Rhône, Seine, Rhine, Elbe and upper Danube, with some scattered settlements in England. Wherever they went, they were alternately privileged and persecuted: privileged, because rulers in need of productive settlers were prepared to reward them with legal immunities; persecuted, because host-communities resented advantaged intruders. Anti-semitism has been traced, especially by Jewish historians, to the influence of Christianity. It is true that medieval anti-semitism exploited Christian prejudices; an unwarranted reading of gospel texts besmirched Jews with collective responsibility for the death of Christ; and Holy Week was at best an expensive and at worst a fatal time for Jewish communities. In general, however, medieval anti-semitism seems part of the antipathy of vertically-ordered societies for unassimilable groups – comparable, for instance, to treatment of lepers, 'Moors' and, later, Gypsies.

As early as the 1320s, in the writings of Asher ben Jehiel, Jews were distinguishing two strands of Jewish culture in Europe, centred respectively in Spain and Germany. The first, called Sephardi, from *Sefarad*, the Hebrew name for Spain, benefited from its location in what had been one of the heartlands of the Roman empire, in close contact with sophisticated centres of learning in both the Latin-Christian and Islamic traditions. Sephardim therefore had access to a potential sense of superiority which has characterized their descendants, at least until very recent times; although now a small minority in world Jewry, Sephardim retain some features of a self-conscious aristocracy, with their own religious hierarchies and, in some places, their own synagogues which retain an exclusive club-like atmosphere. The Jewish culture centred in Germany was called Ashkenazi from *'Ashkenaz'*. This biblical term for a region in or near Armenia was adopted as a rabbinical name for Germany in the 11th century, perhaps because of a phonic resemblance to 'Saxonia' or to the name of the presumed Germanic homeland in 'Scania'. Though Asher ben Jehiel claimed 'to prefer our Ashkenazi ways', Jews living on or beyond the barbarian frontiers of the former Roman world were at a cultural disadvantage compared with the Sephardim. The spread of Ashkenazi communities in northern and eastern Europe gradually ensured that Ashkenazim would establish a huge demographic preponderance; and in the 19th century, when German civilization attained a high level of respect world-wide, the atavistic sense of cultural inferiority began to wear off.

The increasing pace and virulence of persecution in the late Middle Ages drove Jews to new centres. Those who did not convert to Christianity were expelled from England in 1290, from most of France in the early 14th century, from many areas of western Germany in the early 15th century and from Spain and Portugal in the 1490s. The general effect was to shift the main areas of Jewish settlement in Europe eastward, into the central and eastern Mediterranean, Poland and the region of the lower Danube. Yet wherever controls were absent, relaxed or unenforced, movements of counter-colonization re-introduced the Jews or strengthened their communities, and in the early modern period they returned or re-emerged in small numbers in France, the Netherlands, England and most of the formerly inhospitable parts of western Germany.

The Jewish experience in Poland illustrates some of the transformations of this long and unsettled era. Jews were documented in Poland from 1098, when the atmosphere generated by the First Crusade inspired the persecutions which drove them from Bohemia. Their numbers increased after the depredations of the Mongols despoiled and depopulated the land in the 1240s: Jews from Germany were welcomed as colonists and the persecutions of the late 14th and 15th centuries sent more waves in from the west. Poland was not exempt from anti-semitism; some towns had the 'privilege of not tolerating Jews', who were expelled from Cracow in

1490; but neighbouring countries were even less hospitable. Jews were not admitted to Lithuania until 1321; in East Prussia they were banned in 1309 and their settlement was tightly controlled until well into the 16th century. In partial consequence, Jewish population built up in Poland and – once admitted – in Lithuania, until Jews amounted to perhaps 20% of the population in the former territory and a third in the latter by the mid-18th century. As a result of pressure of numbers, opportunities for rural colonization, and exploitation by landowners (who could coerce Jews into serfdom by 'protecting' them from anti-semitism) the Jews in these countries diversified into agriculture and produced Europe's only Jewish peasantry: about a third of Jews were country-dwelling in the 18th century.

The 18th century in Europe generally was an era of religious toleration and 'enlightened' thought, from which Jews – though never entirely at ease nor entirely exempt from victimization – benefited, especially in England, France and the lands of the Austrian Habsburgs. The triumph of 'enlightened' principles in the French Revolution, and their spread in consequence of the Napoleonic wars, extended to Jews the 'rights of man' and led to the general relaxation of the civil disabilities and fiscal disadvantages under which they laboured: notable exceptions were the Iberian peninsula, where, except in Gibraltar, they were still not allowed, and the Russian empire (which had almost no Jews until the annexation of much of Poland in the late 18th century), where they were restricted to a 'pale of settlement' and officially hounded by discriminatory laws, designed to limit their access to education and livelihoods.

The progress of emancipation was matched by demands from within Jewry for an end to the traditional exclusiveness of ghetto and tribe and self-assimilation into mainstream European culture. The transition was fraught with dangers of loss of identity and even of faith: Moses Mendelssohn (1729–86), generally regarded as the first great figure in the movement, was the progenitor of a Christian dynasty; but the practicability of non-traumatic adjustment to the non-Jewish world seemed to be conspicuously demonstrated in the lives of the brother-financiers, Nathan (1777–1836) and James (1792–1868) Rothschild, who established eminent positions respectively in English and French society without ceasing to be Jews. Emergence from the ghetto conferred on individuals opportunities to amass great wealth, as in the Rothschilds' case, and gradually, as civil disabilities waned, political authority too. In the 19th and early 20th centuries, Jewish genius, emancipated both by the laws of host-societies and by Jewish adherence to cosmopolitan values, made its greatest contributions to European civilization since the time of Christ and the apostles – especially in science and political and economic thought, and to a lesser but still remarkable extent in the humanities and the creative and performing arts.

It was a false dawn. The tolerance of host societies cracked as Jewish numbers grew. Demographic trends are hard to assess at every stage of Jewish history, but in general in the 19th century Jewish communities seem to have had higher birth rates and lower death rates than the societies which surrounded them. This coincided with a period in Europe when many forms of pseudo-scientific racism were popularized. Anti-semitic violence, sporadic in the early part of the century, became commonplace in Russia from the 1870s and Poland from the 1880s; under the pressure of numbers of refugees it spread to Germany and even, in the 1890s, to France, where Jews had hitherto seemed well integrated and established at every level of society, and where it could be said that there were 'no Jews or Christians, except at the hour of prayer'.

Like every form of resentment of minorities, anti-semitism was exacerbated by adverse economic conditions. When these were generalized in Europe in the 1920s and early 1930s, anti-semitism became an uncontainable contagion, exploited by politicians, some of whom seem to have believed their own rhetoric and genuinely to have regarded a Jewish presence as incompatible with welfare or security. By demagogues of the right Jews were denounced as indelibly communist and by those of the left as incurably capitalist. Anti-semitic regimes had always tended to seek to 'solve' the Jewish 'problem' by eliminating it – usually through hermetic sealing in ghettos, forced conversion or mass expulsion. The Nazi project for eliminating the Jews by extermination was an extreme development of a long tradition. The Nazi movement seemed, at first, too fantastic and irrational to take seriously. But it mobilized mass support among a despairing and impoverished constituency in the German proletariat and petty bourgeoisie; respectable parties of the right tolerated and even supported it as a bulwark against communism. The Nazi party seized power in Germany in 1933 and German success in the early stages of World War II spread that power over the areas with the biggest concentrations of Jews in Europe. War conditions stimulated an ever more rabid drive by the Nazis to eliminate their Jewish enemies. The Nazis' first plan was to starve Jewish communities to extinction; when that failed, they resorted to mass shootings and gassing. Including those who died resisting or who were tortured or worked to death, about six million Jews perished at Nazi hands in the most purposeful and effective campaign of genocide ever recorded in human history. Throughout Europe, west of the Soviet border, fewer than two million survived.

From a Jewish perspective, the 'solution' to European anti-semitism was flight: to the United States or, to a lesser extent, Argentina, or potentially to Zion, to a Jewish state to be founded, preferably, in the ancient Jewish homeland of Palestine. A trickle of Zionist colonists had begun to flow towards Palestine from the early years of the 19th century; a small but growing minority of Jewish intellectuals and philanthropists gradually came to espouse the project; but only the impact of the pogroms turned zionism into a mass movement, guided by Theodore Herzl (1860–1904) and Chaim Weizmann (1874–1952). During World War I, Weizmann persuaded the British government – which had a long history of sympathy for zionism – to earmark Palestine, plundered from the crumbling Turkish empire, as the site of a Jewish 'national home'. Even then, many – perhaps most – Jews remained aloof; but the holocaust of World War II, followed by the heroic struggles of the Jews in Palestine against British imperialism and Arab irredentism, made the State of Israel, proclaimed in 1948, a magnet for Jewish sentiment. The result has been to refresh the sense of identity of otherwise assimilated European Jews, and further to drain their diminished numbers by migration.

THE JEWS OF EUROPE TODAY ■

In Poland, out of a pre-war population of three million, about 225,000 are thought to have survived the holocaust; but spasms of anti-semitism had driven almost all of them away by the end of the 1960s. In Hungary, where about 200,000 survived or returned in a community historically well integrated (outside frontier areas) with the Magyar population (see p. 258), the numbers declined to about 80 to 90,000 over a similar period; even in Britain, where Jews felt relatively secure, numbers fell, from a peak of 400,000 at the end of World War II, by nearly a quarter by the late 1908s, through demographic debility, emigration and assimilation. From Romania, where for centuries Jews were a vital part of the scene, most survivors of the holocaust and their families decamped to Israel; the once-huge Jewish communities of the Czech and Slovak republics have declined to under 30,000 – about a tenth of their pre-war levels. Today, the only large concentrations, by historic standards, are in France, where the community has grown to over 660,000 (1989), thanks to the influx of North African Jews fleeing from Muslim hostility in the 1950s and 1960s, and the former Soviet Union, where the Jews officially numbered about one and a half million when the union broke up in 1991: here, though Jews were victimized for 'economic crimes' until the mid-1980s, their numbers were kept intact by official discouragement – amounting to prohibition – of emigration. On the other hand, a paradoxical effect of the holocaust was the re-introduction of Jews, as asylum-seekers, into Spain, which now has a scattering of small congregations and a national Jewish organization.

The option evidently preferred by most of those who have chosen to stay in Europe is camouflage: assimilation into the host society at the sacrifice of everything except residual Jewish feeling, minimal sense of kindred with fellow-Jews, discreet religious observance (usually of a liberal kind) and, in most cases, political sympathy with Israel. The dangers of this policy are threefold: first, marriage outside the community attenuates Jewish feeling, generation by generation; secondly, compromises with non-Jewish society facilitate conversions and apostasy; finally, for the dwindling number who remain consciously and recognizably Jewish, the fear of renewed anti-semitic outbursts is never wholly allayed. In a previous generation, even the rich, socially successful, old-established families of Anglo-Jewry, depicted by Somerset Maugham in *The Alien Corn*, could not escape vilification and humiliation in a country where institutionalized anti-semitism was mild and mob violence muted.

THE GYPSIES

Gypsies are conventionally defined as a wandering people of Indian origin, widely scattered throughout the world, though concentrated in Europe. For most of them, long association with Europeans has indelibly marked their language, their culture and their society. At the same time they have tended to stand apart and retain a self-awareness of being Gypsies – or rather, of being different from those whom they call gadjé, *non-Gypsies. Their most common name for themselves is* Roma.

In the heyday of biological determinism, their nomadism was often put down to instinct and atavism. Such views attract few adherents today. In so far as Gypsies have remained nomadic, adequate explanations can be found in social, economic and political factors. The commercial nomadism which they practise is at root an economic phenomenon, catering for intermittent demands which can best be met by mobility. Nowadays, however, sedentarized Gypsies are in the majority. But while perhaps remaining based in the same place for years, even they often maintain their group identity and follow occupations which still involve mobility. Nomadism can be more a state of mind than a reality.

From the 1960s onwards in Europe, there has been a rise of Gypsy national organizations – political, social and cultural – to promote the ideals of self-determination and to struggle against policies of rejection and assimilation. The notion of nationalism is not linked to the idea of a territory or nation state, but rather to winning recognition from the gadjo *world that Gypsies constitute a distinct non-territorial people with a history, language and culture of their own.*

HISTORY AND MIGRATORY PATTERNS ■

For something like half of Gypsy history, obscurity reigns. With few written records to turn to, language and genes must fill the gap. The Gypsies' language, Romani, has been very receptive to borrowings. These provide some indication of the route taken in their westward migration and even of the length of their stay in various countries.

As for the place of origin, linguistic evidence – community of basic vocabulary, similarity of grammatical structure, and regularity of sound correspondence – all points to Romani's affinity with modern Indic languages and its departure from the Indian subcontinent in post-Sanskritic times, probably well over 1000 years ago. The origin and relationships of the speakers do not necessarily match those of the language; but the findings of population genetics, notably data from blood groups, tend to confirm the Indian link between language and original speakers. It seems probable that the Indian component of Gypsy ancestry was made up of Dravidian inhabitants of the subcontinent who came to speak the language of later-arriving Aryan peoples. Since then, however, there has been plenty of time for intermingling of blood-lines.

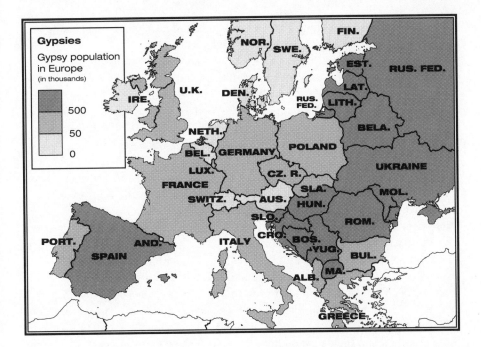

No combination of linguistics and genetics clarifies the circumstances which prompted the original exodus. Its cause – perhaps flight from natural causes, such as famine, or from hostile neighbours or war – can only be guessed at. There is more room for assurance over the migration route itself, at least for the ancestors of those Gypsies who reached Europe: lexical items adopted along the way suggest that these early Romani speakers probably passed through the Hindu Kush, and then through Iranian linguistic territory and the southern Caucasus, and on into the Byzantine Empire. It was a diffusion likely to have occupied a few hundred years. Once Gypsies entered western Byzantine territory, documentary evidence at last begins to appear, and from the 11th century Byzantine texts provide references which, with increasing confidence, can be related to Gypsies.

It appears to have been the Turkish expansion which drove many of them onwards through the Near East and across the Bosphorus and the Dardanelles into Thrace and the Greek mainland and islands. This generated at least part of the impulse for migration into Western Europe as well, when, after the diversion which Tamerlane's invasion created, the Turkish advance was resumed in 1415. Nonetheless, the larger part of Europe's Gypsy population remained in the Ottoman dominions, which would eventually include Transylvania and much of Hungary as well. Some of those who stayed behind had little option, having been subjected to serfdom or to outright slavery, as in Wallachia and Moldavia.

Once Gypsies moved into Western Europe in the 15th century – appearing first in the Holy Roman Empire, then in France and the Low Countries, Italy and Spain –

they told much the same story wherever they passed. Travelling in small bands, and headed by leaders with grandiose titles – duke, count, or earl of Little Egypt or Lesser Egypt (hence the misnomer Egyptian and then Gypsy) – they explained themselves with a tale of a seven-year pilgrimage, imposed as a penance for having once forsaken the Christian religion. At a time when Europe's was a deeply religious culture, the alms this brought them supplemented the living they made from horse-trading, tinkering, entertaining, healing and fortune-telling. More Gypsies spread out from the southeast of the continent. They met with other vagrant classes, some plying small trades along the roads and with lifestyles overlapping their own. But fewer of those were family-based, as the Gypsies were; and still fewer ranged as widely. What united them, Gypsies or not, in the eyes of the settled classes was their rootless and masterless status, an aberration at odds with the dominant schemes of value founded on land ownership. Official attitudes hardened in every country of Christendom, and a tide of repression rose against vagabondage and the sturdy beggar. Country after country faced wandering Gypsies with policies of rejection and expulsion (including, later, transportation to colonies) and sometimes with coerced assimilation. The resultant pressures towards settlement – backed up by draconian penalties – eventually meant that in countries such as Spain and Hungary much of the Gypsy population became sedentarized. It did not follow, however, that they were absorbed into their surroundings. Even in such countries, it was common for settled Gypsies to live in an enclave of their own in a town or village, and Gypsies' love of their own distinctive society, and their dislike of intensive, intimate contact with non-Gypsies, underpinned by their pollution code (see page 398), ensured that their distinctiveness was maintained.

The industrial and social changes which swept much of Europe in the 19th century led to a distinct shift in many Gypsies' patterns of livelihood and travel. Since they relied on settled folk to buy their goods and services, their field of action moved with the market. Their lives became attuned to new seasonal rhythms in which the more densely populated areas loomed larger. They resisted temptations to go over to wage-labour: most, even when settled, clung tenaciously to some ideal of community, independence and self-employment. Urbanization did not prove incompatible with maintaining a degree of nomadism, though the distances covered by peripatetic Gypsies tended to become shorter, reflecting the increased geographical concentration of their clientele.

On the international plane, Gypsies shared in the mass migrations which were encouraged by factors such as economic opportunities in Western Europe and the United States, improved rail communications and faster and cheaper sea travel. In the latter half of the 19th century, several Gypsy tribes sprang to prominence as some of their members began to move out in all directions from the Balkans and Hungary. Notable among them were those who called themselves 'Rom', and whose major sub-divisions included *Kalderasha*, *Lovara* and *Churara*. (These are old occupational denominations – coppersmiths, horse-dealers and sieve-makers respectively. In the 19th century they had more relevance to actual livelihoods than they have today.) The speech of the Rom was permeated by Romanian influences, and they had clearly long been rooted in Romanian-speaking lands. Nowadays, Rom are found in almost every European country, as well as the Americas and elsewhere.

These renewed east-to-west migrations led to intensification of the repressive measures against the Gypsies. In World War II, this turned into outright genocide. Gypsies, like Jews, were designated by National Socialist ideology as a threat to German racial purity and, within allied or occupied territories as well as the expanded frontiers of the Reich, they were consigned to internment camps and, more often, to concentration or death camps. In the military arenas, many were killed on the spot by special SS action groups. Perhaps half-a-million Gypsies fell victim.

The return to peace brought further upheaval, with massive transfers of territory and peoples between countries. For much of the time, however, post-war international Gypsy migrations have been economic in origin. One of the more conspicuous was another of those westward surges out of the Balkans which have punctuated Gypsy history. This one began in the 1960s with its source in Yugoslavia, where frontier regulations became more relaxed than in the rest of Eastern Europe. It was a heterogeneous movement, including both settled and nomadic Gypsies.

Within frontiers, national policies towards Gypsies have tended to curb whatever nomadism still survived. In most communist countries the authorities demanded integration: any group not behaving in accordance with the model disturbed fundamental concepts of central planning. To a large extent communist governments were successful in eliminating full-time nomadism, but less so in exercising control over semi-nomads. Yugoslavia was the one communist state which did not seek to compel nomadic Gypsies to settle. There, pressure to do so came from economic circumstance rather than government coercion, and the transition was like a re-enactment of events which had led to widespread changes a century before in the countries which had been in the van of industrialization.

In Western Europe, the influences were more diffuse, but peripatetic families, increasingly living in caravans drawn by motor-vehicles, found that their way of life fitted uneasily with the voracious demand for land for development and with general laws on vagrancy, public health and town and country planning. Nomadism in itself might no longer be prohibited, but legislative systems designed for settled societies could have much the same effect. Gypsies were simply ordered to move on or perhaps tolerated for a time in shanty-towns or at places such as rubbish tips with no water supply or sanitary facilities. When some national policies turned towards the setting up of authorized camping sites, provision lagged far behind need. In Britain, the government despaired in the end of ever cajoling local authorities into providing an adequate supply, and in 1992 announced proposals to free them of the obligation altogether and to introduce stringent new measures against illegal camping.

The collapse of communism in Eastern Europe in 1989 brought a resurgence of anti-Gypsy feelings. When the emergent democracies slackened their border controls, the rest of Europe experienced an invasion of emigrants, including many tens of thousands of Gypsies from Romania, where antagonism against them ran particularly high. Once Yugoslavia disintegrated into bitter conflict, Gypsies from there swelled the numbers. In Germany – the prime destination for hordes of migrants – xenophobic attacks erupted and in 1992 the government struck a repatriation deal with Romania which opened the way to the deportation of Romanian asylum seekers, many of them Gypsies. Unrest over immigration, both legal and illegal, was also widespread in central European countries, while the European Community moved towards more standardized policing of entry of non-EC nationals and a tougher stance towards asylum seekers.

DISTRIBUTION AND DIALECTS ■

Gypsies are dispersed over the whole of Europe and are also found in the Middle East, North and South America, Australia and parts of Africa. Recent estimates for Europe as a whole vary from about three million to six or even eight million or more. Such ranges reflect lack of reliable figures for particular countries. It is easier to point to regions where numbers are proportionately high, and these are mainly in Eastern Europe. The former Yugoslavia and USSR, Romania, Hungary, Bulgaria and Slovakia together account for over two thirds of Europe's Gypsy population. In the west, Spain and France have the greatest numbers. The birthrate among Gypsies is often higher than in the general population.

In most countries there are several strata: the word Gypsy covers a patchwork of different elements, and a basic distinction has to be made between old-established groups and those which arrived within the past century or so (like the Rom and, more recently, Gypsies from Yugoslavia). The distinction manifests itself in all sorts of ways, language among them. Every Romani speaker, beyond childhood, is bilingual, and in all parts of Europe there have been constant borrowings throughout centuries of exposure to disparate contact languages. The differences between Romani dialects are therefore often considerable, though much reduced in their central core of basic vocabulary. The Romanian colouring which characterizes the speech of the Rom has already been mentioned. Another important dialect grouping is that of the Sinti, which is strongly influenced by German though now spread well beyond German-speaking lands.

GYPSY SOCIETY AND CULTURE ■

Old trappings and customs may die away for some, but that need not destroy the feeling of separateness, for out of whatever is absorbed from the *gadjé* can be constructed typically Gypsy cultures. It is pointless to look for neat patterns applicable to all Gypsies. In matters of social organization, there is a world of difference between, say, the resistance to continuity and structure among Spanish *Gitanos* and the relatively formal social institutions of the Rom, including bride-price in arranging marriages and the *kris romani*, or Romany trial, in settling disputes. What is common is the importance of family values as the cement: Gypsies are a people for whom communal life is of great significance, and where marriages, baptisms, parties, feasts and funerals are major social occasions. Often important, too, is a pervasive concept of defilement which has served to keep Gypsy populations separate. Though the code of taboos which goes with it relates to persons, objects, parts of the body, foodstuffs and topics of conversation, its overwhelming concern is with the potential threat of the female to ritual purity. Wherever it is strictly adhered to, the pollution code influences all interaction between male and female and Gypsy and *gadjé*. By definition, *gadjé* are unclean, being ignorant of the rules of the system. Marriage with *gadjé* presents dangers, though even among Gypsies the permissible marriage choices are restricted.

It is never simple to decide how much of the cultural preserve of Gypsies is unique to them. In the field of folklore, for example, they have adapted elements of the culture of the non-Gypsy community with which they are in contact and integrated them into their own songs and tales. In the course of time, that community's heritage may have sunk into oblivion, leaving the Gypsies as the conservators of what they had originally borrowed. In their folk-tales, they picked up motifs in the different countries which they traversed and gave them a Gypsy colouring. In the musical field, when playing as entertainers rather than for themselves, they turned to the music which was characteristic of their environment, and to instruments typical of the locality. During the 19th century, in three countries in particular – Hungary, Russia and Spain – Gypsies rose to a position of considerable eminence as professional musicians, to a point where they became almost part of the national identity. In many parts of the Balkans, their music is much in demand at weddings, baptisms and other celebrations.

Religion is another sphere where Gypsies reflect the *gadjo* world around them: they have accepted the religions of the countries in which they have lived for some time – Muslim, Orthodox, Catholic, Protestant. A much more recent development is the remarkable extent to which charismatic born-again Christianity has spread among some groups, with the potential for making a radical impact on a committed convert's life-style and on practices and customs regarded as incompatible with the new faith.

One widespread characteristic of Gypsies, of whatever formal religion, is devotion to the memory of the dead, and a dread of the clinging or haunting presence of the disembodied spirit of someone who has died. That has not, however, prevented the details of their funeral rites from becoming considerably varied, for they may often be linked with acceptance of other beliefs or observance of other folk-usages.

OCCUPATIONS ■

In most aspects of Gypsies' life, then, a common theme is adaptability. This tradition of change is evident in their occupations, too. Gypsies prefer trades which avoid prolonged contact with the *gadjé* and safeguard their independence. Services that cater to occasional needs are well suited to their way of life. The means by which they earn a living are legion, and in the course of one lifetime the pattern may alter radically. In many countries Gypsies have shifted away from small-scale trading in new goods and repair services, with a large clientele, towards trade in salvage and construction work, with fewer individual transactions. New livings have emerged or become more widespread; old ones may continue, such as music and other entertainment, fortune-telling, or (generally as an ancillary source of income) contract work in horticulture and agriculture. But if the activities change, what can be said to be unchanging is an underlying propensity for working for themselves.

BIBLIOGRAPHY

Chapter 1
THE MARITIME NORTH

Icelanders
Einarsson, S., *A History of Icelandic Literature* (New York, 1957).

Jones, G., *The Norse Atlantic Saga* (2nd edn, Oxford, 1986).

Magnusson, M., *The Iceland Saga* (London, 1987).

Magnússon, S., *A. Northern Sphinx, Iceland and the Icelanders from the Settlement to the Present* (2nd edition, Reykjavik, 1984).

Scherman, K., *Iceland – Daughter of Fire* (London, 1976).

Faeroese
Heinesen, W., *The Lost Musicians* (New York, 1971).

Schei, L.K. & Moberg, G., *The Faeroe Islands* (London, 1991).

West, J.F., *Faeroe – the Emergence of a Nation* (London, 1972).

West, J.F., *Faeroese Folk-Tales and Legends* (Lerwick, 1990).

Young, G.V.C. & Clewer, C.R. (trs.), *The Faeroese Saga* (Belfast, 1973).

Wylie, J. & Margolin, D., '*Grinadrap*' in Scandinavian Review LXX (1982)

Norwegians
Derry, T. K., *A History of Modern Norway 1814–1972* (Oxford, 1973).

Holt-Jensen, A., '*Norway and the Sea*', Geography Journal X (1985).

Midgaard, J., *A Brief History of Norway* (Oslo, 1979).

Popperwell, R. G., *Norway* (London, 1972).

Selbyg, A., *Norway Today, An Introduction to Modern Norwegian Society* (Oslo, 1986).

Danes
Facts about Denmark, Danish Ministry of Foreign Affairs (Copenhagen, 1987).

Jacobsen, H. S., *An Outline History of Denmark* (Copenhagen, 1986).

Jones, W. Glyn, *Denmark, a Modern History* (London, 1986).

Lauring, P., *A History of Denmark* (Copenhagen, 1986).

Thomasson, E., *Danish Quality Living, the Good Life Handbook* (Copenhagen, 1987).

English & Lowland Scots, Highland Scots
Clark, G. (Ed.), *The Oxford History of England* (15 vols. Oxford, 1930s to 1960s).

Daniell, W., *Voyage Round Great Britain* (2 vols. London 1978).

Daiches, D., *The Paradox of Scottish Culture, The Eighteenth Century Experience* (Oxford, 1964).

Donaldson, G. (Ed.), *The Edinburgh History of Scotland* (Oliver Boyd, Edinburgh, 1960s).

Hoskins, W.G., *The Making of the English Countryside* (London).

O'Dell. A..C. & Walton, K., *The Highlands & Islands of Scotland* (London & Edinburgh 1962).

Elton, G., *The English* (Oxford, 1992)

Hobsbawm, E. & Ranger, T. (Eds.), *The Invention of Tradition* (Cambridge, 1983)

Piehler, H.A., *Walks for Everyman* (London, 1969).

Sampson, A., *The Changing Anatomy of Britain* (London, 1982).

Sampson, A., *The Essential Anatomy of Britain* (London, 1992).

Dutch & Frisians
Boxer, C.R, *The Dutch Seaborne Empire 1600–1800* (London, 1965).

Schama, S., *An Embarrassment of Riches* (London, 1987)

Schama, S., *Patriots and Liberators* (London, 1977)

Normans
Bates, D., *Normandy before 1066* (London, 1982).

Bouard, M., *Histoire de la Normandie* (Toulouse, 1970).

Davis, R. H. C., *The Normans and their Myth* (London, 1976)

Douglas, D. C., *The Norman Achievement* (London, 1969).

Chapter 2
THE ATLANTIC ARC

Portuguese
Birmingham, David, *A Concise History of Portugal* (Cambridge, 1993).

Boxer, C.R., *The Portuguese Seaborne Empire 1415–1825* (London, 1991).

Cutileiro, Jose, *A Portuguese Rural Society* (Oxford, 1971).

Machado, Diamantino P., *The Structure of Portuguese Society. The Failure of Fascism* (New York, 1991).

Galicians, Asturians & Cantabrians
Cabezas, J.A., *Asturias* (Madrid, 1970).

Calderón Gutiérrez, C., *Cantabria en la historia contemporánea* (Santander, 1991.)

Cántabros, astures y galaicos (Subdirección general de arqueología (Madrid, 1982)

Christian, William A. jnr, *Person and God in a Spanish Valley* (1978).

Fabra G., Otero Pedrayo R., González V. et al., *Los gallegos* (Madrid, 1976).

Fraga Iribarne M., *Discurso de investidura, parlamento de Galicia* (Santiago de Compostela, 1990).

García Alvarez, M.R., *Galicia y los gallegos en la alta edad media* (Santiago de Compostela, 1975).
González Echegaray, J., *Cantabria a través de su historia* (Santander, 1977).
Montero Xesús, A., *Galicia vista por los no gallegos* (Madrid, 1974).
Olavarri, R., *Cantabria en el siglo XX* (Santander, 1987).
Otero Pedrayo, R. (Ed.). *Historia de Galicia*, (3 vols. Santiago de Compostela, 1979–80).
Schulten, A., *Los cántabros y astures* (Madrid, 1943).

Basques
Azcona, J., *Etnía y nacionalismo vasco* (Barcelona, 1984).
Basabe Prado, J.M., 'Identidad vasca y biología de la población', *Euskaldunak* V (1985).
Collins, R., *The Basques* (Oxford, 1986).
Heiberg, M., *The Making of the Basque Nation* (Cambridge,1989).
Larronde, J.C., *El nacionalismo vasco* (San Sebastián, 1977).
MacClancy, J., 'Biological Basques, sociologically speaking' in M. Chapman (Ed.) *Social and Biological Aspects of Ethnicity* (Oxford, 1983).

Bretons
Delumeau, J., *Histoire de la Bretagne* (Toulouse, 1969).
Galliou, P. & Jones, M., *The Bretons* (Oxford, 1991).
Hélias, P.-J., *The Horse of Pride* (London, 1978).
Jones, M., *The Creation of Brittany* (London, 1988).

Welsh
Roderick, A.J., *Wales through the Ages* (2 vols. London, 1959)
Williams, D., *Modern Wales* (revised edtn. London, 1977)
Williams, G., *An Introduction to Welsh Poetry* (London, 1953)
Williams, G. (Ed.), *History of Wales* (6 vols. Oxford, in progress).

Irish
Beckett, J.C., *Making of Modern Ireland, 1603–1923* (London, 1966).
Biggs-Davison, J. & Chowdhray-Best, G., *The Cross of St. Patrick* (London, 1984).
Byrne, F.J., Martin, F.X., Moody, T.W. (Eds.), *A New History of Ireland* (Oxford, 1984).
Foster, R., *Modern Ireland* (London, 1989)
Mac Gréil, M., *Prejudice & Tolerance in Ireland* (Dublin, 1977).
Miller, D.W., *Queen's Rebels, Ulster Loyalism in Historical Perspective* (Dublin & New York, 1978).
Robinson, P., *The Plantation of Ulster* (Dublin and New York, 1984).
Sacks, P.M., *The Donegal Mafia* (Yale & London, 1976).
Murphy, J.A., O'Carroll, J.P. (Eds.), *De Valera & his Times* (Cork, 1983).
West, T., *Horace Plunkett & Cooperative Politics* (Gerrards Cross, 1984).

Chapter 3
THE CONTINENTAL NORTHWEST

French
Bonnaud, P., 'Peopling and origins of settlement' in H.
D. Clout (Ed.) *Themes in the Historical Geography of France* (London, 1977).
Braudel, F., *L'Identité de la France* (Paris, 1986).
Claval, P., 'The image of France and Paris in modern times, a historico-geographical problem' in A. R. H. Baker and M. Billinge (Eds.) *Period and Place, Research Methods in Historical Geography* (Cambridge, 1982).
Higounet, C., *Histoire de l'Acquitaine* (Toulouse, 1971).
James, E., *The Origins of France from Clovis to the Capetians, 500–1000* (Oxford, 1982).
James, E., *The Franks* (Oxford, 1988).
Planhol, X. de, *Géographie Historique de la France* (Paris, 1988).
Rickard, P. A , *History of the French Language* (2nd edition. London, 1990).
Todd, E., *The Making of Modern France, Politics, Ideology and Culture* (Oxford, 1991).
Trotter, D. A., 'The French language since 1945' in M. Cook (Ed.) *French Culture since 1945* (London, 1993).
Weber, E., *My France, Politics, Culture, Myth* (Cambridge, Mass. 1991).

Burgundians
Aldrich, R., *Economy and Society in Burgundy since 1850* (London, 1984).
Commeaux, C., *Histoire des Bourguignons* (Vol. 1. Paris, 1977. Vol. 2 Paris, 1980).
Richard, J., *Histoire de la Bourgogne* (Toulouse, 1978).
Vaughan, R., *Valois Burgundy* (London, 1975).

Luxembourgers
Bruch, R., *Précis Populaire de Grammaire Luxembourgeoise* (Luxembourg, 1973).
Calmes, C., *The Making of a Nation, from 1815 to the Present Day* (Luxembourg, 1989).
The Economist Intelligence Unit, *Country Profile, Belgium, Luxembourg* (London, 1986- in progress).
Lef°03ebvre, *Le Musée Luxembourgeoise* (Luxembourg, 1990).
Watelet, M., *Luxembourg en cartes et plans* (Luxembourg, 1989).

Walloons
Genicot, L. (Ed.), *Histoire de la Wallonie* (Toulouse, 1973).
Hasquin, H., *Historiographie et Politique, Essai sur l'Histoire de Belgique et la Wallonia* (Charleroi, 1981).
Huggett, F.E., *Modern Belgium* (London, 1969).
Irving, R.E.M., *The Flemings and Walloons of Belgium* (London, 1980).
Lipjhart, A. (Ed.), *Conflict and Coexistence in Belgium, the Dynamics of a Culturally Divided Society.* (Berkeley, California, 1981).
Quévit, M., *La Wallonie, l'Indispensable Autonomie* (Paris, 1982).
Stephens, M., 'Belgium' in *Linguistic Minorities in Western Europe*, Chapter 2 (Llandysul, 1976).
Thomas, P., 'Belgium's north-south divide and the Walloon regional problem'. *Geography LXVV* (1990).
Willemart, H. Willemart, P. & Van Elzen, S., *La Belgique et ses Populations* (Brusselsh, 1980).
Zolberg, A.R., 'The making of Flemings and Walloons, Belgium 1830–1914'. *Journal of Interdisciplinary History* V (1974).

Flemish

Hermans, T. (Ed.), *The Flemish Movement. A Documentary History 1780–1990*. (London, 1992).
Irving, R.E.M., *The Flemings and Walloons of Belgium*. (London, 1980).
McRae, K.D., *Conflict and Compromise in Multilingual Societies*. Volume 2, Belgium. (Waterloo, Ontario, 1986).
Ruys, M., *The Flemings. A People on the Move, a Nation in Being*. (Tielt, 1973)
Encyclopedie van de Vlaamse Beweging. Edited by J. Deleu, G. Durnez, R. de Schryver & L. Simons. (2 vols. Tielt, 1972).

Germans

Adams, M., *The German Tradition* (Sydney, 1971).
Applegate, C., *A Nation of Provincials, The German Idea of Heimat* (Oxford, 1990)
Ardagh, J., *Germany and the Germans* (London, 1991)
Barraclough, G., *The Origins of Modern Germany* (Oxford, 1966).
Bauml, F.H., *Medieval Civilization in Germany 800–1273* (London, 1969).
Carsten, F., *The Origins of Prussia* (Oxford, 1954)
Conze, W., *The Shaping of the German Nation* (London, 1979).
Craig, G., A, *The Germans* (London, 1982).
Craig, G.A., *The Politics of the Prussian Army* (Oxford, 1955).
Elkins, T., *Germany* (London, 1968).
Gordon Childe, V., *Prehistoric Migrations in Europe* (Oslo, 1950).
Robertson, J., *A History of German Literature* (Edinburgh, 1970).
Sagarra, E., *A Social History of Germany, 1648–1914* (London).
Watson, A., *The Germans, Who are they now?* (London, 1992).

Rhinelanders (see Germans)

Franconians (see Germans)

Chapter 4
THE ALPINE REGIONS

Swiss

Adams, Sir F.O. & Cunningham, C.D., *The Swiss Confederation* (London, 1889).
Allemann, F.R., *25 Mal die Schweiz* (Munich, 1968).
Bonjour E., Offler, H. & Potter, G., *A Short History of Switzerland* (Oxford, 1952).
De Salis, J.R., *Switzerland and Europe* (Leamington Spa & London, 1971).
Gibbon, M., *Swiss Enchantment* (London, 1950).
Hughes, C., *Switzerland* (London, 1973).
Mettler, E., *Switzerland, Past & Future* (Lenzburg, 1963).
Potter, G., *Ulrich Zwingli* (London, 1977).
Siegfried, A., *Switzerland* (London, 1950).
Steinberg, J., *Why Switzerland?* (Cambridge, 1985).
Wraight, J., *The Swiss and the British* (Wilton, 1987).

Bavarians and Swabians

Ammon, U., *Schwäbisch* (Düsseldorf, 1977).

Bosl, K., *Bayern* (Stuttgart, 1961).
Holtmann, E., *Lokale Identität und Gemeindegebietsreform* (Erlangen, 1991).
Hüttl, L., *Marianische Wallfahrten* (Cologne, 1985).
Larson, B., *Your Swabian Neignbours* (Stuttgart, 1980).
Tauber, W., *Munart und Schriftsprache in Bayern* (Berlin, 1993).
Zehetner, L., *Bairisch* (Düsseldorf, 1977).
Zorn, W., *Bayerns Geschichte im 20 Jahrhundert* (Munich, 1986)

Austrians

Austrian History Yearbook (Minneapolis, annually from 1964).
Bruckmüller, E., *Nation Österreich. Sozialhistorische Aspekte ihrer Entwicklung* (Böhlau, Vienna, 1984).
Bruckmüller, E., 'The national identity of the Austrians' in Mikulas Teich & Roy Porter (Eds) *The National Question in Historical Context* (Cambridge, 1993).
Collinson R.L. et al. (General Eds.), *Austria*. World Bibliographical Series 66 (Denver, Colorado and Santa Barbara, California, 1986).
Gulick, C., *Austria from Habsburg to Hitler* (2 vols. Berkeley, California, 1948).
Kann, R.A., *A History of the Habsburg Empire, 1526–1918* (London, 1974).
Rickett, R., *A Brief Survey of Austrian History* (9th edtn. Vienna, 1988) .
Zöllner, E., *Geschichte Österreichs von den Anfängen bis zur Gegenwart* (Vienna, 1992).

Piedmontese

Cox, E.L., *The Eagles of Savoy. The House of Savoy in Thirteenth-Century Europe* (Princeton, 1973).
Cox, E.L., *The Green Count of Savoy. Amadeus VI and Transalpine Savoy in the Fourteenth century.* (Princeton, New Jersey, 1967).
Cameron, E., *The Reformation of the Heretics* (Oxford, 1984).
Hearder, H., *Italy in the Age of the Risorgimento* (London, 1983).
Mack Smith, D., *The Making of Italy 1796–1866* (London, 1968).
Romeo, R., *Cavour e il suo tempo* (4 vols. Bari, 1969–1984).
Passerini, L., *Fascism in Popular Memory. The Cultural Experience of the Turin Working Class.* Translated by Robert Lumley and Jude Bloomfield (Cambridge, 1984).

Lombards

Greenfield, K.R., *Economics and Liberalism in the Risorgimento* (Baltimore, 1965).
Hearder, H., *Italy. A Short History* (Cambridge, 1990).
Romani, M., *L'agricoltura in Lombardia dal periodo delle riforme al 1859* (Milan, 1955).
Sked, A., *The survival of the Habsburg Empire. Radetzky, the imperial army and the class war, 1848.* (London, 1979).
Storia di Milano (Treccani, Milan 1959).
Venturi, F., *Italy and the Enlightenment* (London, 1972).

Slovenes

See Chapter 6

Chapter 5
THE WESTERN AND CENTRAL MEDITERRANEAN

Spanish-speaking Peoples
Barceló, M. (Ed.), *Historia de los pueblos de España* (Barcelona, 1983 – in progress).
Bielza de Ory, V., *Geografía humana de Aragón* (Vilassar, 1987).
Cano Bueso, J. (Ed.), *Comunidades autónomas e instrumento de cooperación* (Madrid, 1990).
Delibes, M., *Castilla, lo castellano y los castellanos* (Barcelona, 1982).
Delibes, M., *Castilla habla* (Barcelona, 1986).
Domínguez Ortiz, A. (Ed.), *Historia de Andalucía* (Madrid, 1983 – in progress).
Floristán Samanes, A. and Martín Duque, A., *Atlas de Navarra* (1981).
García Manrique, E. and Ocaña Ocaña, C., *Geografía humana de Andalucía* (Barcelona, 1986).
Gran atlás de Navarra (Caja de Ahorros de Navarra) (Pamplona, 1986).
Gran Enciclopedia Navarra, (8 vols. Caja de Ahorros de Navarra) (Pamplona, 1990)
Huici Urmeneta, V. et al., *Historia de Navarra desde los orígenes a nuestros días* (Madrid, 1982).
Lacomba Abellán, J., *Regionalismo y autonomía en la Andalucía contemporánea, 1835–1936* (Granada, 1988).
Rodríguez Becerra, S. (Ed.), *Antropología cultural de Andalucía* (Seville, 1984).
Tornos, J., *Legislación sobre comunidades autónomas* (Madrid, 1983).

Catalans, Valencians and Balearic Islanders.
Fernández-Armesto, F., *Barcelona* (Oxford, 1992).
Mascaró Pararius, J. (Ed.), *Historia de Mallorca* (5 vols. Palma, 1970–2).
Soldevila, F., *Història de Catalunya* (3 vols. Barcelona, 1934–5).
Vicens Vives, J., *Los catalanes en el siglo XIX* (Barcelona, 1986).
Vilar, P., *La Catalogne dans l'Espagne moderne* (3 vols. Paris, 1962)
Vilar, P. (Ed.), *Història de Catalunya* (Barcelona, 1977 – in progress).

Provençals
Baratier, E., *Histoire de la Provence* (Toulouse, 1969).
Geary, P. J., *Aristocracy in Provence, the Rhône Basin at the Dawn of the Carolingian Age* (Stuttgart, 1985).
Roche, A. V., *Provençal Regionalism* (Evanston, Illinois, 1954).

Corsicans
Abrighi, P., *Histoire de la Corse* (Toulouse, 1971).
Carrington, D., *This Corsica* (London, 1962).
Thompson, I., *Corsica* (Newton Abbot, 1971).

Sardinians
Clough, S.B., *The Economic History of Modern Italy* (New York, 1964).
Haycroft, J., *Italian Labyrinth. An Authentic and Revealing Portrait of Italy in the 1980s* (London, 1985).
Hearder, H., *Italy in the Age of the Risorgimento* (London, 1983).
Sassoon, D., *Contemporary Italy. Politics, Economy and Society since 1945.* (London, 1986).

Storia d'Italia, Volume III (Turin, 1973).

Ligurians
Clark, M., *Modern Italy 1871–1982* (London, 1984).
Clough, S.B., *The Economic History of Modern Italy* (New York, 1964).
Hearder, H., *Italy in the Age of the Risorgimento* (London, 1984).
Sassoon, D., *Contemporary Italy. Politics, Economy and Society since 1945* (London, 1986).
Woolf, S., *A History of Italy 1700–1860* (London, 1979).

Veneto-Friulians
Clark, M., *Modern Italy 1871–1982* (London, 1984).
Ginsborg, P., *Daniele Manin and the Revolution of 1848–49* (Cambridge, 1979).
Hearder, H., *Italy. A Short History* (London, 1990).
Norwich, J.J., *A History of Venice* (London, 1977).
Pullen, B. (Ed.), *Crisis and Change in the Venetian Economy in the Sixteenth and Seventeenth Centuries* (London, 1968).

Central Italians
Burckhardt, J., *The Civilization of the Renaissance in Italy* (London 1965).
Gross, H., *Rome in the Age of the Enlightenment* (Cambridge, 1990).
Hancock, W.K., *Ricasoli and the Risorgimento in Tuscany* (London, 1926).
Perowne, S., *Rome from its Foundation to the Present* (London. 1971).
Potter, T.W., *Roman Italy* (London, 1987).
Schevill, F., *The Medici* (London, 1949).
Waley, Daniel, *Siena* (London, 1993).

South Italians
Acton, H., *The Bourbons of Naples* (London, 1961).
Acton, H., *The Last Bourbons of Naples* (London, 1961).
Allum, P., *Politics and Society in Post-War Naples* (Cambridge, 1973).
Croce, B., *A History of the Kingdom of Naples* (Ed. H. Stuart Hughes, Trs. Francis Fenaye, Chicago, 1965).
Davis, J., *Società e imprenditori nel regno borbonico 1815/1860* (Bari, 1979).
Ginsborg, P., *A History of Contemporary Italy. Society and Politics 1943–1988* (London, 1990).
Venturi, F., *Italy and the Enlightenment* (London, 1972).

Sicilians
Arlacchi, R., *Mafia, Peasants and Great Estates* (Cambridge, 1983).
Blok, A., *The Mafia of a Sicilian Village* (New York, 1974).
Hilowitz, J., *Economic Development and Social Change in Sicily* (Cambridge, Mass., 1976).
Mack Smith, D., *Cavour and Garibaldi 1860. A study in political conflict* (Cambridge, 1954).
Mack Smith, D., *Medieval Sicily 800–1713* (London, 1968).
Mack Smith, D., *Modern Sicily. After 1713.* (London, 1968).

Maltese

Boiossevain, J., *Saints and Fireworks. Religion and Politics in Rural Malta* (London, 1965).
Blouet, B., *The Story of Malta* (1967).

Chapter 6
THE BALKANS

Turks

Ahmad, F., *The Making of Modern Turkey* (London, 1993).
Lord Kinross, *Atatürk, The Rebirth of a Nation* (London, 1964).
Lewis, B., *The Emergence of a Modern Turkey* (London, 1968).
Lewis, G., *Modern Turkey* (New York and London, 1974).
Özal, T., *Turkey in Europe and Europe in Turkey* (Nicosia, 1991).

Greeks

Andreades, K.G., *The Moslem Minority in Western Thrace* (Thessaloniki, 1956).
Campbell, J. & Sherrard, P., *Modern Greece* (London, 1968).
Clogg, R., *A Concise History of Greece* (Cambridge, 1992).
Poulton, H., *The Balkans, Minorities and States in Conflict* (London, 1991).
Pettifer, J., *The Greeks. The Land and People since the War* (London, 1993).
Stavroulakis, N., *The Jews of Greece. An Essay.* (Athens, 1990).

Albanians

Bihiku, K., *A History of Albanian Literature* (Tirana, 1980).
Hibbert, R., *Albania's National Liberation Struggle, the Bitter Victory* (London and New York, 1991).
Lear, E., *Journals of a Landscape Painter in Greece and Albania* (London, 1988. 1st published 1851).
Mann, S.E., *Albanian Literature, An Outline of Prose, Poetry and Drama* (London, 1955).
Marmallaku, R., *Albania and the Albanians* (London, 1975)
Pano, N.C., *The People's Republic of Albania* (Baltimore, 1968).
Pavlowitch, S.K., *The Albanian Problem in Yugoslavia; Two Views* (London, 1982).
Skendi, S., *The Albanian National Awakening, 1878–1912* (Princeton, New Jersey, 1967)

Macedonians, Serbs, Montenegrins, Croats, Bosnian Muslims & Slovenes

Banac, I. (Ed.), *Eastern Europe in Revolution*, (Ithaca and London, 1992)
Banac, I., *The National Question in Yugoslavia, Origins, History, Politics* (Ithaca and London, 1984 & 1992).
Barker, E., *Macedonia, Its Place in Balkan Power Politics* (London, 1950)
Blue Guide, Yugoslavia (London, 1989)
Cviić, Christopher, *Remaking the Balkans* (London, 1991)
Jelavich, B., *History of the Balkans*, Vol I

Eighteenth and Nineteenth centuries; vol II Twentieth century (Cambridge, 1983).
Glenny, M., *The Fall of Yugoslavia* (London, 1992).
King, R.R., *Minorities under Communism, Nationalities as a Source of Tension among Balkan Communist States* (Cambridge, Mass., 1973).
Kofos, E., *Nationalism and Communism in Macedonia* (New York, 1992).
Magaš, B., *The Destruction of Yugoslavia* (London, 1993).
Poulton, H., *The Balkans; Minorities and States in Conflict* (London, 1991 & 1993).
Rogele, C., 'The Slovenes and Yugoslavism', 1890–1914. East European Quarterly. (Boulder, Colorado 1977)
Thompson, M., *A Paper House, the Ending of Yugoslavia* (London, 1992).
Sugar, P.F., *Southeastern Europe under Ottoman Rule, 1354–1804.* Vol V of a History of East Central Europe (Seattle, 1977).

Bulgarians

Bell, J.D., *Peasants in Power, Alexander Stamboliski and the Bulgarian Agrarian National Union 1899–1923* (Princeton, New Jersey, 1977).
Black, C.E., *The Establishment of Constitutional Government in Bulgaria* (Brunswick, New Jersey, 1954).
Constant, S., *Foxy Ferdinand, Tsar of Bulgaria* (New York & London, 1978).
Crampton, R., *A Short History of Bulgaria* (Cambridge).
Groyeff, A., *The Crown of Thorns, A Biography of King Boris III of Bulgaria* (New Brunswick, New Jersey, 1987).
Macartney C.A., Palmer A.W., *Independent Eastern Europe, A History* (London, 1962).
Miller, M.L., *Bulgaria During the Second World War* (Stanford, California, 1975)
Nissen, O., *Bulgarian Communism, The Road to Power, 1934–1944* (New York, 1971).

Chapter 7
THE CARPATHIANS

Czechs & Slovaks

Crankshaw, E., *The Fall of the House of Habsburg* (London, 1963).
Gorys, E., *Czechoslovakia (Cologne, 1991).*
Hassinger, H., *Die Tschechoslovakei* (Vienna, 1925).
Katzner, K., *The Languages of the World* (London, 1977).
Kirschbaum, S.J., Slovak Politics; *Essays on Slovak History* (Cleveland, 1983).
Lettrich, J., *History of Modern Slovakia* (New York, 1955).
Mastny, V., *The Czechs under Nazi rule* (New York and London, 1971).
Maurice, C.E., *Bohemia from the Earliest Times to the Foundation of the Czechoslovak Republic* (London, 1922).
Polisensky, J.V., *History of Czechoslovakia in Outline* (Prague, 1991).
Seton-Watson, R.W., *A History of the Czechs and Slovaks* (London, 1943).
Thomson, D., *Europe since Napoleon* (London, 1966).
Tranchfort, F.R., *Guide de la Musique Symphonique* (Paris, 1986).

Wallace, W., *Czechoslovakia* (Boulder, Colorado, 1976).
Wolnik, S.L., *Czechoslovakia in Transition* (London, 1991).

Magyars
Drage, G., *Austria Hungary* (John Murray, 1989).
Ignotus, P., *Hungary* (London, 1972).
Kőpeci, Béla (Ed.), *Histoire de la Transylvanie* (Budapest, 1989).
Macartney, C.A., *Hungary* (London 1934).
Macartney, C.A., *The Habsburg Empire 1790–1918* (London, 1968).
Macartney, C.A., *National States & National Minorities* (London 1934).
Sugar, P.F., *A History of Hungary* (London & New York, 1990).

Scattered Germans (See Germans, Chapter 4)

Romanians
Cambridge, R.W., *A History of the Rumanians* (Cambridge, 1934).
Condurachi, E. & Daicoviciu, C., *The Ancient Civilization of Romania* (London, 1971).
Dantazzi, E.G., *Rumania in Light and Shadow* (London, 1921).
Hall D.J., *Rumanian Furrow* (London, 1933).
Handbook of Rumania, Naval Staff Intelligence Unit (London, 1918).
Ionescu, G., *Communism in Rumania, 1944–1962* (Oxford, 1964).
Mitrany, D., *Land & Peasant in Romania* (New York, Greenwood, 1968)
River, T.W., *The Making of the Rumanian State* (London, 1931).
Roberts, H.L., *Rumania, The Problems of an Agrarian State* (Newhaven, 1951).
Stratilesco, T., *From Carpathians to Pindus* (London, 1906).

Ruthenians
Bonkáló, A., *The Rusyns* (Fairview, New Jersey, 1990).

Chapter 8
THE NORTHERN PLAIN

Saxons (See Germans, Chapter 4)

Poles
Bromke, A., *Poland's Politics, Idealism vs. Realism* (Cambridge, Mass., 1967).
Davies, N., *God's Playground, A History of Poland* (2 vols. Oxford, 1981).
Davies, N., *Heart of Europe, A Short History of Poland* (Oxford, 1984).
Dziewanowski, M.K., *Poland in the 20th Century* (New York, 1977).
Gomulka, S. and Polonsky, A. (Eds.), *Polish Paradoxes* (London, 1990).

Lithuanians
The Baltic States, A Reference Book (Tallinn, Riga & Vilnius, 1991).
Brakas, M. (Ed.), *Lithuania Minor* (New York, 1976).
Budreckis, A. (Ed.), *Eastern Lithuania* (Chicago, 1985).

Encyclopedia Lituanica (6 vols. Boston, Mass., 1970–8).

Latvians
The Baltic States, A Reference Book (Tallinn, Riga & Vilnius, 1991).
Rutkis, J. (chief Ed.), *Latvia, Country and People* (Stockholm, 1967)
Schwabe, A., *Histoire du Peuple Letton* (Stockholm, 1953)

Prussians (See Germans, Chapter 4)

Chapter 9
THE NORTHERN BALTIC

Swedes
Elstob, E. C., Sweden, *A Political and Cultural History* (New York, 1979).
Forsberg, M., *The Evolution of Social Welfare Policy in Sweden* (Stockholm, 1984).
Imber, W. & Tietze, W., *Sweden* (New York, 1979).
Kayfetz, V. J., *Sweden in Brief* (Stockholm, 1982).
Ruth, A., 'The Second New Nation, The Mythology of Modern Sweden' in *Daedalus CXIII*, part 2 (1984)
Scott, F. D., *Sweden, the Nation's History* (Minneapolis, 1979).

Swedish-speaking Finns and Ålanders
Liebkind, K., *The Swedish-speaking Minority, a Case Study* (Helsinki, 1985).
Lönnqvist, Bo, 'What does it mean to be a Swedish-speaking Finn?' *A choice between isolationism and cosmopolitanism.'* LEIF, Life and education in Finland, Vol XXVIII (Helsinki, 1991)
Klövekorn, M., *Die Sprachliche Struktur Finnlands 1880–1950* (Copenhagen, 1960).

Lapps
Ahlbäck, *Saami Religion* (Uppsala, 1987).
Aikio, P. et al., 'The Sámi people in Finland' in *Cultural Minorities in Finland, An Overview Towards Cultural Policy* (Ed. Juha Pentikäinen and Veikko Anttonen, Helsinki 1985).
Hill, R.G.P. & Nickul, K. (Eds.), *The Lapps Today in Finland, Norway and Sweden* (Vol I. Paris, 1960; Vol II. Oslo, 1969).
Kasten, E., *Kulturwandel bei den Samen. Eine ethnohistorische Untersuchung zum Kulturkontakt in Schwedisch-Lappland* (Berlin, 1983)
Nickul, K., *The Lappish nation, Citizens of Four Countries* (Bloomington, Indiana 1977).
Paine, R., *Coast Lapp Society* (Vol I. Tromsø, 1957; Vol II. Oslo, 1965)
Vorren, Ørnulf & Manket, Ernst, *Lapp Life and Customs* (London, 1962).
Pelto, P.J., *Individualism in Skolt Lapp Society* (Helsinki, 1962).

Finns
Atlas of Finland (Geographical Society of Finland, Helsinki, 1992).
Hadjú, P. (Ed.), *Ancient Cultures of the Uralian Peoples* (Budapest, 1976).

Jutikkala, E. & Pirinen, K., *A History of Finland* (4th edtn. Espoo, 1984).
Mead, W.R., *An Experience of Finland* (London, 1993).
Vuorela, T. (Ed.), *Atlas of Finnish Folk Culture* (Helsinki, 1976).

Karelians, Veps & Estonians
The Baltic States, A Reference Book (Tallinn, Riga & Vilnius, 1991).
Kirkinen, H., *The Road of Culture from Byzantium to Karelia and the North* (Helsinki,. 1985)
Pimenov, V.V., *Vepsy* (In Russian, Moscow-Leningrad 1965).
Turunen, A., *Über die Volksdichtung und Mythologie der Wepsen* (Studia Fennica Vol 6. Helsinki, 1952).
Uustalu, E. (Ed.), *Aspects of Estonian Culture* (London, 1961).
Vuorela, T., *The Finno-Ugric peoples*. (Bloomington, Indiana 1964).

Chapter 10
THE EASTERN MARCHES

The Marchland Poles (See Poles, Chapter 8)

Belorussians
Vakar, N., *Belorussia, The Making of a Nation* (Cambridge, Mass., 1956).
Zaprudnik, J., *Belarus at a Crossroads in History* (Boulder, 1993).

Ukrainians
Subtelny, O., *Ukraine, A History* (Toronto, 1988).
Ukraine, A Concise Encyclopedia (2 vols. Toronto, 1963–1971).
Zubkewych, O. and Sorokowski, A. (Eds.), *A Thousand Years of Christianity in Ukraine* (New York, 1988)

Russians
Auty, R. and Obolensky, D. (Eds.), *Companion to Russian Studies* (3 volumes. Cambridge, 1976).
Blum, J., *Lord and Peasant in Russia from the Ninth to the Nineteenth Century* (Princeton, 1961).
Bobrick, B., *East of the Sun, The Conquest and Settlement of Siberia* (London, 1993)
Hosking, G., *History of the Soviet Union* (London, 1985)
Mackenzie Wallace, D., *Russia on the Eve of War and Revolution* (Princeton, republished 1984)
Pipes, R., *The Russian Revolution 1899–1919* (Fontana, 1990).
Riha, T. (Ed.), *Readings in Russian Civilisation* (Volumes 1–3 Chicago, 1969).
Shanin, T., *Russia as a 'Developing Society'* (Volumes 1 & 2 Macmillan, 1985).
Schapiro, L., *Russian Studies* (London, 1986).
Vernadsky, G., *Kievan Russia* (New Haven, Conn., 1972).

Chapter 11
THE URALS AND CAUCASUS

The Tatars
Akchura, Y., *L'etat actuel et les aspirations des turco-tatares musulmans en Russie* (Lausanne, 1916).
Allworth, E.(Ed.), *Soviet Nationality Problems* (New York, 1971).
Bennigsen, A. and Lemercier-Quelquejay, C., *Les mouvements nationaux chez les musulmans de Russie. Le 'sultangalievisme' au Tatarstan* (Paris, 1960).
Bennigsen, A. and Lemercier-Quelquejay, C., *Sultan Galiev. Le père de la revolution tiers-mondiste* (Paris, 1986).
Bennigsen Broxup, M., 'The Volga Tatars', in *The Nationalities Question in the Soviet Union,* Graham Smith Ed. (London and New York, 1990) .
Central Asian Survey Volume 9, No 2 (1990). Special issue on Idel-Ural.
Fisher, A. W., *Crimean Tatars* (Stanford, 1978).
Golden, P.B., *An Introduction to the History of the Turkic Peoples. Ethnogenesis and State-Formation in Medieval and Early Modern Eurasia and the Middle East* (Wiesbaden, 1992).
Grousset, R., *L'empire des steppes* (Paris, 1952).
Rorlich, Azade-Ayse, *The Volga Tatars. A Profile in National Resilience* (Stanford, 1986).
Zenkovsky, S. A., *Pan-Turkism and Islam in Russia* (Cambridge, Mass., 1960).

Muslim Turkic and Mongol Peoples of the Volga-Urals and Daghestan
Akiner, S., *Islamic Peoples of the Soviet Union* (London, 1983).
Bennigsen, A. and Broxup, M., *The Islamic Threat to the Soviet State* (London, 1983).
Bennigsen, A. and Wimbush, E., *Muslims of the Soviet Empire. A Guide* (London, 1986).
Bennigsen, A. and Carrère d'Encausse, H., *Une republique soviétique musulmane, Le Daghestan,* (Paris, 1956).
Bennigsen, A. and Wimbush, E., *Mystics and Commissars. Sufism in the Soviet Union* (Hurst & Co, London, 1985)
Bennigsen Broxup, M. (Ed.), *The North Caucasus Barrier. The Russian Advance towards the Muslim World* (London, 1992).
Carrère d'Encausse, H., *The Great Challenge, Nationalities and the Bolshevik State, 1917–30* (New York, 1992).
Central Asian Survey, Volume 10, No 1/2, special issue devoted to the North Caucasus.
Wixman, R., *The Peoples of the USSR. An Ethnographic Handbook* (New York, 1984).

Non-Muslim Peoples of the Volga-Urals
Dugántsy, M. *Erzä-mordwinische rituelle Klagegesänge* (Stockholm, 1991).
Erdal, M. *Die Sprache der wolgabulgarischen Inschriften* (Wiesbaden, 1993).
Jevsevjev, T. et al., *Folklore-Sammlungen aus dem Tscheremissischen Herausgegeben* (Helsinki, 1983).
Latham, R. *Native Races of the Russian Empire* (London, 1854).
Vikár, L. and Bereczki, G. *Votyak Folksongs* (Budapest, 1989) .

Peoples of the Caucasus
Aves, J., *Post-Soviet Transcaucasia* (London, 1993).

Bell, J.S., *Journal of a Residence in Circassia 1837–9* (2 vols. London, 1840).

Benningsen, A. and Wimbush, E., *Muslims of the Soviet Empire* (London, 1985).

Benningsen Broxup, M. (Ed.), *The North Caucasus Barrier* (London, 1992).

Blanch, L., *The Sabres of Paradise* (London, 1960).

Cox, C. and Eibner, J., *Ethnic Cleansing in Progress, War in Nagorno Karabakh*. (Institute for Religious Minorities in the Islamic World, 1993).

Cunynghame, Sir A.A.T., *Travels in the Eastern Caucasus during the summer of 1871* (London, 1873).

Hewitt, B.G., 'Abkhazia, a problem of identity and ownership.' in *Central Asian Survey* 12/3 (1993).

Lang, D.M., *A Modern History of Georgia* (London, 1962).

Lang, D.M., *The Armenians, a People in Exile.* (London, 1980).

Longworth, J.A., *A Year among the Circassians* (London, 1840).

Spencer, Capt. E., *Travels in Circassia, Krim-Tartar, etc.* (2 vols. London, 1837).

Wixman, R., *Language Aspects of Ethnic Patterns & Processes in the North Caucasus.* (Chicago, 1980).

Chapter 12
DISPERSED PEOPLES

Jews

Bacon, J. and Gilbert, M., *The Illustrated Atlas of Jewish Civilization* (London, 1990).

Encyclopedia Judaica (16 vols. Jerusalem, 1971).

Gilbert, M., *Jewish History Atlas* (London, 1992)

Gilbert, M., *The Holocaust* (New York, 1986).

Kochan, L., *The Jew and His History* (London, 1977).

Johnson, P., *A History of the Jews* (London, 1988).

Rosen, L., *The Joys of Yiddish* (Harmondsworth, 1971).

Gypsies

Fraser, Angus, *The Gypsies* (London, 1992).

Journal of the Gypsy Lore Society (Now in 5th series. Since 1888. Cheverley, Maryland).

Sampson, J., *The Dialect of the Gypsies of Wales* (Oxford, 1926).

Vaux de Foletier, F. de., *Mille ans d'histoire des Tsiganes* (Paris, 1970).

Vossen, R., *Zigeuner* (Frankfurt am Main 1983).

INDEX